Charles Anderson

DEATH:

CURRENT PERSPECTIVES

Mayfield
Publishing
Company

DEATH:

CURRENT PERSPECTIVES

SECOND EDITION

Edited by

Edwin S. Shneidman, Ph.D.

Professor of Thanatology

Director, Laboratory for the Study of Life-Threatening Behavior

University of California at Los Angeles School of Medicine

Second edition, 1980

Library of Congress Catalog Card Number: 80-81360
International Standard Book Number: 0-87484-508-4

Manufactured in the United States of America
Mayfield Publishing Company
285 Hamilton Avenue, Palo Alto, California 94301

This book was set in Zapf Book by the Lienett Company and was printed and bound by the George Banta Company. Sponsoring editor was Robert Erhart, Maggie Cutler supervised editing, and manuscript editor was Loralee W. Lowe. Michelle Hogan supervised production, and the book was designed by Nancy Sears. Cover and part title page artwork is by Patrick Korch. Dedication illustration is from an original work by Judith Malkin Watkyns rendered by Mary Burkhardt.

To
Judith Malkin Watkyns
1944-1971
my former Teaching Assistant,
gentle and generous
even in her death

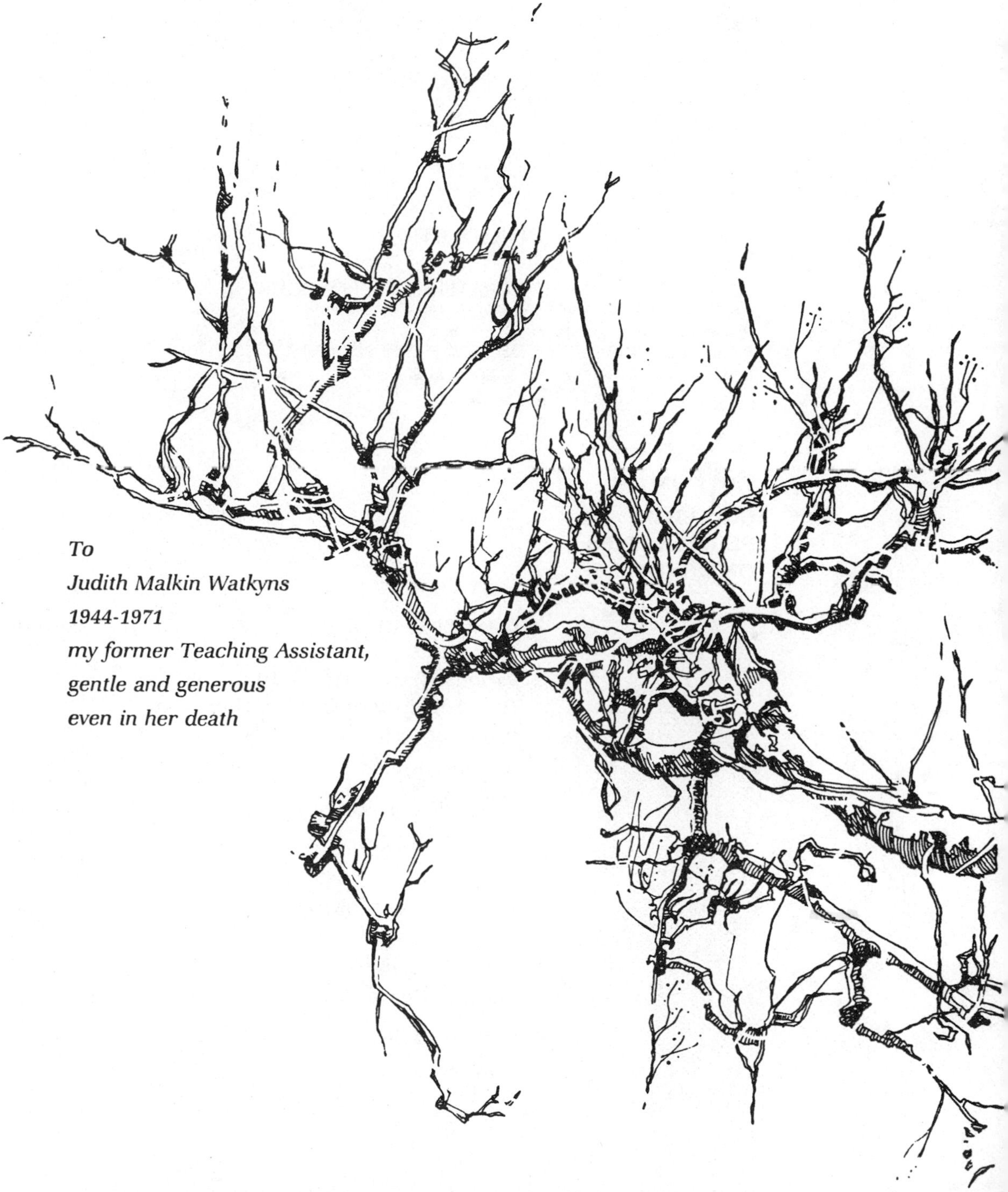

CONTENTS

PART TWO

SOCIETAL PERSPECTIVES ON DEATH

PART THREE
INTERPERSONAL PERSPECTIVES ON DEATH

PART FOUR
PERSONAL PERSPECTIVES ON DEATH

POETIC EPILOGUE

PREFACE

In a well-known letter to his famous friend and fellow author, Nathaniel Hawthorne, Herman Melville, in June of 1851, wrote these intimate lines: "Dollars damn me; and the malicious Devil is forever grinning in upon me, holding the door ajar. . . . What I feel most moved to write, this is banned—it will not pay. Yet, altogether, write the other *way, I cannot." And elsewhere (that same year), Melville exclaimed, "Oh, what quenchless feud is this, that Time hath with the sons of Men!"*

My purpose in quoting these two diverse statements from Melville is not to make the point that either money or time were my *antagonists; rather, my adversary was* space. *The first draft of this book had over three times its present content—much too bulky and thus potentially far too expensive to be practical. To excise fully eligible articles in order to reduce this volume to any manageable size meant to give up many favorites—clear favorites of mine and possible favorites of yours.*

One decision of mine—to limit the selections entirely to those written in the last fifteen years—helped in the process of selection. This was an especially difficult decision to hold to because it meant eliminating some obvious choices—such as Freud's papers on death and mourning and several worthwhile books completed before 1965, including those by Eissler, Fulton, Choron, and many other worthies—but I needed some criterion for restraint, and recency *seemed to be an especially relevant one. Also, I chose mostly from books rather than items from the periodical literature, believing that the latter, in general, tend to be more ephemeral and to become dated more quickly.*

My essential aim in assembling this volume was to provide a representative sample of recent and contemporary writings on the myriad aspects of death and dying. My principal goal was to create a set of materials that would serve as either a primary or a supplementary text for a college undergraduate course relating to death. I have pursued this goal in two ways: first, by structuring the book according to a logic that offers the reader a series of pertinent perspectives with which to build up an understanding of death —death as it relates to our culture and society; death as it relates to our understanding of each other and of ourselves. Secondly, in the interstitial materials (the Introduction and the prefatory comments to each chapter) I have attempted to guide readers—especially readers who may be relatively unsophisticated about the contemporary literature on death—to a wider understanding of the field and to provide them with some conceptual cement to pull together the disparate bricks of concept, opinion, and fact. I trust that some sense of the continuity and interrelatedness will be apparent and that the active reader will be able to sense that the selections do indeed complement one another much as there is a mysterious, complementary relationship between the complexities of human death and the complications of human life.

The goal of this revision was to incorporate the main thrust of suggestions arising from the use of the first edition over the past few years. The major result has been the elimination of several of the more discursive papers and all of the "student papers" and the addition of new materials, particularly in the section "Life after Death?" and a whole new section on that special kind of death, "Self-Destruction." An annotated bibliography has also been added.

All these changes have made the book more comprehensive and timely. I hope that its reception in thanatological classrooms and in studies at home will be even more cordial than that accorded the first edition.

Though it is intended for use as a college text, I hope that this book will also be useful to professionals in medicine, nursing, theology, law, public health and mortuary science, in police academies, and in the social and behavioral sciences in general, especially in the disciplines of psychology and sociology.

A number of people helped me personally, especially Bengt Ljunggren, whose editorial suggestions for the first edition were invariably helpful, and Loralee W. Lowe, whose efficient copy editing of the second edition was most helpful. In the revision, the efforts of my assistant, Anita Navarra, were indispensable.

I wish to thank Ralph B. Hupka, California State University, Long Beach; Harold A. Widdison, Northern Arizona University; Tony Bell, California State University, Fullerton; Kent Bennington, University of California, Davis; June O'Conner, University of California, Riverside; and Robert Hunt, University of Redlands, who reviewed the manuscript in its developmental stages and made valuable comments and suggestions.

I would also like to thank Marie A. Caputi, School of Social Work, University of Wisconsin, Madison, Audrey Gordon, Oakton Community College, Morton Grove, Illinois, Wendy Martyna, University of California, Santa Cruz, and Douglas A. Michell, California State University, Sacramento, for their counsel in preparing the second edition.

Finally, I acknowledge my gratitude to Mrs. Maggie Cutler, Managing Editor at Mayfield Publishing Company, who cheerfully applied a combination of extraordinary skills to the preparation of this revision.

Below, I happily acknowledge the several publishers from whom permis-

sion was obtained to reproduce the selections in this volume. I am grateful to them. Detailed acknowledgement notes are given on the initial page of each selection.

Aldine Publishing Co. for *Awareness of Dying* by Barney G. Glaser and Anselm L. Strauss; and for *Time for Dying* by Barney G. Glaser and Anselm L. Strauss.

George Allen & Unwin Ltd. for *Why I Am Not a Christian* by Bertrand Russell.

Jason Aronson for *Beyond Grief* by Erich Lindemann.

Associated Book Publishers Ltd. for *Bereavement* by C. M. Parkes.

Association of Military Surgeons of the United States for "The Reliability of Mortality Count and Suicide Count in the United States Army" by William E. Datel from *Military Medicine.*

Basic Books for "When, Why, and Where People Die" by Monroe Lerner from *The Dying Patient* edited by Orville G. Brim, Jr. et al.

Baywood Publishing Co., Inc. for "Life Revisited (Parallels in Death Experiences)" by Frederick H. Holck from *Omega.*

Behavioral Publications, Inc. for *On Dying and Denying* by Avery D. Weisman; and for "A Psychiatrist's Response to a Life-Threatening Illness" by Lauren E. Trombley and "Suicide Among the Gifted" by Edwin S. Shneidman from *Life-Threatening Behavior.*

George Braziller, Inc. for *How Could I Not Be Among You?* by Ted Rosenthal.

Commonweal for "Redefining Death" by Walter G. Jeffko.

Death Education for "I Want to Die While I'm Still Alive" by Sylvia Lack and "Altered States of Consciousness: A Form of Death Education?" by Virginia H. Hine.

Doubleday & Company, Inc. for *Death, Grief and Mourning* by Geoffrey Gorer.

Encyclopaedia Britannica, Inc. for "Suicide" by Edwin S. Shneidman.

Harper & Row for *Voices of Death* by Edwin S. Shneidman.

Hemisphere Publishing Corporation for "Children and Death" by Judith Stillion and Hannelore Wass from *Dying: Facing the Facts* edited by Hannelore Wass.

Hodder and Stoughton Ltd. for "Death and Psychical Research" by Rosalind Heywood, and "Various Ways in Which Humans Have Sought to Reconcile Themselves to the Fact of Death" and "The Relation between Life and Death, Living and Dying" by Arnold Toynbee from *Man's Concern with Death* by Arnold Toynbee and others.

The Johns Hopkins University Press for *Western Attitudes toward Death* by Philippe Ariès.

Institute of Society, Ethics and the Life Sciences for "Brain Death" by Robert M. Veatch, from the *Hastings Center Report.*

International Universities Press for *Bereavement* by C. M. Parkes.

Little, Brown and Company, Inc., for *The Aristos* by John Fowles; and for *Population, Modernization and Social Structure* by Calvin Goldscheider.

McGraw-Hill Book Co. for "Death and Psychical Research" by Rosalind Heywood; "Various Ways in Which Humans Have Sought to Reconcile Themselves to the Fact of Death" and "The Relation between Life and Death, Living and Dying" by Arnold Toynbee from *Man's Concern with Death* by Arnold Toynbee and others; "Some Aspects of Psychotherapy with Dying Persons" by Edwin S. Shneidman from *Psychosocial Aspects of Terminal Patient Care* edited by Charles A. Garfield; and "Drug Abuse as Indirect Self-Destructive Behavior" by Calvin J. Frederick from *The Many Faces of Suicide: Indirect Self-Destructive Behavior* edited by Norman L. Farberow.

Macmillan Publishing Co., Inc. for *On Death and Dying* by Elisabeth Kùbler-Ross.

Mockingbird Books for *Life After Life* by Raymond A. Moody, Jr.

Nash Publishing Co. for "Voluntary Euthanasia: The Ethical Aspect" by W. R. Matthews from *Euthanasia and the Right to Death* edited by A. B. Downing.

The New England Journal of Medicine for "Brain Death: An Editorial" by William H. Sweet and for "Patient Autonomy and Death with Dignity" by David L. Jackson and Stuart Youngner.

Harold Ober Associates, Inc. for *Death, Grief and Mourning* by Geoffrey Gorer.

Penguin Books Ltd. for *Dying* by John Hinton; and for *The Twentieth Century Book of the Dead* by Gil Elliot.

Praeger Publishing Co. for *Living and Dying* by Robert Jay Lifton and Eric Olson.

Prentice-Hall, Inc. for *Passing On* by David Sudnow.

G. P. Putnam's Sons for *A Very Easy Death* by Simone de Beauvoir.

Quadrangle The New York Times Book Co. for *Deaths of Man* by Edwin S. Shneidman.

Random House, Inc. for *The Twentieth Century Book of the Dead* by Gil Elliot; and for *Lying: Moral Choice in Public and Private Life*by Sissela Bok; and for *The Savage God* by A. Alvarez.

St. Christopher's Hospice (London) for *Annual Report* by Cicely Saunders.

The Seabury Press for *Death: Meaning and Mortality in Christian Thought and Contemporary Culture* by Milton McC. Gatch.

Anthony Sheil Associates Ltd. for *The Aristos* by John Fowles.

Simon & Schuster, Inc. for *Why I Am Not a Christian* by Bertrand Russell.

Springer Publishing Co., Inc. for *The Psychology of Death* by Robert Kastenbaum and Ruth Aisenberg.

University of California Press for *Cancer, The Wayward Cell* by Victor Richards.

George Weidenfeld and Nicolson, Arthur Barker, Ltd. for *A Very Easy Death* by Simone de Beauvoir.

INTRODUCTION

Perhaps the single most impressive fact about death today—independent of the unchangeable truth that death can never be circumvented—is how much (and in how many different ways) various aspects of death and dying are currently undergoing dramatic changes. Nowadays, there are many breezes in the thanatological wind.[1] *We are experiencing a cultural revolution in many areas of our living. In the last short generation, dozens of our folkways (in dress, behavior, civility, morality, sexuality) and even some of our mores have been changed, often in breathtaking ways. The ethics, and sociology, and psychology, and morality of death have not been exempt from these culturewide changes. This book attempts to reflect these changes in relation to death—changes that have led us to new, and often startling, insights into the very process of dying; into the intricate interactions between the dying and those who care for the dying; into the impact of death on those left behind; even into the need for reexamining such fundamental questions as: When* does *death occur? When* should *death occur?*

In order to place these current trends in thanatology in context, this volume examines death from many perspectives, ranging from cultural strategies for dealing with death as a philosophical concept to individual tactics for dealing with death as an inevitable reality.

What will be discussed here are the threads of change that weave through the various chapters and constitute some of the more important developments in the current thanatological scene.

Consider this paragraph:[2]

> *"Haul in the chains! Let the carcass go astern!" The vast tackles have done their duty. The peeled white body of the beheaded whale flashes like a marble sepulchre; though changed in hue, it has not perceptibly lost anything in bulk. It is still colossal. Slowly it floats more and more away, the water round it torn and splashed by the insatiate sharks, and the air above vexed with rapacious flights of screaming fowls, whose beaks are like so many insulting poniards in the whale. The vast white headless phantom floats further and further from the ship, and every rod that it so floats, what seem square roods of sharks and cubic roods of fowls, augment the murderous din. For hours and hours from the almost stationary ship that hideous sight is seen. Beneath the unclouded and mild azure sky, upon the fair face of the pleasant sea, wafted by the joyous*

breezes, the great mass of death floats on and on, till lost in infinite perspectives.

What is to be especially noted in this superlative passage is the breathtaking shift in mood between the first eight sentences and the last—from horror and rapaciousness to the most pacific calm. Indeed, the last sentence itself contains the same dramatic contrast as seen in the shift in tone between the first three phrases and the last two. Such a combination of opposites is called an oxymoron. *The best known examples of oxymorons in the English language are from* Romeo and Juliet: *"... Feather of lead, bright smoke, cold fire, sick health" and, of course, "... Parting is such sweet sorrow." I have dwelled on the subject of oxymorons because it so aptly describes death in our time. Death is oxymoronic, a paradox made up of contrasting values, opposite trends, and even contradictory facts.*

We live in an oxymoronic century. At the same time we have created the most exquisitely sophisticated technological procedures for saving one individual's life, we have also created lethal technological devices, of at least equal sophistication, with the capacity of exterminating millions, of expunging cultures, of jeopardizing time itself by not only erasing the present but also threatening the future—what Melville, in White Jacket, *called "... the terrible combustion of the entire planet." On the one hand, marvelous devices for emergency surgery, kidney dialysis, and organ transplantations promise life; on the other hand, megadeath bombs constantly aimed from above the clouds and beneath the waves promise death. No one is safe; there is no place to hide (see Kahn's* On Thermonuclear War *[1960] an Lifton's* Death in Life *[1967]).*

We live in paradoxical times. On the one hand, there has been more killing by the state than ever before: over 110 million deaths since 1900 in brutish wars, deliberate famines, planned starvations, police and government executions (see Elliot's The Twentieth Century Book of the Dead *[1972]); on the other hand, there has been no century where so much effort has been put into saving individual lives and increasing the general span of life.*

Even the scientific marvels of our age for saving individual lives are part of the oxymoronic nature of death in our times, for they exist side by side with the frustrating and unfulfilled promises of medicine to save us from the dread maladies of heart disease and cancer. Dubos has referred to this failure of medicine in his book The Mirage of Health *(1971), and others have called it "the mythology of American medicine." We have been overpromised in part because we have oversought. But great strides have been made: in the United States, life expectancy has been extended 28 years in the last 75 years , from 47 years in 1900 to 75 years in 1975 (see Dublin's* After Eighty Years *[1966]). However it is important to note that this remarkable increase has been due not so much to medicine's miracles for adults, as to everyday public health practices in the areas of infant mortality (reduced from 150 to 25 per*

1,000 births in this century), sanitation, immunization, and environmental control—unpretentious activities when compared with the dramatic surgical and medical cures that can increase the life span of the middle-aged and elderly, those very people who tend to be most concerned about death and wish to cling to life.

The elimination of diphtheria, scarlet fever, and typhoid fever and the reduction of mortality from tuberculosis were a million times more effective in increasing general longevity than heart transplants. Conquering the causes of death over 40—cancer, cardiovascular diseases, and accidents—will do an incalculable amount of psychological good, but will not have enormous impact on the total duration of life for the populace as a whole, adding no more than perhaps five or six years to the present average of 75 (Dublin, 1966). Probably the most significant changes in mortality are to be found less in medical and hospital care than they are in health education: simply in voluntary and controllable changes in our routine daily patterns of eating, exercising, and smoking.

Nowadays the great challenge seems to lie in improving the kind of lives we lead. It seems more important than extending life by a year or two to enhance the quality of those seventy or eighty years by elevating the current level of our common courtesy, moral rights, education, employment, and contentment. This refocusing on the quality, rather than the quantity of life has profound implications for our changing views on death and for our treatment of the dying.

Certainly one of the most refreshing currents in the changing thanatological wind is the increasing emphasis on a "humanistic" approach to death—an approach that seems to parallel the humanistic trends in other sectors of society today. This new approach is seen, for example, in an increasing concern that the dying individual live as fully and as richly as possible until death and that communication with the dying be tailored to specific human needs, and in the recognition of a need for special therapies to help those who have suffered the loss of someone close. Indeed, this humanistic trend in the treatment of the dying and those immediately affected by death is causing a complete reexamination of the premises on which we have traditionally based our views on death and dying.

A very impressive aspect of thanatology in the current scene is the dynamic and changing nature of its vital issues. Consider, for example, the swirl of debate around organ transplantation, tied directly to the definition of "death"—does death occur when the heart stops? When the vital signs are gone? Or when the cradle of consciousness, the brain, ceases to generate electrical energy? (The last-named criterion is the one emphasized in the famous Harvard report on "brain death" [Beecher et al., *1968]). One expert (Glaser, 1970) summed it up this way: "The brain is our master control; the heart is just a pump." Or, to put it another way: "No brain, no personality," (Murray, 1951).*

And if there is controversy over the definition of "death"—or "How does one take a live heart from a dead person?"—there is a potential moral and legal storm over the issue of voluntary euthanasia. If, as has been said, war is too important to be left to generals, then is life too precious (or too miserable) to be left solely to the judgment of doctors? Should a weakened citizen, too ill to kill himself, have the right to say, "Enough!" And, considering what we read and know of occasional heinous derelictions in some nursing homes, what are the chances, without any opportunity for redress, of abuses in the practice of voluntary euthanasia? For young readers especially, these questions may become real issues before their time to die.

One additional current trend can be mentioned. Today there is a new permissiveness regarding death, almost an urgency to speak and think about it. In this century death has become, as Gorer (1965) says, the new pornography—a subject banned from polite society and social discourse. Yet, in the last few years there has been a spate of books on death; death has become a respectable field of inquiry, particularly in the social and behavioral sciences; and death has become an acceptable topic of study in the college curriculum.

The cultural revolution that we are experiencing today is effecting sweeping changes in the pattern and texture of our lives, changes that are now reaching to the very threshold of our deaths. The scope and impact of these changes concerning death are the concern of this book.

Notes

1 Thanatology is the study of death and dying, after Thanatos, the mythological Greek god of death, twin of Hypnus, the god of sleep.

2 This passage is from the chapter "The Funeral" in Herman Melville's masterpiece, *Moby Dick.*

References

Beecher, Henry K., *et al*, A Definition of Irreversible Coma. *Journal of the American Medical Association*, 1968, *205*, 85-88.

Dublin, Louis I. *After Eighty Years.* Gainesville: University of Florida Press, 1966.

Dubos, Rene. *The Mirage of Health.* New York: Harper, 1971.

Elliot, Gil. *The Twentieth Century Book of the Dead.* New York: Ballantine Books, 1972.

Glaser, Robert J. Innovations and Heroic Acts in Prolonging Life. In Orville G. Brim, Jr. *et al.* (eds.), *The Dying Patient.* New York: Russell Sage Foundation, 1970.

Gorer, Geoffrey. *Death, Grief and Mourning.* New York: Anchor Books, 1965.

Kahn, Herman. *On Thermonuclear War.* Princeton: Princeton University Press, 1960.

Lifton, Robert Jay. *Death in Life: Survivors of Hiroshima.* New York: Vantage Books, 1967.

Murray, Henry A. Some Basic Psychological Assumptions and Conceptions. *Dialectica,* 1951, *5,* 266-292

EPIGRAMMATIC PROLOGUE

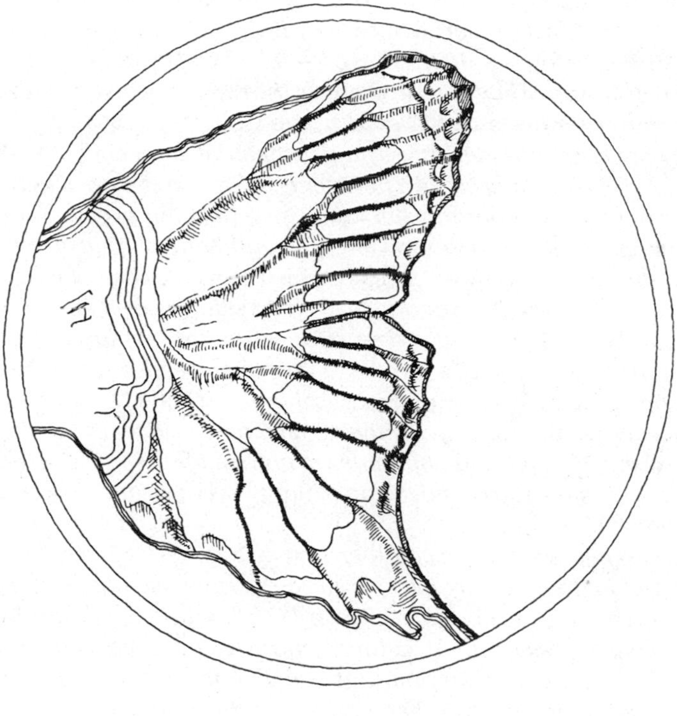

EPIGRAMMATIC PROLOGUE

Among the handful of extraordinary contemporary American and English writers—Anthony Burgess, Saul Bellow, Kurt Vonnegut, John Barth, Christopher Isherwood, Robert Graves, Norman Mailer, John Updike, Peter DeVries, J. D. Salinger—John Fowles must be mentioned quickly and near the top of any list. He is one of the most interesting and vibrant writers alive with five novels to his credit: The Collector (1963), an original tour de force concerning desperate evil and ineffectual innocence; The Magus (1966), a sweeping book that creates a new genre, blurring the lines between the reality of the author's fiction and the latent psychosis in every reader's mind; The French Lieutenant's Woman (1969), an authentic classic, a breathtaking book about the deepest ambivalences between sacred and profane love; The Ebony Tower (1974), a set of psychologically laden stories; and Daniel Martin (1977), a colossal book that spans three continents and explores dozens of human emotions. The theme of sacred and profane love either touches or permeates all of Fowles's work. He explores this theme in each of his works, each time with an original twist, exposing a hitherto unexplored facet of the dualities, ambivalences, ambiguities, and duplicities of human life. In spirit (although surely not in style), he is the most Melvillean of our current writers—and for that reason, perhaps the greatest.

Fowles has written three other books: Islands (1979), a detailed nonfiction report of Britain's Scilly Isles, "where the unconscious grows conscious and the imagination never rests," Trees (1980), an unusual and beautiful prose-photographic essay about nature, and The Aristos(1968; revised 1970). The last is not a work of fiction, but a collection of 761 aphorisms and notes subsumed under twelve chapters. The pronouncements run from two brief lines to almost a full page. It is a veritable catalog of wisdom, and harkens back to Pascal's Pensées. The word aristos, from the ancient Greek, means roughly "the best for a given situation." The Aristos deals with topics where the choices are, at best, often between miserable alternatives: aspects of isolation, anxiety, envy, tension, nationalism, culpability, and death.

A not insignificant number of Fowles's thoughts relate to death. Fowles tells us that the original impetus and many of the ideas for these notes came to him from Heraclitus (500 B.C.); he reprints one fragment of Heraclitus's teaching: "All that we see is death." Fowles himself is not totally focused on this thanatological topic, but he is keenly interested, almost to the point of obsession, with *the dark side of life. His short section on death—only twenty-eight aphorisms subsumed under the more general heading of "Human Dissatisfactions"—provides us with some of the flavor of his work. The reader may wish to look again at Heraclitus's pithy sayings and at Pascal's* Pensées *for other sets of mind-stretching aphorisms from previous centuries.*

1• Human Dissatisfactions

John Fowles

1 Why do we think this is not the best of all possible worlds for mankind? Why are we unhappy in it?

2 What follow are the great dissatisfactions. I maintain that they are all essential to our happiness since they provide the soil from which it grows.

DEATH

3 We hate death for two reasons. It ends life prematurely; and we do not know what lies beyond it.

4 A very large majority of educated mankind now doubts the existence of an afterlife. It is clear that the only scientific attitude is that of agnosticism: we simply do not know. We are in the Bet Situation.

5 The Bet Situation is one in which we cannot have certainty about some future event; and yet in which it is vital that we come to a decision about its nature. This situation faces us at the beginning of a horse race, when we want to know the name of the winner . . .

6 To Pascal, who first made this analogy with the bet, the answer was clear: one must put one's money on the Christian belief that a recompensatory afterlife exists. If it is not true, he argued, then one has lost nothing but one's stake. If it is true, one has gained all.

7 Now even an atheist contemporary with Pascal might have agreed that nothing but good could ensue, in an unjust society where the majority conveniently believed in hellfire, from supporting the idea, false or true, of an afterlife. But today the concept of hellfire has been discarded by the theologians, let alone the rest of us. Hell could be just only in a world where all were equally persuaded that it exists; just only in a world that allowed a total freedom of will—and therefore a total biographical and biological similarity—to every man and woman in it . . .

8 The idea of an afterlife has persistently haunted man because inequality has persistently tyrannized him. It is only to the poor, the sick, the unfortunate underdogs of history, that the idea appeals; it has appealed to all honest men's sense of justice, and very often at the same time as the use of the idea to maintain an unequal *status quo* in society has revolted them. Somewhere, this belief proposes, there is a system of absolute justice and a day of absolute judgment by and on which we are all to be rewarded according to our deserts.

9 But the true longing of humanity is not for an afterlife; it is for the establishment of a justice here and now that will make an afterlife unnecessary. This myth was a compensatory fantasy, a psychological safety valve for the frustrations of existential reality.

10 We are ourselves to establish justice in our world: and the more we allow the belief in an afterlife to dwindle away, and yet still do so little to correct the flagrant inequalities of our world, then the more danger we run.

11 Our world has a badly designed engine. By using the oil of this myth it did not for many centuries heat up. But now the oil level is dropping ominously low. For this reason, it is not enough to remain agnostic. We *must* bet on the other horse: we have one life, and it is ended by a total extinction of consciousness as well as body.

12 What matters is not our personal damnation or salvation in the world to come, but that of our fellow man in the world that is.

13 Our second hatred of death is that it almost always comes too soon. We suffer from an illusion, akin to that of the desirability of an afterlife, that we should be happier if we lived for ever. Animal desires are always for an extension of what satisfies them. Only two hundred years ago a man who reached the age of forty was exceeding the average life span; and perhaps two hundred years from now centenarians will be as common as septuagenarians today. But they will still crave a longer life.

14 The function of death is to put tension into life; and the more we increase the length and the security of individual existence then the more tension we remove from it. All our pleasurable experiences contain a faint yet terrible element of the condemned man's last breakfast, an echo of the intensity of feeling of the poet who knows he is going to die, of the young soldier going doomed into battle.

15 Each pleasure we feel is a pleasure less; each day a stroke on a calendar. What we will not accept is that the joy in the day and the passing of the day are inseparable. What makes our existence worthwhile is precisely that its worth and its while—its quality and duration—are as impossible to unravel as time and space in the mathematics of relativity.

16 *Pleasure is a product of death; not an escape from it.*

17 If it were proved that there is an afterlife, life would be irretrievably spoilt. It would be pointless; and suicide, a virtue. The only possible paradise is one in which I cannot know I did once exist.

18 There are two tendencies in the twentieth century; one, a misguided one, is to domesticate death, to pretend that death is like life; the other is to look death in the face. The tamers of death believe in life after death; they indulge in elaborate after death ceremonial. Their attitude to death is euphemistic; it is "passing on" and "going to a better place." The actual process of death and decomposition is censored. Such people are in the same mental condition as the ancient Egyptians.

19 "Passing on": the visual false analogy. We know that passing objects, such as we see repeatedly every day, exist both before and after the passage that we see: and so we come, illogically and wrongly, to treat life as such a passage.

20 Death is in us and outside us; beside us in every room, in every street, in every field, in every car, in every plane. Death is what we are not every moment that we are, and every moment that we are is the moment when the dice come to rest. We are always playing Russian roulette.

21 Being dead is nothingness, not being. When we die we constitute "God's."* Our relics, our monuments, the memories retained by those who survive us, these still exist; do not constitute "God," still constitute the process. But these relics are the fossilized traces of our having been, not our being. All the great religions try to make out that death is nothing. There is another life to come . . .

22 As one social current has tried to hide death, to euphemize it out of existence, so another has thrust death forward as a chief element in entertainment: in the murder story, the war story, the spy story, the western. But increasingly, as our century grows old, these fictive deaths become more fictitious and fulfill the function of concealed euphemism. The real death of a pet kitten affects a child far more deeply than the "deaths" of all the television gangsters, cowboys, and Red Indians.

23 By death we think characteristically of the disappearance of individuals; it does not console us to know that matter is not disappearing, but is simply being metamorphosed. We mourn the individualizing form, not the generalized content. But everything we see is a metaphor of death. Every limit, every dimension, every end of every road, is a death. Even seeing is a death, for there is a point beyond which we cannot see, and our seeing dies; wherever our capacity ends, we die.

24 Time is the flesh and blood of death; death is not a skull, a skeleton, but a clock face, a sun hurtling through a sea of thin gas. A part of you has died since you began to read this sentence.

25 Death itself dies. Every moment you live, it dies. *O Death where is thy sting, Death I will be thy death.* The living prove this; not the dead.

*EDITOR'S NOTE; *Elsewhere in* The Aristos, *under "God," Fowles says: "'God' is a situation. Not a power, or a being, or an influence. Not a 'he' or a 'she' but an 'it.' Not an entity or nonentity but the situation in which there can be both entity and nonentity."*

26 In all the countries living above a bare subsistence level, the twentieth century has seen a sharp increase in awareness of the pleasures of life. This is not only because of the end of belief in an afterlife, but because death is more real today, more probable, now that the H-bomb is.

27 *The more absolute death seems, the more authentic life becomes.*

28 All I love and know may be burnt to ashes in one small hour: London, New York, Paris, Athens, gone in less time than it takes to count ten. I was born in 1926; and because of what can happen now in ten seconds, that year lies not forty-one years but a measureless epoch and innocence away. Yet I do not regret that innocence. I love life more, not less.

29 Death contains me as my skin contains me. Without it, I am not what I am. Death is not a sinister door I walk toward; it is my walking toward.

30 Because I am a man death is my wife; and now she has stripped, she is beautiful, she wants me to strip, to be her mate. This is necessity, this is love, this is being-for-another, nothing else. I cannot escape this situation, nor do I want to. She wants me to make love, not like some man-eating spider, to consume me, but like a wife in love, so that we can celebrate our total sympathy, be fertile and bear children. It is her effect on me and my effect on her that make all that is good in my time being. She is not a prostitute or a mistress I am ashamed of or want to forget or about whom I can sometimes pretend that she does not exist. Like my real wife she informs every important situation in my life, she is wholly of my life, not beyond, or against, or opposite to it. I accept her completely, in every sense of the word, and I love and respect her for what she is to me.

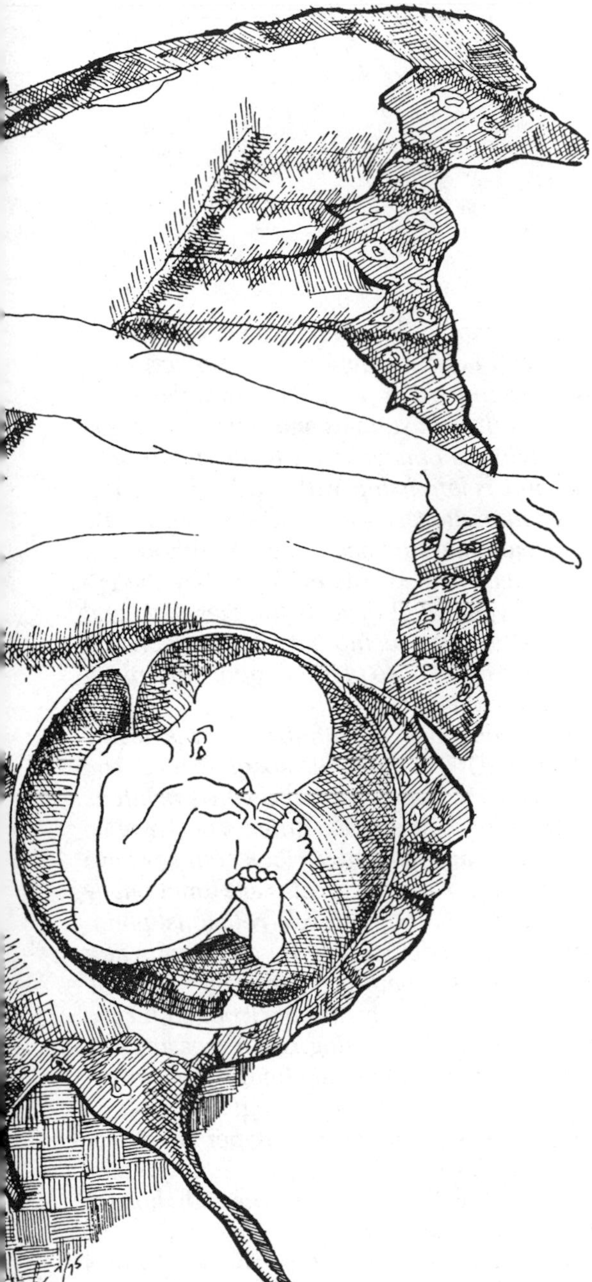

PART ONE

CULTURAL PERSPECTIVES ON DEATH

CONCEPTS OF DEATH

Death, perhaps humanity's greatest mystery and source of fear, has from earliest recorded times been a chief focus of superstitions and beliefs about life and the world (and about other possible lives and places). Thoughts about death have influenced both philosophies and religions. This is not at all surprising inasmuch as religion is concerned with the myths and mysteries of resurrection, rebirth, and relationship with God. In essence, humans seem to generate, in their various cultures, some kind of view of death, what might be called a "strategy" for handling the idea of death. Although in this century death has become vastly secularized—as evidenced by the exalted scientist, the revered doctor, the venerated devices for diagnosis and treatment, and the glorified hospital—the relationship between religion and death is rooted in history and continues, for many, to play an important role in their attitudes (and their behavior) toward death.

Always, and in all cultures, the main questions seem to be: What is death? How shall we think of it? (Fear it? Welcome it?) Is death the absolute end? The selections in this chapter offer the reader a "long view" of death—death as seen from the perspective of various cultures at various times. The Toynbee selection discusses some of the specific strategies that various cultures have worked out for dealing with the fact of death. These strategies are functionally related to, or even functionally dependent on, the culture's religions, philosophies, legal and political institutions, and socioeconomic conditions at a particular period. (As the gods evolve and the pantheons change, so do the concepts of death). Some of these concepts are highly durable from culture to culture and from time to time (e.g., Toynbee's "putting one's treasures in future generations . . ."), while others, such as "physical countermeasures," are less durable, albeit they may be retained today in vestigial form (e.g., peasant funeral rites in China, calling for burning of symbolic paper articles to accompany the dead). The "evolution" of perspectives on death within a major culture can be illustrated by comparing early Christian concepts with those of modern Christianity, as is done in the selection by Gatch.

From the very beginning we sense the oxymoronic quality of death. Death is destroyer and redeemer; the ultimate cruelty and the essence of release; universally feared but sometimes actively sought; undeniably ubiquitous, yet incomprehensibly unique; of all phenomena, the most obvious and the least reportable; feared, yet fascinating.

Various Ways in Which Human Beings Have Sought to Reconcile Themselves to the Fact of Death

Arnold Toynbee

Arnold Toynbee, an internationally famous English historian, is best known for A Study of History, *a ten-volume work written between 1934 and 1954. In this selection taken from his remarkable and scholarly book* Man's Concern with Death, *Professor Toynbee lists and discusses numerous ways in which human beings have denied, accepted, embraced, or "handled" death.*

(a) *Hedonism.* The most obvious way of reconciling oneself to death is to make sure of enjoying life before death snatches it from us. The catchwords *"Carpe diem"*[1] and "Let us eat and drink, for tomorrow we shall die"[2] are notorious, and Herodotus[3] has preserved an Egyptian folktale in which Pharaoh Mycerinus, when the gods had sentenced him to die after enjoying six more years of life, successfully doubled the term arbitrarily allotted to him by turning night into day. This hedonistic solution of the problem of death is, of course, illusory. In reality a human being cannot stay awake, enjoying himself, for twenty-four hours a day, day in and day out, over a span of six years. Nor can he make sure of enjoying himself even for the briefest spells; and, if luck does favor him that far, his foreknowledge that one day he is going to die will be lurking all the time at the back of his mind. The skeleton was simply being brought out of the cupboard in the Egyptian custom, also recorded by Herodotus,[4] of exhibiting a miniature wooden model of a mummy at a feast in order to remind the revellers of the grim fact of death, which they were trying to put out of their minds for the moment. Eating, drinking, and being merry is, like war and revolution, an intrinsically transient activity. It is, in fact, another name for "sowing one's wild oats," and it is only in fairy tales that this conventional escapade is followed by "marrying and living happily after." In prosaic real life, it is followed by the anxieties and fatigues and maladies of adult life—congenital evils of our human condition, which, if they are severe and long drawn out, may make a human being actually look forward to death as an eventual relief on which he can count for certain.

(b) *Pessimism.* The most obvious alternative to the illusory solace of hedonism is to conclude that life is so wretched that death is the lesser evil. In the fifth century B.C., when the Greeks were at the height of their achievement in all fields, the Greek poet Sophocles declared[5] that "it is best of all never to have been born, and second best—second by far—if one has made his appearance in this world, to go back again, as quickly as may be, thither whence he has come." The Greek historian Herodotus attributed the same view to the sixth century B.C. Greek sage Solon.[6] According to Herodotus's story of Solon's conversation with King Croesus, the human beings cited by Solon as having been the happiest, save for one, within his knowledge, were, not Croesus, as Croesus had hoped, but two young men—a pair of brothers —who had died in their sleep at the height of their strength, achievement, and fame, when their mother had prayed to the goddess Hera to bestow on them the best lot that a human being can hope for. The comment that Herodotus puts into Solon's mouth is that the brothers "met with the best possible end that human life can have, and that God took this opportunity for making it manifest that, for a human being, it is better to be dead than to be alive."

"Those whom the gods love, die young."[7] In many military-minded societies, there have been young men who have looked forward, with pride and exaltation, to the prospect of dying prematurely in battle; and it is significant that when, in the seventh and sixth centuries B.C., some Greeks began to transfer their treasure from their community to their own individual lives, the elegiac and lyric poets who gave expression to this psychological revolution harped plaintively on the brevity of the springtime of an individual human being's life, and on the weariness of the long-drawn-out sequel of old age, with its burden of increasing ill health and debility.[8]

However, in this age and in all subsequent ages of ancient Greek history, the Greeks continued to be enthralled by the Homeric epics. These were probably composed, or given their final form, in the eighth century B.C., and the hero of the *Iliad,* Achilles, is not at all reconciled to his foreknowledge that he is doomed to die young, nor does his mother the goddess Thetis take satisfaction, as some Spartan human mothers did in later times, in the prospect of her son's dying young on the field of honor. Young though he still is at the siege of Troy, Achilles has already had time to win matchless glory by his outstanding prowess. But the fame that Achilles has already achieved in a short life does not console him for death's imminence; and his experience after death, in the realm of the shades of the dead, justifies posthumously his reluctance, while alive, to lose his life prematurely. In the eleventh book of the *Odyssey,* his shade is represented as saying to Odysseus that the lot of an agricultural laborer who is the serf of a pauper in the land of the living is preferable to being king of all the dead,[9] and, after making this bitter observation, he strides away, unresigned and indignant, though elated at the same time by the news, given him by Odysseus, of the military prowess of his son.[10]

The repining at the prospect of an early death which is attributed to Achilles in the *Iliad* may have corresponded to the average Greek young man's attitude in real life—even a young man who happened to have been born a Spartan and to have been conditioned by being brought up under the "Lycurgan" regimen. If his mother took the stand of the legendary Spartan mother, his private reaction may have been a wry one. At Sparta, and, *a fortiori,* in other Greek city-states, there is much evidence that the Greeks, even those who paid lip service to pessimism, got much enjoyment out of life; were not eager to exchange it for death; and did not let the edge be taken off their enjoyment by brooding on a death for which they were in no hurry. The Greeks enjoyed passing the time of day in each other's company, discussing anything and everything; they enjoyed beauty; and they had a genius for bringing these two sources of enjoyment together in choral singing and dancing, theatrical performances, religious processions, and talkative political assemblies.

Compared with Greek pessimism, Indian pessimism has been radical, and it has also been sincere, as is demonstrated by the single-mindedness and the austerity with which it has been put into action. Hinduism regards man's universe as being an illusion; the Buddha, anticipating some of the schools of modern Western psychologists by about twenty-four centuries, held that the soul is an illusion too. He saw in the human psyche only a fleeting series of discontinuous psychological states, which are held together only by desire, and which can be dissipated if and when desire is extinguished. In the Buddha's view, the extinction of desire is the proper goal of human endeavor, because the achievement of this brings with it the extinction of suffering, and, for the Buddha, life and suffering were synonymous. Not death, but rebirth, is the arch-ordeal for a human being. The Buddha took it for granted that the effect of desire, precipitated in the form of karma (the cumulative spiritual effects of action taken in a succession of lives up to the present), is to keep a series of rebirths going *ad infinitum*, unless and until, in one of the lives in this chain, the sufferer, by successfully performing the strenuous spiritual exercises that the Buddha has prescribed, manages to bring the series to an end by attaining the state of extinguishedness (nirvana) in which all passion is spent and rebirth ceases because it is no longer brought on by the momentum of karma, now that karma has been worked off. In this spiritual struggle to attain nirvana, death (i.e., the death of the current life in the series) is an unimportant incident. Nirvana may be attained at death, but it may also be attained while the former sufferer is still living what will now have been the last of his successive lives.

One index of pessimism is suicide. In a society in which life is rated at so low a value that death is held to be the lesser evil, suicide will be held to be one of the basic human rights, and the practice of it will be considered respectable and in some cases meritorious or even morally obligatory.

In the Graeco-Roman world, no stigma was attached to suicide, though the practice of it was not so common as it has been in South and East Asian countries in which the prevailing religions and philosophies have been of Indian or Chinese origin. There were cases of Greek statesmen who committed suicide in a political impasse. Demosthenes and King Cleomenes III of Sparta are examples. Under the Principate, Roman nobles were in some cases allowed to commit suicide as an alternative to execution. The Greek philosopher Democritus is said by Lucretius to have exposed himself to death voluntarily (perhaps by starvation) when he found that his mental powers were failing.[11] But the Greek spectators were surprised and impressed when Peregrinus Proteus burned himself to death ostentatiously at Olympia.[12] (A modern Western psychologist might have convicted him, as Lucian does, of exhibitionism.) It is possible that Peregrinus may have been influenced by an Indian precedent that could have been within his knowledge. According to the geographer Artemidorus of Ephesus, an Indian who had accompanied an Indian embassy to the Emperor Augustus had burnt himself to death at Athens. Strabo[13] cites Artemidorus as saying that "some Indians do this because they are finding life a burden, while others — of whom this one is an example — do it because they are finding life so good. The idea is that, when everything has gone as one likes, it is time to be off, for fear that, if one lingers, one may be overtaken by something that one does not like."

According to Artemidorus, this particular Indian "leaped on to the pyre, laughing, with nothing on but a loin cloth and with his body well oiled; and his tomb bears the inscription: 'Zarmanochegas, an Indian from Bargosa (Broach), who made himself immortal by following traditional Indian custom'."

In Hindu society the commonest form of suicide has been *sati*. It used to be deemed a meritorious act for a widow to burn herself to death when her husband died; and, though *sati* was nominally voluntary, it seems often to have been committed under pressure. A widower was under no reciprocal obligation; but male devotees used to throw themselves under the wheels of Juggernaut's car to be crushed to death. In present-day Vietnam, Buddhist monks and nuns have committed suicide by burning themselves as a political protest. In China under the imperial regime, a censor who had felt it to be his official duty to present a memorial to the Emperor, criticizing the Emperor's conduct, might follow up this act by committing suicide—a reconciliation of sincerity with loyalty that would increase the pressure on the Emperor while releasing the censor himself from embarrassment. In Japan, it has been a point of honor to commit suicide, not only as a political protest, but as a sign of respect for a defunct emperor or as atonement for some failure in duty, or for some breach of etiquette, which, in a Westerner's eye, would be a quite inadequate ground for making such drastic and such irrevocable amends, even if the Western observer had no objection to suicide in principle.

There have been cases in which Jews, Phoenicians, and Lycians have committed suicide *en masse* rather than allow themselves to be taken prisoner by a victorious enemy. On the other hand, Christians, whose religion is of Jewish origin, have always felt an inhibition against committing suicide, and have branded a suicide as a *felo de se*, who has debarred himself, by his crime, from being given burial in consecrated ground. The Christian's view of this world as being "a vale of tears" is much the same as the Buddhist's view; but the Christian, unlike the Buddhist, does not consider that he has the right to decide for himself to put an end to his life. For the Christian, this is not man's prerogative; it is God's; and it is impious wilfully to anticipate God's action. If this is a Christian superstition—and it is a superstition in Greek, Roman, Hindu, Buddhist, Confucian Chinese, and Japanese eyes—it is a Christian tradition that dies hard. At the present day, many ex-Christians, who have abandoned almost all the rest of the Christian tradition, still retain the Christian feeling that suicide is shocking.

In a community of Australian natives who live by food gathering and migrate, in search of food, in an annual orbit, the aged will voluntarily drop out and stay behind to die, in order to relieve the community of the burden of continuing to maintain them. In the present-day Western world the average expectation of life has been increased, without any accompanying increase in zest or relief from pressure, while the loosening of family ties has left many old people out in the cold, socially and spiritually. If they had been Australian natives, they would have allowed themselves to die; if they had been Chinese peasants, there would have been a place for them in the home, with their children and grandchildren, as long as they remained alive. Being Christians or ex-Christians, and therefore feeling the traditional Christian inhibition against committing suicide, many old people in the Western world today linger on, lonely and unhappy, until medical ingenuity ceases to be able to keep them physically alive.

The Christian inhibition against suicide applies *a fortiori,* to giving to incurably and painfully ailing human beings the merciful release that humane Christians give, as a matter of course, to animals when these are in the same plight. Hitler was not prevented by the conscience of the German Christian public from murdering millions of Jews; yet the German Christian conscience that did not prove effective for deterring Hitler from committing the crime of genocide did make it impossible for Hitler to carry out his plan of killing off aged, infirm, and feeble-minded Germans in order to relieve physically and mentally fit Germans of the burden of continuing to look after the unfit when Geman energies were being mobilized by Hitler for the waging of the Second World War.

(c) *Attempts to circumvent death by physical countermeasures.* One of the commonest primitive assumptions regarding death is that a dead person's life can be prolonged after death by providing the corpse with the food, drink, paraphernalia, and services that were formerly at the disposal of the person whose living body this corpse once was. The burial with the dead of objects that are useful to the living has been a worldwide practice. Archaeologists have been able to reconstruct a culture from the contents of graves in sites which there has been little or no trace left of the apparatus used by the living. Ancient tombs have been preserved in far greater numbers than ancient dwellings once inhabited by the living. Besides yielding up tools, weapons, ornaments, and clothes, some tombs have been found to contain the remains of slaughtered domestic animals and of human servitors, whose services the dead owner of the tomb was expected still to be able to command.

This naive strategy for circumventing death was carried to extremes in Ancient Egypt. If the tomb representing a dead pharaoh's house was magnified to the dimensions of a gigantic pyramid, if the furniture deposited in his tomb was as lavish in both quantity and quality as the gear that was buried with Tutankhamen; and if the tomb was endowed with lands whose revenues would pay, in perpetuity, for the provision of victuals and for the performance of ritual by priests, it was felt that death could be counteracted and overcome by this massive application of physical countermeasures—in fact, by sheer physical force. Still more naive was the assumption that preserving a dead body by arresting its natural decay was tantamount to keeping the life in it. Mummification was practiced not only in Egypt but in Peru. The dryness of the climate in both coastal Peru and Upper Egypt was an assistance to the embalmer's work, yet this fine art was manifestly just as incapable of keeping life in a corpse as the Zoroastrian practice of exposing corpses to putrefy until they have been consumed by scavenging birds and beasts.

Another strategy for the circumvention of death by physical countermeasures has been to seek for the tree of life or for the elixir of immortality. But the fruitlessness of this quest has been recognised in mythology. When Adam and Eve had eaten of the fruit of the Tree of Knowledge, they were expelled from the Garden of Eden by the angel with the flaming sword before they had had time to baffle Yahweh by eating the fruit of the Tree of Life as well. Translated into present-day prosaic terms, this myth signifies that man's acquisition of science and technology has not enabled him to acquire immortality as well. The outcome of the Sumerian hero Gilgamesh's quest for immortality was likewise ironical. After performing a series of Herculean labors, Gilgamesh was on the last stage of his journey home with a branch of the Tree of Life in his hand when he accidentally dropped this into the water, where it was immediately snapped up by a snake. So Gilgamesh arrived home still mortal. His labors had, after all, been in vain.

The futility of trying to circumvent death by taking physical countermeasures was demonstrated dramatically in Ancient Egypt at the fall of the Old Kingdom. The fall of this regime was accompanied by a social revolution in the course of which the tombs of the pharaohs and of their courtiers were rifled and the funerary wealth accumulated in the course of three-quarters of a millennium was impudently plundered. The irony of this ignominious end of such careful and elaborate physical provision for the circumvention of death is one of the themes of surviving Egyptian works of literature written in the age of the Middle Kingdom. Yet this recognition of the futility of the practice did not deter succeeding generations from persisting with it, and the principal beneficiaries of the costly furnishing of Egyptian pharaohs and nobles came to be, not the dead themselves, but living tomb robbers. Tomb robbing became as fine an art as mummification. The robbers penetrated the most massive and most cunningly contrived defences and eluded the watchful eye of the public authorities. They battened on the Egyptian people's invincible naiveté. Yet it is conceivable that the robbers themselves were not altogether immune from the prevailing superstition. We can imagine them going about their professional business with mixed feelings of cynicism and guilt.

(d) *Attempts to circumvent death by winning fame.* Though a dead body cannot be kept alive by physical measures, the memory of the dead, as they were when they were truly alive, can be transmitted to succeeding generations. In an illiterate society the main media of commemoration are the memorization of genealogies and the composition and recital of oral poetry.

When a society has become literate, poetry can be reduced to writing and can be supplemented by inscriptions engraved on stone or impressed on clay tablets or written on papyrus or parchment or paper or palm leaves or slivers of bamboo, to record the foundation of temples and the annals of reigns. These official records, in turn, can be raised to the level of biographies and historical works of literature which can take their place side by side with poetry.

This attempt to circumvent death by commemoration is more sophisticated than the attempt to circumvent it by physical measures; but the outcome of this attempt is ironical too in ways of its own. For instance, the recorder eventually wins greater fame than the men of action whose fame has been preserved by the recorder's pen. Most of what we know about the Athenian statesman Pericles and the Spartan soldier Brasidas today is due to the fact that a minor naval commander, Thucydides, was given the leisure for becoming a major historian thanks to his having been cashiered and exiled, perhaps unfairly, for having failed to prevent Brasidas from capturing Amphipolis. When Horace wrote "non omnis moriar,"[14] he underestimated the length of the time after his death during which his poetry would preserve the memory of the poet himself. He reckoned that his poetry would continue to be read as long as the ritual of Rome's official religion continued to be performed. This ritual was suppressed by the intolerant Christian Roman Emperor Theodosius I in the last decade of the fourth century of the Christian Era, only four centuries after the date of Horace's death. Yet Horace's poetry is still being read in the twentieth century by readers whose mother tongue is not Latin, and, in the earlier decades of the nineteenth century, it was still being quoted in speeches made in English by members of the parliament at Westminster.

Horace himself, however, has pointed out the precariousness of this circumvention of death by commemoration — sophisticated and ethereal though this method is by comparison with the naive circumvention of death by physical measures.

> Vixere fortes ante Agamemnona
> multi; sed omnes illacrimabiles
> urgentur ignotique longa
> nocte, carent quia vate sacro.[15]

The relics of Agamemnon's predecessors who are not commemorated in the Homeric epic have now been disinterred by modern archaeologists. They have proved to have been mightier monarchs than Agamemnon himself, and whether or not they employed court poets whose works have not yet come to light, we have now retrieved some of their records—not romantic minstrels' lays but prosaic official inventories, corresponding to what present-day governments call "forms." These pre-Agamemnonian Mycenaean official documents are at least four or five centuries older than the *Iliad* and the *Odyssey*, and we have specimens of rudiments of the Sumerian cuneiform script that date from before the close of the fourth millennium B.C. but mankind's first five millennia of literacy are dwarfed by the dark night of the preceding million years during which our ancestors were already human yet have not left any surviving memorial except their tools and their cave paintings—and even those Late Palaeolithic paintings are estimated to be not more than about thirty thousand years old. Our thousand past millennia of oblivion are a long span of time, compared to our subsequent 30,000 years of pictorial commemoration and 5000 years of literacy. But mankind's first million years, as well as his latest 5000 years, are dwarfed by the span of 2000 million years which is reckoned to be the expectation of life on the surface of this planet. It is difficult to imagine that any existing works of man, either monumental or literary, will have survived until the day when this planet becomes no longer habitable. Will any of the now current languages then still be intelligible? Will any works written in these still survive? Will not the pyramids, and the still more durable tumuli and railway embankments, have been worn down flatter than the most archaic of the rocks that now crop out on the earth's surface?

(e) *Self-liberation from self-centeredness by putting one's treasure in future generations of one's fellow human beings.* Another way in which human beings have sought to reconcile themselves to the fact of death has been so ubiquitous and so constant that one might almost venture to infer that it is innate in human nature. Down to this day, since the earliest date to which our surviving records reach back, most human beings have reconciled themselves, to some extent, to their mortality as individuals by putting their treasure in their descendants, while some human beings have expanded their concern to embrace all the other representatives of future generations who, though not their physical descendants, will be their successors and will perhaps be their spiritual heirs.

In the genealogy in the eleventh chaper of the Book of Genesis, the high point in the life of Shem and each of his successive descendants is his age when his first child is born. The remainder of his life, from that red-letter day onwards, till his death, is represented implicitly as being an anticlimax.

In Yahweh's successive promises to Abraham, the god never promises his human client personal immortality. What he promises him is progeny. "I will make of thee a great nation";[16] "I will make thy seed as the dust of the earth, so that, if a man can number the dust of the earth, then shall thy seed also be numbered";[17] "look now toward heaven and tell the stars, if thou be able to number them: and he said unto him, so shall thy seed be";[18] "thou shalt be a father of many nations";[19] Abraham shall surely become a great and mighty nation";[20] "in multiplying I will multiply thy seed as the stars of the heaven, and as the sand which is upon the sea shore."[21] Whether or not this prospect of becoming the ancestor of the Hebrew peoples reconciled Abraham to the prospect of his own death, it is evident that the promises that were held to have been made to Abraham by Yahweh were felt, by the authors and editors of the Book of Genesis, to be more valuable and more satisfying than any promise of personal immortality would have been. If the Israelite writers of these passages believed that, after death, the shades of the dead retained a shadowy existence in Sheol, they will have shared the feelings of the author of the eleventh book of the *Odyssey,* who, as has been remarked earlier, describes the shade of Achilles as exulting, in Hades, at the news of his son's prowess on earth, unreconciled though Achilles himself was to his own state after death.[22]

It is significant that the belief in the resurrection of the dead did not gain a foothold in the Jewish community until the second century B.C. This belief seems to have been introduced to the Jews through their becoming acquainted with a foreign religion, Zoroastrianism. One of the considerations that led some Jews to believe, from the second century B.C. onwards, in the eventual resurrection of some individuals is thought to have been their confidence in Yahweh's sense of justice. They will have felt that this was bound to move Yahweh to reward those Jews who had suffered martyrdom in resisting the Seleucid Emperor Antiochus IV's attempt to coerce the Palestinian Jewish community into adopting the Greek way of life; and these martyrs would not be adequately rewarded if they were not eventually raised from the dead to become living participants in the messianic kingdom when this was eventually established. The belief that, not only the Jewish martyrs, but all the dead, were destined to rise again seems, in the development of Judaism, to have come later.

It is also significant that this addition of a new article to the traditional corpus of Jewish beliefs was not accepted immediately by the Jewish people as a whole. It was adopted, at first, by the Pharisees only. It was rejected by the Sadducees on the ground that there was no warrant for it in the written Mosaic Law, and that the written law alone was valid. The Pharisees were originally dissenters; the Sadducees represented the "establishment." The Sadducees were in control of the temple at Jerusalem, and held at least the key posts in the officiating priesthood. The Sadducees maintained their dominant position in the Palestinian Jewish community, and persisted in their rejection of the belief in resurrection of the dead, until the destruction of the temple in A.D. 70. It was only after this that the Pharisees' hitherto controversial belief became part of the orthodox faith of the Jewish people as a whole; and, among the Jews, this general adoption of the belief in the resurrection of the dead has not weakened the desire for the continuous survival of the Jewish people as a community that perpetuates itself from generation to generation of the mortal men and women who are its successive ephemeral representatives.

The pre-Pharisaic Israelites and Jews were not peculiar in reconciling themselves to the prospect of death by taking comfort in the prospect that their race would be perpetuated in their descendants. A prospect that has caused greater anxiety and distress than the prospect of death has been the prospect of dying without being survived by any descendants. According to the Book of Genesis,[23] Abraham felt that Yahweh's announcement that he was going to be Abraham's "exceeding great reward" was meaningless so long as Yahweh suffered Abraham to go childless; and this passionate desire to have descendants, that is attributed to Abraham in this passage, has been widespread. It has been particularly strong in societies, such as the Hindu and the Chinese, in which it has been held to be important for a human being that, after his death, he should be commemorated and venerated in a cult performed by a surviving son and by this son's descendants in their turn.

Where the cult of ancestors is practiced, this is evidence of a concern about what is going to happen after one's own death, but this concern may not be solely a concern for the perpetuation of the race; it may be partly self-centered. The ancestor who has demanded the cult has presumably sought commemoration for himself in the belief that this will have some posthumous value for him; the descendant who performs the cult may be moved to undertake this burden not only by love of a parent or by a feeling of piety toward a more remote ancestor, but also by a belief that dead ancestors have it in their power to benefit or injure their descendants, and that it is therefore advisable for their descendants to give them satisfaction by carrying on the cult. Abraham's longing to have a child is not un-self-regarding either. He points out to Yahweh that, if he dies childless, the heir who will inherit his estate will be, not one of his own kinfolk, but "one born in my house," i.e. a child of one of Abraham's slaves."[24]

This self-regarding aspect of the desire to be survived by a legitimate successor is likely to be prominent in cases in which the estate that the present holder of it will leave behind him at death does not consist just of private property, such as Abraham's flocks and herds, but is the succession to the throne of a kingdom. In this case, no doubt, the self-regarding desire to be succeeded by a descendant may be accompanied by a concern for the public welfare. The reigning sovereign may forebode that, if no near kinsman of his survives to succeed him, his own death may be followed by a dispute over the succession that might give rise to disorder. If the reigning sovereign has imposed on his subjects reforms that are radical and controversial, and if he is conscious that his own ability and willpower have been the principal agencies by which his reforms have been instituted and have been maintained, his desire that his lifework shall outlast his own lifetime may be stronger than his desire that his successor shall be one of his descendants.

The classic case is Peter the Great's treatment of his son and heir Alexei. After disinheriting Alexei, Peter had him flogged to death. One of Peter's motives for committing this dreadful and unnatural crime was a personal antipathy that was mutual; but Peter was also moved by concern for the future public welfare of the Russian state and people, and this concern of Peter's was justified by facts. Alexei was not, by nature, a man of action; he hated being involved in public affairs and was incompetent in them, and he was under the influence of people who were opposed to Peter's reforms and who would have pressed Alexei to undo these if Alexei had survived Peter and had succeeded him. Posterity will agree with Peter that, for Russia, this would have been a calamity.

The extreme step taken by Peter to ensure that the reforms which he had carried out in Russia should not be undone after his death brings out the truth that it is difficult to feel concern for the future welfare of posterity without also trying to give practical effect to this concern by taking steps to influence or even determine what shall happen after one's death insofar as this lies in one's power. If one feels concern for posterity, one will have one's own ideas about what is going to be beneficial for or detrimental to posterity, and one will then be moved to try to ensure the welfare of these future generations as one sees it, and to secure them against suffering harm as one sees that too. Heads of states who have a lifelong tenure of office are, of course, not the only people whose concern for posterity may incline them to try to make their power last longer than their own lifetime by fixing, while they are still alive, what shall happen after they are dead. This possibility also arises whenever any private person makes his or her will, especially if the testator is making bequests, not only to kinsmen and friends of his, but to religious, educational, or charitable institutions. The exercise, by the dead, of this posthumous power has been found so burdensome for posterity that, in some countries, legislation has been enacted that limits a testator's freedom to dispose of his property altogether as he chooses.

However, neither private testators nor rulers with a lifelong tenure have been so successful in governing the life of posterity as the founders of the historic philosophies and higher religions. Hundreds of millions of human beings who are alive at this moment are being swayed, on many issues, great and small, by the commandments and precepts of Marx, Muhammad, Saint Paul, Jesus, the Buddha, Confucius, and the redactors of the Pentateuch. The posthumous power of these spiritual authorities has been, and continues to be, incomparably great. Yet the exercise of this posthumous spiritual power has its ironical aspect.

Some of the authentic commandments and precepts of these religious leaders were drafted and promulgated by them on the spur of the moment for dealing with some urgent but local and temporary situation. Cases in point are Saint Paul's epistles and the chapters of the Qur'an that were issued by the Prophet Muhammad when he was the head of the government of the city-state of Medina. Both Muhammad and Paul would probably have been disconcerted if they could have foreseen how literally and earnestly even the most casual of their pronouncements were going to be taken by millions of devout posthumous adherents of theirs, and this for hundreds of years to come. There are other zealously obeyed commandments and precepts and statements that have been attributed falsely to the religious leader whose name has lent them their authority, and some of these might have shocked their alleged authors. What would Jesus, for instance, have felt if he could have foreseen that, after his death, his followers were going to worship him, in company with Yahweh and with the Holy Spirit, as one of the members of a divine trinity? On the evidence of the Gospels themselves, Jesus was an orthodox Jew. He is reported to have said to an enquirer: "Why callest thou me good? There is none good save one: that is God."[25] This saying is likely not only to be authentic but to have been notoriously authentic at the time when the Gospel according to Saint Mark was composed. If it had not been, it would surely have been expurgated; for it is a contradiction, out of Jesus's own mouth, of his posthumous Christian followers' thesis that he was God himself.

Peter's murder of Alexei also brings out, through being an extreme case, the truth that the future generations in whom a living human being can put his treasure may comprise a far wider circle than his own physical descendants. The choice that confronted Peter was not, in itself, a unique one. The reigning occupant of an hereditary office—whether he is the sovereign of a state or the director-in-chief of a family business—may feel obliged to disinherit his son, or some less close kinsman, because he judges him to be unfit to take over the duties of the office and because his conscience tells him that the interests of the realm or the business—i.e., the interests of people who are not his relatives but for whose welfare he is responsible—ought to take precedence over his family obligations to his "kith and kin." The disinheriting of an heir who is his heir by virtue of kinship does not normally require that he should put his disinherited kinsman to death. The Roman emperors Nerva, Trajan, Hadrian, and Antoninus Pius each in turn handed on the imperial office to a successor who was his son only by the legal fiction of adoption, and in doing this they were making the future welfare of the Empire and its inhabitants their paramount concern; but none of them murdered any disinherited kinsman of his, as Peter murdered Alexei. On the other hand Marcus Aurelius did a bad service to the Empire when he departed from the consistent practice of his four immediate predecessors by bequeathing the imperial office to his actual son Commodus. For Commodus was not only incompetent in public affairs and uninterested in them, as Alexei was. Unlike Alexei, Commodus was a vicious character.

Peter the Great's concern for the welfare of future generations embraced a nation that was already a large one, but that was, at the same time, only one among a number, with some of which it was at enmity. Marcus Aurelius's four predecessors' concern embraced the whole population of an empire that was a world-state in the eyes of its rulers and their subjects, in the sense that the Roman Empire contained within its frontiers as much of the contemporary civilised world as was within its inhabitants' ken. Today, anyone who is concerned with the welfare of future generations has to expand his concern not only from his family to his nation, but from his nation to the whole human race. For, in our day, "the annihilation of distance" by the progress of technology has linked together, for good or for evil, the fortunes of all sections of mankind, while the invention of the atomic weapon has put the human species in danger of extinction once again for the first time since, in the Later Paleolithic Age, man definitively got the upper hand over all other living creatures on the face of this planet except bacteria. No doubt, Lord Russell was thinking in these ecumenical terms if he said, as he is reported to have said, that, when one has reached old age, it is important to care immensely about what is going to happen after one is dead.

In the present state of military potency, political tension, and scientific knowledge, this means putting one's treasures in seventy million future generations of mankind which will have come and gone, after the present generation has died off, before the surface of this planet will have ceased to be habitable for living creatures. Can a human being reconcile himself to the fact of death by putting his treasure in future generations of all mankind in these almost unimaginably large numbers? Can the transfer of one's concern from one's own puny self to so vast a posterity give meaning, value, and zest to life and deprive death of its sting?

It may seem audacious to say that posterity on this scale is not something great enough to draw a human being competely out of himself, and so to reconcile him entirely to his foreknowledge that he himself is going to die. Yet to sink one's self-centeredness in a concern for all future generations of one's fellow human beings would be wholly satisfying only if one knew that mankind was the be-all and end-all of the universe. We do not know this; we have no means of discovering whether or not it is the truth; and it seems unlikely to be the truth, considering that our own planet, solar system, and galaxy are only minute fragments of a physical universe whose bounds, if it has any bounds, are beyond the reach of our powers of observation. Moreover, there is, within the psyche of any single human being, a psychic universe that is apparently proving to be at least as vast, in its own medium, as the physical universe is. Furthermore, the psychic universe, the physical universe, and the relation between the two are not self-explanatory; they are mysterious; they can hardly be the ultimate reality. Can a human being get into touch with this ultimate reality? And, if he can, can he reconcile himself to death by entering into eternal communion with the ultimate reality or by merging himself in it?

(f) *Self-liberation from self-centeredness by merging oneself in ultimate reality.* To get into touch with ultimate reality and to merge oneself in it has been an Indian quest. In India, this has been the principal quest of philosophers of all schools for the last 3,000 years at least. Round about the turn of the sixth and fifth centuries B.C., the quest produced a sharp cleavage between two schools which gave different reports of the findings of introspection and consequently worked out different prescriptions for reaching spiritual goals that were perhaps identical.

The adherents of one school reported that, when a human being succeeds in bringing into the light of consciousness the very center of his psyche, he finds there a "dweller in the innermost"—a soul—that is identical with ultimate reality itself. This finding has been expressed in the three words "That art thou"—"that" meaning ultimate reality, and "thou" meaning a human soul. Was the recognition of the identity of "thou" with "that" held to be tantamount to the merging of "thou" in "that"? Possibly it was; for the recognition of the identity is not just an intellectual discovery; it is the consummation of long and hard spiritual travail.

The opposing school was the school founded by the Buddha. The Buddha's findings were quite different from those of his contemporaries, and, so far from being the final consummation of long and hard spiritual travail, they were a fresh starting point for this. The Buddha reported that in the psyche there was no soul; he found there only a series of discontinuous psychic states, held together and kept moving only by the momentum of the karma engendered by desire. His prescription for merging the self in ultimate reality was not to penetrate to the self's core and recognise the identity of ultimate reality with this; it was to stop the flow of psychic states by extinguishing desire—i.e., self-centeredness—thus attaining the state of "extinguishedness" (nirvana).

A present-day Western observer is likely to be more conscious of the common ground of these two opposing Indian schools of thought than of the differences that loomed so large in the minds of their respective Indian initiators. Both schools take it for granted that all sentient beings are doomed to go through a round of rebirths which will continue unless and until, in one of the successive lives, the sufferer succeeds in bringing the series of lives to an end. Both schools hold that rebirth is a far greater evil than death, and that to circumvent rebirth, not to circumvent death, ought therefore to be the supreme goal of human endeavors. Both schools also hold that the spiritual exertions required for attaining this goal are long and hard, though their prescriptions for striving to attain it differ. A human being who adheres to either of these schools of Indian philosophy will have little difficulty in reconciling himself to the fact of death. The fact (taken by him for granted) that death is going to be followed by another rebirth will be this man's nightmare. I have never forgotten the radiant smile that came over the face of a Japanese scholar, Professor Anesaki, when, at a conference held in Kyoto in 1929, he announced: "I am from Tokyo, but also from Kyoto, because I am coming here after I am dead." My guess is that Professor Anesaki's smile was evoked by two thoughts: the thought of the natural beauty of the city that was to cherish his mortal remains, and the thought of the ineffable beauty of nirvana.

(g) *The belief in the personal immortality of human souls.* Hindus believe in a suprapersonal immortality (i.e., in the identity of the essence of a human being's psyche with ultimate reality). Buddhists believe in a depersonalized immortality (i.e., in the possibility of extinguishing the self through self-release from self-centeredness). I have suggested that these two beliefs of Indian origin prove, on analysis, to be more closely akin to each other than they might appear to be at first sight and than they have been held to be in Indian philosophical controversies. A further feature that they have in common is that both alike are more credible than the belief in personal immortality.

It is credible that a human being, in his psychic dimension, may be part and parcel of ultimate reality in its spiritual aspect, and it is demonstrable that, in his physical dimension, the same human being is part and parcel of the universe in the material aspect in which we apprehend the universe with our senses and interpret our sense data in scientific terms. On the other hand, no living human being has ever been able to demonstrate conclusively that he has been in psychic communication with a disembodied human psyche (i.e., with the psyche of a human being whose body was, at the time not alive, but was either a corpse or had decomposed into the chemical elements of which the corpse had consisted at the moment at which it had ceased to be a living body). *A fortiori*, no one has ever been able to demonstrate that he has been in psychic communion with an unembodied human psyche that has never yet been embodied or that has, at the time, been temporarily unembodied in an interval between the successive incarnations (a conception that requires the undemonstrated assumption that a psyche can be, and is, repeatedly reembodied in successive living bodies, human or nonhuman, without losing its identity).

Every living human being whom any other living human being has ever encountered has been a psychosomatic entity; and the life of every one of these human psychosomatic entities, like the life of every other sexual living organism inhabiting this planet, has moved, or is in the course of moving, in the time dimension, on a trajectory which describes a course up from birth through infancy to its prime and from its prime through old age down to death, supposing that the human being in question lives out his or her life to the end of its full natural span, and that this particular life is not cut short prematurely by disease, accident, or violent death inflicted by other human beings in war, by law, or by private enterprise.

Death, whatever its cause and its circumstances may be, is an event in which the former living body becomes a corpse which decays (unless its physical decomposition is artificially arrested), while, at the same moment, the psyche passes out of human ken (i.e. ceases to be in communication with the psyche of any human being who is alive at that moment). It is impossible to conceive of a human body being alive without being associated with a human psyche. It has been found possible to imagine a psyche being alive without being associated with a living body. However, this feat of imagination is so difficult that attempts to work outs its implications in detail have run into incongruities, inconsistencies, incompatibilities, and self-contradictions.

When believers in personal immortality have sought to describe the state of disembodied souls, they have found no way of describing this hypothetical state that does not involve the drawing of some analogy with the psychosomatic life on earth of which we have actual experience. The shade that has been consigned to Sheol or to Hades or the underworld as conceived by the Sumerians and their Akkadian and Babylonian cultural heirs is an enfeebled replica of the now dead person who was once alive in psychosomatic form. In fact, the author of the eleventh book of the *Odyssey* takes it for granted that the only condition on which the living visitor, Odysseus, can put himself into communication with the shades of the dead in their shadowy world is by partially and temporarily reendowing them with a modicum of physical life. In order to enable them to talk to him, Odysseus has first to administer to them a physical stimulant. He gives each of them, in turn, a drink of the blood of nonhuman psychosomatic animals—sheep—which Odysseus has slaughtered for this purpose.[26] As for the privileged minority of the departed who are imagined to be enjoying a blissful existence in the Kingdom of the

West or as a star in heaven (if the departed grandee has been an Egyptian pharaoh), or in Elysium (if he has been a pre-Christian Greek hero), or in Valhalla (if he has been a pre-Christian Scandinavian warrior), these favored few are credited with a vitality that is of a superhuman or even godlike exuberance.

This inability to conceive of disembodied spirits in nonpsychosomatic terms also besets those believers in personal immortality who hold that the destiny of the departed is determined, not by their former rank, but by their former conduct. The torments of the damned in hell are depicted on the walls of Etruscan tombs and of Eastern Orthodox Christian refectories in monasteries on Mount Athos, and are described in Dante's *Divina Commedia,* in crassly physical terms—and some of these imaginary torments are so extreme that no living human being could be subjected to them for more than a few seconds without dying of them, though, incongruously, the disembodied spirits that are believed to be suffering these lethal torments are held to have been made immortal in order that their suffering may be everlasting. There have been a number of different conceptions of the nature of the personal immortality of a disembodied or unembodied soul, but they all have one significant feature in common. In some degree, they all involve some incongruities, inconsistencies, incompatibilities, and self-contradictions.

One conception of the immortality of the soul has been that souls are not only immortal but eternal: i.e., that every soul has been in existence eternally before it ever came to be embodied, and that it will remain in existence eternally after having become disembodied once for all. Of all the divers conceptions of the personal immortality of the soul, this is the one that comes nearest to the Indian conception of a suprapersonal or a depersonalized immortality. This belief was held by some pre-Christian Greeks, but never, so far as we can judge, by more than a small sophisticated minority. Another small minority believed that, at death, the soul was annihilated. The majority probably believed, from the beginning to the end of the pre-Christian age of Greek history, that each human soul comes into existence together with the body with which it is associated in life, and that, after death, it continues, as a shade, to lead, in Hades, a shadowy life of the kind depicted in the eleventh book of the *Odyssey.*

The most prominent of the Greek believers in the eternity of souls were the Pythagoreans (an esoteric semiphilosophical semireligious organized fraternity) and the Orphics (an unorganized and unsophisticated sect). Both these Greek sets of believers in the eternity of souls were also believers in the transmigration of souls from one incarnation to another, and this latter belief is so arbitrary and so peculiar that its simultaneous appearace, in the sixth century B.C., in the Greek world and in India can hardly have been fortuitous. One possible common source is the Eurasian nomad society which, in the eighth and seventh centuries B.C., had descended upon India, Southwestern Asia, the steppe country along the north shore of the Black Sea, and the Balkan and Anatolian peninsulas in one of its occasional explosive *völkerwanderungen.*

A belief in the personal immortality of souls which does not involve a belief in their being eternal as well as immortal is bound up with the attempts, noted already, to circumvent death by physical countermeasures. The pre-Christian and pre-Muslim Egyptians, for instance, believed in the conditional immortality of the souls of the dead—or, strictly speaking, in the conditional immortality of one of the several souls that were believed to appertain to a human being. The particular soul known as "ka" was believed to remain in existence, haunting the dead person's tomb, as long as posterity continued to keep the tomb in proper spiritual condition by performing the requisite ritual there and by providing the requisite supplies of food, drink, clothes, and furniture which were conceived of as being necessities of life after death, as they had been before death. This belief was held simultaneously with the incompatible beliefs that the dead person's soul might have migrated to the Kingdom of the West or might have ascended to heaven to shine there as a star or might have descended into the underworld presided over by the god Osiris.

This Egyptian belief in the conditional immortality of souls after death has also been held, though it has not, in all cases, been worked out so systematically, by all the numerous other peoples that have practiced ancestor worship, e.g., the Chinese.

Three other varieties of a belief in the immortality of souls after death that does not involve a belief in their preexistence before birth or in their eternity have been mentioned already. There has been a belief in a dismal habitation of the souls of the dead, which retain a shadowy existence there. This is the Hebrew Sheol, the Greek Hades, and the Sumerian counterpart of these. There has been a belief in a blissful abode for the souls of dead persons who had been in privileged positions in their lifetime. This is the Egyptian Kingdom of the West and the Kingdom of Heaven, the Greek Elysium, the Scandinavian Valhalla. There has also been a belief in the existence of two alternative destinations for the souls of the dead—destinations that are determined, according to this more ethical belief, not be previous rank, but by previous behavior. The souls of the wicked are consigned, as a punishment, to hell—an everlasting abode which is not merely dismal, as Sheol or Hades is, but is excruciating. On the other hand, the souls of the righteous are admitted, as a reward, to Paradise or heaven—an everlasting abode which is as blissful as Elysium or Valhalla, but which, unlike them, is attained in virtue of previous merits, not of previous rank.

For believers in Hades and Elysium, the consignment of a dead person's soul to the one or the other two alternative abodes is automatic. It is decided by the dead person's former social rank in his lifetime. For believers in hell and heaven, the decision depends on the dead person's conduct during his lifetime; his conduct cannot be assessed without being examined and appraised; and this requires the passing of a judgment by some authority. The belief in a judgment of souls after death is a necessary corollary of the belief in heaven and hell.

This belief in a judgment of souls after death made its appearance at two widely different dates at two far apart places (far apart, that is to say, before the very recent "annihilation of distance"). The belief appeared in Egypt perhaps as early as the age of the Old Kingdom in the third millennium B.C., and it also appeared in Northeastern Iran or in the Oxus-Jaxartes basin round about the turn of the seventh and sixth centuries B.C., i.e., in the lifetime of the Prophet Zarathustra, who was the promulgator of the belief in this region. We We have no evidence as to whether the Egyptian and the Iranian belief in a judgment by which the soul, after death, is consigned either to hell or to heaven had a common historical origin. It is noteworthy, however, that the Egyptian and Iranian beliefs have a further feature in common. The judge of the souls of the dead — Osiris in the one case and Ahura Mazdah in the other — is a good god who has triumphed, or who is going to triumph, in a hard struggle with a wicked god or wicked semidivine being. Osiris, after an initial defeat, has been given an eventual victory over his wicked brother and adversary Seth by the prowess of Osiris's son Horus and by the devotion of his sister and wife Isis. Ahura Mazdah is going to be victorious, eventually, over his wicked adversary Ahriman.

The Egyptian belief in a judgment of souls after death, to determine whether they shall be sent to hell or to heaven, was presumably the source of the same belief in the Greek world in the Hellenic Age. Here it was probably a legacy of Egyptian influence in Crete in the Minoan Age. Osiris, in his capacity of serving as the judge of the souls of the dead, has a Cretan counterpart in Rhadamanthus. In Egypt the pyramid texts, inscribed for the benefit of pharaohs in the age of the Old Kingdom, and the later "Book of the Dead," circulated for popular use, are collections of formulae, spells, and instructions designed to help the dead person's soul find its way successfully to a blissful terminus without falling into any of the pitfalls, traps, and obstacles that will beset the soul in the course of its difficult and dangerous passage. The contents of the Orphic tablets are similar and are designed to serve the same purpose.

In both cases the purpose is practical guidance, not edification, and, in so far as purification enters into it, this is purification in the ritual, not in the ethical, sense. In the pre-Christian Greek picture of hell, Tityus, Sisyphus, Tantalus, and Ixion are four classical representatives of the damned who are suffering everlasting torments. The wall paintings in Etruscan tombs show that the Greek picture of hell made a strong impression on the Etruscans; and it may not be fanciful to guess that there may have been an Etruscan component (preserved in subsequent Tuscan folklore), as well as a Christian component, in the medieval Christian Tuscan poet Dante's lurid description of the torments of the damned in the Christian hell.

The Christian and Muslim conceptions of the judgment of souls after death and of the heaven and the hell to which the souls are consigned respectively, in accordance with the verdict, are evidently derived, in the main, not from the pre-Christian religion of Egypt, but from Zoroastrianism —presumably via Pharisaic Judaism, which—unlike the Sadduccan Judaism of the postexilic Jewish "establishment" in Judea—laid itself open to Zoroastrian influences that played upon Judaism after the incorporation of

Babylonia, Syria, Palestine, and Egypt in the Persian Empire in the sixth century B.C.

In Christian belief the individual judgment of souls immediately after death, and their consignment, immediately after judgment, to hell, limbo, or heaven, coexists with the incompatible belief in the universal judgment of all souls—both the souls of the resurrected dead and the souls of the human beings alive at the moment—when the Last Trump sounds to give the signal for the resurrection of the dead and for "the Last Judgment" of living and of resurrected dead human beings alike.

When the belief in personal immortality is associated with a belief in a judgment after death—a judgment that will consign the dead to either eternal bliss or eternal torment—the price of a human being's belief in the survival of his personality after his death is anxiety during his lifetime.

> For we know Him that hath said, "Vengeance belongeth unto me; I will recompense," said the Lord. And again, "The Lord shall judge his people."
>
> It is a fearful thing to fall into the hands of the living God.[27]

(h) *The belief in the resurrection of human bodies.* A disembodied or unembodied soul is more difficult to imagine than a soul that is associated with a living body in the psychosomatic unity with which we are familiar through our acquaintance with ourselves and with our fellow living human beings. This union of soul with body in a life after death is easier to imagine if it is represented as being a reunion, in which the body with which the soul is now associated is the body — reconstituted, reanimated, and resurrected — with which this soul was associated before soul and body were parted by death and the body consequently became a corpse. On the other hand the reconstitution, reanimation, and resurrection of a corpse is virtually impossible to imagine, considering that, after death, a human body immediately begins to decay and eventually decomposes completely, unless the entrails are removed and the rest of the corpse is preserved artificially by being mummified.

The audience that Saint Paul had attracted at Athens listened to him patiently till he made the statement that God had raised a man from the dead; but this assertion brought the meeting to an end. Some of Paul's listeners laughed, while others, more courteously, told him that they would wait to hear more from him till they found another opportunity.[28] If Paul had stated that Jesus had an immortal soul which had preexisted and would continue to exist eternally, his Greek audience might have been willing to hear him out. Personal immortality of souls was a familiar and not incredible hypothesis for Greeks of Saint Paul's generation, but to be asked to believe in the resurrection of the dead was, for them, tantamount to being given notice by the speaker himself that he was wasting their time by talking nonsense.

Paul might have obtained a better hearing for his declaration of belief in bodily resurrection if he had been preaching in contemporary Egypt; for in

Egypt, since at least as far back in time as the third millennium B.C., it had been believed that one corpse had come to life again—and this after it had been cut up into fourteen pieces that had been scattered and had had to be reassembled. In Egypt this story was told of a god—the god Osiris who, since his own bodily resurrection, had become the judge of souls after death. When Paul told the Athenians that Jesus had been raised from the dead, he referred to Jesus as being a man and said that it was God who had raised him; but at the same time Paul cited this act of God's as evidence that God had appointed Jesus to judge all mankind at a future date that was already fixed,[29] and Paul believed that Jesus was in some sense God, though he did not divulge this belief of his on this occasion. It will be recognized that the role of being a god who is put to death and is resurrected in order to become mankind's judge is attributed to both Osiris and Jesus.

The belief that Jesus has risen from the dead, the belief that he is to judge mankind, and the linking of these two beliefs with each other thus have an Egyptian precedent; but there is also another tenet of Christianity in which a belief in resurrection is linked with a belief in judgment, and this tenet appears to be of Zoroastrian, not Egyptian, origin. According to Christian doctrine, Christ's judgment of mankind is not an *ad hoc* judgment of the souls of the dead individually, immediately after the death of each of us; it is a future judgment of all mankind simultaneously, including the people who will be alive at the time, as well as all those who will have lived and died by then; and the dead will be brought to judgment by a resurrection of their bodies, which will be brought back to life for the occasion and will be reunited with their souls. This belief in the bodily resurrection of all dead human beings is common to Christianity and Islam, and, like the belief in judgment, noted earlier, it seems to have been derived by both religions from Zoroastrianism via Pharisaic Judaism. According to Zoroastrian doctrine, the discrimination between the righteous and the wicked at the last and general judgment is to be made by means of a physical ordeal by fire and molten metal; and this indicates that, according to Zoroastrianism, in accordance with Pharisaic Judaism, Christianity, and Islam, the dead are expected to rise again physically.

Zoroastrianism anticipated Christianity in believing in two judgments: a judgment of each soul individually, immediately after death, and a final judgment of all human beings simultaneously, the dead as well as those alive at the time. This belief is so peculiar and involves such incongruities that there surely must be an historical connection between its appearances in these two different religions: i.e., Christianity must have adopted the belief from Zoroastrianism. Zoroastrianism's priority is indicated, not only by the chronological fact that Zoroastrianism is about six centuries older than Christianity, but also by the connection, in Zoroastrianism, between the belief in a future last and general judgment and the belief in a final and conclusive victory of the good god Ahura Mazdah over the evil spirit Ahriman in the current war between these two spiritual powers. Ahura Mazdah's coming victory over Ahriman is to have the general judgment of mankind as its sequel.

This belief that mankind is to be judged twice over, besides being incongruous—it seems superfluous to recall souls from heaven or hell, as the case may be, to earth in order to have the same verdict passed on them for the second time—also raises the question whether heaven and hell are to be thought of as existing in the psychic dimension or in the physical dimension. The locus of disembodied souls is presumably not physical. Yet the agony and the bliss of the souls of the dead before the general resurrection are depicted in physical imagery; and if, for the last and general judgment, the temporarily disembodied souls of the dead will have been reunited with their resurrected bodies, the heaven and the hell to which they will then be consigned must be physical localities, if the human beings who are sent there after this second judgment have been restored to the psychosomatic state in which they lived on earth before their deaths — not to speak of those who are overtaken, still alive, by the sounding of the Last Trump.

In Christianity and Islam, as in Zoroastrianism, the resurrection of human bodies is associated with a last and general judgment, which will consign —or reconsign—the resurrected dead, and will also consign the living to either heaven or hell. Their common mother religion, Pharisaic Judaism, however, seems—at any rate, to begin with—to have adopted the Zoroastrian belief in bodily resurrection in a version that was less close to the original than the Christian-Muslim version is. In this original Pharisaic Jewish version the resurrection is apparently to be a privilege, not an ordeal. The Jewish martyrs who have given their lives for the Jewish faith and for the Jewish people are to rise again from the dead, not to attend a divine judgment which will consign them either to heaven or to hell, but to participate in the reestablishment on earth of the Kingdom of Judah by "the Lord's Anointed" (the Messiah): a scion of the House of David who will not only reinstate his ancestral kingdom up to its Davidic frontiers, but will transform it into a world-empire that will be the millennial Jewish successor of the successive world-empires of the Assyrians, the Persians, and the Macedonians.

This mundane Jewish adoption of a transcendental Zoroastrian belief brings out the truth that the resurrection of the body does not necessarily imply that the reconstituted psychosomatic human being is going to be immortal. The Messiah himself seems to have been thought of originally as being a mortal man who would be distinguished from his fellow mortals only in being the legitimate Davidic heir to the Kingdom of Judah and in bearing rule over a world-empire that would be still more extensive and more mighty than the realm of the Messiah's ancestor David himself. In the course of nature the Messiah would die, like David and like every one of David's successors and the Messiah's predecessors who, from the tenth to the sixth century B.C. had, each in turn, reigned over the Kingdom of Judah as "the Lord's Anointed," i.e., as the legitimate living representative of the Davidic dynasty. If the Davidic restorer of the Davidic kingdom was destined to be mortal, like his ancestor, the resurrected martyrs would presumably prove to be mortal too. They would be resurrected only to die again eventually —dying, in their exceptional case, for the second time.

It will be seen that, in this first phase, the adoption by the Pharisaic Jews of the Zoroastrian belief in bodily resurrection was subordinated to the traditional Jewish view—expressed in the legend of Yahweh's successive promises to Abraham—that the supreme blessing for a mortal man was to be assured, not of securing personal immortality for himself, but of leaving behind him descendants who would perpetuate his race. It was taken as a matter of course that the Jewish martyrs would be raised from the dead expressly for the purpose of witnessing the eventual military and political triumph of Judah to which they would have contributed by having sacrificed their lives. It was assumed that they would be well content to "depart in peace," together with the Messiah himself, when their eyes had seen God's salvation which He had prepared before the face of all peoples[30] — a salvation that would be the corporate salvation of the Jewish people, and a glory that would be the political glory of a reestablished Jewish state which, this time, would be, not a petty local principality, but a veritable world-empire.

(i) *The hope of heaven and the fear of hell.* A Hindu who, as a result of intense introverted contemplation, has attained, as a personal experience, the intution that the essence of his soul is identical with ultimate reality, has presumably been liberated by this experience from all hopes and fears about either life or death. He has become aware of a truth that assures him of the unimportance of life and of death alike. A Buddhist who has learned that it is possible to make a definitive exit into nirvana from the sorrowful series of rebirths, and who has also been instructed in the strenuous spiritual exercises by means of which this goal may be attained, will be too absorbingly preoccupied with the pursuit of his practical spiritual endeavors to concern himself with either life or death or to entertain either hopes or fears. On the other hand, lively hopes and fears about a human being's destiny after death will be aroused by a belief in personal immortality, whether the believer in this expects to survive everlastingly as a disembodied soul or expects his soul to be reunited, at the sounding of the Last Trump, with his resurrected body, to live on everlastingly thereafter as a reconstituted psychosomatic unity: i.e., as a human being constituted like his own present living self and like the living selves of his contemporaries who, like him, have not yet suffered death.

What is the effect of the belief in personal immortality after death on the feelings, attitude, and conduct of the believer? To what degree, if any, does it influence his behavior while he is alive in the psychosomatic form of life which is the only form of it that is known to us in our experience?

The believer in a conditional personal immortality—an immortality that is dependent on the perpetual performance of rites by the believer's descendants — is likely to suffer anxiety. He will be anxious to make sure both that he is going to leave descendants behind him and that these will have both the will and the means to perform, punctiliously, all that is requisite in order to maintain the immortality of this ancestor of theirs. The believer in a personal immortality in the shadowy realm of Sheol or Hades will repine at the brevity of a human being's full-blooded zestful psychosomatic life on earth—unless, of course, he undergoes so much suffering before death that he comes to contemplate even the bleak prospect of Sheol or Hades with resignation. The grandee who is confident that his own destination is not Sheol or Hades but is Elysium or Valhalla may be nerved by his aristocratic self-assurance to face the prospect of personal immortality after death with equanimity, or even with the pleasurable anticipation with which a Buddhist—the polar opposite of the pagan barbarian warrior—looks forward to his exit into a nirvana in which his personality will have been extinguished.

The believer in a personal immortality which he may be going to spend either in heaven or in hell, according to the verdict that will be passed, after his death, on his conduct while he was alive, ought, if he holds this belief *bona fide*, to be the most anxious of all; and his version of the belief in personal immortality ought to have the greatest effect of all on his present behavior. He is committed to the belief that the credit or debit balance of the account of his good and evil deeds during his brief life on earth is going to decide, once and for all, whether his destiny is to be weal or woe in the everlasting future of sentient personal life that awaits him after death.

In practice, there is in some cases a considerable discrepancy between the belief on the one hand—even when the believer believes himself to be sincere—and the believer's state of mind and behavior on the other hand. I have, for instance, known one believer who was intensely afraid of the prospect of death, though he was conscious of having lived righteously in the main and though he was utterly confident that he was one hundred percent correct in his theological tenets. Logically, he ought to have felt assured that, after death, he would not only go to heaven but would be received there as a VIP. All the same, he was unable to face the prospect of death with equanimity. Conversely, there have been people who have believed that the infallible penalty for the commission of serious sins in this life is condemnation, after death, to everlasting torments in hell, yet who have not been deterred by this belief from committing sins that have been so heinous that, according to the sinner's own belief, his condemnation to suffer everlasting torment in hell will be inescapable.

Such discrepancies between belief and behavior indicate that belief has to be supported by experience if its influence on behavior is to be effective. All beliefs, whatever they may be, that relate to what is going to happen or is not going to happen to a human being after death are, intrinsically beyond the range of experience, and they are perhaps even beyond the range of realistic imagination.

Insofar as the belief in personal immortality after death does captivate a living person's imagination, the believer's mental picture of hell seems generally to be livelier than his mental picture of heaven. The torments of the damned in hell have, on the whole, been depicted and described more vividly than the bliss of the salvaged in heaven. Lucretius, in the third book of his *De Rerum Natura*,[31] in which he is arguing that death spells complete and permanent annihilation, presents this as a consoling thought for the living, because the prospect liberates them from the fear that, after death, they may be condemned to suffer the legendary everlasting torments that are believed, by the credulous, to be being inflicted on the mythical archsinners Tantalus, Tityus, Sisyphus, and Ixion.[32] As Lucretius drives his point home at the close of this passage, it is in this world only that life ever becomes hell, and this only for people who are such fools as to believe in the reality of a life in hell after death.

This fear of hell, which Lucretius is seeking to dispel, is offset, of course, by the hope of reunion, after death, with beloved fellow human beings from whom one has been parted either by dying before them or by surviving them. Bereavement through death is harder to face and to bear than death itself; and the pain of bereavement is mitigated if the separation that death brings with it is believed to be not everlasting but only temporary. The coming reunion is usually pictured as a blissful one in heaven; yet even the torments of hell are eased if they are shared. The most moving passage in Dante's *Inferno* is his depiction of Paolo and Francesca[33] locked in each other's arms in everlasting love as they are swept round together in an everlasting wind of anguish.

Notes

1 Horace, *Odes,* Book I, Ode xi, line 8. Cf. Book I, Ode iv, passim.

2 Isaiah 22:13. Cf. Eccles. 3:22.

3 Herodotus, Book II, chap. 133.

4 *Ibid.,* chap. 78.

5 Sophocles, *Oedipus Coloneus,* lines 1224-26.

6 Herodotus, Book I, chap. 31.

7 Byron, *Don Juan,* IV, xii.

8 E.g., Mimnermus, *Nanno,* Elegies I and II.

9 Homer, *Odyssey,* Book XI, lines 489-491.

10 *Ibid.,* lines 538-540.

11 Lucretius, *De Rerum Natura,* Book III, lines 139-141.

12 Lucian, *De Morte Peregrini.*

13 Strabo, *Geographica,* Book XV, chap. 1, §73 (C.720).

14 Horace, *Odes,* Book III, Ode xxx, line 6.

15 Horace, *Odes,* Book IV, Ode ix, line 25-28. "There were mighty men before Agamemnon—there were any number of them; yet, one and all, these are buried in a long, long night, unknown and unmournable—and this just because they had no inspired bard [to commemorate them, as Agamemnon has been commemorated by Homer]."

16 Gen. 12:2.

17 Gen. 13:16.

18 Gen. 15:5.

19 Gen. 17:4.

20 Gen. 18:18.

21 Gen. 22:17.

22 Homer, *Odyssey,* Book XI, lines 538-540.

23 Gen. 15:2-3.

24 *Ibid.*

25 Mark 10:18.

26 Homer, *Odyssey* Book XI, lines 23-50, 82, 88-89, 98, 153, 232, 390.

27 Heb. 10:30-31.
28 Acts 17:32.
29 Acts 17:31.
30 Luke 2:29-32.
31 Lucretius, *De Rerum Natura,* lines 978-1023.
32 Cf. Homer, *Odyssey,* Book XI, lines 582-600.
33 Dante, *Inferno,* Canto Quinto, lines 73-142.

3. The Biblical Tradition

Milton McC. Gatch

Milton McC. Gatch, Professor of English at the University of Missouri, was educated at Haverford College, Episcopal Theological School, and Yale University. This selection, taken from his book Death: Meaning and Morality in Christian Thought and Contemporary Culture, *presents a brief overview of the Old and New Testament views on death—views that may prove surprising to those who are not students of the Bible.*

On the whole, it can be said of the biblical writings that they have no theology of death or of an afterlife. Both Testaments are radically secular in their overriding concern with history, which is to be understood in both in a very special sense as the self-manifestation of God in human events or as the interpretation and judgment of human events in the light of man's highest aspirations—which the Hebraic tradition viewed as the will of God for men.[1] Concerned with the destiny of a People in history, the writers of Scripture had little to say about the significance of the end of the individual's historical existence and were not motivated to speculate about an extrahistorical survival. Passages which seem to belie this generalization must be read very carefully within the special historical circumstances which gave rise to them. Any effort to understand the biblical view of the nature of death and man's destiny must, in other words, keep constantly in mind the resounding silence of the Bible on the subject in general and be tempered by a very careful interpretation of its few specific statements within their historical contexts.

THE OLD TESTAMENT

The Old Testament records the historical and theological reflections of a People for over a millennium, during which time considerable development and alteration of ideas are observable. Despite their wide divergencies of points of view, nevertheless, the Hebrew writers uniformly approached the question of death in a manner quite different from those of either the Greeks or the moderns.[2]

The prevailing opinion concerning death can be expressed in two ways. One might say either that death was regarded as the termination of human existence or that, because the predominant concern was with the People and its historical destiny, the question of the significance of death for the individual rarely arose and was essentially meaningless. From the point of view of the modern world, which is uniquely concerned with the role and identity of the individual, the former restatement of the biblical approach to death is probably the more congenial; historically, the latter is surely the more accurate.

The concerns of the dying patriarch, Abraham, as related in the Yahwist history, touch upon several of the chief themes in the basic biblical understanding of death:

> Abraham was now old, advanced in years; and Yahweh had blessed Abraham in everything.
>
> Abraham said to the senior servant of his household, who had charge of all his possessions, "Place your hand under my thigh, and I will make you swear by Yahweh, God of heaven and God of the earth, that you will not obtain a wife for my son from the daughters of the Canaanites among whom I dwell, but will go to the land of my birth to get a wife for my son Isaac . . . On no account are you to take my son back there! Yahweh God of heaven, who took me from the home of my father and the land of my birth, and who solemnly promised me, saying, "I will give this land to your offspring' — he will send his angel before you that you may bring my son a wife from there . . ." So the servant placed his hand under the thigh of his master Abraham and swore to him concerning this matter. (Gen. 24:1-9)[3]

This account of the death of Abraham is a passage from the Yahwist epic of the history of the Hebrew peoples. The writer of this great narrative was concerned to set out the historical framework within which the present state of the kingdom of Judah was to be understood. He believed that by telling of the nomadic patriarchs, the tribal confederacy, and the emergence of the Davidic kingship, he could explain how it had come to pass that a tribal people had prospered among the other peoples of the ancient Near East, whose cultures and religions contrasted markedly with those of the worshipers of Yahweh. For the Yahwist historian, in other words, history supplanted myth as the means of explaining the meaning of the experience of the People.[4] The account of the life of Abraham holds a pivotal place among the earlier chapters of this epic of the People's history, and the treatment of the death of the patriarch typifies the essential concerns of earlier Hebraic thought in dealing with the termination of life.

At the end of his full and prosperous life, Abraham remembered that one task remained unfinished. He had not provided for the continuation of his line beyond the next generation. Thus, his dying act[5] was to cover this oversight. One can hardly say that he was motivated to this ultimate intervention in Isaac's affairs, after the manner of the dying patriarch of the modern novel, either by a generous desire to see that his son would be cared for when the father was no longer there to oversee his activities or by a malicious compulsion to continue his parental tyranny even in death. Rather, he wanted to see that the achievements of his lifetime would be continued; and this could only be done through Isaac and his progeny.

Abraham believed that he had come to live among the Canaanites through the intervention of Yahweh and that this settlement was not a matter of a generation or two but a permanent one. The Yahwist historian stresses this conviction again and again, but chiefly by means of the quotation of the promise of the "God of heaven and God of the earth." The promise is stated not in terms of Abraham himself but in terms of his "offspring." In other words, the patriarch conceives of the meaning of his life not in terms of his own accomplishments but in terms of the fulfillment of the promise he had received. He is not to be regarded as a remarkable man of unusual and significant achievements but as an actor in the continuing processes of purposeful historical development. He will remain important only insofar as what he has begun in his lifetime is continued in the history of his offspring. He will assume a place in the genealogies of his people and will remain a vital link in the chain which is being forged in the history of the People. The unusual oath which Abraham makes the servant swear upon his genitals probably underlines this general point of view.[6] In those who proceed from his thighs, both his life and his death assume significance.

There is no attempt (indeed, it is not possible) to speak in individual terms for Abraham, for the Hebraic mind does not conceive of the situation as we do. There is no way to separate Abraham from the clan he produces. Even his personality is indistinct from that of the tribe. Thus, one can only speak anachronistically of his death as an end since, even dead, Abraham continues to be an important aspect of the corporate personality. Such was also the meaning of the priestly historian who, in his account of the death of the patriarch (Gen. 25:8), says, "he was gathered to his kin." Like his predecessors, the man who dies becomes one of the fathers, a name in the genealogical list; and as such he never ceases to be a part of the continuing story of the People.[7]

This frame of mind made quite inconceivable the question of an individual afterlife and probably contributed to the fact that Hebrew thought never developed a notion of a soul or life-force which is separable from the historical man.[8] At the same time, the general Old Testament conceptualization is both different from and more profound than the Greek view of political immortality. The Greek notion seems to have been that immortality was earned through one's contribution to the state and that the locus of immortality was in the collective memory of the state. The Hebrew understanding is at once more primitive and more organic. Personality and identity are terms which attach not to the person but to the People; thus, when one dies, personality and identity are not disrupted, for the People continues. Only the possibility that one's line may not be fruitful gives rise to anxiety in the face of death.

In a general way, the kind of view expressed by the Yahwist historian persevered throughout the period of Old Testament writing. The concept of corporate personality tended to be refined (some might say, refined away), but the tradition refrained from assigning to death more than physiological significance and continued to regard the People as the locus both of continuity and of the ultimate meaning of life.

After the fall of the Israelite kingdoms and the period of the exiles, nevertheless, the historical situation of the Jews gave rise to a quite different formulation of the relationship between Yahweh and his People. No longer a member of a nation chosen from among the peoples of the world to fulfill a special calling, the Jew now found himself "essentially an *individual* adrift in the cosmos."[9] The older literature was canonized and reinterpreted so as to provide guidelines for the Jew in this dilemma, and new forms of religious writing emerged to give similar guidance and encouragement.

Chief among these kinds of writings are those of the Wisdom School. Most of the motifs of this literature are found elsewhere in the traditions of the ancient Near East, and they were not unknown to the Hebraic world before the fall of the kingdoms. But the Wisdom tradition came into its own as a theological and literary approach to the problems raised by the new historical situation of the Jews. Psalm 137 is the classic depiction of that situation: the People are captives in an alien land, longing for the familiar ways of Jerusalem (the ways whose importance had been explained by the Yahwist and other epics of the emergence of the People) and not knowing how to worship their God in the foreign place. The situation necessitated a new formulation of the religion (which we know as Judaism) which would guide the individual by instruction and by example and enable him to maintain his integrity in the face of his aloneness in the cosmos.

Thus it is that the Wisdom literature is characterized both by a prescriptiveness which stresses the manner in which the wise man will react to his situation and by a resignation which counsels him to keep the faith in the face of adversity. In its approach to the phenomenon of death, the Wisdom school generally maintained the realism of the Yahwist historian. But the historical hopes of the Yahwist have been dashed: the People is no longer a nation whose emergence and reason for being need to be explained; the individual finds himself without a nation and seeks to understand the nature of his dependence upon Yahweh. Since he has no new picture of the meaning of death, the Wisdom writer tends to counsel resignation and trust in the face of death and other adversities, as in Job. Only occasionally did the school tend toward bitterness over the prospect of the end of life, as in Ecclesiastes and (more characteristically) Psalm 88.

The same phenomena which gave currency to the Wisdom literature gave rise to the apocalyptic literature in which pseudonymous wise men revealed the secrets of the future inbreaking of the divine realm upon the sphere of human life in order to save men. In the book Daniel,[10] for example, the central figure is portrayed as a wise man living among foreigners but strictly adherent to the law of his People. The visions of Daniel reveal that the Son of man will come from the heavenly to the human realm for the purpose of redeeming the latter and counsel the faithful to suffer martyrdom rather than gainsay the commandments and lose their place among the elect.

One of the characteristic teachings of apocalyptic literature (based ultimately upon extrapolations from certain of the exilic and postexilic prophetic books) is the doctrine of resurrection. Whereas Ezekiel, in the vision of the valley of the dry bones (chapter 37), had spoken metaphorically of the restoration of the nation from its deathlike desolation, the writer of Daniel speaks of the resurrection of those Jews who have died in the interim between the collapse of the kingdoms and the forthcoming revival through Yahweh's agency. But this is not his only innovation. Influenced by the priestly notion that salvation depends upon one's adherence to the law (a notion which also tends to undermine the concept of corporate personality), the author also foresees a judgment of those who are raised: "And many of those who sleep in the dust of the earth shall awake, some to everlasting life, and some to shame and everlasting contempt. And those who are wise shall shine like the brightness of the firmament; and those who turn many to righteousness, like the stars for ever and ever" (Dan. 12:2-3 RSV).

Daniel does not, it must be noted, base this hope of a postmortem life upon some notion of the nature of man but upon his faith that, in the divine economy, wisdom and virtue must be rewarded. And he can only conceive of this life as a corporate one within a restored and transformed Israel. His view is radically new, but it is also clearly continuous with the traditions of his heritage. It amounts to saying that one's life is not in vain if it is virtuous because, like the life of Abraham and others before, it has its meaning and continuation in the ongoing history of the People. To be dead or with one's kin is not to have become nothing, for the People will be restored. In this sense, Daniel simply reaffirms the tradition in which the Preacher had seen no grounds for continued confidence. Death gave no more grounds for anxiety to Daniel than to Abraham.[11]

THE NEW TESTAMENT

Much of New Testament teaching[12] concerning death developed from the apocalypticism of the Old Testament and the Apocrypha. Yet, it is a mistake to say that Jesus' teaching follows the spirit of apocalyptic eschatology, which tended to point to the exact time when the divine, restorative intervention might be expected.[13] Rather, Jesus maintained a careful tension between present and future: his proclamation of the imminent futurity of the Kingdom of God, combined with his assertions of the power and significance of his own work, is meant to state that "he who will bring in the Kingdom of God in the future has appeared in the present in Jesus himself, and in him the powers of the coming eon are already at work . . ."[14] Thus, more than that of the apocalyptic school, Jesus' eschatology is unconcerned with speculation concerning the meaning of death or the future destiny of the person.

There is, indeed, no passage in the synoptic Gospels in which Jesus discourses explicitly on the subject of death. The questions which we characteristically ask about the subject simply did not occur to him or to those who gathered his sayings. It is possible, however, to deduce certain aspects of his attitude on the matter of death from several discourses whose chief subjects were quite different. In the following passage, for example, the intent of Jesus' interlocutors was to confound him by posing an impossible and hypothetical legal question:

> "Teacher, Moses wrote for us that if a man's brother dies and leaves a wife, but leaves no child, the man must take the wife, and raise up children for his brother. There were seven brothers; the first took a wife, and when he died left no children; and the second took her, and died, leaving no children; and the third likewise; and the seven left no children. Last of all the woman also died. In the resurrection whose wife will she be? For the seven had her as wife."
>
> Jesus said to them, "Is not this why you are wrong, that you know neither the scriptures nor the power of God? For when they rise from the dead, they neither marry nor are given in marriage, but are like angels in heaven. And as for the dead being raised, have you not read in the book of Moses, in the passage about the bush, how God said to him, 'I am the God of Abraham, and the God of Isaac, and the God of Jacob'? He is not God of the dead, but of the living; you are quite wrong." (Mark 12:18-27 RSV)[15]

Despite the fact that this passage is concerned with a question of legal interpretation, rather than an expostulation on the meaning of death, it will suit our present purpose of examining Jesus' attitude toward death. He does not speak on the subject directly or because death as a topic interests him. Rather it arises as an incident of an effort to entrap him in heretical teaching. He and the Sadducees are agreed on one point: that human life is to be conceived as a unitive phenomenon in which the physical and that which animates the physical (the Greeks would have called it spirit or soul) are inseparable. No more than the Abraham of the Yahwist historian can Jesus or his interlocutors imagine that body and soul are separable or that, as Socrates put it in the *Phaedo,* human life is a condition in which the soul is temporarily entrapped in flesh. Man is that being who exists on the historical plane and whose existence has both a beginning and an end.

But the Sadducees, who did not accept the apocalyptists' doctrine of resurrection, tried to confute that notion by resort to the device of *reductio ad absurdum* with their presentation of the impossible case of the woman married successively to seven brothers; and Jesus parried the question neatly. The doctrine of resurrection in Daniel had been an effort to say that life lived well was not in vain even though it bore no apparent fruit because of the present condition of the People. God would not allow such a life to be "vanity" as the Preacher of Ecclesiastes had thought, but would accept it into the genealogy of the restored Israel. It would be judged acceptable at the coming time of restoration or renewal. "He is not God of the dead, but of the living," and therefore, the literalistic question about life after the resurrection is absurdly beside the point. The God who manifested himself to Moses at the burning bush is concerned with the life of a People, the progeny of Abraham, and not with death.

What exactly Jesus conceived to be the nature of the life of resurrection is unclear, and it is unlikely that he ever considered the problem. His preoccupation was with the urgency of life in the present time: with the signs in his own ministry and in general historical phenomena which proclaimed or would soon proclaim that God is about to do something new, to inaugurate his kingship in a decisive way. This is the motif of the parables,[16] and the synoptic Apocalypse[17] stresses not resurrection but the signs of the end of the present age. The statement: "And then he will send out the angels, and gather his elect from the four winds, from the ends of the earth to the ends of heaven" (Mark 13:27 RSV) is the only sentence (in only two of the three versions) of the Apocalypse which touches on resurrection; and it is very general. The description of the Last Judgment in Matthew 25:31-46 is cast in parabolic form so as to stress rather the importance of being prepared for the impending coming of God's kingship than the nature of the resurrection and its aftermath.[18]

Jesus, in other words, was unconcerned with speculations either about death or about the meaning of resurrection. Nothing he says seems to enlarge upon the traditional Hebraic stance; indeed, he seems to have used the language of apocalyptic literature while withdrawing from the apocalyptic picture of resurrection in favor of a reaffirmation of the kind of assertion made before the historical dislocation of the People. At the time of his crucifixion, there is abundant evidence in the synoptic Gospels that Jesus showed both fear and terror in the face of suffering. Unlike Socrates who faced death with triumphant composure, he took death as a terrible and serious thing.[19] His ultimate appeal was to the will of God, and that same will was his only and bitter comfort.

Jesus was concerned with life, or with the quality of life expected by God of his people, because he believed that the new age was about to begin. Death is the end of historical existence except insofar as one conceives of the dead as being with the fathers or a part of the living heritage of the People. To say that the dead shall be raised is to say that they will, as a part of the living heritage, participate in the life of the restored People which is about to begin.[20]

Of course, Jesus may have had (and probably did have) a more concrete picture than this in mind when he spoke of resurrection. His failure to be much more specific in his pronouncements is, however, made clear by the problems raised almost immediately for his followers in communicating this crucial, eschatological aspect of his teaching. For one thing, the time of the coming of the new order of things, for which Jesus had urged men to prepare, was not so imminent. Thus (rather as the Wisdom and apocalyptic schools emerged to answer questions raised by the historical failure of the expectations of the Hebraic peoples), it became imperative to develop a rationale for life in the interim before the coming of the kingship of God. Furthermore, it was necessary to accommodate Jesus' teaching, addressed only to the Jews, to the universal audience to whom Paul and others came to believe it was appropriate. And, finally, as a consequence of this, a new language was needed to express uniquely Judaic concepts in a society for which the terminology of the followers of Plato was more readily comprehensible.

It is in the writing of Paul,[21] who was attempting to resolve all three of these problems, that the problem of eschatology and the problem of death and the afterlife met and for the first time were made inseparable. Clarification of Jesus' vagueness, the lapse of time and the difficulty of cross-cultural interpretation all loom large in the following passage, which gathers a number of themes familiar in Paul's day and fuses them for the first time.

> . . . There is one glory of the sun, and another glory of the moon, and another glory of the stars; for star differs from star in glory.
>
> So it is with the resurrection of the dead. What is sown is perishable, what is raised is imperishable. It is sown in dishonor, it is raised in glory. It is sown in weakness, it is raised in power. It is sown a physical body, it is raised a spiritual body. If there is a physical body, there is also a spiritual body. Thus it is written, "The first man Adam became a living being"; the last Adam became a life-giving spirit . . . I tell you this, brethren: flesh and blood cannot inherit the kingdom of God, nor does the perishable inherit the imperishable.
>
> Lo! I tell you a mystery. We shall not all sleep, but we shall all be changed, in a moment, in the twinkling of an eye, at the last trumpet. For the trumpet will sound, and the dead will be raised imperishable, and we shall be changed. For this perishable nature must put on the imperishable, and this mortal nature must put on immortality. When the perishable puts on the imperishable, and the mortal puts on immortality, then shall come to pass the saying that is written:
>
> "Death is swallowed up in victory."
> "O death, where is thy victory?
> O death, where is thy sting?" (I Cor. 15:41-55 RSV)

No longer can the question of the nature of the resurrection as a mode of existence for the revivified dead be evaded. It must become what it was only potentially in the apocalyptic tradition: a special kind of corporeal existence which is a reward for the righteous who have died and a punishment for the wicked. To spell out what he means by this, Paul has recourse not only to fundamentally Greek terms like "spiritual" but also to the typological comparison of Christ and Adam and to the logical forms of disputation familiar to the philosophical schools and through them, perhaps, to the rabbinical schools of the Jewish dispersion. The passage is primarily a careful, rhetorical, and logical development of the antitheses of "physical" and "spiritual," constructed so as to show that there can be full life (in the unitive, Hebraic sense) for those who will be raised but that it must be understood symbolically or spiritually (in the dualistic Greek sense) as radically different from historical existence. Just as Jesus was raised, so all men will be raised—or if they are still living, changed—when the time comes. Therefore, the length of the time interval makes little difference; salvation remains universally available.[22]

Death in Paul's view is the "last" and greatest enemy of man, yet an enemy whose power derives from man's own acts of sinfulness. The moment of death is, thus, one of obliteration or of self-obliteration but for the intervention of God in Christ Jesus, whose own resurrection and glorification constitutes man's only hope of victory over death (I Cor. 15:12-22). Death is, then, an event or phenomenon of awful seriousness; Jesus' own reactions to his impending death were not cowardly or unphilosophical but absolutely realistic. But Jesus' own triumph is the assurance of man's triumph whenever God chooses to inaugurate his own reign. Those who die in Christ are, euphemistically, "asleep" and awaiting the ultimate triumph—or the dread judgment —at the resurrection with the rest of the People of God. Ultimately, the dead will be raised, corporeal and yet spiritual; and therefore, we can face death with a sure hope of ultimate triumph by God's grace.

With the possible exception of the radically hellenized Wisdom of Solomon of the Apocrypha, the first consistently developed theology of death in the Judeo-Christian intellectual tradition is that of Paul. Although none of Paul's assumptions were novel in the first century, he seems to have gone beyond what Jesus said on the subject, so far as we can tell from the meager record of the Gospels; and he makes certain concessions in its vocabulary, at least, to common Greek conceptualizations. But the expansions and the concessions are minimal and were necessary in the light of the apologetic problems of explaining the lengthening of the interim and of speaking to a non-Judaic audience. The fundamental elements of the tradition—the lack of distinction between body and spirit and the overriding concern not with the destiny of the individual but with that of the People—are carefully maintained to the absolute exclusion of either the dualistic and metaphysical or the political notion of immortality which the Hellenistic Age had inherited from fifth-century Greece.

Statements like that of Geoffrey Gorer, that "orthodox Christianity is dogmatic that the soul continues to exist after death,"[23] are, then absolutely without biblical foundation. Not only do the biblical writers on the whole have no conception of a soul as a separable element of human existence, but also there is agreement that death is the (often dreadful) termination of existence and that there is no such thing as an individual afterlife. The very urgency of living well in the world arises, in the biblical outlook, from the fact of death and from the high mission of the People of the Covenant, old or new, within which People alone the individual's life has meaning and purpose. At the end of the biblical tradition, the Pauline emphasis upon the general resurrection serves simply to underline these points, that all life is corporeal and that the judgment of mankind is general because the People is indivisible. In this view lay the possibility of a further development in which man could be regarded as entering upon an afterlife in the body of his resurrection after the sleep of the interim.

Against this general understanding of death, the Greek views stand in contrast. Whereas the Judeo-Christians maintained the unity of the human being, the Greek philosophical tradition in general conceived of a soul which might or must continue to exist after its separation from the body. Metaphysically speaking, immortality was a necessary logical deduction for the Greek but an inconceivable construct for the Jews and primitive Christians. And, whereas the Hebraic progenitor was understood as always part of the living heritage of the People, the Greek political hero continued to exist in the memory of his city and thus to be granted immortality.

Notes

1 On the biblical definition of History, see Lloyd G. Patterson, *God and History in Early Christian Thought,* Studies in Early Christian Thought (New York: Seabury Press, 1967), pp. 1-15.

2 For a survey of Old Testament attitudes toward death (with which I disagree at several points), see Robert Martin-Archard, *From Death to Life: A Study of the Development of the Doctrine of the Resurrection in the Old Testament,* trans. John Penney Smith (Edinburgh: Oliver and Boyd, 1960).

3 E. A. Speiser, trans., *The Anchor Bible,* I (Garden City: Doubleday, 1964), p. 174. Used with permission. I am further indebted to Speiser's "Introduction" and "Notes" for helpful suggestions; to the "Introduction" and "Commentary" of C. A. Simpson in *The Interpreter's Bible,* I (Nashville: Abingdon Press, 1952); and to the articles of Edmond Jacob on "Death" and "Immortality" in *The Interpreter's Dictionary of the Bible* (Nashville: Abingdon Press, 1962). Lack of space has prevented me from taking account of the kinds of evidence presented by Roland de Vaux (*Ancient Israel: Its Life and Institutions,* trans. John McHugh [New York: McGraw-Hill, 1961], esp. at pp. 56-61); I am, however, convinced that these considerations do not fundamentally challenge my discussion.

4 Harvey H. Guthrie, Jr., *Wisdom and Canon: Meanings of the Law and the Prophets,* Winslow Lectures, 1966 (Evanston: Seabury-Western Theological Seminary, 1966), pp. 4-5.

5 According to the Yahwist, who is not responsible for Gen. 25:1-11.

6 Here I go beyond other commentators, who are more cautious. The only other reference to this kind of oath is in Gen. 47:29; and it is, significantly, associated with the death of Israel, who is likewise preoccupied with thoughts of the land of the promise of Yahweh.

7 Because of the unique role of Abraham as the first patriarch, "in Abraham's bosom" became a common euphemism for death.

8 *Nephesh,* the Hebrew word which has often been translated "soul," means, rather, "that which is vital in man in the broadest sense" (Gerhard von Rad, *Old Testament Theology,* trans. D. M. G. Stalker, 2 vols. [Edinburgh: Oliver and Boyd, 1962 and 1965], I, p. 153). Although *nephesh* is given to man at his creation and it returns to God at his death, the concept is closer to selfhood or life-force than to soul.

9 Guthrie, *Wisdom and Canon.* My statement of the themes of later Hebrew religious thought is heavily influenced by Guthrie in the work cited and in *God and History in the Old Testament* (New York: Seabury Press, 1960), pp. 117-137. See also von Rad, *Old Testament Theology,* II, pp. 301-315. Not all scholars would agree to their formulation of the relationship between wisdom and apocalyptic literature, but it seems to me proper because of the essential contemporaneity of the traditions to see them as related rather than as antipathetic.

10 See von Rad, *Old Testament Theology,* II, pp. 308-315.

11 I have not treated Wisdom of Solomon, which does incorporate the Hellenistic doctrine of the immortal soul into the Hebraic historical framework, because of its late date (*c.* 100 B.C.-*c.* A.D. 40) and its uniqueness. Obviously, however, it shows the inherent possibilities of accommodation to Hellenism via the Wisdom tradition (and this is doubly significant in the light of its association with Alexandria where Christian philosophical theology was to flower and

represents a significant movement in late Judaism, the importance of which has only recently been recognized). One might argue that Wisdom only translates Hebraic notions into the Greek philosophical idiom (and I have been tempted to do so, claiming for the author a high level of sophistication and remarkable poetic powers); but in the light of the Christian history of the problem of immortality, that seems to be pushing things. It is easy to see why the Fathers were moved by this document. For further commentary, see Bruce C. Metzgar, *An Introduction to the Apocrypha* (New York: Oxford University Press, 1957), pp.65-76.

12 My interpretation is heavily influenced by Oscar Cullmann's Ingersoll Lecture for 1955, "Immortality of the Soul or Resurrection of the Dead," reprinted in Stendahl, ed., *Immortality and Resurrection* (New York: Macmillan, 1965), pp. 9-47; I go somewhat further than he, however.

13 See Dan. 12:5-13.

14 Werner Georg Kümmel, *Promise and Fulfillment: The Eschatological Message of Jesus,* trans. D. M. Barton, Studies in Biblical Theology 23 (London: SCM Press, 1957), p. 153. See also Gunther Bornkamm, *Jesus of Nazareth,* trans. Irene and Fraser McLuskey with James M. Robinson (New York: Harpers, 1960), pp. 90-95.

15 See also Matt. 22:23-33.

16 See Joachim Jeremias, *The Parables of Jesus,* rev. ed. (London: SCM Press, 1963), *passim.*

17 Mark 13:5-37; Matt. 24:4-36; Luke 21:8-36.

18 See Kummel, *Promise and Fulfillment,* pp. 88 ff.

19 See Cullmann in *Immortality and Resurrection,* pp. 12-20.

20 Regretfully, considerations of length prevent us from dealing here with the John Gospel, for it has seemed to many to represent a hellenized point of view. Despite its radically different vocabulary. I regard it more and more as a document in which Hellenic terms are used to present Hebraic notions. Its real sources lie in the Wisdom movement; but its exegetical interpretation has been shaped by the Alexandrian philosophical theologians.

21 Paul's writing, of course, antedates that of the evangelists and in some ways influences them. The present order of discussion is based on the assumption that Mark 12:18 ff. is a comparatively untouched *logion.* The signs of the synoptic Apocalypse are not free from later influences, and even the reference therein to the resurrection may not be authentic.

22 Paul treats this problem more directly in I Thess. 4:13-18.

23 Geoffrey Gorer, *Death, Grief, and Mourning* (Garden City, N.Y.; Doubleday, 1965), p.24.

B

DEATH AS A SOCIAL DISEASE

In this world there are certain positive attributes (beauty, brains, elegance, talent, etc.), and conversely there are certain stigmas. These stigmas include deformity, disease, outcast status (see Erving Goffman's Stigma [1963]), failure, old age, and death. Very few people are permitted to be proud of their aging or dying.

This section represents a tightening of focus on the cultural perspectives of death by concerning itself with death as viewed in contemporary culture. The section is divided into two aspects, each of which talks about death as a disease. The first "disease" aspect is our contemporary treatment of death as a social disease (much like VD) not appropriate to "polite society." This attitude stems from the changing characteristics of death ("controlled mortality" as discussed in the next chapter and the institutionalization of death—both of which pull death away from our immediate view and make it somewhat "sinful," just as a "glimpse of stocking was shocking" at another age) and from an oxymoronic approach to death. This double view of death is underscored by Gorer (whose selection is already a sociological classic), who points out that while violent death is an increasing part of the fantasy life of mass audiences, natural death becomes unmentionable, more taboo in our time than sex was in Victorian days.

Because death is "socially unacceptable," we attempt to interdict it, as the Ariès article shows. In effect we pretend it is not there by "tarting up" the cadaver so that it is not dead but just sleeping. Ariès, a European, attributes this behavior almost entirely to the United States.

Our increasing acceptance of violent death leads us to the second "disease" aspect—a disease of the society, resulting from the inexorable ubiquity of death. The last two selections of the section are about macroviolence. The twentieth century—like the time of the great Asian and European plagues of the fourteenth century (See Ziegler's The Black Death)—can be called a century of death: atomic death is in the air, omnipresent, possible in any spot or at any moment; there is no place to hide.

Our society embraces violent death (witness our avid attention to the butchery on television programs and our relative indifference to the slaughter on our highways) in various ways; but it should be noted that the emphasis here is on violent death as practiced by governments. This killing by governments is the most serious disease of our world. It is the only malady that could kill us all. With the perception of this threat has come a number of psychological concomitants: what Robert Lifton has called "numbing"; Nathan Leites has referred to as "affectlessness"; Kenneth Keniston has called "alienation"; and Henry Murray has labeled "the root mood of an articulate depth-sensitive minority."

These psychological states may be related to recent increases in crime, use of drugs, disaffection, and violence. The resulting disease of society is expressed by the psychic numbing and guilt of survivors highlighted in the Lifton and Olson selection.

Another expression of the disease is a pervasive fear—fear that nothing will last in the face of possible total destruction and that therefore nothing matters. The overriding aspect of this disease of society is represented by the "technological alienation" described by Elliot. (How can any society behave healthily with a loaded atomic gun constantly pointed at its head?) As Lifton and Olson say, in a "sense we are all survivors of this century's holocausts ..."; and it might be added that we all suffer the special sickness characteristic of survivors.

Every once in a while one comes across a book that is so shocking in its simple recitation of horrible facts that it seems both noble and obscene. Elliot's The Twentieth Century Book of the Dead *is such a volume. All he does is detail the 110 million deaths committed by* governments *since 1900—a "nation of the dead," created by man himself. The selection from that work reprinted here is about the agents of death—how the killing is done. Elliot's book is not one for the timid; it is for everyone. Read, shudder, and weep.*

4• The Pornography of Death

Geoffrey Gorer

Geoffrey Gorer is a noted English anthropologist who has written about Africa, Bali and Angkor, Himalayan villages, and the American people. His first book was about the Marquis de Sade. This selection, which is taken from his book Death, Grief and Mourning, *has already become a classic of its kind. In it, Gorer proposes and brilliantly explicates the dramatic thesis that death is treated in our society as obscene and pornographic; that while sex was the pornography of the Victorians, death is the pornography of our times.*

Birth, and copulation, and death.
That's all the facts when you come to brass tacks;
Birth, and copulation, and death.

—T. S. Eliot, *Sweeney Agonistes* (1932)

Pornography is, no doubt, the opposite face, the shadow, of prudery, whereas obscenity is an aspect of seemliness. No society has been recorded which has not its rules of seemliness, of words or actions which arouse discomfort and embarrassment in some contexts, though they are essential in others. The people before whom one must maintain a watchful seemliness vary from society to society: all people of the opposite sex, or all juniors, or all elders, or one's parents-in-law, or one's social superiors or inferiors, or one's grandchildren have been selected in different societies as groups in whose presence the employment of certain words or the performance of certain actions would be considered offensive; and then these words or actions become charged with affect. There is a tendency for these words and actions to be related to sex and excretion, but this is neither necessary nor universal; according to Malinowski, the Trobrianders surround eating with as much shame as excretion; and in other societies personal names or aspects of ritual come under the same taboos.

Rules of seemliness are apparently universal; and the nonobservance of these rules, or anecdotes which involve the breaking of the rules, provoke that peculiar type of laughter which seems identical the world over; however little one may know about a strange society, however little one may know about the functions of laughter in that society (and these can be very various) one can immediately tell when people are laughing at an obscene joke. The topper of the joke may be "And then he ate the whole meal in front of them!" or "She used her husband's name in the presence of his mother!" but the laughter is the same; the taboos of seemliness have been broken and the result is hilarious. Typically, such laughter is confined to one-sex groups and is more general with the young, just entering into the complexities of adult life.

Obscenity then is a universal, an aspect of man and woman living in society; everywhere and at all times there are words and actions which, when misplaced, can produce shock, social embarrassment, and laughter. Pornography on the other hand, the description of tabooed activities to produce hallucination or delusion, seems to be a very much rarer phenomenon. It probably can only arise in literate societies, and we certainly have no records of it for nonliterate ones; for whereas the enjoyment of obscenity is predominantly social, the enjoyment of pornography is predominantly private. The fantasies from which pornography derives could of course be generated in any society; but it seems doubtful whether they would ever be communicated without the intermediary of literacy.

The one possible exception to this generalization is the use of plastic arts without any letterpress. I have never felt quite certain that the three-dimensional *poses plastiques* on so many Hindu temples (notably the "Black Pagoda" at Konarak) have really the highfalutin worship of the life force or glorification of the creative aspect of sex which their apologists claim for them; many of them seem to me very like "feelthy" pictures, despite the skill with which they are executed. There are too the erotic woodcuts of Japan; but quite a lot of evidence suggests that these are thought of as laughter provoking (i.e., obscene) by the Japanese themselves. We have no knowledge of the functions of the Peruvian pottery.

As far as my knowledge goes, the only Asian society which had a long-standing tradition of pornographic literature is China; and, it would appear, social life under the Manchus was surrounded by much the same haze of prudery as distinguished the nineteenth century in much of Europe and the Americas, even though the emphasis fell rather differently; women's deformed feet seem to have been the greatest focus of peeking and sniggering, rather than their ankles or the cleft between their breasts; but by and large life in Manchu China seems to have been nearly as full of "unmentionables" as life in Victoria's heyday.

Pornography would appear to be a concomitant of prudery, and usually the periods of the greatest production of pornography have also been the periods of the most rampant prudery. In contrast to obscenity, which is chiefly defined by situation, prudery is defined by subject; some aspect of human experience is treated as inherently shameful or abhorrent, so that it can never be discussed or referred to openly, and experience of it tends to be clandestine and accompanied by feelings of guilt and unworthiness. The unmentionable aspect of experience then tends to become a subject for much private fantasy, more or less realistic, fantasy charged with pleasurable guilt or guilty pleasure; and those whose power of fantasy is weak, or whose demand is insatiable, constitute a market for the printed fantasies of the pornographer.

Traditionally, and in the lexicographic meaning of the term, pornography has been concerned with sexuality. For the greater part of the last two hundred years copulation and (at least in the mid-Victorian decades) birth were the "unmentionables" of the triad of basic human experiences which "are all the facts when you come to brass tacks," around which so much private fantasy and semiclandestine pornography were erected. During most of this period death was no mystery, except in the sense that death is always a mystery. Children were encouraged to think about death, their own deaths and the edifying or cautionary deathbeds of others. It can have been a rare individual who, in the nineteenth century with its high mortality, had not witnessed at least one actual dying, as well as paying their respect to "beautiful corpses"; funerals were the occasion of the greatest display for working class, middle class, and aristocrat. The cemetery was the center of every old-established village, and they were prominent in most towns. It was fairly late in the nineteenth century when the execution of criminals ceased to be a public holiday as well as a public warning.

In the twentieth century, however, there seems to have been an unremarked shift in prudery; whereas copulation has become more and more "mentionable," particularly in the Anglo-Saxon societies, death has become more and more "unmentionable" *as a natural process*. I cannot recollect a novel or play of the last twenty years or so which has a "deathbed scene" in it, describing in any detail the death "from natural causes" of a major character; this topic was a set piece for most of the eminent Victorian and Edwardian writers, evoking their finest prose and their most elaborate technical effects to produce the greatest amount of pathos or edification.

One of the reasons, I imagine, for this plethora of deathbed scenes—apart from their intrinsic emotional and religious content—was that it was one of the relatively few experiences that an author could be fairly sure would have been shared by the vast majority of his readers. Questioning my old acquaintances, I cannot find one over the age of sixty who did not witness the agony of at least one near relative; I do not think I know a single person under the age of thirty who has had a similar experience. Of course my acquaintance is neither very extensive nor particularly representative; but in this instance I do think it is typical of the change of attitude and "exposure."

The natural processes of corruption and decay have become disgusting, as disgusting as the natural processes of birth and copulation were a century ago; preoccupation about such processes is (or was) morbid and unhealthy, to be discouraged in all and punished in the young. Our great-grandparents were told that babies were found under gooseberry bushes or cabbages; our children are likely to be told that those who have passed on (fie! on the gross Anglo-Saxon monosyllable) are changed into flowers, or lie at rest in lovely gardens. The ugly facts are relentlessly hidden; the art of the embalmers is an art of complete denial.

It seems possible to trace a connection between the shift of taboos and the shift in religious beliefs. In the nineteenth century most of the inhabitants of Protestant countries seem to have subscribed to the Pauline beliefs in the sinfulness of the body and the certainty of the afterlife. "So also is the resurrection of the dead. It is sown in corruption; it is raised in incorruption: it is sown in dishonour; it is raised in glory." It was possible to insist on the corruption of the dead body, and the dishonour of its begetting, while there was a living belief in the incorruption and the glory of the immortal part. But in England, at any rate, belief in the future life as taught in Christian doctrine is very uncommon today even in the minority who make church going or prayer a consistent part of their lives; and without some such belief natural death and physical decomposition have become too horrible to contemplate or to discuss. It seems symptomatic that the contemporary sect of Christian Science should deny the fact of physical death, even to the extent (so it is said) of refusing to allow the word to be printed in the *Christian Science Monitor*.

During the last half century public health measures and improved preventive medicine have made natural death among the younger members of the population much more uncommon than it had been in earlier periods, so that a death in the family, save in the fullness of time, became a relatively uncommon incident in home life; and, simultaneously, violent death increased in a manner unparalleled in human history. Wars and revolutions, concentration camps, and gang feuds were the most publicized of the causes for these violent deaths; but the diffusion of the automobile, with its constant and unnoticed toll of fatal accidents, may well have been most influential in bringing the possibility of violent death into the expectations of law-abiding people in time of peace. While natural death became more and more smothered in prudery, violent death has played an evergrowing part in the fantasies offered to mass audiences—detective stories, thrillers, Westerns, war stories, spy stories, science fiction, and eventually horror comics.

There seem to be a number of parallels between the fantasies which titillate our curiosity about the mystery of sex, and those which titillate our curiosity about the mystery of death. In both types of fantasy, the emotions which are typically concomitant of the acts—love or grief—are paid little or no attention, while the sensations are enhanced as much as a customary poverty of language permits. If marital intercourse be considered the natural expression of sex for most of humanity most of the time, then "natural sex" plays as little role as "natural death" (the ham-fisted attempts of D. H. Lawrence and Jules Romains to describe "natural sex" realistically but high-mindedly prove the rule). Neither type of fantasy can have any real development, for once the protagonist has done something, he or she must proceed to do something else, with or to somebody else, more refined, more complicated, or more sensational than what had occurred before. This somebody else is not a person; it is either a set of genitals, with or without secondary sexual characteristics, or a body, perhaps capable of suffering pain as well as death. Since most languages are relatively poor in words or constructions to express intense pleasure or intense pain, the written portions of both types of fantasy abound in onomatopoeic conglomerations of letters meant to evoke the sighs, gasps, groans, screams and rattles concomitant to the described actions. Both types of fantasy rely heavily on adjective and simile. Both types of fantasy are completely unrealistic, since they ignore all physical, social, or legal limitations, and both types have complete hallucination of the reader or viewer as their object.

There seems little question that the instinct of those censorious busybodies preoccupied with other people's morals was correct when they linked the pornography of death with the pornography of sex. This, however, seems to be the only thing which has been correct in their deductions or attempted actions. There is no valid evidence to suggest that either type of pornography is an incitement to action; rather are they substitute gratifications. The belief that such hallucinatory works would incite their readers to copy the actions depicted would seem to be indirect homage to the late Oscar Wilde, who described such a process in *The Picture of Dorian Gray*. I know of no authenticated parallels in real life, though investigators and magistrates with bees in their bonnets can usually persuade juvenile delinquents to admit to exposure to whatever medium of mass communication they are choosing to make a scapegoat.

Despite some gifted precursors, such as Andréa de Nerciat or Edgar Allan Poe, most works in both pornographics are aesthetically objectionable; but it is questionable whether, from the purely aesthetic point of view, there is much more to be said for the greater part of the more anodyne fare provided by contemporary mass media communication. Psychological Utopians tend to condemn substitute gratifications as such, at least where copulation is involved; they have so far been chary in dealing with death.

Nevertheless, people have to come to terms with the basic facts of birth, copulation, and death, and somehow accept their implications; if social prudery prevents this being done in an open and dignified fashion, then it will be done surreptitiously. If we dislike the modern pornography of death, then we must give back to death—natural death— its parade and publicity, readmit grief and mourning. If we make death unmentionable in polite society—"not before the children"—we almost ensure the continuation of the "horror comic." No censorship has ever been really effective.

5. Forbidden Death

Philippe Ariès

Philippe Ariès is a French writer who specializes in social history. In his book Western Attitudes toward Death, *from which this selection is taken, Ariès traces the development of these attitudes from the Middle Ages to the present. He contends that the modern tendency toward interdicting or in some way denying the presence of death began around the turn of this century. With a view reminiscent of that expressed by Evelyn Waugh in* The Loved One, *Airès attributes this phenomenon almost entirely to America.*

It seems that the modern attitude toward death, that is to say the interdiction of death in order to preserve happiness, was born in the United States around the beginning of the twentieth century. However, on its native soil the interdict was not carried to its ultimate extremes. In American society it encountered a braking influence which it did not encounter in Europe. Thus the American attitude toward death today appears as a strange compromise between trends which are pulling it in two nearly opposite directions.

There is as yet very scanty documentation on this subject, but the little that is available has inspired the following thoughts, which I hope will evoke comments, corrections, and criticism from American historians. When I read for the first time G. Gorer, J. Mitford, H. Feifel, etc.,[1] I thought I was finding in contemporary America traces of the mentality of the French Enlightenment.

"Forest Lawn" is not as futuristic as Evelyn Waugh thought,[2] and it made me think of the descriptions of the cemeteries dreamed of by the French authors of cemetery plans in the late eighteenth century, plans which never materialized owing to the Revolution and which were replaced in the early nineteenth century by the more declamatory and figurative architecture of romanticism. In the United States, everything was happening as if the romantic interval had never existed, and as if the mentality of the eighteenth-century Enlightenment had persisted without interruption.

This first impression, this first hypothesis, was false. It did not take sufficient account of American Puritanism, which is incompatible with confidence in man, in his goodness, in his happiness. Excellent American historians pointed this out to me, and I was very willing to agree with them. Yet the similarities between a part of the current American attitude toward death and that of enlightened Europe in the eighteenth century are no less troubling. We must concede that the mental phenomena which we have just observed occur much later than the French Enlightenment. In America, during the eighteenth and the first half of the nineteenth centuries, and even later, burials conformed to tradition, especially in the countryside: the carpenter made the coffin (the coffin, not yet the "casket"); the family and friends saw to its transport and to the procession itself; and the pastor and gravedigger carried out the service. In the early nineteenth century the grave was still sometimes dug on the family property—which is a modern act, copied from the ancients, and which was unknown in Europe before the mid-eighteenth century and with few exceptions was rapidly abandoned. In villages and small towns the cemetery most frequently lay adjacent to the church. In the cities, once again paralleling Europe, the cemetery had in about 1830 been situated outside the city but was encompassed by urban growth and abandoned toward 1870 for a new site. It soon fell into ruin, and Mark Twain tells us how the skeletons would leave it at night, carrying off with them what remained of their tombs ("A Curious Dream," 1870).

The old cemeteries were church property, as they had been in Europe and still are in England. The new cemeteries belonged to private associations, as the French authors of those eighteenth-century plans had fruitlessly dreamed. In Europe cemeteries became municipal, that is to say public, property and were never left to private initiative.

In the growing cities of the nineteenth century, old carpenters or gravediggers, or owners of carts and horses, became "undertakers," and the manipulation of the dead became a profession. Here history is still completely comparable to that in Europe, at least in that part of Europe which remained faithful to the eighteenth-century canons of simplicity and which remained outside the pale of romantic bombast.

Things seem to have changed during the period of the Civil War. Today's "morticians," whose letters-patent go back to that period, give as their ancestor a quack doctor expelled from the school of medicine, Dr. Holmes, who had a passion for dissection and cadavers. He would offer his services to the victim's family and embalmed, it is said, 4,000 cadavers unaided in four years. That's not bad a rate for the period! Why such recourse to embalming? Had it been practiced previously? Is there an American tradition going back to the eighteenth century, a period in which throughout Europe there was a craze for embalming? Yet this technique was abandoned in nineteenth-century Europe, and the wars did not resurrect it. It is noteworthy that embalming became a career in the United States before the end of the century, even if it was not yet very widespread. We can cite the case of Elizabeth "Ma" Green, born in 1884, who as a young woman began to help the undertaker in her small town. At the age of twenty she was a "licensed embalmer" and made a career of this trade until her death. In 1900 embalming appeared in California. We know that it has today become a very widespread method of preparing the dead, a practice almost unknown in Europe and characteristic of the American way of death.

One cannot help thinking that this long-accepted and avowed preference for embalming has a meaning, even if it is difficult to interpret.

This meaning could indeed be that of a certain refusal to accept death, either as a familiar end to which one is resigned, or as a dramatic sign in the romantic manner. And this meaning became even more obvious when death became an object of commerce and of profit. It is not easy to sell something which has no value because it is too familiar and common, or something which is frightening, horrible, or painful. In order to sell death, it had to be made friendly. But we may assume that "funeral director"—since 1885 a new name for undertakers—would not have met with success if public opinion had not cooperated. They presented themselves not as simple sellers of services, but as "doctors of grief" who have a mission, as do doctors and priests; and this mission, from the beginning of this century, consists in aiding the mourning survivors to return to normalcy. The new funeral director ("new" because he has replaced the simple undertaker) is a "doctor of grief," an "expert at returning abnormal minds to normal in the shortest possible time." They are "members of an exalted, almost sacred calling."[3]

Thus mourning is no longer a necessary period imposed by society; it has become a *morbid state* which must be treated, shortened, erased by the "doctor of grief."

Through a series of little steps we can see the birth and development of the ideas which would end in the present-day interdict, built upon the ruins of Puritanism, in an urbanized culture which is dominated by rapid economic growth and by the search for happiness linked to the search for profit.

This process should normally result in the situation of England today, as it is described, for example, by Gorer: the almost total suppression of everything reminding us of death.

But, and this is what is unique about the American attitude, American mores have not gone to such an extreme; they stopped along the way. Americans are very willing to transform death, to put makeup on it, to sublimate it, but they do not want to make it disappear. Obviously, this would also mark the end of profit, but the money earned by funeral merchants would not be tolerated if they did not meet a profound need. The wake, increasingly avoided in industrial Europe, persists in the United States: it exists as "viewing the remains," the "visitation." "They don't *view* bodies in England."[4]

The visit to the cemetery and a certain veneration in regard to the tomb also persist. That is why public opinion—and funeral directors—find cremation distasteful, for it gets rid of the remains too quickly and too radically.

Burials are not shameful and they are not hidden. With that very characteristic mixture of commerce and idealism, they are the object of showy publicity, like any other consumer's item, be it soap or religion. Seen for example in the buses of New York City in 1965 was the following ad, purchased by one of the city's leading morticians: "The dignity and integrity of a Gawler. Funeral costs no more . . . Easy access, private parking for over 100 cars." Such publicity would be unthinkable in Europe, first of all because it would repel the customer rather than attract him.

Thus we must admit that a traditional resistance has kept alive certain rituals of death which had been abandoned or are being abandoned in industrialized Europe, especially among the middle classes.

Nevertheless, though these rituals have been continued, they have also been transformed. The American way of death is the synthesis of two tendencies: one traditional, the other euphoric.

Thus during the wakes or farewell "visitations" which have been preserved, the visitors come without shame or repugnance. This is because in reality they are not visiting a dead person, as they traditionally have, but an almost-living one who, thanks to embalming, is still present, as if he were awaiting you to greet you or to take you off on a walk. The definitive nature of the rupture has been blurred. Sadness and mourning have been banished from this calming reunion.

Perhaps because American society has not totally accepted the interdict, it can more easily challenge it; but this interdict is spreading in the Old World, where the cult of the dead would seem more deeply rooted.

During the last ten years in American publications an increasing number of sociologists and psychologists have been studying the conditions of death in contemporary society and especially in hospitals.[5] This bibliography makes no mention of the current conditions of funerals and mourning. They are deemed satisfactory. On the other hand, the authors have been struck by the manner of dying, by the inhumanity, the cruelty of solitary death in hospitals and in a society where death has lost the prominent place which custom had granted it over the millennia, a society where the interdiction of death paralyzes and inhibits the reactions of the medical staff and family involved. These publications are also preoccupied with the fact that death has become the object of a voluntary decision by the doctors and the family, a decision which today is made shamefacedly, clandestinely. And this paramedical literature, for which, as far as I know, there is no equivalent in Europe, is bringing death back into the dialogue from which it had been excluded. Death is once again becoming something one can talk about. Thus the interdict is threatened, but only in the place where it was born and where it encountered limitations. Elsewhere, in the other industrialized societies, it is maintaining or extending its empire.

Notes

1 G. Gorer, *Death, Grief and Mourning* (New York: Doubleday, 1965); J. Mitford, *The American Way of Death* (New York: Simon & Schuster, 1963); H. Feifel *et al.*, *The Meaning of Death* (New York: McGraw-Hill, 1959), a pioneering work.

2 E. Waugh, *The Loved One* (Boston: Little, Brown, 1948).

3 From Mitford, *The American Way of Death.*

4 *Ibid.*

5 A bibliography of 340 recent works is to be found in O.G. Brim *et al.*, *The Dying Patient* (New York: Russell Sage Foundation, 1970). It does not include anything to do with funerals, cemeteries, mourning, or suicide.

6• The Nuclear Age

Robert Jay Lifton and Eric Olson

Robert Jay Lifton is Professor of Psychiatry at Yale University and is perhaps most widely known for his book Death in Life: Survivors of Hiroshima, *which won a National Book Award in 1969. This selection, taken from his more recent work* Living and Dying *(written with Eric Olson), discusses the effects of the Hiroshima explosion not only on those who survived that blast and experienced what the authors call "psychic numbing," but on the rest of humanity as well.*

Eric Olson, who was a graduate student at Harvard when he wrote this selection with Dr. Lifton, has earned his Ph.D. degree and is a psychology instructor in the department of psychiatry at Harvard Medical School. He is also affiliated with the Cambridge Hospital.

The 17th century was the century of mathematics, the 18th that of the physical sciences, and the 19th that of biology. Our 20th century is the century of fear.

— Albert Camus, from
Neither Victims Nor Executioners

The sun can't hold a candle to it.

Now we're all sons of bitches.

—Two reactions of nuclear
scientists to the first atomic bomb test

Early in the morning of August 6, 1945, the United States dropped on the Japanese city of Hiroshima the first atomic bomb ever used on a human population. The destruction and chaos wrought by that bomb were so immense that it has never been possible to make a precise count of the number of people killed. Most estimates are in the range of 100,000 to 200,000 people. Even for the hundreds of thousands who experienced the bombing but remained alive, the vision and taint of nuclear holocaust left lifelong scars.

The bomb was unexpected; it came as people went about their morning chores of making and eating breakfast and preparing to go to work. Suddenly a blinding flash cut across the sky. There were a few seconds of dead silence and then a huge explosion. Enormous clouds formed and then rose upward in a gigantic dark column. The clouds leveled off and the whole formation resembled an enormous black mushroom.

Those who have seen atomic explosions speak of their awesome and frightening beauty. On that Japanese summer morning, the beauty was immediately eclipsed by the experience of an overwhelming encounter with death. Normal existence had suddenly been massively invaded by an eerie and unknown force. An area of total destruction was created extending for two miles in all directions, and 60,000 buildings within the city limits were demolished.

The reaction of the survivors was at first a sense of being totally immersed by death. Houses and buildings leveled, the sight of dead bodies, the cries and moans of the severely injured, and the smell of burning flesh all combined to leave a permanent death imprint of staggering power.

Among the survivors there quickly developed a profound kind of guilt. This guilt was related both to having remained alive while others (including loved ones and neighbors) died, and to the inability to offer help to those who needed it. All of this became focused in a question that remained at the center of a lifelong struggle for the survivors: "Why did I remain alive when he, she, they died?" And this question itself sometimes became transformed into the haunting suspicion that one's own life had been purchased at the cost of the others who died: "Some had to die; because they died I could live." This suspicion led to a feeling among survivors that they did not deserve to be alive and that one could justly remain alive only by coming in some way to resemble the dead.

The Japanese survivors became psychologically numb, their sensitivities blunted by guilt and by an inability to resume meaningful activity amid the chaos. The boundary separating life from death no longer seemed distinct. By becoming numb, the survivors blocked their awareness of the pain and suffering and effected a kind of compromise between life and death.

The survivors' lives were made even more difficult by a susceptibility to various forms of disease and weakness to which their exposure to atomic radiation made them vulnerable. Many of those exposed have had to struggle to live with maimed bodies; all have had to live with the incredible end-of-the-world image of nuclear holocaust.

For us, now, the image of Hiroshima symbolizes the possibility that what has happened once can happen again. By today's standards, that first atomic bomb was a very small one. The difficulty of imagining the human suffering that followed in the wake of its use is multiplied many times over in trying to contemplate what a world war with atomic weapons would be like now.

The atomic bomb was the product of an extraordinary research program carried out during World War II. In the beginning there had been little confidence that an atomic bomb could actually be made. But the suspicion that German scientists were attempting to put such a weapon into the hands of Hitler led the United States to undertake an all-out effort.

In 1939, a letter to President Roosevelt was drafted by Albert Einstein encouraging full support for a scientific program that would lead to the development of the atomic bomb. Research installations were established at a number of places throughout the country, and work went ahead with unprecedented commitment. By July 1945, the first atomic bomb was ready for testing in the New Mexico desert. So intense was the effort to create the bomb and so anxious were the scientists about whether it would work that few physicists at Los Alamos were inclined to raise moral questions about the weapon they made.

The bomb worked. Suddenly, it became possible for one plane to deliver a single bomb, the explosive power of which previously would have required two thousand bombs. All who watched were awestruck by what they saw; the experience had a religious quality. Men had released through the bomb a source of power literally beyond imagining. It seemed that the use of this powerful device could bring the war to a rapid conclusion and could in peacetime yield untold energy, and would thus transform the nature of both war and peace.

All these things were possible. But what was immediate and overwhelming was the sheer majesty and power of the bomb itself. Robert Oppenheimer, director of the research project that produced the bomb, later remembered his thoughts at the time of the explosion:

> At that moment . . . there flashed into my mind a passage from the Bhagavad-Gita, the sacred book of the Hindus: "I am become Death, the Shatterer of Worlds!"

Another observer at the time used such phrases as "mighty thunder" and "great silence" to describe his response, and went on to speak in clearly religious language:

> On that moment hung eternity. Time stood still. Space contracted to a pinpoint. It was as though the earth had opened and the skies had split. One felt as though he had been privileged to witness the Birth of the World.

Others had more cynical responses: "Now we're all sons of bitches," and, more simply, "What a thing we've made." Still others spoke of "the dreadful," "the terrible," "the dire," and "the awful."

"This is the greatest thing in history!" was President Truman's response upon hearing of the bomb's successful use in Hiroshima, which seemed to portend a rapid end to the war. And a newspaper report at the time described the force as "weird, incredible, and somehow disturbing."

If we understand the experience of religious conversion as involving a changed image of the cosmos and man's place within it, then certainly the responses of those early witnesses to atomic power would qualify as religious. There was a sense of a "new beginning," of making contact with the infinite and the feeling that life would never be the same again. The bomb took on qualities of a deity, a god whose strange and superhuman power would change the course of human history.

After it became clear that this atomic god was real, the scientists who had unleashed it began to diverge in their responses to the new power. As in any situation, most went on with their professional "business as usual." Some assumed a sense of mission in committing themselves to controlling the use of this threatening force. Others identified themselves with the force, became converts to the religion of nuclearism, and dedicated themselves to propagating the new faith.

Nuclearism is a peculiar, twentieth-century disease of power. We would do well to specify it, trace its roots, and see its connection with other forms of religious and immortalizing expression. Nuclearism is a form of totalism. It yields a grandiose vision of man's power at a historical time when man's precarious sense of his own immortality makes him particularly vulnerable to such aberrations.

Man has always attached deep emotion to his tools. As extensions of his own body and capacities, they have provided him with an image of himself. The centrality of technology to twentieth-century culture has increased this tendency to define life in terms of the tools and techniques that have so deeply transformed the world. In this sense, nuclearism is a manifestation of two underlying contemporary inclinations: to deify tools, and to seize whatever symbols are available in the desperate search for a sense of significance.

The career and personal struggles of Robert Oppenheimer reveal the tensions that have existed in relation to nuclear weapons. Oppenheimer directed the vast and complex research effort at Los Alamos. He and those with whom he worked were convinced that if the bomb could be developed quickly, its availability would hasten the end of the war and could even rid the world of war permanently. Certain nuclear scientists in Chicago who had completed their contribution to the bomb research project tried to raise moral questions about the bomb's use. Oppenheimer, however, remained committed and resisted such reflection. He did not agree that the bomb should merely be "demonstrated" to frighten the enemy into submission rather than be actually used on a human population.

It was not until 1949, when the vastly more powerful hydrogen bomb was nearly completed, that Oppenheimer began to reexamine his convictions. He continued to work on weapons research, and even came to favor the development of small "tactical" hydrogen bombs. But he became concerned that the idea of a "super" H-bomb seemed "to have caught the imagination, both of the congressional and military people, as the answer to the problem posed by the Russians' advance." With his characteristic brilliance, Oppenheimer then began to expose the dangers involved in letting the bomb dominate all thinking on international relations.

Oppenheimer had been a national hero during and just after the war, when he was widely credited with the success of the atomic bomb research project. But when he began to raise questions about nuclearism and underwent what we might call "nuclear backsliding," he was forced to submit to extreme public humiliation in the form of a long government investigation of his "Americanism" and was eventually denied a security clearance. His earlier strong advocacy of the bomb and his national standing made his subsequent doubts all the more dangerous to those who remained proponents of nuclearism.

Edward Teller, another physicist important in early bomb research who later became known as "the father of the hydrogen bomb," is representative of the opposite sequence. In 1945, Teller opposed the use of the atomic bomb without warning. After the war, he vehemently objected to the moral reservations expressed by other scientists toward the idea of making nuclear weapons. Teller advocated maintaining an "adventurous spirit" in fully exploring the possibilities of atomic weapons—which now meant "his" H-bomb—and he believed that "we would be unfaithful to the tradition of Western civilization if we shied away from exploring what man can accomplish." This combination of ethical blindness and extreme technicism, not just in Teller but in many others as well, inspired the subtitle of the film *Dr. Strangelove, or How I Stopped Worrying and Learned to Love the Bomb.*

No one could argue that the power of the atomic bomb is not impressive, or that it does not readily engender a sense of awe both for nature's power and man's capacity for technological mastery. But the danger of the nuclearist position is that the bomb's power and its limitations are never clearly examined. The terms that were used by the scientists in referring to the bomb—terms such as "the gadget," "the thing," "the device," or simply "It"—served to blunt a continuing awareness of the bomb's deadly purpose. The bomb became enmeshed in utopian hopes for total salvation that seemed otherwise unattainable. Man's own place in the scheme of things was devalued and made subordinate to the demands of the weapon.

The early discussion of bomb shelters and diplomacy in the postwar period are examples of the perversions of logic to which the bomb led. It became clear that the United States could not fully defend itself from nuclear attack in case of another major war. An anxious debate ensued in which the chief issue was whether there would be any survivors of a major nuclear conflagration—shelters or no shelters. Also involved was the question of whether, considering the world into which they would emerge, the survivors would envy the dead. Teller argued that there *would* be survivors and that democratic ideals would survive with them. He insisted that "realistic thinking" demanded facing up to the possible consequences of the use of atomic weapons.

Given the experience of those who actually did survive the atomic bomb in Hiroshima, the question about survivors in this debate was never properly posed. The important question is not "Would there be survivors?" or "Would the survivors envy the dead?" but rather "Would the survivors themselves feel *as if* dead?"

Nuclearist thinking pervaded the field of diplomacy. There was a feeling that "the big atomic stick" (as Edward Teller called it) could solve the political problems of the world. There is no doubt that the presence of nuclear weapons did exercise a deterrent effect in international relations immediately following World War II. But a weapon too awesome and frightening to be used could not be a permanently effective deterrent. Statesmen began to realize that an arsenal consisting only of nuclear weapons would make the punishment for international violations more destructive than the crime. As one writer put it, a policeman armed only with an atomic bomb could not even prevent a housebreaking unless he were willing to sacrifice the entire city in doing so. It is even possible that the restraint on all-out war created by nuclear weapons made smaller, more prolonged conflicts like Vietnam more likely.

Nuclearism involves a failure of the imagination—a failure to conceive in human terms the meaning of the weapons—and the embrace as a means of man's salvation of that which most threatens it. Nuclearism provides an apocalyptic alternative to the already impaired modes of symbolic immortality while itself further undermining the viability of these modes. Nuclearism propels us toward use of the weapons and, equally dangerous, undermines man's capacity to confront the problems they raise.

Each of the modes of symbolic immortality has been affected by the dislocations of the nuclear era. Even without the actual deployment of these weapons, their very existence poses a profound threat to our perceptions of living and dying. The possibility that the human species can annihilate itself with its own tools fundamentally alters the relationship of human imagination to each mode of symbolic continuity.

The biological (and biosocial) mode is perhaps most obviously affected. The assumption of "living on" in one's descendants is made precarious. The aspiration of living on in one's nation is also undermined, for no longer do national boundaries offer the protection and security they once did. National security becomes identical with international security, which is dependent upon the partial relinquishment by each nation of its own exclusive claim on the allegiance of its citizens.

Because ultimate issues of life and death have become more urgent and more problematic, the theological mode has also become problematic. A rational-scientific age had already made commitments of religious faith and the meaning of God difficult issues for many people. Theological imagery of transcending death becomes a dubious promise if the assurance of some form of earthly survival is not also given. If there are none (or few) left among the biologically living, then the image of spiritual survival loses much of its symbolic and comforting power. It is precisely these threats to the belief in salvation that may account for the burgeoning of fundamentalist groups and the insistence of these groups upon the most narrow and literal—one might say desperate—forms of biblical faith.

In Japan after the explosion of the atomic bomb, neither Eastern nor Western religious imagery seemed capable of providing an acceptable explanation or formulation of the meaning of the disaster. The bomb experience seems to have wounded that deep layer of human confidence and trust to which religious symbolism appeals. No conventional religious expression was adequate to reestablish a sense of trust and continuity.

Partly as a response to this impasse, religious language has come to emphasize the sacred quality of man's earthly commitments and the religious importance of responsible political action. At the same time, there has been a revival of fundamentalist and occult religion—a manifestation of the increased plausibility of apocalyptic visions. Who can now say that an image of the end of the world is merely a religious pipe dream meant to frighten people into submission?

Theological imagery has developed in two contrasting directions. There has been a movement toward naturalism, in which religious imagery is more humanistic and closer to observable process. But there has also been a rise of visionary and doom-prophesying religious forms, in which salvation is made conditional upon total repentance. In either case, man's new demonic technological capacity (if not demonic human psychological potential) always threatens to overwhelm and render futile the attempt to immortalize man's spiritual attainments.

Immortality through the creative mode depends upon the conviction that one's works will endure. But what lasts anymore? The existence of nuclear weapons, together with the breakdown of the many forms of collective symbolization and ritual we have discussed, raise doubts about the permanence of any contributions to human culture. The fear is that nothing will last and that, therefore, nothing matters.

This concern about the viability of particular social forms and even about historical continuity itself creates an undercurrent of anxiety and mistrust that is generally not directly felt. But this concern is expressed in the increased need of young people to have a sense of the immediate human impact of their work and has resulted in heightened interest in careers involving teaching, legal practice, social work, and medicine. With regard to scientific work, as more questions are raised about the ethics of various scientific projects, the individual scientist is less able to undertake research without consideration of the lethal or life-enhancing potentials of the new knowledge he may unearth.

These questions and threats lead to a greater reliance upon the fourth mode—that of nature—for an image of permanence. But we now know that nature is all too susceptible to both our weapons and our pollution. Joan Baez's mournful tones in the song "What Have They Done to the Rain?" and Bob Dylan's desperate anger in "A Hard Rain's A-gonna Fall" both suggest a vision, shared by all of us in some degree, of ultimate nuclear violation of our planet.

In the face of this vision, explorations of outer space take on a special symbolic urgency. In these explorations we seek to extend our natural environment almost to infinity. But it would be the most wishful kind of illusion to see in these explorations, or in speculation about life on other planets, a solution to the problems of human continuity on our own endangered planet.

The impairment of these four modes of symbolic immortality has led to a greater reliance on the mode of experiential transcendence. This mode is closely related to immediate sensation. It is therefore less vulnerable to being impoverished by misgivings about historical durability, on which the other modes are more dependent. The resort to pleasure seeking or mystical experience is common in historically dislocated times. In our own time, we have witnessed great preoccupation with intensified forms of experience through drugs, sex, music, meditation, dance, nature, and even politics.

Beyond enabling one to live more fully in the present, the experiential mode lends itself to something more—to engaging death anxiety directly by experimenting with risk. Almost as artists become a community's conscience by exploring the extremities of the community's unfaced danger, the active pursuit of experiential transcendence plays with fears of death by inviting them, even encouraging them.

In this respect, there may be a strange parallel between nuclearism and the intense forms of experience that many people are now seeking. The most perverse response to the existence of a doomsday machine would be to love the bomb itself joyously: the nightmare of oblivion experienced as ecstasy. This is the malignant phenomenon that the film *Dr. Strangelove* carries even further and portrays in a powerfully bizarre image: a cowboy euphorically riding an atomic bomb as it soars from the plane toward glorious explosion.

Fanciful as this image appears, it has an eerie psychological plausibility. Expressed boldly, there may be a need to destroy one's world for purposes of imagined rebirth, a need which lends itself either to suicidal obliteration or to transformation and regeneration. This need takes advantage not only of every variety of individual and social aggression, but fits as well with the psychological principle of touching death, either imaginatively or literally, as a precondition of new life. Thus, nuclear weapons can achieve vivid symbolic representation in our minds precisely because of their promise of devastation.

The ultimate threat posed by nuclear weapons is not only death but meaninglessness: an unknown death by an unimaginable weapon. War with such weapons is no longer heroic; death from such weapons is without valor. Meaninglessness has become almost a stereotyped characterization of twentieth-century life, a central theme in modern art, theater, and politics. The roots of this meaninglessness are many. But crucial, we believe, is the anxiety deriving from the sense that all forms of human associations are perhaps pointless because subject to sudden irrational ends. Cultural life thus becomes still more formless. No one form, no single meaning or style appears to have any ultimate claim. The psychological implications of this formlessness are not fully clear; while there seem to be more life choices available, fewer are inwardly compelling.

Such broad historical themes as these can influence even the most fundamental of human relationships—the nurturing bond between mother and child. No mother can fully escape the general threat to the continuity and significance of life, nor the resulting death anxiety. Nor can she avoid transmitting these doubts to her offspring. Erik Erikson has emphasized the importance for the child of gaining a sense of "basic trust" early in life. Lack of such a firm sense of basic trust can undermine one's self-confidence for life and can prevent an individual from fulfilling his creative potential. Such childhood deficiencies may result from a lack of parental trust, from misgivings in the parents about the meaning and significance of their own lives.

Fundamental attitudes like these are communicated to children in subtle ways from their earliest days on. The importance of symbolic impairments in parents, such as a lost sense of immortality, in producing individual-psychological difficulties in children has not been much examined. But it is in such ways as this that the psychohistorical themes that characterize an era—like unfaced death anxiety in our time—become enmeshed in the psychological lives of individuals from one generation to another.

We began this discussion by describing some of the psychological struggles of those who survived the atomic bomb in Hiroshima. Those struggles involved guilt, numbing, and a continuing effort to give form and meaning to radically disrupted lives. Perhaps we can achieve little more than a glimmer of the excruciating tensions such extraordinarily painful lives have involved. But in another sense we are all survivors of this century's holocausts.

In cultivating and making clear to ourselves our own status as survivors, we become more fully part of the century in which we live. In doing so we open ourselves to the experience of pain and to the imagery and anxiety of death. We glimpse at such moments the necessity for personal and social transformation in the interest of continued survival and new meaning. The urgency of the tasks of reconstruction are then pressed upon us—though the forms our efforts must take are never fully clear.

7• Agents of Death

Gil Elliot

Gil Elliot was born in Scotland in 1931 and studied at Glasgow and Sussex universities. In his remarkable work The Twentieth Century Book of the Dead, *from which this selection is taken, Elliot details the 110 million murders committed by governments in this century.*

DEATH MACHINES

In considering violent or untimely death, it is the manner and means of death—not the general phenomenon of death itself—that are of primary philosophical interest.

Can the manner and means of violent death be reduced to a knowable mechanism—a "death machine"?

Of the ways in which we can think of knowing or understanding such a death machine, one is to "know all the facts," another is to ask the question, "how does it relate to me?"

To know the facts is desirable. To know *all* the facts about such a phenomenon as the death machine would clearly be an absurd pretension. Yet, "waiting for science to establish all the facts" is the everyday limbo of the game of factual knowledge. Whilst playing this waiting game we are supposed to suspend the judgment of values, and even to neglect that most sensitive tool of inquiry, sharpened by experience, alert to survive, vivid in its brief life: intuition. Intuition, or the practice of relating oneself to the object in the immediacy of experience, is, like life itself, "unreliable." It seems that the certainties of science are worth waiting for. But when these so-called certainties appear they are pluralistic, as conflicting, as subject to opinion as anything else. In short, the procedures of "objective" inquiry are just as much modified by self and by fantasy as those of subjective inquiry. The difference is that in the first case the part played by the self is concealed from the observer, and often from the would-be scientist himself.

Shelley said that the poet is the "unacknowledged legislator" of the world. In our grim times the chief unacknowledged legislator has been the subjective fantasy of political leaders, academic theorists, social groups masquerading as "objective reality," "historical necessity," "political realism," "value-free judgment," "scientific objectivity," and so forth.

The death machine, then, is partly a factual object—an ever-incomplete accretion of facts; and partly a philosophical object—uncertain of definition yet conceived as a whole to which I relate myself, so intuitively that the "I" itself will become, if necessary, subject to analysis as part of the death machine!

We might manage a preliminary definition, or at least tease out some of the relevant parts, of the death machine if we look at those versions of it which [can be] loosely identified with different areas of macroviolence. The *war machine*, the *total-war machine*, and the *total-state machine* are pretty well factual objects, identifiable in terms of organization, weapons, production, deployment of plans and personnel.

I took the war machine of the First World War as the type of the twentieth-century war machine. What characterizes it most is a change in the nature of the *alienating process*. War was traditionally a conflict between two alienated sides, "enemies." During the First World War even the men in the trenches ceased to believe that the enemy was the men in the other trenches. The alienating process of the modern war machine divides men into two subjective environments: the physical environment of the victim (the death environment) and the technological environment of the systems and machines which produce death. Some have perceived this in terms of class alienation. According to this view, the killing systems and machines are within the conscious control of the leaders and generals, and it is their class alienation from the poor that prevents them from using restraint in the use of these systems against the chief victims, the ordinary soldiers who without their uniforms are, of course, the poor. I am sure that this process—which I shall call *natural alienation* when I discuss it below in the context of the nature machine—is relevant to a discussion of how the modern war machine came into being, or evolved. The other view is that the machines and systems inhabit a faceless environment of their own, and dominate their users.

However it evolved in the first place, it is this, which we can fairly call *technological alienation,* that remains and persists as the most characteristic feature of the twentieth-century war machine.

It is also characteristic of the war machine that the same man, the soldier, operates the killing systems as well as being their victim. The *total-war* machine extends the alienation principle, for here death environments are also created for people who are not themselves involved in operating the killing systems, that is civilians shot, starved, or bombed, soldiers and civilians enclosed in camps. Here the alienation between the environment of the killing system—military or administrative—and the environment of the victim is total. The same is true of the total-state machine, with one additional refinement. The alienated identity of the victim is not merely created by the technological sweep of the machine, as it is in the total-war machine. In this case, before the victim is included in the killing technology (the labor camp, the mass execution, the deportation) a paranthropoid identity, such as class enemy or enemy of the people, is created for him out of the ideology of the total-state machine. That is to say, *ideological alienation* precedes the technological alienation.

The essential difference between the war machine and the total-war machine is one of *consciousness.* Traditionally war was a ritual in which certain qualities such as bravery, generalship, morale, cunning contributed to the symbolic outcome known as "victory." Where ritual and symbol broke down you had chaotic, meaningless conflicts such as the Thirty Years' War. The First World War was *not* this chaotic, meaningless thing, not merely the war of attrition and exhaustion. It was a case—*the* case—of ritual and symbol being outstripped and replaced by a new logic of war. But it was not yet a conscious logic. Total war as it developed thereafter was a *conscious* departure from the natural order provided by ritual and symbol. But how conscious? and how true has the logic of the new order been to the human consciousness?

As we know, the raw material of total war, and hence the chief premises of its logic are, one, vast numbers of people and, two, machines.

The vast numbers were first represented by the figure of the citizen-soldier, who reached his apotheosis in the First World War. By the Second World War he was already outstripped, in numbers participating, by the plain *citizen.* The next total war will involve very few soldiers as against citizens. Thus the logic of numbers reaches its conclusion, that total war is war between citizens not soldiers. But this logic cannot sustain a theory of war. "Soldiers" means a selective, limited number of people who can be used for purposive action. "Citizens" has no such finite, purposive meaning. It can only mean either "all citizens" or "citizens at random to an infinite number." It is an inchoate principle which cannot sustain a theory of conflict.

The responsibility for providing a rationale of total war thus devolves heavily upon the machines, and the logic of the machines is utterly fascinating. We should remember, first, that the machines of modern warfare are not merely horrid excrescences, nightmarish extrusions of the human mind.

That is what they become in action, but purely as machines they are truly representative of us and the times we live in. The force of unprecedented numbers; impersonal answers to the demands of conflicting egos; the development of solutions under pressure; economical concentration of human ingenuity—all of these are represented and symbolized in our machines of warfare. They are our champions on the field of conflict.

It is part of the genius of living things that violence, when not directed to survival (food, protection), is economical in its effects. The biological response to conflict between equals is an instinctive ritual which (a) recognizes and respects the reality of the conflict or disagreement, and (b) reduces the struggle to symbolic dimensions. Animals fighting their own kind have a system of signals symbolizing defeat, victory, submission which allow the conflict to be resolved far short of irreparable physical harm. Human society is far too complex for such patterns to remain in a pure form, but they still survive at the roots of individual behavior. So far as group conflict is concerned, the most economical fighting ritual is that where two champions symbolize two numerous groups of people and fight on their behalf.

When it comes to the *machine as champion*, not only does the machine lack these reductive qualities: its response to the conflict situation is purely quantitative. Where there are two machines confronting one another, there will be soon four, and so on. The symbol or champion becomes greater in importance than what it represents. As the number and power of the machines increase, so does the number of people involved. But . . . the logic of numbers in the context of total war cannot sustain a rationale of conflict. Once again we reach a logical *impasse*. There is only one logical path left, and that is that the machines should fight one another *without the involvement of people.*

There are I think two possible reasons why we do not proceed with this logic and have a War of the Machines. One is the difficulty of arranging it; but I cannot believe this would be an insuperable obstacle. The other reason, and I believe the valid one, is that it would be absurd. For two opposing sides to contemplate arranging a War of the Machines would expose the absurdity of the logic of conflict by destructive machinery, and hence must lead to the dismantling of the machinery. But this is something that we could not bear to contemplate. So great is our spiritual and material investment in the machines, so much do they truly champion our values, so little do we have the wit or resourcefulness to devise other symbols to represent us in our conflicts, that we cannot face up to the logic of what we are doing. So the people and the machines continue to grow in numbers, the function of the people being to lend verisimilitude to the War of the Machines. Thus we achieve the poor man's version of sanity, which is the physical acceptance of whatever happens to exist, supported by whatever rationalization can be concocted at the moment.

. . . How true [has] the logic of total war been to the human consciousness? Well, it is a straightfoward denial of consciousness, of course. If the machines are looked upon as the objective results of thought, and in their development as the repositories of an objective logic, then the objective conclusion they display is, as demonstrated above, the need for their own destruction or dismantling. Consciousness demands that we draw this conclusion and act upon it. Indeed, if looked upon in this way the machines of war might provide the basis for a complete rationale of the place of conflict in human society, and of the destruction of human life in particular. In this case they would perform a useful rationalizing function, and would actually take human practice a progressive step beyond the simple logic of survival which governs the instinctive rituals of fighting. But, in the denial of this consciousness, we leave ourselves in that limbo known as the world of objective reality: a world of external objects in which the human being has no greater value than any other object displacing the same physical volume of space, a mental environment as hostile to the survival of life as a concentration camp.

What is the difference between the "nature machine" and these man-made death machines? Well, the *nature machine* is the mechanics of what used to be called, rather smugly, the balance of nature. It was a kind of long-term death machine for the poor in their environment, in the form of disease, epidemic, and shortage of food; tendencies that were exacerbated from time to time by natural disasters such as flood and crop failure, and by degenerate relationships between alienated classes. But the balance of nature was kept in the sense that life triumphed conspicuously over death.

On the basis of this definition we can draw some comparisons between death in the natural environment and in the man-made environment. By "natural environment" I mean the context of living when the world society as a whole was preindustrial. Many of the same conditions apply to present-day "underdeveloped" countries. But remember that however pre- or nonindustrial a society may be today, it almost certainly possesses two basic ingredients of the man-made environment: modern medicine, which may drastically reduce the deathrate and increase the population; and, at the least, rapid access to sophisticated military technology in the world community. The essential elements of the new man-made life and death.

If we think of untimely deaths in the natural environment as being the "violence of nature" then by far the greatest proportion came from *microviolence,* by which I mean the regular, widely distributed incidence of disease, infant mortality, malnutrition. Because of the gradual, pervasive nature of microviolence we tend to lack direct ways of apprehending its magnitude. For the same reason its impact is taken and absorbed by those directly affected by it: it does not *apparently* affect the structures of society as a whole. The macroviolence of nature—floods, famine, pestilence — had more apparent, dramatic impact, but in fact the quantitative effects were much smaller; and macroviolence was not institutionalized and given a continuous existence as it is in the man-made environment. The same was true of the macroviolent forms of fighting, which retained an inherent *reductive capacity;* whilst in the man-made environment, where the propensity to fight is invested in machines, the problem of reduction is divorced from instinct, ritual, and commonsense and is a problem of men and machines, and which control which.

The chief reason the effects of microviolence are unapparent is because it is an essential *part* of the social structure. The "balance of nature" depends upon it. So does the large-family structure and hence the specialized roles of men and women. Natural microviolence has a macroviolent impact only when the possibility of stopping it is perceived—then it promotes change or revolution; and when it *has* been stopped—then it promotes (in default of birth control) a population explosion with future implications of macroviolence.

The alienation process in the natural environment has the same roots as in the man-made environment, but develops in a radically different way. *Natural alienation* begins as a good and necessary separation of vigorous social elements from their bondage to the earth. As this separation flowers into the skills and arts of social management the classes formed from it, whether aristocratic or middle class, become physically alienated not only from the earthier aspects of themselves but from the people associated with the earth; hence the despised class of *peasants.* In spite of this actual circumstance, of people living as it were in separate worlds, the Christian ethos claims to unite them. The people are spiritually united in God, and even physically united in a romanticized version of nature. When this unified consciousness is challenged or threatened we have *religious alienation,* the victims being in the post-Reformation period *minority Christian* denominations, in the turbulent and insecure seventeenth century *witches,* and persistently throughout the Christian centuries the *Jews.*

Physical and spiritual alienation is thus, in the natural environment, natural and religious, and in the man-made environment, technological and ideological. The victims are similar and the relevant psychological patterns seem to be very much the same. Peasants and Jews are major victims of both types of environment; they are the link as it were between the paranthropoid identities of one kind of society and the other. The great difference is in the kind of violence they bring about. The natural environment contained a continual microviolence which took a regular toll of human life and from time to time escalated sufficiently through plague, famine, and the chaos of war to give society a nasty jolt, but it preserved the balance of nature and never at any time threatened the existence of the human species. The man-made environment has brought microviolence impressively under control, but it threatens to disturb the balance of nature through industrial activity affecting the atmosphere, through the destruction of living species, and through uncontrolled increases in human population; it has brought macroviolence to a level which disastrously upsets the stability of societies, destroys morals, and threatens the continued existence of the human species.

Another link between the two environments is the *death-breeding machine* which at its most chaotic combines the violence of nature with that of technology. If technology is nature moulded by consciousness then we might expect this machine to contain a progression from a less-conscious to a more-conscious process. Certainly human consciousness is embedded in technology, yet apologists of modern war tend to present the technology as a massive simulation of nature about which little can be done; and it does seem more like a progression from blind nature to blind technology. If we extend the meaning of the *death-breeding process* to signify the active principle of all macroviolent systems, we shall see however that some are more conscious than others. Also we should remember that technology proceeds from a knowable first cause: man or, more specifically, scientific man. The death-breeding process leads to the final peak of the *total-death machine,* that which threatens the apocalyptic end and absolutely final appearance of . . . us.

What about . . . us? the celluloid lovers continually ask each other as we catch our breaths in the dark of the cinema, and that is also the question of the total-death machine. I suppose total death is some kind of absolute value and the philosophical core of the man-made death machine. Looking at the death machine as a philosophical entity, we might see the *nature machine* as the basic source of all; the *death-breeding process* as the active principle with its question about consciousness; and *total death* as the final question.

In the natural environment nature is supposed to unite society in happy worship of God. In the man-made environment technology is supposed to unite society in happy worship of Science. But if we look at the technologies of macroviolence we shall soon see that the reality is very different.

TECHNOLOGIES OF MACROVIOLENCE

Of the 110 million man-made deaths calculated in this century, sixty-two million died in conditions of *privation,* forty-six million from guns and bombs, or *hardware,* and two million from *chemicals.* In separating or *chemicals* as a category on its own I am thinking of the future as well as reflecting the century's progress from the heavy metal industries to the advances in the chemical industries which are such a significant part of our present-day scene. The familiar association of large-scale killing with factory production is not merely a colorful metaphor. Given the scale of modern killing technologies, their parallel development with that of industrial research and methods is inevitable. Hence the latest developments in killing methods are those associated with the fashionable science of the moment, biology.

Privation technologies

The basic kinds of privation technologies are I think best expressed as operating in *enclosed, semienclosed* and *diffuse* areas.

Enclosed privation areas

Camp privation is a highly conscious process, involving collection and movement of people, and selective identity of the victim. The systems of the killing technology are various: camp administration, collection or concentration

Deaths from privation technologies 62 million		
ENCLOSED	SEMIENCLOSED	DIFFUSE
Camp privation	City privation	Rural or mixed privation
20 million	16 million	26 million

system, and the wider governmental system directing all. Where the secret police system is a power in the land these functions are vertically integrated. But the people who perform the different functions, even if belonging to the same organization, differ from one another, partly in class and outlook, certainly in their spatial relationship with the victim. Where there is no curb on the power of the state (the first condition for camp privation), the state's victims are passed on *notionally* by those who make the rules, *administratively* by those who run the identification and collection system, and *physically* by the camp administration and guards. They are delivered from one set of people to the next. Arbitrary brutality occurs in those who are brutal by nature. But when the conditions notionally or administratively laid down are inhuman, and are supervised by the kind of people who survive by obeying orders, then the system is brutal and that is a more powerful force than arbitrary brutality. The most powerful force of all is physical neglect.

ENCLOSED PRIVATION AREAS

Camp privation

Enclosed ghetto, 1 m. deaths

Concentration camp, 2.5 m. deaths

Prisoners-of-war camp, 4.5 m. deaths

Labour camp, 12 m. deaths

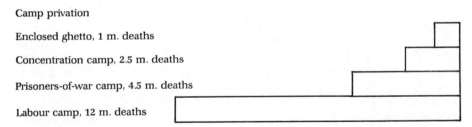

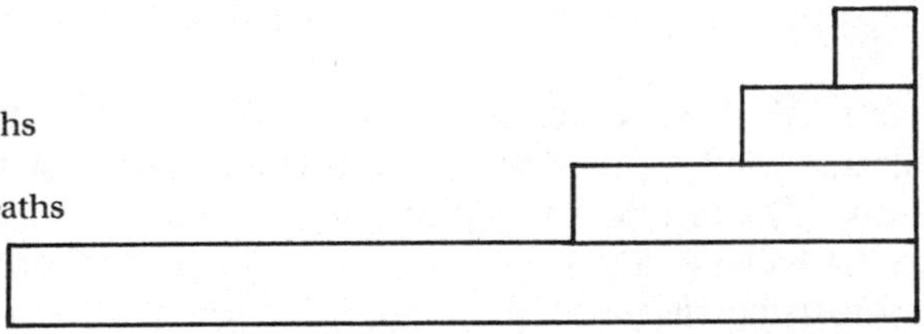

The *enclosed ghettoes* of Poland—Warsaw, Lodz, Lublin—were used as camps. They were sealed off city areas in which people from outside were concentrated. They were virtually total-death environments. They are unique as enclosed privation areas in which the identity of the victim was not selective as to age and sex (although it is true that less severe privations have been suffered by entire families in transit camps for deported populations and in displaced person camps for refugees).

The German *prisoner-of-war camps* for Russians were the only enclosed privation areas with entirely male populations. Some of these camps were certainly places of total death. They are the most extreme example of sheer physical neglect, more powerful in its effects (cannibalism, for instance) than enforced human pressures.

Although the degeneration of conditions in the German *concentration camps* was possibly due to the secret police arm in particular, the German camps as a whole reflected the policy of the government over a period and hence to a very large extent the society as a whole. Racist attitudes were responsible for the ghettoes, and for the treatment of Slav prisoners of war in a way different from people of other races. The German camp system in its developed form was possible only as the result of military conquest, and with military cooperation. Nine-tenths of the victims were foreigners. Any individual actions leading to their presence in the camps were committed in response to military aggression. In the chain of people who pass on victims from one to the other, the military acted as delivery men to the secret police, not only in the case of some of the concentration camp victims, but also in the case of the Russian prisoners of war.

Whilst the German camp system lasted little more than the duration of the war, the Russian *labor camps* have the distinction of being a permanent assertion of a national system of injustice, traditional in its present form for over fifty years. This is the only camp system where privation has been imposed on people for more than about five years. Hence the environments created by the system—virtually a conscious re-creation of the microviolence of nature—are unique. Within the system, all on a large scale, are a survival environment, a random-death environment, and a total-death environment. There are certain special camps where people are deprived of liberty but otherwise not harassed. There are the camps of the survival environment, which Solzhenitsyn's novel describes as *The First Circle.* Beyond this there is the second circle, of the labor camp proper and the random-death environment. Beyond that there is the third circle, the camps of the far north and east and the total-death environment: Komi, Karaganda, Vorkuta.

Semienclosed privation areas Privation technologies in semienclosed areas emphasize the vulnerability of cities. A city cannot adapt itself to military strategies. It cannot pretend it is not a city, disguise itself as a forest, grow its own food on the sly, and so on. Its citizens depend upon organizational structures and if these are interfered with so is the life of the citizen. Once disruption gets beyond a certain stage there is nothing much that can be done about it. Total war and total revolution bring the random-death environment to the city.

SEMIENCLOSED PRIVATION AREAS

City privation

Unenclosed ghetto, 1 m. deaths

Siege, 1 m. deaths

Occupation, 6 m. deaths

Civil dislocation, 8 m. deaths

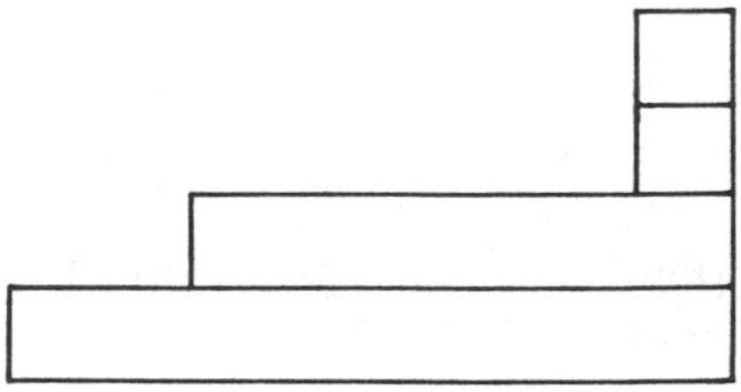

The *unenclosed ghettoes of* eastern Poland and the Baltic States were subject to harassment and pressures from the occupying forces, for racialist reasons, which turned them into total-death environments. The purely military pressures of *siege* almost did the same for Leningrad. On a larger and somewhat more diffuse scale, the cities of Russia became areas of random death from privation during the *dislocation* of the civil war period and again under the pressures of military *occupation* during the Second World War.

The victims of city privation are of course families in their normal habitats; in time of war their identities are selective to the extent that the younger men are being killed elsewhere.

Diffuse privation areas It's amazing in how many different ways the life can be squeezed out of people. It had never occurred to me that a sizable number of people might have died in *transit* — in the sheer bungling inefficiency of forced movement. Think of the way human beings have been driven and herded back and forth across Europe and Russia in our century. Deportation of peasants to Siberia. Trains to the labor camps. Deportation of Russian and Ukrainian slave laborers to Germany. Trains from every corner of Europe to the ghettos and death camps. Rail journeys and forced marches of prisoners of war.

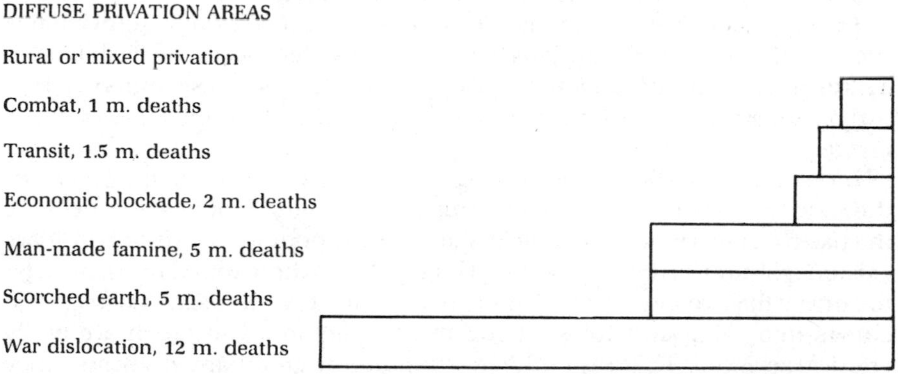

Privation deaths among soldiers in *combat* conditions include the typhus and wound infections of the First World War, the freezing hardship and disease of the Second World War in Russia, the starvation and typhus of the China War and amongst other ill-equipped armies throughout the century, the malarias and jaundices of Western soldiers in the East.

You would imagine that *diffuse* privation would have a larger element of the accidental about it, if only because of the sheer difficulty of getting at people in far-flung rural areas. But not so. *Economic blockade*, as practiced against the Germans in the First World War, against the Biafrans in the Nigerian Civil War; *man-made famine*, as engineered against the Russian peasants during the collectivization; *scorched earth* tactics, as used by the Germans in Russia and the Japanese in China. They are all highly conscious and deliberate methods of destroying people; killing technologies.

Most of these highly conscious technologies tend to produce an immediate random-death environment. In the case of the general *war dislocation* in China and other places where a slow privation was diffused over a vast population, you might say that the privation deaths were an intrusion into a survival environment, that is to say, a social climate in which death is not random but people still have some room to survive by their own efforts.

Listing these technologies, as objective parts of the death machine, is not difficult. But how can I, as an individual, relate myself to these? Perhaps we all tend to feel we ought to attempt to relive the sufferings of the dead. Apart from the self-delusion involved in such an attempt, it is difficult to see what object is served by it. It certainly doesn't bring back the dead or heal their agony or expiate the crimes of which they are the victims. In fact, if you read some of the basic factual accounts of the intensest death environments such as concentration or death camps—as you must do, if you hope to reach any understanding of the human story—you will probably have an *involuntary* "reliving" of suffering in any case. The experience of most people I have talked to on this subject agrees with my own—that the simple factual detail of such accounts is so horrifying that it is only bearable for a few pages at a time. Herein I think lies the salutary and sole purpose of "reliving" such sufferings: the perception of the unbearable. If it is bearable something phony is going on, either on the part of the writer or of the reader.

I cannot then truly relate myself to these technologies of macroviolence through the simulated emotions, feelings, and sufferings of the flesh known as "reliving." But I *can* suffer these structures of reality—these terms descriptive of real event—to enter the mind undistorted by specific color, myth, or image.

Indeed it would be difficult enough to describe the *ghetto,* the *blockade,* the *scorched earth,* the *famine,* in terms of image or metaphor—for these are the basic realities which provide image and metaphor for the rest of ordinary existence. They are the bare bones of reality. Nor is there much need, in order to convey their reality, to explain in great detail how the *siege* or *occupation* comes into being and works its effects, for the bones of death are easily enough achieved. There is nothing extraordinary about any of these—they could be organized by a wise child if there were a wise child willing to organize millions of deaths. If we were describing some complex social fabric where a million conflicting interests were maintained in a living pattern then there would be some call for depth of study . . . but when it comes to the *prison camp,* the *concentration camp,* the *labor camp,* all of these share that cretinous unity of human purpose whereby success and failure achieve the same end of destruction and death. These are the bones, these technologies of the past and those death systems latent in our present, that form the skeleton structure of the death machine.

If it is true that in the twentieth century man has finally come face to face with his own skeleton, it is a structure such as this that he is looking at. I would have the *intellect,* not simulated feelings but the perceiving *mind,* to suffer that skeleton.

Hardware technologies

Military experts tend to assert that in twentieth-century conflicts many more deaths have been caused by the big guns than by small arms. In this generalization there is an important truth and an important untruth. Quantitatively, the statement is not true. According to my calculations deaths from hardware technologies divide roughly as follows:

Deaths from hardware technologies 46 million			
BIG GUNS	AERIAL BOMBS	SMALL ARMS	DEMOGRAPHIC (mixed)
18 million	1 million	24 million	3 million

But the *significant* untruth lies in the implication that as deaths from the big guns increase, deaths from small arms might, or do, or by some logic should, decline in numbers. Not only is this a demonstrably false proposition, but it is the very opposite that is true. As deaths from big guns increase, they also help to bring about an *increase* in deaths from small arms. This is the important truth about the death potential of the big guns. It is not a question of a particular type of weapon being chosen for military reasons, or of one type making another type obsolete. It is a question of big guns *creating an environment* of death on the scale of macroviolence. In this environment small arms and other death technologies not only flourish but also tend to increase to the same scale of macroviolence.

Big guns Basing itself on the general nature of the First World War and on some evidence suggesting the preponderance of wounds to be from the effects of exploding shells, expert opinion concludes that "90 percent" or "three-quarters" of the deaths came from the big guns. We may modify that proportion if we assume that experts tend to think exclusively in terms of combat deaths, chiefly in terms of the major theaters of war and mainly of the most characteristic set-piece battles. On the basis of a ten million total, at least two million deaths (from the economic blockade and from soldier disease) were outside of combat. If we think of the early part of the war when the machine gun was used intensively, of the massed cavalry charges of the Russian front and the heavy losses on the Italo-Austrian front, as well as continuous small engagements and sniping throughout the war, it becomes at least possible that as many as three million may have died from small arms fire.

Even if the proportion of deaths from the big guns was as low as five million out of ten, the experts are certainly correct in emphasizing the overwhelming significance of these weapons. The big guns created a physical and mental environment, a list of whose effects on the human race would break the spirit of any computer. The mechanical scale of the big guns determined strategy and the general context in which twentieth-century conflict would take place. The big guns decided that the characteristic form of killing in the twentieth century would be repetitive massacre, with a minimum of felt conflict. Thus the nature of the *small arms* killings in the First World War was predetermined by the big guns. In the first place, whether they amounted to one or three million, the number was greater than the number killed by small arms in any previous war. Secondly, probably the majority took the form of repetitive massacre in situations created by the logic of the big guns.

BIG GUNS

China, 1 m. deaths

Other conflicts, 2 m. deaths

Rest of the Second World War, 5 m. deaths

Second World War, Russians, 5 m. deaths

First World War, 5 m. deaths

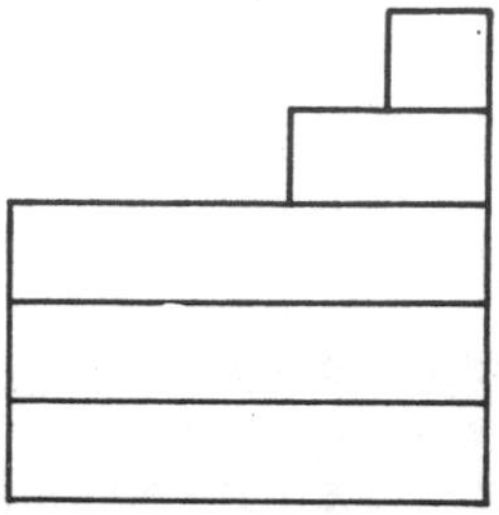

In the First World War the big guns were heavier and the distinction between them and small arms was cruder than in the Second World War. Rifles and machine guns—dominated, like the minds of generals, by the big guns—did the work of big guns. That is to say, they were frequently used for massacre in situations where big guns might as well have been used. In the Second World War big guns were generally lighter and the range of weapons wider. Some were even portable. Weapons had been rationalized to meet the techniques of massacre.

The big guns and, later, the mechanized battlefield created a technological environment which men accepted as a simulation of nature, a force which could not ultimately be controlled by men but only guided in certain directions. We can see this development also in the smaller conflicts of the century. The forces which govern the incidence of conflict and the scale of death are still localized, traditional ones: genuine if senseless conflicts, death occurring on a scale with at least some reference to the objects of struggle. But in the post-Second World War period, as the world situation casts its shadow more and more on local conflicts, so the great technological environment of large-scale death is imported into them and the localized effects diminish in importance.

In China, the physical environment created by the big guns has not existed to a very large extent at all. In China, of course, the natural environment was sufficiently deteriorated not to require the massive technological creation of a death environment.

Small arms The use of small arms is much wider than the limits of formal wars or conflicts. Big guns are used within the context of a formal war, and indeed often dominate the context and create their own environment. This is probably not true of small arms. There is always, I believe, a controlling system or factor stronger than the weapons themselves. This is clearly evident in the case of *formal executions,* where the legal or pseudolegal process decides death for every individual; death is certified in advance. Execution can be by a number of means—strangling, guillotine, hanging—as well as by shooting. But it seems unlikely that the executions of this century would have reached such numbers without the rifle and pistol. Pulling a trigger is so easy. The uniquely twentieth-century characteristic of these killings is the scale on which they have occurred. The sinister auspices of state interrogations, trials, summary executions are not new, they are as old as human records. The scale is quite new, and it is of course the scale of military operations and massacre.

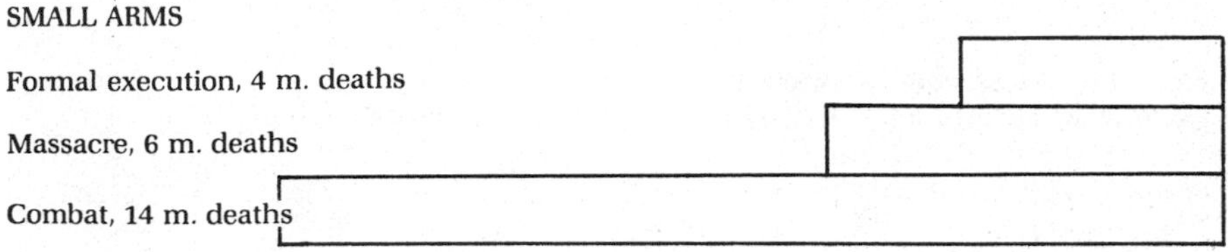

If the massacre by big gun and the massacre by formal execution are rationalized by their apparent connections with traditional human activities —"fighting" and "war," "punishment" and the "legal process"—at least in the massacre by massacre there are no such hypocrisies to obscure the simple truth. Administrative or military orders, men with guns, selected victims, killing: that's the simple recipe. In listing five major areas of massacre with small arms, I shall indicate associated areas where massacres on a smaller scale have occurred, and the approximate figures relate to all the areas mentioned.

The last and largest category of small arms deaths is those that occurred in military *combat.* My impression is that, on the basis of about fourteen million deaths, half of these would be in the two world wars, and the other half in other wars including those of China. Of the small arms deaths in the First World War it is likely the preponderance were in situations where the massed firepower of small arms were used as a means of massacre auxiliary to that of the big guns. This would also be true of Russian combat deaths in the Second World War, and somewhat less true of deaths on other fronts. In the spectrum of smaller wars over the century the pattern would be more erratic. It is probably safe to say that at least half of all the deaths from small arms in the major and minor wars had the characteristics of massacre in environments dominated by big guns.

It becomes necessary to make a distinction between formal combat and what we understand by conflict. Presumably, in conflict in the individual sense, there is some kind of equation such as equal opportunity for both parties or at least a feeling of such, or that the outcome should be dependent on some kind of skill. Conflict in this sense does not exist where people die from privation, or from the big guns, or from the various massacres of small arms. Only in about half the deaths from small arms in combat situations is there the remotest possibility of a conflict situation having existed. If we add to this the category of demographic violence where there is clearly a large element of conflict, we have a figure of about ten million deaths where a situation of conflict *might* have existed; that is to say, in less than 10 percent of all the man-made deaths of the century.

RECIPE FOR MASSACRE

Administrative or military orders	*Men with guns*	*Selected victims*	*Number killed*
Suppression of minority and other *ad hoc* orders	Turkish Army and others in "small" wars	Armenians and others	1m.
Enforced collectivization and other administrative tasks	Russian Secret Police	Peasants, camp prisoners, etc.	1m.
Reprisal orders and other law-and-order measures	German Army	People, random selected	2m.
Orders to suppress and destroy Jewry and other groups	German Secret Police	Jews, Gypsies, old and sick people	1m.
Other *ad hoc* orders	Japanese army and other armies in the Second World War	Peasants and others	1m.
		Approximate total	*6m*

Demographic violence Each of the three cases I have noted, the Russian Bread War, the Chinese antibourgeois campaigns, and the Indian Partition riots—accumulating to a minimum of three million deaths—might be looked upon as escalated forms of microviolence. That is to say, to some extent they have the character of ordinary civil violence. Yet in each case there is a macroelement in the organizational structure of the event as well as in its incidence, in the form of instruction or recommendation from the center. In each case an official pronouncement, coming at a time of transition between two systems of government, leads to a violence which reflects the clash between the two forms of government. This reminds us that even in an age of macroviolence the violence of "the people" remains microviolent, that is taking the form of frequent individual and occasional mob violence which *never* approaches the dimensions of macroviolence *except when organized by the state.* Feelings of violence in the people are only united into a mass in the fantasy of scholar and politician. Thus we have the grotesque paradox that many respectable statesmen, in their fear of "the people" or "the masses" or "disorder," recommend that the best way to keep them off the streets is to put them in uniform—the very action that unites vast numbers of people in the potential of macroviolence!

The very exceptional nature of demographic violence in the spectrum of macroviolence—the fact that it involves hand-to-hand fighting reflecting direct conflict, aggression, fear, and struggle in the individual—leads to a necessary question. Do the technologies of macroviolence, with a few exceptions, lead to situations, and ultimately to a general situation, in which violence may explode or proliferate without reference to conflict, aggression, fear, or struggle? Can macroviolence become completely divorced from human psychology and motivation? If it can, then it calls for a completely new dimension of inquiry, for most studies of violence assume a link with aggression, conflict, frustration, boredom, and other human conditions.

Aerial bombing The number of deaths [from aerial bombing] may be a good deal in excess of the one million I have calculated, but it is most unlikely to be more than two million. The peak level of deaths for an individual city is about 200,000 and the main victims were Dresden, Hiroshima, and Nagasaki, chief targets of Allied terror bombing in the Second World War. The deliberate bombing of civilians was the chief source of deaths in volume, and other cities attacked in this way during the Second World War (including the Sino-Japanese war) were: Coventry and other English cities; Rotterdam and other Dutch cities; Warsaw and other Polish cities; Stalingrad and other Russian cities; Shanghai and other Chinese cities; Frankfurt and other German cities; Tokyo and other Japanese cities.

In the bombing of cities the technologies of violence are destroying the technologies of peace. In the early days, bombing was similar to the shelling of a city, that is the city happened to crop up in the strategic plans. By the time we reach the atom bomb, Hiroshima and Nagasaki, the ease of access to target and the instant nature of macroimpact mean that both the choice of city and the identity of the victim have become completely randomized, and human technology has reached a final platform of self-destructiveness. The great cities of the dead, in numbers, remain Verdun, Leningrad, and Auschwitz. But at Hiroshima and Nagasaki the "city of the dead" is finally transformed from a metaphor into a literal reality. The city of the dead of the future is our city and the victims are—not French and German soldiers, nor Russian citizens, nor Jews—but all of us without reference to specific identity.

Chemicals and other advanced technologies

About the asphyxiation of between one and two million people by poisonous fumes in specifically prepared chambers and vans, there is little to be said that has not already been said. It should be studied in direct physical detail as recorded in several books and the reader will then find if he has not already done so that there is no need to compare it with anything else in order to get it "into perspective." Since then science and technology have proliferated the technologies of macroviolence to the extent that every new technological development has a death application as well as a life use. If you explore the ocean bed and contemplate its human uses you also devise a means of devastating the ocean bed. If you discover how to isolate germs and viruses for protective purposes you also proceed to concentrate them into a technology for killing a million people. If you can deaden the nerves to lessen surgical pain you can also paralyze the nerves for hostile purposes, and modify your technology to produce various degrees of agony and types of death. Whilst scientific discoveries and technologies often remain hypothetical and open ended for a considerable time while their life uses are being explored, the death application has the advantage of unquestionable effectiveness. The technology can thus instantly become a closed system and acquire that aura of magic and power which has been sought through the ages of villains, charlatans, psychopaths, and fools. Thus, for instance, the attempt to connect the subtle detail and variety of human behavior with physiological processes is delicate—difficult—hypothetical—frustrating—open ended. But if you approach it from the angle of the *death application*, you can most certainly by drugs and surgery ensure the deadening of great areas of human behavior, and thus become a magician freed from irritating difficulties.

Such is the romanticization of technology, like the old romanticizing of nature, that the technologies of macroviolence are actually glamorized in modern fiction, with the glossy inanity with which overfed, stupid aristocrats used to dress up as swains and shepherdesses. These corruptions are beginning to eat back at technology so that, in addition to the city of the dead as a future arena of self-destructiveness, we have the possibility of human technology destroying itself at the source . . .

VALUES: NEGATIVE AND POSITIVE

Seeking an *answer to death* is perhaps the greatest wild-goose chase of human existence. Yet from time to time a new attitude if not solution arises out of our experience. Such an attitude is latent in the connection between *violence* and *death* which, although apparently an obvious one, has not yet been fully expressed in terms of recent experience. Violence in the twentieth century has produced the new phenomenon of *total death.* As an *idea,* total death has existed—in mental pictures of *the day of judgment, doomsday, the end of the world*—at least since the formulation of the great religions. As a *reality* attainable by human means, the science of which is a permanent unalterable part of knowledge, it originates in the notorious half century from which we are just emerging. *Can* we emerge from the nightmare of reality and vision created in that period? We cannot create a retrospective order for the chaos of the actual events. Can we escape from the chaos of the idea that is left to us? *Total death* could mean the obliteration of particular cities, or countries, or regions; it could mean the collapse of world civilization or the death of the species; or it could mean the total death of the mind within a variety of physical parameters. *Total death* might be brought about by a wide range of means; by the carefully considered destruction of selected millions; by the direct and secondary effects of pollution or overcrowding; by a death-breeding mixture of every kind of human motivation acting on machineries and systems which are beyond the control of living creatures. *Total death* has a time span overwhelming the convenient human notion of time. It can "happen" in an instant, in a few days; it can have the monthly, yearly rhythms of traditional warfare or it could create a chronic long-term disruption of seasons of nature and the years of human life. Its possibility is tomorrow, or in the next two hundred years, or at any "time" in the future. *Total death* is a hard, scientific, and immediate reality at the same time as being a speculative idea in search of a philosophy. No existing mental structures, of science, philosophy, or religion, are adequate to contain it.

Death after all is a powerful reality. It is one of two or three fundamental ideas that condition the human attitude to existence. I think we should find, if we examined them in the cool comparative way that is now becoming possible, that some of the great religions have gravely distorted truth in order to accommodate the idea of death—to explain it away, to dodge its straightforward implications. A common result is the identification of *death* with *evil*, or with an unknowable darkness or *chaos*. Hence the rejection in the mind of death as a reality. Hence the reluctance of those who write with such vigor the history of the machines and systems of violence to mention the facts of death and to include these in their historical interpretations. Hence *our* need to *reject the assumption that reality is chaos*, to insist on *the possibility of knowing the truth about the deaths that result from our behavior*, to *structure our knowledge of death and deaths and total death* and bring the facts into the light of day. *Bringing into light of day* is what happens to the soul after death, according to the *Egyptian Book of the Dead*. I made a distinction, between ancient books of the dead and the present one, of *necromancy* and *necrology*, as an indication of the different structures of knowledge of different ages. As a deeper level of truth the distinction is, I admit, a mere quibble. *Our* bringing into the light of day is different in structure but reaches the same end.

Our structure of knowledge is founded in fact. Yet the exposition of total death in terms of fact explodes the ethos of factual knowledge that is so characteristic of our age!

Total death explodes the simple *myths* of belligerent nationalism. It reduces the death formulas of *religion* to absurdity. As an idea, it cannot be relegated to those rarefied spheres of *philosophy* where all ideas are made silly and ineffectual by the cleverness of philosophers. There is too much grim reality in it for that. As a practical reality, aspects of total death can be governed on a factual basis by a discipline such as *ecology*. But the full reality cannot, for it is too much beyond the predictable, its time span is too unwieldy, to be contained within the factual parameters of a scientific discipline.

It is not surprising that the idea of total death should crash through established structures of thought. It is the intellectual legacy of a violence that crashed through the physical structures of human societies for half a century. Those who used to live by the *Tibetan Book of the Dead* would not be surprised: yet some of our most "modern," "scientific," "brilliant" minds seem to imagine that we can go on living just as before, with the degradation and nothingness of the public experience expressed in terms of the historical myths and clichés that preceded it! But total death is not simply a myth-destroying reality. It disrupts more than those *intellectual* forms of mediation between man and his surroundings—religion, philosophy, scientific disciplines—already mentioned. It tears apart in the mind some of the forms of *physical* mediation that are most dearly cherished by the advanced societies. Principal among these is the arms pile.

The notion that national "defense" rests in the accumulation of suicidal weaponry is the final surrealism of the factual ethos, for total death is itself the mocking product of this delusion.

And this great scientific proof—that there is no ultimate physical "protection" against one's surroundings—calls in question the whole area of "factual" mediation between man and his surroundings as expressed in technology.

Fact is not superior to myth. Technology is not more efficient than religion. However much factual and technical knowledge we acquire, we shall always have to live with the unpredictable. These are the immediate implications of total death. That is why, although this exploratory study is grounded in fact and systems, the intellectual tools I am most familiar with as a child of my age, it also indicates the possibility of *knowing* this area of reality through myth and through speculative philosophy, and future students may develop the subject in these directions, taking the factual grounding for granted.

It is easy to italicize a few phrases, more difficult to predict how they are to be absorbed into the fabric of existence. The student of total death will not expect immediate technical spin-off from his researches, for he knows the time span of total death is not that of a generation nor of a lifetime, but of a civilization. A great deal of fuss is made about the pace at which "modern ideas" succeed one another. But these are ideas used as technology, as closed systems of thought. The open-ended idea takes longer to absorb, it continues to breed and stimulate further thought. It was in the nineteenth century that the idea of men as gods came to us, and we still do not know what it means. The turbulence of our own century has produced advances in the idea of consciousness which we have hardly begun to absorb. And in the aftermath of that turbulence we have perforce to change our idea of death.

The discoveries of science and the rapid production of ideas-as-technology are very important and powerful and capable of bringing about the most significant historical events, such as the end of the world and endless other adjustments to life. No one can deny the impressiveness of that claim.

But with the above three ideas alone—god, consciousness, death—and the new interpretations of them afforded by recent experience, it would be possible to build a high civilization, and that is something different.

In our own period we are in the midst of a movement to recover inner values. Among these the values of death must be recycled into our vision of totality so that we may live truly in the world of life and death.

PART TWO

SOCIETAL PERSPECTIVES ON DEATH

THE DEMOGRAPHY OF DEATH

The four selections that comprise this section represent a further tightening of our focus on death—death in our society and in our own time. The chapter also extends the oxymoronic aspect of death: the efforts and resources invested by our society in creating a "total death" capability and at the same time the scientific and medical efforts directed toward saving individual lives and extending the average life expectancy.

The first selection is current and encyclopedic, citing up-to-date mortality statistics and providing factual answers to questions about the when, why, and where of death. Historically, the demographic (or actuarial) approach has been identified largely with the names of an Englishman, John Graunt, who in 1662 published an enormously important book on the London bills of mortality—what later evolved into the current death certificate--and of a Prussian clergyman, Johann Süssmilch, who in 1741 made a systematic attempt to correlate figures on mortality—what used to be called "political arithmetic" and what we now call "vital statistics." Lerner's selection reminds us of our indebtedness to Graunt and Süssmilch and also of how science and knowledge develop over the centuries. Lerner discusses how changes of mortality levels effect changes in social structure, one such change being the increasing institutionalization of death resulting from the effects of controlled mortality.

Datel's brief (four-page) article in a recent issue of Military Medicine, is a veritable bomb-shell for statisticians and demographers. In an ingeniously simple study, Datel points out the serious deficiencies of reliability in the elementary task of counting dead bodies within a closed sociological unit—in this case the United States Army—not to mention the disturbingly low reliability in the tabulation and reporting of suicidal deaths. The implications of this simple study for all past and present death data (comparing different cities with each other, different countries, different eras) are enormous.

The benefits of an increased life expectancy do not accrue to all strata of society, as pointed out in the Sudnow selection. In our society today, death is egalitarian only in the ultimate sense; otherwise it is the most undemocratic aspect of life. Sudnow's selection, while not strictly "demographic" in its exposition, can be seen as a companion piece to the Goldscheider selection, because it is, among other grisly things, an extraordinary exploration of the social forces that go into the designation "Dead On Arrival (DOA)." It has been included to give some emotional texture to the "social inequality of death."

The fourth selection, by Goldscheider, deals with the fascinating (and frightening) social inequalities of death. "Mortality differences," he writes, "may be *observed between men and women, young and old, farmers and urbanites, college educated and high school dropouts, professionals and laborers, rich and poor . . ." In this selection, he speaks of the significant social inequities of death specifically related to race and to socioeconomic status. The Surgeon General might well warn us that being black or poor is much more dangerous to your life than smoking.*

We have alluded to the secularization of death in this century. There are implications of this secularization even beyond the shift of death's focus from religion to science, the disciplines where the main "priests" of death are to be found today. (Nowadays, when people pray for a dying loved one, they may pray to God to help the doctor *save the person's life; the realistic appeals are made to medical science.) While we have seen the creation of a megadeath capability in our lifetime, we have also seen, in our crazy oxymoronic century (vis-à-vis death) considerable socioeconomic, political, and especially, technological (medical) advances in the prolongation of human life. Only with the secularization of death has it been possible to effect this increased life expectancy, but "at the price" of rather substantial social changes in various aspects of our attitudes toward death, as we shall see in subsequent chapters touching on the changing character of death in our times.*

8• When, Why, and Where People Die

Monroe Lerner

Monroe Lerner is a professor at the Johns Hopkins University, where he is a member of the Department of Medical Care and Hospital and of the Department of Behavioral Sciences. This selection, which first appeared in the The Dying Patient *edited by Orville Brim, Jr. and others, is both current and encyclopedic in its discussion of the many facts of mortality statistics.*

Perhaps one of man's greatest achievements in his endless quest to extend the limits of his control over nature has been his success in increasing the average duration of his lifetime. This success has been particularly substantial in the modern era, beginning with the mid-seventeenth century, and during the second third of the twentieth century it extended even to the far corners of the globe. During this period, and possibly for the first time in human history, the lifetimes of a substantial proportion of the world's population have been extended well beyond even the economically productive years, so that most people can now reasonably expect to survive at least into their retirement period.

The ability to do this has always been highly valued, at least as an ideal, and perhaps especially in those societies able at best to struggle along only at the subsistence margin and with almost no economic surplus to support life during the barren years. But even in other circumstances, more than one conception of the "good society" has had a component notion that survival beyond the productive years could be within the realm of possibility for all. Nevertheless, only in the technologically advanced Western nations of today does the *average* duration of life reach, and even in some instances exceed, the famous biblical standard of threescore and ten. If the average duration of life—life expectancy, to use the technical term of statisticians and actuaries—is conceived of as an important indicator of man's control over nature and at the same time also as a crucial element in the moral evaluation of society, then surely man's difficult journey down the long paths of history may be described as social progress rather than merely as evolution.

In any case, whether progress or evolution, man certainly has extended his average lifetime. This [selection] first traces that process, as much as it is possible to do so from the inadequate historical data, and only in the most general terms, from prehistory down to the present situation in the United States. Life expectancy, however, is in one sense simply a refined measure of mortality, and for some purposes it is more useful to deal with mortality rates rather than with life expectancy. Mortality, then, becomes the focus of the remainder of the present discussion.

Later, mortality trends in the United States are traced from 1900 to the present, for the total population and separately by age and sex. Young people—infants, children, and young adults—and females of all ages have clearly been the chief beneficiaries of this process, although other segments of the population have also gained substantially. The major communicable diseases—tuberculosis, influenza and pneumonia, gastritis and duodenitis, the communicable diseases of childhood, and so on—have declined as leading causes of death, to be replaced by the "degenerative" diseases, that is, diseases associated with the aging process—heart disease, cancer, and stroke—and by accidental injury.

Populations may be perceived not only as consisting of sex and age groups, but also as individuals and families ranged along a multidimensional, socioeconomic continuum. The problem then becomes: How do people at various points or in various sections of this continuum fare with regard to mortality risk or, in a more literal meaning of the term than was intended by the German sociologist Max Weber who coined it, what are their life chances?

Perhaps the most meaningful way of dealing with this question, if the objective is to identify large groups or strata in the population who actually do experience gross or at least identifiable differences in mortality risk, is to assume the existence of three major socioeconomic strata in this country, each characterized by a distinctive and unique life-style—the white-collar middle class, the blue-collar working class, and the poverty population. Various structural factors in the life-styles of these populations are conducive to different outcomes in mortality risk. In general, the poverty population experiences relatively high mortality rates at the younger ages and from the communicable diseases, while the white-collar middle class, especially its male members, experiences relatively high mortality rates at midlife and in the older ages, from the "degenerative" diseases. The blue-collar working class, to the extent that it avoids both types of disabilities, appears for the moment at least to be experiencing the lowest mortality rates among the three strata.

Finally, the place where death occurs—that is, in an institution, at home, or elsewhere—has long been a neglected area of mortality statistics. From national data presented later in this [selection], it seems clear that the proportion of all deaths in this country occurring in institutions has been rising steadily, at least for the last two decades and probably for much longer than that. It may now be as high as, or higher than, two-thirds of all deaths. Almost 50 percent of all deaths occurring outside an institution in 1958 were due to heart disease, and especially to the major component of this cause-of-death category, arteriosclerotic heart disease, including coronary disease, which accounted for 37 percent of the total. Cancer, stroke, and accidents comprised the remaining major components of the total, accounting for another 30 percent of the out-of-institution deaths.

HISTORY AND THE DURATION OF HUMAN LIFE

Scholars can only estimate, in the absence of direct data, what the average duration of life must have been during prehistory. Such estimates have been made, however, and they appear to be roughly consistent with the fragmentary data available from the few surviving contemporary primitive groups, in Africa and elsewhere, whose conditions of life resemble those of our remote ancestors at least in some of their major relevant aspects. Prehistoric man lived, according to these estimates, on the average about eighteen years (Dublin, 1951:386–405); life during the prehistory was, in the Hobbesian sense, indeed nasty, short, and brutish. Violence was the usual cause of death, at least judging from the many skulls found with marks of blows, and man's major preoccupation was clearly satisfying his elemental need for survival in the face of a hostile environment including wild beasts and other men perhaps just as wild. Survivorship in those days was very seldom beyond the age of forty. Persons who reached their midtwenties and more rarely their early thirties were *ipso facto* considered to have demonstrated their wisdom and were, as a result, often treated as sages.

With the rise of the early civilizations and the consequent improvements in living conditions, longevity must surely have risen, reaching perhaps twenty years in ancient Greece and perhaps twenty-two in ancient Rome. Life expectancy is estimated to have been about thirty-three years in England during the Middle Ages, about thirty-five in the Massachusetts Bay Colony of North America, about forty-one in England and Wales during the nineteenth century, and 47.3 in the death-registration states of the United States in 1900.[1] Thus a definite upward progression in life expectancy has been evident in the Western world throughout its history, and this progression is, furthermore, one in which the pace has clearly accelerated with the passage of time.

The upward progression has continued during the twentieth century and, at least in the United States, its rate of increase has accelerated even further. Thus, life expectancy continued to rise in this country after 1900, even if somewhat erratically; by 1915 it had reached a temporary peak at 54.5 years. The 1918 influenza epidemic caused a sharp drop in life expectancy, to just below forty years, a level probably typical of "normal" conditions in the United States during the first half of the nineteenth century (Lerner and Anderson, 1963:317–326). But thereafter the upward trend in life expectancy resumed and, between 1937 and 1945 and following the development of the sulfa drugs and the introduction of penicillin during World War II, its increase was extraordinarily rapid. From 1946 to 1954, however, although life expectancy in this country continued upward, the *rate* of increase tapered off. And from 1954, when life expectancy was 69.6 years, to 1967[2] when it had reached only to 70.2, the gain was at a snail's pace compared to what it had been during the earlier period.

In broader perspective, that is, during the first two-thirds of the twentieth century that we have now experienced, life expectancy rose by almost twenty-three years, an average annual gain of about one-third of a year. This is a breathtaking pace compared to any period of human history prior to this century, and it clearly could not be sustained over a long period of time without enormous social disruption. In line with this, however, life expectancy in the country may now have reached a plateau at, or just above seventy years.

Where does the United States stand in life expectancy compared with other nations, and what can we anticipate as the reasonable upper limit, or goal, that this country *should* be able to attain in the present state of the arts? Although international comparisons of this type appear to be a hazardous undertaking, in large part because of the substantial obstacles to comparability, a number of other nations clearly have higher life expectancies than we do, and at least in some instances the differences are fairly substantial. Even cursory observation of a recent international compendium of demographic statistics (United Nations, 1967:562–583) reveals, for example, that in Australia, Denmark, The Netherlands, New Zealand, Norway, and Sweden life expectancy may be as much as two to three years higher than the comparable figure in the United States. Countries such as Belgium, France, East Germany, the Federal Republic of Germany, Switzerland, England and Wales, and many others, also exceed us in life expectancy, but not by so wide a margin. Surely this country should at least be able to reach the level of those listed above, if not to exceed them. It is possible that these countries may be nearing an upper limit, however, one that may persist unless some major medical breakthrough occurs. Returning to our own country, future projections of life expectancy and mortality made prior to 1954 now appear to have been much too conservative (Dorn, 1952); on the other hand, those made subsequent to

1954 were clearly too optimistic. Tarver (1959), for example, projected a life expectancy of about 73.5 years in 1970, but it now appears that we may be a long time in reaching this goal.

Life expectancy by definition is equivalent to the average duration of life. But how are the numbers obtained for this measure? Starting with a hypothetical cohort of one hundred thousand persons at birth, the mortality rates by age and by sex of a given population in a given year are applied to this cohort as it ages and moves through its life cycle, reducing it in number until no survivors of the original cohort remain (Spiegelman, 1968:293). The number of years lived by the *average* person in this cohort is termed the given population's life expectancy. Clearly then, the life expectancy figure thus obtained is simply the inverse of mortality experience; it depends entirely upon age-and-sex-specific mortality rates. Employment of the measure of "life expectancy" as an indicator of the mortality experience of a population is useful for comparison purposes both currently and across time. This is especially true because this measure eliminates the disturbing influence on the mortality rate of variation in the age-and-sex composition of populations. It is precisely because of this characteristic that life expectancy was used in the preceding discussion to make comparisons across the long span of history. For discussion of the immediate past and current situations, however, it is perhaps best to shift the locus of the discussion from life expectancy to mortality.

MORTALITY IN THE UNITED STATES, 1900 TO 1967: TRENDS AND DIFFERENTIALS, OVERALL AND BY AGE AND SEX

Paralleling inversely the increase in life expectancy from 1900 to the present, the mortality rate (deaths per 1,000 population) of the United States population has declined sharply during this century. Thus in 1900 the mortality rate was 17.2 per 1,000 population, but by 1954 had dropped to 9.2 per 1,000, the lowest ever recorded in the United States. Since that time it has fluctuated between 9.3 and 9.6, and in 1967 the rate was 9.4, representing a decline of about 45 percent since 1900. These figures understate the extent of the "true" decline, however, primarily because the age composition of the United States population has changed drastically since 1900. This change has generally been in the direction of increasing the high-mortality-risk age segments of the population as a proportion of the total and at the expense of the low. With age composition held constant, that is, using the 1940 age composition of the United States population as a standard, the hypothetical "age-adjusted" death rate in this country declined between 1900 and 1967 from 17.8 to 7.2 per 1,000, a drop of about 60 percent.

Age and sex

The pattern of mortality rates by age in this country during 1900 was generally similar to that prevailing today (see Table 1). Thus in 1900 the mortality rate was high during infancy, 162.4 per 1,000, in comparison to the rates at other ages; it dropped to the lowest point for the entire life cycle, 3.9, at ages five through fourteen; but thereafter it rose steadily with increasing age until at

TABLE 1
MORTUARY RATES PER 1,000 POPULATION BY AGE AND SEX, UNITED STATES, 1900 AND 1966

	1900			*1966*		
Age (in years)	*Both sexes*	*Males*	*Females*	*Both sexes*	*Males*	*Females*
All ages	17.2	17.9	16.5	9.5	11.0	8.1
Under 1	162.4	179.1	145.4	23.1	25.7	20.4
1-4	19.8	20.5	19.1	1.0	1.0	0.9
5-14	3.9	3.8	3.9	0.4	0.5	0.4
15-24	5.9	5.9	5.8	1.2	1.7	0.6
25-34	8.2	8.2	8.2	1.5	2.0	1.0
35-44	10.2	10.7	9.8	3.1	3.9	2.3
45-54	15.0	15.7	14.2	7.3	9.7	5.1
55-64	27.2	28.7	25.8	17.2	23.6	11.2
65-74	56.4	59.3	53.6	38.8	52.0	28.1
75-84	123.3	128.3	118.8	81.6	98.5	69.5
85 and over	260.9	268.8	255.2	202.0	213.6	194.9

ages eighty-five and over the mortality rate was 260.9 per 1,000 population. In 1966 the comparable rate was only 23.1 per 1,000 during infancy; the low point was 0.4 at ages five through fourteen; and again the rates rose steadily with increasing age, to 202 per 1,000 at ages eighty-five and over. Between 1900 and 1966 the largest *relative* declines in the mortality rates took place at the younger ages, especially during infancy and childhood. Although the declines at the older ages are less impressive percentages, they are, nevertheless, very substantial in absolute numbers. For example, at ages eighty-five and over the mortality rate dropped by about 59 deaths per 1,000 population, that is, from 261 to 202 per 1,000.

Although the mortality rates for both males and females in the United States population declined substantially since 1900, the *rate* of decline was much sharper for females. Thus the mortality rate for females dropped from 16.5 in 1900 to 8.1 in 1966, a decline of 51 percent. For males the corresponding drop was from 17.9 to 11.0, or by 39 percent. The male death rate has been significantly higher than the female death rate in this country throughout the twentieth century, but the relative excess of male over female rates has increased over the years from 8.5 percent in 1900 to 36 percent in 1966. When these rates are age adjusted to a standard population, the excess of male over female rates in 1966 is considerably larger, about 70 percent.

In 1900, the relative excess of male over female mortality rates by age was largest during infancy, at 23 percent. At ages five through fourteen, the mortality rates for males were actually slightly lower than the comparable rates for females; at ages fifteen through thirty-four, rates were about the same for each sex; and in each of the age groups at thirty-five and over, the mortality rates for males exceeded the comparable rates for females only by a relatively slight amount, that is, by from 5 to 11 percent. By 1966, however, although the mortality rates at each age were lower for each sex than the comparable rates in 1900, the decline in almost all cases was larger for females. As a result, the percentage excess of male mortality rates over female rates was larger in most age groups during 1966 than it had been during 1900. It was largest (an excess of almost 200 percent in 1966), at ages fifteen through twenty-four.

MORTALITY IN THE UNITED STATES, 1900 TO 1967: TRENDS AND DIFFERENTIALS BY CAUSE OF DEATH

One of the most significant changes in the mortality experience of this country since 1900 has been the decline in the major communicable diseases as leading causes of death[3] and the consequent increase in *relative importance* of the so-called chronic degenerative diseases, that is, diseases occurring mainly later in life and generally thought to be associated in some way with the aging process. Accidents, especially motor vechicle accidents, have also risen in relative importance as causes of death during this period, but mortality during infancy and maternal mortality, that is, mortality associated with childbearing, have declined sharply.

The communicable diseases

The leading cause of death[4] in 1900 was the category: "influenza and pneumonia, except pneumonia of the newborn." This major communicable disease category was listed as the cause of 202.2 deaths per 100,000 population in 1900 (see Table 2), and it accounted for 11.8 percent of all deaths in that year. By 1966, however, the mortality rate for this category was down to 32.8, it ranked fifth among the leading causes of death, and it now accounted for only 3.4 percent of all deaths during the year.

Tuberculosis (all forms) and the gastritis grouping[5] second and third leading causes of death, respectively, in 1900, were both reduced so significantly and to such low rates during the course of this century that neither category was listed among the ten leading causes of death in 1966. Tuberculosis had caused 194.4 deaths per 100,000 in 1900, or 11.3 percent of all deaths, while the gastritis grouping, with 142.7 deaths per 100,000, had accounted for 8.3 percent of the total. By 1966 the comparable rates for these two categories were 3.9 and 3.3, respectively, with each accounting for substantially less than one-half of 1 percent of all deaths in that year. The percentage declines for each from 1900 to 1966 were by 98 percent.

Diphtheria had been listed as tenth leading cause of death in 1900, with 40.3 deaths per 100,000 population. In 1966 this condition accounted for only forty deaths all told in this country, that is, considering the entire United States population as at risk, so that the death rate was about one death per five million persons. Other major communicable diseases with impressive declines in mortality were some of the other communicable diseases of childhood, such as whooping cough, measles, scarlet fever, and streptococcal sore throat, and syphilis, typhoid and paratyphoid fevers, rheumatic fever, and typhus.

TABLE 2

THE TEN LEADING CAUSES OF DEATH, BY RANK, UNITED STATES, 1900 AND 1966

1900

Rank	*Cause of death*	*Deaths per 100,000 population*	*Percent of all deaths*
	All causes	1,719.1	100.0
1	Influenza and pneumonia	202.2	11.8
2	Tuberculosis (all forms)	194.4	11.3
3	Gastritis, duodenitis, enteritis, etc.	142.7	8.3
4	Diseases of the heart	137.4	8.0
5	Vascular lesions affecting the central nervous system	106.9	6.2
6	Chronic nephritis	81.0	4.7
7	All accidents	72.3	4.2
8	Malignant neoplasms (cancer)	64.0	3.7
9	Certain diseases of early infancy	62.6	3.6
10	Diphtheria	40.3	2.3

1966

Rank	*Cause of death*	*Deaths per 100,000 population*	*Percent of all deaths*
	All causes	954.2	100.0
1	Diseases of the heart	375.1	39.3
2	Malignant neoplasms (cancer)	154.8	16.2
3	Vascular lesions affecting the central nervous system	104.6	11.0
4	All accidents	57.3	6.0
5	Influenza and pneumonia	32.8	3.4
6	Certain diseases of early infancy	26.1	2.7
7	General arteriosclerosis	19.5	2.0
8	Diabetes mellitus	18.1	1.9
9	Cirrhosis of the liver	13.5	1.4
10	Suicide	10.3	1.1

Hillery *et al.* (1968), comparing recent mortality data from forty-one countries, have shown that the communicable diseases ("infectious diseases" in their terminology) as causes of death decline significantly as a proportion of all deaths in each country as these countries move "up" in the demographic transition, that is, as their birth and death rates decline, and as they concomitantly become at least presumably more "advanced" technologically and socially. Thus, in the "transitional" countries (low death rates but high birth rates), communicable diseases account for about one-third of all deaths on the average, while in the demographically "mature" countries (both death rates and birth rates low), the comparable proportion is about one in twelve of all deaths. This finding is generally in conformity with past experience in this country and elsewhere.

The degenerative diseases

"Diseases of the heart" ranked fourth among the leading causes of death in this country during 1900; this category caused 137.4 deaths per 100,000 and accounted for 8.0 percent of all deaths. By 1966, however, it had risen so far in importance that it had become the leading cause of death, far outranking all others. Its mortality rate had risen to 375.1 deaths per 100,000 population, and it accounted for nearly 40 percent of all deaths in that year. Between 1900 and 1966 the unadjusted death rate from this disease rose by 173 percent; the rise was much less if the age-adjusted rates for these two years are compared, but even this rise was very substantial.

The pattern of increase for malignant neoplasms (cancer) as a cause of death was generally quite similar. This disease ranked eighth among the leading causes of death in 1900. It accounted for 64 deaths per 100,000 population and less than 4 percent of all deaths. By 1966, however, its rank among the leading causes had risen to second, its rate per 100,000 to 154.8, and its proportion of the total of all deaths exceeded 16 percent. Vascular lesions of the central nervous system, although remaining relatively stable in number of deaths per 100,000 (106.9 in 1900 and 104.6 in 1966), nevertheless rose in rank (fifth to third) and as a proportion of all deaths (6 to 11 percent).

How can we account for the increases, in both absolute and relative terms, in these "degenerative" diseases as causes of death? As the classification implies, these are diseases occurring later in life and closely associated with the aging process. Whereas formerly people died on the average much earlier in life, victims primarily of the communicable diseases, they survive today to a much later age, only to succumb in due time to the degenerative conditions. Hillery and his associates (1968) in their interesting study have generalized this trend also. Thus in their demographically transitional countries (low death rates but high birth rates) the degenerative diseases account for less than one-third of all deaths, whereas in their demographically mature countries (both death rates and birth rates low) these diseases account for just under two-thirds of the total. The net overall gain has clearly been an extension of life by many years.

MORTALITY AND SOCIOECONOMIC STATUS

There appears to be a good deal of confusion in this country today, and perhaps especially among social scientists, demographers, and health statisticians, as to the precise nature of the relationship between mortality and socioeconomic status. This confusion has existed, and perhaps will continue to exist for some time, despite the fact that quite a few studies in the past, and a number of ongoing studies, have attempted to clarify the relationship. Part of this confusion may be occasioned by what is perhaps the changing nature of that relationship, a change which in turn may have been brought about by the tremendous improvements in medical technology and therapies during the past century and by the increasing general affluence of the American population. But part of it results from the lack of a generally accepted method for the construction of an overall index of socioeconomic status (Lerner, 1968).

In turn, the failure of social scientists to develop a generally accepted method for the construction of an overall index reflects their lack of general agreement on the number or composition of social classes or social strata in the United States, especially when this entire culturally diverse country is considered as the unit of analysis. Different numbers of classes or strata have been identified, depending on definitions and operational purposes, but none of these is a real entity. Various measures of socioeconomic status have been related to mortality, and the results of one very large study along these lines are now beginning to appear (Kitagawa, 1968). Nevertheless, the overall pattern continues to remain quite unclear at this writing.

For present purposes—to relate socioeconomic status to mortality—it appears that the most meaningful division of the United States population from a conceptual, rather than an operational, standpoint is into three socioeconomic strata. These strata are set apart from one another, in the most general terms, by a distinctive and unique life-style, even though the boundaries between these strata are not sharp, and there may be a considerable movement of individuals and families among them. The life-styles of these strata, in turn, are dependent upon or associated with income, wealth, occupation and occupational prestige, dwelling, ethnic origin, educational attainment, and many other factors, all of which, in some as yet unspecified way, add up to the total. The life-styles, in turn, are directly relevant to the health level, and more specifically the mortality experience of each stratum. The structural factors in each of the three major life-styles through which the relationship to mortality operates include at least these four: the level of living (food, housing, transportation, or other factors); degree of access to medical care within the private medical care system; occupation of the family head (sedentary or involving physical activity); and the nature of the social milieu for that stratum (that is, its degree of economic or social security).

The highest stratum consists of those who are usually designated as the middle- and upper-class white-collar business executives at all levels and professionals, and all those who are above this category. It even includes the highest echelons of skilled blue-collar workers (tool-and-die makers), foremen, supervisors, or the like. Although the range of variation *within* this stratum is great, the group as a whole shares the essential elements of a "middle-class" way of life, that is, residence in "better" neighborhoods and suburbs, general affluence, and so on.

The second stratum consists of this country's blue-collar working class —mainly the semiskilled and unskilled workers in the mass-production and service industries, but also small farmers and possibly even farm laborers, and lower level white-collar workers. These people are also relatively affluent, but not to the same extent as the middle class. Again, although the range of variation *within* this stratum is great, they also share a unique style of life distinctively different from that of the higher stratum. This group will subsequently be designated in the present discussion as the working class.

The lowest of the three strata includes those who are generally designated as the poverty population. By definition, these people generally do not share in the affluence characteristic of this country. It consists of the poor in large-city ghettoes and the rural poor (residents of Appalachia or the Deep South, as well as others); the Negro, Puerto Rican, Mexican, and French Canadian populations, and the other relatively poor ethnic minorities in this country; Indians on reservations; the aged, migratory laborers; and the dependent poor.

Although, as stated above, this mode of classification of socioeconomic status appears to be the most meaningful from a conceptual standpoint in terms of relating it to mortality, it clearly lacks merit from the operational point of view. This is because there would appear to be no ready way of segregating these groups from one another in the available national statistical data, relating either to population data or health statistics, and especially to study their respective mortality experiences. Nevertheless, here and there some attempts have been made, and some studies, mostly local and regional in character and particularly of the poverty population, have been carried out (cf. Chicago Board of Health, 1965; and Lerner, 1968). What follows, therefore, is to be understood as more of an overall gross impression and prediction, rather than anything else, and one based on a general familiarity with the literature of what would be found if the data were available in the form required by the present framework.

The poverty populations generally are likely to have the highest death rates of the three strata on an overall basis, but especially from the communicable diseases. This has been true historically between rich and poor nations in the modern era and still represents the situation in the world today at various levels of wealth and technological advancement (Pond, 1961; Anderson and Rosen, 1960). Within this country, a considerable amount of evidence exists to show that mortality rates among the poverty population are likely to be highest during infancy, childhood, and the younger adult ages. The communicable diseases of childhood, gastrointestinal diseases, and influenza and pneumonia are still a relatively serious health problem among this population, even where public health facilities and services are relatively adequate, as, for example, in the slums of large cities in this country today. What this population lacks most, perhaps, is adequate access to personal health services within the private medical care system. Although these services are to some degree available under other auspices (Strauss, 1967), they may be relatively ineffective and not oriented to the life-style of their recipients, while the cultural impediments to their use appear to be substantial.

In contrast, the white-collar middle class does enjoy relatively adequate access to personal health services under the private medical care system, and their mortality rates during infancy, childhood, and even young adulthood are substantially lower than that of the poverty populations. This is especially true for mortality from the communicable diseases, but appears to extend almost to the entire spectrum of causes of death. The higher levels of living enjoyed by this stratum in general buttress its advantage during the younger years. During midlife and especially during the later years, however, its mortality rates appear to become substantially higher than those of the rest of the population, primarily for the "degenerative" diseases, especially heart disease, cancer, and stroke.

One possible hypothesis that has been offered in explanation of this phenomenon merits comment here. It may be that, because of improved survival by members of this stratum at the younger ages, many persons are carried into midlife with a lower "general resistance" factor than that which characterizes persons in the poverty stratum, and that these individuals are perhaps therefore more vulnerable to the diseases and hazards most prevalent at midlife and beyond. At the moment, at least, there seems to be no possible way of testing this hypothesis.

Another hypothesis is that this excess mortality at midlife is a concomitant of the general affluence characterizing the life-styles of the middle class and of their sedentary occupations (executive and white-collar). Both of these, in turn, may result in obesity, excessive strains and tensions, excessive cigarette smoking, and perhaps ultimately premature death. Men aged forty-five through sixty-four (midlife), especially white men, appear to be particularly vulnerable to coronary artery disease and respiratory cancer. Middle-class women, on the other hand, appear to be less affected by these affluence-related forms of ill health than middle-class men, perhaps because of innate resistance, social pressures to avoid obesity, cigarette smoking without inhalation, and generally less stressful lives, or perhaps some combination of these factors. In any case, women in this stratum appear to have the best of all possible worlds, that is, they have none of the health disabilities associated with the sedentary occupations characteristic of their spouses while at the same time enjoying adequate medical care.

The blue-collar working class appears to have the best overall mortality record. This group appears to have relatively low mortality during the younger ages and from the communicable diseases, especially because they do have access to good medical care in the private medical care system. At midlife, moreover, they appear to suffer from relatively few of the disabilities associated with middle-class affluence.

WHERE DEATH OCCURS

Where people die—in a hospital or other institution, at home, or in a public place—has been a relatively neglected aspect of mortality statistics in this country during the past few years. Although this information is contained on each death certificate and relatively little additional effort or expense would be required to code and tabulate it, this has not been done, perhaps because it has not been at all clear that the returns would be commensurate to the additional expense. As a result, the last national tabulation of these data based on the regular vital statistics data-collection system relates to 1958, and these data were far from complete; many of the cross-tabulations that could have been made were not, in fact, carried out. Some of these states and cities here and there have published tabulations since that time, however.

Recently, some new interest has been expressed in this question among public health circles, possibly stimulated by the coming into being of Regional Medical Programs throughout the country. These in turn were set up under the Heart Disease, Cancer, and Stroke Amendments of 1965 (P.L. 89–239), which provided for the establishment of regional cooperative arrangements for improvement of the quality of medical care through research and training, including continuing education, among medical schools, research institutions, and hospitals, and in related demonstrations of patient care. The new legislation was aimed generally at improving the health, manpower, and facilities available, but one specific purpose was to make new medical knowledge available, as rapidly as possible, for the treatment of patients (Yordy and Fullarton, 1965). The assumption in public health circles was that the place of occurrence of some deaths, and the circumstances, may have been related to an inability to obtain proper medical care either at the moment of death or immediately preceding it, as in cases of sudden death, or at some point during the illness or condition leading to death in other cases. The extent to which this assumption is true is, of course, difficult to test given the present paucity of relevant data.

In 1958, according to the most recent *national* data available (see Table 3), 60.9 percent of all deaths in this country occurred in institutions, that is, in hospitals, convalescent and nursing homes, and in hospital departments of institutions or in other domiciliary instititions. This figure represented a considerable rise over the comparable 49.5 percent recorded in 1949, the

TABLE 3
NUMBER AND PERCENT OF DEATHS OCCURRING IN INSTITUTIONS BY TYPE OF SERVICE OF INSTITUTION, UNITED STATES, 1949 AND 1958

	1958		*1949*	
	Number	*Percent*	*Number*	*Percent*
Total deaths	1,647,886	100.0	1,443,607	100.0
Not in institution	644,548	39.1	728,797	50.5
In institution	1,003,338	60.9	714,810	49.5
General hospital	784,360	47.6	569,867	39.5
Maternity hospital	1,862	0.1	2,249	0.2
Tuberculosis hospital	9,097	0.6	13,627	0.9
Chronic disease, convalescent and other special hospitals	24,180	1.5	12,402	0.9
Nervous and mental hospitals	57,675	3.5	45,637	3.2
Convalescent and nursing homes, homes for the aged, etc.	98,444	6.0	22,783	1.6
Hospital department of institutions, and other domiciliary institutions	3,646	0.2	41,841	2.9
Type of service not specified	24,074	1.5	6,404	0.4

most recent preceding year for which a national tabulation was made. On the basis of these data it appeared that the proportion was rising by an average of better than 1 percent annually.

National data to test whether the trend continued beyond that year are unavailable, but state and local data appear to indicate that this, in fact, may have been the case. In New York City, for example, the proportion of deaths occurring in institutions rose steadily, with only one very slight fluctuation, from 65.9 percent in 1955 to 73.1 percent in 1967 (see Table 4). These same data indicate that the proportion of deaths occurring at home dropped commensurately during these years, from 31.4 percent to 24.2 percent. The proportion of deaths occurring elsewhere, primarily in public places, remained relatively constant. Data from the Maryland State Department of Health also indicate a substantial upward progression in the proportion of all deaths occurring in institutions, from 64.4 percent in 1957 to 71.8 percent in 1966 (Maryland State Department of Health, 1967).

Most of the deaths occurring in "institutions," as the data of Table 3 indicate, occurred in hospitals, the vast majority of which were general hospitals. Nervous and mental hospitals during each of the two years to which the table relates, however, accounted for somewhat more than 3 percent of all deaths. The proportion occurring in convalescent and nursing homes, homes for the aged, and similar establishments increased substantially between 1949 and 1958, from 1.6 percent to 6.0 percent.[6]

TABLE 4
NUMBER AND PERCENT OF DEATHS BY PLACE OF DEATH, NEW YORK CITY, 1955-1967

	Number of deaths				*Percentage*			
	Total	*In institution*	*At home*	*Other*	*Total*	*In institution*	*At home*	*Other*
1955	81,612	53,746	25,598	2,268	100.0	65.9	31.4	2.8
1956	81,118	54,716	24,193	2,209	100.0	67.5	29.8	2.7
1957	84,141	57,141	24,609	2,391	100.0	67.9	29.2	2.8
1958	84,586	57,946	24,230	2,410	100.0	68.5	28.6	2.8
1959	85,352	58,859	24,127	2,366	100.0	69.0	28.3	2.8
1960	86,252	59,413	24,341	2,498	100.0	68.9	28.2	2.9
1961	86,855	60,061	24,524	2,270	100.0	69.2	28.2	2.6
1962	87,089	60,409	24,315	2,365	100.0	69.4	27.9	2.7
1963	88,621	61,588	24,677	2,356	100.0	69.5	27.8	2.7
1964	88,026	62,391	23,602	2,033	100.0	70.9	26.8	2.3
1965	87,395	62,308	22,879	2,208	100.0	71.3	26.2	2.5
1966	88,418	63,599	22,576	2,243	100.0	71.9	25.5	2.5
1967	87,610	64,083	21,222	2,305	100.0	73.1	24.2	2.6

Source of basic data: Personal communication from Mr. Louis Weiner, New York City Department of Health.

TABLE 5
PERCENT OF DEATHS OCCURRING IN INSTITUTIONS BY COLOR AND GEOGRAPHIC DIVISION, UNITED STATES, 1949 AND 1958

	1958			*1949*		
Geographic division	*Total*	*White*	*Nonwhite*	*Total*	*White*	*Nonwhite*
United States	60.9	61.9	53.2	49.5	50.4	43.2
New England	64.2	64.0	72.4	52.2	52.0	67.1
Middle Atlantic	62.8	62.3	68.9	53.2	52.2	69.0
East North Central	63.6	63.2	67.9	51.5	50.9	59.7
West North Central	63.8	63.9	61.5	50.7	50.6	54.4
South Atlantic	55.8	58.6	48.4	42.5	45.3	36.3
East South Central	47.6	51.8	37.3	34.6	37.8	27.6
West South Central	54.9	57.7	44.2	42.8	45.3	34.3
Mountain	63.5	63.4	64.1	55.2	54.9	61.0
Pacific	66.5	66.3	68.8	58.5	58.1	65.5

Table 5 shows the percent of deaths, by color, that occurred in institutions in 1949 and 1958, for the entire country and for each geographic division. In both years the proportion of deaths occurring in institutions was substantially lower for the nonwhite population than for the white when the country as a whole is considered as the unit. However, for the New England, Middle Atlantic, and East North Central states in both years and the West North Central states in 1949 the reverse pattern was true, that is, the proportion of deaths occurring in institutions was higher for the nonwhite population than for the white. In general, the proportions in both years for the East South Central, West South Central, and South Atlantic states, and especially for their nonwhite populations, were very low in comparison to the rest of the country. In Mississippi, even as late as 1958, only 31.0 percent of the nonwhite deaths occurred in institutions. (These data are not shown in Table 5.)

By cause of death, as Table 6 indicates, the most important categories in which the proportion of deaths occuring in institutions was relatively small were the external causes of death (accidents, suicide, and homicide), diseases of the heart, influenza, and the catchall category "symptoms, senility, and ill-defined conditions." Less than one-half of all deaths following accidents occurred in the hospital, and the comparable figure was only 44 percent for motor vehicle deaths. Only about one-half of all deaths from diseases of the heart occurred in an institution, and somewhat less than that figure for arteriosclerotic heart disease, including coronary disease. In the case of each of these conditions, as well as for suicide and homicide, it seems likely that the short time interval between onset of the condition and death is probably a major reason for the relatively small proportions occurring in hospitals. Finally, only about one-fourth of all deaths for which a cause could not clearly be delineated (deaths attributed to symptoms, senility, and ill-defined conditions) occurred in hospitals.

TABLE 6
TOTAL DEATHS AND PERCENT OCCURRING IN INSTITUTIONS BY CAUSE, FOR SELECTED CAUSES OF DEATH, UNITED STATES, 1958

Cause of death	*Total deaths, number*	*Percent in institutions*
Tuberculosis, all forms	12,361	80.0
Syphilis and its sequelae	3,469	71.7
Dysentery, all forms	407	62.4
Scarlet fever and streptococcal sore throat	139	57.6
Whooping cough	177	60.5
Meningococcal infections	746	87.9
Acute poliomyelitis	255	91.8
Measles	552	63.8
Malignant neoplasms, including neoplasms of lymphatic and hematopoetic tissues	254,426	67.7
Benign neoplasms	4,961	82.5
Asthma	5,035	55.4
Diabetes mellitus	27,501	68.6
Anemias	3,195	72.4
Meningitis, except meningococcal and tuberculous	2,247	91.8
Vascular lesions affecting central nervous system	190,758	65.8
Diseases of heart	637,246	50.4
Arteriosclerotic heart disease, including coronary disease	461,373	48.5
Other hypertensive disease	13,798	68.5
General arteriosclerosis	34,483	61.8
Other diseases of circulatory system	17,204	79.5
Chronic and unspecified nephritis, etc.	13,827	67.6

Considering the almost 645,000 deaths that occurred outside an institution in 1958, almost one-half (49 percent) were accounted for by diseases of the heart (see Table 7). (Within this category, arteriosclerotic heart disease, including coronary disease, accounted for about 37 percent of the total.) The next three most important causes of death in accounting for all deaths outside of institutions were malignant neoplasms, 13.1 percent; vascular lesions, 10.1 percent; and accidents, 7.4 percent. These first four categories combined accounted for about 80 percent of all deaths occurring outside institutions, but other causes of death—for example, influenza and pneumonia, suicide, general arteriosclerosis, and so on—were also important in the total.

CONCLUSIONS AND IMPLICATIONS

It would appear, at least from the point of view and focus of the preceding discussion, that the implicit goal of the health establishment in this country to "assure for everyone the highest degree of health attainable in the present

TABLE 6 *(Continued)*

Cause of death	*Total deaths, number*	*Percent in institutions*
Influenza and pneumonia	57,439	68.6
Influenza	4,442	43.1
Pneumonia, except pneumonia of newborn	52,997	70.7
Bronchitis	3,973	61.7
Ulcer of stomach and duodenum	10,801	88.2
Appendicitis	1,845	94.5
Hernia and intestinal obstruction	8,853	90.5
Gastritis, duodenitis, enteritis, etc.	7,838	78.7
Cirrhosis of liver	18,638	79.3
Cholelithiasis, cholecystitis and cholangitis	4,720	90.0
Acute nephritis, and nephritis with edema, etc.	2,203	76.0
Infections of kidney	6,889	85.5
Hyperplasia of prostate	4,627	81.1
Deliveries and complications of pregnancy, childbirth, and the puerperium	1,581	85.5
Congenital malformations	21,411	86.5
Certain diseases of early infancy	68,960	94.5
Svmptoms, senility, and ill-defined conditions	19,729	25.2
Accidents	90,604	47.6
Motor-vehicle accidents	36,981	44.0
Other accidents	53,623	50.0
Suicide	18,519	18.5
Homicide	7,815	34.1

state of the arts" has been far from realized. For example, with regard to mortality and its derivative, life expectancy, other nations have clearly outdistanced us, and by a substantial margin. It is true that most of these countries are smaller and more homogeneous, and the environmental hazards plaguing them may not be operative in the same manner and to the same degree as they are among us. Nevertheless, we do appear to have fallen short of what has been achieved elsewhere, and it is therefore appropriate to raise questions about the reasons for this apparent failure.

Three broad lines of inquiry have been suggested as possible approaches in this [discussion], and a fourth influencing and possibly underlying the others will be mentioned. When one considers the entire spectrum of causes of death and their "places of occurrence," it is not unreasonable to assume *as a working hypothesis* that many deaths are occurring from causes—disease conditions—that are amenable, at least under optimum conditions in the present state of the arts, to medical management and control. Of course, the sex and age of the patient, the general state of health and degree of "resistance" of the organism, and many other factors should be considered in the evaluation of each case before any death is characterized as needless or

TABLE 7
DEATHS OCCURRING OUTSIDE INSTITUTIONS BY CAUSE, FOR SELECTED CAUSES OF DEATH, UNITED STATES, 1958

Cause of death	*Number*	*Percent*
All causes	644,548	100.0
1. Diseases of the heart	316,074	49.0
Arteriosclerotic heart disease, including coronary disease	237,607	36.9
2. Malignant neoplasms, including neoplasms of the lymphatic and hematopoietic tissues	84,724	13.1
3. Vascular lesions affecting the central nervous system	65,239	10.1
4. Accidents, all forms	47,476	7.4
Motor-vehicle accidents	20,709	3.2
Other	26,767	4.2
5. Influenza and pneumonia	18,036	2.8
Pneumonia	15,528	2.4
Influenza	2,508	0.4
6. Suicide	15,093	2.3
7. General arteriosclerosis	13,173	2.0
8. Diabetes mellitus	8,635	1.3
9. Homicide	5,150	0.7

preventable. Furthermore, it may be very difficult to refrain from setting up, as working standards, ideal conditions that are unattainable anywhere, given the realities and the imperatives of social organization, the relatively low priority of health in the hierarchy of human values and "needs," the "mass" nature of society, and the vagaries and irrational elements in what is colloquially described as "human nature." Nevertheless, the social and economic differentials in mortality discussed in this [selection] would appear to argue that there is much room for improvement, that the low mortality rates now attained by some could be attained, theoretically at least, by all.

If this is true, and if our goal is indeed to assure the highest degree of health attainable *for everyone*, then we must ask ourselves whether the social organization for the provision of health services to the population in some degree shares responsibility for the discrepancy between goal and reality. If responsible inquiry is directed toward this problem, the unknowns in this vital area of public policy may be reduced, and we may begin to reexamine the place of health in our presently implicit hierarchy of values as opposed, for example, to education, other forms of welfare, space exploration, urban crowding, rural poverty, national security, and the myriad national concerns to which we allocate community resources. We may even be able to move toward calm and rational discussion of some alternative forms of social organization of the health care system, including their economic and perhaps social costs, hopefully with the result that we ultimately arrive at intelligent decisions.

Notes

1 All life expectancy and mortality figures presented in this section pertaining to the United States in 1900 or subsequent years, unless otherwise specified, are based on various published reports of the National Vital Statistics Division of the National Center for Health Statistics (formerly the National Office of Vital Statistics), U.S. Public Health Service. The reports themselves are not specifically cited here, but the source for each figure is available upon request. Rates for years prior to 1933 are based on the "death-registration states" only. In 1900 this group consisted of ten states, primarily in the northeastern part of the country, and the District of Columbia. However, the number of states included in this registration area gradually increased over the years, and by 1933 all states in the continental United States were part of it. For comparison purposes, figures for the death-registration states are customarily considered as satisfactorily representing the experience of the entire country, and this practice is followed in the present discussion.

2 All 1966 and 1967 figures shown in this selection are provisional. Based on past experience, however, the provisional rates are likely to be identical, or nearly so, to the final rates.

3 Cause of death in United States mortality statistics is currently determined in accordance with World Health Organization Regulations, which specify that member nations classify causes of death according to the International Statistical Classification of Diseases, Injuries and Causes of Death, 1955. Besides specifying the classification, World Health Organization Regulations outline the form of medical certification and the coding procedures to be used. In general, when more than one cause of death is reported, the cause designated by the certifying physician as the underlying cause of death is the cause tabulated (cf. World Health Organization, 1957).

4 The method of ranking causes of death used here follows the procedure recommended by *Public Health Conference on Records and Statistics* at its 1951 meeting. Only those causes specified in the "List of 60 Selected Causes of Death" were included in the ranking, and the following categories specified in that list were omitted: the two group titles, "major cardiovascular-renal diseases" and "diseases of the cardiovascular system"; the single title, "symptoms, senility, and ill-defined conditions"; the residual titles, "other infective and parasitic diseases," "other bronchopulmonic diseases," "other diseases of the circulatory system," and "all other diseases"; and all subtitles represented within a broader title. Causes of death are ranked on the basis of rates unadjusted for age or to a specific Revision of the International List of Diseases and Causes of Death, and the above discussion is based on these "crude" rates. But the *titles* used, and the 1966 rates, are those of the Seventh Revision.

5 The full title of this cause-of-death grouping, in the nomenclature of the Seventh Revision of the International List of Diseases and Causes of Death, is: gastritis, duodenitis, enteritis, and colitis, except diarrhea of the newborn.

6 However, there is some lack of comparability between these two figures, and this increase, although undoubtedly substantial, may not be quite as large as these figures indicate.

References

Anderson, Odin W., and George Rosen.
1960 An examination of the concept of preventive medicine. *Health Information Foundation, Research Series No. 12.* New York: Health Information Foundation.

Chicago Board of Health; Planning Staff of the Health Planning Project.
1965 *A Report on Health and Medical Care in Poverty Areas of Chicago and Proposals for Improvement.*

Dorn, Harold F.
1952 Prospects of further decline in mortality rates. *Human Biology* 24, 4 (December): 235–261.

Dublin, Louis I., in collaboration with Mortimer Spiegelman.
1951 *The Facts of Life—From Birth to Death.* New York: Macmillan.

Hillery, George A., Jr. *et al.*
1968 Causes of death in the demographic transition. Paper presented at the Annual Meeting of the Population Association of America, Boston, Mass.

Kitagawa, Evelyn M.
1968 Race differential in mortality in the United States, 1960 (corrected and uncorrected). Paper presented at the Annual Meeting of the Population Association of America, Boston, Mass., April.

Lerner, Monroe.
1968 The level of physical health of the poverty population: a conceptual reappraisal of structural factors. Paper presented at Conference on New Dimensions in Health Measurements, sponsored by Washington Statistical Society and American Marketing Association, Washington, D.C., January 25.

Lerner, Monroe, and Odin W. Anderson.
1963 *Health Progress in the United States: 1900-1960.* Chicago: University of Chicago Press.

Maryland State Department of Health, Division of Biostatistics.
1967 *Annual Vital Statistics Report: Maryland, 1966.* Also, same annual reports for earlier years to 1957. Baltimore.

Pond, M. Allen.
1961 Interrelationship of poverty and disease. *Public Health Reports 76* (November): 967–974.

Spiegelman, Mortimer.
1968 Life tables. Pp. 292–299 in *International Encyclopedia of the Social Sciences.* New York: Free Press.

Strauss, Anselm L.
1967 Medical ghettos: medical care must be reorganized to accept the life-styles of the poor. *Trans-action* 4(May):7–15 and 62.

Tarver, James D.
1959 Projections of mortality in the United States to 1970. *The Milbank Memorial Fund Quarterly 37,* 2(April): 132–143.

United Nations.
1967 *Demographic Yearbook, 1966.* New York.

World Health Organization.
1957 *Manual of the International Statistical Classification of Diseases, Injuries, and Causes of Death: Based on the Recommendations of the Seventh Revision Conference, 1955.* Vol. I. Geneva, Switzerland.

Yordy, K.D., and J.E. Fullarton.
1965 The heart disease, cancer, and stroke amendments of 1965 (P.L. 89–239). Reprint from *Health, Education and Welfare Indicators.* November.

9 ·

The Reliability of Mortality Count and Suicide Count in the United States Army

William E. Datel

William E. Datel is a (civilian) research psychologist with the United States Army, working at the Walter Reed Army Hospital in Washington, D.C. Dr. Datel is concerned with the reliability of military demographic data and with the reliability of demographic data in general. In this summarized article—military policy did not permit direct reproduction of the entire article—Datel, in a simple and ingenious study, reports some data about "unreliability" that have extremely important implications for every producer and consumer of mortality and morbidity data anywhere in the world.

From William E. Datel, "The Reliability of Mortality Count and Suicide Count in the United States Army," Military Medicine *144, no. 8 (August 1979): 509–512. Summarized and commented on by Edwin S. Shneidman. Permission to extract and quote given by the Association of Military Surgeons of the United States.*

The copyright policy of *Military Medicine,* the official journal of the Association of Military Surgeons of the United States, does not permit the reprinting of any of their articles in entirety. That journal does however "grant the privilege of extraction of generous quotation of portions of the article with proper acknowledgement of prior publication. The following is a précis of William E. Datel's recent article, "The Reliability of Mortality Count and Suicide Count in the United States Army."

Datel's article has implications of the first importance for the reliability of all demographic and epidemiological suicidal data—from the beginning of suicidal statistics (with Graunt and Süssmilch) in every locale in the world.

In brief, Datel's succinct article tells us that historically there are two independent systems within the United States Army that report all soldier (officer and enlisted personnel) deaths, including of course suicide, to the Pentagon. The two systems are the medical arm of the army, the Office of the Surgeon General (OTSG), and the forensic and legal arm of the army, Office of the Adjutant General (OTAG). Datel states: "The two data systems are separate and distinct from each other, arising from differing sets of requirements and performing different missions." One system was begun in 1971, the other in 1961.

Datel had the brilliant idea of simply comparing the two lists of army deaths for two calendar years, specifically 1975 and 1976. The data are dead military personnel of the United States Army. Datel does not explicitly state a hypothesis—it was hardly an experimental study—but he does say, "the army epidemiologist is blessed with a work environment wherein two institutionalized independently operated data systems record the same phenomenon—the occurence of death." One can legitimately assume that, *a priori,* the null hypothesis would be implied; that is, that there would be *no* difference between the two lists or that the names on the two lists ought to be identical.

Under "Findings," Datel indicates that the death count from the Army medical data base (OTSG) was 1,828; the death count according to the OTAG's accounting system was 2,178. "Common to both death lists was a total of 1,561 persons. Appearing on one list only was a total of 884 persons, 267 of whom were unique to the OTSG list and 617 of whom were present only on the OTAG list. Thirteen additional deaths appeared on [another] suicide list and were not found in either the OTSG or OTAG lists."

Under "Suicide Enumeration," Datel reports a previous study by him and Johnson for the same years (1975 and 1976) which reported 255 cases of army active duty suicide.

> "The OTSG list was found to contain 132 deaths labeled as due to intentionally self-inflicted wounds, and the OTAG list contained 172 such deaths for the same two-year period. These three lists produced a total of 302 individuals whose death was reported as suicide by one or more of the three tabulators . . . These reliability data can be further elaborated by noting that, of the 302 soldiers whose death was labeled as suicide by one or more of the three tabulators, only 236 (78.1 percent) appeared as a death at all on the OTSG list and only 248 (82.1 percent) were found as a death due to any cause whatsoever on the OTAG list. The varying suicide counts produce a greater than two-to-one difference in the range of resultant annual suicide rates."

The data show the following for the same years: OTSG, 8.4 (per 100,000); OTAG, 11.0; Datel and Johnson, 16.3.

The first two paragraphs of Datel's "Discussion" section read as follows:

> How many American soldiers died during the years 1975 and 1976? The Adjutant General reported 2,178 deaths, some 16 percent more than the Surgeon General count of 1,828. Together, both systems reported 2,445, a gain of 11 percent over the higher single-system count. Thirteen more deaths, not recorded in either system were also discovered.
>
> *There was only 63.5 percent commonality in the mortality lists of the two independent electronic data-processing systems studied.* (Italics added.) The casualty reporting system contained 89 percent of the 2,458 total (?) deaths, and the medical data base contained only 74 percent of the total number of deaths. These results are judged to represent an unsatisfactory degree of reliability for scientific purposes. Presumably, they are also unsatisfactory for administrative, planning, or legal use of the information as well.

Under the heading "Implications of Unsatisfactory Reliability," Datel continues:

Some of the implications of an unreliable death record system are painfully obvious and need not be delineated. For the epidemiologist, the most destructive implication is the one of suspicion. If mortality cannot be counted reliably, how then must go morbidity? As regards death, we have a quite hard criterion for case definition; case finding in morbidity is much more influenced by observer differences. How reliable are our counts of mental illness? Of hypertension? Of battle wounds?

Attribution of suicide is a cause of death question—not unlike matters of differential diagnosis. To ask how reliable was the obtained count on suicide, then, is to inquire into the data reliability on a matter akin to that involved in the study of morbidity. The results give little cause for rejoicing.

Of 302 persons labeled suicide by at least one of the three record systems, unanimous agreement on suicide as the cause of death occurred for only 22.5 percent of the cases. (Italics added.) In 40 percent more instances, two of the three lists agreed with each other. Thirty-seven percent of the time, the persons appeared as a suicide on only one of the three lists.

Considering the OTSG and OTAG lists only, a total of 232 persons were labeled as suicides by one or both of the two systems. *Of this number, only 72 (or 31 percent) were mutually labeled as suicide by the two systems.* (Italics added.)

Even more discouraging was the finding that, of the 132 persons labeled suicides by the OTSG, only 77 percent could be found in the OTAG list as having died at all; and of the 172 persons labeled suicides by the OTAG, only 75 percent could be found in the OTSG list as having died at all.

That seems to be the essence of Datel's interesting findings. If any reader has concluded that the extended reference to Datel's article in this setting is meant as an indictment of the United States Army—which admittedly needs to get its mortality count act together—that reader has missed the main point entirely. This article is a *caveat emptor* to all users of all mortality statistics, especially of statistics relating to suicide, however carefully those data *seem* to have been generated. The results of Datel's brilliant study have profound and systematic implications for all statisticians and demographers to the best of possible tactics, in general, to pursue.

10 • Death, Uses of a Corpse, and Social Worth

David Sudnow

David Sudnow is Associate Professor in the Sociology Department at Brooklyn College. This selection is taken from his book Passing On *and describes the rather startling treatment accorded both the living and the dead as they pass through a hospital's emergency room.*

From David Sudnow, Passing On, ©1967, pp. 95–107. Reprinted by
permission of Prentice-Hall, Inc., Englewood Cliffs, New Jersey.

In County's Emergency Ward, the most frequent variety of death is what is known as the "DOA" [dead on arrival] type. Approximately forty such cases are processed through this division of the hospital each month. The designation "DOA" is somewhat ambiguous insofar as many persons are not physiologically dead upon arrival, but are nonetheless classified as having been such. A person who is initially classified as "DOA" by the ambulance driver might retain such a classification even though he might die some hours after his arrival at the hospital.

When an ambulance driver suspects that the person he is carrying is dead, he signals the Emergency Ward with a special siren alarm as he approaches the entrance driveway. As he wheels his stretcher past the clerk's desk, he restates his suspicion with the remark "possible," a shorthand reference for "Possible DOA." The use of the term *possible* is required by law which insists, primarily for insurance purposes, that any diagnosis unless made by a certified physician be so qualified. The clerk records the arrival in a logbook and pages a physician, informing him, in code, of the arrival. Often a page is not needed as physicians on duty hear the siren alarm and expecting the arrival wait at the entranceway. The "person" is rapidly wheeled to the far end of the ward corridor and into the nearest available foyer or room, supposedly out of sight of other patients and possible onlookers from the waiting room. The physician arrives, makes his examination and pronounces the patient dead or alive. A nurse then places a phone call to the coroner's office, which is legally responsible for the removal and investigation of all DOA cases.

Neither the hospital nor the physician has medical responsibility in such cases. In many instances of clear death, ambulance drivers use the hospital as a depository for disposing of a body, which has the advantages of being both closer and less bureaucratically complicated a place than the downtown coroner's office. The hospital stands as a temporary holding station, rendering the community service of legitimate and free pronouncements of death for any comers. In circumstances of near-death, it functions more traditionally as a medical institution, mobilizing lifesaving procedures for those for whom they are still of potential value, at least as judged by the ER's [emergency room] staff of residents and interns. The boundaries between near-death and sure-death are not, however, altogether clearly defined.

In nearly all DOA cases, the pronouncing physician, commonly that physician who is the first to answer the clerk's page or spot the incoming ambulance, shows, in his general demeanor and approach to the task, little more than passing interest in the event's possible occurrence and the patient's biographical and medical circumstance. He responds to the clerk's call, conducts his examination, and leaves the room once he has made the necessary official gesture to an attending nurse (the term "kaput," murmured in differing degrees of audibility depending upon the hour and his state of awakeness, is a frequently employed announcement). It happened on numerous occasions, especially during the midnight-to-eight shift, that a physician was interrupted during a coffee break to pronounce a DOA and returned to his colleagues in the canteen with, as an account of his absence, some version of "Oh, it was nothing but a DOA."

It is interesting to note that while the special siren alarm is intended to mobilize quick response on the part of the ER staff, it occasionally operates in the opposite fashion. Some ER staff came to regard the fact of a DOA as decided in advance, and exhibited a degree of nonchalance in answering the siren or page, taking it that the "possible DOA" most likely is "D," and in so doing gave authorization to the ambulance driver to make such assessments. Given that time lapse which sometimes occurs between that point at which the doctor knows of the arrival and the time he gets to the patient's side, it is not inconceivable that in several instances patients who might have been revived died during this interim. This is particularly likely as apparently a matter of moments may differentiate the reviveable state from the irreversible one.

Two persons in "similar" physical condition may be differentially designated as dead or not. For example, a young child was brought into the ER with no registering heartbeat, respiration, or pulse and was, through a rather dramatic stimulation procedure involving the coordinated work of a large team of doctors and nurses, revived for a period of eleven hours. On the same evening, shortly after the child's arrival, an elderly person who presented the same physical signs, with what a doctor later stated, in conversation, to be no discernible differences from the child in skin color, warmth, etc., "arrived" in the ER and was almost immediately pronounced dead, with no attempts at stimulation instituted. A nurse remarked later in the evening: "They (the doctors) would never have done that to the old lady (attempt heart stimulation) even though I've seen it work on them too." During the period when emergency resuscitation equipment was being readied for the child, an intern instituted mouth-to-mouth resuscitation. This same intern was shortly relieved by oxygen machinery and when the woman "arrived," he was the one who pronounced her dead. He reported shortly afterwards that he could never bring himself to put his mouth to "an old lady's like that."

It is therefore important to note that the category "DOA" is not totally homogeneous with respect to actual physiological condition. The same is generally true of all deaths, death involving, as it does, some decisional considerations, at least in its earlier stages.

There is currently a movement in progress in some medical and lay circles to undercut the traditional distinction between "biological" and "clinical" death, and procedures are being developed and their use encouraged for treating any "clinically dead" person as potentially reviveable.[1] This movement, unlike late nineteenth-century arguments for life after death, is legitimated by modern medical thinking and technology. Should such a movement gain widespread momentum, it would foreseeably have considerable consequence for certain aspects of hospital social structure, requiring, perhaps, that much more continuous and intensive care be given "dying" and "dead" patients than is presently accorded them, at least at County. At Cohen Hospital, where the care of the "tentatively dead" is always very intensive, such developments would more likely be encouraged than at County.

Currently, at County, there seems to be a rather strong relationship between the age, social backgrounds, and perceived moral character of patients and the amount of effort which is made to attempt revival when "clinical death signs" are detected, as well as the amount of effort given to forestalling their appearance in the first place. As one compares practices at different hospitals, the general relationship seems to hold, although at the private, wealthier institutions, like Cohen, the overall amount of attention given to "initially dead" patients is greater. At County, efforts at revival are admittedly superficial, with the exception of the very young and occasionally wealthier patient, who by some accident, ends up at County's ER. No instances have been witnessed, at County, where external heart massage was given a patient whose heart was stethoscopically inaudible, if that patient was over forty years of age. On the other hand, at Cohen Hospital heart massage is a normal routine at that point, and more drastic measures, such as injection of adrenalin directly into the heart, are not uncommon. While these practices are undertaken for many patients at Cohen if "tentative death" is discovered early, as it generally is because of the attention "dying" patients are given, at County they are reserved for a very special class of cases.

Generally, the older the patient the more likely is his tentative death taken to constitute pronounceable death. Before a twenty-year-old who arrives in the ER with a presumption of death, attached in the form of the ambulance driver's assessment, will be pronounced dead by a physician, very long listening to his heartbeat will occur, occasionally efforts at stimulation will be made, oxygen administered, and oftentimes stimulative medication given. Less time will elapse between initial detection of an inaudible heartbeat and nonpalpable pulse and the pronouncement of death if the person is forty years old, and still less if he is seventy. As well as can be detected, there appeared to be no obvious difference between men and women in this regard, nor between white and Negro "patients." Very old patients who are considered to be dead, on the basis of the ambulance driver's assessment, were seen to be put in an empty room to "wait" several moments before a physician arrived. When a young person is brought in as a "possible," the ambulance driver tries to convey some more alarming sense to the arrival by turning the siren up very loud and continuing it after he has already stopped, so that by the time he has actually entered the wing, personnel, expecting "something special," act quickly and accordingly. When it is a younger person that the driver is delivering, his general manner is more frantic. The speed with which he wheels his stretcher in, and the degree of excitement in his voice as he describes his charge to the desk clerk, are generally more heightened than with the elderly "DOA." One can observe a direct relationship between the loudness and length of the siren alarm and the considered "social value" of the person being transported.

The older the person, the less thorough is the examination he is given; frequently, elderly people are pronounced dead on the basis of only a stethoscopic examination of the heart. The younger the person, the more likely will an examination preceding an announcement of death entail an inspection of the eyes, attempt to find a pulse and touching of the body for coldness. When a younger person is brought to the hospital and while announced by the driver as a "possible" is nonetheless observed to be breathing slightly, or have an audible heart beat, there is a fast mobilization of effort to stimulate increased breathing and a more rapid heart beat. If an older person is brought in in a similar condition there will be a rapid mobilization of similar efforts; however, the time which will elapse between that point at which breathing noticeably ceases and the heart audibly stops beating, and when the pronouncement of death is made, will differ according to his age.

One's location in the age structure of the society is not the only factor which will influence the degree of care he gets when his death is considered to have possibly occurred. At County Hospital a notable additional set of considerations can be generally termed as the patient's presumed "moral character." The detection of alcohol on the breath of a "DOA" is nearly always noticed by the examining physician, who announces to his fellow workers that the person is a drunk, and seems to constitute a feature he regards as warranting less than strenuous effort to attempt revival. The alcoholic patient is treated by hospital physicians, not only when the status of his body as alive or dead is at stake, but throughout the whole course of medical treatment, as one for whom the concern to treat can properly operate somewhat weakly. There is a high proportion of alcoholic patients at County, and their treatment very often involves an earlier admission of "terminality" and a consequently more marked suspension of curative treatment than is observed in the treatment of nonalcoholic patients. In one case, the decision whether or not to administer additional needed blood to an alcoholic man who was bleeding severely from a stomach ulcer was decided negatively, and that decision was announced as based on the fact of his alcoholism. The intern in charge of treating the patient was asked by a nurse, "Should we order more blood for this afternoon?" The doctor answered, "I can't see any sense in pumping it into him because even if we can stop the bleeding, he'll turn around and start drinking again and next week he'll be back needing more blood." In the DOA circumstance, alcoholic patients have been known to be pronounced dead on the basis of a stethoscopic examination of the heart alone, even though that person was of such an age that were he not an alcoholic he would have likely received much more intensive consideration before being so designated. Among other categories of persons whose deaths will be more quickly adjudged, and whose "dying" more readily noticed and used as a rationale for palliative care, are the suicide, the dope addict, the known prostitute, the assailant in a cr1me of violence, the vagrant, the known wifebeater, and other persons whose moral characters are considered reproachable.

Within a limited temporal perspective at least, but one which is not necessarily to be regarded as trivial, the likelihood of "dying" and even of being "dead" can thus be said to be partially a function of one's place in the social structure, and not simply in the sense that the wealthier get better care, or at least not in the usual sense of the fact.[2] If one anticipates having a critical heart attack, he best keep himself well-dressed and his breath clean if there is a likelihood he will be brought into the County Emergency Unit as a "possible."

There are a series of practical consequences of publicly announcing that a patient is dead in the hospital setting. His body may be properly stripped of clothing and jewelry, wrapped up for discharge, the family notified of the death, and the coroner informed in the case of DOA deaths. In the Emergency Unit there are a special set of procedures which are partially definitive of death. DOA cases are very interestingly "used" in many American hospitals. The inflow of dead bodies, or what can properly be taken to be dead bodies, is regarded as a collection of "guinea pigs," in the sense that a set of procedures can be performed upon those bodies for the sake of teaching and research.

In any "teaching hospital" (in the case of County, I use this term in a weak sense, a hospital which employs interns and residents; in other settings a "teaching hospital" may mean systematic, institutionalized instruction), the environment of medical events is regarded not merely as a collection of treatable cases, but as a collection of experience-relevant information. It is a continually enforced way of looking at the cases one treats under the auspices of a concern for experience with "such cases." This concern can legitimately warrant the institution of a variety of procedures, tests, and inquiries which lie outside and may even, on occasion, conflict with the strict interests of treatment; they fall within the interests of learning "medicine," gaining experience with such cases and acquiring technical skills. A principle for organizing medical care activities in the teaching hospital, and perhaps more so in a county hospital where patients' social value is often not highly regarded, is the relevance of any particular activity to the acquisition of skills of general import. Physicians feel that among the greatest values of such institutions is the ease with which they can selectively organize medical attention so as to maximize the benefits to knowledge and technical proficiency which working with a given case expectably afford. The notion of the "interesting case" is, at County, not simply a casual notion, but an enforced principle for the allocation of attention. The private physician is in a more committed relation to each and every one of his patients, and while he may regard this or that case as more or less interesting, he ideally cannot legitimate the interestingness of his patients' conditions as bases for devoting varying amounts of attention to them. His reward for treating the uninteresting case is, of course, the fee, and physicians are known to give more attention to the patients who will be paying more.

At County Hospital, a case's degree of interest is a crucial fact, and one which is invoked to legitimate the way a physician does and should allocate his attention. In surgery I found many examples. If on a given morning in one operating room a "rare" procedure was scheduled, and in another a "usual" procedure planned, there would be no special difficulty in getting personnel to witness and partake in the "rare" procedure, whereas work in the "usual" case was considered as merely work, regardless of such considerations as the relative fatality rate of each procedure or the patient's physical condition. It is not uncommon to find interns at County interchange among themselves in scrubbing for an appendectomy, each taking turns going next door to watch the skin graft or chest surgery. At Cohen[3], such house staff interchanging was not permissible. Interns and residents were assigned to a particular surgical suite and required to stay throughout the course of the procedure. On the medical wards, on the basis of general observation, it seems that one could obtain a high order correlation between the amount of time doctors spent discussing and examining patients and the degree of unusualness of their medical problems.

I introduce this general feature to point to the predominant orientation, at County, to such matters as "getting practice," and the general organizational principle which provides for the propriety of using cases as the basis for this practice. Not only are live patients objects of practice, so are dead ones.

There is a rule, in the Emergency Unit, that with every DOA a doctor should attempt to insert an "endotracheal" tube. This should be done only after the patient is pronounced dead. The reason for this practice (and it is a rule on which new interns are instructed as part of their training in doing emergency medicine) is that such a tube is extremely difficult to insert, requiring great yet careful force and, insofar as it causes great pain, cannot be "practiced" on live patients. The body must be positioned with the neck held at an angle so that this large tube will go down the proper channel. In some circumstances when it is necessary to establish a rapid "airway" (an open breathing canal), the endotracheal tube can apparently be an effective substitute for the tracheotomy incision. The DOA's body, in its transit from the scene of the death to the morgue constitutes an ideal experimental opportunity. The procedure is not done on all deceased patients, the reason apparently being that it is part of the training one receives on the Emergency Unit, and to be learned there. Nor is it done on all DOA cases, for some doctors, it seems, are uncomfortable in handling a dead body whose charge as a live one they never had, and handling it in the way such a procedure requires. It is important to note that when it is done, it is done most frequently and most intensively with those persons lowly situated in the social structure. No instances were observed where a young child was used as an object for such practice, nor where a well-dressed, middle-aged, middle-class adult was similarly used.

On one occasion a woman, who had seemingly ingested a fatal amount of Clorox, was brought to the Emergency Unit and after her death several physicians took turns trying to insert an endotracheal tube, after which one of them suggested that the stomach be pumped to examine its contents to try to see what effects the Clorox had on the gastric secretions. A lavage was set up and the stomach contents removed. A chief resident left the room and gathered together a group of interns with the explanation that they should look at this woman because of the apparent results of such ingestion. In effect, the doctors conducted their own autopsy investigation without making any incisions.

On several similar occasions, physicians explained that with these cases they didn't really feel like they were prying in handling the body, but that they often did in the case of an ordinary or "natural death" of a morally proper person. Suicidal victims are frequently the object of curiosity, and while among the nursing staff there is a high degree of distaste in working with such patients and their bodies, doctors do not express such a high degree of distaste. There was a woman who came into the Emergency Unit with a self-inflicted gunshot wound, which ran from her sternum downward and backward, passing out through a kidney. She had apparently bent over the rifle and pulled the trigger. Upon her "arrival" in the Emergency Unit she was quite alive and talkative, and while in great pain and very fearful, was able to conduct something of a conversation. She was told that she would need immediate surgery, and was taken off to the OR. She was followed by a group of physicians, all of whom were interested in seeing what damage the path of the bullet had done. One doctor said aloud, quite near her stretcher, "I can't get my heart into saving her, so we might as well have some fun out of it." During the operation, the doctors regarded her body much as they would during an autopsy. After the critical damage was repaired and they had reason to feel the woman would survive, they engaged in numerous surgical side ventures, exploring muscular tissue in areas of the back through which the bullet had passed but where no damage requiring special repair had to be done, with the exception of tying off bleeders and suturing. One of the operating surgeons performed a side operation, incising an area of skin surrounding the entry wound on the chest, to examine, he announced to his colleagues, the structure of the tissue through which the bullet passed. He explicitly announced his project to be motivated by curiosity. One of the physicians spoke of the procedure as an "autopsy on a live patient," about which there was a little laughter.

In another case, a man was wounded in the forehead by a bullet, and after the damage was repaired in the wound, which resembled a natural frontal lobotomy, an exploration was made of an area adjacent to the path of the bullet, on the forehead proper below the hairline. During this exploration the operating surgeon asked a nurse to ask Dr. X to come in. When Dr. X arrived, the two of them, under the gaze of a large group of interns and nurses, made a further incision, which an intern described to me as unnecessary in the treatment of the man, and which left a noticeable scar down the side of the temple. The purpose of this venture was to explore the structure of that part of the face. This area of the skull, that below the hairline, cannot be examined during an autopsy because of a contract between local morticians and the Department of Pathology, designed to leave those areas of the body which will be viewed, free of surgical incisions. The doctors justified the additional incision by pointing out that since he would have a "nice scar as it was, a little bit more wouldn't be so serious."

During autopsies themselves, bodies are routinely used to gain experience in surgical techniques, and many incisions and explorations are conducted that are not essential to the key task of uncovering the cause of the death. On frequent occasions, specialists-in-training came to autopsies having no interest in the patient's death. They would await the completion of the legal part of the procedure, at which point the body is turned over to them for practice. Mock surgical procedures are staged on the body, oftentimes with two coworkers simulating actual conditions, tying off blood vessels which obviously need not be tied or suturing internally.

When a patient died in the Emergency Unit, whether or not he had been brought in under the designation "DOA," there occasionally occurred various mock surgical procedures on his body. In one case a woman was treated for a chicken bone lodged in her throat. Rapidly after her arrival via ambulance a tracheotomy incision was made in the attempt to establish an unobstructed source of air, but the procedure was not successful and she died as the incision was being made. Several interns were called upon to practice their stitching by closing the wound as they would on a live patient. There was a low peak in the activity of the ward, and a chief surgical resident used the occasion to supervisorily teach them various techniques for closing such an incision. In another case the body of a man who died after being crushed by an automobile was employed for instruction and practice in the use of various fracture-setting techniques. In still another instance several interns and residents attempted to suture a dead man's dangling finger in place on his mangled hand.

Notes

1 There is a large popular and scientific literature developing on efforts to "treat the dead," the import of which is to undercut traditional notions of the nonreversibility of death. Some of this discussion goes so far as to propose the preservation of corpses in a state of nondeterioration until such time as medical science will be able to do complete renovative work. See particularly R. Ettinger, *The Prospect of Immortality* (Garden City: Doubleday & Company, Inc., 1964). The Soviet literature on resuscitation is most extensive. Soviet physicians have given far more attention to this problem than any others in the world. For an extensive review of the technical literature, as well as a discussion of biomedical principles, with particular emphasis on cardiac arrest, see V. A. Negovskii, *Resuscitation and Artificial Hypothermia* (New York: Consultants Bureau Enterprises, Inc., 1962). See also, L. Fridland, *The Achievement of Soviet Medicine* (New York: Twayne Publishers, Inc., 1961), especially Chapter Two, "Death Deceived," pp. 56-57. For an account of the famous saving of the Soviet physicist Landau's life, see A. Dorozynski, *The Man They Wouldn't Let Die* (New York: The Macmillan Company, 1956).

For recent popular articles on "bringing back the dead" and treating death as a reversible process, see "The Reversal of Death," *The Saturday Review,* August 4, 1962; "A New Fight Against Sudden Death," *Look,* December 1, 1964.

Soviet efforts and conceptions of death as reversible might be seen to have their ideological basis in principles of dialectics:

> For everyday purposes we know and can say, e.g., whether an animal is alive or not. But, upon closer inquiry, we find that this is, in many cases a very complex question, as the jurists know very well. They have cudgelled their brains in vain to discover a rational limit beyond which the killing of the child in its mother's womb is murder. It is just as impossible to determine absolutely the moment of death, for physiology provides that death is not an instantaneous, momentary phenomenon, but a very protracted process.
>
> In like manner, every organized being is every moment the same and not the same . . .

From F. Engels, *Socialism: Utopian and Scientific* (New York: International Publishers Co., 1935), p. 47.

For a discussion of primitive conceptions of death with particular attention to the passage between life and death, see I. A. Lopatin, *The Cult of the Dead Among the Natives of the Amur Basin* (The Hague: Mouton and Company, 1960), pp. 26-27 and 39-41.

2 The "DOA" deaths of famous persons are reportedly attended with considerably prolonged and intensive resuscitation efforts. In Kennedy's death, for example, it was reported:

> Medically, it was apparent the President was not alive when he was brought in. There was no spontaneous respiration. He had dilated, fixed pupils. It was obviously a lethal head wound.
>
> Technically, however, by using vigorous resuscitation, intraveneous tubes and all the usual supportive measures, we were able to raise the semblance of a heartbeat.

The New York Times, November 23, 1963, p. 2.

3 *A private hospital in the same city.*—ED.

11• The Social Inequality of Death

Calvin Goldscheider

Calvin Goldscheider's work explicates, in a fascinating and frightening manner, the social inequalities of death. In this selection Professor Goldscheider focuses on the inequalities as they relate specifically to race and socioeconomic status.

SOCIOECONOMIC STATUS AND MORTALITY

On April 14, 1912, the maiden voyage of the *Titanic* met with disaster. However, not all the passengers died at sea. The official casualty lists revealed that only 4 first-class female passengers (3 voluntarily chose to stay on the sinking ship) of 143 were lost; among second-class passengers, 15 of 93 females drowned; among third-class female passengers, 51 out of 179 died.[1] The social class selectivity among females on the *Titanic*—from 3 percent to 45 percent who died—dramatically illustrates the general inequality in death associated with social class levels.

The unequal distribution of death for various social classes has been observed regularly since the turn of the twentieth century. Sir Arthur Newsholme wrote in 1910 about England that "no fact is better established than the deathrate, and especially the deathrate among children, is high in inverse proportion to the social status of the population." In a review of infant mortality conditions in the United States during the first quarter of this century, Woodbury notes that low socioeconomic status, particularly low-income earnings, is the "primary cause" of excess mortality.[2]

Let us review briefly the relationship between social class and mortality for several European countries, where data have been more accurate and more readily available for a longer period of time, and for the United States. The countries to be considered include Scotland, England and Wales, The Netherlands, Denmark, the United States, and one underdeveloped country, Chile.

In Scotland, infant and fetal mortality rates for all social classes (defined by father's occupation) have declined over the last three decades, but the mortality differential between the lowest and highest social class has widened. In 1939, the fetal deathrate of the lowest occupation class was 1¼ times as high as that of the highest occupational class grouping; in 1963, it was 2⅓ times as high. Similarly, in 1939, the highest social class had a neonatal mortality rate of 30 per 1,000 live births, whereas the lowest social class had a neonatal mortality rate of 40 per 1,000 live births; in 1963, the gap widened with the highest social class having a neonatal mortality rate of 9.5, and the lowest social class a rate of 22.3. Moreover, the gap between these two class extremes was most evident in the postneonatal period, where socioeconomic environmental conditions clearly outweigh biological factors. In 1939, postneonatal deaths in the lowest occupational class were six times that of the highest occupational class, whereas in 1963, the differential more than doubled, and postneonatal deathrates were more than thirteen times as great among the lowest than among the highest social classes.[3]

Since 1911, British statistics have repeatedly shown this same inverse relationship between parental social class (father's occupation) and infant mortality. Although significant declines in infant mortality *within* each social class during the first half of the twentieth century have been reported, the relative differences *between* classes have not decreased.[4] The gap is indeed large: mortality among infants born into families of unskilled laborers is 2½ times that of infants born into families of professionals and rates of infant deaths among the lowest class lag thirty years behind infant deathrates among the highest class.[5] This has occurred in Britain and Scotland even when medical care is readily available to the entire population and where maternity hospital accommodations are ample. Moreover, some evidence shows that the steep mortality gradient from the highest to the lowest occupational class has widened in England and Wales, as in Scotland, precisely during the same period when the gap between the incomes of these class extremes has decreased.

The Danish evidence reveals the same pattern of considerable mortality differences from one occupational group to another. In a 1967 report, data derived in 1954-1955 show that 2½ times as many children of "domestic workers" (lowest occupational rank) died in their first year of life when compared to the children of self-employed persons in professional services.[6] The widening of class inequalities in life chances, particularly between the highest and lowest social classes, has also been observed for Denmark.

The Netherlands data provide an interesting confirmation of the persistence of inequality in deathrates between social classes. Infant mortality in The Netherlands (15 per 1,000 live births in 1964) is one of the lowest recorded in the world (second only to Sweden) and probably one of the lowest recorded in world history. After World War II, the Netherlands became one of the western European welfare states characterized by social security for the great masses, moderate wages increasing with the living standard, relatively little unemployment, and no real poverty. Yet, despite the fact that infant loss has reached low levels, the classic rule still prevails: unfavorable social conditions increase prenatal and postnatal mortality. Mortality is lowest in the highest social class and increases more or less progressively with decreases in social class. Data for 1961-1962 show a wide mortality range by social class in the Netherlands. Neonatal and postneonatal mortality among children with parents in the highest occupational class was about 20 percent below the averages for the country as a whole, whereas in the lowest occupational class, the mortality rates were 10 percent above the national average. The influence of father's occupation on infant mortality is unmistakable. Infant mortality in the lowest social class shows a lag of about seven years in reaching the level attained by the highest social class. The lag would be even greater if the highest income group included in the highest occupational class were compared with the lowest income group in the lowest occupational class. The decline in infant mortality has been fairly uniform for all occupational groups and, at least over the last decade, no appreciable increase in the gap between the highest and lowest class has been observed.[7]

Most European data available on social class differences in general mortality are based on the occupation of father. For overall mortality, it is difficult to separate deaths associated with the "risks" or hazards of various occupations from deaths due to the social and economic implications of life-styles associated with occupational class. But the data on infant mortality classifed by the occupation of father unmistakably reflect life-style and social class factors. In addition, information in England on social class differentials in mortality of women classified by the occupation of their husbands show the same mortality gradient by social class. In these cases, the relationship found could only be a function of differential social and economic life styles indicted by occupational groupings.[8]

Comparable data on socioeconomic class differences in mortality are unavailable for the United States. The several community, ecological studies (ranking census tracts by some measure of socioeconomic status and correlating census tract mortality measures), direct studies for New York State and California, and preliminary national estimates based on death record-census matching of 1960 have all noted the inverse relationship of social class indicators and mortality. These findings, based on various methodologies, gain in reliability not only because of the consistency of results but because of the overall similarity with the European evidence, which is based on more accurate data for a longer period of time. Several United States studies illustrate similar findings using the three methodologies cited.

First, one of the most carefully executed ecological-correlation studies, of Providence, Rhode Island, found infant mortality to be less a sensitive indicator of socioeconomic status as it was in the past. However, when neonatal mortality was separated from postneonatal mortality, i.e., where the major causes of death are farther removed from the physiological processes of gestation and birth, the findings point clearly to an inverse relationship between postneonatal mortality and socioeconomic status.[9]

In a 1961-1963 special study of health problems associated with poverty in New York City, sixteen poverty areas were identified by low income and high frequency of social problems. In 1961-1963, infant mortality in New York City was 26 per 1,000 live births, but in the sixteen poverty areas the rate was 35 per 1,000. The maternal mortality rate for the sixteen poverty areas was almost 2½ times that of the rest of New York City. When health districts were grouped by housing quality in New York City, districts with poor housing had an infant mortality rate over twice that of districts with good housing and a maternal mortality rate almost four times as high.[10]

Studies of upstate New York, for the 1950–1952 period, reaffirm the inverse relationship between level of father's occupation and infant deaths. Neonatal mortality ranged from 14 per 1,000 births among the children of professionals to 20 per 1,000 among the children of laborers; postneonatal mortality (28 days to 11 months per 1,000 survisors to 28 days among births) ranged from 3.5 to 3.7 among professionals and managers to 9.6 among nonfarm laborers.[11]

Finally, carefully matched death and census records (350,000) in the United States resulted in the following estimates of mortality (twenty-five years of age and older) by years of school completed and family income.[12]

1. Among white males with no schooling, mortality was about 10 percent higher than among the college educated; among females mortality was about 50 percent higher among those with no schooling than among those with some college education. The inverse gradient characterizes both sexes and most age groups.
2. Among white males with family incomes below $2,000 a year, mortality was over 50 percent higher than among males with incomes $10,000 a year or more; among females mortality was slightly less than 50 percent greater among those with the lowest family incomes than among those with the highest family incomes.
3. A strong inverse relationship between mortality and level of educational attainment was found for the 1960 nonwhite population. Among nonwhite males, from twenty-five to sixty-four years of age, mortality was 31 percent higher for those with less than five years of schooling when

compared to males with some high school or college education. Poorly educated nonwhite females from twenty-five to sixty-four years of age had mortality rates 70 percent higher than better-educated nonwhite females.

Health can be measured not only by length of life but also by positive elements of good health. Information from the United States National Health Survey clearly confirms the generally accepted positive relationship between poor health and low income.[13] People in families with a total income of less than $2,000 a year (in 1961) had twenty-nine restricted days of activities per year, per person; for those with family incomes of $2,000 to $4,000 a year, disability days dropped to eighteen, and in families with incomes of $4,000 a year and over the number was thirteen. To some extent income may be low because of greater illness just as illness may be low because of higher income—but it is clear that the two misfortunes exist together.

The National Health Survey in the United States further reveals that lower income persons, despite their increased level of illness and greater need for health care, receive fewer health services than people with higher incomes. Information gathered between 1963 and 1964 shows that 59 percent with family incomes below $2,000 a year consulted a physician at least once during the preceding year, compared with 66 percent of those with annual incomes between $4,000 and $7,000 a year and 73 percent of those with annual incomes of $10,000 a year. Finally, twice as many of those with higher incomes ($7,000 a year or more) avail themselves of medical specialists when compared to those with the lowest income status (below $2,000 a year).

In sum, the evidence from several European countries and the United States points consistently to the social inequality of death for members of different social strata. Some evidence, by no means universal or documented fully, also indicates an increased mortality discrepancy between the highest and lowest classes since World War II, paralleling the findings for racial mortality differentials in the United States and South Africa. Sufficient materials are not yet available to account for these increased mortality discrepancies, if they do in fact exist. Two points of conjecture are worthy of intense and rigorous testing. First, social class mobility may result in the movement out of the lower classes of persons who are healthier and more motivated to achieve a positive state of health. In the process, the lower classes, over time, may become composed of social and physical "rejects," whose mortality patterns may be consequently higher. This selective upward mobility may have increased after World War II, and, in part, may account for increased discrepancies between the lowest and higher classes. A second possibility relates to processes of urbanization and changing environmental densities since the end of World War II. The increasing urbanization of the lower classes, especially Negroes, as a result of rural-to-urban and interurban mobility, and the increasing concentration of urban residents among the poor in substandard housing and deprived social environments, may have increased mortality rates between classes and races. Although static areal measures show lower mortality rates in overall urban areas, more refined measures that subdivide urban areas into homogeneous socioeconomic sections are needed. A contributing and interrelated factor beyond the changing social-environmental situation of millions of poor persons relates to the differential availability of health and medical facilities and services and, more significantly perhaps, differential motivation to utilize services when they are available. Whether these motivational elements have changed in the last decades requires careful research. These suggestions for research may illuminate the specific problem of the social inequality of death, its persistence and increase, and in the process may suggest alternative solutions for diminishing such inequalities.

Notes

1 Cited in Aaron Antonovsky, "Social Class, Life Expectancy and Overall Mortality," *Milbank Memorial Fund Quarterly,* 45 (April 1967), pt. 1, p. 31.

2 Both Newsholme and Woodbury are cited in Edward G. Stockwell, "Infant Mortality and Socio-Economic Status: A Changing Relationship," *Milbank Memorial Fund Quarterly,* 40 (January 1962), pp. 102–103.

3 The data for Scotland are based on a report by Dr. Charlotte Douglas reviewed in U.S. Department of Health, Education and Welfare, *Report of the International Conference on the Perinatal and Infant Mortality Problem of the U.S.,* National Center for Health Statistics, ser. 4, no. 3 (June 1966), p. 3. (Similar findings are cited for France and Hungary.) Although Dr. Douglas notes the difficulty in understanding the widening class differential in infant mortality in Scotland, she suggests that nutrition, housing, economic conditions, and general life-styles conspire to produce the class gap.

4 See the summary by Dr. Katherine M. Hirst, in ibid., pp. 4–5; Cf. K. Hirst et al., *Infant and Perinatal Mortality in England and Wales,* National Center for Health Statistics, ser. 4, no. 12 (November 1968), pp. 31–32; Helen Chase, *International Comparison of Perinatal and Infant Mortality,* National Center for Health Statistics, ser. 3, no. 6 (March 1967), p. 67.

5 See R. K. Kelsall, *Population* (London: Longmans, Green, 1967), pp. 47–50; for earlier reports, see R. M. Titmuss, *Birth, Poverty and Wealth* (London: H. Hamilton Medical Books, 1943); J. N. Morris and J. A. Heady, "Social and Biological Factors in Infant Mortality," *Lancet,* 268 (March 1955), pp. 554–560; and several studies cited in Kelsall, *Population,* p. 98.

6 P. C. Matthiessen et al., *Infant and Perinatal Mortality in Denmark,* National Center for Health Statistics, ser. 3, no. 9 (November 1967), pp. 15–16, and tables S and 12, p. 55. The same pattern was observed in earlier years.

7 Data on the Netherlands were derived from J. H. de Haas-Posthuma and J. H. de Haas, *Infant Loss in the Netherlands,* National Center for Health Statistics, ser. 3, no. 11, pp. 16–24 and table 11. Social class differences in mortality remain practically the same when adjustment is made for parity and age of mother. See ibid., p. 32.

8 Cf. Harold Dorn, "Mortality" in *The Study of Population,* ed. Philip Hauser and Otis D. Duncan (Chicago: University of Chicago Press, 1959)

9 Stockwell, "Infant Mortality and Socio-Economic Status," pp. 101–111.

10 Eleanor Hunt and Earl Huyck, "Mortality of White and Non-White Infants in Major U.S. Cities," *Health, Education and Welfare Indicators* (January 1966), pp. 1-18.

11 Chase, *International Comparison of Perinatal and Infant Mortality,* pp. 67–68.

12 Evelyn Kitagawa and Philip Hauser, "Education Differentials in Mortality by Cause of Death, United States, 1960," *Demography,* 5:1 (1968), pp. 318–353; Evelyn Kitagawa, "Social and Economic Differentials in Mortality in the United States, 1960" (paper presented to the General Assembly, International Union for the Scientific Study of Population, London, 1969).

13 Data from the National Health Survey have been presented in Forrest E. Linder, "The Health of the American People," *Scientific American,* 214 (June 1966), pp. 21–29.

THE DETERMINATION OF DEATH

Among the many current changes in the "thanatological wind," we have already noted the increase in general longevity and in the secularization of death. In this section, we deal with several additional changes in our attitudes toward death: (a) an appreciation of the increasing complexity of what constitutes "death" and a concomitant concern with a refinement of the precise definition of death; (b) the advent of organ transplantation and the obvious implications for defining legally and ethically when a "viable" organ can be taken from a "dead" body, a topic touched on in the selection by Veatch; (c) as part of the general secularization of death, the "institutionalization" of death in hospitals; and (d) a new concern with reconceptualizing the psychological dimensions of death in light of changes in our understanding of the human condition.

From the standpoint of knowledge about the dying process (especially in the hospital), no discipline has contributed more in the past ten years than has sociology. Contemporary sociologists like Sudnow or Glaser and Strauss have actually gone into hospitals and emerged to "tell it like it is." They have revealed the impersonal methods used in regimenting the activity of dying. They have documented the cruel isolation of the dying person and described the tactics that hospital personnel use to avoid dealing with dying and death. It is clear that death has become a legitimate topic for serious sociological study; what is surprising is that it took so long.

Long before death became as secular as it has in this century, death and dying were associated primarily with the physician, and not unreasonably so. The doctor treated life-threatening illnesses and served as the goalie between the quick puck of death and the awful, irretrievable score. Today, more than ever, the physician has become the arbiter of death, although not everyone (including many physicians) believes that this is best. Nevertheless, the physician deals with such questions as what *is death,* who *is dead,* when *is one dead, and* how long *should a human being in pain and in obvious indignity be kept alive. These questions obviously burden the physician—and all of us—with deep moral and ethical issues.*

Walter Jeffko closely examines the physiological definitions of death and defines death finally as the total and irreversibly permanent cessation of personhood and rationality (cerebral function and brain stem function) and the cessation of the activity of the organism as a whole. The main point of all this definitional activity is to "enable us to indicate what kind of human life is significant and worth saving," without having any special definition of death solely for the purpose of organ transplantations.

Dr. William Sweet also concerns himself with defining death. He asks, "What are the crucial clinical criteria for death?" In this connection, he reports the findings of an international multidisciplinary interagency committee on irreversible coma and brain death. The major point of agreement among members of that committee was that "permanent functional death of the brain stem—the site of the respiratory center, the source of the cranial nerves, the locus of the neural tracts to the spinal cord, etc.—"constitutes brain death." Dr. Sweet also comments on the corroborating role of the electroencephalogram (EEG) in diagnosing brain death in a person whose heart is still beating.

The "determination of death" in the five selections of this section relates to plotting the path to, and defining the point of, death. In the last selection the approach to death and the meaning of the expression "determining death" undergo a mutation. "Determining" now relates to the state of mind of the person approaching death, and we shift from the relatively cold institutional approach to reintroduce human beings to their own deaths. The Shneidman selection reviews the traditional approach to the certification of death and foreshadows discussion in later chapters in which people are treated as "more than biological machines to which things happen."

12· Initial Definitions of the Dying Trajectory

Barney G. Glaser and Anselm L. Strauss

Barney G. Glaser and Anselm L. Strauss are both Professors of Sociology at the University of California School of Nursing in San Francisco. This selection, taken from their book Time for Dying, *discusses how hospitals seek to project the path that a terminal patient takes on the way to death.*

When the dying patient's hospital career begins—when he is admitted to the hospital and a specific service—the staff in solo and in concert make initial definitions of the patient's trajectory. They expect him to linger, to die quickly, or to approach death at some pace between these extremes. They establish some degree of certainty about his impending death—for example, they may judge that there is "nothing more to do" for the patient. They forecast that he will never leave the hospital again, or that he will leave and perhaps be readmitted several times before his death. They may anticipate that he will have periods of relative health as well as severe physical hardship during the course of his illness. They predict the potential modes of his dying and how he will fare during the last days and hours of his life.

They anticipate how much relative control the patient, the family, and they, the staff, will have over different stages of his dying trajectory, thus anticipating who will shape the dying patient's existence, and in what way, as the trajectory runs its course. For example, during what stages, if any, in the trajectory will the family feel it necessary to search for a cure—a "reprieve"—from any quarter of the medical community? And the staff, even at the outset, may begin considering which would be the best place for the patient's life to end—in the hospital or at home?—and, if in the hospital, how to manage the death watch, the constant care before death, and the family.

At this early stage of rehearsing these aspects and critical junctures of the dying patient's trajectory, the staff may perceive a temporally determinant trajectory—its total length with clearcut stages—or an indeterminant trajectory—its stages or length or both are unclear. Although they assign as complete a trajectory as possible to the dying patient, the clarities and vagaries of the several aspects of any trajectory generate differentials in definitions among the various staff members. The legitimate definitions . . . come from the doctor. Since the definition of trajectory influences behavior, these differing definitions may create inconsistencies in the staff's care of and interaction with the patient, with consequent problems for the staff itself, family, and patient.

No matter how full and clear they may appear at the patient's admission, the initial definitions of the dying trajectory seldom remain unchanged. The staff is continually redefining the trajectory as the patient's hospital career proceeds and his condition changes. Defining the dying trajectory is, then, an open-ended process, which continually explains to the staff what they must do now, next, and in the future in caring for the dying patient. Changes in definition cause them to revise their ideas of hospital organization to help in this care, and reformulate their feelings about the patient as he proceeds toward death. Defining and redefining the dying trajectory is, in effect, a process by which the staff maps the care of the hospitalized dying patient over long and short periods of time.

The defining process allows the staff to *temporalize* every aspect of the hospital career of the dying patient. They can temporally organize their work, its associated activities and interactions, and their sentiments. Without this temporalization afforded and guided by the dying trajectory, they could neither follow nor keep up with the constant shifting and changing condition of the patient as he dies. Without this temporalization, the hospital organization, the organization of the service, and the sentimental order of the ward would be under constant threat of breaking down, and often in a state of disarray. By defining trajectories, the staff establish for themselves a *broad-range "explanation"* of what will happen to the patient, and thereby provide an *organizing perspective* on what they will do about handling the impending flow of events.

They also engage in what we shall call a *structural process.* As the dying trajectory proceeds, it generates the need for various structural aspects of hospital organization to be brought into play (the patient is, say, sent to the Intensive Care Unit or is put through dismissal procedures). Each such action moves the trajectory along, and changing conditions force other structural aspects of the hospital to be brought into play—some of them routine, as procedures for disposing of the body or for readmitting the patient, and others created to handle infrequent events, such as the announcement of a surprise death to an unsuspecting family. As the trajectory runs its course, its process is linked with the hospital organization as a structure in process. At different stages of the trajectory, different aspects of hospital procedures and facilities become relevant for the care and handling of the dying patient. These "structural relevancies" in turn become conditions and processes tied to the staff's work and mood in caring for the patient. The open-ended redefinition of the trajectory, and its linkage with the structural processes of hospital care, come to an end in any given case when the body is removed and the family sent home. However, it must be kept in mind that the hospital is usually dealing with a number of dying trajectories at once, each with various staff definitions. Hence there is a constant tendency toward disorder in the work and sentiments of staff.

GOING TO THE HOSPITAL

There is an old adage that people in general no longer believe, but that is well understood by hospital staffs: "Never go to the hospital, because hospitals are a place where people die." It is clear to most of us that large numbers of people go to hospitals to recover; it is clear to staff members that more people than ever before are going to hospitals to die. In either case, hospitalization delegates considerable responsibility to the hospital and the medical staff. Determination of what is going to happen to the patient and the style in which it will happen become an institutional-professional, rather than a personal, issue. The degree of delegation of responsibility and control over the patient is in the beginning never quite appreciated by the patient or his family, for they are typically rather ignorant of hospital structure, hospital staff, and hospital careers.

In the case of dying patients, the family is perhaps even less willing to recognize the extent of the delegation, for they tend to see the hospital as a custodial institution that is taking over the management of the patient's dying. In their eyes the hospital will protect them from the ordeal of having the patient at home and will structure and limit the ordeal of his dying for all concerned. The dying patient may be delegating more control over his style of living while dying than he wishes. When they realize this, some patients leave the hospital without their doctor's advice. But most stay (unless sent home), supporting the loss of control over their living as best they can, while trying to learn to be acceptable dying patients. Of course, at some point in their dying trajectory, their physical condition may require the staff to manage their existence completely, no matter what they may wish.

In the case of patients who are expected to recover, the patient's and family's delegation of responsibility and control to the hospital is made "in the service of recovery." They see the hospital as a rehabilitating institution —a concentration of equipment and know-how designed to produce a cure. To reject going to the hospital is, perhaps, to risk dying. If such a patient dies, the bewildered family is likely to accuse the hospital and staff of negligence, questioning their curative ability and pretensions. This point is made clear by the following extreme example: A family in Greece sent a relative to the hospital to get well; however, he died—a complete surprise to everyone involved. The family gathered and stoned the hospital, breaking several windows. (In the United States, the family considers a malpractice or negligence suit.)

In sum, even when seen as a place for recovery, the hospital sometimes serves as the locus of dying. Its resources are better organized to handle the problems of dying, however, when the patients comes to it to die. Yet even under this condition, as we shall show, staff and organization preparations for the social-psychological problems of dying are not as adequate as those for recovery.

ENTERING THE HOSPITAL

Entering a hospital juxtaposes a hospital career and a dying trajectory. The doctor, patient, or family who chooses the hospital must anticipate some kind of career in the hospital suitable to the patient's dying trajectory. Hospitals vary in their ability ot mobilize the resources necessary to cope with all stages of a trajectory. For example, when a hospital does not have a particular piece of equipment, such as a kidney machine, it can mean potential death to the patient who suddenly requires one. In one such case, it was discovered that a well-known private hospital did not have such a machine (which everyone assumed it ought to have). When a dying patient suffered a renal failure, he had to be rushed to a nearby medical center. A hospital's resources—its adequacies and limitations—must be considered when linking a dying trajectory to a hospital career.

Hospital resources significantly influence the staff's initial definition of the patient's dying trajectory, and they plan accordingly for his hospital career. They have a good idea of what hospital care they can provide, and this knowledge sets limits on how they define his dying trajectory. The doctor, the patient, and the family may or may not consider this hospital career and trajectory acceptable. If not acceptable, they will seek another hospital that can, by virtue of its resources, provide a more favorable career and dying trajectory. This process of fitting resources, careers, and trajectories together accounts in large measure for the drift of patients toward the large, research-oriented, medical centers whose resources permit more optimistic dying trajectories—either longer or less certain to end in death.

Some patients who would wish it cannot be moved to a medical center because their dying is too rapid or because their physical condition or their dependence on a machine does not allow them to be moved. They are locked in a particular hospital career until the end of their trajectories. Other patients prefer a career in a hospital where excessive heroics are not possible. They prefer not to be subjected to unique machines, equipment or drugs that may prolong their trajectories painfully. These patients and their families do not consider moving but focus on living and preparing themselves for a trajectory shaped only by the resources of their current hospital. With still other patients, the dying trajectory does not permit a move to any hospital, and they must remain at home to die. In such cases, a hospital may send equipment into the home to ease or prevent the dying for a time, and a nurse may attend the patient. These patients experience, out of context, some aspects of a hospital career.

Moving between hospitals is also contingent on the type of dying trajectory. If a patient is dead on arrival, his hospital career starts with the end of trajectory—usually a very short one, occasioned, for example, by a heart attack or accident. Trajectories that last a few days or weeks typically do not allow time for more than one hospital career, unless a nearby hospital can provide an emergency measure deemed advisable. The patient either dies in the first hospital or is sent home to die. With their typical pattern of entry and reentry, trajectories and occasional reprieves may last over several months or years. This long duration allows much time for "hospital hopping," especially in the search of new cures or more reprieves. Thus the lingering dying patient may have several different hospital careers before he dies. On the other hand, the lingering patient in a large urban center may keep returning to the same hospital, and even the same ward, throughout the course of his dying trajectory.

In sum, different hospitals may provide different hospital careers and different initial definitions of dying trajectories. When the patient or his family chooses the hospital, they are exercising a measure of control over the patient's trajectory—how he will fare as a human being and as a patient. The more their decision is based on experience with hospitals, the more control they exercise over the differentials associated with dying in them. To be sure, frequently the patient simply goes to the hospital with which his doctor is affiliated, and no control is exercised, Sometimes control may be sought by changing to a doctor with access to the hospital preferred by the patient or family. Some doctors can take a patient to several hospitals and so allow their patients a choice; by briefly reviewing the conditions at the various hospitals, they give a patient a basis of control over his impending hospital career. In the case of short trajectories, the only choice may be the nearest hospital, chosen with the hope that its facilities can handle the emergency.

ADMITTANCE TO A WARD

There is an acceptable dying trajectory for each ward in a hospital. Upon entering, the dying patient is assigned to the appropriate ward on the basis of initial definitions of his trajectory; and the ward staff accept him or not on the basis of *their* initial definitions of his trajectory. When the initial definitions of ward staff and admitting personnel or private doctor differ significantly, the patient may be refused admittance to the ward. In this section we shall examine admission processes to several different kinds of wards—emergency, intensive care, cancer, medical, and premature baby—particularly the relationship of the ward staff's initial definitions of the dying trajectory to the admission requirements and procedures.

Generally, we are concerned here exclusively with admission to United States hospitals that separate illnesses by ward or departments within wards. In most large American hospitals, patients are placed on the basis of some notion of an "ideal" trajectory for each ward. This approach helps the hospital and ward staff codify their initial and subsequent definitions of the patient's dying trajectory. In contrast, European and Asian hospitals in the main have large, open wards that admit *all* patients, no matter what their trajectories may be. It is harder for the staff in these hospitals to maintain clear definitions of the diverse multiple dying trajectories; open wards create many problems in handling the dying situation. American hospitals, however, introduce an initial orderliness by screening patients on the basis of initial definitions of trajectory.

There are, to be sure, exceptions. Some county hospitals in rural areas in the United States have large open wards. On the other hand, the university hospital in one Italian city has separate wards for each department specializing in particular classes of illness. Each doctor-professor in this hospital has his own ward. Some are so jealous of their realms that they pass no records on to another ward when a patient is moved. Thus, upon being admitted to the new ward the patient's trajectory must be defined anew, repeating the whole process of examinations and history taking. The trajectory of a patient who must pass from ward to ward is repeatedly being "initially" defined, in contrast to the redefinition process in American hospitals, where some records are usually passed along with the patient who must travel between wards.

Not all wards have the space or personnel to accept appropriate dying patients; this can have drastic consequences for the unaccepted patient. He may be sent to a ward not accustomed to his particular trajectory, which cannot offer the suitable hospital career. For example, if a patient needing constant care is placed in a ward where he can receive only periodic care, he may die between routine checks, unattended. We found precisely this situation in a county hospital whose emergency ward has a rule prohibiting accepting patients once all beds are full, regardless of consequences. Some patients are sent home to await a bed and, while waiting, become sicker or even die. Other patients, nearer death, are sent to appropriate wards. For example, a patient in danger of dying from a drug was sent for the night to the "psych" ward, where being "drugged" qualified him for admittance as suicidal. Patients on the "psych" ward, once asleep, are not checked until morning. The staff member reporting this observed: "If he did have a bad reaction there, he was as good as dead. Do you realize that just that sort of thing happened a hundred and some-odd times last year?" On the wrong ward, even a recoverable patient can become a dying patient. Another patterned hospital condition that might put the patient on the wrong ward appears when the inexperienced aide, under doctor's orders, takes a patient who needs oxygen periodically down to X ray, where there is no oxygen supply. Conditions such as these, which mate a dying trajectory with an inappropriate hospital career, can increase both the likelihood and the speed of dying . . .

Where and how a patient is placed on the ward upon admission or soon after can also be for him a very telling indicator of his chances for recovery, especially if he has had some experience in hospitals either as a patient or visitor. For example, being placed in a room alone with the door left ajar, being screened off immediately after being placed in a multipatient room, or being placed as close to the nursing station as possible can lead to realization that perhaps he is dying. These realizations are based both on comparisons with other patients, indicating that the common ward career does not entail isolation, and on the recognition that isolation prevents one's dying from disturbing other patients. In short, the patient's trajectory is not quite acceptable, and he is being provided a slightly different career. Explaining to themselves the unusual placements may easily lead both patient and family to formulate definitions of a dying trajectory.

The definitions of a dying trajectory that may occur to a patient as he passes through the conditions and procedures of entering a hospital and ward are just beginning and concern mostly the certainty (or uncertainty) of dying. Definitions of time, mode and shape of trajectory come later. Whether or not correct, the initial definitions will be imbued with doubt, and are, therefore, liable to much redefinition as the patient's trajectory and hospital career proceed with their attendant changing conditions.

13· Redefining Death

Walter G. Jeffko

Walter G. Jeffko is a professor of philosophy at Fitchburg State College in Massachusetts. In his article, "Redefining Death," printed in Commonweal, *Jeffko evolves a new definition of death by synthesizing the various present physiological definitions.*

Walter G. Jeffko, "Redefining Death." From Commonweal, *6 July 1979, pp.394–397.*

Traditionally, defining death was simple. It occurred when breathing and heartbeat stopped. Without oxygen, the brain quickly died, and the organism as a whole ceased to exist. In the last twenty years or so, however, two developments in biomedical technology have raised problems for this traditional, cardiopulmonary definition. First, artificial life-support systems have maintained respiration and circulation in irreversibly comatose individuals whose brain function is totally destroyed. The only reason these brain-dead individuals are "alive" is that they are attached to a mechanical respirator. But are they really alive, or are they actually dead?

The second development concerns organ transplants. To preserve the vitality of the organs to be transplanted, there should be no unnecessary delay in declaring a person dead. At the same time, one would obviously not want to declare organ donors dead prematurely and thus remove organs from the living.

Faced with these two problems, the famous Ad Hoc Committee of the Harvard Medical School issued an influential and controversial report in 1968, advocating a "new" definition of death, that of "brain death." Essentially it said that an individual should be judged dead when his total brain is dead (such an individual is often called "decerebrate"), even if his respiration and circulation could be maintained artificially. It proposed four criteria for determining when an individual fulfilled this definition: (1) total unreceptivity and unresponsitivity—even to the most painful of stimuli; (2) no movements for one hour as observed by a physician and no breathing for three minutes when taken off a mechanical respirator; (3) no reflexes, e.g., fixed and dilated pupils, and no brain stem activity; (4) a flat electroencephalogram (EEG)—an indication considered of great confirmatory value. The Committee recommended that the patient be declared dead before the respirator is turned off. This would guarantee that, in organ transplants, organs would be removed from the dead and not from the living.

Two additional factors govern the valid application of these four criteria. First, all of the above tests are to be repeated at least twenty-four hours later with no change. Second, two conditions must be excluded from these criteria: hypothermia (body temperature 90°F); and the presence of central nervous system depressants, such as barbiturates. Both conditions are known causes of *reversible* coma, and the application of the criteria to them may yield similar results as in irreversible coma.

There are those, however, who feel that the Harvard Report did not go far enough. According to this group, once you begin down the road of defining the death of a *person* in terms of brain death, then the only logical alternative is to define death in terms of that part of the human brain which is the seat or locus of man's consciousness and of his higher, rational activities—in short, of that part of the brain which is associated with his personhood. They consider this part of the brain to be the neocortex, which, in general, is the outer surface of the cerebrum. According to them, a person should be judged dead when his neocortex, and not his total brain, has permanently ceased to function. A neocortically dead individual, like a decerebrate one, will suffer irreversible coma and will register a flat EEG. Unlike the decerebrates, however, the neocortically dead may still be able to breathe spontaneously—off the respirator—and exhibit reflex activity such as eye opening and yawning, for their brain stem may still be intact. Consequently, insofar as these individuals are able to perform such lower functions, society in general still judges them to be alive, although it is customarily said that they exist only in a "vegetative" state rather than in a truly human state. On the other hand, the neocortical position maintains that, since what is at issue here is the life or death of a human being and not of a "vegetable," these individuals are really dead—considered, that is, precisely as human beings. If a person is neocortically dead, then, he should be declared dead, even if he is exhibiting *spontaneous* respiration, circulation and other reflex activity. Admittedly, such cases are uncommon, but they do occur. Karen Quinlan is a notable example.

Thus, there are three major competing definitions of death today. Let us call them the "cardiopulmonary," the "decerebrate," and the "neocortical." Is any one by itself completely valid? Which are invalid? Does it make sense to have more than one definition of death, as is the case in some of the states which have adopted definition of death statutes? Is a synthesis among these definitions possible?

I

To answer these questions, we need to make some distinctions, an activity that unfortunately strains the patience of a great many people and yet ought to be seen as inevitable when society approaches a matter as delicate and central as the definition of death. Above all, we must recognize that the process of defining death occurs at different levels. We have already seen, for example, that the Harvard Report distinguishes between its "new" definition of death proper and the criteria, tests and procedures used to determine whether or not an individual has in fact died in accordance with this definition. The significance of this distinction becomes obvious as soon as we realize that the criteria, tests and procedures might change (with the advance of medical capabilities) while the definition remained the same.

But in fact the Harvard "decerebrate" definition of death, and the rival "cardiopulmonary" and "neocortical" notions, are all definitions at the *physiological level.* Since these physiological definitions concern the death of human beings, they will inevitably rest on certain philosophical presuppositions concerning what a human being, or human nature, is. And a philosophical concept of humanness, in turn, implies a philosophical concept or definition of what constitutes the death of a human being. In other words, another level of definition.

This philosophical definition will be distinct from, but oriented toward a particular physiological definition of death. For example, the neocortical physiological definition presupposes a philosophical definition of death something like, "permanent cessation of the consciousness and rational activities characteristic of the personhood of a human being." This definition, in turn, presupposes a concept of human nature which identifies the totality of man's being with his personhood and thus effectively writes off his lower biological nature. On the other hand, since the cardiopulmonary definition at the physiological level explicitly focuses on man's respiration and circulation rather than on his brain activity as such, it appears to rest on a concept of human nature which holds that man's biological dimension is primary and his rationality or personhood is secondary.

But we must go further. A philosophical definition of human death in particular presupposes a philosophical definition of death in general. This is the first of the four levels of definition—and the starting point for an analysis that I hope will justify a new definition of death and synthesize the decerebrate, neocortical and cardiopulmonary definitions that are now pitted against one another.

On the first level, that of philosophical definition of death in general, it is necessary to consider what its contrary, life in general, is. In its most proper sense, life is something that applies to organisms. It applies to other contexts either analogously (organ, cells) or metaphorically (a language, a music). Death here is defined as *the total and permanent cessation of the spontaneous activity of an organism as a whole.* Two elements of this defintion require a brief explanation: (1) "spontaneous," and (2) "organism as a whole."

Spontaneous activity is essential to an organism, and is distinguished from the transient activity of non-living, or inanimate, beings. Spontaneous activity—for example, nutrition—originates, continues and terminates within the organism. It is an immanent activity which either maintains or develops the individual organism or else propagates its species. (In the case of propagation, even though its final state, in some instances, terminates outside the organism by reproducing another one of its kind, its preparatory stages terminate within the organism.) On the other hand, transient activity—say, a stone rolling down a hill—is wholly external to its object. It neither originates, continues nor terminates *within* the inanimate object. It does not maintain the object in existence, much less develop it or propagate its "species." Indeed, the term, "propagate its species," does not even apply here. If, then, an organism completely lacked spontaneous activity (or function), it would not be a living organism. It would be dead.

The phrase "organism as a whole" is distinguished from "each and every part of the organism." To illustrate this distinction, let us suppose that someone has just died according to the traditional, cardiopulmonary definition. For a period of time after his death, isolated cells and tissues may continue to manifest biochemical activity in the form of slight hair and fingernail growth. Not each and every part of his organism has died. Yet no one would claim that this individual is still alive. For his organism as a whole has died: those systems which pervade and sustain his whole organism have irreversibly ceased—the respiratory, circulatory and nervous systems.

Turn now to the second level of defining death: a philosophical definition of *human* death, which presupposes a philosophical definition of human nature. Aristotle's widely accepted definition of human nature will be our touchstone: "Man is a rational animal (or organism)." Man's rationality is his primary or higher dimension. It includes everything that distinguishes him, as one species of animal, from all other species of animal. As such, it covers such activities as thought, self-consciousness, intentionality, culture-making and language and other forms of symbolization, the distinctively human feelings such as love, compassion and kindness, and everything all of these imply—science, philosophy, religion, art, morality, mathematics, politics, technology, etc. Man's rationality roughly corresponds to what is often called personhood or his spirtual nature. Man's animality or organicity, on the other hand, is his secondary or lower dimension. It refers to the fact that he has a biological body, a fact that he shares in common with all other animals. Our philosophical definition of human death based on the foregoing definition of man is: *the permanent cessation* primarily *of man's rationality and* secondarily but necessarily *of his animality (or organicity).* The implications of this definition will be developed as we turn now to the next level of defining death.

Level three is a physiological definition of human death. It must adequately reflect both man's rationality (or personhood) and his animality (or organicity). The question before us is this: how do we translate the philosophical concepts of rationality and animality into corresponding physiological concepts? In other words, what is the physiological seat or locus, as far as death is concerned, of man's rationality and animality? The cerebrum, or higher brain, would seem to be the sufficient physiological locus of man's rationality. If the cerebrum is destroyed, there is permanent loss of consciousness and a flat EEG. There is no chance that an individual will ever again perform a rational activity.

If, however, the brain stem is still intact, even though the cerebrum is destroyed, an individual may be able to breathe spontaneously even while existing only in a vegetative state. In turn, breathing controls circulation, which are the two fundamental activities with respect to man's animality in the sense that, without them, man dies within minutes. Therefore, man's brain stem, his respiratory system, and his circulatory system are the three physiological loci of man's animality insofar as a definition of death is concerned. Bearing in mind that, although both rationality and animality are essential dimensions of humanness, rationality is the primary dimension and animality secondary, I propose the following physiological definition of human death. Death is *the irreversible cessation* primarily *of cerebral function; and* secondarily but necessarily *of (a) lower brain function, including that of the brain stem; (b) spontaneous respiratory function; and (c) spontaneous circulatory function.*

Finally, level four of defining death involves the various criteria, procedures, and tests for determining when death has occurred. They are essentially the business of the medical profession and, as I said, may change with time. For the moment the Harvard criteria are widely accepted as sufficient evidence of brain death. They are certainly sufficient evidence of cerebral death, although there is some question whether a flat EEG by itself is. Therefore, until this question is resolved, the more inclusive Harvard criteria should be employed as criteria of cerebral death, even though they measure more than that. There is certainly no justification for holding, as some do, that a flat EEG by itself is a sufficient criterion of the death of a human being. As of now, it should be used merely as a confirmatory adjunct to other criteria. In spite of the enormous development of medical technology, the fact remains that most people continue to die as they always have. In general, the traditional cardiopulmonary criteria are still quite adequate and are the ones most physicians employ. Nevertheless, as one neurosurgeon-philosopher observes: "Clinical unresponsiveness to any external or internal stimuli, lack of spontaneous respiration, fixed dilated pupils, lack of brain-stem reflexes, an isoelectric electroencephalogram or absence of cerebral blood flow may one day mean 'death' as clearly as an absent heartbeat does today."

II

At this point we may shift about restlessly and ask exactly what has been gained by this painstaking exercise in definition, and in particular by my own physiological definition.

What, for example, is the practical purpose or benefit of distinguishing between primary and secondary attributes of a definition of death? For a man is not dead until all of them are fulfilled; and if one of them is not fulfilled—whether primary or secondary—he is still alive. The practical benefit of the distinction is this. It enables us to indicate what kind of human life is *significant* and worth saving. In my opinion, if an individual meets the primary attribute of death but not the secondary ones, he no longer possesses significant human life (although, to be sure, he is still alive), and his life is no longer worth prolonging—at least by the use of extraordinary means.

Beyond this, my physiological definition is an attempt to synthesize the cardiopulmonary, the decerebrate and the neocortical definitions by keeping their strengths and omitting their weaknesses.

The strength of the traditional, cardiopulmonary definition is that it still adequately covers the vast majority of individuals, who die "naturally." Without respiration and circulation, the whole brain soon dies, and the organism as a whole is dead. But this definition has two weaknesses. First, to count someone as alive, it does not require that respiration and circulation be spontaneous. Therefore, on this definition, a totally brain-dead individual who can respirate and circulate blood only because he is attached to a respirator may still be considered alive. Therefore, in order not to call such an individual alive, I have modified the traditional cordiopulmonary definition by insisting that respiration and circulation be spontaneous. As we have seen, spontaneous activity is an essential characteristic of an organism. Secondly, by explicitly defining death in terms of respiration and circulation, and specifically excluding not only the brain in general but the cerebrum in particular, the cardiopulmonary definition, unlike mine, implies that man's animality is primary and his rationality or personhood is secondary.

The strength of the decerebrate definition is twofold. First, it focuses on the organ which is the physiological locus of man's rationality or personhood—his brain. Secondly, to count someone as alive, it asserts that respiration must be spontaneous and therefore implies that circulation must be spontaneous. A decerebrate individual who is breathing only because he is attached to a mechanical respirator but who needs no additional device for circulation, such as a heart-lung machine, should not be regarded as having spontaneous circulation. His heartbeat should be regarded as an "artifact," which is sustained only by continued artificial respiration. The nonspontaneity of respiration, then, guarantees the nonspontaneity of circulation. The reason the decerebrate definition insists that respiration be spontaneous is that spontaneous respiration (and circulation) is always evidence that the brain is not totally dead. The weakness of this definition, however, is that it does not distinguish between the cerebrum and the lower brain, particularly the brain stem. Therefore, it fails to recognize that man's rationality or personhood is the primary dimension of his being. Instead, it implicitly treats his personhood and organicity as coequal dimensions of human nature.

The strength of the neocortical definition is the emphasis it places upon the neocortex and cerebrum as the locus of human death. Herein lies its weakness. It forgets that, although man is primarily a person, he is not exclusively so. It forgets that organicity is an essential dimension of humanness and that until organicity dies, a man is still alive.

I also believe that this physiological definition can provide the basis of a uniform legal definition of death. Levels one and two of the definition are too broad and too philosophical for legislation; level four is too medical and technological, and is best left to the determination of the medical profession. Yet is seems reasonably clear that death statutes are needed. Because of the current confusion as to when someone should be judged dead, the courts are being asked more and more to make decisions that properly belong to the legislative process and, ultimately, to an informed public opinion. Admittedly, some of the statutes enacted to date have been unfortunate. In Kansas, for example, the first state to enact a death statute, two alternative definitions of death were adopted. The first is a cardiopulmonary definition; the second, a brain definition. The apparent purpose of the latter definition is the facilitation of organ transplants. The Kansas statute, however, raises two problems. First, human death is a single phenomenon. There are not two separate phenomena of death, as the statute seems to imply. On the Kansas statute, an individual could be declared dead by the second definition and still be alive on the first. But it is absurd to say someone is both dead and alive. Secondly, it is fraudulent and unethical to have a "special" definition of death for the purpose of organ transplants. If someone is really alive, he is not made dead simply by a legal declaration of death. There is a world of moral difference between removing organs from the living and removing them from the dead—especially when the organ donors have given their express consent to have them removed only after they die. What is needed, then, is a statute which embodies one definition of death and which uniformly applies to everyone.

14• Brain Death

Robert M. Veatch

Robert M. Veatch is the Associate for Medical Ethics and Director of the research group on Death and Dying at the Hastings (New York) Institute of Society, Ethics and the Life Sciences. Dr. Veatch's article reports a fascinating and poignant case (involving a heart transplant) that touches on morality, religion, law, science, praxis, and prejudice.

Robert M. Veatch, "Brain Death: Welcome Definition . . . or Dangerous Judgment?" Hastings Center Report, *Vol. 2, No. 5 (November 1972). Reprinted by permission.*

CASE NO. 23 The following case, decided by a Virginia jury, may be a crucial one for medical ethics. It may be used as precedent in deciding *when a patient is dead* and for establishing *where the proper authority lies* for changing public policy regarding such fundamental decisions as those of human life and death. It appears that there were serious mistakes, both in interpretation and in judgment, by all involved. A more thorough exploration is certainly called for.

On May 25, 1968, at the beginning of the era of transplantation, Bruce Tucker was brought to the operating room of the hospital of the Medical College of Virginia. Tucker, a fifty-six-year-old black laborer, had suffered a massive brain injury the day before in a fall. He sustained a lateral basilar skull fracture on the right side, subdural hematoma on the left, and brain stem confusion.

The following timetable is taken from the summary of the case by Judge A. Christian Compton:

6:05 P.M.	Admitted to the hospital.
11:00 P.M.	Emergency right temporoparietal craniotomy and right parietal burr hole.
2:05 A.M.	Operation complete; patient fed intravenously and received "medication" each hour.
11:30 A.M.	Placed on respirator, which kept him "mechanically alive."
11:45 A.M.	Treating physician noted "prognosis for recovery is nil and death imminent."
1:00 P.M.	Neurologist called to obtain an EEG with the results showing "flat lines with occasional artifact. He found no clinical evidence of viability and no evidence of cortical activity."
2:45 P.M.	Mr. Tucker taken to the operating room. From this time until 4:30 P.M. "he maintained vital signs of life, that is, he maintained, for the most part, normal body temperature, normal pulse, normal blood pressure and normal rate of respiration."
3:30 P.M.	Respirator cut off.
3:33 P.M.	Incision made in Joseph Klett, heart recipient.

3:35 P.M. Patient pronounced dead.
4:25 P.M. Incision made to remove Tucker's heart.
4:32 P.M. Heart taken out.
4:33 P.M. Incision made to remove decedent's kidneys.

Tucker's heart and kidneys were removed by the surgical team. The heart was transplanted to Joseph G. Klett, who died about one week later.

William E. Tucker, brother of the dead man, sued for $100,000 damages, charging the transplant team was engaged in a "systematic and nefarious scheme to use Bruce Tucker's heart and hastened his death by shutting off the mechanical means of support." According to the judge's summary, "a close friend of the deceased was searching for him and made an inquiry at three of the hospital information desks, all without success." Tucker's brother was "at his place of business, located within fifteen city blocks of the hospital, all day on May 25th until he left his business to go find his brother in the afternoon when he heard he had been injured. Among the personal effects turned over to the brother later was a business card which the decedent had in his wallet which showed the plaintiff's (brother's) name, business address and telephone number thereon." The suit charged that the removal of organs was carried out with only minimal attempts to notify the victim's family and obtain permission for use of his organs.

This case is one of the most complicated and significant in the current debate about the brain locus for death. Whether or not it should, in fact, be treated as a "brain death" case we shall consider later, but certainly that is the way the principals in the case and the press have handled it. The Internal Medicine News Service headed the report, "'Brain Death' Held Proof of Demise in Va. Jury Decision." The *New York Times'* headline said, "Virginia Jury Rules That Death Occurs When Brain Dies." *Internal Medicine News,* in one of the best stories covering the case, claimed—quite accurately—that "the landmark decision is not binding elsewhere but it is certain to be cited as precedent in related cases." In fact, not one news story with which we are familiar saw this as other than a brain death case.

The surgeons who removed Tucker's heart evidently also interpreted it as a case of deciding when a patient is dead. Dr. Hume is quoted as saying that the court's decision in favor of the physicians "brings the law up to date with what medicine has known all along—that the only death is brain death."

Asked to decide whether the physicians were guilty of causing the death of the heart donor, the jury in the Tucker case were in effect being asked to make a public policy judgment about whether the irreversible loss of brain function is to be equated for moral, legal, and public policy purposes with the death of an individual.

The task of defining death is not a trivial exercise in coining the meaning of a term. Rather, it is an attempt to reach an understanding of the philosophical nature of man and that which is essentially significant to man which is lost at the time of death. When we say that a man has died, there are appropriate behavioral changes; we go into mourning, perhaps cease certain kinds of medical treatment, initiate a funeral ritual, read a will, or, if the individual happens to be president of an organizaton, elevate the vice president to his presidency role. According to many, including those who focus on the definition of death as crucial for the transplant debate, it is appropriate to remove vital, unimpaired organs after, but not before, death. So there is a great deal at stake at the policy level in the definition of death.

CANDIDATES FOR "DEATH"

There are several plausible candidates for the concept of death. All are attempts to determine that which is so significant to man that its loss constitutes the change in the moral and legal status of the individual. The traditional religious and philosophical view in Western culture was that a man died at the time when his soul left the body. This separation of body and soul is difficult to verify experimentally and scientifically and is best left to the religious traditions, which in some cases still focus upon the soul-departure concept of death.

Traditional secular man has focused on the cessation of the flow of the vital body fluids, blood and breath; when the circulatory and respiratory functions cease, the individual is dead. This is a view of the nature of man which identifies his essence with the flowing of fluids in the animal species.

There are also two new candidates. One of these is the complete loss of the body's integrating capacities, as signified by the activity of the central nervous system. This is the now-popular concept frequently though inaccurately given the name "brain death." Most recently in the literature there are those who are beginning to question the adequacy of this notion of brain death, claiming that it already has become old-fashioned. They ask why is it that one must identify the entire brain with death; is it not possible that we are really interested only in man's consciousness: in his ability to think, reason, feel, experience, interact with others, and control his body functions consciously? This is crucial in rare cases where the lower brain function might be intact while the cortex, which controls consciousness, is utterly destroyed.

MORAL, NOT TECHNICAL

The public policy debate about the meaning of death involves a choice among these several candidates for death. The Harvard Ad Hoc Committee to Examine the Definition of Brain Death established operational criteria for what it called irreversible coma, based on very sound scientific evidence. These four criteria are: 1. unreceptivity and unresponsivity; 2. no movements or breathing; 3. no reflexes; 4. flat electroencephalogram ("of great confirmatory value").

What the committee did not do, however, and what it was not capable of doing, was establishing that a patient in irreversible coma is "dead," i.e., that we should treat him as if he were no longer a living being who is the possessor of the same human moral rights and obligations as other human beings. While it may be the case that a patient in irreversible coma, according to Harvard criteria, has shifted into that status where he is no longer to be considered living, the decision that he is "dead" cannot be derived from any amount of scientific investigation and demonstration. The choice among the many candidates for what is essential to the nature of man and, therefore, the loss of which is to be called "death," is essentially a philosophical or moral question, not a medical or scientific one.

This being the case, it is troubling, indeed, to hear physicians say as Dr. Hume did, that the Virginia legal decision "brings the law up to date with what medicine has known all along—that the only death is brain death." If some physicians have believed this (and certainly there is no consensus among medical professionals), they know it from their general belief system about what is valuable in life and not from their training as medical scientists. It is therefore distressing that "expert" witnesses, including Dr. William Sweet of Harvard Medical School, were called by the defense to testify before the jury. Dr. Sweet said, "Death is a state in which the brain is dead. The rest of the body exists in order to support the brain. The brain is the individual." This may or may not be a sound moral philosophical argument. It is certainly not a medical argument. And to ask a chief of neurosurgery at Massachusetts General Hospital to make the moral argument is certainly a kind of special pleading on the part of legal counsel for the defense. This led to the *New York Times'* story which began, "A medical opinion that death occurs when the brain dies; even if the heart and other organs continue to function, has been reinforced by a jury here in a landmark heart transplant suit." The claim that death occurs when the brain dies is opinion to be sure, but it is not, and by the very nature of the case cannot be, medical opinion. To leave such decision making in the hands of scientifically trained professionals is a dangerous move.

Especially in such a fundamental matter as life and death itself, it is very difficult to see how the rest of society can shirk its responsibility in deciding what concept of death is to be used. To be sure, the scientific community can and should be asked to establish the criteria for measuring such things as irreversible coma, once the public, acting through its policy-making agencies in the legislature, has determined that irreversible coma is to be equated with death.

But let us return to the Tucker trial to see how this confusion between social and medical responsibilities developed. In the state of Virginia, according to the judge, there was a definition of death operative and that definition was specifically "the cessation of life; the ceasing to exist; a total stoppage of the circulation of the blood, and a cessation of the animal and vital functions consequent thereto such as respiration and pulsation." On a motion for summary judgment for the defendants, the judge ruled that the lawbook definition of death must take precedence over medical opinion. In this opinion, Judge Compton directed that the court was bound by the legal definition of death in Virginia until it was changed by the state legislature. Three days later, however, after considerable debate, Judge Compton may have backtracked on his commitment to the publicly established concept of death. He instructed the jury:

> In determining the time of death, as aforesaid. . . .you may consider the following elements none of which should necessarily be considered controlling, although you may feel under the evidence that one or more of these conditions are controlling: the time of the total stoppage of circulation of the blood; the time of the total cessation of the other vital functions consequent thereto, such as respiration and pulsation; the time of complete and irreversible loss of all functions of the brain; and whether or not the aforesaid functions were spontaneous or were being maintained artificially or mechanically.

This instruction is ambiguous, to say the least. It could be that Judge Compton meant no innovation here. It could be that the "complete and irreversible loss of all function of the brain" might have been merely the "cause" of death traditionally defined, i.e. "a cessation of the animal and vital functions." Presumably if the head injury to Tucker led to the cessation of all brain function and thereby to the cessation of all other vital functions, death could have occurred in the traditional sense without or prior to the intervention of the surgeons. This almost certainly would have been the case if Mr. Tucker had received no medical attention. The (traditional) death would have occurred and the "complete and irreversible loss of all function of the brain" would have been simply a relevant factor.

But it also is possible to interpret the judge's instructions as authorization for the jury to use a new concept of death—one based directly on brain function—in determining the time of the patient's death. If this is the case it is a complete reversal of the judge's earlier statement and a major change in public policy. It would appear that this contradicts Judge Compton's earlier conclusion that "if such a radical change is to be made in the law of Virginia, the application should be made therefore not to the courts but to the legislature wherein the basic concept of our society relating to the preservation and extension of life could be examined and, if necessary, reevaluated." Let us hope that the judge's later instruction to the jury should not be taken as backing down from this important principle.

WHO SHOULD HAVE MADE THE DECISION?

The other candidates for decision making in this case obviously are the relatives of the patient. While it is the state's obligation to establish fundamental policy in this area, it would seem reasonable and in the interest of the state that they would judge that no organs may be removed from an individual after death unless there is some authorization by the individual patient, such as is now called for in the Uniform Anatomical Gift Act, or by the patient's relatives, also as provided by that act. If it is true, in this case, that the relatives of the patient were not consulted and sufficient time was not taken to establish that relatives were available, this would seem to have been a most serious infringement upon the rights of the patient and the patient's family.

The removal of organs in the rare situations where relatives cannot be found raises a serious, if rather unusual, problem for transplant surgeons. It would appear to be far wiser to avoid the risk of abuse in these cases, which will frequently involve indigent and lonely patients, by simply forbidding the use of organs. Certainly four hours (from the time Mr. Tucker was placed on a respirator until the respirator was turned off) was not sufficient time to seek permission from the next of kin.

WAS THIS REALLY A DEFINITION OF DEATH CASE?

Up to this point, we have assumed that the defense, the prosecution, and the press were correct in interpreting this case as one focusing upon the meaning and concept of death. Yet the case record, as presented to the court, leaves open some very serious questions. The medical team was operating with a definition of death which focused on the brain. Medical witnesses for the defense claimed that Mr. Tucker was "neurologically dead" several hours before the transplant operation. Yet according to the records presented of the case, at 11:45 A.M. Mr. Tucker's physician says prognosis is nil and death imminent. At 1:00 P.M. the neurologist took an EEG reading and found it "showing flat lines with occasional artifact" and he "reports no evidence of viability and no signs of cortical activity." Presumably, according to a brain-oriented concept of death, Mr. Tucker was thought to be dead at the time by the surgeons. Yet we are told by the surgeons that at 3:30 P.M. they turned the respirator off. One must ask what possible moral principle would justify turning off a respirator on a dead patient. Presumably if one is dealing with a corpse, the moral imperative would be to preserve the organs for the benefit of the living in the best possible condition—by continuing the respiration process until the heart could be removed. We would find no moral problems with such behavior; in fact, one would say that it would be morally irresponsible to run the risk of damaging the tissue. Yet the respirator was turned off—from which one can only surmise that it must have been done in order to permit the heart and lungs to stop functioning. The only plausible reason for this would be that there was some lingering doubt about whether or not Mr. Tucker was dead. Of course, to introduce this dimension is to place doubt on the claim that the patient was dead at 1:00 P.M. when the EEG showed a flat tracing, "with occasional artifact."

If, however, the purpose was to turn the respirator off in order to allow the patient to die all the way, the case is not one of a new definition of death at all; it is instead the common one of morally, and possibly legally, deciding to continue treatment no longer on an irreversibly terminal patient. The morality of ceasing treatment on such a terminal patient has been accepted widely in medical ethics. Such procedures are practiced and accepted by Catholic, Protestant, and Jewish moral traditions alike. It could be, then, that this is really a case of deciding when it is morally acceptable to stop treatment on a dying patient, rather than a case of deciding when a patient was dead. This seems to be the most plausible and morally acceptable reason for turning off the respirator under law then existing in Virginia. It is very important to note that the jury never announced that the brain-oriented concept of death is now appropriate or that they themselves used such a concept. They were not asked or permitted to do this. They merely concluded that they found the defendants not guilty of wrongful death of the decedent. It may well be that at least some of them reasoned that the physicians did indeed hasten the dying process by turning off the respirator, but given the patient's condition this was an acceptable way to behave, i.e., they may have considered that the physician could have justifiably decided to withdraw the mechanical means of support as "extraordinary for a patient in Tucker's irreversibly dying condition." We do not know this of course, but we also do not know that the jury accepted a brain-oriented concept of death.

At 3.35 P.M., five minutes after the respirator was turned off, the patient was pronounced dead. One would think this was because there had been a cessation of heartbeat and respiratory function and the death was pronounced according to the traditional heart/lung criteria. If this were the case, the physicians would be operating under the traditional moral and legal requirements, and the removal of organs for transplantation, presumably with the permission of the next of kin, would be an acceptable procedure. They would not be using the brain-oriented concept of death at all.

WAS HE NEUROLOGICALLY DEAD?

There is one final problem which must be resolved. The summary of the proceedings raises some doubt as to whether the patient was dead even according to the concept of brain death which focuses upon the brain. The Harvard criteria call for the use of irreversible coma. But the Harvard report appeared in the *Journal of the American Medical Association* dated August 5, 1968, and the surgeons at the Medical College of Virginia had to make their decision two months earlier, on May 25, 1968. Obviously they could not be expected to have followed the Harvard criteria precisely. Nevertheless, Mr. Tucker definitely could not have been declared dead according to the criteria since established by the Harvard Committee and widely used as being the minimal tests for establishing irreversible coma. At the very least, the tests were not repeated twenty-four hours later. The patient was pronounced dead less than two hours and thirty-five minutes after the electroencephalogram reading.

In order to accept the jury's decision in this case and accept it as demonstrating that the physicians were justified in the use of brain evidence of death, one would have to accept four highly questionable premises. The first is that the jury did indeed base its decision on a brain-oriented concept of death. Second, that a man is really dead when he no longer has any capacity for brain activity. The third is that it was reasonable under 1968 conditions to conclude that the patient had irreversibly lost the capacity for any brain activity based on the EEG reading without repetition. Such a conclusion is premature even for the scientific evidence which exists today, [several] years later. Finally, one would have to accept that individual medical professionals should be vested with the authority to change public policy on an area as fundamental as life and death. This no one should be willing to tolerate.

15 · Brain Death: An Editorial

William H. Sweet

William H. Sweet is a distinguished neurosurgeon (now Professor Emeritus) at Harvard Medical School and the Massachusetts General Hospital. He was a Rhodes Scholar and received his M.D. cum laude at Harvard. Among his many writings is his book, Pain and the Neurosurgeon: A Forty Year Experience. *In this editorial published in* The New England Journal of Medicine, *Dr. Sweet addresses the question of how to make a clinical diagnosis of death.*

William H. Sweet, M.D., D.Sc., "Brain Death," Reprinted by permission of The New England Journal of Medicine *299, no. 8 (1978): 410–411.*

The inescapable logic of the concept that death of the brain is equivalent to death of the person has not achieved widespread acceptance. In the decade since a Harvard Ad Hoc Committee enunciated the view and gave specific guidelines for making such a diagnosis,[1] a vast literature has developed on this subject. The Medical Progress article by Dr. Peter Black appearing in the last two issues of the *Journal* is a superb summary of various facets of this subject ranging through medicine, law, ethics and public opinion. The title of the Harvard report was: "A Definition of Irreversible Coma: Report of the Ad Hoc Committee of the Harvard Medical School to examine the definition of brain death." As Black and others point out, it is essential that a clear distinction be made between death of the brain and a prolonged or irreversible state of coma but with some evidence of brain-related bodily function. Not only are the two terms not synonymous, but they describe two different states that do not overlap. Once a person is dead, he is no longer in coma.

It is the condition of brain death that physicians can now diagnose with a confidence sufficient to have resulted in legislation embodying such a concept in eighteen states by mid-1977. The courts in the remainder of the states may well be willing to abide by the decision made on appeal to the Supreme Judicial Court of Massachusetts: "Brain death occurs when, in the opinion of a licensed physician, based on ordinary and accepted standards of medical practice, there has been a total and irreversible cessation of spontaneous brain functions and further attempts at resuscitation or continued supportive maintenance would not be successful in restoring such functions."[2]

Indeed, it is clear that a person is not dead *unless* his brain is dead. The time-honored criteria of stoppage of the heartbeat and circulation are indicative of death only when they persist long enough for the brain to die.[3]

Black's article points out that validation of the clinical diagnosis may be provided by two types of evidence—i.e., demonstration that when certain clinical criteria of brain death have been met, either somatic death inevitably follows despite assiduous resuscitative measures or certain structural changes will be seen in the brain post mortem. Black points out major difficulties with the latter type of validation that are worth reemphasizing. In an enormous number of clinical problems the pathologist's postmortem studies provide not only the final but the most conclusive data on which to base decisions. The problem of validating the diagnosis of brain death is an unequivocal exception to this rule. The anatomic substrate of the mechanisms occurring in a living brain is so delicate that it deteriorates with extraordinary rapidity. Currently, hours to a day or more elapse between pronouncement of death and the placement of the brain in chemical fixatives. Yet in patients who die from failure of other systems the cerebral tissues are usually classified as "normal" by gross and light microscopial appearances. The electron microscopist is aware of the rapidity of ultrastructural deterioration after death; hence his adamant demand for absolutely fresh tissue fixed seconds after it leaves the living brain. A graphic illustration of the vulnerability of central neural tissues to rapid postmortem change is given by the recently discovered monoaminergic neural structures. Three independent but widely pervasive sets of nerve cells and fiber systems have been found in the brain, one for each of the three neurotransmitters, dopamine, norepinephrine and serotonin. These substances lose their in vivo characteristic chemical affinities so rapidly that they cannot even be seen by the necessary fluorescence histochemical methods in central nervous tissues processed more than one hour after death! Hence, current knowledge of this structure in man has been obtained from nondiseased fetuses removed by cesarean section.[4] Although the light microscopical appearances post mortem of a decomposing brain are decisive evidence that it was indeed dead, a postmortem brain normal by light microscopy is obviously also dead. The role of the pathologist here is a subsidiary one.

What, then, are the crucial clinical criteria? To answer that question in this country an "Inter-Agency Committee on Irreversible Coma and Brain Death" was set up with representatives from the main United States national neurologic, neurosurgical, neuropathologic and electroencephalographic societies. We on this committee have agreed on broad "guidelines" to make the diagnosis,[5] but have not yet agreed on certain minutiae. Virtually all the practical problems related to making a *clinical* diagnosis of brain death have in my view been discussed in an excellent detailed article in the *Lancet,* [6] which I heartily recommend to every interested physician. It represents the combined thinking of a broadly representative British group and before its publication it had been unanimously approved by the Conference of Medical Royal Colleges and their Faculties in the United Kingdom. This huge group was able to agree that "permanent functional death of the brain stem constitutes brain death." This unassailably logical statement is followed by a precise operational account of what the physician actually does to make the diagnosis with no risk to the patient; it also involves no electroencephalogram. To the diagnostic tests for confirmation of death of the brain stem many of the United States Inter-Agency Committees' members would add, "Decerebrate or decorticate responses anywhere should not occur spontaneously or be elicited by noxious or other stimuli. The decerebrate position is one of adduction of arm, extension and often hyperpronation of forearm, extension of thigh, leg and foot, possibly with extension of head and spine. In the decorticate position one or both arms or one or both legs may be in flexion rather than extension."

The British criteria do not insist on "an irreversible loss of all brain function" or on "total brain death." It makes no practical difference if some hundreds of thousands of the many millions of brain cells are still functional, and it is certainly impractical at present to test the function of all brain-cell clusters.

The Inter-Agency Committee has not been able to agree on the role here of the electroencephalogram. The experience of testifying in court on three different cases when a person was accused of homicide in connection with brain death has made me acutely aware of the objective value of the judge and the jury of extensive tracings revealing electrocerebral silence. When the technics rigidly prescribed by the American Electroencephalographic Society are followed[7] in a patient definitely without exogenous or endogenous intoxication, one can be sure that at least the cerebral hemispheres are dead. Clearly, such a person is as certainly dead as one with a dead brain stem. This statement rests primarily on the carefully planned and monitored "Collaborative Study of Cerebral Survival" of 503 patients.[8] If all drug-induced comas were eliminated, no patient survived after having a single thirty-minute record of electrocerebral silence. In a previous longer series of the American Electroencephalographic Society's Committee on Cerebral Death, only three of 1665 persons with a flat record recovered. All three had drug intoxication.[9]

The electroencephalogram, then, adds graphic confirmatory evidence of death. Although I have no quarrel with our British colleagues that such confirmation is not necessary, I would point out that in this country a climate of general public uneasiness about brain death exists, partly engendered by sensational fiction. Moreover, juries considering murder cases in this country will usually be exposed to as massive a dose of skepticism about the brain death of the victim as the defendant's attorney can muster. The latter may be able to find an electroencephalographer who will testify that the demonstration of electrocerebral silence is essential for the diagnosis. In view of these facts, as well as the increasingly litigious trends in the population, it may be prudent in this country to have two electroencephalograms that make the diagnosis of brain death trebly sure. The Inter-Agency Committee recommends that the clinical criteria should have persisted for at least six hours after the first tracing. All criteria should be reexamined and confirmed on a second occasion at least six hours later. Some jurisdictions require that two physicians collaborate in the diagnosis, a further useful precaution for both him and his patient. Armed with both the clinical and the electroencephalographic evidence, physicians are now in a position to be 100 percent sure of this diagnosis.

References

1 Beecher HW, Adams RD, Barger AC, et al: A definition of irreversible coma: report of the Ad Hoc

Committee of the Harvard Medical School to examine the definition of Brain Death. JAMA 205:337–340, 1968
2 Commonwealth v. Golston, 1977. Mass. Adv. Sh. 1778–1791
3 Executive Committe of the Netherlands Red Cross Society: Memorandum on organ transplantation. Presented at the third International Congress of the Transplantation Society, The Hague, Netherlands, September 7-11, 1970
4 Nobin A, Björklund A: Topography of the monoamine neuron systems in the human brain as revealed in fetuses. Acta Physiol Scand (Suppl) 388:1–40, 1973
5 Report of the Inter-Agency Committee on Irreversible Coma and Brain Death. Trans Am Neurol Assoc 100:280–282, 1975
6 Diagnosis of brain death. Lancet 2:1069–1070, 1976
7 Bennett DR, Hughes JR, Korein J, et al: Atlas of Electroencephalography in Coma and Cerebral Death. New York, Raven Press, 1976
8 An appraisal of the criteria of cerebral death: a summary statement. JAMA 237:982–986, 1977
9 Silverman D, Saunders MG, Schwab RS, et al: Cerebral death and the electroencephalogram: report of the Ad Hoc Committee of the American Electroencephalographic Society on EEG Criteria for Determination of Cerebral Death. JAMA 209:1505–1510, 1969

16 • The Death Certificate

Edwin S. Shneidman

Edwin S. Shneidman is Professor of Thanatology and Director of the Laboratory for the Study of Life-Threatening Behavior at the University of California at Los Angeles. In this selection, which is taken from his book Deaths of Man, *Dr. Shneidman discusses the development, the uses, and the main deficiencies of the death certificate. He notes that the contemporary death certificate fails to reflect the psychological role of the decedents in their own demise.*

As this book is about death, so this selection is about a unique document that memorializes death. We have seen that death is an epistemologically curious event that cannot be experienced and never has been directly reported. The document of which we speak is one that must, without exception, be completed (in due time) for each reader, and which, under no possible circumstances in this world, can readers ever see completed for themselves. The document is, of course, the death certificate.

That interesting document is much more than just a document. It is better understood as that special form which gives operational meaning to death and which, in fact, defines its current dimensions. It reflects the ways in which people—administrative and forensic people, at any rate—think about death and the ways in which they believe it occurs.

The impact of the death certificate is considerable. It holds a mirror to our mores; it reflects some of our deepest taboos; it can directly affect the fate and fortune of a family, touching both its affluence and its mental health; it can enhance or degrade the reputation of the decedent and set its stamp on his or her postself career. But if the impact of the death certificate is great, its limitations are of equal magnitude. In its present form the death certificate is a badly flawed document.

Today most states follow the format of the U.S. Standard Certificate of Death. Most relevant to our present interests is the item which reads: "Accident, suicide or homicide (specify)." When none of these is checked, a natural mode of death is, of course, implied. Only two states, Delaware and Virginia, have made all four of these modes of death explicit on the death certificate (and have included "undetermined" and "pending" categories as well). Curiously enough, Indiana included these modes of death on the death certificate form from 1955 to 1968, but then revised the form in 1968 and now provides no item for mode of death; nor, surprisingly, does the current Massachusetts death certificate contain an accident-suicide-homicide item.

In addition to the U.S. Standard Certificate, the International Classification of Diseases and Causes of Death plays a major role in determining the way a specific death may be counted—and thus in the apparent change in statistical causes of death from decade to decade. For example, the definitions of suicides and accidents were changed in the Seventh Revision (1955) and Eighth Revision (1966) of the International Classification, and the numbers of suicides and accidents changed along with the definitions. When the Seventh Revision was put into effect for the data year 1958, the death rate for suicides increased markedly over 1957. In part, one can find the explanation in this paragraph (U.S. Department of Health, Education and Welfare, 1965):

> About 3.3 percent of the total suicide rate for 1958 as compared with that for 1957 resulted from the *transfer of a number of deaths from accidents to suicide.* In 1958 a change was made in the interpretation of injuries where there was some doubt as to whether they were accidentally inflicted or inflicted with suicidal intent. Beginning with the Seventh Revision for data year 1958, "self-inflicted" injuries with no specification as to whether or not they were inflicted with suicidal intent and deaths from injuries, whether or not self-inflicted, with an indication that it is not known whether they were inflicted accidentally or with suicidal intent, are classified as suicides. The change was made on the assumption that the majority of such deaths are properly classified as suicide *because of the reluctance of the certifier to designate a death as suicide unless evidence indicates*

suicidal intent beyond the shadow of a doubt. The magnitude of the comparability ratios for suicide varied considerably with means of injury, from 1.02 for suicide by firearms and explosives to 1.55 for suicide by jumping from high places. [Emphasis added.]

It would seem that this redefinition led to an apparent 55 percent increase from one year to the next in suicides by jumping from high places. Even more interesting is the official observation that the death certifier would be reluctant to indicate suicide "unless evidence indicates suicidal intent beyond the shadow of a doubt." Clearly the certifier plays an important role in the process of generating mortality data. It is the certifier who makes the subjective judgment of what constitutes conclusive evidence of the decedent's intent. The Eighth Revision (1966), which made the category "Undetermined" available, introduced still further problems, apparently shifting many suicidal deaths to the Undetermined category. What is urgently needed is an explanation and description of the current practices of certifying deaths, especially deaths by suicide. We need a uniform system that would eliminate such inconsistencies (or confirm the differential unequivocally) as for example, 10.9 deaths by suicide per 100,000 population for Idaho versus 20.2 for Wyoming. What is required is a "correctional quotient" for each reporting unit—county, state, and nation. Until such information is obtained, available suicidal statistics are highly suspect.

That is what the situation is now. At the turn of the century, an early reference book of the medical science (Abbot 1901) urged reliable death registration bookkeeping:

The objects secured by a well-devised system of death certification are manifold and may be enumerated as follows:

1. Questions relating to property *rights* are often settled by a single reference to a record of a death.
2. The official certificate of a death is usually required in each case of claim for *life insurance.*
3. Death certificates settle many disputed questions in regard to *pensions.*
4. They are of great value in searching for records of *genealogy.*
5. A death certificate frequently furnishes valuable aid in the *detection of crime.*
6. Each individual certificate is a contribution *causa scientiae.* Taken collectively they are of great importance to physicians, and especially to health officers, in the study of disease, since they furnish valuable information in regard to its causes, its prevalence, and its geographical distribution.

All that is well and good. But that was three-quarters of a century ago. It is time to take full account of the enormous scientific and intellectual developments of the twentieth century, especially the psychiatric revolution that began with Freud and has grown steadily during the past three generations. At least four more functions for the death certificate might be added to the half-dozen listed in 1901:

7. The death certificate should reflect the dual nature of death; that is, its private nature (as it is almost experienced by the decedent) and its public nature (as it is experienced and accounted for by others).
8. It should reflect the type of death that is certified—for example, brain death (a flat electroencephalographic record), or somatic death (no respiration, heartbeat, reflexes).
9. It should include space for the specification of death by legal execution, death in war or military incursions, death by police action, and others of the sort.
10. Perhaps most important, it should abandon the anachronistic Cartesian view of humans as passive biological vessels on which the fates work their will, and instead reflect the contemporary view of humans as psycho-socio-biological organisms that can, and in many cases do, play a significant role in hastening their own demise. This means that the death certificate should contain at least one item on the decedent's *intention* vis-á-vis death. It is not enough to state that a death was natural, accidental, suicidal, or homicidal; we should know too whether it was intentioned, subintentioned, or unintentioned.

Let us look at the typical death certificate reproduced here. What is there seems fairly straightforward. The items for themselves. But not everything is so obvious. For example, it is possible to think of the items on the death certificate as being divided into three groups: The top third of the certificate has to do with identification of the decedent. It establishes exactly who that person was: name, date of birth, place of birth, spouse's name, mother's maiden name, Social Security number, etc.—items calculated to distinguish one person from any other.

The middle section of the certificate relates to cause or causes of the death. There is some worldwide agreement as to what causes are to be listed. Indeed, . . . there is an international classification of diseases and causes of death: an Abbreviated List of 50 Causes and an Intermediate List of 150 Causes. The International Conference for the Eighth Revision of the International Classification of Diseases, held in Geneva in 1965 (U.S. Department of Health, Education and Welfare 1966), considered compilation of a longer list of 250 to 300 causes.

The bottom third of the death certificate contains a number of items usually related to injury and to such miscellaneous items as place of burial or cremation, name of funeral director or embalmer, and so on—none of which interests us especially. But there is one item of very special interest in this section, usually relative to "violent death," which typically contains only three words: accident, suicide, homicide. The important point is this: If none of these three is checked, it is implied that the death was natural. These four terms, then, represent the four traditionally implied modes of death: natural, accidental, suicidal, and homicidal—what, acronymically, I have called the NASH classification (Schneidman 1963). (The use of modifications and combinations of these terms to yield other labels, such as "probable suicide," "probable accident," "suicide-accident undetermined," and so on, does not change the fact that there are only four main modes of death stated or implied on the present certificate.)

INDIANA STATE BOARD OF HEALTH
DIVISION OF VITAL RECORDS
MEDICAL CERTIFICATE OF DEATH

Local No.________________ State No.________________

1. PLACE OF DEATH a. COUNTY
2. USUAL RESIDENCE (Where deceased lived. If institution: Residence before admission) a. STATE b. COUNTY
b. CITY, TOWN, OR LOCATION | c. Length of Stay in 1b
c. CITY, TOWN, OR LOCATION
d. NAME OF HOSPITAL OR INSTITUTION (If not in hospital, give street address)
d. STREET ADDRESS
e. IS PLACE OF DEATH INSIDE CITY LIMITS? YES☐ NO☐
e. IS RESIDENCE INSIDE CITY LIMITS? YES☐ NO☐ | f. IS RESIDENCE ON A FARM? YES☐ NO☐
3. NAME OF DECEASED (Type or print) First Middle Last | 4. DATE OF DEATH Month Day Year
5. SEX | 6. COLOR OR RACE | 7. MARRIED☐ NEVER MARRIED☐ WIDOWED☐ DIVORCED☐ | 8. DATE OF BIRTH | 9. AGE (In years last birthday) | IF UNDER 1 YEAR Months Days | IF UNDER 24 HRS. Hours Min.
10a. USUAL OCCUPATION (Give kind of work done during most of working life, even if retired) | 10b. KIND OF BUSINESS OR INDUSTRY | 11. BIRTHPLACE (State or foreign country) | 12. CITIZEN OF WHAT COUNTRY?
13. FATHER'S NAME | 14. MOTHER'S MAIDEN NAME
15. WAS DECEASED EVER IN U. S. ARMED FORCES? (Yes, no, or unknown) (If yes, give war or dates of service) | 16. SOCIAL SECURITY NO. | 17a. INFORMANT'S NAME
17b. INFORMANT'S ADDRESS | 17c. RELATIONSHIP TO DECEASED

MEDICAL CERTIFICATION

18. CAUSE OF DEATH [Enter only one cause per line for (a), (b), and (c).]
PART I. DEATH WAS CAUSED BY:
IMMEDIATE CAUSE (a)________________
Conditions, if any, which gave rise to above cause (a) stating the underlying cause last.
DUE TO (b)________________
DUE TO (c)________________
INTERVAL BETWEEN ONSET AND DEATH
PART II. OTHER SIGNIFICANT CONDITIONS CONTRIBUTING TO DEATH BUT NOT RELATED TO THE TERMINAL DISEASE CONDITION GIVEN IN PART I (a). | 19. WAS AUTOPSY PERFORMED? YES☐ NO☐
20a. ACCIDENT ☐ SUICIDE ☐ HOMICIDE ☐ | 20b. DESCRIBE HOW INJURY OCCURRED. (Enter nature of injury in Part I or Part II of item 18.)
20c. TIME OF INJURY Hour a. m. p. m. Month Day Year
20d. INJURY OCCURRED WHILE AT WORK☐ NOT WHILE AT WORK☐ | 20e. PLACE OF INJURY (e. g., in or about home, farm, factory, street, office bldg., etc.) | 20f. CITY, TOWN, OR LOCATION COUNTY STATE

21. ATTENDING PHYSICIAN: I certify that I attended the deceased from________________, to________________ and last saw her/him alive on________________ Death occurred at ________________M (C.S.T.) on the date stated above; and to the best of my knowledge, from the causes stated.
22. HEALTH OFFICER: I certify that I investigated cause of death of deceased and find that death occurred at________________M (C.S.T.) from causes stated and on above date.
23a. Signature of Attending Physician or Health Officer. | 23b. ADDRESS | 23c. DATE SIGNED
24a. BURIAL, CREMATION, REMOVAL (Specify) | 24b. DATE | 24c. NAME OF CEMETERY OR CREMATORY | 24d. LOCATION
DATE REC'D BY LOCAL HEALTH OFFICER | SIGNATURE OF HEALTH OFFICER | 25. FUNERAL DIRECTOR ADDRESS

EMBALMER'S NAME________ LICENSE No.________
FUNERAL DIRECTOR'S LICENSE No.________

S.B.H.—6-24-3—Revised 1955 U. S. Department Health, Education and Welfare. Form Approved Budget Bureau No. 68-R375

It should be immediately apparent that the cause of death stated on the certificate does not automatically carry with it information as to the specific mode of death. One example should suffice: Asphyxiation due to drowning in a swimming pool does not clearly communicate whether the decedent struggled and drowned (accident), entered the pool with the intention of drowning (suicide), or was held under the water until drowned (homicide).

In the Western world death is given its administrative dimensions by the death certificate. It is the format and content of this document that determines and reflects the categories in terms of which death is conceptualized and death statistics reported. The ways in which deaths were described and categorized in John Graunt's day[1] and earlier set deep precedents for ways of thinking about death, and they govern our thoughts and gut reactions to death to this day . . . Deaths were then assumed to fall into one of two categories: there were those that were truly adventitious—accidents, visitations of fate or fortune (called natural and accidental)—and there were those that were caused by a culprit who needed to be sought out and punished (called suicidal and homicidal deaths). In the case of suicide, the victim and the assailant were combined in the same person and the offense was designated as a crime against oneself, a *felo de se*. England did not cease to classify suicide as a crime until 1961, and in this country it remains a crime in nine states to this day (Litman 1970).

The importance of the certification of the mode of death—of the coroner's function—can now be seen: it not only set a stamp of innocence or stigma upon the death, but also determined whether the decedent's estate could be claimed by the legal heirs (natural or accidental deaths) or by the crown or local lord (a suicide or a murderer). That was certainly one important practical effect of the death certificate. This bias (in relation to suicide, at any rate) is reflected today in the ways insurance policies are written. I would assert that the NASH categories of death were implied as early as the sixteenth century in English certification, and that this submanifest administrative taxonomy of death has beguiled most people into thinking that that is the way death phenomena really are; which, of course, is not necessarily so at all.

Although it may be platitudinous to say that in each life the inevitability of death is an inexorable fact, there is nothing at all inexorable about our ways of dimensionalizing death. Conceptualizations of death are man-made and mutable; what people can make they can also clarify and change. Indeed, changes in the conceptualizations of death are constantly occurring, notwithstanding the NASH notions of death that have held on for centuries after they became anachronistic. Each generation becomes accustomed to its own notions and thinks that these are universal and ubiquitous.

From the time of John Graunt and his mortality tables in the seventeenth century through the work of Cullen in the eighteenth century and William Farr in the nineteenth century, the adoption of the Bertillon International List of Causes of Death in 1893, and the International Conference for the Eighth Revision of the International Classification of Diseases as recently as 1965, the classification of causes of death has constantly been broadening in scope, the changes characterized primarily by attempts to reflect additions to knowledge, particularly those contributed by the new professions as they have developed — anesthesiology, pathology, bacteriology, immunology, advances in obstetrics and surgery, and most recently, the behavioral sciences.

The traditional natural-accident-suicide-homicide classification of modes of death is demonstrably insufficient: certain deaths cannot be classified as other than equivocal. This can be true, of course, even when *cause* of death is clearly established. Indeed, in the modern medical examiner-coroner's office, it is a very rare case—given the available skills of pathologist, microscopist, and toxicologist—in which the cause of death cannot be determined. But it does not follow at all that mode of death can be so clearly stated; . . . an estimated 10 to 15 percent of all coroner's cases are equivocal as to mode of death, the alternatives usually being accident or suicide.

The most serious fault in the certification of equivocal death is the lack of any attempt to establish the *intention* of decedents in regard to their demise. The decedents' intentions—not their stomach or lung contents or their brain pathology—is what operationally distinguishes suicide from the other three modes. And the decedents' intentions cannot be found in the test tube or under the microscope. Often, however, they can be discovered by conscientious interviewing of people who knew various aspects of their life-styles and specific behavior immediately prior to their deaths. A total autopsy ought to include the services of the behavioral scientists—psychologist, psychiatrist, sociologist, social worker. We call this procedure the "psychological autopsy."

Much of what I have had to say about the NASH classification of death has impugned its heuristic and scientific usefulness. What, in fact, is its major shortcoming? By far its greatest inadequacy lies in the fact that it emphasizes relatively trivial elements in the death of human beings while omitting altogether the psychological role they may have played in their own demise. The NASH classification, Cartesian and apsychological in spirit, implies that human beings are biological machines to which things happen, rather than vital, introspective, unique individuals who often unconsciously play a decisive role in their own fate. In other words, it leaves the person out.

I propose that we put the person in. We could begin by adding the item I have already suggested—an indication of the decedent's intention regarding his or her own death. This item might be labeled "Imputed Lethality," since this judgment can only be inferential, and I suggest that it consist of four designations: "High," "Medium," "Low," "Absent."

High imputed lethality would indicate that the decedent definitely wanted to die, and played a direct and conscious role in his or her own death. The death was due primarily to the decedent's conscious wish to be dead, and to his or her actions in carrying out that wish either by some recognized means of suicide (jumping from a high place, shooting in the head) or by deliberately goading someone to kill him or her, refusing life-saving procedures, stopping a prescribed medical regimen, or some other act of commission or omission that the decedent knew would result in death.

Medium imputed lethality would indicate that the decedent played an important role in effecting his or her own death. The decedent's behavior in some degree hastened the event—carelessness, foolhardiness, neglect of self, rash judgment, gambling with death, laxness in following a prescribed life-saving medical regimen, active resignation to death, drug abuse, habitual drunkenness, "tempting fate," "asking for trouble."

Low imputed lethality would indicate that the decedent played some small but insignificant role in effecting or hastening his or her own demise. The difference between medium and low imputed lethality is one of degree, not of kind.

When imputed lethality is absent, the decedent has played no role in effecting his or her own death. The death was due entirely to assault from outside the body (in no way invited by the decedent) or to failure within the body (in a decedent who unambivalently wished to continue to live).

This is a classification that seems to me to be meaningful; it is more fair than the NASH categories alone. At present, individuals of higher social status who commit suicide are more likely to be assigned the mode of accident or natural death than are individuals of low social status whose suicidal intent appeared no less ambiguous. If the term is to have any meaning at all, it should be used fairly across the board, measured by the individual's intention.

Perhaps more important from the larger view, the lethality-intention item would provide an unexampled source of information by means of which biostatisticians, public health officials, and social scientists could assess the mental health of any community. It is obvious that the number of deaths that are caused, hoped for, or hastened by the decedents themselves is a measure of the prevalence of psychological disorder and social stress. At present we do not have this measure, and we need it.

It might be protested, inasmuch as the assessments of these intention states involve the appraisal of unconscious factors, that some workers (especially lay coroners) cannot legitimately be expected to make the kinds of psychological judgments required for this type of classification. But medical examiners and coroners throughout the country are making judgments of precisely this nature every day of the week. When coroners must evaluate a possible suicide, they act, perhaps without realizing it, as psychiatrist and psychologist, as both judge and jury: any certification of death as suicide implies some judgment or reconstruction of the victim's motivation or intention. But it would be far better if these psychological dimensions of death were made explicit through use of a lethality-intention scale than to allow them to remain implicit and be used in an influential manner. The dilemma is between the present usable, oversimplified classification on the one hand, and a somewhat more complex but more precise classification on the other.

In Marin County, California, the coroner's office[2] is currently assessing each death processed by that office terms of both the traditional NASH classification of mode of death and the lethality intention of the decedent.

For a two-year period, 1971-1972 (978 cases), the breakdown was as follows:

(1) Natural deaths (630): high lethality intent, none; medium lethality, 33 (5 percent); low, 37 (6 percent); absent, 560 (89 percent).

(2) Accidental deaths (176): high lèthality intent, 2 (1 percent); medium; 77 (44 percent); low, 40, (22 percent); absent, 57 (33 percent).

(3) Suicidal deaths (131): high lethality intent, 131 (100 percent).

(4) Homicidal deaths (37): high lethality intent, none; medium, 20 (54 percent); low, 9 (24 percent); absent, 8 (22 percent). Four deaths were of unknown origin.

The first thing we notice is that *some* natural, accidental, and homicidal deaths were classified as having *some* degree of lethal intention. If the medium- and low-intention categories are combined, then over one-fourth (26 percent) of all natural, accidental, and homicidal deaths (216 of 847) were deemed to be subintentioned. If one adds the suicidal deaths (in which the decedent obviously has played a role), then only 64 percent—or 625 of 978—of all deaths were deemed to have been totally adventitious; or conversely, 36 percent were deemed to have some psychological components.

Also of special interest in these Marin County data is the finding that coroners can, with no more apparent difficulty than they experience in assigning death to the NASH categories, simultaneously (and by essentially the same processes of inference and induction) assign deaths to psychological (intentional) categories as well. It is an important pioneer effort that deserves widespread emulation.

Notes

1 John Graunt, a London tradesman, published in 1662 a small book of observations on the "bills of mortality" that were published in London at the end of each year. Graunt separated the various bits of information contained in these bills into categories and organized them into tables. He focused on individual causes of death and on the subject of population estimation, and constructed a mortality table which was the first attempt to organize data in this manner. Of greatest significance was his success in demonstrating the regularities that can be found in medical and social phenomena when one is dealing with large numbers. John Graunt's book was to have great social and medical significance.

2 I am especially grateful to Keith C. Craig, coroner's deputy, Marin County, for his interest and help in supplying these data.

References

Abbott, Samuel W. Death Certification. In Albert H. Buck (Ed.), *Reference Handbook of the Medical Sciences.* New York: William Wood, 1901.

Litman, Robert E. Medical-Legal Aspects of Suicide. In Edwin S. Shneidman, Norman L. Farberow and Robert E. Litman, *The Psychology of Suicide.* New York: Science House, 1970.

Shneidman, Edwin S. Orientations toward Death: A Vital Aspect of the Study of Lives. In Robert W. White (Ed.), *The Study of Lives.* New York: Atherton, 1963.

World Health Organization, *Manual of the International Statistical Classification of Diseases, Injuries, and Causes of Death: Based upon the Recommendations of the Seventh Revision Conference, 1955.* Geneva: World Health Organization, 1957.

PART THREE

INTERPERSONAL PERSPECTIVES ON DEATH

THE PARTICIPANTS OF DEATH

Rarely is the drama of dying played by a single actor. Usually some supporting cast is involved and, as a result, the drama partakes of the complications (and shortcomings) of all human interaction, including such reactions and emotions as withdrawal, fear, disgust, shame, guilt, and ambivalence. Interactions between a dying person and the survivors-to-be —loved ones, doctors, nurses and others—are rather complicated because parties on both sides are participating in an unusual and extraordinarily stressful situation. One of the most important developments in the current thanatological scene is a growing awareness and understanding of how terminal persons view their condition and how they seek to cope with the prospect and process of dying; and further, how these awarenesses and understandings are reflected in the new approaches being used (by the medical profession in general and by thanatologists in particular) to treat and help terminal patients. We now are beginning to recognize, for example, that dying persons are human beings who dislike being abandoned as much as anyone else and that wanting human contact while facing death is biologically and psychologically sound and normal.

In this section too there is a shift of focus, this time centering on those immediately concerned with death. A concomitant of the institutionalization of death is the creation of a set of relationships between the institution (as represented by the hospital staff) and the dying. This, in turn, gives rise to a set of interpersonal interactions. How these interactions are structured is discussed in the first selection of this section (Glaser and Strauss), in which "implicit understandings" that patients and staff often have with each other in relation to the patient's death are explicated. This selection describes a sort of courtly dance of death, a grisly ballet in which unspoken "contracts" are carried out, sometimes by mutual consent, but often unilaterally without the patient's knowledge and perhaps at the cost of the patient's life, days or weeks or months sooner than he or she otherwise might have lost it.

In "Lies to the Sick and Dying," Sissela Bok discusses the role of deception in therapy, life from the perspective of the patient, and the topics of respect and truthfulness. The new humanistic approach theme is continued by the Hinton selection, which addresses the importance of communication tailored to the specific needs of the dying or death-contemplating individual.

Another set of interpersonal reactions—those between the terminal patient and a therapist—is discussed by Elisabeth Kübler-Ross. Her selection not only contains practical suggestions on how to handle a terminal illness, but also points up the current changes toward a more humanistic approach which, in effect, helps offset some of the problems created by the trend toward institutionalizing death.

It is interesting to speculate how the increasingly humanistic approach by and toward the "participants of death" is related to the general humanistic trend in other sectors of society (for example, as in humanistic psychology developed by Henry Murray, Abraham Maslow, Carl Rogers, Gordon Allport, and others) and to wonder whether this approach may return to death and dying a portion of the human dimension that has been lost as death has become increasingly institutionalized and desacralized.

The final selection, "Some Aspects of Psychotherapy with Dying Persons," first delineates the difference between ordinary talk, hierarchical exchanges, psychotherapy, and clinical thanatology; it asserts that interaction with a dying person, which is called clinical thanatology, is psychologically and philosophically different from any other kind of human interaction. The author then labels and describes the dozen or so particular characteristics of clinical thanatology in the hope of providing clinicians with suggestions and clues about conducting the special kind of interchange that seems to be required with dying persons.

17 • The Ritual Drama of Mutual Pretense

Barney G. Glaser and Anselm L. Strauss

This selection, taken from the book Awareness of Dying *by Barney G. Glaser and Anselm L. Strauss, reflects some of the current thinking of the "new sociology" concerning death and discusses an "implicit mutual understanding" about death between terminal patients and hospital staffs.*

When patient and staff both know that the patient is dying but pretend otherwise—when both agree to act as it he were going to live—then a context of mutual pretense exists. Either party can initiate his share of the context; it ends when one side cannot, or will not, sustain the pretense any longer.

The mutual-pretense awareness context is perhaps less visible, even to its participants . . . because the interaction involved tends to be more subtle. On some hospital services, however, it is the predominant context. One nurse who worked on an intensive care unit remarked about an unusual patient who had announced he was going to die: "I haven't had to cope with this very often. I may know they are going to die, and the patient knows it, but (usually) he's just not going to let you know that he knows."

Once we visited a small Catholic hospital where medical and nursing care for the many dying patients was efficiently organized. The staff members were supported in their difficult work by a powerful philosophy—that they were doing everything possible for the patient's comfort—but generally did not talk with patients about death. This setting brought about frequent mutual pretense. This awareness context is also predominant in such settings as county hospitals, where elderly patients of low socioeconomic status are sent to die; patient and staff are well aware of imminent death but each tends to go silently about his own business.[1] Yet, as we shall see, sometimes the mutual pretense context is neither silent nor unnegotiated.

The same kind of ritual pretense is enacted in many situations apart from illness. A charming example occurs when a child announces that he is now a storekeeper, and that his mother should buy something at his store. To carry out his fiction, delicately cooperative action is required. The mother must play seriously, and when the episode has run its natural course, the child will often close it himself with a rounding-off gesture, or it may be concluded by an intruding outside event or by the mother. Quick analysis of this little game of pretense suggests that either player can begin; that the other must then play properly; that realistic (nonfictional) action will destroy the illusion and end the game; that the specific action of the game must develop during interaction; and that eventually the make-believe ends or is ended. Little familial games or dramas of this kind tend to be continual, though each episode may be brief.

For contrast, here is another example that pertains to both children and adults. At the circus, when a clown appears, all but the youngest children know that the clown is not real. But both he and his audience must participate, if only symbolically, in the pretense that he is a clown. The onlookers need do no more than appreciate the clown's act, but if they remove themselves too far, by examining the clown's technique too closely, let's say, then the illusion will be shattered. The clown must also do his best to sustain the illusion by clever acting, by not playing too far "out of character." Ordinarily nobody addresses him as if he were other than the character he is pretending to be. That is, everybody takes him seriously, at face value. And unless particular members return to see the circus again, the clown's performance occurs only once, beginning and ending according to a prearranged schedule.

Our two simple examples of pretense suggest some important features of the particular awareness context to which we shall devote this [discussion]. The make-believe in which patient and hospital staff engage resembles the child's game much more than the clown's act. It has no institutionalized beginning and ending comparable to the entry and departure of the clown; either the patient or the staff must signal the beginning of their joint pretense.

Both parties must act properly if the pretense is to be maintained, because, as in the child's game, the illusion created is fragile, and easily shattered by incongruous "realistic" acts. But if either party slips slightly, the other may pretend to ignore the slip.[2] Each episode between the patient and a staff member tends to be brief, but the mutual pretense is done with terrible seriousness, for the stakes are very high.[3]

INITIATING THE PRETENSE

This particular awareness context cannot exist, of course, unless both the patient and staff are aware that he is dying. Therefore all the structural conditions which contribute to the existence of open awareness (and which are absent in closed and suspicion awareness) contribute also to the existence of mutual pretense. In addition, at least one interactant must indicate a desire to pretend that the patient is not dying and the other must agree to the pretense, acting accordingly.

A prime structural condition in the existence and maintenance of mutual pretense is that unless the patient initiates conversation about his impending death, no staff member is required to talk about it with him. As typical Americans, they are unlikely to initiate such conversation; and as professionals they have no rules commanding them to talk about death with the patient, unless he desires it. In turn, he may wish to initiate such conversation, but surely neither hospital rules nor common convention urges it upon him. Consequently, unless either the aware patient or the staff members break the silence by words or gestures, a mutual pretense rather than an open awareness context will exist; as, for example, when the physician does not care to talk about death, and the patient does not press the issue though he clearly does recognize his terminality.

The patient, of course, is more likely than the staff members to refer openly to his death, thereby inviting them, explicitly or implicitly, to respond in kind. If they seem unwilling, he may decide they do not wish to confront openly the fact of his death, and then he may, out of tact or genuine empathy for their embarrassment or distress, keep his silence. He may misinterpret their responses, of course, but . . . he probably has correctly read their reluctance to refer openly to his impending death.

Staff members, in turn, may give him opportunities to speak of his death, if they deem it wise, without their directly or obviously referring to the topic. But if he does not care to act or talk as if he were dying, then they will support his pretense. In doing so, they have, in effect, accepted a complementary assignment of status—they will act with pretense toward his pretense. (If they have misinterpreted his reluctance to act openly, then they have assigned, rather than accepted, a complementary status.)

Two related professional rationales permit them to engage in the pretense. One is that if the patient wishes to pretend, it may well be best for his health, and if and when the pretense finally fails him, all concerned can act more realistically. A secondary rationale is that perhaps they can given him better medical and nursing care if they do not have to face him so openly. In addition, as noted earlier, they can rely on common tact to justify their part in the pretense. Ordinarily, Americans believe that any individual may live —and die—as he chooses, so long as he does not interfere with others' activities, or, in this case, so long as proper care can be given him.

To illustrate the way these silent bargains are initiated and maintained, we quote from an interview with a special nurse. She had been assigned to a patient before he became terminal, and she was more apt than most personnel to encourage his talking openly, because as a graduate student in a nursing class that emphasized psychological care, she had more time to spend with her patient than a regular floor nurse. Here is the exchange between interviewer and nurse:

INTERVIEWER: Did he talk about his cancer or his dying?

NURSE: Well, no he never talked about it. I never heard him use the word cancer . . .

INTERVIEWER: Did he indicate that he knew he was dying?

NURSE: Well, I got that impression, yes . . . It wasn't really openly, but I think the day that his roommate said he should get up and start walking, I felt that he was a little bit antagonistic. He said what his condition was, that he felt very, very ill that moment.

INTERVIEWER: He never talked about leaving the hospital?

NURSE: Never.

INTERVIEWER: Did he talk about his future at all?

NURSE: Not a thing. I never heard a word . . .

INTERVIEWER: You said yesterday that he was more or less isolated, because the nurses felt that he was hostile. But they have dealt with patients like this many many times. You said they stayed away from him?

NURSE: Well, I think at the very end. You see, this is what I meant by isolation . . . we don't communicate with them. I didn't, except when I did things for him. I think you expect somebody to respond to, and if they're very ill we don't . . . I talked it over with my instructor, mentioning things that I could probably have done; for instance, this isolation, I should have communicated with him . . .

INTERVIEWER: You think that since you knew he was going to die, and you half suspected that he knew it too, or more than half; do you think that this understanding grew between you in any way?

NURSE: I believe so . . . I think it's kind of hard to say but when I came in the room, even when he was very ill, he'd rather look at me and try to give me a smile, and gave me the impression that he accepted . . . I think this is one reason why I feel I should have communicated with him . . . and this is why I feel he was rather isolated . . .

From the nurse's account, it is difficult to tell whether the patient wished to talk openly about his death, but was rebuffed; or whether he initiated the pretense and the nurse accepted his decision. But it is remarkable how a patient can flash cues to the staff about his own dread knowledge, inviting the staff to talk about his destiny, while the nurses and physicians decide that it is better not to talk too openly with him about his condition lest he "go to pieces." The patient, as remarked earlier, picks up these signals of unwillingness, and the mutual pretense context has been initiated. A specific and obvious instance is this: an elderly patient, who had lived a full and satisfying life, wished to round it off by talking about his impending death. The nurses retreated before this prospect, as did his wife, reproving him, saying he should not think or talk about morbid matters. A hospital chaplain finally intervened, first by listening to the patient himself, then by inducing the nurses and the wife to do likewise, or at least to acknowledge more openly that the man was dying. He was not successful with all the nurses.

The staff members are more likely to sanction a patient's pretense than his family's. The implicit rule is that though the patient need not be forced to speak of his dying, or to act as if he were dying, his kin should face facts. After all, they will have to live with the facts after his death. Besides, staff members usually find it less difficult to talk about dying with the family. Family members are not inevitably drawn into open discussion, but the likelihood is high, particularly since they themselves are likely to initiate discussion or at least to make gestures of awareness.

Sometimes, however, pretense protects the family member temporarily against too much grief, and the staff members against too immediate a scene. This may occur when a relative has just learned about the impending death and the nurse controls the ensuing scene by initiating temporary pretense. The reverse situation also occurs: a newly arrived nurse discovers the patient's terminality, and the relative smooths over the nurse's distress by temporary pretense.

THE PRETENSE INTERACTION

An intern whom we observed during our field work suspected that the patient he was examining had cancer, but he could not discover where it was located. The patient previously had been told that she probably had cancer, and she was now at this teaching hospital for that reason. The intern's examination went on for some time. Yet neither he nor she spoke about what he was searching for, nor in any way suggested that she might be dying. We mention this episode to contrast it with the more extended interactions with which this [selection] is concerned. These have an episodic quality—personnel enter and leave the patient's room, or he occasionally emerges and encounters them—but their extended duration means that special effort is required to prevent their breaking down, and that the interactants must work hard to construct and maintain their mutual pretense. By contrast, in a formally staged play, although the actors have to construct and maintain a performance, making it credible to their audience, they are not required to write the script themselves. The situation that involves a terminal patient is much more like a masquerade party, where one masked actor plays carefully to another as long as they are together, and the total drama actually emerges from their joint creative effort.

A masquerade, however, has more extensive resources to sustain it than those the hospital situation provides. Masqueraders wear masks, hiding their facial expressions; even if they "break up" with silent laughter (as a staff member may "break down" with sympathy), this fact is concealed. Also, according to the rules ordinarily governing masquerades, each actor chooses his own status, his "character," and this makes his role in the constructed drama somewhat easier to play. He may even have played similar parts before. But terminal patients usually have had no previous experience with their pretended status, and not all personnel have had much experience. In a masquerade, when the drama fails it can be broken off, each actor moving along to another partner; but in the hospital the pretenders (especially the patient) have few comparable opportunities.

Both situations share one feature—the extensive use of props for sustaining the crucial illusion. In the masquerade, the props include not only masks but clothes and other costuming, as well as the setting where the masquerade takes place. In the hospital interaction, props also abound. Patients dress for the part of not-dying patient, including careful attention to grooming, and to hair and makeup by female patients. The terminal patient may also fix up his room so that it looks and feels "just like home," an activity that supports his enactment of normalcy. Nurses may respond to these props with explicit appreciation—"how lovely your hair looks this morning"—even help to establish them, as by doing the patient's hair. We remember one elaborate pretense ritual involving a husband and wife who had won the nurses' sympathy. The husband simply would not recognize that his already comatose wife was approaching death, so each morning the nurses carefully prepared her for his visit, dressing her for the occasion and making certain that she looked as beautiful as possible.

The staff, of course, has its own props to support its ritual prediction that the patient is going to get well: thermometers, baths, fresh sheets, and meals on time! Each party utilizes these props as he sees fit, thereby helping to create the pretense anew. But when a patient wishes to demonstrate that he is finished with life, he may drive the nurses wild by refusing to cooperate in the daily routines of hospital life—that is, he refuses to allow the nurses to use their props. Conversely, when the personnel wish to indicate how things are with him, they may begin to omit some of those routines.

During the pretense episodes, both sides play according to the rules implicit in the interaction. Although neither the staff nor patient may recognize these rules as such, certain tactics are fashioned around them, and the action is partly constrained by them. One rule is that dangerous topics should generally be avoided. The most obviously dangerous topic is the patient's death; another is events that will happen afterwards. Of course, both parties to the pretense are supposed to follow the avoidance rule.

There is, however, a qualifying rule: Talk about dangerous topics is permissible as long as neither party breaks down. Thus, a patient refers to the distant future, as if it were his to talk about. He talks about his plans for his family, as if he would be there to share their consummation. He and the nurses discuss today's events—such as his treatments—as if they had implications for a real future, when he will have recovered from his illness. And some of his brave or foolhardy activities may signify a brave show of pretense, as when he bathes himself or insists on tottering to the toilet by himself. The staff in turn permits his activity. (Two days before he returned to the hospital to die, one patient insisted that his wife allow him to travel downtown to keep a speaking engagement, and to the last he kept up a lively conversation with a close friend about a book they were planning to write together.)

A third rule, complementing the first two, is that each actor should focus determinedly on appropriately safe topics. It is customary to talk about the daily routines—eating (the food was especially good or bad), and sleeping (whether one slept well or poorly last night). Complaints and their management help pass the time. So do minor personal confidences, and chatter about events on the ward. Talk about physical symptoms is safe enough if confined to the symptoms themselves, with no implied references to death. A terminal patient and a staff member may safely talk, and at length, about his disease so long as they skirt its fatal significance. And there are many genuinely safe topics having to do with movies and movie stars, politics, fashions—with everything, in short, that signifies that life is going on "as usual."

A fourth interactional rule is that when something happens, or is said, that tends to expose the fiction that both parties are attempting to sustain, then each must pretend that nothing has gone awry. Just as each has carefully avoided calling attention to the true situation, each now must avert his gaze from the unfortunate intrusion. Thus, a nurse may take special pains to announce herself before entering a patient's room so as not to surprise him at his crying. If she finds him crying she may ignore it or convert it into an innocuous event with a skillful comment or gesture—much like the tactful gentleman who, having stumbled upon a woman in his bathtub, is said to have casually closed the bathroom door, murmuring "Pardon me, sir." The mutuality of the pretense is illustrated by the way a patient who cannot control a sudden expression of great pain will verbally discount its significance, while the nurse in turn goes along with his pretense. Or she may brush aside or totally ignore a major error in his portrayal, as when he refers spontaneously to his death. If he is tempted to admit impulsively his terminality, she may, again, ignore his impulsive remarks or obviously misinterpret them. Thus, pretense is piled upon pretense to conceal or minimize interactional slips.

Clearly then, each party to the ritual pretense shares responsibility for maintaining it. The major responsibility may be transferred back and forth, but each party must support the others's temporary dominance in his own action. This is true even when conversation is absolutely minimal, as in some hospitals where patients take no particular pains to signal awareness of their terminality, and the staff makes no special gestures to convey its own awareness. The pretense interaction in this case is greatly simplified, but it is still discernible. Whenever a staff member is so indelicate, or so straightforward, as to act openly as if a terminal patient were dying, or if the patient does so himself, then the pretense vanishes. If neither wishes to destroy the fiction, however, then each must strive to keep the situation "normal."[4]

THE TRANSITION TO OPEN AWARENESS

A mutual pretense context that is not sustained can only change to an open awareness context. (Either party, however, may again initiate the pretense context and sometimes get cooperation from the other.) The change can be sudden, when either patient or staff distinctly conveys that he has permanently abandoned the pretense. Or the change to the open context can be gradual: nurses, and relatives, too, are familiar with patients who admit to terminality more openly on some days than they do on other days, when pretense is dominant, until finally pretense vanishes altogether. Sometimes the physician skillfully paces his interaction with a patient, leading the patient finally to refer openly to his terminality and to leave behind the earlier phase of pretense.

Pretense generally collapses when certain conditions make its maintenance increasingly difficult. These conditions have been foreshadowed in our previous discussion. Thus, when the patient cannot keep from expressing his increasing pain, or his suffering grows to the point that he is kept under heavy sedation then the enactment of pretense becomes more difficult, especially for him.

Again, neither patient nor staff may be able to avoid bringing impending death into the open if radical physical deterioration sets in, the staff because it has a tough job to do, and the patient for other reasons, including fright and panic. Sometimes a patient breaks his pretense for psychological reasons, as when he discovers that he cannot face death alone, or when a chaplain convinces him that it is better to bring things out into the open than to remain silent. (Sometimes, however, a patient may find such a sympathetic listener in the chaplain that he can continue his pretense with other personnel.) Sometimes he breaks the pretense when it no longer makes sense in light of obvious physical deterioration.

Here is a poignant episode during which a patient dying with great pain and obvious bodily deterioration finally abandoned her pretense with a nurse:

> There was a long silence. Then the patient asked, "After I get home from the nursing home will you visit me?" I asked if she wanted me to. "Yes, Mary, you know we could go on long drives together . . ." She had a faraway look in her eyes as if daydreaming about all the places she would visit and all the things we could do together. This continued for some time. Then I asked, "Do you think you will be able to drive your car again?" She looked at me, "Mary, I know I am

daydreaming; I know I am going to die." Then she cried, and said, "This is terrible, I never thought I would be this way."

In short, when a patient finds it increasingly difficult to hang onto a semblance of his former healthy self and begins to become a person who is visibly dying, both he and the staff are increasingly prone to say so openly, whether by word or gesture. Sometimes, however, a race occurs between a patient's persistent pretense and his becoming comatose or his actual death —a few more days of sentience or life, and either he or the staff would have dropped the pretense.

Yet, a contest may ensue when only one side wishes to keep up the pretense. When a patient openly displays his awareness but shows it unacceptably, as by apathetically "giving up," the staff or family may try to reinstate the pretense. Usually the patient then insists on open recognition of his own impending death, but sometimes he is persuaded to return to the pretense. For instance, one patient finally wished to talk openly about death, but her husband argued against its probability, although he knew better; so after several attempts to talk openly, the patient obligingly gave up the contest. The reverse situation may also occur: the nurses begin to give the patient every opportunity to die with a maximum of comfort—as by cutting down on normal routines—thus signaling that he should no longer pretend, but the patient insists on putting up a brave show and so the nurses capitulate.

We would complicate our analysis unduly if we did more than suggest that, under such conditions, the pretense ritual sometimes resembles Ptolemy's cumbersomely patched astronomical system, with interactants pretending to pretend to pretend! We shall only add that when nurses attempt to change the pretense context into an open context, they generally do this "on their own" and not because of any calculated ward standards or specific orders from an attending physician. And the tactics they use to get the patient to refer openly to his terminality are less tried and true than the more customary tactics for forcing him to pretend.

CONSEQUENCES OF MUTUAL PRETENSE

For the patient, the pretense context can yield a measure of dignity and considerable privacy, though it may deny him the closer relationships with staff members and family members that sometimes occur when he allows them to participate in his open acceptance of death. And if they initiate and he accepts the pretense, he may have nobody with whom to talk although he might profit greatly from talk. (One terminal patient told a close friend, who told us, that when her family and husband insisted on pretending that she would recover, she suffered from the isolation, feeling as if she were trapped in cotton batting.) For the family—especially more distant kin—the pretense context can minimize embarrassment and other interactional strains; but for closer kin, franker concourse may have many advantages . . . Oscillation between contexts of open awareness and mutual pretense can also cause interactional strains. We once observed a man persuading his mother to abandon her apathy—she had permanently closed her eyes, to the staff's great distress—and "try hard to live." She agreed finally to resume the pretense, but later relapsed into apathy. The series of episodes caused some anguish to both family and patient, as well as to the nurses. When the patient initiates the mutual pretense, staff members are likely to feel relieved. Yet the consequent stress of either maintaining the pretense or changing it to open awareness sometimes may be considerable. Again, both the relief and the stress affect nurses more than medical personnel, principally because the latter spend less time with patients.

But whether staff or patient initiates the ritual of pretense, maintaining it creates a characteristic ward mood of cautious serenity. A nurse once told us of a cancer hospital where each patient understood that everyone there had cancer, including himself, but the rules of tact, buttressed by staff silence, were so strong that few patients talked openly about anyone's condition. The consequent atmosphere was probably less serene than when only a few patients are engaged in mutual pretense, but even one such patient can affect the organizational mood, especially if the personnel become "involved" with him.

A persistent context of mutual pretense profoundly affects the more permanent aspects of hospital organization as well. (This often occurs at county and city hospitals.) Imagine what a hospital service would be like if all terminal patients were unacquainted with their terminality, or if all were perfectly open about their awareness—whether they accepted or rebelled against their fate.[5] When closed awareness generally prevails the personnel must guard against disclosure, but they need not organize themselves as a team to handle continued pretense and its sometimes stressful breakdown. Also, a chief organizational consequence of the mutual pretense context is that it eliminates any possibility that staff members might "work with" patients psychologically, on a self-conscious professional basis. This consequence was strikingly evident at the small Catholic hospital referred to a few pages ago. It is also entirely possible that a ward mood of tension can be set when (as a former patient once told us) a number of elderly dying patients continually communicate to each other their willingness to die, but the staff members persistently insist on the pretense that the patients are going to recover. On the other hand, the prevailing ward mood accompanying mutual pretense tends to be more serene—or at least less obviously tense—than when open suspicion awareness is dominant.[6]

Notes

1 Robert Kastenbaum has reported that at Cushing Hospital, "a Public Medical Institution for the care and custody of the elderly" in Framingham, Massachusetts, "patient and staff members frequently have an implicit mutual understanding with regard to death . . . institutional dynamics tend to operate against making death 'visible' and a subject of open

communication . . . Elderly patients often behave as though they appreciated the unspoken feelings of the staff members and were attempting to make their demise as acceptable and unthreatening as possible." This observation is noted in Robert Kastenbaum, "The Interpersonal Context of Death in a Geriatric Institution," abstract of paper presented at the Seventeenth Annual Scientific Meeting, Gerontological Society (Minneapolis: October 29–31, 1964).

2 I. Bensman and I. Garver, "Crime and Punishment in the Factory," in A. Gouldner and H. Gouldner (eds.), Modern Society *(New York: Harcourt, Brace and World, 1963), pp.593–96.*

3 A German communist, Alexander Weissberg, accused of spying during the great period of Soviet spy trails, has written a fascinating account of how he and many other accused persons collaborated with the Societ government in an elaborate pretense, carried on for the benefit of the outside world. The stakes were high for the accused (their lives) as well as for the Soviet. Weissberg's narrative also illustrated how uninitiated interactants must be coached into their roles and how they must be cued into the existence of the pretense context where they do not recognize it. See Alexander Weissberg, *The Accused* (New York: Simon and Schuster, 1951).

4 A close reading of John Gunther's poitnant account of his young son's last months shows that the boy maintained a sustained and delicately balanced mutual pretense with his parents, physicians and nurses. John Gunther, *Death Be Not Proud* (New York: Harper and Bros., 1949). Also see Bensman and Garver, *op. cit.*

5 For a description of a research hospital where open awareness prevails, with far-reaching effects on hospital social structure, see Renée Fox, *Experiment Perilous* (New York: Free Press of Glencoe, 1959).

6 EDITOR'S NOTE: Contrast this paper with selections 18, 21 and especially 36, below.

18• Lies to the Sick and Dying

Sissela Bok

Sissela Bok holds a Ph.D. degree in philosophy. She is at Harvard University. This selection is taken from her recent book, Lying: Moral Choice in Public and Private Life. *The book is a brilliant text on the philosophical and ethical aspects of non-truth-telling. The selection reprinted here deals with the subject in relation to dealing with the dying patient.*

The face of a physician, like that of a diplomatist, should be impenetrable. Nature is a benevolent old hyprocrite; she cheats the sick and the dying with illusions better than any anodynes. . .

Some shrewd old doctors have a few phrases always on hand for patients that will insist on knowing the pathology of their complaints without the slightest capacity of understanding the scientific explanation. I have known the term "Spinal irritation" serve well on such occasions, but I think nothing on the whole has covered so much ground, and meant so little, and given such profound satisfaction to all parties, as the magnificent phrase "congestion of the portal system."

Oliver Wendell Holmes, *Medical Essays*

This deception tortured him—their not wishing to admit what they all knew and what he knew, but wanting to lie to him concerning his terrible condition, and wishing and forcing him to participate in that lie. Those lies—lies enacted over him on the eve of his death and destined to degrade this awful, solemn act to the level of their visitings, their curtains, their sturgeon for dinner—were a terrible agony for Ivan Ilych.

Leo Tolstoy, *The Death of Ivan Ilych*

When a man's life has become bound up with the analytic technique, he finds himself at a loss altogether for the lies and the guile which are otherwise so indispensable to a physician, and if for once with the best intentions he attempts to use them he is likely to betray himself. Since we demand strict truthfulness from our patients, we jeopardize our whole authority if we let ourselves be caught by them in a departure from the truth.

Sigmund Freud, *Collected Papers, II*

DECEPTION AS THERAPY

A forty-six year-old man, coming to a clinic for a routine physical checkup needed for insurance purposes, is diagnosed as having a form of cancer likely to cause him to die within six months. No known cure exists for it. Chemotherapy may prolong life by a few extra months, but will have side effects the physician does not think warranted in this case. In addition, he believes that such therapy should be reserved for patients with a chance for recovery or remission. The patient has no symptoms giving him any reason to believe that he is not perfectly healthy. He expects to take a short vacation in a week.

For the physician, there are now several choices involving truthfulness. Ought he to tell the patient what he has learned, or conceal it? If asked, should he deny it? If he decides to reveal the diagnosis, should he delay doing so until after the patient returns from his vacation? Finally, even if he does reveal the serious nature of the diagnosis, should he mention the possibility of chemotherapy and his reasons for not recommending it in this case? Of should he encourage every last effort to postpone death?

In this particular case, the physician chose to inform the patient of his diagnosis right away. He did not, however, mention the possibility of chemotherapy. A medical student working under him disagreed; several nurses also thought that the patient should have been informed of this possibility. They tried, unsuccessfully, to persuade the physician that this was the patient's right. When persuasion had failed, the student elected to disobey the doctor by informing the patient of the alternative of chemotherapy. After consultation with family members, the patient chose to ask for the treatment.

Doctors confront such choices often and urgently. What they reveal, hold back, or distort will matter profoundly to their patients. Doctors stress with corresponding vehemence their reasons for the distortion or concealment: not to confuse a sick person needlessly, or cause what may well be unnecessary pain or discomfort, as in the case of the cancer patient; not to leave a patient without hope, as in those many cases where the dying are not told the truth about their condition; or to improve the chances of cure, as where unwarranted optimism is expressed about some form of therapy. Doctors use information as part of the therapeutic regimen; it is given out in amounts, in admixtures, and according to timing believed best for patients. Accuracy, by comparison, matters far less.

Lying to patients has, therefore, seemed an especially excusable act. Some would argue that doctors, and *only* doctors, should be granted the right to manipulate the truth in ways so undesirable for politicians, lawyers, and others.[1] Doctors are trained to help patients; their relationship to patients carries special obligations, and they know much more than laymen about what helps and hinders recovery and survival.

Even the most conscientious doctors, then, who hold themselves at a distance from the quacks and the purveyors of false remedies, hesitate to forswear all lying. Lying is usually wrong, they argue, but less so than allowing the truth to harm patients. B. C. Meyer echoes this very common view:

> [O]urs is a profession which traditionally has been guided by a precept that transcends the virtue of uttering truth for truth's sake, and that is, "so far as possible, do no harm."[2]

Truth, for Meyer, may be important, but not when it endangers the health and well-being of patients. This has seemed self-evident to many physicians in the past—so much so that we find very few mentions of veracity in the codes and oaths and writings by physicians through the centuries. This absence is all the more striking as other principles of ethics have been consistently and movingly expressed in the same documents.

The two fundamental principles of doing good and not doing harm—of beneficence and nonmaleficence—are the most immediately relevant to medical practitioners, and the most frequently stressed. To preserve life and good health, to ward off illness, pain, and death—these are the perennial tasks of medicine and nursing. These principles have found powerful expression at all times in the history of medicine. In the Hippocratic Oath physicians promise to:

> use treatment to help the sick . . . but never with a view to injury and wrongdoing.[3]

And a Hindu oath of initiation says:

> Day and night, however thou mayest be engaged, thou shalt endeavor for the relief of patients with all they heart and soul. Thou shalt not desert or injure the patient even for the sake of thy living.[4]

But there is no similar stress on veracity. It is absent from virtually all oaths, codes, and prayers. The Hippocratic Oath makes no mention of truthfulness to patients about their condition, prognosis, or treatment. Other early codes and prayers are equally silent on the subject. To be sure, they often refer to the confidentiality with which doctors should treat all that their patients tell them; but there is no corresponding reference to honesty toward the patient. One of the few who appealed to such a principle was Amatus Lusitanus, a Jewish physician widely known for his skill, who, persecuted, died of the plague in 1568. He published an oath which reads in part:

> If I lie, may I incur the eternal wrath of God and of His angel Raphael, and may nothing in the medical art succeed for me according to my desires.[5]

Later codes continue to avoid the subject. Not even the Declaration of Geneva, adopted in 1948 by the World Medical Association, makes any reference to it. And the Principles of Medical Ethics of the American Medical Association[6] still leave the matter of informing patients up to the physician.

Given such freedom, a physician can decide to tell as much or as little as he wants the patient to know, so long as he breaks no law. In the case of the man mentioned at the beginning of this chapter, some physicians might feel justified in lying for the good of the patient, others might be truthful. Some may conceal alternatives to the treatment they recommend; others not. In each case, they could appeal to the AMA Principles of Ethics. A great many would choose to be able to lie. They would claim that not only can a lie avoid harm for the patient, but that it is also hard to know whether they have been right in the first place in making their pessimistic diagnosis; a "truthful" statement could therefore turn out to hurt patients unnecessarily. The concern for curing and for supporting those who cannot be cured then runs counter to the desire to be completely open. This concern is especially strong where the prognosis is bleak; even more so when patients are so affected by their illness or their medication that they are more dependent than usual, perhaps more easily depressed or irrational.

Physicians know only too well how uncertain a diagnosis or prognosis can be. They know how hard it is to give meaningful and correct answers regarding health and illness. They also know that disclosing their own uncertainty or fears can reduce those benefits that depend upon faith in recovery. They fear, too, that revealing grave risks, no matter how unlikely it is that these will come about, may exercise the pull of the "self-fulfilling prophecy." They dislike being the bearers of uncertain or bad news as much as anyone else. And last, but not least, sitting down to discuss an illness truthfully and sensitively may take much-needed time away from other patients.

These reasons help explain why nurses and physicians and relatives of the sick and the dying prefer not to be bound by rules that might limit their ability to suppress, delay, or distort information. This is not to say that they necessarily plan to lie much of the time. They merely want to have the freedom to do so when they believe it wise. And the reluctance to see lying prohibited explains, in turn, the failure of the codes and oaths to come to grips with the problems of truth-telling and lying.

But sharp conflicts are now arising. Doctors no longer work alone with patients. They have to consult with others much more than before; if they choose to lie, the choice may not be met with approval by all who take part in the care of the patient. A nurse expresses the difficulty which results as follows:

> From personal experience I would say that the patients who aren't told about their terminal illness have so many verbal and mental questions unanswered that many will begin to realize that their illness is more serious than they're being told . . .
>
> Nurses care for their patients twenty-four hours a day compared to a doctor's daily visit, and it is the nurse many times that the patient will relate to, once his underlying fears become overwhelming . . . This is difficult for us nurses because being in constant contact with patients we can see the events leading up to this. The patient continually asks you, "Why isn't my pain decreasing?" or "Why isn't the radiation treatment easing the pain?" . . . We cannot legally give these patients an honest answer as a nurse (and I'm sure I wouldn't want to) yet the problem is still not resolved and the circle grows larger with the patient alone in the middle.[7]

The doctor's choice to lie increasingly involves coworkers in acting a part they find neither humane nor wise. The fact that these problems have not been carefully thought through within the medical profession, nor seriously addressed in medical education, merely serves to intensify the conflicts.[8] Different doctors then respond very differenty to patients in exactly similar predicaments. The friction is increased by the fact that relatives often disagree even where those giving medical care to a patient are in accord on how to approach the patient. Here again, because physicians have not worked out to common satisfaction the question of whether relatives have the right to make such requests, the problems are allowed to be haphazardly resolved by each physician as he sees fit.

THE PATIENT'S PERSPECTIVE

The turmoil in the medical profession regarding truth-telling is further augmented by the pressures that patients themselves now bring to bear and by empirical data coming to light. Challenges are growing to the three major arguments for lying to patients: that truthfulness is impossible; that patients do not want bad news; and that truthful information harms them.

The first of these arguments . . . confuses "truth" and "truthfulness" so as to clear the way for occasional lying on grounds supported by the second and third arguments. At this point, we can see more clearly that it is a strategic move intended to discourage the question of truthfulness from carrying much weight in the first place, and thus to leave the choice of what to say and how to say it up to the physician. To claim that "Since telling the truth is impossible, there can be no sharp distinction between what is true and what is false"[9] is to try to defeat objections to lying before even discussing them. One need only imagine how such an argument would be received, were it made by a car salesman or a real estate dealer, to see how fallacious it is.

In medicine, however, the argument is supported by a subsidiary point: even if people might ordinarily understand what is spoken to them, patients are often not in a position to do so. This is where paternalism enters in. When we buy cars or houses, the paternalist will argue, we need to have all our wits about us; but when we are ill, we cannot always do so. We need help in making choices, even if help can be given only by keeping us in the dark. And the physician is trained and willing to provide such help.

It is certainly true that some patients cannot make the best choices for themselves when weakened by illness or drugs. But most still can. And even those who are incompetent have a right to have someone—their guardian or spouse perhaps—receive the correct information.

The paternalistic assumption of superiority to patients also carries great dangers for physicians themselves—it risks turning to contempt. The following view was recently expressed in a letter to a medical journal:

> As a radiologist who has been sued, I have reflected earnestly on advice to obtain informed consent but have decided to "take the risks without informing the patient" and trust to "God, judge, and jury" rather than evade responsibility through a legal gimmick . . .
>
> [In] a general radiologic practice many of our patients are uninformable and we would never get through the day if we had to obtain their consent to every potentially harmful study.
>
> . . . We still have patients with language problems, the uneducated and the unintelligent, the stolid and the stunned who cannot form an informed opinion to give an informed consent; we have the belligerent and the panicky who do not listen or comprehend. And then there are the Medicare patients who comprise 35 percent of general hospital admissions. The bright ones wearily plead to be left alone . . . As for the apathetic rest, many of them were kindly described by Richard Bright as not being able to comprehend because "their brains are so poorly oxygenated."[10]

The argument which rejects informing patients because adequate truthful information is impossible in itself or because patients are lacking in understanding, must itself be rejected when looked at from the point of view of patients. They know that liberties granted to the most conscientious and altruistic doctors will be exercised also in the "Medical Mills"; that the choices thus kept from patients will be exercised by not only competent but incompetent physicians; and that even the best doctors can make choices patients would want to make differently for themselves.

The second argument for deceiving patients refers specifically to giving them news of a frightening or depressing kind. It holds that patients do not, in fact, generally want such information, that they prefer not to have to face up to serious illness and death. On the basis of such a belief, most doctors in a number of surveys stated that they do not, as a rule, inform patients that they have an illness such as cancer.

When studies are made of what patients desire to know, on the other hand, a large majority, say that they *would* like to be told of such a diagnosis.[11] All these studies need updating and should be done with larger numbers of patients and non-patients. But they do show that there is generally a dramatic divergence between physicians and patients on the factual question of whether patients want to know what ails them in cases of serious illness such as cancer. In most of the studies, over 80 percent of the persons asked indicated that they would want to be told.

Sometimes this discrepancy is set aside by doctors who want to retain the view that patients do not want unhappy news. In reality, they claim, the fact that patients say they want it has to be discounted. The more someone asks to know, the more he suffers from fear which will lead to the denial of the information even if it is given. Informing patients is, therefore, useless; they resist and deny having been told what they cannot assimilate. According to this view, empirical studies of what patients say they want are worthless since they do not probe deeply enough to uncover this universal resistance to the contemplation of one's own death.

This view is only partially correct. For some patients, denial is indeed well established in medical experience. A number of patients (estimated at between 15 percent and 25 percent) will give evidence of denial of having been told about their illness, even when they repeatedly ask and are repeatedly informed. And nearly everyone experiences a period of denial at some point in the course of approaching death.[12] Elisabeth Kübler-Ross sees denial as resulting often from premature and abrupt information by a stranger who goes through the process quickly to "get it over with." She holds that denial functions as a buffer after unexpected shocking news, permitting individuals to collect themselves and to mobilize other defenses. She describes prolonged denial in one patient as follows:

> She was convinced that the X rays were "mixed up"; she asked for reassurance that her pathology report could not possibly be back so soon and that another patient's report must have been marked with her name. When none of this could be confirmed, she quickly asked to leave the hospital, looking for another physician in the vain hope "to get a better explanation for my troubles." This patient went "shopping around" for many doctors, some of whom gave her reassuring answers, others of whom confirmed the previous suspicion. Whether confirmed or not, she reacted in the same manner; she asked for examination and reexamination . . .[13]

But to say that denial is universal flies in the face of all evidence. And to take any claim to the contrary as "symptomatic" of deeper denial leaves no room for reasoned discourse. There is no way that such universal denial can be proved true or false. To believe in it is a metaphysical belief about man's condition, not a statement about what patients do and do not want. It is true that we can never completely understand the possibility of our own death, any more than being alive in the first place. But people certainly differ in the degree to which they can approach such knowledge, take it into account in their plans, and make their peace with it.

Montaigne claimed that in order to learn both to live and to die, men have to think about death and be prepared to accept it.[14] To stick one's head in the sand, or to be prevented by lies from trying to discern what is to come, hampers freedom—freedom to consider one's life as a whole, with a beginning, a duration, an end. Some may request to be deceived rather than to see their lives as thus finite; others reject the information which would require them to do so; but most say that they want to know. Their concern for knowing about their condition goes far beyond mere curiosity or the wish to make isolated personal choices in the short time left to them; their stance toward the entire life they have lived, and their ability to give it meaning and completion, are at stake.[15] In lying or withholding the facts which permit such discernment, doctors may reflect their own fears (which, according to one study,[16] are much stronger than those of laymen) of facing questions about the meaning of one's life and the inevitability of death.

Beyond the fundamental deprivation that can result from deception, we are also becoming increasingly aware of all that can befall patients in the course of their illness when information is denied or distorted. Lies place them in a position where they no longer participate in choices concerning their own health, including the choice of whether to be a "patient" in the first place. A terminally ill person who is not informed that his illness is incurable and that he is near death cannot make decisions about the end of his life: about whether or not to enter a hospital, or to have surgery; where and with whom to spend his last days; how to put his affairs in order—these most personal choices cannot be made if he is kept in the dark, or given contradictory hints and clues.

It has always been especially easy to keep knowledge from terminally ill patients. They are most vulnerable, least able to take action to learn what they need to know, or to protect their autonomy. The very fact of being so ill greatly increases the likelihood of control by others. And the fear of being helpless in the face of such control is growing. At the same time, the period of dependency and slow deterioration of health and strength that people undergo has lengthened. There has been a dramatic shift toward institutionalization of the aged and those near death. (Over 80 percent of Americans now die in a hospital or other institution.)

Patients who are severely ill often suffer a further distancing and loss of control over their most basic functions. Electrical wiring, machines, intravenous administration of liquids, all create new dependency and at the same time new distance between the patient and all who come near. Curable patients are often willing to undergo such procedures; but when no cure is possible, these procedures merely intensify the sense of distance and uncertainty and can even become a substitute for comforting human acts. Yet those who suffer in this way often fear to seem troublesome by complaining. Lying to them, perhaps for the most charitable of purposes, can then cause them to slip unwittingly into subjection to new procedures, perhaps new surgery, where death is held at bay through transfusions, respirators, even resuscitation far beyond what most would wish.

Seeing relatives in such predicaments has caused a great upsurge of worrying about death and dying. At the root of this fear is not a growing terror of the *moment* of death, or even the instants before it. Nor is there greater fear of *being* dead. In contrast to the centuries of lives lived in dread of the punishments to be inflicted after death, many would now accept the view expressed by Epicurus, who died in 270 B.C.:[17]

> Death, therefore, the most awful of evils, is nothing to us, seeing that, when we are, death is not come, and, when death is come, we are not.

The growing fear, if it is not of the moment of dying nor of being dead, is of all that which now precedes dying for so many: the possibility of prolonged pain, the increasing weakness, the uncertainty, the loss of powers and chance of senility, the sense of being a burden. This fear is further nourished by the loss of trust in health professionals. In part, the loss of trust results from the abuses which have been exposed—the Medicaid scandals, the old-age home profiteering, the commercial exploitation of those who seek remedies for their ailments;[18] in part also because of the deceptive practices patients suspect, having seen how friends and relatives were kept in the dark; in part, finally, because of the sheer numbers of persons, often strangers, participating in the care of any one patient. Trust which might have gone to a doctor long known to the patient goes less easily to a team of strangers, no matter how expert or well-meaning.

It is with the working out of all that *informed consent*[19] implies and the information it presupposes that truth-telling is coming to be discussed in a serious way for the first time in the health professions. Informed consent is a farce if the information provided is distorted or withheld. And even complete information regarding surgical procedures or medication is obviously useless unless the patient also knows what the condition is that these are supposed to correct.

Bills of rights for patients, similarly stressing the right to be informed, are now gaining acceptance.[20] This right is not new, but the effort to implement it is. Nevertheless, even where patients are handed the most elegantly phrased bill of rights, their right to a truthful diagnosis and prognosis is by no means always respected.

The reason why even doctors who recognize a patient's right to have information might still not provide it brings us to the third argument against telling all patients the truth. It holds that the information given might hurt the patient and that the concern for the right to such information is therefore a threat to proper health care. A patient, these doctors argue, may wish to commit suicide after being given discouraging news, or suffer a cardiac arrest, or simply cease to struggle, and thus not grasp the small remaining chance for recovery. And even where the outlook for a patient is very good, the disclosure of a minute risk can shock some patients or cause them to reject needed protection such as a vaccination or antibiotics.

The factual basis for this argument has been challenged from two points of view. The damages associated with the disclosure of sad news or risks are rarer than physicians believe; and the *benefits* which result from being informed are more substantial, even measurably so. Pain is tolerated more easily, recovery from surgery is quicker, and cooperation with therapy is greatly improved. The attitude that "what you don't know won't hurt you" is proving unrealistic; it is what patients do not know but vaguely suspect that causes them corrosive worry.

It is certain that no answers to this question of harm from information are the same for all patients. If we look, first, at the fear expressed by physicians that informing patients of even remote or unlikely risks connected with a drug prescription or operation might shock some and make others refuse the treatment that would have been best for them, it appears to be unfounded for the great majority of patients. Studies show that very few patients respond to being told of such risks by withdrawing their consent to the procedure and that those who do withdraw are the very ones who might well have been upset enough to sue the physician had they not been asked to consent beforehand.[21] It is possible that on even rarer occasions especially susceptible persons might manifest physical deterioration from shock; some physicians have even asked whether patients who die after giving informed consent to an operation, but before it actually takes place, somehow expire because of the information given to them.[22] While such questions are unanswerable in any one case, they certainly argue in favor of caution, a real concern for the person to whom one is recounting the risks he or she will face, and sensitivity to all signs of distress.

The situation is quite different when persons who are already ill, perhaps already quite weak and discouraged, are told of a very serious prognosis. Physicians fear that such knowledge may cause the patients to commit suicide, or to be frightened or depressed to the point that their illness takes a downward turn. The fear that great numbers of patients will commit suicide appears to be unfounded.[23] And if some do, is that a response so unreasonable, so much against the patient's best interest that physicians ought to make it a reason for concealment or lies? Many societies have allowed suicide in the past; our own has decriminalized it; and some are coming to make distinctions among the many suicides which ought to be prevented if at all possible, and those which ought to be respected.[24]

Another possible response to very bleak news is the triggering of physiological mechanisms which allow death to come more quickly—a form of giving up or of preparing for the inevitable, depending on one's outlook. Lewis

Thomas, studying responses in humans and animals, holds it not unlikely that:

> . . . there is a pivotal movement at some stage in the body's reaction to injury or disease, maybe in aging as well, when the organism concedes that it is finished and the time for dying is at hand, and at this moment the events that lead to death are launched, as a coordinated mechanism. Functions are then shut off, in sequence, irreversibly, and, while this is going on, a neural mechanism, held ready for this occasion, is switched on . . .[25]

Such a response may be appropriate, in which case it makes the moments of dying as peaceful as those who have died and been resuscitated so often testify. But it may also be brought on inappropriately, when the organism could have lived on, perhaps even induced malevolently, by external acts intended to kill. Thomas speculates that some of the deaths resulting from "hexing" are due to such responses. Lévi-Strauss describes deaths from exorcism and the casting of spells in ways which suggest that the same process may then be brought on by the community.[26]

It is not inconceivable that unhappy news abruptly conveyed, or a great shock given to someone unable to tolerate it, could also bring on such a "dying response," quite unintended by the speaker. There is every reason to be cautious and to try to know ahead of time how susceptible a patient might be to the accidental triggering—however rare—of such a response. One has to assume, however, that most of those who have survived long enough to be in a situation where their informed consent is asked have a very robust resistance to such accidental triggering of processes leading to death.

When, on the other hand, one considers those who are already near death, the "dying response" may be much less inappropriate, much less accidental, much less unreasonable. In most societies, long before the advent of modern medicine, human beings have made themselves ready for death once they felt its approach. Philippe Ariès describes how many in the Middle Ages prepared themselves for death when they "felt the end approach." They awaited death lying down, surrounded by friends and relatives. They recollected all they had lived through and done, pardoning all who stood near their deathbed, calling on God to bless them, and finally praying. "After the final prayer all that remained was to wait for death, and there was no reason for death to tarry."[27]

Modern medicine, in its valiant efforts to defeat disease and to save lives, may be dislocating the conscious as well as the purely organic responses allowing death to come when it is inevitable, thus denying those who are dying the benefits of the traditional approach to death. In lying to them, and in pressing medical efforts to cure them long past the point of possible recovery, physicians may thus rob individuals of an autonomy few would choose to give up.

Sometimes, then, the "dying response" is a natural organic reaction at the time when the body has no further defense. Sometimes it is inappropriately brought on by news too shocking or given in too abrupt a manner. We need to learn a great deal more about this last category, no matter how small. But there is no evidence that patients in general will be debilitated by truthful information about their condition.

Apart from the possible harm from information, we are coming to learn much more about the benefits it can bring patients. People follow instructions more carefully if they know what their disease is and why they are asked to take medication; any benefits from those procedures are therefore much more likely to come about.[28] Similarly, people recover faster from surgery and tolerate pain with less medication if they understand what ails them and what can be done for them.[29]

RESPECT AND TRUTHFULNESS

Taken all together, the three arguments defending lies to patients stand on much shakier ground as a counterweight to the right to be informed than is often thought. The common view that many patients cannot understand, do not want, and may be harmed by, knowledge of their condition, and that lying to them is either morally neutral or even to be recommended, must be set aside. Instead, we have to make a more complex comparison. Over against the right of patients to knowledge concerning themselves, the medical and psychological benefits to them from this knowledge, the unnecessary and sometimes harmful treatment to which they can be subjected if ignorant, and the harm to physicians, their profession, and other patients from deceptive practices. we have to set a severely restricted and narrowed paternalistic view—that *some* patients cannot understand, *some* do not want, and *some* may be harmed by knowledge of their condition, and that they ought not to have to be treated like everyone else if this is not in their best interest.

Such a view is persuasive. A few patients openly request not to be given bad news. Others give clear signals to that effect, or are demonstrably vulnerable to the shock or anguish such news might call forth. Can one not in such cases infer implied consent to being deceived?

Concealment, evasion, withholding of information may at times be necessary. But if someone contemplates lying to a patient or concealing the truth, the burden of proof must shift. It must rest, here, as with all deception, on those who advocate it in any one instance. They must show why they fear a patient may be harmed or how they know that another cannot cope with the truthful knowledge. A decision to deceive must be seen as a very unusual step, to be talked over with colleagues and others who participate in the care of the patient. Reasons must be set forth and debated, alternatives weighed carefully. At all times, the correct information must go to *someone* closely related to the patient.

The law already permits doctors to withhold information from patients where it would clearly hurt their health. But this privilege has been sharply limited by courts. Certainly it cannot be interpreted so broadly as to permit a general practice of deceiving patients "for their own good." Nor can it be made to include cases where patients might calmly decide, upon hearing their diagnosis, not to go ahead with the therapy their doctor recommends.[30] Least of all can it justify silence or lies to large numbers of patients merely on the grounds that it is not always easy to tell what a patient wants.

For the great majority of patients, on the contrary, the goal must be disclosure, and the atmosphere one of openness. But it would be wrong to assume that patients can therefore be told abruptly about a serious diagnosis —that, so long as openness exists, there are no further requirements of humane concern in such communication. Dr. Cicely Saunders, who runs the well-known St. Christopher's Hospice in England, describes the sensitivity and understanding which are needed:

> Every patient needs an explanation of his illness that will be understandable and convincing to him if he is to cooperate in his treatment or be relieved of the burden of unknown fears. This is true whether it is a question of giving a diagnosis in a hopeful situation or of confirming a poor prognosis.
>
> The fact that a patient does not ask does not mean that he has no questions. One visit or talk is rarely enough. It is only by waiting and listening that we can gain an idea of what we should be saying. Silences and gaps are often more revealing than words as we try to learn what a patient is facing as he travels along the constantly changing journey of his illness and his thoughts about it.
>
> . . . So much of the communication will be without words or given indirectly. This is true of all real meeting with people but especially true with those who are facing, knowingly or not, difficult or threatening situations. It is also particularly true of the very ill.
>
> The main argument against a policy of deliberate, invariable denial of unpleasant facts is that it makes such communication extremely difficult, if not impossible. Once the possibility of talking frankly with a patient has been admitted, it does not mean that this will always take place, but the whole atmosphere is changed. We are then free to wait quietly for clues from each patient, seeing them as individuals from whom we can expect intelligence, courage, and individual decisions. They will feel secure enough to give us these clues when they wish.[31]

Above all, truthfulness with those who are suffering does not mean that they should be deprived of all hope: hope that there is a chance of recovery, however small; nor of reassurance that they will not be abandoned when they most need help.

Much needs to be done, however, if the deceptive practices are to be eliminated, and if concealment is to be restricted to the few patients who ask for it or those who can be shown to be harmed by openness. The medical profession has to address this problem. Those who are in training to take care of the sick and the dying have to learn how to speak with them, even about dying. They will be helped to do so if they can be asked to consider alternative approaches to patients, put themselves in the situation of a patient, even confront the possibility of being themselves near death.

Until the day comes when patients can be assured that they can trust what doctors tell them, is there anything they can do to improve the chances for themselves? How can they try to avoid slipping into a dependent relationship, one in which they have no way of trusting what anyone tells them? Is there any way in which they can maintain a degree of autonomy, even at a time of great weakness?

Those who know who will take care of them when they become seriously ill or approach death can talk this matter over well ahead of time. If they do, it is very likely that their desires will be respected. Growing numbers are now signing statements known as *living wills*, in which they can, if they so wish, specify whether or not they want to be informed about their condition. They can also specify conditions under which they do not want to have their lives prolonged.[32] Still others, who may not have thought of these problems ahead of time, can insist on receiving adequate information once they are in need of care. It is the great majority—those who are afraid of asking, of seeming distrustful—who give rise to the view that patients do not really want to know since they never ask.

The perspective of needing care is very different from that of providing it. The first sees the most fundamental question for patients to be whether they can trust their caretakers. It requires a stringent adherence to honesty, in all but a few carefully delineated cases. The second sees the need to be free to deceive, sometimes for genuinely humane reasons. It is only by bringing these perspectives into the open and by considering the exceptional cases explicitly that the discrepancy can be reduced and trust restored.

Notes

1 Plato, *The Republic*, 389 b.

2 B.C. Meyer, "Truth and the Physician," *Bulletin of the New York Academy of Medicine* 45 (1969): 59–71 . . .

3 W. H. S. Jones, trans, *Hippocrates*, Loeb Classical Library (Cambridge, Mass.: Harvard University Press, 1923), p. 164

4 Reprinted in M. B. Etziony, *The Physician's Creed: An Anthology of Medical Prayers, Oaths and Codes of Ethics* (Springfield, Ill.: Charles C. Thomas, 1973), pp. 15–18.

5 See Harry Friedenwald, "The Ethics of the Practice of Medicine from the Jewish Point of View," *Johns Hopkins Hospital Bulletin*, 318 (August 1917): 256–61.

6 "Ten Principles of Medical Ethics," *Journal of the American Medical Association* 164 (1957): 1119–20.

7 Mary Barrett, letter, *Boston Globe*, 16 November 1976, p. 1.

8 Though a minority of physicians have struggled to bring them to our attention. See Thomas Percival, *Medical Ethics*, 3d ed. (Oxford: John Henry Parker, 1849), pp. 132–41; Worthington Hooker, *Physician and Patient* (New York: Baker and Scribner, 1849), pp. 357–82; Richard C.

Thank you Dr. Anderson
for the information you gave
me. It was very
helpful - esp. the articles
about Debbie. You'll be
happy to know (at least
I was) that I got an A
Thanks- again

Jennifer

Cabot, "Teamwork of Doctor and Patient Through the Annihilation of Lying," in *Social Service and the Art of Healing* (New York: Moffat, Yard & Co., 1909), pp. 116–70; Charles C. Lund, "The Doctor, the Patient, and the Truth," *Annals of Internal Medicine* 24 (1946): 955; Edmund Davies, "The Patient's Right to Know the Truth," *Proceedings of the Royal Society of Medicine* 66 (1973): 533–36.

9 Lawrence Henderson, "Physician and Patient as a Social System," *New England Journal of Medicine* 212 (1955).

10 Nicholas Demy, Letter to the Editor, *Journal of the American Medical Association* 217 (1971): 696–97.

11 For the views of physicans, see Donald Oken, "What to Tell Cancer Patients," *Journal of the American Medical Association* 175 (1961): 1120–28: and tabulations in Robert Veatch, *Death, Dying, and the Biological Revolution* (New Haven and London: Yale University Press, 1976), pp. 229–38. For the view of patients, see Veatch, *ibid.;* Jean Aitken-Swan and E. C. Easson, "Reactions of Cancer Patients on Being Told Their Diagnosis," *British Medical Journal* (1959): 779–83; Jim McIntosh, "Patients' Awareness and Desire for Information About Diagnosed but Undisclosed Malignant Disease," *The Lancet* 7 (1976): 300–303; William D. Kelly and Stanley R. Friesen, "Do Cancer Patients Want to Be Told?" *Surgery* 27 (1950): 822–26.

12 See Avery Weisman, *On Dying and Denying* (New York: Behavioral Publications, 1972); Elisabeth Kübler-Ross, *On Death and Dying* (New York: Macmillan Co., 1969); Ernest Becker, *The Denial of Death* (New York: Free Press, 1973); Philippe Ariès, *Western Attitudes Toward Death,* trans. Patricia M. Ranum (Baltimore and London: Johns Hopkins University Press, 1974); and Sigmund Freud, "Negation," *Collected Papers,* ed. James Strachey (London: Hogarth Press, 1950), 5:181–85.

13 Kübler-Ross, *On Death and Dying,* p. 34.

14 Michel de Montaigne, *Essays,* bk. 1, chap. 20.

15 It is in literature that these questions are most directly raised. Two recent works where they are taken up with striking beauty and simplicity are May Sarton, *As We Are Now* (New York: W. W. Norton & Co., 1973); and Freya Stark, *A Peak in Darien* (London: John Murray, 1976).

16 Herman Feifel et al., "Physicians Consider Death," *Proceedings of the American Psychoanalytical Association,* 1967, pp. 201–2.

17 See Diogenes Laertius, *Lives of Eminent Philosophers,* p. 651. Epicurus willed his garden to his friends and descendants, and wrote on the eve of dying: "On this blissful day, which is also the last day of my life, I write to you. My continual sufferings from strangury and dysentery are so great that nothing could augment them; but over against them all I set gladness of mind at the remembrance of our past conversations." (Letter to Idomeneus, *Ibid,* p. 549).

18 See Ivan Illich, *Medical Nemesis* (New York: Pantheon, 1976), for a critique of the iatrogenic tendencies of contemporary medical care in industrialized societies.

19 The law requires that inroads made upon a person's body take place only with the informed voluntary consent of that person. The term "informed consent" came into common use only after 1960, when it was used by the Kansas Supreme Court in *Nathanson v. Kline* 186 Kan 393, 350 P2d 1093 (1960). The patient is now entitled to full disclosure of risks, benefits, and alternative treatments to any proposed procedure, both in therapy and in medical experimentation, except in emergencies or when the patient is incompetent, in which case proxy consent is required.

20 See, for example, "Statement on a Patient's Bill of Rights," reprinted in Stanley Joel Reiser, Arthur J. Dyck, and William J. Curran, *Ethics in Medicine* (Cambridge, Mass., and London: MIT Press, 1977), p. 148.

21 See Ralph Aphidi, "Informed Consent: A Study of Patient Reaction," *Journal of the American Medical Association* 216 (1971): 1325–29.

22 See Steven R. Kaplan, Richard A. Greenwald, and Arvey I. Rogers, Letter to the Editor, *New England Journal of Medicine* 296 (1977): 1127.

23 Oken, "What to Tell Cancer Patients"; Veatch, *Death, Dying and the Biological Revolution;* Weisman, *On Dying and Denying.*

24 Norman L. Cantor, "A Patient's Decision to Decline Life-Saving Treatment: Bodily Integrity Versus the Preservation of Life," *Rutgers Law Review* 26: 228–64; Danielle Gourevitch, "Suicide Among the Sick in Classical Antiquity," *Bulletin of the History of Medicine* 18 (1969): 501–18; for bibliography, see Bok, "Voluntary Euthanasia."

25 Lewis Thomas, "A Meliorist View of Disease and Dying," *The Journal of Medicine and Philosophy* 1 (1976): 212–21.

26 Claude Lévi-Strauss, *Structural Anthropology* (New York: Basic Books, 1963), p. 167; See also Eric Cassell, "Permission to Die," in John Behnke and Sissela Bok, eds., *The Dilemmas of Euthanasia* (New York: Doubleday, Anchor Press, 1975), pp. 121–31.

27 Ariès, *Western Attitudes Toward Death,* p. 11.

28 Barbara S. Hulka, J. C. Cassel, et al., "Communication, Compliance, and Concordance between Physicians and Patients with Prescribed Medications," *American Journal of Public Health,* Sept. 1976, pp. 847–53. The study shows that of the nearly half of all patients who do not follow the prescriptions of the doctors (thus forgoing the intended effect of these prescriptions), many will follow them if adequately informed about the nature of their illness and what the proposed medication will do.

29 See Lawrence D. Egbert, George E. Batitt, et al., "Reduction of Postoperative Pain by Encouragement and Instruction of Patients," *New England Journal of Medicine,* 270, (1964): 825–27. See also Howard Waitzskin and John D. Stoeckle, "The Communication of Information about Illness," *Advances in Psychosomatic Medicine,* 8 (1972): 185–215.

30 See Charles Fried, *Medical Experimentation: Personal Integrity and Social Policy* (Amsterdam and Oxford: North Holland Publishing Co. 1974), pp. 20–24.

31 Cicely M. S. Saunders, "Telling Patients," in Reiser, Dyck, and Curran, *Ethics in Medicine,* pp. 238–40.

32 "Personal Directions for Care at the End of Life," Sissela Bok, *New England Journal of Medicine* 295 (1976): 367–69.

19 · Speaking of Death with the Dying

John Hinton

John Hinton is an English physician and professor of psychiatry at Middlesex Medical School. In this selection, taken from his indispensable book, Dying, *Dr. Hinton discusses the issues involved in speaking with a terminal patient and notes that* how *one speaks with the dying is far more important than* what *one says.*

The frequently debated question "Should the doctor tell?" tends to carry a false implication that the doctor knows all about the patient's approaching death and the patient knows nothing. The resultant discussion and controversy [are] therefore often irrelevant or, at least, tangential to the real problem. Doctors are far from omniscient. Even if they have no doubt that their patients' condition will be fatal, they can rarely foretell the time of death with any accuracy unless it is close at hand. Furthermore . . . patients are not necessarily unaware of what is happening; many have a very clear idea that they are dying.

Rather than putting a choice between telling or not telling, it would be more useful to ask other questions. Should we encourage or divert a patient who begins to speak of matters that will lead to talk of dying? How freely should we speak to him about it? Should we lie to him if we suspect he only wants to be told that all will be well? If he sincerely wishes to know if his illness will be fatal, should his suppositions be confirmed? If he never asks outright, have we a duty to tell him? Is it right to deny knowledge of dying to those who ask, or wrong to tell those who show no wish to know? Should we allow the awareness of dying to grow gradually, or should patients who are mortally ill know this early on, so that they may attain greater acceptance of dying? If they are to be told more openly, how should such knowledge be given? How do people react to being told? These questions—all part of that oversimplified "Should the doctor tell?"—can have no universally accepted answer. Individuals differ, and ethical beliefs or current opinions will influence judgment.

TO SPEAK FREELY?

There are some good reasons for speaking freely about the possibility of dying to those with fatal conditions. An ill person who strongly suspects that he is dying, but is denied the least opportunity to question or discuss this, can feel cruelly isolated if he does not want this conspiracy of silence. He may be surrounded by people whose every manifest word or action is designed to deny or avoid the fact that he is dying, and he is aware of the artificiality of their deception. How can he gain the ease of wholly sincere talk with others if all maintain the pretence that his imminent departure from life, his leaving them forever, is just not taking place? It would be thought preposterous and cruel if throughout a mother's first pregnancy and delivery all around conspired to treat it as indigestion and never gave her an opportunity to voice her doubts.

The view that we all have a duty to inform the dying man has some support on material and spiritual grounds. If a doctor conceals from a patient that he is mortally ill, the person may fail to order his family affairs or may embark on business ventures which he would not contemplate if he knew his likely fate. The doctor's legal responsibility to warn the dying person appears to be a matter of debate. Most doctors, however, will bear in mind how far a person needs to set his affairs in order, when considering what they should tell a dying patient. Imparting advice to a man that it might be a wise precaution to tidy up business arrangments serves more than that single function. (Kline & Sobin, 1951). Conveyed with tact, it is a hint that an ill man can discuss further with his doctor if he is of a mind to know more, or it is advice he can just accept at its face value.

The spiritual need for a man to know that he is dying may well take precedence over material matters in the terminal phase. Frequently the dying person spontaneously turns or returns to his religious beliefs. He may already have prayed for help in his serious illness, perhaps with rather unfamiliar voice. If it appears that recovery is unlikely, most ministers hold strongly that the patient should know this, so that he can prepare for eternal life.

At times there is an increasing need to be frank with a patient over his prognosis, because he has short periods of feverish hopes followed by long periods of despairing misery. He may waste effort and money on unjustified and quite hopeless treatments, only to have bitter disappointment as proclaimed panaceas fail. If a patient is seriously ill and appears to be getting worse, while his physician appears content with ineffective remedies, he may feel that opportunities of cure are being lost. This may lead to a feeling of frustration or a desperate tour of other doctors. Of course, a second opinion from a respected source may be a great help to all concerned. This may bring assurance that no important possibility is being neglected. When a troubled patient who has been seeking fruitlessly for cure comes to a better understanding with his doctor on the nature of his disease and how much hope is justifiable, he may regain confidence and find greater peace.

In spite of these arguments which favor frankness with the dying, many doctors are reluctant to speak with them of death. They feel that most patients do not wish to raise the subject except to get reassurance, and that the truth is likely to be hurtful. This common medical attitude is uncomfortably combined with a considerable hesitation over practicing deliberate evasion and deceit on patients who have put their trust in the doctor, even if the "white lies" are intended to avoid distress. Some forthright physicians, however, make plain their belief that it does patients no good to be told that they are dying (Asher, 1955). It is a viewpoint easy to attack on theoretical grounds; but when truth can give rise to considerable distress, when kindly half-truths do not materially alter the course of death, and when dying people would like to hear that they will recover, it takes a very convinced man to condemn evasion or even the occasional untruth. Many scrupulous people who care for the dying find themselves concealing the truth in a manner they always wished to avoid.

In practice, relatively few doctors tell patients that there is no hope of recovery. In one study of medical opinion, for example, a group of over two hundred doctors, working in hospital and private practice, were asked if they favored informing those patients found to have a cancer very likely to prove fatal (Oken, 1961). Patients so defined would include, of course, some whose symptoms were investigated early while they were in reasonable general health, with death some way off. Such patients might have little reason at this stage to suspect their illness to be mortal, and if a doctor did tell them, it would give some unanticipated bad news. Eighty-eight percent of these doctors would not tell the patient, although some of them would make exceptions. The doctors felt that usually the patient's questions were pleas for reassurance. The other 12 percent usually told the patients that they had cancer, especially if the latter were intelligent and emotionally stable. Most of the doctors felt that they should inform a relative and were glad to share the burden of their knowledge. Incidentally, no less than 60 percent of these same doctors said that they would like to be told if they themselves had an equally sinister form of cancer. This inconsistency of opinion between imparting and receiving such information was explained by the doctors on the basis of their own greater fortitude or responsibilities. It might be so, but it is more likely to be the emotionally determined attitude found among lay and medical people alike. This was indicated by the fact that these physicians were not any more frank with doctors whom they treated for cancer than any other patients with cancer. Equally, lay people are more in favor of themselves being told they have developed a cancer than of recommending that others in a similar condition should be told (Kelly & Friesen, 1950).

Although the majority of practicing doctors may believe that it is better for them to be reticent with the dying, this opinion must be reconsidered in the light of the fact that an equally large proportion of lay people say that they would like to be told. On the surface, it seems quite perverse that 80 or 90 percent of physicians say that they rarely, if ever, tell patients that their illness is mortal (Oken, 1961), whereas about 80 percent of patients say they would like to be told (Gilbertsen & Wangensteen, 1961). If a doctor sees the question in rather unreal black-and-white terms of either pressing unpleasant news of impending death upon a patient or keeping him in happy ignorance of his fate, this will sway him towards expressing an opinion against telling. This travesties the usual situation, however, where the dying person, with gathering doubts and clues, becomes increasingly suspicious that his condition is mortal.

It is often suggested that the very high percentage of people who give the theoretical answer that they would like to know if they had cancer, do so because they feel secure in their present state of good health. They might be less confident if there was an immediate possibility of having a fatal illness. Albeit, almost as high a proportion of patients actually being treated for cancer in Manchester were just as much in favor of being told of their diagnosis (Aitken-Swan & Easson, 1959). They had been told they had a treatable cancer and later on were asked if they approved or disapproved of being informed. Two thirds were glad to have been told, only 7 percent disapproved, and 19 percent denied having been told—the familiar phenomenon of failing to hear or remember what one does not wish to learn. This particular group of patients, however, had curable cancers. Is it the same for those with incurable cancers?

The answer appears to be that they equally wish to know. In the university hospitals at Minnesota it is the practice of doctors to tell their patients the diagnosis (Gilbertsen & Wangensteen, 1961). A group of patients with advanced cancer were asked if they knew their diagnosis and 86 percent did know. Most had been told by their doctor, although some found out in other ways. Many of the remaining 14 percent, who did not know, had asked at one time and been given evasive answers. As many as four-fifths of these very ill patients thought that cancer patients should be told. They said it had helped them understand their own illness and given them peace of mind. It also allowed them to plan for further medical care, religious matters and for other aspects of their families' and their own lives.

HOW TO SPEAK OF DYING?

There are, therefore, several good reasons justifying considerable candor with people who are fatally ill. If this were to be more widely accepted in principle, how and when should such sincere conversation take place? Clearly an abrupt statement to every patient with incurable disease that he is going to die is likely to do more harm than good.

Some wish to know only a little of their illness. As with nonfatal disease, a person may be helped by simple explanations of the illness, together with a general plan of investigating or treating the condition. An intelligent young woman, who was admitted to hospital with an obviously growing lump on one rib, was very troubled while investigations were done and treatment started without anyone telling her what it was. There was not much reassuring information to give her, as it was the sign of a widespread cancer. She wanted to know something, however. She was told that it was a tumor and that the X rays had shown up one or two smaller ones. They would be treated by radiotherapy and, it was correctly said, her condition would improve considerably. This was as much as she wanted to know at that time. She had been very anxious, but after this talk she was less so. She was quite sad for a day or two, and then her spirits recovered. This sort of response of sorrow on learning of having serious disease, followed by greater equanimity as acceptance grows, is the usual understandable reaction.

Some dying patients want to know even less than this sort of edited version of the truth. They may not want to hear a word about the nature of their condition. They may well have a hidden suspicion and gladly enter a tacit conspiracy to avoid the whole subject. They wish others to take over all responsibilities, anxieties, and decisions. This total surrender of all decision to the doctor may be somewhat less common now, especially as doctors tend to lose a little of their former authoritative manner, and more patients refuse to put up with it. But when seriously ill, it can be easier for a patient to relinquish all control, all knowledge, to his doctor. If the dying person indicates openly that he does not want to know, if he shows by his manner or by his talk that he does not wish to regard his illness as fatal, it would be uncharitable to force the truth upon him. The aim is to make dying a little easier, not to apply a dogma of always divulging truth (Alvarez, 1952).

It is not an easy problem when a patient asks about his incurable illness in a way that indicates his need for reassurance or, at least, hope. He is probably more likely to ask such questions as "It's not cancer, is it, doctor?" if his doctor has shown no sign of giving any spontaneous comment about his condition. If a patient does blurt out this loaded question, or suddenly asks, "Will I get better?" of someone ill prepared to answer, the situation is potentially distressing to both. The result is often a hasty untruthful reassurance. If this is given in an atmosphere of doubt and anxiety, present in both their minds, little good will be done to the ill person's morale. If the question has been met with a hasty denial or a misleadingly optimistic view, this may be accepted with gratitude. Sometimes it is taken as a more definite answer than was intended. The ill person may even, by a series of further questions based on the first slanted answer, wring out a more emphatic denial of fatal disease than one would wish to give. This is disturbing, but is not necessarily a catastrophe, even if the patient later comes to realize that his first misgivings were well founded. Nevertheless, an emotional balance achieved on a basis of assurances bound to be proved false, is no stable adjustment. When the original loaded question is put, it is often better not to answer the dying person's anxious inquiry straight away. Returning the question, asking him to describe more fully what anxieties he has in mind, and listening sympathetically to his doubts and fears will meet some of his needs. Then the fuller description may show the basis of his anxiety. It may be a totally unwarranted fear which can be allayed, such as an anticipation of prolonged agony. It may be a well-founded apprehension, but one that can be borne with help. In the long run, especially if there is someone at hand to help with any subsequent doubts, allowing a person to discuss his fears may prove more valuable than a hasty, consoling, but untrue, answer.

In practice, probably the best and easiest way to broach the matter of dying with a mortally ill person is just to allow him to speak of his suspicions or knowledge of the outcome. If necessary, he can be asked how he feels and shown that more than the polite stereotyped answer is wanted. If the patient mentions that he feels upset he can be encouraged to talk about it. Then frequently the doctor will find that there is little for him to "tell," all that is required is for him to listen with sympathy. In these circumstances the dying person does not usually ask for reassurance or praise for his courage. He may glance up for confirmation of mutual understanding. He may want to know a little more to clarify some aspect of the situation. It is quite possible for the doctor to be uncertain of the exact course of an illness and yet, when asked, to give an honest qualified answer without lying or undue prevarication. To many people this brings firmer comfort than the flimsy props of obviously false promises or the chaos of apparently bewildered ignorance. In treating any disease it is common enough to be thinking in terms of probabilities and possibilities rather than certainties. As compensation for our having to endure uncertainty, it is uncommon to be in a position where there is no comforting straw of hope for survival.

If it is unclear if an ill person desires to know the whole truth, it is possible to start by giving gentle hints. A simple explanation of the disease, mentioning the favorable aspects of treatment and touching upon the other serious possibilities, will enable the ill person to take up the aspects he wishes and ignore others (Aldrich, 1963). The beginnings of awareness may be started early. A surgeon before operating upon a suspected cancer will often tell the patient that if the condition is serious he will need to perform an extensive operation. The patient who has such an operation can then pursue the matter with the doctor as much as he wishes. He can apprehend the threat of the illness, or concentrate on the curative value of the treatment.

Many doctors prefer to use an oblique approach for letting the patient know that he may be dying. Without any deception or lies, they aim to allow an awareness of the outcome to grow. If need be, a germ of realization is planted, but hope is never utterly excluded. Discussion can be reasonably frank, but the emphasis is on the favorable aspects (Gavey, 1955). If, indeed, the awareness of dying is going to grow, those who care for the patient must be prepared to keep pace with this increasing realization. They should be ready to listen and let the patient know that some of his surmises are true and some of his fears are unjustified. In this way the dying person should not feel too lonely, too uncertain, nor plunged into acute emotional distress.

Although it is not an infallible guide to how much the dying patient should be told, his apparent wishes and questions do point the way. This means that the manner in which he puts his views should be revealing. It also means that he must be given ample opportunity to express his ideas and ask questions. If the questions are sincere, however, then why not give quiet straight answers to the patient's questions about his illness and the outcome? It makes for beneficial trust (Leak, 1948).

It is to be remembered that while doctors are trying to judge their patients' capacity to stand unpleasant news, many patients are equally making their intuitive judgments of whether their doctor can bear sincere but difficult questions. They often have a very accurate idea of what doctor is quite accustomed or unsuited to being frank about fatal illness to the person most concerned. I have often been told by understanding people, toward the end of their life, that they knew that the doctor looking after them could not easily talk about this. "He feels he's got to get people well, and I couldn't very well talk to him about not getting better," said a woman who knew she would soon die. If a patient is firmly insistent and his doctor is honest, frank conversations do take place. "I asked him what they'd found and then I asked him if it was cancer. And now I know it's cancer, and they haven't been able to take it all away. There's only one in a thousand chance of recovery." The physician who had been questioned by this man said that he felt that he had probably been more perturbed by this conversation than the patient had.

Occasionally those concerned with a patient's care hold conflicting views over his need to be told. Such unpleasant disagreements, when they do occur, are not resolved as often as they should be by discovering what the patient already knows. Nor do those with his interest at heart meet as often as they should to see what common ground they have between their seemingly opposed and entrenched beliefs.

It is perhaps strange that there is so much more agreement over talking frankly to the members of the family about their relative's fatal illness rather than to the patient himself, even if he shows a wish to know. It reverses the usual convention of the doctor keeping confidential the information concerning an adult and telling other people only if the patient agrees. A few doctors, if they tell the patient the serious nature of the illness, do discuss with them who else should be informed. Usually the next of kin is told, but often it is clear that some other responsible member of the family is better able to receive the information and pass on the appropriate knowledge to the rest. As with the patient, the families receiving these tidings often need more than just a bulletin of bad news.

REACTIONS TO SPEAKING OF DEATH

Many patients have said what a relief they have felt when at last they have had a chance to talk openly about the probability that they are dying. As so many gain comfort from this, it is clearly unkind to deny them the opportunity. They do not get the chance because people are fearful of embarking on such conversations. In the book *Awareness of Dying* by Glaser and Strauss (1965), the authors refer to the fact that some people who care for patients are recognized by their colleagues to have an aptitude for speaking easily and honestly to the dying and bring them comfort. I am sure that many more people could do this if the climate of opinion changed toward greater frankness, and more people realized how much they could help in this way. Most nurses, medical students, and young doctors do not receive as much help as they should, during their training, over the problems raised in caring for the dying.

If more people become prepared to speak freely with the dying there will be a need for caution, because although many would benefit, some would react adversely. A proportion of people, nearing the end of life, are very distressed by implicit or explicit references to death's coming. A little exploratory conversation may indicate a patient's likely reaction. He may say quite clearly what he wants. A man who was pretty sure that he had abdominal cancer said, "I want them to tell me if they *are* going to operate. If they aren't, I want them to give me the wire. Then I'll know what to make of it." It was clear that he was not one who only wanted to know as long as the news was good.

There can be some intuitive judgment of how much particular individuals should be told. Their habitual manner of life can be a useful guide, their style of facing former difficulties or attaining their social position (Ogilvie, 1957). This was illustrated by one equable man who had risen to a position supervising a group of shops. He had always coped well with problems in life, once he knew what was needed to be done. The previous year he had had a kidney removed and had been told that all should be well after the operation. His wife, however, had been told that he had a cancer and also warned, according to his doctor's usual policy, not to tell the patient. When the patient entered hospital again with a spread of his cancer, he insisted on being told the true state of affairs. He took it very well, but regretted that he had not been told before, so that he and his wife could have openly acknowledged that he might have little time to live. Naturally, a patient's expressed wishes and clues from his past life as to his manner of facing difficulties give no perfect prediction. The man who has succeeded in life, developing strong friendships and warm family ties may, in spite of his apparent stability, be unable to cope with the threat of so much loss. The less happy person may be better prepared to give up his life (Aldrich, 1963). Nevertheless, the view that a stable person will probably retain this characteristic when facing death usually proves correct.

In general, learning that an illness is likely to be fatal produces a period of disquiet, even dismay, although this may be effectively concealed. However well the knowledge has been conveyed, it is almost bound to cause some emotional reaction. If frank discussions were often to result in patients becoming severely or persistently distressed, even suicidal, few doctors would wish to speak to them of dying. There does tend to be an exaggerated fear that dying patients will kill themselves if they are told that their illness may be fatal. The chances are that the suicidal acts which occur in those with mortal disease are due to the suffering and the spiritual isolation when the sick are lonely, rather than any despair following a sympathetic discussion of their outlook. Although suicide remains a threatening possibility, inhibiting some from frank discussion with the dying, it is hard to find a case where a humane conversation on these lines precipitated any suicidal act. It is much more likely to have prevented it. "I knew what I'd got," said a young woman who had attempted suicide, "I'd seen it in my notes. I'd looked it up in the medical books and I knew I couldn't recover. I wanted to talk about it with the doctor, but he always seemed too busy, or just called it inflammation."

Clumsy telling of a fatal illness can cause great distress, but this extreme is generally avoidable. There is an account of one Veteran's Administration Hospital in North America where it was the practice to tell the patient the nature of his illness, including fatal illness (Glaser & Strauss, 1965). Many of the patients in this hospital were from a low social class or destitute, and, it seems, not necessarily treated with much dignity. Some of the doctors made a practice of short, blunt announcements to the patients and walking away. Some softened it a little and assured the patient that pain would be controlled. Although they could justify telling the truth because the patients become "philosophical" about it after a few days, this technique seems hard. The sociologists describing the situation wrote that the abrupt disclosure tended to result in a more immediate profound depression. As a result the patients were more apt to try and cope with such potential distress by denying the reality of their situation, rather than being helped to accept it.

In order to evaluate more reliably the effect of telling patients that they have a mortal illness, a careful and courageous investigation was carried out by some of the medical staff at Lund University (Gerle et al., 1960). Some patients with an incurable illness were told and others were not. Personal contact was maintained throughout the further course and treatment of their illness, taking care to note if the greater frankness or reticence was more helpful to them. A psychiatrist made a preliminary assessment of the patients to see if there were any indications of emotional instability in the past or present to contraindicate telling. In the overwhelming majority of those he thought it suitable to tell, the patients maintained their emotional balance and did not regret being told. In some patients it was suspected that they would be upset initially, but later regain composure; and this was largely borne out. Among both those who were told and those who were not, there were equally small groups who never achieved serenity in this last illness. None of the patients in this group, told with care, reacted in a dramatic or excessive way on learning that they had incurable cancer. On the contrary, the social worker, who continued visiting the patient and family throughout the illness, was impressed by the improved family relationships among those who had been told. There appeared to be less tension and desperation at the progressive deterioration in health.

This maintenance of contact and care by people who have imparted tidings of fatal illness is most helpful. People cannot take in all such information of emotional importance immediately. They must be given the opportunity to ask again. Indeed the patient with a serious disease may ask the same questions about his condition again and again, while gradually coming to terms with it. Others deny that they have ever been told (Aitken-Swan & Easson, 1959). There would seem little kindness in insisting that they realize it if they do not want to hold it in their consciousness. At a later time they may wish to know more. It is a chilling, cruel experience to be told of having an incurable disease and then to be apparently dismissed with no further mention of further care, just discarded. Those who confirm a patient's suspicion that he now has little time to live should surely see that he can return to them or some other suitable person who knows of the situation, if he wishes to talk more of the matter. Then he will gain comfort from this honesty.

References

Aitken-Swan, J., and Easson, E. C. Reactions of Cancer Patients on Being Told Their Diagnosis. *British Medical Journal,* 1959, 1, 779.

Aldrich, C. K. The Dying Patient's Grief. *Journal of the American Medical Association,* 1963, 184, 329.

Alvarez, W. C. Care of the Dying. *Journal of the American Medical Association*, 1952, 150, 86.

Asher, R. Management of Advanced Cancer. *Proceedings of the Royal Society of Medicine*, 1955, 48, 373.

Gavey, C. J. Discussion on Palliation in Cancer. *Proceedings of the Royal Society of Medicine*, 1955, 48, 703.

Gerle, B., Lunden, G., and P. Sandblom. The Patient with Inoperable Cancer from the Psychiatric and Social Standpoints. *Cancer*, 1960, 13, 1206.

Gilbertsen, V. A., and Wangensteen, O. H. Should the Doctor Tell the Patient that the Disease is Cancer? In *The Physician and the Total Care of the Cancer Patient*. New York: American Cancer Society, 1961.

Glaser, B. G., and Strauss, A. L. *Awareness of Dying*. Chicago: Aldine, 1965.

Kelly, W. D., and Friesen, S. R. Do Cancer Patients Want to Be Told? *Surgery*, 1950, 27, 822.

Kline, N. S., and Sobin, J. The Psychological Management of Cancer Cases. *Journal of the American Medical Association*, 1951, 146, 1547.

Leak, W. N. The Care of the Dying. *Practitioner*, 1948, 161, 80.

Ogilvie, H. Journey's End. *Practitioner*, 1957, 179, 584.

Oken, D. What to Tell Cancer Patients. *Journal of the American Medical Association*, 1961, 175, 1120.

20 • Therapy with the Terminally Ill

Elisabeth Kübler-Ross

In this selection from her book On Death and Dying, *Dr. Elisabeth Kübler-Ross discusses, with characteristic gentleness and concern, therapy for the terminally ill and concludes with a memorable phrase about the care that can be given in "the silence that goes beyond words."*

Death belongs to life as birth does.
The walk is in the raising of the foot as in the laying of it down.

Tagore, from *Stray Birds*, CCXVII

The terminally ill patient has very special needs which can be fulfilled if we take the time to sit and listen and find out what they are. The most important communication, perhaps, is the fact that we let him know that we are ready and willing to share some of his concerns. To work with the dying patient requires a certain maturity which only comes from experience. We have to take a good hard look at our own attitude toward death and dying before we can sit quietly and without anxiety next to a terminally ill patient.

The door-opening interview is a meeting of two people who can communicate without fear and anxiety. The therapist—doctor, chaplain, or whoever undertakes this role—will attempt to let the patient know in his own words or actions that he is not going to run away if the word cancer or dying is mentioned. The patient will then pick up this cue and open up, or he may let the interviewer know that he appreciates the message though the time is not right. The patient will let such a person know when he is ready to share his concerns, and the therapist will reassure him of his return at an opportune time. Many of our patients have not had more than just such a door-opening interview. They were, at times, hanging onto life because of some unfinished business; they cared for a retarded sister and had found no one to take over in case of their death, or they had not been able to make arrangements for the care of some children and needed to share this worry with someone. Others were guilt-ridden about some real or imagined "sins" and were greatly relieved when we offered them an opportunity to share them, especially in the presence of a chaplain. These patients all felt better after "confessions" or arrangements for the care of others and usually died soon after the unfinished business was taken care of.

Rarely an unrealistic fear prevents a patient from dying, as earlier exemplified in the woman who was "afraid to die" because she could not conceive of "being eaten up alive by the worms." She had a phobic fear of worms and at the same time was quite aware of the absurdity of it. Because it was so silly, as she herself called it, she was unable to share this with her family who had spent all their savings on her hospitalizations. After one interview this old lady was able to share her fears with us and her daughter helped her with arrangements for a cremation. This patient, too, died soon after she was allowed to ventilate her fears.

We are always amazed how one session can relieve a patient of a tremendous burden and wonder why it is so difficult for staff and family to elicit their needs, since it often requires nothing more but an open question.

Though Mr. E. was not terminally ill, we shall use his case as a typical example of a door-opening interview. It is relevant because Mr. E. presented himself as a dying man as a consequence of unresolved conflicts precipitated by the death of an ambivalent figure.

> Mr. E., an eighty-three-year-old Jewish man, was admitted to the medical service of a private hospital because of severe weight loss, anorexia, and constipation. He complained of unbearable abdominal pains and looked haggard and tired. His general mood was depressed and he wept easily. A thorough medical workup was negative, and the resident finally asked for a psychiatric opinion.
>
> He was interviewed in a diagnostic-therapeutic interview with several students present in the same room. He did not mind the company and felt relieved to talk about his personal problems. He related

how he had been well until four months before admission when he suddenly became "an old, sick, and lonely man." Further questions revealed that a few weeks before the onset of all his physical complaints he lost a daughter-in-law and two weeks before the onset of his pains his estranged wife died suddenly while he was on a vacation out of town.

He was angry at his relatives for not coming to see him when he expected them. He complained about the nursing service and was generally displeased with the care he received from anybody. He was sure that his relatives would come immediately if he could promise them "a couple of thousand dollars when I die," and he elaborated at length about the housing project in which he lived with other old people and the vacation trip they all were invited to attend. It soon became evident that his anger was related to his being poor and that being poor meant that he had to take the trip when it was planned for his place of residence, i.e., he had no choice in the matter. On further questioning it became clear that he blamed himself for having been absent when his wife was hospitalized and tried to displace his guilt on the people who organized the vacation.

When we asked him if he did not feel deserted by his wife and was just unable to admit his anger at her, an avalanche of bitter feelings poured out in which he shared with us his inability to understand why she deserted him in favor of a brother (he called him a Nazi), how she raised their only son as a non-Jew, and finally how she left him alone now when he needed her most! Since he felt extremely guilty and ashamed about his negative feelings toward the deceased, he displaced his feelings on the relatives and nursing staff. He was convinced that he had to be punished for all those bad thoughts and that he had to endure much pain and suffering to alleviate his guilt.

We simply told him that we could share his mixed feelings, that they were very human and everybody had them. We also told him bluntly that we wondered if he could not acknowledge some anger at his former wife and express it in further brief visits with us. He answered to this, "If this pain does not go away I will have to jump out of the window." Our answer was, "Your pain may be all those swallowed feelings of anger and frustration. Get them out of your system without being ashamed and your pains will probably go away." He left with obvious mixed feelings but did ask to be visited again.

The resident who accompanied him back to his room was impressed with his slumped posture and took notice of it. He reinforced what we had said in the interview and reassured him that his reactions were very normal, after which he straightened up and returned in a more erect posture to his room.

A visit the next day revealed that he had hardly been in his room. He had spent much of the day socializing, visiting the cafeteria, and enjoying his food. His constipation and his pain [were] gone. After two massive bowel movements the evening of the interview, he felt "better than ever" and made plans for his discharge and resumption of some of his former activities.

On the day of discharge, he smiled and related some of the good days he had spent with his wife. He also told of the change in attitude toward the staff "whom I have given a hard time" and his relatives, especially his son whom he called to get acquainted a bit better, "since both of us may feel lonely for a while."

We reassured him of our availability should he have more problems, physical or emotional, and he smilingly replied that he had learned a good lesson and might face his own dying with more equanimity.

The example of Mr. E. shows how such interviews may be beneficial to people who are not actually ill themselves, but—due to old age or simply due to their own inability to cope with the death of an ambivalent figure—suffer a great deal and regard their physical or emotional discomforts as a means of alleviating guilt feelings for suppressed hostile wishes toward dead persons. This old man was not so much afraid to die as he was worried about dying before he had paid for his destructive wishes toward a person who had died without giving him a chance "to make up for it." He suffered agonizing pains as a means of reducing his fears of retribution and displaced much of his hostility and anger onto the nursing staff and relatives without being aware of the reasons for his resentment. It is surprising how a simple interview can reveal much of this data and a few statements of explanation, as well as reassurance that these feelings of love and hate are human and understandable and do not require a gruesome price, can alleviate much of these somatic symptoms.

For those patients who do not have a simple and single problem to solve, short-term therapy is helpful, which again does not necessarily require the help of a psychiatrist, but an understanding person, who has the time to sit and listen. I am thinking of patients like Sister I., who was visited on many occasions and who received her therapy as much from her fellow patients as she did from us. They are the patients who are fortunate enough to have time to work through some of their conflicts while they are sick and who can come to a deeper understanding and perhaps appreciation of the things they still have to enjoy. These therapy sessions, like the brief psychotherapy sessions with more terminally ill patients, are irregular in time and occurrence. They are individually arranged depending on the patient's physical condition and his ability and willingness to talk at a given time; they often include visits of just a few minutes to assure them of our presence even at times when they do not wish to talk. They continue even more frequently when the patient is in less comfort and more pain, and then take the form of silent companionship rather than a verbal communication.

We have often wondered if group therapy with a selected group of terminally ill patients as indicated, since they often share the same loneliness and isolation. Those who work on wards with terminally ill patients are quite aware of the interactions that go on between the patients and the many helpful statements that are made from one very sick patient to another. We are always amazed how much of our experiences in the seminar are communicated from one dying patient to another; we even get "referrals" of one patient from another. We have noticed patients sitting together in the lobby of the hospital who have been interviewed in the seminar, and they have continued their informal sessions like members of a fraternity. So far we have left it up to the patients how much they choose to share with others, but we are presently looking into their motivation for a more formal meeting, since this seems to be desired by at least a small group of our patients. They include those patients who have chronic illnesses and who require many rehospitalizations. They have known each other for quite a while and not only share the same illness but they also have the same memories of past hospitalizations. We have been very impressed by their almost joyful reaction when one of their "buddies" dies, which is only a confirmation of their unconscious conviction that "it shall happen to thee but not to me." This may also be a contributing factor why so many patients and their family members . . . get some pleasure in visiting other perhaps more seriously ill patients. Sister I. used these visits as an expression of hostility, namely, to elicit patients' needs and to prove to the nursing staff that they were not efficient . . . by helping them as a nurse, she could not only temporarily deny her own inability to function, but she could also express her anger at those who were well and unable to serve the sick more effectively. Having such patients in a group therapy setup would help them understand their behavior and at the same time help the nursing staff by making them more accepting of their needs.

Mrs. F. was another woman to be remembered as she started informal group therapy between herself and some very sick patients, all of whom were hospitalized with leukemia or Hodgkin's disease, from which she had suffered for over twenty years. During the past few years she had an average of six hospitalizations a year, which finally resulted in her complete acceptance of her illness. One day a nineteen-year-old girl, Ann, was admitted, frightened of her illness and its outcome and unable to share this fear with anyone. Her parents had refused to talk about it, and Mrs. F. then became the unofficial counselor for her. She told her of her sons, her husband, and the house she had taken care of for so many years in spite of the many hospitalizations, and finally enabled Ann to ventilate her concerns and ask questions relevant to her. When Ann was discharged, she sent another young patient to see Mrs. F., and so a chain reaction of referrals began to take place, quite comparable to group therapy in which one patient replaces another. The group rarely consisted of more than two or three people and remained together as long as the individual members were in the hospital.

THE SILENCE THAT GOES BEYOND WORDS

There is a time in a patient's life when the pain ceases to be, when the mind slips off into a dreamlike state, when the need for food becomes minimal, and the awareness of the environment all but disappears into darkness. This is the time when the relatives walk up and down the hospital hallways, tormented by the waiting, not knowing if they should leave to attend the living or stay to be around for the moment of death. This is the time when it is too late for words, and yet the time when the relatives cry the loudest for help—with or without words. It is too late for medical interventions (and too cruel, though well meant, when they do occur), but it is also too early for a final separation from the dying. It is the hardest time for the next of kin as he either wishes to take off, to get it over with; or he desperately clings to something that he is in the process of losing forever. It is the time for the therapy of silence with the patient and availability for the relatives.

The doctor, nurse, social worker, or chaplain can be of great help during these final moments if they can understand the family's conflicts at this time and help select the one person who feels most comfortable staying with the dying patient. This person then becomes in effect the patient's therapist. Those who feel too uncomfortable can be assisted by alleviating their guilt and by the reassurance that someone will stay with the dying until his death has occurred. They can then return home knowing that the patient did not die alone, yet not feeling ashamed or guilty for having avoided this moment which for many people is so difficult to face.

Those who have the strength and the love to sit with a dying patient in the *silence that goes beyond words* will know that this moment is neither frightening nor painful, but a peaceful cessation of the functioning of the body. Watching a peaceful death of a human being reminds us of a falling star; one of the million lights in a vast sky that flares up for a brief moment only to disappear into the endless night forever. To be a therapist to a dying patient makes us aware of the uniqueness of each individual in this vast sea of humanity. It makes us aware of our finiteness, our limited lifespan. Few of us live beyond our three score and ten years and yet in that brief time most of us create and live a unique biography and weave ourselves into the fabric of human history.

> The water in a vessel is sparkling; the water in the sea is dark.
> The small truth has words that are clear; the great truth has great silence.
>
> Tagore, from *Stray Birds,* CLXXVI

21• Some Aspects of Psychotherapy with Dying Persons

Edwin S. Shneidman

In this selection Dr. Shneidman outlines the ways in which working with a dying person (called clinical thanatology) is different from ordinary psychotherapy.

From the psychosocial point of view, the primary task of helping the dying person is to focus on the *person*—not the biochemistry or pathology of the diseased organs, but a human being who is a living beehive of emotions, including (and especially) anxiety, the fight for control, and terror. And, with a dying person, there is another grim omnipresent fact in the picture: time is finite. The situation is dramatic, unlike that of psychotherapy with an essentially physically healthy person, where time seems "endless" and there is no push by the pages of the calendar. One of the main points of this chapter is that just as psychotherapy is, in some fundamental ways, clearly different from "ordinary talk," so working psychotherapeutically with a dying person involves some important differences from the usual modes of psychotherapy.

I

At the outset it is only reasonable that I indicate some issues that are fundamental to understanding any list of therapeutic suggestions. The "rules" for psychotherapy are rather easy to comprehend but their more meaningful application within the context of a stressful dying scenario has to take into account certain subtleties that lie behind the obvious and visible drama. We must look behind the apparent dying scenario if we wish to encompass the powerful and poignant psychological richness inherent in the dying drama. To be specific, I shall suggest that there are three aspects of the dying process that need to be kept in mind.

A. PHILOSOPHIC (MORAL-ETHICAL-EPISTEMOLOGICAL) ASPECTS OF THE DYING PROCESS

One can begin with the assertion that, typically, a death is a dyadic event, involving the chief protagonist (the dying person) and the survivors—basically an I-thou relationship. Toynbee (1969) has stated it succinctly:

> The two-sidedness of death is a fundamental feature of death . . . There are always two parties to a death; the person who dies and the

survivors who are bereaved . . . the sting of death is less sharp for the person who dies than it is for the bereaved survivor. This is, as I see it, the capital fact about the relation between living and dying. There are two parties to the suffering that death inflicts; and in the apportionment of this suffering, the survivor takes the brunt.

Often the situation is even more complicated, involving several persons as in the two vignettes below.

1. A physician asks me to see one of his patients. He tells me, beforehand that her numerous physical pains and complaints have absolutely no organic basis. I see her and talk with her. As much as I try to eschew simplistic diagnostic labels for a complicated human being, the tag of "agitated depression" seems to describe her rather accurately. She is complaining, pain filled; she wrings her hands; her brow is furrowed; she is restless; fidgety, tearful, woebegone. She looks older than her forty years.

   The story is this: Her wealthy husband has a terminal disease. He may very well be dead in a few years or even much sooner. He has told her that she makes him nervous and that he cannot stand her. He has placed her in a private nursing home. She hates that nursing home and wants to return to her own home. Coincidentally, he has employed a practical nurse to massage his muscular pains and also to act as chauffeur and "keeper" for his wife.

   At the end of my session with the wife, the nurse comes into the office to take her back to the nursing home. She is rather heavily made up, and has a striking figure. The picture is suddenly clear to me. The practical nurse is the husband's mistress. The wife has been evicted from her own home. "But, after all," says the doctor, "the poor man is dying."
2. A seventy-year-old man has cancer of the esophagus. He received a course of chemotherapy, which made him excruciatingly uncomfortable—nausea, vertigo, vomiting. Several weeks after the treatment he began to show memory loss, some confusion, and uncharacteristic irritability. A thorough neurological examination disclosed a malignant brain tumor. Another course of treatment was suggested. His son—a physician (neurologist) in another city (who was in daily telephone communication with his parents)—asked his father's doctor to forgo the treatments. To me, on the telephone, the son said: "What is the point of an unknown amount of possible good compared to an onerous treatment of absolutely uncertain benefit imbedded in a procedure which will give him a substantial amount of certain torture?" The local treating physician was incensed. The wife was in a quandary. The treating physician demanded that the patient be told "all the facts" and be permitted to make up his own mind. The physician-son retorted that his father, not being medically trained, was in no position to evaluate "all the facts," and more than that, his mind—specifically his brain—was no longer able to make the ordinary judgments of which he had been previously capable. As the mother's

psychotherapist, I marveled at the sad game of what I called "Who owns the body?"

Toynbee raises the question of who, in the total suffering a death inflicts, is hurt the most? The two criteria are comfort and dignity—their opposites are pain and humiliation (degradation).

Imagine for each of the two vignettes cited above, a chart in the shape of a circle. In each there seem to be four characters: in the first, the husband, the wife, the mistress, and the doctor; in the second, the father, the mother, the son, and the doctor. The second case is compounded by the fact that we do not know, from day to day, what the father can think or experience. How should the calculations of the percentages of dignity, self-esteem, well-being, comfort, sense of accomplishment, freedom from pain, and so on be made? Who should be given the largest percentage; who the least? Should, in the first case, the wife be scapegoated—given electric shocks for her "depression?" In the second case, should the treating physician's wishes—who may have the patient on some research protocol as part of a grant—supersede, in the name of science and possible help for future patients (not to mention the physician's narcissistic and professional investment in his research), the physician-son's emotional feelings about his father's dignity and comfort?

Far from being esoteric abstractions, these philosophic points touch on the deepest questions relating to death: Who have become the priests of death? What are the citizen's rights to "death with dignity?" When can a spouse or grown child say for a loved one, "Enough?"

B. SOCIOLOGICAL (SITUATIONAL) ASPECTS OF THE DYING PROCESS

Inasmuch as nowadays, the majority of terminally ill persons die in institutions—hospitals or nursing homes—it is appropriate to ask: What are the constraints of the social environment? The recent observations and reports of field sociologists such as David Sudnow, author of *Passing On* (1967) (an intriguing description of "what actually happens" in hospitals, especially in emergency rooms and the various uses to which fresh corpses are put), and Barney Glaser and Anselm Strauss, authors of *Awareness of Dying* (1965) and *Time for Dying* (1968) (with their enlightening concepts of "mutual pretense" and "dying trajectory"), teach us that a great deal "goes on" in the institutional interplay that is neither in the organizational chart nor in the brochure given to visitors.

Whether or not a person is resuscitated; how many minutes doctors and nurses spend in a dying person's room; whether a person will be "pronounced dead" on this hospital shift or that; whether or not interns will practice surgery on the dead body—all these occurrences, and others, are what realistic sociologists tell us about—and it behooves us to listen. In an understanding of the dying person, we need to include a keen situational view of the events.

Glaser and Strauss's concept of "the dying trajectory" deserves our close attention. In *Time for Dying* they say:

> When the dying patient's hospital career begins—when he is admitted to the hospital and a specific service—the staff in solo and in concert make initial definitions of the patient's trajectory. They expect him to linger, to die quickly, or to approach death at some pace between these extremes. . . . Since the definition of trajectory influences behavior, these differing definitions may create inconsistencies in the staff's care of and interaction with the patient, with consequent problems for the staff itself, family and patient.

When ordinary, well-functioning individuals are asked about what they consider to be most important to them if they were dying, they usually list "control"—having some measure of "say" over their own treatment and management—as the most important item (followed by relief from pain, which can, in the last analysis, also be subsumed under control). But we see that there are often conflicting agendas between the dying person and his or her fight for dignity (self-control, autonomy) and the hospital staff and their interest in assigning that person (called "patient") to certain roles, including even the pace or rate at which those roles are to be played.

In order to be a "good patient," one has to die on schedule, in accordance with the dying trajectory mapped by the staff. To die too early, unexpectedly, is an embarrassment to hospital staff; but what is more surprising (and of psycho-social interest), is that to linger too long, beyond the projected trajectory, can be an even greater embarrassment to hospital staff—and a great strain on the next of kin who may have premourned and set their mind's clock for a specific death date, which, if not met, becomes painfully overdue.

C. PSYCHOLOGICAL (CHARACTEROLOGICAL) ASPECTS OF THE DYING PROCESS

For the terminally ill person, the time of dying is a multiscened drama, with elements of Shakespearean tragedy and historical (introspective) pageant. It is probably true that each person dies idiosyncratically alone, "in a notably personal way," but nonetheless there are generalizations that can be made about the dying process. From a psychological point of view, the most interesting question is what are the psychological characteristics of the dying process.

In the current thanatological scene there are those who write about fewer than a half-dozen stages lived through in a specific order—not to mention the even more obfuscating writing of a life after death. My own experiences have led me to rather different conclusions. In working with dying persons I see a wide range of human emotions—few in some people, dozens in others—experienced in a variety of orderings, reorderings, and arrangements. The one psychological mechanism that seems ubiquitous is denial, which can appear or reappear at any time. (See Avery Weisman's *On Dying and Denying* (1972).) Nor is there any natural law that an individual has to achieve closure before death sets its seal. In fact, most people die too soon or too late, with loose threads and fragments of agenda uncompleted.

My own notion is more general in scope; more specific in content. It borrows from Adolph Meyer and Henry A. Murray in its spirit. My general hypothesis is that a *dying person's flow of behaviors will reflect or parallel that person's previous segments of behaviors, specifically those behaviors relating to threat, stress, or failure.* There are certain deep *consistencies* in human beings. Individuals die more-or-less characteristically as they have lived, relative to those aspects of personality which relate to their conceptualization of their dying. To put it oversimply: The psychological course of the cancer mirrors certain deep troughs in the course of the life—*oncology recapitulates ontogeny.*

What is especially pertinent is how individuals have behaved at some of the most stressful, least successful times in their lives—whether those incidents relate to stress in school, job, marriage, separations, loss, or whatever. The hypothesis further holds that people's previous macrotemporal patterns and coping mechanisms will give clues about their patterns of behavior when dying—fighting illness or surrendering to it, despairing, denying, and their combinations, as they become increasingly aware of the life-threatening situation.

II

I believe that working intensively with a dying person is different from any other human encounter. The main point is that when a clinical thanatologist (physician, psychologist, nurse, social worker, or any trained person) is working with a dying person, he or she is not just "talking." (There is, of course, an enormously important place for mere *presence*—which, after all, may be the most important ingredient in care—or for sitting in communicative silence, or for seemingly just talking about what may appear to be trivial or banal topics.)

Working with the dying person is a special task. A person who systematically attempts to help a dying individual achieve a more psychologically comfortable death or a more "appropriate death"—given the dire, unnegotiable circumstances of the terminal disease—is either a psychotherapist or is acting in the role of a psychotherapist. That role cannot be escaped. (This is not to say that many others—relatives, church members, neighbors—cannot also play extremely important roles). But the distinction between a *conversation* and a *professional exchange* is crucial; more than that, I now believe that working with dying persons is different from working with any other kind of individual and demands a different kind of involvement; and I am willing to propose that there may be as important a conceptual difference between ordinary psychotherapy (with individuals where the life span is not an issue) and psychotherapy with dying persons as there is between ordinary psychotherapy and ordinary talk. The following paragraphs outline what I feel are some of the important nuances of these differences.

1. Ordinary talk or conversation

   In this kind of exchange which makes up most of human discourse, the focus is on the surface content (concrete events, specific details, abstract issues, questions and answers of content). The individuals are talking about what is actually being said: the obvious, stated meanings, and the ordinary interesting (or uninteresting) details of life. Further, the social role between the two participants is one of essential equality, sometimes tempered somewhat by considerations of age, status or prestige. But each of the two parties has the social right to ask the other the same kind of questions which he or she has been asked. Some examples of ordinary talk might be two friends conversing with one another about the events of the day, or two lovers whispering intimate thoughts to one another, or two businessmen closing a deal, or two neighbors simply chatting.

2. A hierarchical exchange

   In this kind of exchange the entire focus (like in a conversation) is on the manifest content—on what is being said—but the situation is marked by an explicit or tacit acknowledgment by the two parties that there is a significant difference of status between them; one of them is "superior" to the other. Questions asked or suggestions made or information transmitted or orders given by one would seem inappropriate if attempted by the other party. Examples would be the verbal exchange between a supervisor and subordinate, between an army officer and enlisted man, or between an oncologist and a patient in the doctor's office. The officer can order the enlisted man, but not vice versa; the doctor can examine the patient, but not vice versa. The doctor-patient relationship is an hierarchical one in that a doctor and a patient do not exchange roles.

3. A professional (e.g., psychotherapy) exchange

   Here the focus is on feelings, emotional content and unconscious meanings, rather than primarily on what is apparently being said. The emphasis is on the latent (between-the-lines) significance more than on the manifest and obvious content; on unconscious meanings, including double entendre, puns and slips of the tongue; on themes that run as common threads through the content rather than on the concrete details for their own sake. Perhaps the most distinguishing aspect of the professional exchange (as opposed to ordinary talk) is the occurrence of "transference"—wherein the patient projects onto the therapist certain deep expectations and feelings. These transference reactions often stem from the patient's childhood and reflect earlier patterns of reaction (of love, hate, dependency, suspicion, etc.) to whatever the therapist may or may not be doing. The therapist (like the doctor) is often invested by the patient with almost magical healing powers, which, in fact, can serve as a self-fulfilling prophecy and thus help the interaction become therapeutic for the patient. The roles of the two participants, unlike those in a conversation, are not coequal. The situation is hierarchical but the focus is not on the manifest content.

4. A thanatological exchange

   A person who systematically attempts to help a dying individual achieve a psychologically comfortable death (or a more "appropriate" death or an "ego-syntonic" death)—given the dire, unnegotiable circumstances of the situation—is acting in a special role. (This is not to say that many others—doctors, nurses, relatives, dear friends, specially trained volunteers—cannot also play extremely important roles.) If the distinction between a conversation and a professional exchange is crucial, certainly the distinction between working with dying persons as opposed to working with any other kind of individual is a vital one. Working with a dying person demands a different kind of involvement. My position is that there may be as important a conceptual difference between ordinary psychotherapy and working with dying persons as there is between ordinary psychotherapy and ordinary talk. Below, I have attempted to limn out some of the important nuances of these differences.

III

I believe that every physician should be a clinical thanatologist, at least once (preferably early) in his or her career, dealing intensively (five or six days, for an *hour* each day) with the personal-human-psychological aspects of a dying person. This means sitting unhurriedly by the bedside and coming to know the dying person as a person—over and above the biochemistry, cytology, medicine, and oncology of the "case." This also means not avoiding the dying and death aspects of the situation, but learning about them, sharing them, being burdened by them, (and their enormous implications)—in a word, to share the intensity of the thanatalogical experience. It also means (1) working with the survivor-victims to help them survive better; (2) interacting with ward staff personnel (doctors and nurses) to help them cope better; and (3) being mindful of one's own countertransference so the thanatologist can survive better.

The reward of this onerous event—treating one person intensively as a paradigm of how one might optimally (if there were unlimited time and one had infinite psychic reserves) treat every dying person—is an enrichment experience that will illuminate all the rest of one's practice and will enable admittedly busy physicians to be enormously more effective in the necessarily briefer encounters with all their patients, terminal or otherwise. The proper role of the physician in the twentieth century is not only to alleviate pain and cure the sick but, when the situation requires it, to help people die better. And how can the physician really know "on the pulses" unless he or she carves out the time to gain the *intimate* experience of the psychological details of at least one or two intensive dying experiences?

Let me now list some of the specific characteristics of working with dying persons—as opposed to those who are "only" critically ill, sick, diseased, injured, or disturbed. What these add up to is the prefiguring of a new specialty—of import to all care givers and not limited to physicians—called thanatology.

What is special about thanatological work?

1. *The goals are different.* Because the time is limited, the goals are more finite. The omnipresent goal is the psychological *comfort* of the person, with, as a general rule, as much alleviation of physical pain as possible. With a terminal person, addiction is not the issue—yet many physicians are niggardly or inappropriately moral about the use of pain-relieving substances. We have much to learn from Dame Cicely Saunders, founder of St. Christopher's Hospice (near London), about the humane uses of morphine, alcohol, and other analgesics. Nor is psychological insight the goal. There is no rule that states that an individual must die with any certain amount of self-knowledge. In this sense, every life is incomplete. The goal—fighting the calendar of the lethal illness—is to "will the obligatory"; to make a chilling and ugly scene go as well as possible; to give psychological succor; to permit the tying off of loose ends; to lend as much stability to the person as it is possible to give.
2. *The rules are different.* Because there is a foreseeable (although tentative) death date in the finite future—a matter of months or weeks—the usual rules for psychotherapy can realistically be modified. The celerity with which the relationship between therapist and patient is made and the *depth* of that relationship can be of a nature that would be totally appropriate for a dying person, but, with an ordinary (non-dying) patient might appear unseemly or even unprofessional. But the "love" that flows between patient and therapist (and in the opposite direction also) when the patient is a dying person can be sustaining, even ennobling. One might ask what would happen if the patient were to have a remission, even recover. That is an embarrassment devoutly to be wished; in that rare case, the therapist would simply have to "renegotiate" the "contract" or understanding between the two of them. But intensive work with a dying person generally permits a depth of transference and countertransference that should not be done nor countenanced in perhaps any other professional relationship.
3. *It may not be psychotherapy.* Obviously, working with a dying person should, for that person, be psychotherapeutic. (Anything that might be iatrogenic should be avoided). But the process itself may be sufficiently

different from ordinary psychotherapy that it might very well merit a label of its own. What is important is that the process be flexible —which is somewhat different from eclectic—and be able to move with the dying person's shifts of needs and mood, efforts toward control, detours into denial, and so on. Working with a dying person contains elements of rather traditional psychotherapy, but it also is characterized by other kinds of human interaction, including rapport building, interview, conversation, history taking, just plain talk, and communicative silences.

4. *The focus is on benign intervention.* In thanatological work, the therapist need not be a *tabula rasa;* nor need the therapist be inactive. There can be active intervention, as long as it is in the patient's interests. These interventions can take the form of interpretations, suggestions, advice (when asked for), interacting with doctors and nurses on the hospital ward, interacting with members of the family, arranging for social work services, liaison with clergy, and so on. The notion that any intervention is an incursion into the patient's rights and liberties is rejected as a blunt idea that does not make the distinction between benign and malign activities. The clinical thanatologist can act as the patient's ombudsman in many ways—on the ward, in the hospital, and within the community.
5. *No one has to die in a state of psychoanalytic grace.* Putting aside the Jehovah or "savior complex" that is understandably present in many psychotherapists, there is underlying concern with "success" in the motivational system of any effective therapist. With a dying patient, therapists must realign their notions of what they can realistically do for that person. It is a process that no matter how auspiciously begun or effectively conducted always ends in death. We hear phrases like "death work," but we need to appreciate that very few individuals die right on psychological target with all their complexes and neuroses beautifully worked through. The therapist needs to be able to tolerate incompleteness and lack of closure. Patients never untangle all the varied skeins of their intrapsychic and interpersonal life; to the last second there are psychical creations and recreations that require new resolutions. Total insight is an abstraction; there is no golden mental homeostasis.
6. *"Working through" is a luxury for those who have time to live.* It follows from the above that people die either too soon or too late with incompleted fragments in their life's agenda. The goal of resolving life's problems may be an unattainable one; the goal of an "appropriate death"—Avery Weisman's felicitous concept—of helping the dying person to "be relatively pain free, suffering reduced, emotional and social impoverishments kept at a minimum . . . resolving residual conflicts, and satisfying whatever remaining wishes are consistent with his present plight and with his ego ideal." The best death is one that an individual would choose for himself or herself if the choice

were possible (even though the disease remained unnegotiable). Dying people can be helped to put their affairs in order—although everyone dies more-or-less intestate, psychologically speaking.

7. *The dying person sets the pace.* Because there are no specific substantive psychological goals (of having this insight or coming to that understanding), the emphasis is on process and on the thanatologist's continued presence. Nothing *has* to be accomplished. The patient sets the pace. This even includes whether the topic of death is ever mentioned—although, if permitted, it almost always will be. The therapist will note the usefulness of "the method of successive approximations," in which a dying person may say, over the course of many days, "I have a problem, an illness, a tumor, a malignancy, a cancer, a terminal metastasis." This is not a litany that needs to be recited. Different individuals get in touch with their illness at various points of candor. Any one of these points is equally good, as long as it is comfortable for that person.
8. *Denial will be present.* We have already characterized the notion of a half-dozen stages of dying as being oversimplistic and not true to life. In the most popular explication of this approach, denial is listed as the first stage ("No, it can't be me!"). But our disavowal of the idea of a half-dozen fixed stages of dying should not lead us into the error of neglecting the importance of the psychological mechanism of denial itself. Denial is not a stage of dying; it is rather a ubiquitous aspect of the dying process, surfacing now and again (at no predetermined regular intervals) all through the dying process. It is only human for even the most extraordinary human beings occasionally to blot out or take a vacation from their knowledge of their imminent end. It is probably psychologically necessary for dying people intermittently to rest their own deathful train of thoughts on a siding, off the main track that leads only to blackness or mystery. This means that the clinical thanatologist must be prepared for the dying person to manifest a rather radical change of pace. If the therapist will only ride with this transient denial, the dying person will—as surprisingly as he or she began it—abandon it and come back to some of the realities of the present moment.
9. *The goal is increased psychological comfort.* The main point of working with the dying person—in the visit, the give-and-take of talk, the advice, the interpretations, the listening—is to increase that individual's psychological *comfort.* The criterion of "effectiveness" lies in this single measure. One cannot realistically be Pollyannish or even optimistic; the therapist begins in a grim situation that is going to become even grimmer. The best that the therapist can hope to accomplish is to have helped the ill person in whatever ways it takes to achieve some increased psychological comfort. However, hope should never be totally abandoned.
10. *The importance of relating to nurses and doctors on the ward.* If the

dying work is done in a hospital—or wherever it is done—it cannot be conducted as a solo operation. It is of key importance that relatives and personnel on the ward be kept informed of the dying person's condition and needs, and more, that they be kept informed as to the guiding concepts that underlie this special therapeutic exchange. Like clinical research on a ward, thanatological work often goes best with the full cooperation of the chief nurse. It is understood that no one approaches a patient as a "patient care specialist"—the euphemism for clinical thanatologist—unless he or she has been asked to do so by the physician in charge of the case. Then such a person—who has been introduced to the patient by the regular doctor—acts as any consultant would act, the difference being in the frequency and duration of the visits.

11. *The survivor is the victim—and eventually the patient: the concept of postvention.* Arnold Toynbee wrote eloquently about his view that death was essentially a two-person event and that, in the summation of anguish, the survivor bore the brunt of the hurt. All that has been said above should now be understood in the context of advocating that almost from the beginning of working with the dying person, the clinical thanatologist ought to become acquainted with the main survivor-to-be, to gain rapport with that person, and to have an explicit understanding that the survivor will be seen in the premourning stages and then for a while, at decreasing intervals, for perhaps a year or so after the death. *Postvention*—working with survivor-victims—ought to be part of any total health-care system. It is not only humane; it is also good medical practice, for we know—especially from the work of Colin Murray Parkes (1972)—that a population of survivors (of any adult age) is a population at risk, having elevated rates of morbidity (including surgeries and other hospitalizations) and mortality (from a variety of causes of death) for at least a year or so after the death of a mourned person. Postventive care relates not only to "losses" in the survivor's life but also to other aspects of stress from which that mourner may be suffering.
12. *Just as the role of transference is paramount, the place of countertransference bears careful watching, and a good support system is a necessity.* A terminal person's dying days can be made better by virtue of "the joys of transference" that are projected on the thanatological therapist. The therapist, if able, should work for an intense transference relationship. But there is a well-known caveat: where there is transference, there is also countertransference—the flow of feeling from the therapist to the patient. The therapist is invested in the patient's welfare and is thereby made vulnerable. When the patient dies, the therapist is bereaved. And during the dying process, the therapist is anguished by the prospect of loss and a sense of impotence. Dealing with a dying person is abrasive work. The therapist is

well advised to have good support systems in his or her own life: loved ones, dear friends, congenial work, and peer consultants.

The other side of these injunctions is that a physician needs to take vacations from death. A gynecological oncologist, for example, might intersperse his or her practice with obstetrical cases, delivering babies as a balance for those patients who are dying of cancer of the uterus. Moreover, a physician in oncological practice should not fail to seek out psychological or psychiatric consultation for patients if they are significantly depressed or otherwise disturbed about dying and for *himself* (or herself) if there is any sense that one's own equanimity has been touched. This type of psychotherapeutic help might well be made a routine part of a physician's dealing with dying person's, lest the physician fall prey to the predictable consequences of the unusual psychological stresses that come from working constantly around and against death. (Shneidman, 1974, 1980)

References

Glaser, Barney G., and Strauss, Anselm. *Awareness of Dying.* Chicago: Aldine Publishing Company, 1965.

Glaser, Barney G., and Strauss, Anselm. *Time for Dying.* Chicago: Aldine Publishing Company, 1968.

Hinton, John. *Dying.* Baltimore: Penguin Books, 1967.

Parkes, Colin Murray. *Bereavement: Studies of Grief in Adult Life.* New York: International Universities Press, 1972.

Shneidman, Edwin S. *Deaths of Man.* Baltimore: Penguin Books, 1974. (First published by Quadrangle Books, 1973.)

Shneidman, Edwin S. Aspects of the Dying Process. *Psychiatric Annals* 7, no. 3 (March 1977).

Shneidman, Edwin S. *Voices of Death.* New York: Harper & Row, 1980.

Sudnow, David. *Passing On.* Englewood Cliffs, N.J.:Prentice-Hall, 1967.

Toynbee, Arnold *et al. Man's Concern with Death.* New York: McGraw-Hill Book Company, 1969.

Weisman, Avery D. *On Dying and Denying.* New York: Behaviorial Publications, 1972.

THE SURVIVORS OF DEATH

To be a survivor, to have suffered a grievous loss of someone close, is a terrible plight. If grief is not an illness, often its effects are so severe that it might as well be one. Grief and mourning are powerful and stressful emotional states that can touch off unconscious psychological reactions that actually jeopardize the individual's life. A recent study shows that loss of a loved one is absolutely at the top of the list of stressful, abrasive, and disruptive events that can happen to one. (A reader interested in the general topic of stress can refer to the substantial works of Hans Selye.) For a while —at least a year or so—the grieving person is an individual "at risk," more apt not to take adequate care of self, more apt to be sick and hospitalized, and even more apt to die or be killed.

Currently there is much-needed and overdue concern with widows and widowers, bereaved parents, orphaned children, who have, by and large, been a rather neglected group. This section concerns itself with the psychological needs of the mourners and grievers who are left behind.

Toynbee's selection sets the tone for this chapter in his emphasis on death as an essentially dyadic event—an event in which there are always "two parties to the suffering that death inflicts; and, in the apportionment of this suffering, the survivor takes the brunt." This, for Toynbee is the heart of the relation between the living and the dying, between life and death. As a corollary of his notion about the greater burden on the survivor, Toynbee suggests that if one truly loves one's spouse one would wish for one's spouse to die first so that the spouse can be spared the anguish of bereavement.

Perhaps the most impressive systematic studies in the field of bereavement have been done by Parkes. His selection can be said to offer factual grounds for Toynbee's fears by documenting some of the practical perils of being a survivor. Parkes and his associates studied a number of London widows, under the age of sixty-five, for thirteen months following the deaths of their husbands. His interesting findings indicate that the widows have a "search" for their dead spouses, an inner push toward aggressive behavior, and, compared to non-widows, a greater number of unexplained illnesses and deaths. He calls his piece "The Broken Heart."

This "peril of survivorship" leads Shneidman in the next selection to talk about "survivor-victims" and "postvention." A growing appreciation of the survivor as a victim has led to the development of special postventive therapies for the survivors. The goal of postvention is to reduce the possible harmful physical and psychological aftereffects from the death of a loved one.

The impact of watching the dying and experiencing the death of another are important thanatological topics. It is important to understand the psychological stresses of those in daily contact with a human being who is dying. We can note their inner tensions, their premourning—made up of deep concern and understandable "pulling away"—and, after the death, their grief and mourning. Dr. Bugen's contribution focuses on the emotional *realities of helpers —doctors, nurses, psychologists, social workers, health educators, clergy —who interact, often on a rather constant and sometimes intimate basis, with a dying person.*

The death of a child is somehow felt to be more poignant than any other death, and it was difficult to choose from among the hundreds of articles and dozens of books on this admittedly painful topic. The article by Drs. Stillion and Wass seems to be a good representative offering, because it contains a great deal of helpful information on, for example, the reactions of terminally ill children to their own terminality, helpful guidelines for caregivers and the family, anticipatory mourning by parents, and the healthy child's views of death. The authors provide a list of twelve classic books in which death is imbedded in the main theme, and an annotated bibliography of twenty-six books (by age levels) in which death is the main theme.

22 • The Relation Between Life and Death, Living and Dying

Arnold Toynbee

In the moving Epilogue to his book Man's Concern with Death *from which the following essay is excerpted, Professor Toynbee introduces us to the concept that the suffering of death is a dyadic event, involving two parties. These passages serve excellently to introduce the other selections in this section.*

Premature death may be incurred in various ways. It may be inflicted by human hands deliberately either by public enterprise (war and the execution of judicial death sentences) or by private enterprise (murder). It may be inflicted by nonhuman living creatures (bacteria, sharks, man-eating tigers). It may be caused by hunger, thirst, exposure to the elements—defeats of man by nonhuman nature that have been becoming less frequent in the economically "developed" minority of mankind, though the reduction of the rate of premature deaths from these causes among this minority is being offset by an increase in the rate of premature deaths caused by accidents—particularly in the form of miscarriages of our increasingly high-powered machinery which, in its application to our means of locomotion, has enabled us to "annihilate distance" at the price of a high toll of deaths in road vehicles and in aeroplanes. (The toll taken by the now obsolescent railway train was comparatively light.)

Since death is irretrievable, the deliberate infliction of premature death by one human being on another is surely a heinous offense—and this not only in murder and in war, but also in the execution of judicial death sentences. Murder has been almost universally condemned—though there have been, and still are, some exceptional societies in which a youth does not qualify for being accepted as a man until he has taken another man's life. Killing in war has, till now, been almost universally regarded as being respectable—though a misgiving about its respectability is betrayed in the euphemistic use of the word "defense" to signify war and preparation for war, however aggressive the intention. For instance, the Spartan official formula for a mobilization order with the object of invading a foreign country was "to declare a state of defense" (*phouran phainein*); and the costs of genocidal atomic weapons are entered under the rubric "defense" in the budgets of present-day states. The infliction of premature death by process of law has been approved of still more widely and confidently than the infliction of it by act of war. When the abolition of the death penalty has been mooted, this has usually aroused violent controversy; yet the abolition of it is now an accomplished fact in some states in the present-day world. The reason for this obstinately resisted abandonment of an age-old practice is that "while there is life there is hope." A change of heart may be experienced by even the most apparently hardened criminal.

We ought not to be reconciled to premature death when this is caused by human design or callousness or incompetence or carelessness. Yet there are cases in which even premature death is acceptable—the cases in which it has been risked and suffered voluntarily for the benefit of some fellow human being or of mankind in general. Voluntary premature death in war is the form of heroic self-sacrifice that has been both the most frequently performed and the most enthusiastically applauded; yet this is also the form of heroism that is the most ambivalent, since a man who is killed in war dies prematurely in the act of trying to inflict premature death on some of his fellow human beings. There is nothing questionable about the heroism of the premature death of someone who sacrifices his or her life in trying to save a fellow human being from meeting death by, say, drowning or burning; and we can also accept, while we lament, the premature death of pioneers and inventors who have deliberately risked their lives in the cause of making life better for mankind as a whole.

Many men have sacrificed their lives prematurely in winning for mankind, by daring and dangerous experimentation, the art of domesticating wild animals, the art of navigation, the art of aviation. (Scaling the Matterhorn, reaching the poles, and breaking out of the earth's air-envelope into outer space do not seem to me to be objectives for which lives ought to have been risked and lost.) Many physicians have sacrificed their lives prematurely by tending the victims of deadly contagious diseases, or by experimenting perilously on themselves. My grandfather, who was a doctor, killed himself, unintentionally, when he was at the height of his powers, by experimenting on himself, in the early days of the use of anaesthetics, in order to discover what the right degree of dosage was. So there are circumstances in which premature death is not unacceptable, however grievous it may be.

What are we to say about the premature death of the spirit in a human body that still remains physically alive? I am familiar with this form of premature death too—the death-in-life of insanity and senility. I have been at very close quarters with a human being who lived on physically to a higher age than I have reached now for more than thirty years—about three-eighths of his total span of physical life—after he had suffered the death of the spirit. I have also known intimately three persons—two of them dominating personalities and the third a robust one—who have succumbed to senility in old age. This premature death of a human spirit in advance of the death of its body is more appalling than any premature death in which spirit and body die simultaneously. It is an outrage committed by nature on human dignity. "Slay us," nature or God, if you choose or if you must, but slay us "in the light."[1] Allow the light of reason—the faculty that makes a human being—to survive in us till the end of the life of the body. The spectacle of insanity and senility has always appalled me more than the witnessing or the hearing of a physical death. But there are two sides to this situation; there is the victim's side, as well as the spectator's; and what is harrowing for the spectator may be alleviating for the victim.

It will not, of course be alleviation for him if the failure of his mental faculties overtakes him only gradually and then only to a degree that leaves him aware of what is happening to him. I can think of no worse fate than this, and I have seen it befall my oldest and closest friend—a man three months younger than myself. Our friendship had begun at school when we were thirteen years old and had continued for more than sixty years before he died. One could hardly suffer a greater loss than I suffered in losing him. Yet I could not and cannot regret his death, grievously though I miss him; for his death was, for him a merciful release from a distress that was irremediable and that was becoming excruciating for him. As for those other three friends of mine, they did not suffer as my poor school fellow suffered; for their mental eclipse was, not partial, but total—as complete as if they had been dead physically as well as mentally—and, for two of the three, this mental death, so far from being a torment, was a release from acute unhappiness. One of these two had previously been in a constant state of painful anxiety, fretfulness, and tension; and, for her, senility brought with it a serenity that she had not enjoyed since her early years. The other, who was love incarnate, had been inconsolable for the loss of her husband till she was released from her unbearable grief by oblivion—a mental death which was a merciful anticipation of the physical death that was tardy in coming to her rescue.

This two-sidedness of death is a fundamental feature of death—not only of the premature death of the spirit, but of death at any age and in any form. There are always two parties to a death; the person who dies and the survivors who are bereaved.

Death releases its prey instantly from all further suffering in this world —and from any further suffering at all, if one does not believe in personal immortality or in metempsychosis, but believes either that death spells annihilation or that it spells reabsorption into the Ultimate Spiritual Reality from which the life of a human personality is a temporary aberration.

Lucretius believed that death spells annihilation, and that it therefore confers on the dead a total and everlasting immunity from suffering, either mental or physical. He preaches the nihilist gospel of salvation with a passionate conviction and a fervent concern for the relief of his fellow mortals that make this passage of his poem[2] particularly memorable.

> Death, then is null for us—null and irrelevant—in virtue of the conclusion that the spirit of man is mortal. We felt no ill in that past age in which the Phoenicians were flocking to battle from all quarters—an age in which the whole earth was rocked by the fearful turmoil of war, rocked till it quaked horrifyingly under the lofty ceiling of the air; an age in which the fate of all mankind was trembling in the balance. One of the two contending powers was going to win worldwide dominion on both land and sea, and none could foresee which of the two would be the winner. Well, we felt no ill in that age, and we shall feel no ill, either, when we have ceased to exist—when once soul and body, whose union constitutes our being, have parted company with each other. We shall have ceased to exist; that is the point; and this means that, thenceforward, nothing whatsoever can happen to us, that nothing can awaken any feeling in us—no, not even if land were to fuse with sea, and sea with sky . . .[3]
>
> We can feel assured that, in death, there is nothing to be afraid of. If one is nonexistent, one is immune from misery. When once immortal death has relieved us of mortal life, it is as good as if we had never been born . . .[4]
>
> So, when you see someone indulging indignantly in self-pity [at the thought of his body's destiny after death], you may be sure that, though he himself may deny that he believes that, in death, he will retain any capacity for feeling, his profession of faith does not ring true. It is belied by a latent emotion that is subconscious. As I see it, he is not really conceding his premise and its basis. He is not removing and ejecting himself from life radically. Unconsciously he is making some vestige of himself survive . . . He is not dissociating himself fully from his castaway corpse; he is identifying himself with it and is infusing into it his own capacity for feeling, under the illusion that he is standing there beside it. This is the cause of his indignant self-pity at having been created mortal. He fails to see that, in real death, he will have no second self that will be still alive and capable of

lamenting to itself over its own death, or of grieving, as he stands, in imagination, over his prostrate self, that he is being mangled by beasts of prey or is being cremated.[5]

Lucretius goes on to put his finger on the difference between the fate of the dead and the fate of the survivors. He pictures a dead man's wife and children saying, as they stand by his funeral pyre:

"Poor wretch, what a wretched fate. One cruel day has deprived you of all the blessings of life." But, in this pass, they do not go on to say: "However, death has simultaneously released you from any desire for these blessings." If they realised this truth clearly and matched it in what they said, they would be able to release their souls from a heavy burden of anguish and fear. "You," they would say, "are now oblivious in death, and in that state you will remain until the end of time, exempt from all pain and grief. It is we who are the sufferers; it is we who, standing by you, reduced to ashes on the appalling pyre, have mourned you to the limit of human capacity for grief, and find ourselves still inconsolable. Our sorrow is everlasting. The day will never come that will relieve our hearts of it."[6]

From this Lucretius draws the following conclusion in the lines that immediately follow.

So this man [who feels an indignant self-pity in contemplating his future after death] has to be confronted with the question: What is there that is particularly bitter in this future, if it is just a return to sleep and quiet? What is there in this prospect that should make anyone pine away in everlasting grief?[7]

This lapse of a sensitive spirit into such obtuse complacency pulls up Lucretius's reader with a jerk. Is a man who is feeling distress at the prospect of his own death going to be totally relieved by the realization that his death will automatically bring with it an immunity from suffering from himself? Is he going to feel no concern for the grief of his bereaved wife and children? Is his certainty of "everlasting" peace and quiet for himself in death going to console him for the "everlasting" sorrow of the survivors?

It may be answered that, though the poet has used—and perhaps deliberately used—the same word "everlasting" to describe the respective states of the survivors and of the dead, the application of the word to the survivors is an exaggeration, considering that they, in their turn, are going to attain, sooner or later, "the return to sleep and quiet" that death brings to every mortal in the end. Meanwhile, they are going, on Lucretius's own showing, to experience the extreme of suffering; and Lucretius has denied himself the license to play this suffering down on the ground that it will be only temporary; for in a later passage,[8] he argues, eloquently and convincingly, that the fancied everlasting torments of the damned in hell after death are fabulous projections of genuine torments—mostly self-inflicted—which we experience in this life. "It is here, in this world," he sums up the argument of this passage in its last line, "that people make life hell through their own stupidity." Yet he has admitted that bereavement makes life hell, here in this world, for the bereaved. Is he prepared to write off their torment, too, as the self-inflicted penalty for a stupidity that is avoidable and reprehensible?

The truth is that Lucretius has been preoccupied by his characteristically impetuous effort to deprive death of its sting and the grave of its victory for the person who is dreading the prospect of death for himself. He has overlooked the crucial fact that, in death, there are two parties to the event. "For none of us liveth to himself and no man dieth to himself."[9] Man is a social creature; and a fact of capital importance about death's sting is that it is two-pronged. Lucretius may have succeeded in excising the sting for the person who dies, but he has failed to excise it for the dead's survivors. It looks, indeed, as if he has been blind to the significance of the pain of bereavement that he has described incidentally in such moving words. Euripides had been more perceptive. After asking if the experience that we call dying is not really living, and if living is not really dying,[10] he immediately goes on to observe that the spectators of a death are not saved from suffering by their awareness that the dead are exempt from all suffering and from all ills.

When, therefore, I ask myself whether I am reconciled to death, I have to distinguish, in each variant of the situation, between being reconciled to death on my own account and being reconciled to it on the account of the other party. Supposing that I am really reconciled to the prospect of my own death at a ripe old age, am I also reconciled to the prospect of the sorrow and the loneliness that death is going to bring upon my wife if she survives me? Supposing that I feel that people who have risked and suffered premature death deliberately for the sake of fellow human beings have found a satisfactory fulfilment of the possibilities of life for themselves, am I reconciled to the loss that their premature deaths have inflicted on mankind, including me? (This question is the theme of George Meredith's novel *Beauchamp's Career.*) Supposing that I feel that the oblivion conferred by senility or insanity has been a boon for someone who was suffering spiritual agony so long as he was in full possession of his mental and spiritual faculties, am I reconciled to my loss of this friend through his lapse into a death-in-life? And, apart from my personal loss, am I reconciled to the brutal affront to human dignity that nature has committed in choosing this humiliating way of releasing a human being from spiritual suffering?

Finally, am I reconciled to the prospect that I may survive my wife, even supposing that she lives to a ripe old age in full possession of her faculties and without suffering more than the minimum of physical pain that is the normal accompaniment of death even in its easiest forms, with the exception of instantaneous deaths and deaths in sleep? The hard fact is that the ways of dying that impose the lightest ordeal on the person who dies are, by their very nature, the ways that inevitably make the shock for the survivors the severest. I have mentioned an old friend of mine whose unbearable grief for the death of her husband was eventually obliterated by the oblivion of senility. The shock that she had suffered had been extreme. She had found her husband lying dead in his bed one morning. He had appeared to be in normal health the day before; but for some years his heart had been weak, and he had died from heart failure in his sleep—peacefully and almost certainly painlessly; I myself recently had the experience of receiving a severe shock from learning of the sudden death of someone with whom my life had once been intimately bound up, though, in this case too, the death had not been a lingering one or been physically painful, and had come at an age—six months younger than mine—at which death is to be expected.

If one truly loves a fellow human being, one ought to wish that as little as possible of the pain of his or her death shall be suffered by him or by her, and that as much of it as possible shall be borne by oneself. One ought to wish this, and one can, perhaps, succeed in willing it with one's mind. But can one genuinely desire it in one's heart? Can one genuinely long to be the survivor at the coming time when death will terminate a companionship that is more precious to one than one's life—a companionship without which one's life would be a burden, not a boon? Is it possible for love to raise human nature to this height of unselfishness? I cannot answer this question for anyone except myself, and, in my own case, before the time comes, I can only guess what my reaction is likely to be. I have already avowed a boastful guess that I shall be able to meet my own death with equanimity. I have now to avow another guess that puts me to shame. I guess that if, one day, I am told by my doctor that I am going to die before my wife, I shall receive the news not only with equanimity but with relief. This relief, if I do feel it, will be involuntary. I shall be ashamed of myself for feeling it, and my relief will, no doubt, be tempered by concern and sorrow for my wife's future after I have been taken from her. All the same, I do guess that, if I am informed that I am going to die before her, a shameful sense of relief will be one element in my reaction.

My own conclusion is evident. My answer to Saint Paul's question "O death, where is thy sting?" is Saint Paul's own answer: "The sting of death is sin." The sin that I mean is the sin of selfishly failing to wish to survive the death of someone with whose life my own life is bound up. This is selfish because the sting of death is less sharp for the person who dies than it is for the bereaved survivor.

This is, as I see it, the capital fact about the relation between living and dying. There are two parties to the suffering that death inflicts; and, in the apportionment of this suffering; the survivor takes the brunt.

Notes

1 *Iliad,* Book XVII, line 647.

2 Lucretius *De Rerum Natura,* Book III, lines 830–930, minus lines 912–18, which have been misplaced in the surviving manuscripts.

3 *Ibid.,* lines 830–42.

4 *Ibid.,* lines 866–69.

5 *Ibid.,* lines 870–87.

6 *Ibid.*, lines 898-908.
7 *Ibid.*, lines 909–11.
8 *Ibid.*, lines 973–1023.
9 Rom. 14:7.
10 Fragment from Euripides' lost play *Phrixus*....

23 · The Broken Heart

Colin Murray Parkes

Colin Murray Parkes is a psychiatrist at Tavistock Institute of Human Relations in London and is on the staff of St. Christopher's Hospice. Dr. Parkes and his associates have conducted perhaps the most impressive systematic study in the field of bereavement with an investigation of twenty-two London widows for a period of thirteen months, following the deaths of their husbands. In this selection, Dr. Parkes relates some of his more significant findings concerning the impact of death on survivors.

He only without framing word, or closing his eyes, but earnestly viewing the dead body of his son, stood still upright, till the vehemence of his sad sorrow, having suppressed and choaked his vitall spirits, fell'd him starke dead to the ground.

Montaigne's description of the death of John, King of Hungaria

Is grief a cause of death? You will not find grief on a death certificate, not today. But the notion that one may die of grief is a popular theme among novelists and it is not long ago that it was a recognized cause of death.

Thus, in Dr. Heberden's Bill classifying the causes of death in London during the year 1657 we find:

Flox and Small Pox	835
Found dead in the streets, etc.	9
French Pox	25
Gout	8

Griefe	10
Griping and Plague in the Guts	446
Hang'd and made away 'emselves	24

Such figures would today be dismissed as examples of medical mythology, but is there in fact any evidence that grief is sometimes a cause of death?

There is, of course, no doubt that psychological factors play a part in many illnesses, but it is only in rare cases of "vagal inhibition" and in so-called voodoo deaths that they appear to be the sole cause. Vagal inhibition is a pseudoscientific term sometimes used by doctors for the cause of death following a sudden emotional shock. A classic example is provided in the story of some students who held a mock trial and sentenced a man to death. He was led to the place of execution, blindfolded, and hit on the back of the neck with a towel—whereupon he died. Not dissimilar are the numerous well-authenticated cases of death from witchcraft. Although the witchcraft can take many different forms, such deaths seem to follow a general pattern. The "victim" is told that the appropriate ritual curse has been carried out; if he has faith he at once becomes deeply depressed, stops eating, and within a few days is dead. In neither the vagal inhibition type of death nor death from witchcraft is there any postmortem finding that explains the phenomenon.

Such occurrences are fortunately very rare, but there is other evidence of the effect of psychological factors on mortality among the unhealthy and aging. Aldrich and Mendkoff, for instance, discovered a major increase in mortality among chronically sick patients when a Chicago Home for Incurables was closed for administrative reasons. Of 182 patients who were relocated in other homes, thirty were dead within three months—a mortality rate five times greater than expectation. Mortality was highest among those patients whose grasp on reality was most tenuous, particularly among the thirty-eight whom Aldrich rated as "psychotic" before relocation, of whom twenty-four died within a year (Aldrich & Mendkoff, 1963).

Apart from a few isolated cases of doubtful authenticity, I have come across no evidence that phenomena such as these are responsible for death following bereavement. The examples have been quoted simply to remind the reader that psychological factors can have profound effects even on healthy people.

For many years it has been known that widows and widowers have a higher mortality rate than married men and women of the same age. But then so have bachelors and spinsters, and it is not unreasonable to suspect that some of the fitter widows and widowers remarry, thereby ensuring that those who remain will have a relatively high mortality rate.

This explanation might certainly account for an increased mortality rate among the widowed population as a whole but it would not explain the peak of mortality in widowers during the first year of bereavement as discovered by Michael Young and his colleagues (Young, Benjamin & Wallis, 1963). They found an increase in the death rate among 4,486 widowers over the age of fifty-four of almost 40 percent during the first six months of bereavement.

This dropped off rapidly thereafter to around the mortality rate for married men of the same age.

Independent confirmation of this observation has more recently come from a study of a semirural community in Wales (Rees & Lutkins, 1967). A survey of 903 close relatives of 371 residents who died during 1960–65 showed that 4.8 percent of them died within one year of bereavement compared with only 0.7 percent of a comparable group of nonbereaved people of the same age, living in the same area. The mortality rate was particularly high for widows and widowers, 12 percent of whom died during the same period.

These two studies established a statistical relationship between bereavement and an increase in the deathrate, but they did not explain this association, and it is still not known why bereaved people tend to die more readily than the nonbereaved.

Several diseases seem to contribute to the higher mortality but recent work has indicated that the most frequent cause of death is heart disease. The paper by Young *et al.* (1963) on the deathrate among widowers was used as the basis of a further study (carried out by Parkes, Benjamin & Fitzgerald, 1969) of the causes of death among these same widowers as revealed on their death certificates. It was soon apparent that three-quarters of the increased deathrate during the first six months of bereavement was attributable to heart disease, in particular to coronary thrombosis and arteriosclerotic heart disease.

The origin of the term "broken heart" goes back to biblical times. "Bind up the broken hearted," says Isaiah, and the idea seems to have persisted ever since that severe grief can somehow damage the heart. Benjamin Rush, the American physician and signatory of the Declaration of Independence, wrote in his *Medical Inquiries and Observations upon the Diseases of the Mind* (1835): "Dissection of persons who have died of grief, show congestion in, and inflammation of the heart, with rupture of its auricles and ventricles." Rupture of the heart is, of course, a rare condition, but when it does occur it is usually caused by a coronary thrombosis. All of which leads us to suspect that the old physicians may not have been as foolish as we suppose. (In case any bereaved reader is now clutching his chest and preparing to call an ambulance may I hasten to point out that palpitations and a feeling of fullness in the chest are normal concomitants of anxiety and that bereaved people often experience them without developing heart disease.)

The fact that bereavement may be followed by death from heart disease does not prove that grief is itself a cause of death. We do not even know whether bereavement causes the illness or simply aggravates a condition that would have occurred anyway. Perhaps bereaved people tend to smoke more or to alter their diet in a way that increases their liability to coronary thrombosis. Even if emotional factors are directly implicated we still have to explain how they affect the heart. Stress is known to produce changes in the blood pressure and heartrate, in the flow of blood through the coronary arteries and in the chemical constituents of the blood. Any of these changes could play a part in precipitating clotting within a diseased coronary artery and thereby produce a coronary thrombosis, but without further research we can only speculate.

It may be that measures aimed at reducing the stress of bereavement will help to prevent such consequences. If so, then giving help to the bereaved is a practical contribution to public health.

What other effects does bereavement have upon health? Many physical and mental illnesses have been attributed to loss. Usually the attribution is based on the observation that the illness in question came on shortly after a loss. But since losses of one sort or another occur in the lives of all of us, a chance association between illness and loss is always possible. Furthermore, the distinction between physical and psychological symptoms soon breaks down. In this selection I discuss, first, the types of condition that are commonly brought to the attention of a physician or general practitioner, and I then go on to look at the symptoms of bereaved psychiatric patients. But it will soon be obvious that there is a considerable overlap.

Some of the better studies of the psychosomatic effects of loss have come from the Strong Memorial Hospital in Rochester, USA, where a group of psychiatrists have developed the theory that it is the feelings of helplessness and hopelessness that may accompany loss that are responsible for physical illness. In one remarkable study, women suspected of having cancer of the womb were "diagnosed" by a psychiatrist with striking accuracy (Schmale and Iker, 1966). These women had been admitted for investigation after a routine vaginal smear had revealed the presence of ugly-looking cells which might or might not indicate cancer. At this stage nobody knew whether a cancer was present or not, and a minor operation was necessary to prove or disprove such a diagnosis. The psychiatrist, who was as ignorant as anyone of the true situation, interviewed each woman and asked her about her feelings about any recent losses in her life. When he found evidence of both loss and feelings of helplessness or hopelessness, he predicted that this woman would, in fact, be found to have cancer. In 71 percent of cases his diagnosis proved to be correct.

The skeptic will point out that perhaps unbeknown to the doctor, these women did have an inkling of their true diagnosis and it was this knowledge that influenced their feelings or their tendency to recall recent losses in their lives. Similar bias could conceivably explain the high rates of loss which have been reported in cases of leukemia, ulcerative colitis, and asthma. But these results cannot be ignored and it is to be hoped that the necessary work will soon be done to establish the chain of causation. It will indeed be remarkable if psychiatrists have discovered a cause of cancer.

In studies of this type the investigator starts with a person who is sick, or suspected of being sick, and attempts to find out whether he has suffered a loss prior to the onset of his illness. Such studies always carry a risk of retrospective bias. Another way of proceeding is to start with a person who is known to have suffered a loss and to find out what illnesses he contracts thereafter. This approach has been adopted in several studies of bereaved people. For example, seventy-two East London widows were interviewed by Peter Marris on average two years after they had been bereaved; thirty-one (43 percent) thought that their general health was now worse than it had been before bereavement (Marris, 1958). In another study by Hobson (1964), a similar proportion of widows (seventeen out of forty) from a midland market town made the same assertion. According to both these studies the number of complaints attributed to bereavement was very large. Headaches, digestive upsets, rheumatism, and asthma were particularly frequent.

But such symptoms were common enough in any group of women and might have occurred by chance alone. Moreover, "general health" is a woolly concept of doubtful validity. In a study of twenty-two London widows (referred to henceforth as the London study) I attempted to obtain a number of different estimates of general health. I asked the widows to rate their own health as "good," "indifferent," or "bad" at each of five interviews carried out at intervals during their first year of bereavement. I also counted the number of consultations each widow had with her GP in the course of the year, and in addition checked off on a standard list the symptoms she claimed to have suffered each time I visited her. Naturally I anticipated that the widows who said that their general health was bad would be the ones who had consulted their GP most frequently and suffered the largest number of symptoms. It came as a surprise to find that this was not the case. The only thing that was found to distinguish the widows who said that their health was bad was a quite separate series of assessments of irritability and anger. Anger and irritability, it seemed, were accompanied by a subjective feeling of ill health which was not reflected in any particular symptom or in a tendency to consult the doctor (Parkes, 1970).

There is evidence, nevertheless, that newly bereaved people do consult their doctors more often than they did before bereavement. In one study of the case records of eight London general practitioners I was able to identify forty-four widows who had been registered[1] with their GP for 2 years before and 1½ years after bereavement.

Three-quarters of these widows consulted their GP within six months of bereavement and this was a 63 percent increase over the number who had consulted him in a similar period prior to bereavement. The largest increase was in consultations for anxiety, depression, insomnia, and other psychological symptoms, which were clearly attributable to grief. But it was surprising to find that the rise in consultations for such symptoms was confined to widows under 65 years of age. Older people did not, apparently, consult their doctor about these matters.

Consultations for physical symptoms, however, had increased in all age groups, most notably for arthritis and rheumatic conditions. Psychological factors are known to play a part in rheumatism but many of these widows had osteoarthritis, a condition that takes years to develop. It seems therefore that, as with coronary thrombosis, the bereavement probably did not originate the condition but aggravated one that was already present. It is possible, too, that the widows were using their arthritis as an excuse to visit their doctor and that the higher consultation rate reflected a need for help which had little to do with their physical state (Parkes, 1964b).

A useful series of studies which does not rely on the widow consulting her doctor has been carried out by Professor Maddison from the University of Sydney, Australia (Maddison and Viola, 1968). Maddison has devised a postal questionnaire which asks respondents fifty-seven questions about their health over the preceding year. This has now been completed by 132 American and 221 Australian widows thirteen months after bereavement, and by control groups of married women. All were under the age of sixty. Of the total sample of widows, 28 percent obtained scores indicating "marked" deterioration in health, compared with only 4.5 percent of the married women.

Symptoms that were commoner in the bereaved than in the married groups included: nervousness, depression, fears of nervous breakdown, feelings of panic, persistent fears, "peculiar thoughts," nightmares, insomnia, trembling, loss of appetite (or, in a few, excessive appetite), loss of weight, reduced working capacity, and fatigue. All these symptoms are features of "normal" grief, and it is not surprising to find them complained of by a group of newly bereaved widows. But Maddison found also, in the widows, excessive incidence of symptoms that were less obviously features of grieving. These included headaches, dizziness, fainting spells, blurred vision, skin rashes, excessive sweating, indigestion, difficulty in swallowing, vomiting, heavy menstrual periods, palpitations, chest pains, shortness of breath, frequent infections, and general aching.

Many of Maddison's findings have subsequently been confirmed in a study of sixty-eight Boston widows and widowers under the age of forty-five, which I have been carrying out with Ira Glick, Robert Weiss, Gerald Caplan, and others at Harvard Medical School (Glick, Weiss and Parkes, 1974). (This study is henceforth referred to as the Harvard study.) These unselected widows and widowers were interviewed fourteen months after bereavement and compared with a control group of sixty-eight married men and women of the same age, sex, occupational class, and family size. The bereaved group showed evidence of depression and of general emotional disturbance as reflected in restlessness and insomnia, and in having difficulty in making decisions and remembering things. Also, they consumed more tranquilizers, alcohol, and tobacco than they had done prior to bereavement. They were distinguished from the nonbereaved group by the frequency of their complaints of physical symptoms indicative of anxiety and tension; however, they did not show, as older bereaved subjects have shown in other studies, a large increase in physical ailments. The incidence of headaches, for instance, and of muscular and joint affections was no greater in the bereaved than in the control group.

Four times as many bereaved as nonbereaved had spent part of the preceding year in hospital, and the bereaved group sought advice for emotional problems from ministers, psychiatrists, and (occasionally) social workers more often than did the nonbereaved. But it came as a surprise to find that there was no difference between the two groups as regards the number of outpatient or private consultations they had had with a doctor. Clearly, the physician is not the person to whom the young Boston widow or widower turns for help. As far as the widows are concerned, financial considerations may play a part here. Like her British counterpart, the American widow tends to suffer a sharp drop in income; unlike the British widow, however, she has to pay her own medical bills. Although three-quarters of the American widows had health insurance, this does not usually cover the cost of private consultation with a physician which, in Britain, would be obtainable without charge. Inpatient services, on the other hand, are covered by health insurance and it did not appear that American widows and widowers were deterred from entering hospital for treatment (see Parkes and Brown, 1972).

In presenting evidence gleaned from several different studies concerning the effects of bereavement on physical health, I may be producing confusion when my aim is to dispel it. It would be so much simpler if one could state dogmatically that bereavement is a cause of headaches, osteoarthritis, and coronary thrombosis, and leave it at that; or, better still, go on to explain how it causes such conditions. But the evidence (which is reviewed fully in Parkes, 1970a) does not yet justify dogmatism. So what conclusions are possible?

I think we can justly claim that many widows and widowers seek help during the months that follow the death of their spouse, and that the professional persons they most often go to are medical practitioners and ministers of religion. I accept the evidence that bereavement can affect physical health, and that complaints of somatic anxiety symptoms, headaches, digestive upsets, and rheumatism, are likely, particularly in widows and widowers in middle age. Finally, there are certain potentially fatal conditions, such as coronary thrombosis, blood cancers, and cancer of the neck of the womb, which seem in some cases to be precipitated or aggravated by major losses.

Beyond this we cannot go. I have no doubt that further research in these areas will soon be undertaken and that many of the questions raised by these findings will be answered.

Is there also evidence that bereavement can produce frank mental illness? Here it is possible to speak with more confidence since grief has been a subject of detailed study in recent years. Nevertheless we shall soon enter the realms of speculation when we try to explain why one person recovers more easily than another from the psychological effects of bereavement. The only safe course is to review the evidence as concisely as possible so that the reader can make up his or her own mind what conclusions are justified.

From the case summaries of 3,245 adult patients admitted to two psychiatric units during 1949–51, I was able to identify ninety-four (2.9 percent) whose illness had come on within six months of the death of a parent, spouse, sibling, or child. No doubt there were others among these patients who had been bereaved, but this fact was not mentioned in the case summary; and I am sure that there would be others again in whom the onset of mental illness had been delayed for more than six months after the bereavement that caused it. However, it was necessary to confine attention to those patients whose illness could reasonably be supposed to have something to do with bereavement.

Since bereavement is not an uncommon event, it was necessary to discover first whether the association between bereavement and mental illness could be due to chance alone. That is to say, would the patient have become ill at this time whether he had been bereaved or not? I compared the number of spouse bereavements which had actually occurred in the psychiatric population with the number that could have been expected to occur by chance association. The expected number of spouse bereavements was calculated from the registrar general's mortality tables for England and Wales covering the same years as the study. It transpired that thirty of the ninety-four patients had been admitted for illnesses which had come on within six months of the death of a spouse, whereas only five spouse-bereaved patients would have been expected by chance alone (see Parkes, 1964a).

Similar conclusions were reached by Stein & Susser (1969) in two carefully conducted studies of psychiatric care in Salford, England. These studies showed an abnormally large proportion of widows and widowers among people coming into psychiatric care for the first time in their lives and an abnormally large proportion of recently bereaved among these widowed patients.

To return to the ninety-four bereaved psychiatric patients identified from their case notes: the diagnoses made by the psychiatrists in these cases were ascertained and compared with the diagnoses made on the 3,151 patients who had not, according to their case records, been bereaved. Two main findings were: first, that the bereaved patients had been diagnosed as suffering from many different types of psychiatric illness; and, second, that the most common single diagnosis in this group was reactive or neurotic depression. This was the diagnosis for 28 percent of the bereaved patients and for only 15 percent of those who had not been bereaved.

From the case records of the bereaved patients it became apparent that, at the time of their admission to hospital, which was usually about a year after bereavement, many of them were still suffering from grief. Grief, which one normally expects to occur shortly after bereavement and to fade gradually in intensity as time passes, was not only still being experienced by these patients but was an integral part of the illness that had brought them into psychiatric care.

In other cases, however, the mental illness did not seem to involve grieving. For instance, several patients who had always been heavy drinkers had developed alcoholic psychoses after the death of a close family member. Here the symptoms were the symptoms of alcoholism and if there was any persisting tendency to grieve this was not an obvious part of the clinical picture. Bereavement, in these cases, had been the "last straw," resulting in the breakdown of individuals whose previous adjustment had been precarious.

This study (henceforth referred to as the case-note study) revealed quite clearly the important part that bereavement can play in producing mental illness. It also indicated that the mental illnesses that follow bereavement often seem to comprise pathological forms of grieving. But case notes are not the most reliable source of research data and, while many of the case histories contained a full and convincing account of the patient's reaction to bereavement, there were others in which the reaction was not described in any detail. Obviously, a more systematic investigation of bereaved psychiatric patients was required. Research was needed, too, to determine what is a "normal" or "typical" reaction to bereavement.

Two studies were undertaken with these aims in view, the Bethlem study and the London study. . . . The London study, to which reference has been made above, was carried out after the Bethlem study but it will simplify matters if it is discussed first.

It is sometimes said that psychiatrists get a distorted view of life because they see only people who have failed to master the stresses they encounter. The London study was an attempt to find out how an unselected group of twenty-two London widows under the age of sixty-five would cope with the stress of bereavement. It was undertaken with the intention of establishing a picture of "normal grief" among young and middle-aged widows. Older widows were excluded because . . . there is reason to regard grief in old age as a rather different phenomenon from the grief of younger people. Whatever the cause of this, it would have confused the overall picture too much to include older people in this survey.

Widows who agreed to help were brought to my attention by their general practitioners. These GPs had been asked to refer every woman in their practice who lost her husband and not to pick out those with special psychological difficulties. However, there were some widows who were not referred, either because they refused to take part or because the GP did not want to upset them. On subsequent inquiry, GPs did not think that these widows differed to any marked extent from those who were referred and it appears that those who were interviewed were a fairly representative sample of London widows.

They were seen by me at the end of the first month of bereavement, and again at the third, sixth, ninth, and thirteenth months, a minimum of five interviews in all. Essentially I was studying the first year of bereavement. However, in order to include but not be overinfluenced by the anniversary reaction, I carried out the "end-of-year" interview one month late. This enabled me to obtain an account of the anniversary reaction and also to get an idea of how the widow was adjusting now that this crisis was past.

At the outset I had some misgivings about the entire project. It was not my wish to intrude upon private grief and I was quite prepared to abandon the study if it seemed that my questions were going to cause unnecessary pain. In fact, discussion of the events leading up to the husband's death and of the widow's reaction to them did cause pain, and it was quite usual for widows to break down and cry at some time during our first interview; but with only one exception they did not regard this as a harmful experience. On the contrary, the majority seemed grateful for the opportunity to talk freely about the disturbing problems and feelings that preoccupied them. The first interview usually lasted from two to three hours, not because I had planned it that way but because the widow needed that amount of time if she was to "talk through" the highly charged experiences that were on her mind. Once she found that I was not going to be embarrassed or upset by her grief she seemed to find the interview therapeutic and, although I took pains to explain that this was a research project, I had no sense of intrusion after the first few minutes of the initial contact. (Statistical findings are given in Parkes, 1970b.)

The aim of the Bethlem study was to investigate atypical reaction to bereavement. Interviews were obtained between 1958 and 1960 with twenty-one bereaved patients at the Bethlem Royal and Maudsley Hospitals. Of the twenty-one patients, four were male and seventeen female. Most of them were seen soon after entering psychiatric treatment, at which time they had been bereaved for an average of seventy-two weeks (the range was from four to 367 weeks). (For further details see Parkes, 1965.)

In both the London Study and the Bethlem Study bereaved people were asked to tell me, in their own words, about their bereavement and how they reacted to it. Questions were kept to a minimum and simply ensured that comparable information about critical events was obtained in each case. Some notes, particularly records of significant verbatim statements, were taken at the time and some assessments were made immediately after the interview. These were recorded on a survey form which was also used as an *aide-mémoire* during the interview.

Following these two studies, which revealed, respectively, typical and atypical forms that the reaction to bereavement can take, the Harvard study was carried out. This investigation had a rather different object in view. It had been established from earlier work that grief normally follows a certain pattern but that pathological variants sometimes occur, and a group of us now wanted to discover why most people come through the stress of bereavement unscathed whereas others break down with some physical or mental illness. We also wanted to see if it was possible to identify, at the time of a bereavement, those who would be likely to get into difficulties later. Since previous research had shown that the health risk was greatest in young widows, we focused our attention on people under the age of forty-five who had lost a spouse. And because widowers had rarely featured in earlier investigations we included a group of them in this one. We contacted forty-nine widows and nineteen widowers by letter and telephone, and visited them in their homes three weeks and six weeks after bereavement, and again fourteen months after they had been bereaved when an assessment was made of their health. Our aim was to discover whether we could predict, from the evidence of the earlier interviews, how our subjects would be feeling and behaving a year later.

The Harvard study confirmed my expectation that American widows would be found to react to bereavement in a similar manner to the British widows who had been the subjects of my earlier studies. These studies were not carried out to prove or disprove any particular theory, but inevitably I felt constrained to group certain features together and to attempt an explanation of the process of grieving which would make sense of the data.

When, in 1959, I first reviewed the scientific literature on loss and grief I was struck by the absence of any reference in it to the common observation that animals, in their reaction to loss, show many of the features that are evident in human beings. One of the few people who have made this point is Charles Darwin who, in *The Expression of the Emotions in Man and Animals* (1872), described the way in which sorrow is expressed by animals, young children, and adult human beings. His work caused me to formulate a "biological theory of grief" which has been developed over the last decade but has not required major modification.

My preliminary formulation, which formed part of a dissertation for the Diploma in Psychological Medicine, had no sooner been submitted to the examiners when I was lent a duplicated copy of a paper which showed that many of the conclusions I had reached had been reached quite independently by John Bowlby (1951, 1961, 1963, 1969). Bowlby's review of the effects of maternal deprivation in childhood had appeared as a World Health Organization monograph in 1951 and has been followed by a series of papers aimed at clarifying the theoretical questions to which it gave rise. By 1959 Bowlby was well set in working out a comprehensive theory, the first part of which was already in print. I sent him a copy of my own dissertation at that time and subsequently (in 1962) joined his research staff at the Tavistock Institute of Human Relations. Since that time our collaboration has been close and I have made use of many of his ideas. These biographical details are mentioned because I am no longer sure which of us deserves the credit (or blame) for originating many of the ideas that make up the overall theory on these pages. All that I can say, with confidence, is that my debt to John Bowlby is great.

Note

1 Under the National Health Service each member of the British population is registered with a general practitioner who keeps a medical record on an envelope-card designed for the purpose. Most wives are registered with the same GP as their husbands.

References

Aldrich, C. K. and Mendkoff, E. (1963). Relocation of the Aged and Disabled: a Mortality Study, *J. Amer. Geriat. Soc.* II:185.

Bowlby, J. (1951). *Maternal Care and Mental Health.* WHO Monograph 2.

——— (1960). Grief and Mourning in Infancy and Early Childhood, *Psychoanal. Study Child* 15:9.

——— (1961a). Processes of Mourning. *Int. J. Psycho-Anal.* 44:317.

——— (1961b). Childhood Mourning and Its Implications for Psychiatry: the Adolf Meyer Lecture. *Amer. J. Psychiat.* 118:481.

——— (1963). Pathological Mourning and Childhood Mourning. *J. Amer. Psychoanal. Ass.* 11:500.

——— (1969). *Attachment and Loss.* Vol I, *Attachment.* London: Hogarth; New York: Basic Books.

Darwin C. (1872). *The Expression of the Emotions in Man and Animals.* London: Murray.

Glick, Ira O., Weiss, Robert S., and Parkes, C. M. (1974). *The First Year of Bereavement.* New York: John Wiley & Sons.

Hobson, C. J. Widows of Blackton. (1964). *New Society,* September 14.

Maddison, D. and Viola, A. (1968). The Health of Widows in the Year Following Bereavement. *J. Psychosom. Res.* 12:297.

Marris, P. (1958). *Widows and their Families.* London: Routledge.

Parkes, C. M. (1959). Morbid Grief Reactions: a Review of the Literature. Dissertation for DPM, University of London.

______ (1964a). Recent Bereavement as a Cause of Mental Illness. *Brit. J. Psychiat.* 110:198.

______ (1964b). The Effects of Bereavement on Physical and Mental Health: A Case Study of the Case Records of Widows. *Brit. Med. J.* (2)274.

______ (1965). Bereavement and Mental Illness. Pt. I, A Clinical Study of the Grief of Bereaved Psychiatric Patients. Pt. 2, A Classification of Bereavement Reactions. *Brit. J. Med. Psychol.* 38:1.

______ (1970a). The Psychosomatic Effects of Bereavement. In Oscar W. Hill (ed.), *Modern Trends in Psychosomatic Medicine.* London: Butterworth.

______ (1970b). The First Year of Bereavement: a Longitudinal Study of the Reaction of London Widows to the Death of their Husbands. *Psychiatry* 33:444.

Parkes, C. M., Benjamin, B., and Fitzgerald, R. G. (1969). Broken Heart: a Statistical Study of Increased Mortality among Widowers. *Brit, Med. J.* (I):740.

Parkes, C. M. and Brown, R. J. (1972). Health after Bereavement: A Controlled Study of Young Boston Widows and Widowers. *Psychosomatic Medicine,* 34:449-61.

Rees, W. D. and Lutkins, S. G. (1967). Mortality of Bereavement. *Brit. Med. J.* (4):13.

Rush, B. (1835). *Medical Inquiries and Observations upon the Diseases of the Mind.* Philadelphia: Grigg & Elliott.

Schmale, A. H. J. and Iker, H. P. (1966). The Affect of Hopelessness and the Development of Cancer. I, Identification of Uterine Cervical Cancer in Women with Atypical Cytology. *Psychosomat. Med.* 28:714.

Stein, Z. and Susser, M. W. (1969). Widowhood and Mental Illness. *Prev. & Soc. Med.* 23:106.

Young M., Benjamin, B., and Wallis, C. (1963). Mortality of Widowers. *Lancet* (2):454.

24· Postvention and the Survivor-Victim

Edwin S. Shneidman

The following selection is taken from Deaths of Man. *Here Dr. Shneidman introduces the view of the survivor as a victim and discusses working with survivors for several months after the death of a loved one—a type of therapy he calls "postvention."*

A person's death is not only an ending: it is also a beginning—for the survivors. Indeed, in the case of suicide the largest public health problem is neither the prevention of suicide (about 25,000 suicides are reported each year in the United States but the actual number is much higher, probably twice the reported rate) nor the management of suicide attempts (about eight times the number of reported committed suicides), but the alleviation of the effects of stress in the survivor-victims of suicidal deaths, whose lives are forever changed and who, over a period of years, number in the millions.

This is the process I have called "postvention": those appropriate and helpful acts that come *after* the dire event itself (1971, 1974, 1975). The reader will recognize prevention, intervention, and postvention as roughly synonymous with the traditional health concepts of primary, secondary, and tertiary prevention, or with concepts like immunization, treatment, and rehabilitation. Lindemann (1944) has referred to "preventive intervention in a four-year-old child whose father committed suicide"; it would be simpler to speak of postvention.

Postvention, then, consists of activities that reduce the aftereffects of a traumatic event in the lives of the survivors. Its purpose is to help survivors live longer, more productively, and less stressfully than they are likely to do otherwise.

It is obvious that some deaths are more stigmatizing or traumatic than others: death by murder, by the negligence of oneself or some other person, or by suicide. Survivor-victims of such deaths are invaded by an unhealthy complex of disturbing emotions: shame, guilt, hatred, perplexity. They are obsessed with thoughts about the death, seeking reasons, casting blame, and often punishing themselves.

The recent investigations of widows by Dr. C.M. Parkes (1970) are most illuminating. The principal finding of his studies is that independent of her age, a woman who has lost a husband recently is more likely to die (from alcoholism, malnutrition, or a variety of disorders related to neglect of self, disregard of a prescribed medical regimen or commonsense precautions, or even a seemingly unconscious boredom with life) or to be physically ill or emotionally disturbed than a nonwidowed person. The findings seem to imply that grief is itself a dire process, almost akin to a disease, and that there are subtle factors at work that can take a heavy toll unless they are treated and controlled.

These striking results have been intuitively known long before they were empirically demonstrated. The efforts of Erich Lindemann (1944), Gerald Caplan (1964), and Phyllis R. Silverman (1969) to aid survivors of "heavy deaths" were postventions based on the premise of heightened risk in bereaved persons. Lindemann's work (which led to his formulations of acute grief and crisis intervention) began with his treatment of the survivors of the tragic Coconut Grove nightclub fire in Boston in 1942, in which 499 persons died. Phyllis Silverman's projects, under the direction of Gerald Caplan, have centered around a widow-to-widow program. These efforts bear obvious similarities with the programs of "befriending" practiced by the Samaritans, an organization founded by the Reverend Chad Varah (1966; 1973) and most active in Great Britain.

On the basis of work with parents of adolescent (fifteen- to nineteen-year-old) suicides in Philadelphia, Herzog (1968) has enumerated three psychological stages of postventive care: (1) resuscitation: working with the initial shock of grief in the first twenty-four hours; (2) rehabilitation: consultations with family members from the first month to about the sixth month; and (3) renewal: the healthy tapering off of the mourning process, from six months on.

A case can be made for viewing the sudden death of a loved one as a disaster and, using the verbal bridge provided by that concept, learning from the professional literature on conventionally recognized disasters—sudden, unexpected events, such as earthquakes and large-scale explosions, that cause a large number of deaths and have widespread effects. Martha Wolfenstein (1957) has described a "disaster syndrome": a "combination of emotional dullness, unresponsiveness to outer stimulation and inhibition of activity. The individual who has just undergone disaster is apt to suffer from at least a transitory sense of worthlessness; his usual capacity for self-love becomes impaired."

A similar psychological contraction is seen in the initial shock reaction to catastrophic news—death, failure, disclosure, disgrace, the keenest personal loss. Studies of disastrous ship sinking by P. Friedman and L. Lum (1957) and of the effects of a tornado by A. F. Wallace (1956) both describe an initial psychic shock followed by motor retardation, flattening of affect, somnolence, amnesia, and suggestibility. There is marked increase in dependency needs with regressive behavior and traumatic loss of feelings of identity, and, overall, a kind of "affective anesthesia." There is an unhealthy docility, a cowed and subdued reaction. One is reminded of Lifton's (1967) description of "psychic closing off" and "psychic numbing" among the *Hibakusha,* the survivors of the atomic bomb dropped on Hiroshima:

> Very quickly — sometimes within minutes or even seconds — *Hibakusha* began to undergo a process of "psychic closing off"; that is, they simply ceased to feel. They had a clear sense of what was happening around them, but their emotional reactions were unconsciously turned off. Others' immersion in larger responsibilities was accompanied by a greater form of closing off which might be termed "psychic numbing." Psychic closing off could be transient or it could extend itself, over days and even months, into more lasting psychic numbing. In the latter cases it merged with feelings of depression and despair . . . In response to this general pattern of disintegration, *Hibakusha* did not seem to develop clearcut psychiatric syndromes. To describe the emotional state that did develop they frequently used a term which means a state of despondency, abstraction or emptiness, and may be translated as "state of collapse" or "vacuum state." Also relevant is a related state. . . a listlessness, withdrawn countenance, "expression of wanting nothing more," or what has been called in other contexts "the thousand-mile stare." Conditions like the "vacuum state" or "thousand-mile-stare" may be thought of as apathy but are also profound expressions of despair: a form of severe and prolonged psychic numbing in which the survivor's responses to his environment are

> reduced to a minimum—often to those necessary to keep him alive—and in which he feels divested of the capacity either to wish or will. . . . related forms of psychic numbing occur in people undergoing acute grief reactions as survivors of the deaths of family members—here vividly conveyed in a psychiatric commentary by Erich Lindemann (1944):
>
> "A typical report is this, 'I go through all the motions of living. I look after my children. I do my errands. I go to social functions, but it is like being in a play; it doesn't really concern me. I can't have any warm feelings. If I would have any feelings at all I would be angry with everybody'. . . . The absence of emotional display in this patient's face and actions was quite striking. Her face had a masklike appearance, her movements were formal, stilted, robotlike, without the fine play of emotional expression."

All this sounds remarkably like Henry Murray's (1967) description of partial death, those "psychic states characterized by a marked diminution or near-cessation of affect involving both hemispheres of concern, the inner and the outer world."

Postventive efforts are not limited to this initial stage of shock, but are more often directed to the longer haul, the day-to-day living with grief over a year or more following the first shock of loss. Postvention is in the honored tradition of holding a wake or sitting *shiva;* but it means more. Typically it extends over months during that critical first year, and it shares many of the characteristics of psychotherapy: talk, abreaction, interpretation, reassurance, direction, and even gentle confrontation. It provides an arena for the expression of guarded emotions, especially such negative affective states as anger, shame, and guilt. It puts a measure of stability into the grieving person's life and provides an interpersonal relationship with the therapist which can be genuine, in that honest feelings need not be suppressed or dissembled.

An example may be useful: Late one afternoon a beautiful nineteen-year-old girl was stabbed to death by an apparent would-be rapist in a government building. Within an hour her parents were hit between the eyes with the news (and this is the way these matters are usually handled) by two rather young, well-meaning, but inexperienced policemen. The victim was the couple's only child. Their immediate reactions were shock, disbelief, overwhelming grief, and mounting rage, most of it directed at the agency where the murder had occurred.

A few days later, right after the funeral, they were in the office of a high official who was attempting to tender his condolences when the mother said in an anguished tone: "There is nothing you can do!" To which, with good presence of mind, he answered that while it was true the girl could not be brought back to life, there was something that could be done. Whether he knew the term or not, it was postvention that he had in mind.

I began seeing the parents, usually together, sometimes separately. The principal psychological feature was the mother's anger. I permitted her to voice her grief and to vent her rage (sometimes even at me), while I retained the role of the voice of reason: empathizing with their state, recognizing the legitimacy of their feelings when I could, but not agreeing when in good conscience I could not agree. I felt that I was truly their friend, and I believed they felt so too.

A few months after the brutal murder, the mother developed serious symptoms that required major surgery, from which she made a good recovery. I had insisted that each of them see a physician for a physical examination. Although the mother had had similar difficulty some years before, the situation raises the intriguing (and unanswerable) question in my mind whether or not that organic flurry would have occurred in her body if she had not suffered the shock of her daughter's death. Whatever the answer to that may be, I doubt very much that she would have recovered so well and so rapidly if she had received no postventive therapy.

The parents had an extraordinarily good marriage. Many relatives gave them emotional support. The husband, more laconic and more stoic, was my principal cotherapist—although I did not forget his needs and saw him alone occasionally, when for example, his wife was in the hospital.

Several months after the tragedy the parents seemed to be in rather good shape, physically and emotionally, everything considered. They still had low-level grief, and no doubt always will. But what is most important for this discussion is that each of them has stated that the process of working through their grief was made easier for them and that the outcome was better and more quickly achieved (though not with undue haste) as a result of our postventive sessions, that something of positive value had been done for them, and that they felt that something of this nature ought to be done for more people who found themselves in similar situations.

Quite a few months have passed since the homicide, and the murderer has still not been apprehended. If an arrest is ever made, it will inevitably present renewed conflicts for the girl's parents, and a new question will be raised: Should someone also be concerned with the welfare of the parents of the accused after his arrest?

Most deaths occur in the hospitals, and the dying patient is often isolated and his awareness clouded by drugs. (We nowadays rarely see our loved ones die "naturally" at home—a common event a few generations ago.) The topic of death is an especially unpleasant one for medical personnel. Death is the enemy; death represents failure. It has been noted that physicians constitute one of the few groups (along with policemen and combat solidiers) licensed to take lives in our society; at the same time, however, relatively few physicians deal with dying patients (consider the vast numbers of orthopedists, dermatologists, obstetricians, pediatricians, psychiatrists, and other specialists who deal with conditions that only rarely result in death) and are therefore ill equipped to teach others about death comfortably and meaningfully.

From the point of view of the staff-patient relationship vis-á-vis death, there are essentially three kinds of hospital wards or services. They can be labeled benign, emergent, and dire. A benign ward is one on which deaths are not generally expected and the relationship between staff and patient may be of short or long duration: obstetrical services, orthopedic wards, psychiatric wards. A death on such a service is a sharp tragedy and cause for special self-examination. The reaction is both to loss of a person and to loss of control. The staff, typically, is not so much in mourning as in a state of shock at administrative and professional failure.

Emergency services are quite different. These are the hospital emergency room and the intensive care unit. Here death is not an uncommon experience but the relationship between staff and patient is short lived; the patient is hardly known as a person, and there is typically no time for meaningful interpersonal relationships to develop: the focus is on physiological functioning. Patients are often unconscious and almost always acutely ill. Death on such a service is not mourned as deep personal loss. It is a "happening," distressing but seldom totally unexpected. The staff—often self-selected—must be inured to the constant psychological toll of working in such a setting. The dangers are callousness, depression, and even acting out, especially in the forms of alcoholism, drug abuse, and heightened sexual activity.

It is the dire service that poses the most stressful problems for physicians and nurses. On such a ward the patients have grim prognoses (and are often doomed when they come to the ward, their illnesses diagnosed as cancer, leukemia, scleroderma, or whatever), and they remain there for an extended period of time, long enough for personal relations to be formed and for them to be known, loved, and then mourned as "real" human beings. Physicians practicing specialties dealing with fatal conditions—certain hematologists, oncologists, radiologists, and so on—know death all too intimately. Often there is not a week that is free of a death. The psychological stresses on such a service may be even greater for nurses, for they face the problem of giving intimate care, risking personal investment, and then dealing with loss.

Consider the following case: A thirty-year-old man was admitted to a hospital ward diagnosed as having leukemia in the terminal stage. He had an unusual combination of physical and personality characteristics that made him an especially "difficult" patient—not difficult in behavior, but difficult to see grow more ill and die: he was handsome, good-natured, alert; he had a keen sense of humor and was flirtatious with nurses, and through intermittent spells of depression and concern with dying he was remarkably brave, reassuring doctors and nurses and telling them not to worry about him or take it so hard. (It would have been much easier for them if he had been difficult in the usual sense—querulous, demanding, complaining; then they might have accommodated more easily to his death.)

As a consultant on the ward, I visited him each day, having been asked to see him because of his depression. He talked openly about the topic of death and his fears of pain, aloneness, and loss, and specifically about his own death and its meaning for his wife and children. These sessions were, by his own account, very meaningful to him. It was the kind of death work that is not unusual in this kind of circumstance. But what was of special professional interest was the behavior, both before and after his death, of a nurse and of his physician.

The nurse, an exceptionally attractive young woman, grew to like the patient very much, with feelings that seemed to strike deeper than routine professional countertransference. I once witnessed a fascinating scene in which the nurse was massaging the patient's back while his wife stood stiffly off to one side; it was an interesting question as to who, at that moment, "owned" the dying patient. (But this nurse was extraordinarily good with the wife, taking her out to dinner, helping her with her young children, making, in a friendly and noncompetitive way, a number of practical arrangements for her.) After the young man's death there were several mourners for whom postvention was necessary, and the nurse was one of them. She grieved for one she had loved and lost, and her grief was sharpened and complicated by its somewhat secret and taboo nature.

The reaction of the physician in the case, a hematologist in this forties, was rather different but no less intense. We had planned to get together after the patient's death to discuss, I thought, interesting features of the case and possible plans for future collaborative efforts. Instead, he came into my office and announced that the young man's death had been the last straw. He was sick and tired of having all the doctors in the country dump their dying patients on him. He wondered how I could bear to see the young man every day while he was dying, and I countered candidly that I had wondered the same thing about him. Mainly he wanted a safe arena in which to vent his feelings about having had enough of death and dying for a while. Within a few weeks he followed his announced intention of making a major change in his professional life: he accepted a faculty position in a medical school in another state and in a specialty other than hematology.

In my own postventive work I have come to at least a few tentative conclusions:

1. Total care of a dying person needs to include contact and rapport with the survivors-to-be.
2. In working with survivor-victims of dire deaths, it is best to begin as soon as possible after the tragedy; within the first seventy-two hours if possible.
3. Remarkably little resistance is met from survivor-victims; most are willing to talk to a professional person, specially one who has no ax to grind and no pitch to make.
4. The role of negative emotions toward the deceased—irritation, anger, envy, guilt—needs to be explored, but not at the very beginning.
5. The professional plays the important role of reality tester. He or she is

not so much the echo of conscience as the quiet voice of reason.

6. Medical evaluation of the survivors is crucial. One should be alert for possible decline in physical health and in overall mental well-being.

Three brief final points: Postvention can be viewed as prevention for the next decade or for the next generation; postvention can be practiced by nurses, lawyers, social workers, physicians, psychologists, and good neighbors and friends—thanatologists all; and a comprehensive total health program in any enlightened community will include all three elements of care: prevention, intervention and postvention.

References

Caplan, Gerald, *Principles of Preventive Psychiatry.* New York: Basic Books, 1964.

Friedman, Paul, and Lum, L. Some Psychiatric Notes on the *Andrea Doria* Disaster. *American Journal of Psychiatry* 114 (1957):426–32.

Herzog, Alfred A. Clinical Study of Parental Response to Adolescent Death by Suicide with Recommendations for Approaching the Survivors. In Norman L. Faberow (Ed.), *Proceedings of the Fourth International Conference for Suicide Prevention.* Los Angeles: Delmar Publishing Co., 1968.

Lifton, Robert Jay. *Death in Life: Survivors of Hiroshima.* New York: Random House, 1967.

Lindemann, Erich. Symptomatology and Management of Acute Grief. *American Journal of Psychiatry* (1944): 141–48.

Murray, Henry A. Dead to the World: The Passions of Herman Melville. In Edwin S. Shneidman (Ed.), *Essays in Self-Destruction.* New York: Science House, 1967.

Parkes, Colin Murray. The First Year of Bereavement: A Longitudinal Study of the Reaction of London Widows to the Death of Their Husbands. *Psychiatry* 33 (1970):444–67.

Shneidman, Edwin S. Prevention, Intervention and Postvention of Suicide. *Annals of Internal Medicine* 75 (1971):453–58.

Shneidman, Edwin S. *Deaths of Man.* New York: Penguin Books, 1974.

Shneidman, Edwin S. Postvention: The Care of the Bereaved. In Robert O. Pasnau (Ed.), *Consultation-Liaison Psychiatry.* New York: Grune and Stratton, 1975.

Silverman, Phyllis R. The Widow-to-Widow Program: An Experiment in Preventive Intervention. *Mental Hygiene.* 53 (1969):333–37.

Varah, Chad. *The Samaritans.* New York: Macmillan, 1966.

Varah, Chad. *The Samaritans in the 70's.* London: Constable, 1973.

Wallace, A. F. *Tornado in Worcester: An Exploratory Study of Individual and Community Behavior in an Extreme Situation.* Washington, D.C.: National Research Council, 1956.

Wolfenstein, Martha. *Disaster: A Psychological Essay.* New York: Macmillan, 1957.

25• Emotions: Their Presence and Impact upon the Helping Role

Larry A. Bugen

Larry A. Bugen is Director of Psychological Services at St. Edwards University, Austin, Texas, and co-founder of the Austin Stress Clinic.

To document the emotional realities of *helpers* who *interact with* persons needing services, I will explore the impact of emotions on caregivers working with people forced to confront a life-threatening illness. Two points should be made clear at the outset. First, a *helper* is a nurse, psychologist, physician, social worker, health educator, member of the clergy, or any other professional whose function it is to promote the health and well-being of people requesting aid. Second, to understand the impact of emotions on the helping role, it is necessary to view the professional not alone, but in interaction with persons needing help.

In most helper-patient relationships, each person values the other person in the interaction. A patient certainly values the training and expertise of the professional, whereas the professional values the health of the patient. They may differ, however, in the extent to which they value various issues related to health care. Dr. Sanchez, for instance, may value a bone marrow transplant, whereas Mrs. Clifton may not. Or Mrs. Clifton may desire to have her fears and emotional needs regarding treatment alleviated, whereas Dr. Sanchez may be either unable or reluctant to do so.

We can see that a triangular "network" is formed in these situations, consisting of (1) the professional, (2) the patient/client, and (3) some issue related to patient care. When a patient with emotional needs interacts with a professional who does not choose to acknowledge them, their network is out of balance.[1] In the case cited Mrs. Clifton is likely to experience additional stress and frustration as a result of her physician's failure to meet her needs. Since this particular network is out of balance, Mrs. Clifton will need to cope by (1) modifying her physician's willingness and/or ability to deal with emotions, (2) modifying her own need for emotional expression, or (3) meeting her needs in another network.

People who work with persons facing a life-threatening illness are quite aware of the presence of emotions. How do we as professionals cope with patient/client emotional expression or lack of it? Which emotions are most difficult to respond to? If a helper does have difficulty responding to someone with emotional needs, what resources are available to facilitate the process? When we work with the terminally ill, are we aware of how we feel during the moments we are with them? To whom can we turn when we have difficulty handling our own feelings? Can your emotional reaction to a person with a life-threatening illness affect your perception and treatment of that person?

To summarize:

1. All patients or clients have significant emotional needs that they must cope with to make successful progress.
2. All professionals have significant emotional needs that they must cope with to ensure successful intervention.
3. The helping network established by patients and professionals will not function well unless all of these emotional needs are faced.
4. Emotions, particularly anxiety, can affect professional perceptions, diagnosis, and even treatment of patients.

EMOTIONAL STATES OF PATIENTS

The emotional states of a person facing a life-threatening illness have received much attention in this volume and elsewhere; I will therefore discuss them only briefly. Three models for viewing the dying person exist: (1) the *stage model* proposed by E. Kübler-Ross,[12] (2) the *hive of affect model* proposed by E. Shneidman,[17] and (3) the *stereotyped model* suggested by A. Hutschnecker[8] and O. C. Simonton and S. S. Simonton.[18]

Kübler-Ross suggests that a person facing a life-threatening illness progresses through five relatively predictable stages: denial, anger, bargaining, depression, and acceptance. When first confronting the realization of death, people refuse to believe such a calamity could happen to them. They then become angry about the possibility of dying and may even demand to know "Why me?" Since hope is a powerful dynamic force throughout the dying process, they eventually attempt to make bargains with significant others such as physicians, nurses, or even God, "If I take my medication religiously, Doctor, can you promise that I will have another year?" When their futuristic hopes no longer appear viable, a depression sets in but it does not remain indefinitely. Finally the dying person begins to accept his or her lot and feel at peace both within and with the world around. It is at this time that he or she is ready to die.

The second view, proposed by Shneidman, suggests that a dying person manifests a "hive of affect" in which any one of a number of emotional states may emerge for a while. The dying person wavers between denial and acceptance, between disbelief and hope. One day the person may be ready for last rites and the next day be planning a trip to San Francisco. The extent of pain and the presence of symptoms are certainly powerful forces determining the vicissitudes of rage and envy alternating with acquiescence.

The third view of the dying person, provided by Hutschnecker and the Simontons, holds that the dying patient, even in the face of death, remains true to his or her personality.* In addition it is possible to distinguish cardiac patients from cancer patients and cancer patients from one another—all on the basis of personality or emotional expression. For instance, Hutschnecker classifies cancer patients as emotionally passive, dependent, and regressive. In contrast, cardiac patients are characterized as striving for success, aggressive and rebellious.

The three approaches described have come under close scrutiny. Bugen,[2] for instance, has questioned the validity of the need for distinct stages as proposed by Kübler-Ross. It is nevertheless safe to conclude that there is some truth in each of the models. One important element common to all three is the recognition that persons facing a life-threatening process all experience powerful emotions. However, professionals must understand that diversity, rather than sameness, is the rule. They must also be available or make resources available to promote sharing, talking, crying, or screaming if necessary.

EMOTIONAL STATES OF CAREGIVERS

Interaction with seriously ill people is of course a two-way street. Not only are the progress and welfare of the patient dependent on the attitudes and behaviors of the caregiver; the reverse appears to be true too: The emotional status of caregivers seems to be affected by interaction with persons suffering from life-threatening illnesses. What is the evidence for this contention? Reviews of the clinical literature by both Shady[16] and Schultz and Aderman[15], reach the same conclusion that caregivers must deal with their own feelings about death in order to effectively and comfortably deal with a person facing death. Without self-awareness, persons in a helping role are vulnerable to a wide variety of unpleasant, negative manifestations of anxiety. These aversive states include anger, guilt, helplessness, frustration, and feelings of inadequacy. If you are a caregiver, you might take a moment to reflect on whether you have experienced any of the above emotional states. Or perhaps the more relevant questions are "When was the last time?" and "How did you manage your feelings that time?"

In considering the impact of emotions on caregivers, a more detailed look at the literature seems appropriate. Most of the investigations on the helping role refer primarily to nurses. This is probably so because nurses are more willing to assume daily responsibility for seriously ill persons than other professionals. This is a testimonial to both the nurses' dedication to service and the need for making solid training in this area available to other health-care professionals.

*EDITOR'S NOTE *The author does not have these three views quite right. Shneidman also clearly believes that "each individual tends to die as he or she has lived, especially as he or she has previously reacted in periods of threat, stress, failure, challenge, shock and loss." The point is that the individual beehive of a person's way of dying mirrors or reflects the beehive of that person's life. (See E. Shneidman,* Voices of Death. *New York: Harper & Row, 1980, pp. 112–113).*

Research shows that many hospital staff members typically avoid dying persons. In one study, Waechter[19] found that nurse contacts with fatally ill children decreased as the condition worsened. The nurses both visited the children less often and spent less time with them per visit. Feelings of helplessness combined with increased anxiety are possible explanations for this kind of behavior.

We might think that, the more experience a caregiver has with dying persons, the more manageable his or her feelings and behaviors would become. However, a study by Pearlman and others[14] refutes this belief. In their examination of nursing personnel in a variety of institutions—from state hospitals to nursing homes—they found that those nurses who had more experience with the dying persons were *more* likely to avoid the dying and felt more uneasy about discussing death. In fact, 77 percent reported "having difficulty" or avoided discussing matters related to death. Another study by LeShan also documents nurses' avoidance of terminal patients. Using a stopwatch, LeShan recorded how long it took nurses to respond to bedside buzzer calls. He found that it took them significantly more time to respond to terminally ill patients than to less seriously ill persons. These studies suggest that all caregivers, including experienced ones, avoid contact with patients who are dying.

One explanation for this avoidance is that the medical staff members harbor great anxiety about death and as a result tend to avoid discussions of the subject as well as interactions with patients who are dying. Feifel[4] has reported that physicians are more concerned about death and more afraid of dying than medical students and control groups. A number of observers have noted that, because of this high level of anxiety, physicians, like nurses, avoid a patient once he or she begins to die.

A study conducted by Kastenbaum[10] pinpointed the strong impact of emotions on the behaviors of caregivers. Kastenbaum was interested in how 200 nurses attendants might respond to a dying person who says, "I think I'm going to die soon" or "I wish I could just end it all." Five general categories of responses were established:

1. Reassurance: "You're doing so well now. You don't have to feel this way."
2. Denial: "You don't really mean that . . . You're not going to die."
3. Changing the subject: "Let's think of something more cheerful."
4. Fatalism: "When God wants you, He will take you."
5. Discussion: "What makes you feel that way today? Is it something that happened, something somebody said?"

Most of the actual responses fell into the categories of denial, changing the subject, and fatalism. You will note that all three of these categories are a form of avoidance. Only 18 percent of the total group of 200 responded by opening up a discussion. As Kastenbaum points out, the "clear tendency was the 'turn off' the patient as quickly and deftly as possible." He offered two reasons for this reaction. First, the nurses wanted to make the patients happy and believed that the best way to accomplish this was to change the subject. Second, most nurses felt very uncomfortable and wanted to protect themselves.

ANXIETY EFFECTS ON PERCEPTION

The foregoing discussion indicates that aversive *emotional states* can affect the *behaviors* of caregivers in very significant ways. A helper who feels anxious being around persons with life-threatening illnesses will tend to avoid or verbally turn off those patients. The implication is that emotions directly affect behavior. However, the relationship between the two may not be so clear-cut.

I have found that emotional states directly affect *perception*, which in turn may affect behavior.[3] In other words, perception may be a key mediating factor in understanding caregiver behaviors. As part of this study, I invited a guest with acute leukemia to speak to a seminar on death and dying composed of thirty-one students. The topic for that day was "the realities of having a life-threatening illness." Just before the guest speaker arrived all of the students completed Spielberger's (1967) State Anxiety measure; this questionnaire assesses how anxious people feel at the moment rather than in general.

One might think that anxiety would not be a very vivid emotion during this experience since participants were asked only to listen to the guest speaker and ask questions they wished. I found, however, that the range of anxiety among the participants was quite great: Some persons reported very high anxiety, whereas others reported almost none.

When the guest speaker arrived, she discussed a variety of issues and emotional processes typifying her illness and style of coping. She spoke of the effects of chemotherapy, fears of dying, the importance of having good friends and available resources, and ethical/legal issues relating to the "right to die." She openly and candidly answered the numerous questions asked throughout the presentation.

Once the forty-five-minute presentation had been completed, the guest speaker departed and all the participants were asked to rate her in the following manner: "To what extent do you believe the following characterizes this person's response to dying?"

	Definitely not true				*Definitely true*
Denial	1	2	3	4	5
Anger	1	2	3	4	5
Bargaining	1	2	3	4	5
Depressions	1	2	3	4	5
Acceptance	1	2	3	4	5
Hope	1	2	3	4	5

Note that the first five characteristics are the stages of dying described by Kübler-Ross. Since I was interested in the effects of anxiety on the perception of dying stages, the ratings of the ten most anxious persons were compared to the ratings of the ten least anxious persons. Significant statistic differences were found. (For a complete statistical report, see reference 3.) The most anxious participants rated this dying person significantly: (1) *more* denying, (2) *more* angry, (3) *less* accepting, and (4) *less* hopeful. Even though all of the participants observed the same person, at the same time, in the same place, their perceptions of this person varied with their own emotional response, that is, their own anxiety.

This study raises some extremely important questions, particularly for helpers involved in the care of persons with life-threatening illness. As a caregiver are you likely to respond differently to someone you perceive is denying death, compared to someone you perceive is not? For instance, are you more willing to avoid discussing death-related matters in order to "respect the patient's denial?" Similarly are you more likely to avoid persons you perceive to be more angry, less accepting, and less hopeful? Are you more likely to prescribe different medications for such persons? For instance, you may choose to prescribe a tranquilizer to deal with the perceived anger or perhaps a mood elevator to combat the perceived lack of acceptance and hope. To what extent would your behavior as a caregiver affect your patients' responses for coping with death and the progress of the disease process itself?

These questions become vital issues when we stop to realize that our perceptions and our behavior toward persons with a life-threatening illness may well reflect our own discomfort and not theirs. The possibility that we may be projecting our own anxieties onto the dying in ways that affect the course of their treatment mandates that caregivers, as well as caretakers, receive help in coping with their own emotions.

MANAGING THE EMOTIONAL RESPONSES OF CAREGIVERS

This chapter has revealed that it is necessary for helpers to be aware of their emotional state while working with patients suffering from life-threatening illness. The emotional realities of such work can be staggering. ICU nurses, for instance, must deal with the constant threat and frequent reality of death, the repetitive routine of close observation (for example, checking vital signs every fifteen minutes), complex life-support machinery, frequent acute emergencies, distraught families, frightened patients, and a sometimes unobliging or unsupportive staff. How can they possibly cope in such a situation?

In order for caregivers to manage their emotional responses, two kinds of resources are needed.[1] *Internal* resources are those abilities, attitudes, values, beliefs, or techniques that help people handle difficult moments or periods of time. These resources enable them to develop problem-solving strategies that hopefully move them through crises. *External* resources are those people, agencies, customs, or environmental characteristics that facilitate the handling of stressful situations. A friend next door, a counselor, a local widow-to-widow program, and a neighborhood crisis center can all be effective external resources. The table below lists both internal and external resources that may be helpful in dealing with life-threatening illness. It is important to remember that coping involves two tasks: handling the demand of the external situation and controlling the internal emotional response to it.

MANAGING THE EMOTIONAL RESPONSES
OF CAREGIVERS

Internal resources	*External resources*
1. Give up idealism and perfectionist goals.	1. Actively invoke help from others.
2. Accept feelings.	2. Find group support.
3. Analyze the problem.	3. Secure a full-time physician or psychologic ombudsman.
4. Maintain self-trust.	4. Carefully design the physical work setting.
5. Focus selectively.	5. Reschedule time commitments.
	6. Maintain inservice training.

As the table points out under internal resources, effective caregivers must do the following:

1. Give up idealism and perfectionist goals. While working with the terminally ill or other populations, it is essential to distinguish between process and outcome. Is it possible to invest totally in the process of helping without expecting some guaranteed outcome such as regeneration of nerve tissue or even life itself? Health-care workers certainly cannot save the life of every person with a life-threatening illness. They can, however, help those people live as satisfying a life as possible.
2. Accept feelings. Health professionals are bound to have strong emotional reactions to their work regardless of whether they are therapists, interacting with an aggressive client, physicians sharing a dismal prognosis, or nurses working in an ICU. They may at times feel angry, frustrated, depressed, or joyful. Such emotions are the by-products of healthy, caring involvement. Once caregivers can accept the fact that they have these feelings, they can begin the process of sharing them with others.
3. Analyze the problem. Helpers who are reluctant to face their emotions squarely think certain feelings are unacceptable, believe they are unable to handle certain emotions, find that the work setting does not sanction the expression of feelings, or perhaps do not have a support group or person to whom they can turn. As caregivers, we should ask "When do I feel this way? How often? What alternatives are available? Which one should I attempt first? How will I know if it is effective?" This kind of active exploration of reality will encourage us to solve problems rather than hide them.
4. Maintain self-trust. Persons who cope well in a variety of situations have

a robust self-esteem. They generally like themselves and what they do. They believe in themselves and rely on this foundation of trust to work through the feelings or difficult moments that may inevitably arise.

5. Focus selectively. La Rochefoucauld has said that we can't stare directly at the sun or death for any length of time. Helpers who find themselves dwelling excessively on death or other aversive qualities of their work may need to concentrate selectively on the satisfactions of the job or the assets of their patients. Such a constructive use of denial may have the added benefit of focusing attention on the problems of living rather than on those of dying. Caregivers who use this tactic may be able to confront situations in which they can effect change rather than being blocked with feelings of helplessness.

In addition to perfecting these techniques, caregivers can utilize external resources:

1. Actively invoke help from others. Anyone in the helping professions is aware that each individual usually believes he or she is unique in having a particular feeling or a concern. Caregivers involved with life-threatening illness are no different. Social workers, physicians, nurses, or orderlies may consider their feelings of helplessness or depression unusual without checking the validity of this belief with others. Just as helpers interact with their patients, they must also interact with each other to maintain a dynamic and effective problem-solving system.
2. Find group support. If finding help from colleagues can be useful, organizing for such help is also a good idea. The deliberate creation of a supportive structure has been suggested by Kastenbaum,[9] who believes that "a mutual support network should exist among the staff, encompassing both the technical and the socioemotional dimensions of working with the terminally ill." It is not necessary to have the participation of everyone to organize an effective support group. Even a few like-minded people can be effective. They should try to get block time and administrative approval for the group. The success of the group may well depend on the consistency with which all members use one another as resources. Ideally membership in such a group will not come from any single discipline but will offer an opportunity for all persons with an emotional stake in life-threatening illness to give and take.
3. Secure a full-time medical or psychological ombudsman. The decision-making that is constantly required in the care of the terminally ill can be quite stressful to caregivers, especially if knowledgeable authorities are not available to examine patients and provide information, advice, and support. This is particularly true in hospital settings such as the ICU. The presence of a full-time physician could ease the burdens of the immediate tasks at hand. The availability of a full-time psychologist, social worker, or psychiatrist with expertise in emotional responses to

terminal illness would be an additional valuable resource in hospital and clinical settings.

4. Carefully design the physical setting. Staff members should have a place to go that ensures privacy and a break from routines. The use of a lounge should be built into work schedules; otherwise such an area may never be used at all. The unpredictable nature of emotions will also require the unscheduled use of such a facility in intervening with grieving relatives or in recovering emotional stability after the death of a patient.
5. Reschedule time commitments. *Burnout* is a phenomenon common to all helping disciplines. It occurs when demands and emotional pressures of work cause staff to become so calloused, frustrated, or anguished that they are forced to change jobs. One way to prevent burnout while maintaining vitality within a work setting is to schedule shorter rotations for shifts on which intense and emotionally draining interaction is the rule rather than the exception.
6. Maintain inservice training. The need for staff members to assimilate new information and upgrade their skills is constant in organizations that are vital and changing. Caregivers working with the terminally ill may have special needs in understanding loss and grief, learning techniques of bereavement intervention, and exploring the emotional response of helpers. Internal consultants from the work agency itself or external consultants from neighboring facilities should be a component of any health-care delivery system. A useful examination of the emotional needs of staff members who interact with persons facing life-threatening illness may require an experiential workshop format. The appropriateness of such methods will become clearer once the goals for inservice training have been elaborated.

It seems best to conclude this discussion by distinguishing between the *role of saving* and the *role of helping*. A helper who takes on the role of saving has an emotional investment in those persons with whom he or she interacts. Such a helper believes that his or her efforts determine the consequences for the patient or client. The logical extension of this attitude is that, the more the caregiver does, the more likely he or she will prolong or even save a life. Health workers who subscribe to the saving role may find themselves the victims of a double-edged sword. The more involved they get in their efforts to save, the more likely they will experience the feelings of failure. It is perhaps these feelings of failure—a concomitant of the role of saving—that account for so much of the avoidance behavior discussed earlier in this chapter.

The role of helping is an alternative to the dilemma. Like the role of saving, the role of helping stresses the need for emotional investment in seriously ill patients and their families. However, helpers do not believe that their efforts are *necessary* to achieve certain desired outcomes. They do not come to work thinking that they have a life to prolong or save. Instead, they believe in a present-oriented involvement by which they give as much of themselves *now* as they possibly can. A patient's welfare at the present time is what matters. If a person's physical, emotional, or spiritual health can be enhanced in any way, a helper will find the means to do so. In contrast to people who take on the role of saving, helpers do not experience a double-edged sword. The more involved they get, the more successful they feel, since the criterion for success is the process of giving and *not* the product of saving.

I believe that caregivers who take on the role of helping are (1) less likely to avoid the emotional needs of those they serve, (2) more likely to be aware of their own emotional responses, (3) less likely to misperceive the needs of the patient/clients, and (4) more likely to utilize the internal and external resources. The task of accepting major responsibility for caring for another person's physical needs and investing energy in the emotional and psychological welfare of another *is* involvement. There is no way to avoid involvement as a helper. There are ways, however, to nurture it and make it flourish through the process of interaction.

References

1 Bugen, L. A.: Fundamentals of bereavement intervention. In Bugen, L. A., ed.: Death and dying: theory, research and practice. Dubuque, 1978, William C. Brown Co. Publishers.

2 Bugen, L. A.: Human grief: a model for prediction and intervention. American Journal of Orthopsychiatry 47:2, 1977.

3 Bugen L. A.: State anxiety effects upon perceptions of dying stages. Unpublished manuscript. University of Texas, Austin, 1977.

4 Feifel, H., Hanson, S., and Jones, R.: Physicians consider death. Proceedings of the 75th Annual Convention of the American Psychological Association, 2:201-2, 1967.

5 Friedman, M., and Rosenman, R. H.: Type A behavior and your heart. New York, 1974. Alfred A. Knopf, Inc.

6 Glaser, B., and Strauss, A.: Awareness of dying. Chicago, 1965, Aldine Publishing Co.

7 Heider R.: The psychology of interpersonal relations. New York, 1958, John Wiley & Sons, Publishers.

8 Hutschnecker, A.: Personality factors in dying patients. In Feifel, H., ed.: The meaning of death, New York, 1959, McGraw-Hill Book Co.

9 Kastenbaum, R.: Death, society, and human experience. St. Louis, 1977, the C. V. Mosby Co.

10 Kastenbaum, R.: Multiple perspectives on a geriatric "death valley." Community Mental Health Journal 3:21-29, 1967.

11 Kastenbaum, R., and Aisenberg, R.: The psychology of death. New York, 1972, Springer-Verlag, Inc.

12 Kübler-Ross, E.: On death and dying. New York, 1969, Macmillan Inc.

13 Livingston, P., and Zimet, C.: Death anxiety, authoritarianism, and choice of specialty in medical students. Journal of Nervous and Mental Disease 140:222-30, 1965.

14 Pearlman, J., Stolsky , B., and Dominick, J.: Attitudes toward death among nursing home personnel. Journal of Genetic Psychology 114(1):63-75, 1969.

15 Schulz, R., and Aderman, D.: How medical staff copes with dying patients: a critical review. Omega 7(1):11-21, 1976.

16 Shady, G.: Death anxiety and care of the terminally ill: a review of the clinical literature. Canadian Psychological Review 17(2):137-42, 1976.

17 Shneidman, E.: Death: current perspectives. Palo Alto, 1976, Mayfield Publishing Co.

18 Simonton, O. C., and Simonton, S. S.: Belief systems and management of the emotional aspects of malignancy. Journal of transpersonal psychology 7:1, 1975.
19 Waechter, E.: Death anxiety in children with fatal illness. Dissertation Abstracts 29:2505, 1969.

26 · Children and Death

Judith Stillion and Hannelore Wass

Judith Stillion is professor and chairperson of the Department of Psychology, Western Carolina University, Cullowhee, North Carolina. Hannelore Wass is professor of educational psychology and an associate in the Center for Gerontological Studies and Programs at the University of Florida in Gainesville.

INTRODUCTION

Children and *death*—the two words seem contradictory. Children symbolize life and growth whereas death marks decay, the end of growing and being. Why, then, when the subject is so foreign to the nature of children should we try to educate them about the inevitability of death? In the twentieth century the answer of U.S. culture to this question has been, we should not. Many well-intentioned adults fear that facing the facts of death straightforwardly with children will rob them of their essential innocence and, therefore, of their childhood. Some adults go so far as to believe that children, confronted with the concept of death, will become so terrified that they will not be able to face living in a courageous way. A third reason that adults fail to face the question of death with children relates to the adult's own needs for denial and repression of the inevitability of death. Finally, many adults feel that since death is an unknown it is unrealistic to try to teach anyone to prepare for it.

HISTORICAL PERSPECTIVE

That death and children have not always been so foreign to each other is evident in children's games, prayers, and chants that have been passed on from generation to generation. Peek-a-boo, a game that delights infants, is said to be derived from an old English word meaning "dead" or "alive" (1). It teaches babies their first lessons in object permanence. One of the first games children learn, ring-around-the-rosie, with its chant, "ashes, ashes, all fall down," grew out of children's reaction to death during the great plague of the Middle Ages (2). Even today children very commonly learn as their first prayer, "now I lay me down to sleep, I pray the Lord my soul to keep. If I should die before I wake, I pray the Lord my soul to take." Public awareness of death anxiety has caused the latter line to be changed by many teaching agents. However, its original form serves as a reminder that in earlier days children were supposed to recognize life as transient and death as a constant possibility at a very young age. A rope-skipping chant familiar to many children contains the lines, "Doctor, Doctor, will I die? Yes, my dear, but do not cry," or a variation of this rhyme, "Doctor, Doctor, will I die? Yes, my child, and so will I." Many other games, including hide-and-seek and many tag games, have been offered as evidence of children's lasting tendency to explore the contradictory nature of life and death (2, 3).

Until this century children were common witnesses to death. Infant mortality was high, and it was a rare firstborn who did not experience the death of a younger sibling. Similarly, life expectancy was significantly shorter. According to Lerner (4), life expectancy in 1900 in the United States was 47.3 years. Children often attended the funerals of their parents as well as siblings before they reached adulthood. In earlier days death occurred most often at home and children were aware of it in all its aspects. They helped care for the sick family member, were often present at the moment of death, and were included in the planning of the funeral and attended it. In short, children lived continuously with the fact of death from infancy through adulthood.

As medicine became more specialized and sophisticated, as infectious diseases and others were conquered, death became more and more remote. The past two generations are the first in known history in which many middle-aged adults have not experienced the death of an immediate family member.

ADULTS' DEATH DENIAL AND THE CHILD

Death has come to be viewed as an unwelcome stranger rather than an expected companion, and many adults refuse to discuss it or even think about it. Their denial of death has extended to their children. In a survey by Wass 144 high school seniors were asked, among other questions: "When you were a child how was death handled in your family?" Death was never talked about responded 39 percent. An additional 26 percent said that death was talked about only when absolutely necessary, and even then only briefly. The majority of students reported that this death taboo in the family was true for the present time as well. It is safe to say that in the United States parents, as a rule, do not discuss the topic of death with their children. This avoidance of death stems largely from the adults' own discomfort and anxiety concerning dying and death. It is difficult, for example, for the mother of a four-year-old to provide a calm and well-deliberated answer to the child's totally unexpected question "Mommy, do I have to die?" What mother is not horrified at the prospect of her child's death? Even if she managed a straightforward answer such as "Yes, everybody has to die sometime, but we hope you will not die for a long long time, not for many many years," she is likely to communicate a great deal of anxiety to the questioning child. Such transmission of anxiety from adults to children may be unavoidable, and the best we can strive for is to keep the amount of anxiety at a manageable level. In addition to anxiety, adults frequently feel frustrated and sometimes angry about these death questions, and when these feelings are communicated the child may come to feel guilty as well as anxious.

Avoidance of the topic of death on the part of parents is well intentioned. Most parents have a great need to shield their children from the harsh realities of death. In fact, until recently adults generally believed that children are not concerned about death and that those who are need psychiatric help. The fact, however, as shown in many studies and supported by the authors' experiences, is that children are very much concerned. This interest in death is a normal part of human development. The question of life and death is an existential question and an expression of the child's basic curiosity and search for meaning. Children, like other people, seek to understand themselves, their relationship with others, and the world in which they find themselves. Even very young children ask existential questions such as: Where do babies come from? Where was I before I was born? Do I have to die? Who deaded Grandpa? And in their everyday world, children experience death by coming in contact with dead insects, birds, and other animals. With their all-encompassing curiosity, children try to understand the difference between the warmth, motion, and vitality that marks life and the cold, pallor, and silence that marks death. All too often when they broach their questions to adults they are met with not only evasive but often incomplete answers or disapproving silence. In this way a child learns that death is a taboo subject, and a child may well come to believe that death must be a horrifying, terrible thing, too awful even to mention.

Attempting to protect the child from the facts of death is a futile exercise. In addition to their real life experiences with dead animals, children observe death on television news and inordinate amounts of fictional death in movies and television plays. Much of the death portrayed by the media creates a totally unrealistic picture in the mind of child viewers. For example, Wiley Coyote on "Road Runner" is smashed, mashed, blown up, dropped into ravines, shot, stabbed, and run over, and yet he emerges with nothing worse than a frazzled coat and a new determination to catch the Road Runner.

In the human television world, children frequently see a central character on a soap opera die a drawn-out death only to appear on a different soap opera within a week or two. On "cops and robbers" shows characters die violently every night but are seen on other shows the next day or week. Perhaps even more disturbing, actors such as Freddie Prinze die and their deaths are publicized, but they continue to appear on reruns and syndications for years following their deaths. What impression of the nature of death can a child glean from such exposure? While realistic attempts to deal with death, bereavement, and grief are not widespread in our media, at least one notable exception is that of the Emmy award-winning show produced by Family Communications, in which death and grief were both explored at a level preschool children could understand and to which they could relate (5).

CHILDREN'S VIEWS OF DEATH

In order to answer children's questions concerning death, an adult must be aware of the child's age, experience, and prior understanding. In general, children's understandings of death seem to follow the cognitive developmental model rather closely. This model, developed by the acclaimed Swiss psychologist Jean Piaget, states that a child's level of reasoning is dependent upon both maturation and learning. Children pass through certain cognitive stages as their mental structures mature and as they interact with the world around them (6). Thus a child of three confronted with the death of a parent will not react or understand in the same manner as will a child of twelve, even if he or she is given the same explanations and treatment.

Developmental stages in understanding death

Nagy (7), in the now classical study done with Hungarian children between the ages of three and ten years of age, concluded that there are three stages in children's understanding of death and that these three stages are age-related. The *first stage* in understanding death encompasses the age ranges of three to five years and is similar to what Piaget calls the preoperational stage (6) in that it reflects the egocentric mind of the preschool child. Because children know that they need to eat and breathe, they cannot imagine a human body without those characteristics. Therefore, they describe death either as a kind of sleep or as a gradual or temporary state. While there is a recognition that death differs from life (for example, most young children know that dead people are buried in the ground [8]), there is an incomplete and almost wistful tone to the child's understanding. Nagy (9) illustrates this point by recording a preschool child's remarks:

> CHILD: It can't move because it's in the coffin.
> ADULT: If it weren't in the coffin, could it?
> CHILD: It can eat and drink. (p. 274)

Similarly, a small child may urge a parent to take a dead puppy to the doctor to make it well.

This stage in the child's cognitive development is also characterized by magical thinking. The lines between fact and fantasy are often blurred, and for small children many things are possible. A small child believes that flowers whisper and that mountains open up if you tell them to, and that princes turn into frogs and vice versa. Fairy tales support the child's unrealistic concept of death: The beautiful princess sleeps for a hundred years and then a prince awakens her with a kiss (10). While young children are saddened by death, they do not yet grasp the finality and irreversibility of death at this first stage.

The *second stage,* beginning around age five or six and lasting through age eight, is comparable to the stage of concrete operations in Piagetian theory. Piaget describes this stage as the age of the scientist. During this period, children are consumed with questions concerning the workings of the world around them. They are sorting out impressions, classifying objects, and discovering laws of cause and effect (6). Their understanding of death reflects the growing awareness of the way the world operates. They now recognize that death is final. Nagy's children frequently personified death as a skeleton or powerful monster, perhaps in an attempt to bring the topic into a more easily understandable cause-effect relationship. Death personified comes to get you, but if you are fast enough or clever enough you may get away. At this stage, children worry about the mutilation of the body brought about by the death monster. This is well illustrated in poems written by children (11). Obviously the six- to eight-year-old child, while recognizing that death is final, also sees it as capricious. The child has not yet incorporated the ideas that death is inevitable, natural, and universal. A typical conversation with one of Nagy's (9) children reveals this lack of understanding:

ADULT: Do you often think of death?
CHILD: I often do. But such things as when I fight with death and hit him on the head and death doesn't die. (p. 273)

Nagy described the *third stage* of death as that of mature understanding. In Piaget's theory this stage reflects the complex integration of the formal operational stage of cognitive development. Nagy's study indicates that this stage may begin as early as nine years of age. Children who have reached this level of reasoning realize that death is inescapable and universal; "Death is the termination of life. Death is destiny. Then we finish our earthly life. Death is the end of life on earth" (9, p. 273). In addition, children view death as personal. It is no longer something done to people from the outside (except in case of accident) but rather the result of a natural, internal destruction process that will happen to everyone including themselves. Childers and Wimmer (12) conducted a study of the awareness of two aspects of death, universality and irrevocability, in children from ages four to ten. Of the four-year-olds, 11 percent recognized that death is universal, but by the age of nine, 100 percent recognized death as universal. Of the ten-year-olds, 63 percent as compared to 33 percent of four-year-olds recognized death as irrevocable.

However, even strict Piagetian theorists do not maintain that very young children have no concept of death. Being and nonbeing seem to be one of the first differences to which a child attends and tries to understand. Kastenbaum (13) tells the story of a sixteen-month-old boy who is engrossed in watching a caterpillar moving along a path. When the foot of a passing adult crushes the caterpillar, the child looks to his father and says, "No more."

Kastenbaum maintains that the solemnity of the tone and the facial expression of the child are powerful indications that the child comprehends (at least at a preconceptual level) the state of death. Such everyday experiences with death can provide the impetus for an informal death education program within the home.

The influence of life experiences in understanding death

Children vary by age in their understanding of death, but their views are also shaped by their life experiences. For example, two fifteen-year-olds sharing similar backgrounds and IQs can vary greatly in understanding depending upon their religious background and their firsthand dealings with death or lack of them. One fifteen-year-old might have learned at a young age that talking about death made the adults in his family uncomfortable. By circumstance he may not have confronted death among family or close friends. He may even have trained himself to deny curiosity about the subject. When contrasted with a fifteen-year-old who has had to cope with the death of a parent, sibling, or friend, there may be as much difference in comprehension of the topic as we would expect to find between the five- and the nine-year-old of Nagy's study. A replication of Nagy's study (14) showed that children in the United States, in contrast to the Hungarian children of nearly thirty years ago, express concepts of death that could be classified into four categories:

1. Relative ignorance of the meaning of death (ages zero-four).
2. Death as a temporary state. Death is not irreversible and the dead have feelings and biological functions (ages four-seven).
3. Death is final and irreversible but the dead have biological functioning (ages five-ten).
4. Death is final. It is the cessation of all biological functioning (ages six and beyond).

Other attempts to replicate Nagy's findings in this country (12, 14-16) have generally found a relationship between age and breadth of death awareness but have not found the personification of death among six- to nine-year-olds that Nagy found. This may lend support to the idea that cultural beliefs and experiences also shape concepts of death. Nagy's children were all firsthand witnesses of a terrifying, bloody war in which death could be delivered from the skies unexpectedly. Most of them undoubtedly knew families who had lost loved ones during the war. Perhaps it was more natural for those children to try to make the concept of death more understandable by personifying it. However, their words may also reflect a personification tendency more prevalent in Europe than in the United States.

Family and social class influences

The importance of the family in the development of ideas and feelings about death was also demonstrated in a study by Wass and Scott (17). They found that children aged eleven to twelve whose fathers were college educated theorize and verbalize more about death than do children whose fathers only completed high school. Interesting also was the wide variability found in the sample concerning concepts of death. They ranged from an "immature" belief that death is a long rest to a "mature" belief that death is a natural, irreversible, and universal event. It is important to note that the need to discuss death and dying should be viewed as a sign of normal, healthy development rather than as an indication of morbid preoccupation with abnormal material. Older children in particular welcome the chance to discuss their views of death and dying. The protocols that follow are typical of responses made by eleven- and twelve-year-olds who were invited to tell what they thought and felt about what happens when one dies.

GIRL AGE TWELVE: I would like to die of old age. Just go to sleep and never wake up, a nice quiet way to go. I would like to be buried. Then whatever the spirits wanted to do with me they could do.

BOY ELEVEN YEARS: I think if death came slowly I would just fade out. But if it was instant, I would suddenly be gone. I believe that after you die, you have another life and you might come back from anything like a cockroach to a royalty.

GIRL ELEVEN YEARS: I think when someone knows they are going to die, they are very scared. I would be. I think after someone dies they just lie there forever and disintegrate. I hope I never die.

GIRL TWELVE YEARS: When you die, you lay there wondering if you will go to Heaven or Hell. I get scared and don't want to die. Whenever I think about it, I get all spooked out. I don't know about you, but I am going to Heaven.

GIRL TWELVE YEARS: When I die, some people will probably come and put me in a coffin with cobwebs in it; and they'll put me in a dark hearse, and the spiders will probably eat me beflore they get me in the ground. Next they'll put the coffin in a real deep hole and let me rot!

GIRL TWELVE YEARS: I think you would be surrounded by darkness. You would be absolutely without movement. You couldn't talk or see or use any of your senses. You would be that way forever. It's like taking a very long rest.

BOY TWELVE YEARS: Well, to me death is a natural thing. Everybody has to die sometime. Nobody can live forever. I know that my mother and father will die sometime. I just hope it's not soon. Then, later, I myself will be threatened by this natural thing called death (17).

A 1974 study (18) supported the impact of the environment in children's conceptualization of death. These authors studied 199 children between the ages of three and nine. They grouped the children by age according to socioeconomic class. The results showed that lower class children, whose environment is more violent, tend to be more aware of death at younger ages. They concluded that "The lower class children's fantasy content indicates that they are attempting to deal in a realistic, sensible manner with their environment" (p. 19).

In summary, whereas there is ample support for the cognitive-developmental approach to children's concepts of death, it should be remembered that development involves more than maturation; it results from an interaction of biological readiness with environmental factors. Life experiences, intelligence levels, family attitudes and values, self-concepts, and many other as yet unexamined factors all seem to play a part in each child's individual attainment of meaning for death.

LOSS, ANXIETY, AND DEATH IN CHILDREN

Children begin to experience loss at a very young age. Birth itself might be regarded as a form of loss as it involves giving up one state of being (the protective womb) to enter another (the world, which requires many adaptations). Weaning represents the loss of the major source of comfort, security, and pleasure in an infant's life. Toilet training also is a milestone away from the comfortable dependency of babyhood. Each loss might be thought of as representing a "small death" to the child and each loss brings with it anxiety. The toddler moves out of the soft security of his mother's lap in an uncertain, vaguely worried way. The five-year-old worries over the loss of her first tooth until the adult mollifies her by assuring that the "tooth fairy" will pay for the loss. The early teen watches with anxiety as the well-known, compact child body begins to assume new proportions.

The process of growing is intimately tied in with loss; and loss produces anxiety. The very young child, from infancy through preschool, manifests this anxiety over separation. The need for mother is almost equivalent to the need for survival and so to be separated arouses a form of death anxiety in the infant. The child between five and nine years old, who is rapidly gaining a strong self-image, shows mutilation anxiety (fear of destruction of some part of his or her body) but is not yet able to verbalize death anxiety per se. It is the adolescents, with their newly acquired ability to think symbolically, who can torture themselves with the concept of nonbeing.

Even strong adults cannot regard nonbeing with equanimity. As children become more mature in their view of death, it is reasonable to suppose that they also become more anxious. Wahl (19) has suggested that many of his child patients' "anxieties, obsessions and other neurotic symptom formations are genetically related to the fear of death or its symbolic equivalents . . ." (p. 27). Von Hug (20) found support for Wahl's suggestion when he obtained a curvilinear relationship between age and death anxiety in normal children but a linear relationship with neurotic children. However, there is evidence that supports the environmental point of view, namely that a child's death anxiety is also largely influenced by the environment. Wass and Scott (17) found that children with college-educated fathers theorized more about death than those whose fathers only completed high school. And children who theorized showed less death anxiety than those who did not theorize.

Positive self-regard is generally viewed as a sign of mental health. Bluebond-Langner (21) suggested that the self-concept may be an important factor in children's concepts of death. It may relate importantly to children's management of death anxiety. This hypothesis is supported in the Wass and Scott study (17) in which it was found that the self-concepts of eleven- and twelve-year-olds were inversely related to their death anxieties, that is, the higher their self-concepts the lower their death anxiety.

It seems possible that healthy children can grow toward low death anxiety, especially if they are provided with adult models who have worked through their own attitudes toward death and who encourage children to express their fears rather than repress or deny them. Neurotic children, on the other hand, tend to grow more anxious as their concept of death matures.

Implications for parents

During the early years, parents can help most by merely being available to children and assuring the child that he or she is loved and will not be abandoned (22). Children need honest answers no matter how unpleasant, offensive, or seemingly morbid their questions may be, Grollman (23) points out that parents should answer their children's questions factually and uncompromisingly and at a level they can understand. To tell fairy tales about death to children is not only misleading but may create serious problems in trust between the parents and the child as the child grows older. One of the problems with parental answers is that they are frequently spiritual answers to children's physical-chemical questions. Children want to know what happens after a person has died, but they are equally curious about the physical aspects of dying, particularly in the middle years. They ask questions such as: Why do people die with their eyes open? Why does the blood turn blue? Do people get buried alive? Could a doctor say a person is dead when he really isn't? How long does it take for the body to disintegrate? If parents do not know the answers to such questions it is all right to admit to ignorance. It would be wise to consult a physician or books. Evasiveness or refusal to answer children's questions may also lead to heightened anxiety (22).

Adolescents may clothe themselves in an illusion of invulnerability in order to deny anxiety brought about by their mature understanding of death (24). Kastenbaum (25) has reported that about 75 percent of the adolescents he studied shut the idea of death out of their minds. They were interested in living fully in the present, seeking their identity in the here and now. Adults working with teenagers may find invitations to discuss death go unanswered. However, meaningful dialogues on grief and life after death are also possible if and when the adolescent seeks them out.

Terminally ill children

How they view death Since children's firsthand knowledge of death is a powerful environmental influence for learning about death, it would follow that the terminally ill child should have a far different conception of death than would a healthy child of the same age and intelligence. At least one researcher, Bluebond-Langner (21), makes a case for the idea that terminally ill children not only become aware that they are dying but also understand death as adults do. She discusses five stages in the process of the acquisition of information that are progressive and lead to concomitant changes in self-concept. These changes are dependent upon significant cumulative events occurring throughout the course of the illness but follow the sequence as outlined below:

Information acquisition	*Self-concept changes*
"It" is a serious illness	Seriously ill
Names of drugs and side effects	Seriously ill, but will get better
Purposes of treatment and procedures	Always ill, but will get better
Disease as a series of relapses and remissions minus death	Always ill, and will never get better
Disease as a series of relapses remissions plus death	Dying

Death anxiety Other researchers working with terminally ill children have found support for Bluebond-Langner's view (21) that many know of the seriousness of their illness. Waechter (26) reported that anxiety scores of a group of fatally ill children were twice as high as those of other hospitalized children. She suggested that the fatal nature of a child's illness is communicated to the child by the changed way that persons react to him or her after the diagnosis is made. She stated that it is meaningless to argue about whether a child should be told that his or her illness is fatal. Rather, "the questions and concerns which are conscious to the child should be dealt with in such a way that the child does not feel further isolated and alienated from his parents and other meaningful adults" (26, p. 172). Her study reported a significant relationship between children's projective anxiety scores and the degree to which the child has been allowed to discuss his fears and prognosis. She concluded that accepting and permitting dying children to discuss any aspect of their illness may decrease feelings of isolation, alienation, and the sense that the illness is too horrible to discuss completely. Her final plea is that helping professionals not allow the existence of "a curtain of silence around the child's most intense fears" (p. 171).

In another supporting study (27) fatally ill children between the ages of six and ten who were treated as outpatients were compared to a group of chronically but not fatally ill outpatient children. The dying children told stories that revealed significantly more preoccupation with threats to body function and body integrity as well as significantly higher general anxiety than the stories of the less severely ill children.

Most of the studies examining the attitudes of fatally ill children have included storytelling or the use of projective techniques in order to circumvent the child's initial reluctance to discuss death. Vernick and Karon (28) state that "the initiative for talking about death must come from the adult who is in possession of more emotional strength" (p. 395). These authors are representative of many health workers who feel that fatally ill children know more than they feel safe in saying. Yudkin (29) points out that children signal deep anxiety about the possibility of death in many unspoken ways: "Depression out of keeping with the effects of the illness itself; unspoken anger and resentment toward his doctors; resentment toward his parents of a child old enough not to be affected by mere separation in the hospital. These all suggest anxiety about death" (p. 39).

In children under five years of age, death awareness often takes the form of separation anxiety. Natterson and Knudson (30) define death awareness as the "individual's consciousness of the finiteness of his personal existence" (p. 457). Young children, totally dependent on their parents for physical and emotional comfort, often equate separation of parents to physical death. Such separation fear is not dependent upon strong ego and intellectual development. Separation anxiety is most commonly seen in children who have not yet attained language skills but may be the most prevalent fear up to five years of age (31). Terminally ill children between the ages of six and ten often display mutilation fear. Children during this period are still working to develop a concept of death but they have well-developed body images. Threats to that image, whether from medical intervention or from the disease itself, cause severe anxiety. The third and final maturational step in death awareness is death anxiety per se. When death is certain, death anxiety must be regarded as a rational fear rather than as a neurotic symptom.

Viewpoints for working with terminally ill children The medical profession in the past decade has begun to address itself to caring for the psychological health of dying children as well as their physical health. Many health practitioners (32-35) are advocating open honesty in dealing with dying children. Certainly, if it is true that a child may well understand that he is going to die long before he can say it (31), it would seem productive to open lines of communication as fully as possible so as to prevent loneliness, depression, and inward anger in the dying child.

However, the stance of total honesty is not shared by all health professionals. Evans and Edin (34) reflect the more widespread practice of attempting to shield the dying child from death and the fears involved in dying. They believe that this approach is advisable for the following reasons: (a) the fear of death is real and cannot be dissipated by discussion; (b) suppression and rejection cannot be used as mechanisms for dealing with fear if open discussion is encouraged; and (c) children need the support of their parents during terminal illness and parents frequently cannot cope with their children's awareness of imminent death. Evans and Edin appear to favor a less direct method of dealing with children rather than encouraging them to meet the fears head on.

There is a midway position between total honesty and encouraging denial, which is reflected by Green (36). He encourages doctors to remain open to children's questions and to plan for time to talk with their parents. Basically three questions are generally asked by the child between the ages of six and twelve. The first is: "Am I safe?" The second is: "Will there be a trusted person to keep me from feeling helpless, alone, and to overcome pain?" and the third is: "Will you make me feel alright?" (p. 496). Successfully dealing with these three questions may be enough to allow the child to explore his own potential for growth in the time remaining. Even young children need an atmosphere of psychological safety in which to express themselves. Green relates a story of a four-year-old who, though sheltered from the prognosis of his terminal illness, nevertheless told the doctor that he was afraid to die. Allowing the child to express that fear is an important part of total care for the dying child as it results in direct comfort to the child and in freeing up of energy that the child can then use to fight the illness or to engage in intensive living in the time remaining.

Care giving and the dying child In caring for a dying child the natural core conflict of compassion and nurturance for one in pain versus repulsion against impending shock of separation and loss is heightened (37). Somehow death of a child evokes depths of anger, guilt, and frustration that adult deaths do not raise. Perhaps the child's death awakens one of our deepest fears: death before fulfillment (36). Furthermore, patients' failure to get well often leads to feelings of frustration on the part of the health care workers, since one of their primary goals and needs is to restore health. Frustration may lead to feeling angry toward the dying one, which in turn leads to guilt feelings. Since one of the reactions to grief is to become angry at those who invoked the guilt feelings, "a self-sustaining emotional chain reaction" may ensue (37, p. 509). This reaction may be fully conscious, partially conscious, or unconscious to the care giver, but it affects treatment of the dying child, perhaps leading to overprotection and overindulgence or to isolating the child emotionally and caring only for his or her physical needs.

Helping parents How much more pronounced these feelings must be in the caring parents of the dying child! One father, in a letter to a friend, expressed his anguish in the following way:

> As you are probably interested, Brian is quite bad. We wait each day for him to die. His discomfort and ours is now so great that I believe we now hope each day for him to die. But the human body does not die easily. We're like weeds in a garden. It's ironic, but waiting for a baby to die is quite similar to having a baby: you wait helplessly, you can't do anything to speed it up or slow it down, it's too late to change the course of things, you call home wondering what stage you're in, doctors and hospitals are involved, you wonder what you're going to do with the other kids when it happens, you have to call the grandparents, your friends are anxious, you want it to happen and you don't want it to happen, you're afraid and yet you desire relief from the long wait. So alike and yet so different. (38)

Friedman (39), in discussing care of the terminal child, points out that there is probably no other area in which "anticipatory guidance" is so helpful in promoting rapport between the physician and the patient's parents. A few authors (40, 41) have offered suggestions for working with parents of the dying child. At the base of all suggestions are the dual principles of open honesty and support. A summary of points to be covered with parents after the initial diagnosis is known includes the following:

1. Recognize the depth of shock and despair the parents must be feeling.
2. Explain the basis for the diagnosis and the nature and type of disease.
3. Explain the fatal outcome and type of therapy to be undertaken. Make every attempt to gain parental support both in the physical and emotional care of the child.
4. Assure parents that medical support will always be available in times of need.
5. Try to help parents anticipate problems involved in the initial telling of others and during the child's illness. Go over possible reactions of siblings (e.g., anger, jealousy, fear, guilt).
6. Discuss causes of the problem with emphasis on relieving possible parental guilt.
7. Emphasize any hope possible. If there is hope for remission, dwell on that. If there is not, discuss scientific research going on, if appropriate. If nothing is available, emphasize the support the child will get throughout the illness from the medical staff. While the good physician will discourage excessive optimism (42), parents must be allowed some hope, especially during the early stages of a disease.
8. Discuss anticipatory grief both as an attempt to educate parents about their own feelings in the coming days and to prepare them to recognize stages their child may be passing through.
9. Stress the importance of maintaining continuity in raising the child. It is essential that parents assume the child will live to adulthood and raise him or her consistent with their prior values and ideals. The alternative is that parents in their grief and guilt will indulge the child, who in turn will become confused and often test new limits until parents are forced to discipline him or her. This often leads to greater feelings of guilt both for the child and the parents. Children need the security of consistency in their parents' behavior.
10. Try to assess family's strengths and weaknesses and encourage building on the strengths. It is important to ask each parent how the other will accept the death, thus encouraging empathy and visualizing problems in advance.
11. Finally, there is evidence that a follow-up talk after the death of the child is often appreciated by the family in order to provide closure for the family and to permit them to express feelings after the death.

Parents are an integral part of total treatment of the dying child. Morrissey (43) showed that high-quality parent participation leads to better adjustment in hospitalized children. Not only can parents be of help to the ward staff throughout their child's illness, but also by doing this they work off some of their own anxiety, guilt, and grief before the child's death (30). In almost all cases of children who survived four months or more after the initial hospitalization, the caregiving parents (usually the mother) reacted with calm acceptance and some were even able to express relief at their child's death. There was a triphasic response among mothers whose children survived at least four months. In the first phase there was shock and denial often accompanied by anger, excessive weeping, and a tendency toward overprotection. In the second phase there was an acceptance of the situation coupled with the parent's willingness to expend energy in realistic ways that offered hope of saving the child. During this phase the psychological separation of the mother from the child often began. The third phase coincided with the terminal phase of the child's illness. Mothers directed their energy toward other sick children as well as their own. Sublimation was often evident in their desire to give physical and psychological comfort to parents of other terminally ill children. It is noteworthy that in cases where mothers reacted hysterically or clung to hope unrealistically, their child's death usually occurred less than three months after the fatal prognosis was given. It would appear that four months is the critical period for the working through of anticipatory grief (30).

CHILDREN AND GRIEF

There are at least three distinct types of grief reactions that are appropriate to examine in a discussion of children and death. The first is preparatory grief, the emotional reaction of a child becoming aware that he or she is dying. The second is bereavement as a child faces the fact of the death of a loved one. The third is anticipatory grief as the parents of the terminally ill child attempt to cope with the realization that their child is dying.

Preparatory grief

Preparatory grief seems to be a universal aspect of the dying process if the person has adequate warning of his or her condition. It involves the following emotions: denial ("This cannot be happening to me"); anger ("How can you let this happen to me?"); resentment ("Why me? Why not you?"); fear ("What will dying be like? Will I suffer? Will I be alone? What will happen after I die?"). Sometimes guilt also is a part of preparatory grieving, as in the case of children who feel that their disease is punishment for earlier behavior. The idea of death as punishment as well as the child's assumption of parents' omnipotence is chillingly portrayed in Hailey's *Airport* (44) when the child in the crashing plane is heard to say "Mummy! Daddy! Do something! I don't want to die . . . Oh, Gentle Jesus, I've been good . . . Please, I don't want to . . ." (p. 142). If care givers can recognize the complexity of these interrelated emotions and encourage the child to verbalize them according to his needs, the child may be able to work through some of them, thus freeing up energy to be spent in more positive ways. Even if the child cannot work through the emotions, he or she will not feel so cut off and alone during the illness. Often, creation of a positive climate for communication with a dying child stems from the way the disease is presented to the child in the beginning. Foley and McCarthy (35) describe a typical physican's explanation to a leukemic child as follows:

> You have a serious blood disease, leukemia. Ten years ago, there was no treatment for leukemia and many people died. Now there are a number of drugs which can be used to treat leukemia. There are several types of leukemia and the type that you have is the one for which there are the most drugs.
>
> Treatment to keep the leukemia cells away will last three years. You'll miss at least a month of school, the time needed to get the disease in control. The main problem right now is infection. If you stay free of infection you will be out of the hospital in about five days, if an infection occurs, you'll be hospitalized for at least two weeks." (pp.1115–1116)

Allowing children to ask questions after such an explanation and making time to talk even when they have no questions creates the setting of mutual trust so necessary for growth during the final period of life.

Death as loss

Death is above all else loss. The young child (aged three to five) usually has experienced only temporary loss, as when a parent leaves for a short time. These children do not understand permanent loss but they know the discomfort of being without their caretakers. Bowlby's work (45) suggests that since preschool grieving and adult grieving are very similar in their intensity, the longing and mourning that are intrinsic to the grief process may be largely instinctive rather than cognitive. Spitz (46) described a syndrome that he called "hospitalism," in which the young child from infancy through preschool reacts to separation from his mother first with anger, then with a kind of quiet, resigned despair. Some of the children actually refused nutrition, turned their faces to the wall, and died. This was not learned behavior. Rather it was a natural response on the part of the child who had suffered an overwhelming loss.

Dying children suffer not only from physical separation from their home and parents but also from pain and loss of function as the disease progresses. Older children (six years and beyond) begin to have the cognitive capacity to grieve over the loss of the future. They can understand that their tomorrows are numbered. It is difficult for the child as well as the adult to make sense of such an intrinsically unfair situation. However, many children have a need to discuss these feelings. If, when they first mention them, they are met with embarrassment, disapproval, or emotional outburst, the children learn that this is not a safe area for discussion. They must deny those feelings in themselves and retreat into the loneliness of their own loss without the support of those they love. Preparatory grief is real and it can become debilitating. Many health workers today agree that the final cruelty added to the already unbelievably cruel dying situation is to encourage these children to pretend they are *not* suffering the greatest loss of all. In dying the child loses everything: possessions, friends, parents, personality, and self. It is right to grieve then, if he or she realizes even a bit of this loss. Health workers can facilitate the grieving process not by silence but by being available to listen, empathize, and support the child in attempting to cope with the illness.

The bereaved child

Just as dying children profit from being able to communicate their feelings of grief, loss, anger, and bewilderment, so children who have lost a loved one profit from communication. The death of a parent can be particularly tragic for a child (47). Mingled with all the other negative emotions is a feeling of betrayal. It is almost as though the young child feels that if the parent had loved him or her enough, the parent would not have left. Bereavement is accompanied by physical symptoms including feelings of panic, insomnia, lack of appetite, nightmares, and others. Unresolved grief, especially in children, can lead to ongoing somatic illness as well as deep psychological problems. In one study (48) 41 percent of the population of 3216 depressed adult patients had lost a parent through death before age fifteen. In a later study (49) 27 percent of patients in a highly depressed group reported the loss of a parent before the age of sixteen as compared with 12 percent of adults in a nondepressed group. Furthermore, an appreciably larger number of patients in the highly depressed group lost a parent before the age of four. It appears that the loss of a parent is a traumatic psychological event for a child and that the earlier that loss occurs, the more potentially devastating the effect can be.

Parness (50), in working with preschool children who have sustained the loss of a parent or sibling, points out that "very young children have resiliency and fortitude in the face of some of the painful and unpredictable experiences life has to offer" (p. 7). However, she goes on to say that death and loss must be worked through with children. She points out that teachers and mental health workers can encourage healthy coping in children by beginning work with the assumption of loss as a universal human emotion. The adult must also be willing to share feelings of grief honestly and in a positive way that communicates faith in the children's "resources, resiliency, and power over their future lives—in spite of the unexpected" (50, p. 7).

Parental anticipatory mourning

The final type of grief to be considered in this chapter is parental anticipatory mourning. Futterman and Hoffman (51) defined it as "a set of processes that are directly related to the awareness of the impending loss, to its emotional impact and to the adaptive mechanisms whereby emotional attachment to the dying child is relinquished over time" (p. 130). It involves the following steps:

1. *Acknowledgement:* growing awareness of the approach of the inevitable moment of death accompanied by alternating feelings of hope and despair.
2. *Grieving:* the emotional reaction to loss that starts off as an intense undifferentiated response but gradually mellows in quality and the intensity becomes subdued.
3. *Reconciliation:* one step advanced from mere acceptance, it involves attempting to find meaning for the child's life and death and moving beyond that to a stage where the parents can be grateful for their blessings.
4. *Detachment:* this is the process whereby the parents gradually withdraw their emotional investment from the child.

   One parent has described a very rapid detachment reaction in the following way: "As soon as the doctor told me that B. had neuroblastoma (a fatal form of the infantile cancer) I looked at him in the bed and felt like he was already dead. Later on, hope revived for a while with a change in medication, but as the disease progressed, I protected myself from too much feeling by viewing him as already lost to us" (38).

   This process, so necessary to the mental health of the parents, sometimes can result in the tragic condition referred to as the "living dead" (52). If parents complete the detachment process too soon or if the child has an unexpected late remission, the family may have completed the detachment process and the child may find himself dying alone or receiving an unwelcome greeting from a family that has already resolved his death.
5. The final stage in anticipatory grieving is called *memorialization.* It involves idealizing the child and results in the parents' developing a mental image of the child which will live beyond his death.

PROFESSIONALS AND THE FAMILY OF THE DYING CHILD

Professionals working with parents of terminally ill children can do little to lessen the sorrow that is the dominant emotion from the time the diagnosis is made until the child dies. They can, however, help the parents to anticipate and deal effectively with accompanying emotions such as anger, guilt, and anxiety.

Powerful feelings of anger often threaten to overcome parents of fatally ill children. The obvious unfairness of the situation coupled with their impotence to do anything to change it leads to feelings of frustration that can be destructive. The important question for helping professionals must be: How can the parents be helped to express their anger in positive ways? Sometimes, especially in cases of genetically transmitted diseases, one parent will turn his or her anger on the other one, thus adding to the stress of the situation (53). Other family members, including siblings and grandparents, may also have to bear the brunt of displaced parental anger. Other common recipients of anger include God, the doctors, nurses, and other caretakers, and even inanimate objects such as the hospital bed and machines used in treating the child. If parents turn their explosive anger inward, it can result in depression, suicidal urges, and even psychotic breakdown.

Parents need to be helped to find appropriate channels for venting anger. Such channels might include ongoing group or individual therapy, joining an organization to raise funds for medical research, forming parent support groups, and physical activities to discharge tension.

The second major emotion that parents should be helped to anticipate is guilt. Since the child's birth the parents' role has been that of protection and nurturance. When parents are not able to protect their child from a fatal disease, they may feel irrational guilt. In addition, if the parent-child relationship has been strained, the parents may feel guilt for the negative feelings they have had toward the child. As the illness proceeds, guilt may be compounded as the parents experience recurring wishes for the child to die. Guilt is also exacerbated as the parents become aware of hidden feelings of relief that it is not they who have the fatal illness. Folk tales and scattered heroic stories tell of parents who willingly give their lives for their children. However, it is the exceptional person who would willingly choose to exchange places with one who is suffering through a lingering death, even if that person is one's own child. Guilt can be tolerated better if the parent can be encouraged to express these feelings openly. The helping professional can then accept the parents' feelings of guilt and join them in attempting to understand those feelings as natural parts of most intimate relationships.

Commonly, parents of fatally ill children experience a third emotion, anxiety, which arises from at least five sources (53):

1. *Lack of mastery of the protective parental role,* resulting in the need to reorganize self-concept, self-esteem, and feelings of potency. Any major threat to the stable self-concept arouses anxiety.
2. *Inability to cope with the situation effectively,* resulting in feelings of an imminent breakdown. Whenever environmental stress threatens to overwhelm a person, the major emotion is that of anxiety. It is hard to envision a situation more stressful than having to watch your child suffer and die.
3. *Feelings of isolation and loneliness* caused by the parents' new identity as the parent of a doomed child. Parents have said that after finding out the diagnosis they did not want to see friends who had healthy children. They experienced feelings of resentment that the world continued to go on as though nothing had happened while their whole world was collapsing. In short, they felt that theirs was a unique position in the world, which no one else could understand; they were alone.
4. *Separation anxiety* as the parents anticipated the child's death and its psychological cost. Parents have reported feelings of loss so keen that it felt as though they had lost a limb or some other part of themselves.

5. *Death anxiety* as the realization of their own inevitable death hits home more acutely than ever before because of identification with the child.

Anxiety is best counteracted by action, and much of a parent's anxiety can be constructively channeled into caring for the dying child (54). However, parents need to know that sleeping and eating disturbances often accompany anxiety and that anxiety, like anger, can be displaced, resulting in irrational fears concerning their own health or the health of their other children.

Siblings and the dying child

Siblings of a dying child also suffer, often in lonely confusion, as they watch their brother or sister die and their parents grieve. Often parents react to grieving children in an overprotective and secretive manner. Green and Solnit (55) have coined the term "vulnerable child" syndrome to refer to such children. Studies done with adults who lost a sibling in childhood have indicated some support for this syndrome. As early as 1943, Rosenweig and Bray (56) found that patients suffering from schizophrenia had a higher than expected number of siblings who died in childhood. Perhaps the one axiom that will promote the best adjustment in the brothers and sisters of the dying child is quite simply, include them. They need to know some details about the illness if they are old enough; they need to visit the sibling in the hospital and be encouraged to express their thoughts, fears, and guilt feelings just as the parents are. Young children especially need to be reassured that no hostile thought of theirs is responsible for their brother or sister's illness, as magical thinking is still very much a part of their cognitive method of operation.

SUMMARY

Death is a natural event and it is normal for children to want to know about and understand it. Many parents have a need to protect their children from the harsh realities of life, but by doing so they contribute to misconceptions and increased anxieties.

The understanding of what death and dying means develops as the child grows older. The preschool child is believed to understand death as a temporary stage, a long sleep or departure. During the early school years, the child comes to recognize that death is final, but at the same time it is also personified, seen perhaps as a skeleton or a powerful monster who capriciously snatches people and kills them. Usually by the age of nine the child understands that death is final but also natural and universal. A number of studies have shown that there is extreme variability with respect to the age at which a child reaches a mature understanding of death. These variations are due to cultural and subcultural factors, family background, personal encounters, and very likely a number of other as yet unidentified factors.

Children experience loss at a young age. Loss produces anxiety. As children become more aware of the reality of death, it is reasonable to assume that they become more anxious. Caring and patient adults can help alleviate a good deal of a child's death anxiety.

The terminally ill child usually becomes aware of his or her dying and experiences fears, but researchers find that these fears are often unspoken or couched in symbolic language. In the very young terminal child the fear of separation from parents is the predominant fear. Older children fear mutilation of their bodies.

Caring for the dying child is the most difficult task. The death of a child evokes depths of anger, guilt, frustration, and helplessness that are difficult to cope with. An important aspect of care of the terminal child is for physicians or other care givers to work with parents to help them cope with this impending loss and the feelings these bring about. When parents are an integral part of the total treatment of the dying child, it is found that parents are able to work off some of their own anxiety, guilt, and grief, while at the same time filling a need for closeness on the part of the dying child as well as assisting the staff.

There are at least three different identifiable types of grieving. First, preparatory grief or the emotional reaction of children who become aware of their own dying. Second is bereavement, as a child faces the loss of a loved one, and third is anticipatory grief, or the feeling that parents of the terminally ill child experience as they attempt to cope with the fact of their child's impending death.

References

1 Crase, D. R., & Crase, D. Helping children understand death. *Young Children,* 1976 (November), 21–25.

2 Kastenbaum, R. J. *Death, society and human experience.* St. Louis: Mosby, 1977.

3 Maurer, A. Maturation of concepts of death. *British Journal of Medicine and Psychology,* 1966, *39,* 35–41.

4 Lerner, M. When, why, and where people die. In E. S. Shneidman (Ed.), *Death: Current perspectives.* Palo Alto: Mayfield Publishing, 1976, 138–162.

5 Sharapan, H. Mister Rogers' neighborhood: Dealing with death on a children's television series. *Death education: 1,* 1977, 131–136.

6 Piaget, J. *The origins of intelligence in children.* New York: Harcourt, Brace and World, 1932.

7 Nagy, M. The child's theories concerning death. *The Journal of Genetic Psychology,* 1948, *73,* 3–27.

8 Koocher, G. P. Talking with children about death. *American Journal of Orthopsychiatry,* 1974, *44,* 404–411.

9 Wilcox, S. G., & Sutton, M. *Understanding death and dying: An interdisciplinary approach.* Port Washington, NY: Alfred Publishing, 1977.

10 Wass, H. How children understand death. *Thanatos,* 1976, *1,* 4, 18–22.

11 Arnstein, F. I met death one clumsy day. *English Journal,* 1972, *61,* 6, 853–858.

12 Childers, P., & Wimmer, M. The concept of death in early childhood. *Child Development,* 1971, *42,* (4), 1299–1301.

13 Kastenbaum, R. Childhood: The kingdom where creatures die. *Journal of Clinical Child Psychology*, 1974, *3*, (2), 11–14.

14 Melear J. D. Children's conceptions of death. *Journal of Genetic Psychology*, 1973, *123*, (2), 359—360.

15 Gartley, W., & Bernasconi, M. The concept of death in children. *The Journal of Genetic Psychology*, 1967, *110*, 71–85.

16 Hansen, Y. Development of the concept of death: Cognitive aspects. *Dissertation Abstracts International*, 1973, *34*, (2—3), 853.

17 Wass, H., & Scott, M. Middle school students' death concepts and concerns. *Middle School Journal*, 1978, *9*, (1), 10—12.

18 Tallmer, M., Formaneck, R., & Tallmer, J. Factors influencing children's concepts of death. *Journal of Clinical Child Psychology*, 1974, *3*, (2), 17—19.

19 Wahl, C. W. The fear of death. In H. Feifel (Ed.), *The meaning of death*. New York: McGraw-Hill, 1959.

20 Von Hug, H. H. The child's concept of death. *Psychoanalytic Quarterly*, 1965, *34*, 499–516.

21 Bluebond-Langner, M. Meanings of death to children. In H. Feifel (Ed.), *New meanings of death*. New York: McGraw-Hill, 1977.

22 Wass, H., & Shaak, J. Helping children understand death through literature. *Childhood Education*, 1976, (November-December), 80–85.

23 Grollman, E. A. (Ed.) *Explaining death to children*. Boston: Beacon Press, 1967.

24 McCandless, B. R. *Adolescents—Behavior and development*. Hinsdale, Ill.: Dryden Press, 1970.

25 Kastenbaum, R. Time and death in adolescence. In H. Feifel (Ed.), *The meaning of death*. New York: McGraw-Hill, 1959.

26 Waechter, E. H. Children's awareness of fatal illness. *American Journal of Nursing*, 1971, *71*, 1168–1172.

27 Spinetta, J. J., & Maloney, L. J. Death anxiety in the outpatient leukemic child. *Pediatrics*, 1975, *56*, (6), 1034–1037.

28 Vernick, J., & Karon, M. Who's afraid of death and leukemia ward? *American Journal of Diseases of Children*, 1965, *109*, 393–397.

29 Yudkin, S. Children and death. *The Lancet*, 1967, 37–41.

30 Natterson, J. M., & Knudson, A. G. Observations concerning fear of death in fatally ill children and their mothers. *Psychosomatic Medicine*, 1960, *23*, (6), 456–465.

31 Spinetta, J. J., Rigler, D., & Karon, M. Personal space as a measure of a dying child's sense of isolation. *Journal of Consulting and Clinical Psychology*, 1974, *42*, (6), 751–756.

32 Singher, L. J. The slowly dying child. *Clinical Pediatrics*, 1974, *13*, (19), 861–867.

33 Karon, M., & Vernick, J. An approach to the emotional support of fatally ill children. *Clinical Pediatrics*, 1968, *7*, (5), 274–280.

34 Evans, A. E., & Edin, S. If a child must die . . . *The New England Journal of Medicine*, 1968, *278*, (3), 138–142.

35 Foley, G. V., & McCarthy, A. M. The child with leukemia in a special hematology clinic. *American Journal of Nursing*, 1976, *76*, (7), 1115–1119.

36 Green, M. Care of the dying child. In *Care of the child with cancer*. Proceedings of a conference conducted by the Association for Ambulatory Pediatric Services in conjunction with the Children's Cancer Study Group A on November 17, 1966. Edited by A. B. Bergman, & C. J. A. Schultle, 1966, 492–497.

37 Rothenburg, M. B. Reactions of those who treat children with cancer. In Cancer. Proceedings of a conference conducted by the Association for Ambulatory Pediatric Services in conjunction with the Children's Cancer Study Group A on November 17, 1966. Edited by A. B. Bergman, & C. J. A. Schultle, 1966.

38 Dorsel, T. Personal communication, 1976.

39 Friedman, S. B. Care of the family of the child with leukemia. Proceedings of a conference conducted by the Association for Ambulatory Pediatric Services in conjunction with the Children's Cancer Study Group A on November 17, 1966. Edited by A. B. Bergman, & C. J. A. Schultle, 1966.

40 Ablin, A. R., Binger, C. M., Stein, R. C., Kushner, J., Zoger, S., & Mikkelson, C. A conference with the family of a leukemic child. *American Journal of Disabled Child*, 1971, *122*, 362–364.

41 Friedman, S. B., Chodoff, P., Mason, J. W., & Hamburg, D. A. Behavioral observations on the parents anticipating the death of a child. *Pediatrics*, 1963, *33*, 610–625.

42 Lascari, A. D., & Stephbens, J. A. The reactions of families to childhood leukemia: An evaluation of a program of emotional management. *Clinical Pediatrics*, 1973, *12*, (4), 210–214.

43 Morrissey, J. R. Children's adaptation to fatal illness. *Social Work*, 1963, *8*, 81–88.

44 Hailey, A. *Airport*. New York: Doubleday, 1968.

45 Bowlby, J. *Attachment and loss. Vol. II: Separation anxiety and anger*. New York: Basic Books, 1960.

46 Spitz, R. A. Hospitalism: An inquiry into the genesis of psychiatric conditions in early childhood. In *The Psychoanalytic Study of the Child, Volume I*. New York: International University Press, 1945.

47 LeShan, E. *Learning to say goodbye: When a parent dies*. New York: Macmillan, 1976.

48 Brown, F. Depression and childhood bereavement. *Journal of Mental Science*, 1961, *107*, 754–777.

49 Beck, A. T., Sethi, B. B., & Tuthill, R. Childhood bereavement and adult depression. *Archives of General Psychiatry*, 1963, *9*, 129–136.

50 Parness, E. Effects of experiences with loss and death among preschool children. *Children Today*, 1975, *4*, 2–7.

51 Futterman, E. H., & Hoffman, I. Transient school phobia in a leukemic child. *Journal of the American Academy of Child Psychiatry*, 1970, *9*, (3), 477–494.

52 Easson, W. M. *The dying child*. Springfield, Ill.: Thomas, 1970.

53 McCollum, A. T., & Schwartz, H. A. Social work and the mourning parent. *Social Work*, 1972, *17*, (1), 25–36.

54 Martinson, I. M. *Home care for the dying child: Professional and family perspectives*. New York: Appleton-Century-Crofts, 1976.

55 Green, M., & Solnit, A. J. Reactions to the threatened loss of a child. A vulnerable child syndrome. Paediatric management of the dying child. *Paediatrics*, 1964, *37*, 53–66.

56 Rosenweig, S., & Bray, D. Sibling death in anamnesis of schizophrenic patients. *Archives of Neurology and Psychiatry*, 1943, *49*, (1), 71–92.

ANNOTATED BIBLIOGRAPHY

We must all face death, our own or that of a loved one or both. Preparation for facing death is not only possible but appears to be necessary in light of physical and emotional hazards that can arise from ineffectual handling of death and grief. Since children are aware of death from an early age, parents and helping professionals need only create a climate of tolerance toward the subject and direct children's natural curiosity. In addition, parents' and teachers' books can be excellent sources of information and comfort. The topic of death has concerned humankind from time immemorial, and for this reason death has been written about not only in the context of various theologies, philosophies, and recently the sciences, but also in the general literature, including children's books. There are, of course, the all-time favorites in which the subject of death is imbedded in the main theme but not specifically concentrated upon, such as the following books:

Armstrong, W. *Sounder.* New York: Harper & Row, 1969.
Buck, P. *The big wave.* New York: John Day, 1948.
Cleaver, V. *Where the lilies bloom.* Philadelphia: Lippincott, 1969.
Gipson, F. *Old yeller.* New York: Harper & Row, 1956.
Hunt, I. *Up a road slowly.* Chicago: Follett, 1966.
Lawson, R. *Rabbit hill.* New York: Viking Press, 1944.
O'Dell, S. *Island of the blue dolphins.* Cambridge: Riverside, 1960.
Rawlings, M. *The yearling.* New York: Scribners, 1939.
Salten, F. *Bambi.* New York: Grosset & Dunlap, 1929.
Speare, E. *The bronze bow.* New York: Houghton Mifflin, 1961.
Sperry, A. *Call it courage.* New York: Macmillan, 1940.
White. E. B. *Charlotte's web.* New York: Harper & Row, 1952.

Also, in recent years in particular, a number of gifted authors have chosen death as the main theme of their stories. These books can be informative as well as therapeutic not only for children but for adults as well. Wass and Shaak (22) have compiled a brief selected annotated bibliography of such books by age groups. That bibliography is reproduced below.

Preschool through age 7

Brown, M. W. *The dead bird.* Glenview, Ill.: Scott, 1965. A group of children find a bird and feel its heart not beating. They have a funeral for it before returning to their play. Life continues.

Buck, P. *The beech tree.* New York: John Day, 1958. The metaphor of a beech tree is used by an elderly man to help explain his impending death.

De Paola, T. *Nana upstairs and nana downstairs.* New York: Putnam's, 1973. Tommy is heartbroken when his bedridden great-grandmother, with whom he has spent many happy hours, dies. He comes to realize that both the Nana that lived upstairs and the Nana that lived downstairs are "upstairs" in Heaven. The hope of life after death brings satisfaction.

Fassler, J. *My grandpa died today.* New York: Behavioral Publications, 1971. A description of Grandpa sleeping away to a peaceful death in his rocking chair is presented. Knowing his Grandpa was not afraid to die, David is able to continue "running and laughing and growing up with only fond memories of Grandpa." Written in simple story line but with such factual detail that it could be classed as a nonfiction book.

Grollman, E. *Talking about death.* Boston: Beacon, 1970. The finality of death is presented uncompromisingly in simple direct language without softening the blow. Grollman's intent is to protect the child from destructive fantasy and a distorted view of death as well as guilt that often arises when a child is denied information.

Harris, A. *Why did he die?* Minneapolis: Lerner, 1965. A mother's heartfelt effort to speak to her child about death is portrayed. Death is likened to the leaves falling in autumn with new leaves to come in the spring, and to a worn-out motor. Emphasis is on the fact that, no matter what happens, memories of the deceased will never die.

Kantrowitz, M. *When Violet died.* New York: Parents', 1973. A story of the funeral preparations and ceremony for a dead bird, emphasizing the children's reactions, fascination and fun children get out of ceremonies, even funerals. The children are consoled in the continuity of life as shown through their pregnant cat. Life goes on!

Kuskin, K. *The bear who saw the spring*. New York: Harper & Row, 1961. A story of changing seasons and the changes living things go through as they are born, live, and die.

Miles, M. *Annie and the old one*. Boston: Little, Brown, 1971. Annie's Navajo grandmother says she will be ready to die after the new rug is woven. Annie tries to keep the rug from being finished, but her wise grandmother tells her that is wrong, that the "earth from which good things come is where all creatures finally go." Death is a part of life.

Stein, S. B. *About dying*. New York: Walker, 1974. A "shared" and open story about everyday dying, the kind every child meets early in his own life—the death of a pet and a grandparent. Actual photographs accompany the text of death, funeral, and mourning of Snow, a pet bird, and the Grandpa who had given him to the children. The accompanying adult text serves as a resource for handling the questions and discussions arising from the child's natural curiosity. The book explains reality, guiding a child toward the truth even if it is painful, and gives the children the inner strength to deal with things as they are. Preventive mental health!

Tresselt, A. *The dead tree*. New York: Parents', 1972. The life cycle of a tall oak tree is poetically described, showing that in nature nothing is ever wasted or completely dies.

Viorst, J. *The tenth good thing about Barney*. New York: Atheneum, 1971. The rituals of burial and mourning are observed for Barney, a pet cat. The child is led to understand that dying is as usual as living. Death is a part of life. Some readers may question whether young children will be able to comprehend the abstract idea of Barney's future role as fertilizer.

Warburg, S. S. *Growing time*. Boston: Houghton Mifflin, 1969. Jamie learns to accept the reality and meaning of the death of his dog with the help of his sympathetic and understanding family. He finds out that "death is not easy to bear." Something you love never dies; it lives in your heart.

Zolotow, C. *My grandson Lew*. New York: Harper & Row, 1974. The shared remembrances between a mother and a small child of a sadly missed grandfather keep both mother and son from being lonely. Memories keep the deceased alive in your mind.

Ages 8 through 11

Cleaver, V. *Grover*. Philadelphia: Lippincott, 1970. Ten-year-old Grover is forced to handle the changes that the suicide of his ailing mother brought about in his own groping ways, as his father is too grief-stricken to help. He finds out that there is no formula for overcoming grief other than time, friends, and maturity.

Cohen, B. *Thank you, Jackie Robinson*. New York: Lothrop, 1974. The story of the slowly deepening friendship between twelve-year-old Sam Greene and the elderly black cook in Mrs. Greene's restaurant. After following their "main man"—Jackie Robinson—Sam is bereft when Davy suffers a fatal heart attack. Because their relationship seems solid, readers too will mourn Davy's death and sympathize with an honestly grieving Sam.

Lee, V. *The magic moth*. New York: Seabury, 1972. A very supportive family bravely copes with ten-year-old Maryanne's illness and death from a heart defect. A moth bursting from its cocoon as Maryanne dies and seed sprouting just after her funeral symbolize that "life never ends—it just changes."

Orgel, D. *Mulberry music*. New York: Harper & Row, 1971. The efforts of a young girl's parents to protect her from the knowledge of her adored grandmother's impending death result in turmoil, both within the girl and around her, when in her rash and rebellious actions the girl searches for her beloved grandmother. Keeping the truth of an impending death from a child can cause misunderstanding and fear.

Smith. D. B. *A taste of blackberries*. New York: Crowell, 1973. Jamie dies of a bee sting. His best friend is confronted with grief at the loss and comes to terms with a guilty feeling that somehow he might have saved Jamie. After a period of grief, life goes on.

Zim, H., & Bleeker, S. *Life and death*. New York: Morrow, 1970. This is an answer book for questions young people have about death. The physical facts, customs, and attitudes surrounding life and death are discussed. Death is described as part of living.

Age 12 and over

Corburn, J. *Anne and the sand dobbies*. New York: Seabury, 1967. Danny's father tries to answer questions about the death of Danny's sister.

Gunther, J. *Death be not proud*. New York: Harper & Row, 1949. The author writes of the courage of his seventeen-year-old son while facing death. The book is a celebration of life. It is more difficult for his parents than for Johnnie to accept his death.

Hunter, M. *A sound of chariots*. New York: Harper & Row, 1972. Bridie McShane's happy early childhood during World War I in Scotland is interrupted by the death of her beloved father whose favorite child she was. As she matures, her life is marred by her sorrow, leading her to morbid reflections on time and death, which she finally learns to deal with through her desire to write poetry.

Klein, S. *The final mystery*. New York: Doubleday, 1974. The meaning of death is explored and how people of different religions have coped with it. The ongoing war against death is discussed.

Rhodin, E. *The good greenwood*. Philadelphia: Westminster, 1971. A tense and moving story of Mike who lost his good friend, Louie. After time and grief pass, Mike came to realize that Louie was really dead and was not going to reappear around the next corner. He came to remember Louie for the clown and dreamer that he was and for the good times they had together. He was not building another Louie as the grownups were, one that was almost perfect.

PART FOUR

PERSONAL PERSPECTIVES ON DEATH

G PSYCHOLOGICAL ASPECTS OF DEATH

As we shall see in each of the remaining chapters, the patient who is dying is very much a person; so we have a final shift of focus, this time to a concentrated look at the dying person. A standard textbook of clinical medicine states that "each man dies in a notably personal way." It may not be inaccurate to say that individuals are never more like themselves than when they are dying. People come to death with a variety of beliefs, attitudes, superstitions, fears, and hopes. Furthermore, there are deep and important unconscious orientations toward death or cessation, different perhaps in each person, some of which move the dying toward death and some that pull them away. Today, many behavioral scientists believe that there are definite psychological components in the dying process. In many cases, death can be considered to be a psychosomatic disease. Further, many deaths can be thought of as being subintentioned, that is, they are deaths in which the decedents have played an indirect, covert, latent, unconscious role in hastening their own demise. Examples of subintended deaths would be any deaths (excluding clear-cut suicide or absolutely adventitious accident or failure of a vital body part) in which the decedent has acted with some imprudence, excessive risk taking, disregard of medical regimen, abuse of drugs including alcohol, and so on. One can see immediately that subintentioned deaths include many deaths now labelled as natural, accidental, or homicidal. We all know people who are "prone" to accidents, and we can now add the concept of "victim-precipitated homicide" in which individuals play some conscious or unconscious part in creating their own fate.

In general, it is possible to say that there are two main approaches to the topic of death: the sociological and psychological, identified with Emile Durkheim and Sigmund Freud, respectively. In the last several years there have been many psychologists and psychologically oriented physicians who have concerned themselves directly with death. These psychologists and psychiatrists of death (thanatologists) are concerned with the individual's attitudes, development, mental states and orientations, and what are called "psychic mechanisms." The four selections in this chapter touch on different aspects of the psychology of death.

The Kastenbaum and Aisenberg selection can be thought of as background material. Kastenbaum and Aisenberg acquaint the reader with the various stages of the life cycle that individuals pass through in acquiring their personal understanding about the meaning of death. It is important to note that there are considerable variations in the manner in which individuals gain an under-

standing of death—variations that are often reflected in their approaches to dying.

There is a tragic sense of aloneness among terminal patients. Some of this isolation stems from a number of "common fallacies about dying patients," which are discussed in the Weisman selection. Once again the humanistic theme is picked up as Weisman urges against stereotyping people and recommends that each patient be treated as a special case.

"Depersonalization in the Face of a Life-Threatening Danger," by Russell Noyes and Roy Kletti, focuses on the "psychological mechanism of defense" called depersonalization, *a mental phenomenon characterized by a feeling of unreality and strangeness about one's self or one's environment. Its function seems to be to hold in check certain potentially disorganizing emotions, such as an overwhelming fear of death. Such an experience may have metaphoric, even mystical, and seemingly spiritual overtones and appearances, followed by a sense of "rebirth." The authors present their ideas as a partial explanation for the sizable number of seemingly mystical and spiritual experiences that have been reported in certain segments of the thanatological literature over the past thousands of years, including the last decade.*

Shneidman continues and expands the theme of humanistic treatment of the dying by discussing the unique way in which each person prepares for death—"death work." This selection points up the need to understand the interplay of certain coping mechanisms such as acceptance and denial. Understanding these coping mechanisms is important to every student of death inasmuch as they are vital tactics for the person wrestling with the specter of death.

The last selection is by Erich Lindemann, a well-known and much loved psychiatrist. His now-famous paper on the tragic 1942 Boston Coconut Grove fire, "Symptomatology and Management of Acute Grief," created, almost by itself, the important specialty of crisis intervention. The selection in this section is from his posthumously published book, Beyond Grief *(1979). It is the transcript of a talk that he gave to the staff of the radiology (X-ray) department at the Stanford University Medical Center where he was receiving treatment for a malignancy called sacral chordoma. In that talk, Lindemann spoke of the deep psychological investment that dying persons have in themselves, of the ways in which one can grieve for oneself, and of the ways one can transcend the grief of anticipating one's own death. He also spoke of the importance of sharing and of intimacy—a veritable partnership—between doctors and other helpers and dying patients. The talk, by a remarkable gentle giant, is an extraordinary* ave atque vale.

27. Death as a Thought

Robert Kastenbaum and Ruth Aisenberg

Robert Kastenbaum is Superintendent of the Cushing Hospital in Framingham, Massachusetts, and Editor of Omega *and Ruth Aisenberg is a Research Psychologist at the Children's Hospital Medical Center in Boston. This selection, taken from their book* The Psychology of Death, *discusses what "death" may mean to a person and delineates the various life stages that a person passes through in acquiring a fully formed concept about death.*

D-e-a-t-h. This sequence of five letters is fixed and familiar. It is easy to assume that the *meaning* of this term is also fixed (unvarying) and familiar (truly known to us). Furthermore, one is tempted to assume that d-e-a-t-h refers to a "real something" (or a "real nothing") *out there.*

These assumptions will not be honored in the present discussion. For the moment we are setting aside most of what we know or think we know about "real death." Instead we will try to become aware of those mental operations through which we develop and utilize concepts of death. The elementary logic we are invoking here might be stated as follows:

1. Terms such as "dying," "dead," and "death" generally are *intended* by us to *refer* to phenomena that are outside of or beyond our minds. For example, I *think* of Socrates as dead—but the important point is that Socrates *really is* dead.
2. But we never "really" know what is *out there.* We never even know (beyond the possibility of plausible counterargument) that there is an *out there* out there. We live within and by our own psychological processes. The correspondence between our personal thoughts and feelings and anything else in the universe is a matter for conjecture (as it has been for centuries).
3. We do know that concepts of death have a particular form of existence that is amenable to analysis and understanding. It is even amenable to controlled empirical investigations. Concepts of death are *concepts.* We can study the development and structure of death concepts in the individual. We can learn how death concepts get along within the individual's entire community of concepts. We can attempt to discover relationships between concepts of death and such covert states as anxiety or resignation. We can attempt to discover relationships with overt behaviors, such as risk-taking actions or the purchase of "life"

insurance. We can examine cultures and subcultures with respect to their concepts of death and their implications for social structure and function.

4. This level of analysis is highly relevant because it is clearly within the realm of psychology. Even if our present knowledge is quite limited, there is some security perhaps in the feeling that we are looking at death from a perspective that is germane to our scientific background.

In short, we are attending to death first as a psychological concept. It is at least a psychological concept, even if it is more . . .

A FEW GENERAL PROPOSITIONS

Perhaps we should expose some of our conclusions ahead of time. In this way the reader may be better prepared to dispute or disagree with the materials to come.

1. *The concept of death is always relative.* We will emphasize its relativity to *developmental level,* although a case could be made for other frameworks of relativity. By developmental level we do not necessarily mean the individual's chronological age. It is obvious that chronological age provides important clues to the person's mode of thinking. But we are concerned with developmental level in a structural sense that will already be familiar to those acquainted with the writings of Heinz Werner (1), Jean Piaget (2), and some others. The point, in any event, is that the concept of death should be interpreted within its organismic context.
2. *The concept of death is exceedingly complex.* In most instances it is not sufficient to express the death concept in one or two propositions. Along with the sheer complexity of the death concept we find it does not invariably hold together as a unified, internally consistent structure. In short, we must be cautious in thinking about somebody having a concept of death in the same way that he has a Social Security number or a big toe.
3. *Concepts of death change.* This proposition is implied by those already mentioned. When we characterize a person's concept of death at a particular point in time we should not suppose that this description will continue to hold true for him indefinitely.
4. *The developmental "goal" of death concepts is obscure, ambiguous* or *still being evolved.* It is customary to trace growth curves from starting point to apex. To mention one of the clearest examples, we expect the child's height to increase until it attains its "goal": adult height. (One might also persevere to trace the decline of the growth curve after a period of relative stability during the early and middle years of adulthood.)

   Conceptions of death cannot be graphed with the same degree of confidence. Technical reasons for this limitation include difficulties in assessing conceptions of death, and in establishing appropriate quantitative units by which progress or lack of progress can be demonstrated. But the more crucial problem has to do with content, not method: we just do not know what constitutes the most mature or ideal conception of death. There are opinions, of course (too often passed off as though established facts). These opinions represent value orientations rather than inexorable conclusions derived from systematic theory or research. Seldom are attitudinal components distinguished from the more purely cognitive aspects of the conception. Is there, in fact, one and only one mature conception of death? And how can we be certain that the individual does not achieve a mature conception of death relatively early in life, but then retreat to a socially sanctioned position that is less adequate from a developmental standpoint? These questions are merely illustrative. We are suggesting that too little is known at the present time to assume that there is an obvious developmental goal toward which early conceptions of death advance inch by inevitable inch.

5. *Death concepts are influenced by the situational context.* How we conceptualize death at a particular moment is likely to be influenced by many situational factors. Is there a dying person in the room with us? A corpse? Does the situation contain a possible threat to our own life? Are we alone or with friends? Is it bright noon, or black midnight? The situation may selectively draw out one type of death cognition among the several we possess. Or, the situation may even stimulate us to develop new or modified death conceptions.

6. *Death concepts are related to behavior.* Most immediately, perhaps, we think of a person engaging in an action that is directly and positively related to his death cognition. He comes to the conclusion, for example, that death is the gateway to eternal bliss. Suicide follows as his relevant behavior. But the relationship is seldom, if ever, that simple. Similar death cognitions can lead to different behaviors, just as similar behaviors can be preceded by different sequences of psycho-logic. Another person with the "eternal bliss" conception of death stays alive so that he can bring his message of hope and comfort to others. Still another person commits suicide without giving much thought to the prospect of an afterlife; he is totally absorbed in his need to escape from unbearable life stress.

   One's concept of death can influence behavior in remote and complex ways. Behavior patterns that do not seem to have anything in particular to do with death may nevertheless be influenced by these cognitions. Insomnia, for example, or panic upon temporary separation from a loved one, sometimes can be traced to death concerns. Clinicians Hattie Rosenthal (3) and Herman Feifel (4) are among the experienced observers who have discovered death thoughts to be closely interwoven with many types of behavior.

KNOWING AND RELATING

It is difficult, in practice, to maintain a clear distinction between concepts and attitudes. In this selection, we concentrate upon the ways in which we explain or interpret death to ourselves [rather than] upon our attitudes or orientations toward death.

Illustration: We ask a child what a shaggle-toothed boondoggler would look like, were there such an animal. He provides us with a vivid drawing or verbal description. He has, in effect, conveyed his understanding of the boondoggler. Now we inquire what he would do if he saw one of them coming down the street. Here he has the opportunity to express his attitude or orientation ("I would run away—fast!" or "I'd say, 'Here snaggle-tooth, here's some nice milk for you. Will you give me a ride on your back?'")

Our total relationship with any object involves both conceptual and attitudinal components. The mere fact that we know, or think we know something about this object, is sufficient to guarantee some kind of relationship. We are related to this object *through our own cognitive activity.* Similarly, the existence of an orientation (e.g., approach or avoidance) presumes some cognitive component. At the least, we have performed the mental operation of classifying the object as something to be avoided.

We shall not insist upon an artificial separation of death concepts from our total organismic relationship to death. But it will be useful to begin with an emphasis upon death as a psychological concept. Taken by itself, the topic is complex enough. And consideration of this specific problem will provide helpful perspective for the variety of other problems that lie ahead.

"YOU ARE DEAD"

At least two forms of the death conception should be clearly distinguished at the outset. The first of these is death of the other. There is reason to believe that the cognition "You are dead" develops more rapidly than the inward-looking "I will die." Later, both types of death conception will be considered in some detail from a developmental viewpoint. At the moment, we are interested only in sketching some of their implications.

"You are dead" is a proposition that is related to the following considerations:

1. You are *absent.* But what does it mean to be absent? We must appreciate the observer's frame of reference. For a young child, the frame of reference is largely perceptual. Absence means *not* here and now. The child is not yet equipped to distinguish adequately between spatial and temporal distance. Suppose that you are "away," in another city. From an adult frame of reference, you have a spatial existence at the present time. But the child experiences your absence (5). You are not in *his* perceptual space at this time, therefore you are *not.* (There will be an important amendment to this statement later.)
2. I am *abandoned.* This statement is almost a reciprocal of the preceding

proposition. Your disappearance from my perceptual frame of reference has an effect upon my sense of security. As a parent or other crucial person, you constitute a significant aspect of the universe that is known to the child. As the child, I am not merely aware of *your absence,* but of the *presence of discomfort feelings within myself.*

3. Your absence plus my sense of abandonment contributes to the general sense of *separation.* I have been alienated from one of my most important sources of contact and support. If this separation is sufficiently critical to me, then I may experience a pervasive sense of losing contact with the environment, not just with you. Furthermore, I may also have the impression of being wrenched away from you. This trauma could intensify the already bleak picture of absence and abandonment.
4. The separation has *no limits.* The young child does not grasp the concept of futurity, or of time in general, in the way that most adults have come to develop these concepts. This is a multidimensional problem. It may be sufficient at this point to say that the child's immediate sense of separation is not modulated by future expectations. He cannot tell himself, "Mother has gone away . . . but she will return in five days." He cannot distinguish among short-term, long-term, and final (irreversible) separations. Once the separation experience has been induced, he has no dependable way of planning, estimating, or anticipating its conclusion. What the outsider may regard as a brief separation (based upon consensual clock or calendar time) may be indistinguishable in the child's mind from the prospect of prolonged separation.
5. The child's involvement in *recurring psychobiological rhythms* complicates his relationship to separation and death. He is not fully a knowing participant in the world of "objective" time that moves unit by standard unit from the past, through the present, to the future (6). His time begins each morning when he awakes. His midday nap signals a "time out." External rhythms of night and day and internal rhythms of hunger-satiation, sleep-activation, etc., exert a strong influence over his appreciation of time.

How does this relationship to time affect his conception of death of the other? The four preceding points emphasize, in various ways, the child's vulnerability to separation. He cannot, for example, distinguish well between the prospect of moderate-length and long-term or final separation. Now we must add a factor that might seem contradictory. Bear in mind these two points: a) the child's time experience is conditioned by cyclical rhythms, and b) he is apt to experience sensations of absence, abandonment, and separation in situations where adults would argue that the child had not "really" been abandoned.

We see that the sense of *limitless* separation or the *endlessness* of any experience conflicts with the periodic nature of his experiences. It is a bit difficult to express this relationship. As a child who feels abandoned, I have no way of establishing a future limit upon my present experience. In fact, one of the reasons I am so distressed is that this unpleasant experience shows no signs of being self-limiting. Nevertheless, my psychobiological state is always in transition. I am becoming hungry or sleepy. And the environment in which I am embedded is also in transition. The sun is coming up or it is going down. Various periodic household routines are being started or completed. Concretely, as a cyclical creature in cyclical environment, I am not likely to maintain a constant frame of reference over a protracted period of (clock or calendar) time. There are breaks and interruptions in even my most steadfast thought and behavior patterns. In other words, despite my inability to posit *limits* to the separation experience, I do not actually have a continuous experience. Periodic changes in my inner state and my external environment distract and rest me. There will be more to say later about the relationship we have been proposing here.

What is relevant now is the connection between periodicity and the child's vulnerability to separation experiences. Again, as a child I may "misinterpret" your temporary departure as being a consequential separation. By this same token, however, I may underestimate a consequential separation—even your death. My cyclical patterns of functioning lead me to anticipate that every end has a fresh beginning, just as every beginning has an end. You have been away a long time now (by clock-calendar as well as subjective time). But I do not "know" how long this has been. And I have deeply rooted within me the expectation that the familiar pattern of separation-reunion will be completed. This is another point that we will want to keep in mind when we attempt to trace the entire developmental sequence of death conceptions. The proposition, for now, is that the child is more vulnerable to the death implications of trivial separations, and more protected from the death implications of substantial separations than what might appear to be the case from the viewpoint of an observing adult.

"I WILL DIE"

This proposition assumes that one has developed quite a constellation of abstract concepts. The set we offer below is not intended to be exhaustive. The statement "I will die" implies such related concepts as the following:

1. I am an individual with a life of my own, a personal existence.
2. I belong to a *class* of beings one of whose attributes is mortality.
3. Using the intellectual process of logical deduction, I arrive at the conclusion that my personal death is a *certainty*.
4. There are *many possible causes* of my death, and these causes might operate in many different combinations. Although I might evade or escape one particular cause, *I cannot evade all causes.*
5. My death will occur in the *future*. By future, I mean a time-to-live that has not yet elapsed.

6. But I do not know *when* in the future my death will occur. The event is certain; the timing is uncertain.
7. Death is a *final* event. My life ceases. This means that I will never again experience, think, or act, at least as a human being on this earth.
8. Accordingly death is the *ultimate separation* of myself from the world (7).

"I will die" thus implies self-awareness, logical thought operations, conceptions of probability, necessity, and causation, of personal and physical time, of finality and separation. It also seems to require the bridging of a tremendous gap: from what I have experienced of life to the formulation of a death concept. It is a good deal easier to develop a concept of a shaggle-toothed boondoggler; I have had contact with many different animals, so it is just a matter of selecting and combining attributes. Death, however, essentially is a nonexperience. I have not been dead (the state). I have not experienced death (the process of life coming to a final halt). The very mental operations I use in my efforts to fathom death falsify as they proceed. The mind's own modus operandi equips it for interpreting life or lifelike processes better than the alien void. Perhaps now and then I permit myself to believe that I have actually perceived or formed a concept *of* death. Closer to the truth, however, is the realization that I have simply observed my mind as it scurries about in the dark.

Having seen a dead person, animal, or plant is likely to contribute to my conception of death. Yet these perceptions do not truly bridge the gap. The deadness is perceived from the outside only. What it feels like not to feel eludes me. Furthermore, under some circumstances I am liable to misinterpret my perceptions, seeing the living as dead, or vice versa. Experiences with the dead, however, is another one of those topics we will keep in mind as we attempt to understand the development of death conceptions . . .

SOME CONCEPTS RELATED TO DEATH

Animism

Now let us consider a few of the other concepts whose developmental careers intertwine with the concept of death. One of the most relevant concepts is *animism*, or the tendency to impute life to nonliving entities. This, of course, is not identical with the idea of death per se. It is the distinction between living and nonliving that concerns us at the moment.

Perhaps we should begin by recognizing that the term most typically is meant to imply immature or deviant thinking. If the child declares that the squirrel running across the lawn is alive, we would not ordinarily describe this as an "animistic" concept; it is simply being "accurate." But we would consider him to be animistic if he attributed life to a mechanical squirrel, the lawnmower, a squirrel-tailed cap, etc.

The observations and theoretical formulations of Jean Piaget are important with respect to this as with respect to so many other topics in mental development. Piaget maintains that animism is one of the earliest characteristics of the child's thought (8). It is, in fact, based on a "primitive mental structure." The young child does not differentiate between mental and physical realms as clearly as he will when he becomes an adult. Among other implications, this means that he is likely to see external objects in his own image, that is, as live and conscious beings. There is a converse side to this animism: the child is also likely to treat mental phenomena as though they were physical. (We have already touched upon a related phenomenon: the child's tendency to respond as though his angry thoughts had *caused* somebody to die.)

Piaget views animism as undergoing a developmental transformation that is very much in keeping with the general pattern of mental growth. We move, in other words, from the relatively diffuse and undifferentiated to the specific and differentiated. In broad outline, this is also the position of the other premier mental developmentalist of our day, Heinz Werner (9). The young child is said to interpret most activity as the activity of living creatures. Almost everything is alive, or could be alive under the right conditions (water, when it flows; clouds, when they move, etc.). Gradually, the child learns to restrict this category. He progressively excludes certain phenomena from the ranks of the living. He also reduces the amount of consciousness and purpose he is willing to attribute to the nonalive objects he still regards as living. For example, no longer does he regard a table as being alive in any sense of the word, but the moon may retain a more limited kind of "aliveness" because it floats up in the sky "on its own."

Research stimulated by Piaget's ideas has been conducted on Chinese (10) and Swedish (11) as well as American (12) children. The results confirm at least part of Piaget's thesis, namely, that children, especially young children, do have difficulty in distinguishing living from nonliving objects. However, Piaget, as we have seen, had more than this limited proposition in mind. It would appear that his broader formulations have not been as clearly confirmed, at least not in the opinions of some of the independent investigators. A Swedish researcher, Gote Klingberg (13), has offered an alternative explanation of findings in this area. Instead of assuming that the child fundamentally thinks differently and more "primitively" than the adult, why not simply say that the child begins in ignorance and must learn gradually how to make the distinction between living and nonliving? In other words, we should not exaggerate the difference between the basic mental structure of child and adult. It is more a question of learning and experience.

Klingberg's view does seem consistent with some of the findings obtained both by herself and by other investigators. The data indicate that the younger the child, the more likely he is to make errors of overinclusion. The data do not show precisely that children *think* that much differently from adults. There are some indications that children abandon their "animistic" thinking somewhat earlier than Piaget reckoned. (But Piaget himself was more interested in establishing the basic stages through which animistic thought passes than in pinning down a standard timetable by which one traverses the stages.) Another interesting trend is the apparent close similarity between children of different nations (as different as the Swedes and the Chinese) in their designation of particular objects as living or nonliving.

We suggest that theories and research on the topic of "animistic" thinking in children may have the following implications for our understanding of the concept of death:

1. By adult standards, the child begins with "inaccurate" interpretations of both life (or perhaps we should say "livingness") and death. These interpretations become increasingly more "accurate" with age, i.e., they come to resemble the concepts of the parental generations.
2. The directionality of the "error" in both instances may possibly reflect the same underlying bias in the child's mind. It is bias in favor of life. All that is active pertains to life, or is not distinguishable from "livingness." And all that is alive now will continue to be alive (even though subject to disappearances and interruptions).
3. With both concepts, it remains unclear how much of the discernible change reflects an intrinsic, more-or-less built-in developmental program, and how much is a function of learning experiences within a particular psychosocial milieu. Those who emphasize the intrinsic developmental-stages approach tend to regard the young child as fundamentally more different from his elders than do those who attribute the changes to learning and experience. One's position on this question is likely to affect both the nature and the extent of educational or other efforts to influence the child's conceptions of life and death.
4. Surprisingly, there do not seem to have been any developmental studies directed at examining the relationship between concepts of life and death in the same children. Therefore, we do not know, for example, if those children who lag in their tendency to differentiate between the living and the nonliving also are slower or otherwise idiosyncratic in their attainment of death concepts. We have very little information on the general relationship between these two sets of concepts during the early years of life—only separate studies that cannot really be combined.
5. Theoretically, we should expect the relationship between the two concepts to change with age. The child "should" at first be unable to differentiate between the question: living or nonliving? and the question: what is it for living to become dead? The more specific distinction between nonliving and dead should take even longer to become clear to the child (e.g., the stone is not alive, but is not dead; the bird is dead). The discrimination between nonliving and dead is another problem that seems to lack for research attention. And the general theoretical expectation we have suggested here remains in limbo because of the neglect of research into the relationship between the development of life and death concepts, already mentioned.

6. Data regarding both concepts (and general theory on mental development) suggest that the adult versions usually are attained by the preadolescent or early adolescent years. It is taken for granted that there are individual differences. It would appear that the "mature" or adult concepts for both life and death occur at about the same time.
7. There is evidence of various kinds to suggest that the concept of death is quite important both in the child's daily life and in his future personality. But we know very little about the significance of the living/nonliving ("animistic") distinction for the child's current adjustment and subsequent maturation.

OBJECT AND SELF CONSTANCY

We continue our sampling of death-related concepts with one of the most elusive ideas in both philosophy and individual experience. This mystery has been given many names (none of which, however, truly provides a solution). By speaking here of *self constancy* we mean only to make it a little easier to relate this concept to material that is more familiar to specialists in developmental psychology. *Object constancy* or "conservation" is, of course, a household, or laboratory word among developmentalists these days. There is abundant theory and research on this topic (again, much of it derived from Piaget). Much less attention in the form of systematic theory and controlled research has been given to the development of *self* constancy.

Let us first have a word or two about object constancy. For thousands and thousands of words on this topic, the reader will have no difficulty in finding expert treatises (14). The moon is a traditional example here. Sliver, crescent, half, or full, no matter how this object in the sky presents itself to our eyes we recognize it as moon. To update this example a little, we are also capable of identifying the lunarity of the lunar body whether it is viewed in its customary guise as a relatively small object displayed within the larger visual field of the evening sky, or in its new aspect: a television-screen-filling expanse of detailed bleakness. Whether we see the "full" moon as a discrete object within its celestial context or a bit of the moon displayed over our entire visual field, moon it remains.

But it was not always thus. As children, presumably we had to learn to identify those varying shapes in the sky as all being the same. Even earlier in our development, we had to recognize that yesterday's moon and tonight's are the same. A number of observers have pointed out that some children tend to speak of "moons" even at a time when they have already begun to apply the singular/plural distinction correctly in regard to other objects. In any event, a period of development of learning experience is required before we appreciate the constancy of an object through its various transformations. Some objects are trickier than others. Piaget-type experiments often are designed to learn if a child can see his way through the visual manipulations and distractions that are presented to him, and demonstrate his command of the true constancy of the object or object-dimension in question.

Now here is what we wish to say on the topic of object constancy:

1. Disappearance or destruction of the object—"death of the object," if you will permit this phrase—cannot be conceived or appreciated unless the constancy of the object has already been established. We cannot experience the disappearance of an object unless we have already acknowledged its existence as a relatively enduring entity.
2. But constancy of the object itself has little or no meaning, if the child has not already come to appreciate the phenomena of change, destruction, disappearance. The basic notion of constancy implies the possibility of nonconstancy.
3. In other words, we are suggesting that the child must develop the concepts of constancy and change in tandem. Each concept is in a sense "prior" to the other. Right from the start, the concept of enduring qualities is intimately related to the concept of transient or oscillating qualities. This proposition links research and theory on object constancy with . . . the child's early experience of time as periodical and circular. It is also related to . . . our interrelated thoughts of birth and death, and our tendencies to "kill the thing we love." *We are proposing that "the death of the object" is one of the earliest and most fundamental protoconcepts in the child's long progression toward mature cognitive functioning; it is not really to be separated from development of object constancy.*
4. The distinction between death of the object, and death of the object that was once alive probably requires developmental and learning preconditions. The general theoretical expectations that applied to the concepts of "livingness" and of death should apply here as well. We would expect, for example, that all three concepts are fused together in a very general cognitive orientation, and only gradually differentiated from each other.
5. In infancy and early childhood, the disappearance or destruction of objects probably is experienced as a partial loss of the individual himself. In a sense, he disappears, too, when his mother leaves the room. We do not intend to exaggerate the significance of all object losses. Many of these "losses" are trivial, and are replaced by other objects that are fully as satisfying to the child. In principle, however, the child experiences sense of self-loss whether it is a crucial or trivial object that has disappeared. That facet of the child (or that quanta of "libidinal energy") that he invested in the object has become stranded. This cognitive and affective investment of his *self*—is defunct until reinvested elsewhere. He may even "feel dead" when the object has become dead within his own perceptual and phenomenological field.
6. Suppose that a visual field were to be presented in a perfectly stable or static array. Would it be perceived or experienced as unchanging? The answer probably is in the negative, especially if we are concerned with the human eye and the human mind. Our eyes move to transverse the visual field, therefore we bring change and movement to the static array.

Furthermore, what we have in mind by "mind" is mental *activity*, events, processes, currents of perception and thought. To the extent, then, that we do perceive and think, to that extent we introduce a certain level of activity and change into even a hypothetically static external world.

But there is another step to be taken here. We ourselves change over time. The changes are especially rapid and profound during precisely those years of early development that have been our concern in this discussion. Our perceptual, cognitive, and affective orientations are in transition—how, then, can *object* constancy be achieved or maintained? We raise this conundrum only to emphasize the intimate relationship between development of *self* constancy or identity and *object* constancy. A comprehensive account of human development must, we think, give full attention to both aspects, and with apprecation for their mutual influences. Even if we liked to believe that we were interested only in object constancy, we would be unlikely to develop a profound understanding of this topic without also concerning ourselves with what is happening to the self that is achieving or failing to achieve object constancy.

We turn now to a brief consideration of self constancy as this relates to the development of death concepts. (If at this point, the wary reader is expecting another of those apparently obsessive little lists to which he has been exposed so far . . . his expectation is all too well justified.)

1. It seems unlikely to us that object constancy can run very far ahead of self constancy. There are two related but not identical implications. One implication pertains to the constancy of objects. The other implication is concerned with the constancy of the concepts themselves—but we are going to ignore that problem here.

   Whatever interferes with the development of a firm sense of self constancy will make it difficult for the child to comprehend constancy external to himself. More accurately, perhaps, he will be too preoccupied with his unsettled internal state to make adequate distinctions between the enduring and transient qualities in his perceptual field. We might expect such a child to have more than the usual difficulty in achieving clear distinctions between living and nonliving objects, and in moving toward the adult concept of death.

2. The . . . suggestion of Alexander and Adlerstein (15) . . . seems relevant here. These researchers reasoned that death becomes a more significant or salient concept when the individual's identity is challenged by psychosocial stress. They noted that, in American culture at least, certain periods of early development are more likely to be stressful than others. Threat to the child's self constancy might well arouse more salient thoughts of death. Yet, as we have proposed, problems in achieving or maintaining self constancy might be expected to make it more difficult for the child to understand death and related matters. There is the possibility of a "vicious circle" here: Formidable losses, challenges, or demands shake up the child's sense of identity. This turbulence

tends to bring throughts of death and destruction to mind. But the cognitive effects of this shaky self constancy may be such as to increase his difficulties with death and related concepts.

3. It is likely that difficulties could *begin* from the death-loss-separation axis. In the present discussion, we have been regarding death concepts as the function of self constancy, which itself is influenced by role expectations, psychosocial stress, developmental level, and physical condition. But the child who has experienced painful separations from important people may develop a kind of death concern that interferes with the development of both self and object constancy. Some earlier material in this selection is consistent with this proposition. Moriarty's motherless mothers (16) for example, may have difficulty in deciding whether they are themselves, their dead mothers, or their own children.

4. We move deeper into the thicket. Forget the child and his vulnerabilities for the moment. Consider the adolescent or the young adult. The adolescent's *individuality* is likely to be a salient aspect of his total identity. It has taken him a long time to become as individual as he now feels himself to be, and he may be aware that he still has a way to go. But what does it mean to experience oneself as an individual, especially when the experience is of recent vintage? It means to experience onself as *alone.*

   To be individual and to be alone is also to be in a new kind of relationship to death. One is likely to feel more vulnerable to death, or so we believe. And the death to which he is vulnerable is itself more threatening in some respects. . . . The acute perception of individuality-aloneness seems to invite a sharpened sense of personal mortality. Although he has achieved a higher level of integration than he possessed as a child, the adolescent or young adult has not eluded the relationship between self constancy and the prospect of death. The relationship has changed, however, and it will continue to be subject to change throughout life.

Futurity

What remains of our lives is "in" the future. But death is "there," too. Small wonder, then, that we may, at times, have mixed feelings about futurity.

Thoughts of time and death have a natural affinity for each other. It is difficult to imagine how we could form any conception of death without some conception of time. To keep this section within limits, we will concentrate upon *futurity,* referring to other aspects of time only for background and context. The interested reader will find an extensive literature on the more general topic of the meaning of time in human experience (17). Here, our purpose is simply to explore a few mutual implications of futurity and death concepts in cognitive development.

The young child's relationship to time and death has been touched upon several times in this discussion. We will not repeat what has already been ventured, especially under the rubrics of "You are dead," and "I will die." Let us move ahead to that station in his developmental career which marks the child's attainment of culturally mature time concepts.

As one might expect, there is a lack of agreement among researchers concerning the precise age at which it is customary for a child to achieve a solid grasp on time. In their pioneering investigation of this topic, E. C. Oakden and Mary Sturt (18) concluded that the adult's conception of time is not achieved until about thirteen or fifteen. This estimate is probably close to the mark. Futurity and other basic time concepts probably are attained by most boys and girls somewhere between late childhood and early adolescence. We are assuming approximately normal intellectual endowment, and a reasonably adequate psychosocial environment. There are some reasons for believing that intellectual level and social milieu are related to concepts of futurity (19).

We are considering now the older child who knows that future time is *qualitatively* different from past and present time. Things that have already happened have happened in one particular way. They will never rehappen or unhappen. What is *yet* to happen? That is a different story. The future is indeterminate, a zone of possibility, of contingency. This is an exciting discovery for the child. The future is really different from what one has already experienced, from what one already *is*. We leave this discovery for a moment, but place an identification tag on it: both "hope" and "dread" begin with the appreciation of futurity as qualitatively distinct from "used" time.

Our sophisticated child also appreciates the existence of world or "objective" time. There is a constant pulse and flow of time apart from his own personal experiences. His thoughts neither initiate nor terminate external time. If this were not true, then he would never be "late," "early," "impulsive," or "dawdling": his own phenomenological world would justify any tempo at which he cared to function. He knows that he cannot truly take "time out." This insight perhaps bestows special meaning on certain organized games in which one legitimately can suspend time. Even in the game situation, however, he comes to realize that the "time out" must be taken in accordance with consensual rules that govern the total situation.

The discovery of objective time may be one of the major psychic events that force magical thinking into the mind's darker and more remote crevices. If external time is impervious to his control, then how is he to influence events in the world simply by doing things inside his head?

From this point on, it becomes difficult (and perhaps arbitrary) to distinguish between what the individual *knows* about futurity and how he *uses* what he knows. Unlike the younger child, he does not seem limited by lack of basic comprehension. The adolescent is quite capable of engaging in high level mental operations, of "thinking about thought" (20). How he orients himself to time is as much a matter of attitudes and personality structure as it is of cognitive development *per se*. Consider, for example, the results of a multidimensional study of time perspective in normal adolescents (21). Three findings are of particular relevance:

1. Typically, these young people directed their thoughts to the future

—but only to the near future. Almost everything important in life was "just up the road a piece." The second half of their life span was almost barren. It was uncommon for these people to express any thoughts regarding the fourth or fifth decades of their own lives, let alone the seventh, eighth, or ninth decades.

2. The past was neglected or "blanked out" as well. Not only was scant attention given to one's personal past, but there was the strong impression that these adolescents felt uneasy when asked to turn their thoughts toward where they had been, in contrast to where they were going.
3. There was a prevailing sense of rapid movement from the present to the future. The adolescents felt they were moving somewhere, and in a hurry. However, there was *not* a strong relationship between the sense of forward motion and the extent to which the individual actually was thinking ahead into the future. It will be recalled that for this population in general there was a disinclination to conceptualize the later years of life. One hurtled from "now" to "next" with all possible speed—but what comes after "next"? Few ideas were expressed on this subject.

All of these adolescents could conceive of futurity. But why did they, as a group, limit themselves to the immediate future? Why did they tend to exclude the past? And why were there important individual differences within this group, as well as within other groups that have been studied? Possible explanations are offered both in the study cited above, and in related investigations (22). The most relevant point here is that any explanation must take motivational and socioemotional factors into account. It is not enough that the adolescent can think about the future. He must also develop a personal orientation toward his future.

Mention has already been made of the likelihood that heightened awareness of one's self as an individual also tends to heighten one's concern about death (an hypothesis that is almost begging for empirical investigation). Studies such as the one summarized above suggest that the adolescent's identity is closely linked to the who he will be in the near future. Seen from this viewpoint, death becomes much more than an abstract logical concept. The prospect of death is a threat to who the adolescent is now because it clouds the possibility that he will ever become the self that he values and is moving toward. Threatened loss of futurity (premature death) confronts the adolescent with an implicit denial of his basic identity. He cannot look back upon a full lifetime to bolster his sense of individual identity, nor is he at a relatively stable point in his present existence. He is emerging. But what is the point of emerging if one is never to attain his full development?

From this line of reasoning we should expect that the adolescent and the elderly adult would differ markedly in their conceptions of death even though both appreciate the same basic conceptual dimensions (e.g., death is inevitable, final, personal). They would be expected to differ because, among other circumstances, they stand in different relationships to futurity. We will touch upon the older person's view of death and futurity in a moment. Let us remain a little longer with the adolescent—just how concerned is he with the prospect of a foreshortened life? What has been learned about the relationship between conceptions of futurity and conceptions of death?

Psychologists Louis Dickstein and Sidney Blatt studied the relationship between preoccupation with death and two measures of future-time perspective or anticipation (23). The death questions were quite straightforward, for example: "I think about my own death . . . more than once a week, once a week, once a month, once every few months." One of the futurity measures was a set of four story roots from which the subject is requested to construct a story. A sample story root: "Joe is having a cup of coffee in a restaurant. He is thinking of the time to come when. . ." (24). The subjects, all of them Yale undergraduates, were also given the picture arrangment subtest of the Wechsler Adult Intelligence Scale, which is regarded by some psychologists as a measure of the capacity to anticipate future events.

Students who scored very high or very low on the death questionnaire were compared with respect to their futurity scores. It was found that young men with *low* manifest death concern showed significantly *greater* extension into the future. Putting it the other way around, high manifest concern over death was associated with a more limited tendency to project into the future.

This finding is based upon correlational techniques, thus it does not tell us much about the processes involved. Nevertheless, it does allow us to ponder a bit further. Is it possible that apprehension about death is one of the main factors in the (apparently typical) adolescent tendency to rein in his thoughts of futurity? Perhaps one does not care to gaze too far down the road because he just might see something (i.e., *nothing*) there. If death concern does serve to restrain one's view of the future, then it may also impair the ability to plan ahead, to anticipate both hazards and opportunities. One might appear from the outside to be impulsive or short-sighted—even blundering or stupid —when there is in fact no actual cognitive impairment involved. It is just that one has averted his attention from an important source of information (futurity) in consequence of an emotionally aversive reaction to one component of the future (annihilation of the self).

This argument can also be put into reverse. It is possible that the individual's general strategy for organizing his temporal experience is the most relevant factor. The person who organizes his life around one hour or one day at a time may, as a result, be more easily dismayed by the prospect of death. He does not have as much insulation from death as does the person who projects many events, goals, and experiences between his present situation and the remote prospect of his own gravestone.

It is pertinent to remind ourselves that while both of these alternatives seem especially germane to adolescence, the dynamics that are involved can also occur at later points in the life span. Perhaps the adolescent has more built-in reason for fearing death than does his elder. The young person has the task of conceptualizing a longer future, and must do so, of course, from the base of a shorter past. It is likely that he has not had as much occasion to exercise his ability to schedule and organize events in time—this will come later as he moves into occupational, parental, and other social obligatory realms. At any adult age, however, there is probably an important relationship between ability to conceptualize futurity and one's orientation toward death, and the reverse. Again, more research is needed if we are to evaluate the relative significance of the directions: (a) death concern affecting futurity, and (b) futurity affecting death concern.

For another window on the adolescent's relationship to futurity and death, let us consider an investigation by Neil McLaughlin and Robert Kastenbaum (25). The subjects in this study were also college students, in this case all were co-eds. Each subject was asked to write six personal essays. The conditions included: a pleasant future event, pleasant past event, unpleasant future event, unpleasant past event, your earliest memory, and the day of your death. The young women were also asked to rate each of their essays on a five-point scale of engrossment or self-involvement. Those who felt objective and detached, as though they were writing about somebody else, would have a low engrossment score. Those who felt so involved with themselves as depicted in their essay that they were vicariously reliving or preliving the situation would have a high engrossment score. The remainder of the experimental design need not concern us here.

The most relevant point is that the subjects tended to describe their own deaths in a rather tranquil—and distant—manner. The day of death was seen as being a long way off, into their sixties. Not much emotional conflict was expressed, in fact, not much emotion at all. Graceful, peaceful acceptance and resignation were the general themes. The reported engrossment for the death projections was the lowest of all the essays written.

It would seem that college-age women are not nearly as concerned with death as we might have expected from the preceding discussion. In contrast with a number of other studies that might be mentioned, they did tend to project ahead into the fairly remote future (setting their own deaths in the sixth decade of life). But there was more to this piece of research.

After completing the above procedures, the subjects were then asked to imagine the day of their death in a *different* way. Having obtained and, in a sense removed, the image that came most readily to their minds, the investigators attempted to learn what alternate image, if any, was available to them.

The second projected day of death was markedly different from the first. Death was now viewed as a much more proximate event. Many of the young women described deaths that would occur within the next few years. For the total group,, the distance between one's present situation and death *decreased* by more than twenty years.

The specific form taken by death also changed. Accidents and acts of violence became much more frequent. The death situations were described more vividly, in greater detail, with more use of emotion-laden words. The writing style became less restrained and proper—apparently, the subjects were now expressing themselves more spontaneously and idiosyncratically. Emotions and emotional conflicts were much in evidence. Judges who read both set of stories ("blind") had no trouble in determining that the second set conveyed more emotional impact and seemed to represent a greater sense of involvement on the part of the authors.

Yet the subjects themselves reported, through their self-ratings, that they were even *less* engrossed in these essays than they had been in the first set! There was thus a major contradiction between the form and content of the essays as they appeared to outsiders, and as the subjects themselves evaluated them. At the same time that these young women were depicting their deaths as being closer to them in time and in raw affective impact, they were reporting that they felt very little involvement in the situation.

Methodologically, this study underscores the importance of going beyond the subject's first or most accessible response. The subject's total orientation toward death and futurity would have been badly and incompletely represented had the inquiry been limited to their first responses only.

What does this study suggest about the relationship between concepts of death and futurity in young adults? Futurity is stretched out when the topic of personal death is first introduced. Time serves as an insulation between the one's present self and eventual death. The reasonable success of this insulation may be judged by the fact that other aspects of the personal death essay were neutral and tranquil. The subject could rely upon readily available stereotyped expressions. But the requirement to deal twice with the same question forced the respondents to find an alternative organization of thought and feeling within themselves. This turned out to be a more personal kind of response. It was especially interesting to see that as the future shrank, the subject simultaneously introduced a greater *psychological* distance between herself and death. The day of death was seen as much closer at hand, but who was dying? A character on a piece of paper, somebody with whom the writer preferred not to identity.

Which conception of futurity and death was the "real" or "basic" one for those subjects? Perhaps it is more appropriate to inquire: how are these two types of conception related within the same individual? Do adolescents and young adults (and the rest of us) understand our own internal complexity? Is there a clear gap between the conceptions of death and futurity that we have developed on a social expectation level, and our more personal, less often communicated thoughts? It would be useful to know more about this topic.

Let us take up one further point regarding death and futurity in adolescence. One's expectation of personal longevity is an aspect of his future perspective. A series of interrelated studies (26) has been looking into both personal expectations of longevity and their correlates. One of the more interesting findings thus far concerns the relationship between expectations and *preferences*. In all of the adolescent/young adult populations studied to date, there have been an appreciable number of subjects who expect to live longer than they care to live. The (projected) value of being alive seems to run out sooner than life itself. There is some further evidence that people who have this pattern of expectation and preference are relatively less likely to come to the aid of other people who are in life-endangering situations (27).

We see once again that conceptions of time and death are difficult to separate from attitudes or preferences, especially after we leave the early years of childhood. (It is not that easy to differentiate cognitions from attitudes in children, but there, at least, we have the developmental progression of thought to use as a guideline.) We also see that the relationship between futurity and death can be complex within the same individual, let alone from one individual to another. For example, the same young person may (a) feel himself moving rapidly into the future, (b) look forward to this future self as being the "real me," yet (c) think very little about the second half of his life span, and (d) even be convinced that he has more future ahead then he cares to use. Additionally, his #1 expectation that he has a long life span ahead may alternate with a strong secondary expectation that sudden, violent death will snuff out his life in the near future.

We move now to a brief exploration of futurity and death conceptions in elderly adults. It is true that some aged people are afflicted by chronic brain syndrome or senility. Suffering from organic impairments or deficits, they are not able to think very clearly about the future, or about other matters that require high-level cognitive activity. Some observers may prefer to interpret the deterioration of future-oriented thought as a "natural" accompaniment of the aging process. There is no hard evidence for such an interpretation. It is based upon an inclination to regard the pathology of later life as identical with normal aging.

This is not an idle point. If loss of futurity is part of an inevitable and intrinsic biological process, then it may be as "natural" for the elder to turn away from the future realm as it is for the child to discover this same realm. We prefer to distinguish between (a) a general syndrome of age-related decline in which futurity is but one of the psychological casualties, and (b) the thought and behavior of individuals who are not incapacitated by massive organic changes as they move into their later years of life. In the former situation, the impaired elderly person is likely to show obvious difficulty in recalling the recent past and registering the present. He may not even be able to distinguish reliably young past, present, and future. In the latter situation, the "normal" aging person may perhaps think and speak less of futurity, but he does not exhibit a general pattern of deterioration.

There is the implication that reduction in future orientation in later life, when it does occur, may be related as much to socioemotional as to cognitive factors. One study has found that mentally alert geriatric patients could use futurity successfully as a category for organizing experience—providing it was not their personal experience at stake (28). But this same study revealed that the elders in question could not (or, at least, did not) offer much about futurity within a personal framework.

If an elder can "work with the future" (as shown by his performances on story construction tasks), why, then, does he not show a propensity to "live in the future?" The investigator proposed two alternative explanations:

A particular elderly person happens to be depressed, institutionalized

> or fearful of death. This quasi-Aristotelian application of the term "accident" is intended to suggest that elderly people do not *necessarily* have to be limited in their future outlook. . . . Specific conditions have occurred in the particular individual's total life situation which have brought about the observed restriction. That such a restriction might be rather common would be no argument for its necessity. By analogy, even when all oak trees in a given area are blighted with the same disease, no one suggests that this affliction is a necessary and intrinsic characteristic of being an oak tree. This view has practical implications: There would be the prospect that "something could be done" to prevent or remedy this "unfortunate accident" of restriction of future outlook.
>
> An alternative explanation is that there is a certain "necessity" involved in the observed restriction of personal futurity. This might be an individual matter, i.e., not every elderly person would "necessarily" possess this "necessity"—but for those who did, its structuring power would be great. What we mean to suggest here is that certain life-styles imply rather definite self-contained limits. Some elderly people consider that they have lived out their life plan, and thus exist on a sort of "surplus time" that is not part of their lifelong system of values (29).

With respect to the latter point, we are reminded of those young adults who believe they are doomed to an undesired longevity. There are some elders who also seem to feel that they are somewhere between a completed life and a delayed death. (But these orientations are subject to change in both young and old as the conditions of present life change—health, finances, and interpersonal relationships, for example.)

The scarcity of objective future time is likely to confront the elderly person with a problem as fundamental, though qualitatively different, as that which he faced as an identity-conscious adolescent. Should he "write off" the future because so little remains of it? Or should he value the future all the more for precisely the same reason? Again, perhaps he should alter his scale of values and meanings so that *small futures* (tomorrow, not ten years from now) become the relevant frame of reference? Should he retreat into the past? Project himself into a vicarious future through the lives of younger relatives or personally significant endeavors? Bury himself in the present moment, denying both past and future? Whatever solution a particular individual may adopt, it must be acknowledged that the whole pattern of his life is operating within the lengthening shadow of death.

References

1 Werner, H. *Comparative psychology of mental development.* New York: International University Press, 1957.

2 Piaget, J. *The psychology of intelligence.* New York: Littlefield, 1960.

3 Rosenthal, H. R. The fear of death as an indispensable factor in psychotherapy. *American Journal of Psychotherapy,* 1963, *17,* 619–630.

4 Feifel, H. Symposium comments, Gerontological Society, Oct., 1965. Cited by R. Kastenbaum: Death as a research variable in social gerontology: An overview. *Gerontologist,* 1966, *7,* 67–69.

5 Kastenbaum, R. Engrossment and perspective in later life. In R. Kastenbaum (Ed.), *Contributions to the psychobiology of aging.* New York: Springer, 1965. Pp. 3–18.

6 Schecter, D. E., Symonds, M., & Bernstein, I. Development of the concept of time in children. *Journal of Nervous and Mental Diseases,* 1955, *21,* 301–310.

7 Kastenbaum, R. The child's understanding of death: How does it develop? In E. Grollman (Ed.), *Explaining death to children.* Boston: Beacon Press, 1967. Pp. 89–110.

8 Piaget, J. *The construction of reality in the child.* New York: Basic Books, 1954.

9 Werner, *op. cit.*

10 Huang, I., & Lee, H. W. Experimental analysis of child animism. *Journal of Genetic Psychology,* 1945, *66,* 69–74.

11 Klingberg, G. The distinction between living and not living among 7–10 year-old children with some remarks concerning the so-called animism controversy. *Journal of Genetic Psychology,* 1957, *105,* 227–238.

12 Russell, R. W. Studies in animism: II. The development of animism. *Journal of Genetic Psychology,* 1940, *56,* 353–366.

13 Klingberg, *op. cit.*

14 Piaget, *Construction of reality in the child;* Smedslun, J. The acquisition of conservation of substance and weight in children. I. Introduction. *Scandinavian Journal of Psychology,* 1960, *1,* 49–54.

15 Alexander, I. & Adlerstein, A. M. Affective responses to the concept of death in a population of children and early adolescents, *Journal of Genetic Psychology,* 1958, *93,* 167–177.

16 Moriarty, D. *The loss of loved ones.* Springfield, Ill.: Charles C. Thomas, 1967.

17 Fraisse, P. *The psychology of time.* (Translated by Jennifer Lieth.) New York: Harper & Row, 1963; Poulet, G. *Studies in human time.* (Translated by Elliott Coleman.) New York: Harper Torchbooks, 1959; Campbell, J. (Ed.), *Man and time.* New York: Pantheon, 1957.

18 Sturt, M. *The psychology of time.* New York: Harcourt, Brace, 1925.

19 LeShan, L. Time orientation and social class. *Journal of Abnormal and Social Psychology,* 1952, *47,* 589–592; Schneider, L., & Lysgaard, S. The deferred gratification pattern: A preliminary study. *American Sociological Review,* 1953, *18,* 142–149.

20 Piaget, J., & Inhelder, B. *The growth of logical thinking from childhood to adolescence.* New York: Basic Books, 1958.

21 Kastenbaum, R. Time and death in adolescence. In H. Feifel (Ed.), *The meaning of death.* New York: McGraw-Hill, 1959. Pp. 99–113.

22 Kastenbaum, R. The dimensions of future time perspective, an experimental analysis. *Journal of Genetic Psychology,* 1961, *65,* 203–218; McLaughlin, N., & Kastenbaum, R. Engrossment in personal past, future and death. Presented at annual meeting, American Psychological Association, New York City. September, 1966.

23 Dickstein, L., & Blatt, S. Death concern, futurity, and anticipation. *Journal of Consulting Psychology,* 1966, *31,* 11–17.

24 Wallace, M. Future time perspective in schizophrenia. *Journal of Abnormal and Social Psychology,* 1956, *52,* 240–245.

25 McLaughlin & Kastenbaum, *op. cit.*

26 Center for Psychological Studies of Dying, Death and Lethal Behavior. Detroit: Wayne State University.

27 Branscomb, A., & Kastenbaum, R. Orientations toward protecting, extending and forshortening the lifespan: A preliminary study. Center for Psychological Studies of Dying, Death, and Lethal Behavior. Detroit: Wayne State University, 1969, unpublished manuscript.

28 Kastenbaum, R. Cognitive and personal futurity in later life. *Journal of Individual Psychology*. 1963, *19*, 216–222.

29 *Ibid.*

28 • Common Fallacies about Dying Patients

Avery D. Weisman

Avery D. Weisman is a psychoanalyst, physician, and professor of psychiatry at the Harvard Medical School and at the Massachusetts General Hospital where he heads Project Omega—the study of dying persons. He is one of the most thoughtful writers in the field of thanatology today. In this selection from his book On Dying and Denying, *he attacks some of the myths and fallacies concerning the attitudes and actions of the dying.*

The plight of the dying awakens everyone's sense of dread and annihilation. Yet, as Swift said, "It is impossible that anything so natural, so necessary, and so universal as death, should ever have been designed by providence as an evil to mankind." Nevertheless, our common belief, augmented by cultural bias, is that death is a deplorable, evil, unnecessary and premature event. Death is encased by custom. Our rituals, formal and spontaneous, reflect an enormous concern about being in the presence of the dying and the soon-to-be dead.

In this section I use the physician as the prototype for anyone who is forced to consider the interface between life and death. As a professional, however, the physician influences the way that other people approach death. Because dying people are simply living people who have reached an ultimate stage, the doctor's misconceptions may distort their image of death.

Medicine is only partially scientific. Much of what a practitioner does depends upon empirical procedures, ethical precepts, sanctioned mythology, and much, much magic. Were any doctor to depend wholly upon scientific knowledge, he would be as constrained and disabled as anyone who could act only upon proven principles: He would be lost and ineffectual.

To be a responsive and responsible physician is almost an impossible profession, in the presence of incurable disease and dying. Just at the time when a doctor needs his skill and knowledge, they fail him, out of the nature of things. He is forced to improvise, and at times, his art becomes artifice.

Fortunately, patients tend to endow physicians with the aura of the priest and medicine man, both of whom can perform magic. The advantage of magic over science is that it does not need to be true. Magic and sorcery have nothing to do with truth and proof. They are strategies for dealing with special beliefs about reality. Medical practice draws upon folk-wisdom, and it is as indebted to folk-fallacies as to folk-truths. In the realm of death and dying, magical formulas and incantations frequently pass as principles. Consequently, physicians can readily, even inadvertently, call upon their prejudices and act upon preconceptions. As a result, fallacies about dying patients may be perpetuated from one generation to the next, insulated by a tradition that exempts these beliefs from investigation.

Here are a few typical, widespread fallacies about the dying:

1. Only suicidal and psychotic people are willing to die. Even when death is inevitable, no one wants to die.
2. Fear of death is the most natural and basic fear of man. The closer he comes to death, the more intense the fear becomes.
3. Reconciliation with death and preparation for death are impossible. Therefore, say as little as possible to dying people, turn their questions aside, and use any means to deny, dissimulate, and avoid open confrontation.
4. Dying people do not really want to know what the future holds. Otherwise, they would ask more questions. To force a discussion or to insist upon unwelcome information is risky. The patient might lose all hope. He might commit suicide, become very depressed, or even die more quickly.
5. After speaking with family members, the doctor should treat the patient as long as possible. Then, when further benefit seems unlikely, the patient should be left alone, except for relieving pain. He will then withdraw, die in peace, without further disturbance and anguish.
6. It is reckless, if not downright cruel, to inflict unnecessary suffering upon the patient or his family. The patient is doomed; nothing can really make any difference. Survivors should accept the futility, but realize that they will get over the loss.
7. Physicians can deal with all phases of the dying process because of their scientific training and clinical experience. The emotional and psychological sides of dying are vastly overemphasized. Consultation with psychiatrists and social workers is unnecessary. The clergy might be called upon, but only because death is near. The doctor has no further obligation after the patient's death.

Fallacies lead physicians into inconsistencies, and to judgments that confuse the clinical with the moralistic. Precepts help to rationalize assumptions and to shelter the doctor from undue anxiety. Assumptions, particularly false assumptions, decide conclusions in advance. For example, these seven fallacies are, in effect, tacit justifications for not getting involved with death. Were the physician openly to confess his reluctance, he might paraphrase the fallacies like this: "Anyone who is willing to die must be out of his mind. Death is a dreadful business, because I am afraid of dying. I have done everything for this patient that I know. I wish I could do more. I don't want to be blamed, but I can't stand being around anyone who is going to die, especially if I know him. Even though we all know what is going to happen, let's pretend that all is well or soon will be. Maybe he doesn't know, after all. He hasn't ever asked me about his sickness, and certainly never mentioned dying. If he suspects, and he may, I suppose he would rather not know. Leave well enough alone. If we did force him to talk about the future, maybe he'd be more discouraged, or even take matters into his own hands. The family is pretty helpless, too, but I'll make sure that his pain is under control. Why did that family think I was going to upset him when we first found out what was wrong? We've never mentioned it, so far as I can tell. Now, the best thing to do is keep him comfortable, let him die in peace. We don't want to make anyone suffer unnecessarily. The facts are there, but it will do no good to dwell on death. The family seems to be taking it pretty well, but they'll get over it, they always do. Nature will take its course, if things can just be kept quiet. I don't need a psychiatrist to tell me what I know already. When the time comes, I'll ask the family minister to get in on this and offer some consolation. He'll be taking over soon, anyway!"

Dying patients who are attended by physicians who feel this way are probably fortunate. The scene is sympathetic, compared with the bleak prospect of dying alone and unattended. My point, however, is not to argue the merits of one kind of doctor as opposed to the management of another. Compassion and concern are in this mythical doctor's words, but the management he advocates is primarily intended to comfort and console himself.

Only someone who is extremely apprehensive himself would fail to see that many dying patients accept death with equanimity and without mental disturbance. To regard acceptance of death as a sign of being suicidal or psychotic amounts to believing that anyone who attempts suicide is insane and, therefore, beyond help, just as psychotics are beyond help—egregious fallacies, all.

To be more specific about these seven fallacies: the first three rationalize withdrawal and establish more distance between doctor and patient. The fourth fallacy infers that the patient is also disinclined to talk about death. Unwise confrontation is, by definition, apt to cause mental disturbance. We cannot assume, as this doctor does, that someone who asks no questions has no questions to ask. He may have no opportunity to ask, or he may be afraid to ask, lest he repel people on whom he depends. Families cannot decide judiciously about what to tell. They rely upon the expert for advice and can be swayed according to the doctor's beliefs. The fifth and sixth fallacies presuppose that when the patient is not regarded as responsible, with eyes to see and ears to hear, his silence is assumed to mean that he is both ignorant and complacent. Withdrawal does not necessarily mean serenity, nor is open accessibility equivalent to inflicting "unnecessary suffering." It is commonly heard that physicians do not talk about death with very sick patients in order to keep up their hope. But they usually add that the patients are probably already aware of their condition, and so do not need to be told! If there are rationalizations ready for any contingency, how can anyone be wrong?

Let us continue: survivors do not always get over a serious loss and return to "normal," without first suffering a great deal. Sometimes, bereavement leads to serious somatic and psychological symptoms during the next year or two.[1] Mourners may become patients. Yet, some doctors continue to believe that anticipatory bereavement is peripheral to more genuine medical concerns.

What is "unnecessary suffering," that is so often cited as a reason for nonintervention? Who is to judge what varieties of suffering are necessary or not? Whose suffering are we concerned about? During the terminal phase, not many patients ask for miracles, only for evidence of care and concern.

The most damaging and lethal fallacy in this, as in most other situations, is that of stereotyping people and problems. When we categorize anyone, doctor or patient, we reduce them to a least common denominator, and they become less than what they are or could be. The alternative, then, is to look for the exceptions, and meanwhile, to treat everyone as a special case.

Note

1 Colin M. Parkes, "The Psychosomatic Effects of Bereavement," in *Modern Trends in Psychosomatic Medicine,* ed. Oscar W. Hill London: Butterworth, 1970). See also "The Broken Heart," this volume.

29 • Death Work and Stages of Dying

Edwin S. Shneidman

In this selection from Deaths of Man, *Dr. Shneidman discusses what, if any, are the discernible "stages" of dying. He notes that there are certain psychological features of the dying process, characteristic of almost every dying person, that must be understood if one is to comprehend the mind and behavior of those approaching death.*

. . . Death is the most mysterious, the most threatening, and the most tantalizing of all human phenomena. Death is destroyer and redeemer; it is the ultimate cruelty and the essence of release. Death is universally feared but, paradoxically, sometimes is actively sought. Although undeniably ubiquitous, death is incomprehensibly unique. Of all phenomena it is the most obvious and the least reportable; it encompasses the profoundest of people's perplexities and ambivalences. Over the ages death has been the source of fear, the focus of taboo, the occasion for poetry, the stimulus for philosophy—and remains the ultimate mystery in the life of each person.

"Death is the one thing you don't have to do. It will be done for you." So said philosopher Abraham Kaplan to me. But there is more to that statement than first meets the mind. Admittedly it implies that everyone dies, that no one can circumvent death. But it makes no attempt to explicate certain lesser truths: that persons die at various rates (from sudden to protracted), at various ages, and with various degrees of participation in their own death. In those special cases—nowadays rather frequent—in which sensitive adults have been told (or know) that they will die of a fatal disease within a relatively short time, they have the opportunity (and the chore thrust upon them) of preparing for their own death, that is, doing their own "death work."

In the phrase "know that they will die" the word "know" has a special connotation that is critical in any discussion of death. To "know" that one is doomed to die soon is epistemologically different from "knowing" almost anything else about oneself or about the world. It is a kind of "knowing" infused not only with uncertainty but also with several layers of conscious and unconscious mental functioning. Of course, everyone "knows" he or she is going to die ("Life is a fatal disease"; "No one gets out of life alive"), but when one is seriously ill and has been informed that he or she is moribund, then "knowing" about imminent death is typically mixed with magic, hope, disbelief, and denial. After all, death has never happened before.

No one can ever really "know" that he or she is about to die. There is always the intermittent presence of denial. The recurrent denial of death during the dying process seems to be the manifestation of the therapeutic gyroscope of the psyche. (We must not forget that one of the principal functions of the personality is to protect itself against itself—against its own ravages, assaults, and threats.) And yet seemingly contradictorily—but not really contradictorily, because we are dealing with different levels of the human mind—people often do seem to "know" at some deep unconscious or primitive level when they are about to die and then, in a very special and identifiable way, they withdraw, perhaps to husband their last energies, to put themselves together and prepare for their end.

One implication of this view of "knowing" relates to the question "To tell or not to tell?" In the situation of a person with a fatal disease—as in many aspects of psychotherapy—there is almost anything that can be done badly and almost anything that can be done well. The issue of telling is thus not so much a question of whether or not, but of how, how much, how often, how euphemistically, how hopefully, and how far beyond what the patient (and various members of the family) already "knows" at that moment. Hinton (1967) and Weisman (1972) present excellent discussions of this complicated issue.

Death work imposes a two-fold burden: intrapsychic (preparing oneself for death) and interpersonal (preparing oneself in relation to loved ones and, simultaneously, preparing the loved ones to be survivors). The task is further compounded by pervasive emotional states: grief and anguish over the death to come; anger at one's impotence, at fate, and often, by unconscious extension, at key persons in one's life who are not dying, especially the young; and beneath these, a low-grade anxiety related to fear of pain, to loss of competence, to loneliness and abandonment, to fear of the unknown. But always, intermittently coming and going, is the fervent denial that death will really occur to oneself.

Dr. Elisabeth Kübler-Ross has delineated five psychological stages in the process of dying based on her work with terminally ill patients in a Chicago hospital. Her deep concern with their welfare is evident; her book *On Death and Dying* (1969) is a clear manifesto of care for those who are benighted by the shadow of death. At the least, it stands as an antidote to some of the callous conventional hospital procedures surrounding the dying patient, described so well by Sudnow in *Passing On* (1967) and by Glaser and Strauss in *Awareness of Dying* (1965) and *Time for Dying* (1968)

Her book grew out of an interdisciplinary seminar at the University of Chicago, in the course of which dying patients were interviewed, or more accurately, were invited to speak of their fears and hopes, dreams and nightmares. The results of this unexampled open discussion were strikingly salutary for both the stressed dying person and the stressed hospital personnel. The interviews often have an evocative and haunting quality, resonating deep within one and stirring buried aspirations and fears. One cannot help being moved by the great human spirit in the voices of these dying fellow beings.

Kübler-Ross explicates five psychological stages of dying, or sets of reactions to one's awareness of imminent death. Categorized primarily "in terms of coping mechanisms at the time of a terminal illness," these stages are defined as: (1) denial and isolation ("No, not me; it can't be true!"); (2) anger—rage, envy, resentment ("Why me?"); (3) bargaining ("If you'll . . . then I'll . . ."); (4) depression ("What's the use?"); and (5) acceptance (the final rest before the long journey). According to her analysis, "the one thing that persists through all these stages [is] hope" ("I will not die"). One is reminded of Maurice Farber's *Theory of Suicide* (1968), in which self-destruction is seen as "a disease of hope," and of Kobler and Stotland's *The End of Hope* (1964), a case study of the death of a hospital.

Dr. Kübler-Ross does not tell us what percentages of the dying patients lived through each of these five stages or what the consequences were if any were cut off before they achieved the last stage. One key question is how one makes the transition from the negative affective states (which characterize the first four stages) to a state of acceptance. One might wish that she had extended her explorations of the nature of acceptance, as Henry Murray did so superbly in "Dead to the World: The Passions of Herman Melville" (1967). The last of Murray's five "psychic stages" in Melville's psychological development vis-à-vis death is "I accept my annihilation." But Murray then ponders the possible meanings of this acceptance, demonstrating that "acceptance" obviously has many dimensions:

> Did this last station of Melville's pilgrimage constitute a victory of the spirit, as some think? an ultimate reconciliation with God at the end of a lifelong quarrel? or was it a graceful acquiescence to the established morality and conventions of his world with Christian forgiveness toward those who had crushed him in their name? or a forthright willing of the obligatory? or was it an acknowledgement of defeat? a last-ditch surrender of his long quest for a new gospel of joy in this life? or was it a welcoming of death?

My own limited work has not led me to conclusions identical with those of Kübler-Ross. Indeed, while I have seen in dying persons isolation, envy, bargaining, depression, and acceptance, I do not believe that these are necessarily "stages" of the dying process, and I am not at all convinced that they are lived through in that order, or, for that matter, in any universal order. What I do see is a complicated clustering of intellectual and affective states, some fleeting, lasting for a moment or a day or a week, set, not unexpectedly, against the backdrop of that person's total personality, his or her "philosophy of life" (whether an essential optimism and gratitude to life or a pervasive pessimism and dour or suspicious orientation to life).

Philosophers—all but the twentieth-century analytic so-called philosophers—have traditionally taken life and death as their core topics. In relation to death and philosophy, the interested reader can turn to Choron's *Death and Western Thought* (1963) for a résumé of what major philosophers have thought about death. As the tie between philosophic reflection and easing the burden of one's own death, I know of nothing more illuminating than Pepper's crisp and insightful essay, "Can a Philosophy Make One Philosophical?" (1967).

What of that nexus of emotions manifested by the dying person? Rather than the five definite stages discussed above, my experience leads me to posit a hive of affect, in which there is a constant coming and going. The emotional stages seem to include a constant interplay between disbelief and hope and, against these as background, a waxing and waning of anguish, terror, acquiescence and surrender, rage and envy, disinterest and ennui, pretense, taunting and daring and even yearning for death—all of these in the context of bewilderment and pain.

One does not find a unidirectional movement through progressive stages so much as an alternation between acceptance and denial. Denial is a most interesting psychodynamic phenomenon. For a few consecutive days a dying person is capable of shocking a listener with the breathtaking candor of a profound acceptance of imminent death and the next day shock that listener with unrealistic talk of leaving the hospital and going on a trip. This interplay between acceptance and denial, between understanding what is happening and magically disbelieving its reality, may reflect a deeper dialogue of the total mind, involving different layers of conscious awareness of "knowing" and of needing not to know. Weisman's recent book, *On Dying and Denying* (1972), focuses on these complicated psychodynamics of dying, especially on the role of denial.

The optimal working techniques for the clinical thanatologist (the professional or lay person, staff or volunteer) who deals directly with the death-laden aspects of the dying person have yet to be evolved. Admittedly, working with a dying person is a very special kind of intervention and would seem to require some special approaches and skills. As a beginning, one might say that the primary goals of such thanatological efforts are to help the dying person achieve a better death ("an appropriate death") and to help the survivors deal better with their loss, specifically to forestall morbidity or mortality. The interactions with the dying person are, understandably, different from almost any other therapeutic exchange, though they contain typical elements of rapport building, interview, conversation, psychotherapy (including interpretation), history taking, just plain talk, and communicative silences.

There are many ways in which a clinical thanatologist can find an appropriate occasion to speak with a dying person of feelings about death. Even dreams can be used to this end. (On a closely related topic, Litman, in 1964, wrote of the almost prophetic role of dreams in suicide). An example: A singularly beautiful and serene young woman, rapidly dying of metastasized cancer, had not talked about the possibility of her own death. One day, immediately after I came into her hospital room, she stated that she had had a dream the night before that she wanted to tell me. In her dream, she wandered down a street that she almost recognized but had never traveled, in a city that was vaguely familiar but one that she had never visited, and went to a house that seemed like home but clearly was not hers. In response to her ringing the bell, her mother answered the door, but that person was definitely no longer her mother. She then woke up.

"What does it all mean?" she asked me. In turn, I asked her what her mood had been during her dream. She said that it was one of pervasive sadness and nostalgia. She volunteered that perhaps the dream reflected her wish to be more independent of her mother, to lead her own life, living by her own standards. I asked her under what circumstances her mother might not be her mother. To this, she answered if her mother were dead, but she certainly did not wish for that; or, if it turned out that her mother were really not her biological parent, that she had been adopted, but that did not seem to make any sense. I went one step further: I asked if there might be any other circumstance. No, she said, she could not think of any. Her face then clouded and with some surprise she whispered, "If *I* were dead!" After she said this, her expression seemed to brighten. "Of course!" she said, and then asked, "Is that what I've been trying to keep from myself?" In the following few days she spoke of many details of her life, but intermittently, at a pace which she herself set, she talked about the realistic possibility of her death, her fear of dying, her concern for her loved ones, her deep regret at having to die, and the many joys she had had in her brief life. She said that she was glad that she and I could talk "honestly." Five days after her dream of death she died.

Thanatologists, if they examine their own minds, may very well discover that they are almost constantly aware of the expected "death trajectory" of their patients, and they govern the intensity of the sessions, their movement, the climaxes, the protective plateaus, and so on, over that projected time span—just as a skilled psychotherapist tries to control the intensity of the flow of material within any psychotherapeutic hour, trying not to leave the patient disturbed at the end of the session. The benign interventionist always needs to keep a hand on the rheostat governing the intensity of affect. The best results are achieved by turning affective intensity up gradually during the session and shading it down somewhat toward the end. So it is in the thanatological treatment of a dying person over the last months, weeks, days, hours, of life.

In my belief, the transference and countertransference aspects of death work are unique, different in subtle ways from any other human exchange; both Hinton and Kübler-Ross mention this point.[1] For one thing, the situation itself, because of its obvious poignant quality and its time-limited feature, permits a depth of investment which in any other circumstances might border on the unseemly, yet in this setting is not only appropriate but perhaps even optimal. We can love a dying person, and permit a dying person to love us, in a meaningful way that is not possible in any other psychotherapeutic encounter.

It is difficult (and admittedly complicating) to speak meaningfully about Thanatos and its theoretical opposite, Eros. (Nor, parenthetically, do I view these concepts as anything other than figurative metaphoric polarities. I do not at all believe in a death instinct.) But considering the special nature of the transference and countertransference with dying persons, one might ask: Is it possible to fight death with love, or with loving care as a kind of substitute for love? Is it appropriate? Can it work? In some cases of dying persons I have worked with there was little question in my mind that Eros had helped to sustain them in their terminal periods and to lighten their dying days, that is, if by Eros we mean sympathy, support, and concern, all the opposite of neglect.[2] One cannot always give the necessary transfusions of hope, but one should not fail to transmit one's honest feelings of interest, affection, and respect for the other's dignity—presaging one's own real sense of grief at the loss to come.

Working with dying persons seems to have some curious attractions and mystiques, some akin, I believe, to those associated with the very beginnings of life, the primal scene. In a sense the mysteries connected with sexuality are not as great as those lifelong uncertainties about the components of ideal love. In somewhat the same way, one can be continually intrigued, mystified, and even voyeuristic about working with individuals who are in the process of dying. As I see a dying person moving from day to day toward that ultimate moment, I hope that perhaps I can learn something about how dying is done, something about the arcane mysteries of the magic moment of transition from life to nonlife, something about the components of an ideal death, and even, if the gods are gracious, some guidelines that will teach me how to die well when my own turn comes.

Notes

1 Hinton: "Often we came to know each other well—friendships grew fast in these circumstances and sometimes, it seemed difficult to believe we met only a few times"; and "The physician who had been questioned by this man [with cancer] said that he felt that he had probably been more perturbed by the conversation than the patient had" (1967, pp. 96, 134). Kübler-Ross: "We find the same to be true among many patients who developed strong positive feelings toward us and were still able to pass through a stage of rage and anger often displaced onto others in the environment who reminded them of their own failing strength, vitality and functioning" (1972, p. 57).

2 Arnold Toynbee, at eighty, says, "Love cannot save life from death, but it can fulfill life's purpose."

References

Choron, Jacques. *Death and Western Thought.* New York: Collier Books, 1963.

Farber, Maurice. *Theory of Suicide.* New York: Funk & Wagnall, 1968.

Glaser, B. G., and Strauss, A. *Awareness of Dying.* Chicago: Aldine, 1965.

Glaser, B. G., and Strauss, A. *Time for Dying.* Chicago: Aldine, 1968.

Hinton, John. *Dying.* Baltimore: Penguin Books, 1967.

Kobler, Arthur, and Stotland, Ezra. *The End of Hope.* New York: Free Press, 1964.

Kübler-Ross, Elisabeth. *On Death and Dying.* New York: Macmillan, 1969.

Kübler-Ross, Elisabeth. Review of Hinton's *Dying. Life-Threatening Behavior,* 1972, *2,* 56–58.

Litman, Robert E. Immobilization Response to Suicidal Behavior. *Archives of General Psychiatry,* 1964, *11,* 282–285.

Murray, Henry A. Dead to the World: The Passions of Herman Melville. In Edwin S. Shneidman (Ed.), *Essays in Self-Destruction*. New York: Science House, 1967.
Pepper, Stephen C. Can a Philosophy Make One Philosophical? In Edwin S. Shneidman (Ed.), *Essays in Self-Destruction*. New York: Science House, 1967.
Sudnow, David. *Passing On*. Englewood Cliffs, N.J.: Prentice-Hall, 1967.
Toynbee, Arnold *et al*. *Man's Concern with Death*. New York: McGraw-Hill, 1969.
Weisman, Avery D. *On Dying and Denying*. New York: Behavior Publications, 1972.

30 • Reactions to One's Own Fatal Illness

Erich Lindemann

Dr. Lindemann was, for many years, professor of psychiatry at Harvard and medical director of the Wellesley project, a landmark study in community psychiatry. He is most noted for his pioneer work in crisis intervention (which began with his working with the survivors of the infamous Coconut Grove fire). He died of cancer in Palo Alto, California, in 1974. The preliminary remarks (in italics), below, were written by his widow, Elizabeth B. Lindemann.

Even if he had said nothing worthwhile, the scene would have been impressive: the professor who was also a patient standing in the narrow, windowless room in the basement of the Stanford Medical School, where he had recently been undergoing radiation therapy, before a small group of residents, technicians, and nurses. He had had a sacral chordoma for six years and would have two more years of unspeakable suffering. He could have been excused for withdrawing, but giving came as naturally to him as breathing.

Those present on that February morning in 1972 heard him thank them for their unsuccessful efforts at curing him. If they had been trying to avoid thinking about what having terminal cancer meant to some of the people they were treating, they now heard of several ways to help these patients come to better terms with prospective death.

David Satin has called this chapter "the ultimate expression of Dr. Lindemann's characteristic openness with others and the clearest statement of his companionship and sharing with the patient as his therapeutic stance."

I am delighted to have the opportunity to express my appreciation for the fact that I am able to be here, without much discomfort, and able to be an active participant in academic life again. I came here last November looking for help; I was quite crippled as far as my activities went because of pain and general discomfort. It would be only natural for me, since I am in that branch of medicine that deals with experiences and subjective states, to talk a bit about how patients feel, in general, when they are confronted with approaching death, mediated through a malignancy or other conditions; and say a little how a particular kind of person, of my age and attitude and values, reacted to the confrontation with the situation. I should like to mention that it was Mrs. Lutzker, the department social worker, who first suggested that I talk about this theme. Her daily presence in the radiation service was one of the very important items of the treatment experience, to which I shall refer later.

How does one get to the problem, confrontation with death? At the Massachusetts General Hospital, where I worked for thirty years, we came to it through our interest in how people react to losing part of their body —partial death. We studied women who had had a hysterectomy. They found themselves reacting with surprising distress to this event: Instead of being grateful to their surgeon, they were furious with him! One of these women was admitted to our psychiatry service after having knocked her surgeon flat on the floor on the follow-up visit; she was so scared that her fist would fly out again that she said, "Help me against this violent impulse!" And so we became interested, and our first study was of a series of women who had had hysterectomies, comparing them with patients who had had cholecystectomies. And it turned out that indeed they experienced a heightened level of violence and hostile feelings, in most cases quite unspecific and not directed to the surgeon—being irritable, snappy, disliking people more, not being able to stand scenes in the movies where violence was displayed, etc.

The second stage of our interest occurred when the surgeons had to deal with a large number of people after the Coconut Grove fire in Boston who had severe burns and would not cooperate. They were very angry with their well-meaning surgeons, kicked the nurses away, tore off their transplantations and their infusions, and were just nasty patients. On inspection it turned out that those people who were upset in this manner were people who were confronted with death, but not their own: They were afraid that their wife or husband, as the case might be, had been caught in the fire; often they didn't yet know what had happened. They had a high level of uncertainty, and they were concerned with the flood of imagery which comes to the griever about somebody lost.

We then had an opportunity to study what a grieving person does. One of these grievers, before we had learned how to help them, jumped out of a window. It turned out that he wanted to be with his wife. Other patients then gave us a whole variety of the basic ingredients of the grief process. And only when we helped them to do their grieving—once they knew with certainty that the loved one had died in the fire—were we able to make it possible for them to be as cooperative with their physician as I guess I have been here!

Now, what did one have to watch for? This confrontation with death meant induced rage: Who has been the villain? "Was I the villain? I should not have taken my wife to that club. Somebody should have seen that there were proper protections against the fire."—and so on. First, accusations. Accusations, we learned later, often go against the surgeon who lost the patient or against the funeral director. So, increased hostility. Second, waves of sorrow and preoccupation with the image of the deceased. This image was often very disturbing—for instance, being in the fire. A variety of images in one's mind—and really, one of the worst pains there is, is sorrow. Having to suffer this, one gradually masters this pain, and gradually gets away from the inclination one has not to think about it, to be busy with getting the deceased out of one's mind—forgetting it—putting things away which belonged to him; moving into another place so that one will not be reminded of him. Or, one is busy with this aggression against people, looking for the villain but avoiding thinking of the patient. On the other hand, one may suffer through his mourning, and while one does that, do the essentials of grief work, which now becomes important for all people who are faced with a loss, including *losing themselves.*

This grief work has to do with the effort of reliving and working through in small quantities events which involved the now-deceased person and the survivor: the things one did together, the roles one had vis-à-vis each other, which were complementary to each other and which one would pass through day by day in the day's routine. Each item of this shared role has to be thought through, *pained* through, if you want, and gradually the question is raised, How can I do that with somebody else? And gradually the collection of activities which were put together in this unit with the person who has died can be torn asunder and be put onto other people. So it can be divided among other future role partners, who then become loved a little—not much, perhaps, at first—but become tolerable, with whom one can do things and have companionship.

This process is something which can be learned. Thus one can see some people do well, while others never learn it. If they don't learn it they often remain stuck in this early period of grieving, in the first phase of the grief process, in which one has a global relationship to the person lost—perhaps in heaven, perhaps in a picture on the wall. One speaks or prays to that image, sets a place for the person as an imaginary companion at the breakfast table, speaks to the children as if the person were still there, and cannot abandon the total image in favor of partial relationships to parts of that person.

Now I began with parts, when I spoke of losing one's uterus, rather than losing one's whole person. And I think it is important to keep in mind that this problem of relationship to a total entity of a person as compared to partial aspects of one's doing, or to parts of his or her own body, is one of the major themes which occurs in people who are confronted with impending death and who have in their body a dangerous tumor—or, for that matter, have had a heart attack or an amputation of the leg, lose their eyes, etc. In each of these situations, the "job," what we call *grief work,* arises: to think out the aspects of the new role which one has to play in life. With our uterus-deprived women, the question of a new sexual role arises: will I be a cold partner to my husband, or will he think I am, even if I'm not? And so the sexual role relationship threatens to be altered, has to be worked through, and often is neglected to be worked through. The person who loses a leg and has to be rehabilitated has to learn the role of a legless person, who will be received by other people in new role constellations—which must be acceptable to him and to the other persons because one of the ingredients of comfortable living is to have a reference group that accepts one's identity and accepts that network of roles in which one relates to them.

And so in a variety of medical events, which are witnessed by various departments, this process of grieving and of learning new roles takes place, and has to be achieved if one wants to be a mentally healthy griever. Out of this study of grief arose what is now called *community mental health*, where, instead of waiting for illnesses, one tries to find people who are in grief states in response to losses of various kinds, including medical losses, and helps them with these processes. This work is a form of preventive psychiatry or preventive medicine. If they get stuck in this process without knowing it, people then find themselves in a condition of being neurotics, or often psychotics, or angry, ugly persons whom nobody likes. They then become the patients from whom one turns away in the ward, to whom one doesn't talk, and who are so unpleasant and hostile that the social network which is necessary, on the ward perhaps more than in a good many other places, cannot be reestablished with them.

The patient who is caught in the confrontation with a severe impending loss, in this case of his own self, and who has to do *anticipatory grieving*, as we call it now, is facing a psychological job, which can be facilitated by those who look after him or be impeded inadvertently because one doesn't know what is going on; and so one comes out with some of the casualties of maladaptive grief processes. They then have to be handled one way or the other, and usually one is very unhappy with these people.

Now let us turn away from partial losses and think about losing of oneself in threatening death. Some time left, a little time left, a long time left?—how much, one doesn't know. How many impeding aspects are there in the situation? And one of the big things is uncertainty, as it was with our burn patients—the uncertainty about the timing of one's own loss. The problem then is the reaching out and clamoring for information from the physician that he often cannot give. One of the tensions between the patient and yourselves is that you cannot give the information which he wants and which in some way you really ought to be able to give him; but you have a lot of misgivings about giving him that. I went through this in a very big way indeed with my illness and the threat in my system. And so it is a matter of knowledge: information seeking is an essential part of the mentally healthy effort of adapting to a crisis situation.

Around this matter of information getting so many issues have arisen that a whole book has been written about it by Anselm Strauss, a sociologist, and a nurse friend of his. They write in great detail, having studied various hospitals, about the habitual "culture pattern" of communication of the doctors, nurses, and social workers vis-à-vis one another, the patient, and the family. The problem is what information to give to whom, to avoid contradictory information to different participants in a social orbit. Problems arise such as who ought to be the bearer of good or bad news. The relevant participants in this social orbit are likely to receive opposing messages, and the patient is confronted with contradictory information. Then his task is not to adapt to information, period!—but to figure out what is right and what is wrong. And so information getting and transmission is one of the important things.

The second thing is, what does one do with so row, the bad feelings? Patients who are confronted with impending loss are busy with weeping, with painful experiences; and there is an inclination in many medical cultures to consider the good patient as a brave patient, who doesn't show any misery and who—you might almost say—is nice to the doctor by not showing how upset he is because he doesn't want to make his friend the doctor upset. This is a very common reaction among patients. And so the problem is, how does one deal with the masses of emotion? Well, the important thing is that emotions can be displayed and emotions can be shared. Often the nurses are the ones who are the most skillful in this, in sharing the emotions, and who, however, then need a little backing from *their* friends in their social orbit when they go through too much of that. The nurses in the intensive care unit are especially endangered in that way, with such an immediate threat of death. And all these things happen very rapidly, over and over again, and they need help. For instance, in some of the intensive care units we now have nurses' groups, in which they tell each other about feelings such as "I killed that patient—I didn't watch out at the right moment," and that sort of thing, this sense of guilt about not having been properly available or not having used the right judgment. And so the problem of emotions arising and being displayed has to do not only with the patient but also with the caretaking staff: doctor, nurse, social worker, etc. —with their responses and with their sharing, with the patient and with their colleagues, and with themselves. And this emotional impact is a job to be done which takes time . . . And if you have to come to terms with your own demise, it also takes time.

A number of studies have now been done under the heading of terminal care, trying to figure out carefully what is the mode by which this job is done by patients under various circumstances. How is it different in the case of mentally healthy versus neurotic patients, and what devices does one learn from one patient that one can give to another patient. This matter of learning from sufferers and communicating with new sufferers about it has now become a part of psychiatry called *research on coping.* How do people cope with stress situations, such as impending death? And how can one tell other people confronted with such stress how it has been done by successful persons? And how can the means be taught most effectively?

Now, what sort of things have I, for instance, learned, and which did I use in my own coping? One thing which impressed me very much was a book by Hans Zinsser, who was a faculty member at Stanford some years ago—a man who died of leukemia at a relatively young age, when he thought he had only done about a third of what he was going to do. He had to grieve about himself. Since grieving means to review shared experiences, he reviewed those experiences which he had had with Hans Zinsser! He looked him up very carefully, and reconstructed his life, and out of this came one of the most fascinating books, called *As I Remember Him.* In it he describes this partly idealized, partly odd sort of person who was that wonderful guy Hans! Putting him there and loving him—and perhaps sometimes while he was writing, sorrowing a lot—he came to terms with the fact that this *was* once, and lives in memory, but in the future will not be there as an identity. It can only be represented by symbols, such as a book, or—there is a building named for me in Boston, the Lindemann Mental Health Center, which means an awful lot. So you have something which continues your identity's existence by a global attribute, a book or a building which then allows the survivors to remember those things which are pertinent to *you*, the particular person, just as at various stages of your anticipatory grieving you think about various aspects of that life which you are now reconstructing.

Now the reading of this book was a revelation to me and led me to wonder, in looking at grief patients, if they have similar tasks? They don't write books, but with members of their families, or the nurse, they have confidential exchanges about the sort of things they did with other people. They like to be visited by a lot of friends, as long as they don't feel too embarrassed about their emotions, and would like to pick up items in their lives which they shared with the future survivors. And they will rub in these experiences with the family and friends, so that they will be sure to remember when they are gone. So this constructing a collective surviving image of oneself which still will be there when one happens not to be there any more in the flesh is the core of grieving, which, if it is done well, is apt to become an admirable process—a fascinating process if one is lucky enough to witness it.

And every once in awhile one hears about some person who is confronted with a severe illness and is not going to live, who is an inspiration to somebody else. And from our observations, it is these people who do such a good job of recalling their own lives and their own shared experiences, constructing an image which is a tenable image of a human being.

Now if that is so, one can understand why in books dealing with terminal care, the authors are concerned that there is not enough contact between the patient and his family. The family gets into a conflict over whether to stay or not, how much to share in the patient's illness; whether these sometimes trite things which the patient brings up are worth the time of the patient and everybody else. And for the family, a very important problem may come up, which may have been mentioned here by David Kaplan and Dr. Fishman in connection with the mothers of leukemic children—namely, that one does one's grieving so well that one emancipates oneself from the person who is going to die and then has no relationship any more. The parents don't know whether to visit or whether to stay away; if they try to pull themselves out of the bondage they will feel they are disloyal. This problem of a relationship which may be severed too successfully becomes a difficult one for the anticipatory griever. Sometimes patients who have a terminal illness come to terms with this illness, are all settled; and then when people still come, they don't want to see them any more. One wonders what is the matter with them unless one is aware of the fact that a process has been going on, and one has to tap at what phase this process now is.

The next point is the problem of the model for this new kind of endeavor, coming to terms with one's own death. How have other people done it? Does one know somebody who was a good terminal patient? Therefore, the need to know other patients, knowing other people in a similar predicament, becomes so important. That's why some departments have developed groups of patients who meet each other, and why I found the experience in your waiting room helpful, where we got together in our funny little gowns and where you can see the typical evolution of a group process. People when they first come there are very stiff, they don't talk, "they really aren't sick but have just come in order to be irradiated"; finally someone dares to speak about leukemia; what a remarkable place this department is compared to other clinics where they may have been treated; *they* don't know yet what's wrong, but *they* are surely going to find out. So they are proud of the place, and having something to be proud of, they gradually begin to be proud of themselves, telling each other what good patients they are. And a little later, the problem is, can they tell each other what good grievers they are, and how they can come to terms with their death. That comes only after quite a while; it is likely to come first in a dyadic relationship; with a nurse or with a doctor whom one trusts. On the other hand, the learning from a model, perhaps doing it better than a model who doesn't do so well—that's the kind of thing one can have only in a group. And that is where the information we have assembled in psychiatry about group process is very important here, in this particular section of general medicine.

Having a model, then, for the grief process is the third item one hopes will be successfully managed in the person exposed to this need in his life. If it is done successfully, we rejoice with the patient; if he fails to do it, we hope there will be somebody who knows this sort of thing. And we have made great efforts to have not only psychiatrists but also our medical colleagues and our clergymen, who are often the persons chosen as communicators by physicians, know some of these aspects. I think . . . the thing that hits you is that . . . it is not just a naughty patient, or one who doesn't know what it is all about, but a patient who is caught up in not knowing how to do a certain psychological task.

Now I'm sure you don't often have a patient who is also a physician and a psychiatrist and who went through this, and so I shall say a little about some of these items of the work which indeed I have done somewhere, otherwise I couldn't talk with ease about it. They happened to align themselves in confrontation with a chordoma, one of the worst forms of tumor, which was discovered during an exploratory operation three years too late, having been misdiagnosed for three years as a virus or a disc. The surgeon, when he came to send me to radiation, saying he couldn't remove it, was so unhappy that *I* had to comfort *him,* that he had missed the boat. And he said, well, you have three or four years now, can you do with three or four years? Then it really hits you, and the thing that hits you is that you are not immortal. Because there is a curious conviction in some way in everybody that one is immortal. We can't really imagine ourselves dead. When you dream about death, you dream you are a perceiving dead person, and not a person who is nonexistent. And so you search for an image of what that is. There is a story about three clergymen who decided to check with each other, being sure that they would come back after three days; and one of them, being resurrected somehow, is supposed to tell his friends how it was, but all he can report is "totaliter aliter"—absolutely different!

And so one has to recoil from the nonexistence—and then say, what existence? Then the Zinsser model comes to one's mind—namely, the existence is the memory of the person who one was. One thinks back about the past, like mad! All the childhood experiences, boyhood experiences. I began to recall German poems I had memorized, and in terms of this poetry, relive past experiences. And as an older person looks back to an earlier period, just as Goethe in *Faust* looks back to the Ur-Faust, when he was a young man, he sees that that self which was there was interacting with other people as I do now, and I really am a chain of selves; one of them I am now, and in the future there will probably be just an agglomeration of these selves in the memory of other people.

And the next thing I did, which was so important for me as an anticipatory griever, was to actually look at the places of former experiences. I went to Germany and visited the places where I had grown up, the house of my birth; tried to find some people whom I had known then; went back to Heidelberg where I started my career; and did something which I should have done if I had stayed in Heidelberg instead of coming to the United States—that is, I gave a lecture to the medical students. It seemed important to make up for this opportunity which had been missed and which might not occur again. This making up for missed opportunities is a very important element, which anticipatory grievers can't do if they don't know they are going to die. As one knows from grief studies, unrelieved hostile relationships and quarrels which have not been redeemed are just as difficult an aspect of grieving as loving relationships which have led to a great attachment and a great loss of instinctual fulfillment. And therefore, getting quarrels straightened out with the people who are concerned is good not only for oneself who goes, but also for the people who stay afterwards. And to allow some people to have a fight with some of their relatives, maybe on the ward or in an appropriate room when they are in this particular period of life, rather than think "I must stop this right away and intervene" is a good thing to know.

And so, after dealing with the past and the present, the next thing is to get somehow a structure of the remaining future. Now that is where doctor, nurse, and the patient have to be so much together. So often you don't know exactly what to say. The problem is, how can you formulate the future in such a way that it is emotionally tolerable, that it is possible still to do certain things, and that there is an acceptable image of what happens after I am gone—that the people who are left here will have a tolerable life without me. What happens to the other people's grieving after I am gone, and what happens to the empty spot in the social system. Parents who leave children want to know how their children will grieve about them; what happens with the particular job and the particular income—that's where the social worker comes in—and with the particular place which one happens to have had as a buffer person between other people in a complicated social system. For example, one may have felt quite sure "that as long as I am there nothing can go wrong with the others." So one has to straighten that out. In other words, there has to be an opportunity to think about, recollect, and then enact those scenes which are unfinished business.

I really became hypomanic, in the sense that I raced around and wanted to do all the things that would be wonderful to do once more. In other words, see that people who are confronting death are not in an environment which is restrictive of *doing* possibilities; that they are still as mobile as is compatible with their ailments, and still as rich in possible experiences for a little while. I guess it isn't silly to make up for the things you won't have any more of later, and token fulfillment along that line can make an enormous difference.

These are the things to be worked at; and one can be a knowledgeable accomplice in this, as doctor, nurse and social worker, or one can stand there and be baffled: Why is the patient so ununderstandable? If the patient feels that you don't understand him, of course he often won't do certain aspects of his share of the treatment. Now one serious difficulty is that in an institution you don't have any time—I was amazed at how much time you people were able to take with me—and don't have the emotional resources to think of the patient as a suffering person who is going to die and lose himself, rather than as a specimen of a biological species with certain impairments which I luckily am able to fix up to a certain extent. "Maybe he, in my statistics, isn't one of the lucky ones, but I have a lot more who gradually can make up for him." Only "biological statistics" doesn't work for the patient; that is one of the things which requires an awful lot of altruism on the part of the patient who is just now very busy with narcissistic endeavors. But I think that once one understands this process, one can be surprised at how little actual time expenditure is needed to say the right word at the right time, and not too much; the right kind of affirmation that one accepts the patient with his particular style of coping; and in doing so forms what we call a therapeutic alliance with the patient—a companionship with the patient in the effort which he is making, rather than having him as the target of our ministrations.

DEATH AND DIGNITY

Is it true that the most ignominious event, the ultimate indignity that can happen to any person, is to have his or her life taken away, and that dying is often a "degradation ceremony"? We know that overburdened and harried personnel sometimes fail to find time or energy for the moments of civility that could impart dignity to the person; and dying people themselves may oscillate between moments of rebellion, terror, and despair and moments of courage, resolve, and dignity. Always, as Hinton says, "The aim is to make dying a little easier."

It doesn't take much imagination to see some of the ways in which the advent of recent technological advances have affected those aspects of death related to legality, ethics, and civility (dignity). In organ transplantation: when can an organ legally and morally be removed? In kidney dialysis: who shall be given dialysis when the number of needful people exceeds the number of available machines? With heart pacemakers and intravenous feedings: how long should a comatose terminal person be kept alive? And should these issues be decided only by physicians, or should family members, lay groups, or legislators also be a part of the decision-making process? And what about the dying themselves (who may be weak, confused, frightened, or constricted by pain or unconsciousness): what should their voice be in their own death? Should they be permitted to die without their consent or, conversely, should they be forced to stay alive against their express wishes?

The eight selections in this section treat the topics of dying with dignity and the search for an "appropriate death." The Richards selection introduces dignity and dying with a description of how the ordinary person approaches death, oscillating between acceptance and rebellion with moments of great dignity and courage, and presages the idea of an appropriate death by suggesting that death can be a positive experience. Richards also touches on euthanasia as a means of preserving identity and dignity.

Drs. Jackson and Youngner draw our attention to a few of the complex "specific clinical and psychological problems that may complicate the concept of patient autonomy and the right to die with dignity." They focus especially on cases where pain and depression may temporarily distort the person's ability to make irreversible life-and-death decisions. It is important, they believe, that physicians maintain sound clinical evaluation and judgment in spite of (or because of) the dramatic circumstances.

In general, doctors and churchmen in England have taken a stronger leadership role than their counterparts in the United States in the current discussion of euthanasia and suicide. The selection by Reverend Matthews presents a cogent argument, based on church morality, for voluntary euthanasia. The editor's purpose in displaying these selections is not so much an attempt to persuade the reader as it is to acquaint him with the complexities of the basic issues of who and what should determine whether life be prolonged or terminated, and to provide some background materials as a basis for further reflection.

Every once in a while, some gifted student of human nature enunciates an especially felicitous and powerful concept. Weisman's concept of an "appropriate death" seems to belong in that category. It is illuminating, elevating, just right, and eminently humanitarian. In essence, the basic notion—resting on the realistic observation that some deaths are better than others (just as some lives are better than others)—is that individuals who are in fact dying should, as much as possible, be helped to a better death. Weisman has defined an appropriate death as "one in which there is reduction of conflict, compatability with the ego ideal, continuity of significant relationships, and consummation of prevailing wishes. In short, an appropriate death is one which a person might choose for himself had he an option. It is not merely conclusive; it is consummatory." It is probably safe to say that dying with dignity is integral to the concept of an appropriate death.

In this light the Trombley selection can be seen as a fascinating description of how one person attempted to negotiate an appropriate death for himself. It is an extraordinary "death document" written during the last few months in the life of a young psychiatrist dying of leukemia. In interesting ways it touches some of the same themes—but is dramatically different in its style—as the death poem that constitutes the epilogue to this volume.

The contemporary American hospital is probably the best place for care if one is severely ill or badly injured, but perhaps the worst place to be if one is dying. The human being gets lost in the treatment of the disease and, as we have seen, the social system of the hospital often works against closeness and appropriate psychological care as the person moves closer to actually dying. The selection by Dame Cecily Saunders shows how death can be both institutionalized and appropriate. She is the medical director of a hospice near London and, as I have seen, conducts a fervent vendetta against the unnecessary pain and needless indignity often associated with death.

Sylvia Lack's paper continues the discussion of hospice care for the dying. The point here—which is perhaps not as explicit as it might have been—is that two qualities distinguish a good hospice setting (or palliative care service, as it is sometimes called in the United States). One of these is staff civility, *including courtesy, politeness, and attention to the patient as a person, and lack of pomposity, emotional distance, and "medical discourtesies." The other is* respect for the dignity of the ill person, *which is accomplished in part through the immediate control of pain and in part through the reduction of the patients' realistic anxieties for themselves and their families' future.*

It is possible to take the position that no death is appropriate; that death comes too soon or too late and is always intrusive and corroding. In the last selection Simone de Beauvoir describes the difficult death of her mother, a death painful for the mother and immensely complicated for the daughter. She is puzzled about why her mother's death shook her so deeply. The sentence with which de Beauvoir concludes her book (and this selection) openly brands death as the enemy. In it she speaks the language of her lifelong friend, Jean Paul Sartre and of other existential philosophers whose concerns were the topics of death and despair. She says: "All men must die: but for every man his death is an accident and, even if he knows it and consents to it, an unjustifiable violation."

All these selections are part of the current scene of changes in our approach to the dying person, with special emphasis on the desirability of ensuring that the terminal person lives until he dies. They are all part of the oxymoronic climate of our century: the massive destruction of our fellow humans and the concomitant movement toward the more humanitarian treatment of the dying individual, where the latter is, in turn, an integral part of the many current humanistic movements that one sees in various sectors of our society.

31 · Death and Cancer

Victor Richards

Victor Richards is chief of surgery at the Children's Hospital in San Francisco and clinical professor of surgery at both the University of California School of Medicine and the Stanford University School of Medicine. In this selection taken from his book Cancer, the Wayward Cell, *Dr. Richards, speaking with the insight of a modern physician and the wisdom of an ancient priest, discusses the attitudes and behaviors of dying patients.*

From Cancer, the Wayward Cell: Its Origins, Nature and Treatment *by Victor Richards. Originally published by the University of California Press, 1972. Reprinted by permission of the Regents of the University of California.*

"The beauty of failure
is the only lasting beauty.
Who does not understand failure
is lost." Jean Cocteau

In the world of medicine where all efforts are dedicated to success—the overcoming of illness, the restoration of the sick to a healthy life—the admission of failure may seem absurd. Failure? An insult, almost, to doctors and patients alike. Even if it is at times accepted as unavoidable, failure is always acknowledged as unfortunate. But if one examines the meaning of failure more closely one may come to quite different conclusions.

Where there is failure there has also been effort. Without effort failure would make no sense. Effort leads to success and to failure, and indeed many successes are failures in disguise. They do not leave the successful man with a feeling of fullness, of completeness, but with a feeling of emptiness and sometimes of fear. Success, to be complete, must satisfy the beholder. Paradoxically, failure may, and at times does, satisfy the person who has failed, because it brings with itself the realization of the attempt, a particular quality of fulfillment.

We fail only because and after we have tried. We reach the destination of failure not because we are inert or powerless, but for just the opposite reasons. It is often because we have looked in all directions and tried all avenues available to us. We are not powerless: our power finds limits within and without. After many a failure, the best of us, and the best in each of us, rises again. But there comes a time when we have to confront the ultimate failure, or death and the death of others. If we know how to transform this apparent failure into an accomplishment, we shall have defeated death itself, at least to the limits of our individual capacities. How does one defeat death? How does one prove stronger than annihilation?

Perhaps if we understand what death really is we shall also find the answer to our other question, how to defeat death: for understanding alters our point of view and therefore allows attitudes which were unknown to us, or appeared impossible. Although we may see death as a clear termination of life, a definite break with living, an irreversible event which happens once and only once, it may be denied to be that simple. For one does not actually die once, never to return again. Like life, death is a continuing process, as the process of aging and dying of our body cells demonstrates. From the time of birth one grows into death at a slow but steady pace: this growing into death encompasses psychological and spiritual as well as physical changes. The physical changes, viewed as the natural process of growth, are not necessarily painful. The discovery of one's separateness from others, of pain, of sickness, even of joy and happiness are often incommunicable and increase our sense of being alone. The fear of being alone contains the germ of our death, the ultimate separation.

Some people go through the changes and small deaths of their lives with a completely natural acceptance. Few or no questions are asked. People like these are steeped in life and its vicissitudes so thoroughly that, like healthy children, they remain largely untouched. They have an innocence which protects them through their years and the suffering common to all does not find them rebellious.

A woman who was told by her doctor that her cancer was probably incurable reacted in a way which exemplifies this fundamental trust in life, and the acceptance of the end of life. She said that it was all very interesting, that she was looking foward to this new experience, that since it was unavoidable she was determined to enjoy it in the sense of embarking on an unknown and therefore fascinating voyage. She would welcome drugs or sedatives only when the pain became too difficult to bear, and she hoped she would be conscious of all that lay ahead of her, including her own death. This woman was not trying to impress her doctor, she was not pretending to be superior to fate, for she actually maintained her attitude quite naturally until her death. There was an innate grandeur in her faith in herself which carried her through the ordeal exactly as she had foreseen.

Not everyone is capable of instinctive faith in all the processes of life, including death. The extreme neurotic attitude toward life and death, which we all share at times, confuses death and life, takes one for the other, and searches for death where it is not, and for life where it is not either. Fear dominates, not the natural fear of frightful realities, but a fear detached from actual happenings, free-floating and always ready to invade the psychic life. For the neurotic "what is called death . . . mainly because it is dark and unknown, is a new life trying to break into consciousness; what he calls life because it is familiar is but a dying pattern he tries to keep alive" (Hillman, 1964). He clings to the past, to habitual reactions, out of fear of what has never been experienced. The small deaths of his universe do not find him ready and accepting, but fill him with apprehension and resistance. Facing real death may thus prove extremely difficult for him and his confusion may be extreme. He may desire death, he may feel an impulse to suicide: but this is entirely different from the true facing of death: he runs to death out of his need for annihilation, out of his fears, whereas, for facing the death which comes to him, at its own time and place, he would need presence of mind and body; it is a conscious confrontation which is required of him, and of which he is incapable, for his very need is to flee and disappear.

Midway between the attitude of total acceptance and that of total refusal lies the attitude of the ordinary man, who is neither completely at ease with life and death, nor entirely in rebellion. The ordinary man oscillates between yes and no, and he will do the same if he is faced with death from an incurable illness. This ordinary man is depicted to perfection by Pirandello in his play *The Man With The Flower in His Mouth*. The man has an epithelioma: "Death passed my way. It planted this flower in my mouth and said to me: 'Keep it, friend, I'll be back in eight or ten months.'" An ordinary man (in the play he does not even have a name, he is just "the man"), the sick hero oscillates between cheerful sarcasm, amused acceptance, and terror. He struggles for peace through his imagination. "I never let my imagination rest, even for a moment. I use it to cling continually to the lives of others. . . . If you only knew how well it works! I see somebody's house and I live in it. I feel a part of it. . . ." But later he says: "In fact I do it because I want to share everyone else's troubles, be able to judge life as silly and vain. If you can make yourself feel that way, then it won't matter if you have to come to the end of it." He has now oscillated to the no. But the yes comes back to him. He remembers the sensuous joys of life: "These wonderful apricots are in season now . . . How do you eat them? With the skin on, don't you? You break them in half, you squeeze them in your fingers slowly. . . . Like a pair of juicy lips. . . . Ah, delicious'" Then he returns to resentful rage: "We all feel this terrible thirst for life, though we have no idea what it consists of. But it's there, there, like an ache in our throats that can never be satisfied. . . . Life, by God, the mere thought of losing it—especially when you know it's a matter of days. . . ."

The ordinary man's death, which is the death that most of us will encounter, is described at length by Thomas Bell (1961). His book is the record of his last year. Bell, a not very successful writer as he admits himself, has a malignant tumor near his liver and his pancreas. He knows that he will die. After an exploratory operation his surgeon has decided that the excision of the tumor is impossible. The X-ray treatments Bell receives are ineffectual, the drugs he takes have no power. What is his reaction? He is sometimes frightened and discouraged, disgusted at the sight of his body invaded by the tumor, sad for himself and his wife, puzzled by the mystery of fate, but above all courageous and dignified. His book opens with the words: "I said to myself: 'I'll make a journal of it, a book; put down all these thoughts and fears as they come and so get rid of them. Once they're written out in words they won't be confined inside my skull, making trouble.'" Not everyone is a writer, but everyone may decide to face his own thoughts and fears. All through the book one witnesses the author's love of life, which both sustains and saddens him. ("My curiosity is insatiable, my pleasure in reading undiminished . . . I like, as I always have, privacy and solitude, they are as necessary to me as air . . . My appetite is excellent and my pleasure in food has never been greater.")

According to Weisman and Hackett (1961) when we are near death a new world opens up to our perception. While "the fear of dying is the sense of impending dissolution or disintegration of all familiar ways of thought and action," while "the world normally at one with our perceptions suddenly becomes alien, disjointed, and runs along without us," while "few patients save the truly predilected, approach death without despair," it is also "frequently clear that in the terminal phase the sharp antithesis of living and dying gradually become modulated into a dampened harmonic line," and that "for the majority of dying patients, it is likely that there is neither complete acceptance nor total repudiation of the imminence of death."

The fear and rebellion experienced at the coming of one's own death is admittedly stronger in young people who have not yet lived full lives, whose hopes, expectations, and responsibilities are threatened beyond their endurance, whose sense of an unjust fate cannot easily be dismissed. Fortunately "during the decades from fifteen to forty years, there is a relatively low . . . toll of deaths, largely due to fatal accidents and a few cancers" (Hinton, 1967). However, for the young, there is no comfort in statistics. One's life is unique and precious. To younger people the sense of failure from an imminent death cannot be anything but acute. Yet there must be some way to prove stronger than one's fate. When Cocteau writes that the "beauty of failure is the only lasting beauty" doesn't he offer us the solution? In other words everything eventually deserts us, and at a time that we have not chosen; but the power to face our bankruptcy remains our privilege: in so doing we penetrate it and master it, we transmute it through imagination, understanding, and the will to stay in control. The beauty and grandeur of such mastery is exemplified at its most sublime in the death of Christ, in the death of Socrates.

Failure, the success in reverse, can be the success of the ordinary men, who, like Bell and many others, feel "a kind of despairing, dragged-by-the-hand unwillingness," and also, "for no obvious reason . . . smile in the darkness." It is not easy to "smile in the darkness" if one has no previous experience of what that darkness is. In Francis Bacon's words "Man fears death as the child fears the dark," and truly the child in us will always fear the dark until he has gone through it once and for all, willingly and thoroughly. What is this darkness? Is it not the unknown in us, the unresolved, the intricacies and mysteries of an inner life not totally adult, and does not this darkness take its most vivid and its most valid symbol in death, the last question, the perfect unknown? But the exploration of our night can bring strength and a peaceful acceptance of life and of death. In the effort at understanding oneself and one's fears, the frightening bugbear, death, appears in a much gentler light. Death may remain the image of all the unattainables. However, these unattainables, these unreachables, these failures, can become a simple question mark, troubling, but incapable of destroying one any longer.

Hope, "The thing with feathers," in Emily Dickinson's words, almost always "perches in the soul," regardless of our nearness to death, regardless of the mortal quality of our illness, regardless of how small a material hope we harbor. For hope is a quality of being, rather than a rational expectation. And in that sense hope can and must be implanted in the person who is fatally ill.

The quantity and the quality of care that a dying patient receives are powerful adjuvants to the growth of hope, of openness to whatever future may be his. This case is dependent upon the kind of persons physicians are—or nurses, psychiatrists, social workers, family, and friends—all of those who are in contact with the patient in the terminal stage of his illness. Certain qualities are demanded. A profound sense of right judgments. A subtle and supple mind. No preconceived or unchangeable opinions. A willingness to meet the patients on their own terms. No moralistic or religious zeal on the part of the "believing" doctor, nurse, or relative. No skepticism or hardened professional "scientism" from the unbelievers. The first thing to remember about dying patients is that it is *their* death.

Some patients do not want to know of their impending death. Many studies indicate that this wish is rare. Yet in the words of Dr. Paul R. Rhoads "Honesty should often be tempered with optimistic uncertainty" (Ross, 1965). He illustrates the necessity of this attitude: two patients present the same type of cancer at the same time: both have a retroperitoneal lymphosarcoma of about the same size in the same site; they receive the same X-ray treatment. One dies within three months, the other lives an active life for nine years. The future is unpredictable, even in some apparently desperate cases, and optimism and hope can be maintained in many instances, perhaps even when they do not seem warranted by the facts known to the physician, or by his experience.

Dr. Alvarez writes (1952): "I doubt if a physician who has examined an old man and found an inoperable cancer of the prostate gland need always tell about it. Especially when the man has high blood pressure and heart disease or has had some minor strokes, it may be that he will die of one of these before the cancer kills him, and then it may be best to let him live in mental peace."

A reasonable and perceptive openness to the improbable does not mean dishonesty. However, when patients indicate that they desire to know that they may die in the near future, there is little doubt that they must be told the truth. It is a great comfort to some people to be given the time and opportunity to put their affairs in order, to arrange material details with their families, to explore their thoughts, to deepen and enjoy their relationships. Yet even in those who wish to confront their own death, fears still exist, and they should be encouraged to speak freely about themselves, and about everything and anything that troubles them. "Many a dying man," writes Dr. Alvarez (1952), "would like to discuss the problems that are in his mind, but he would like to do this dispassionately, much as if it were someone else whose troubles were being talked about."

Dr. John Hinton has explored many aspects of the act of dying, many attitudes toward death, and a number of ways to make the end of a life more peaceful and more comfortable, mentally and physically (Hinton, 1967). He points out that if a patient receives all the relief from pain to which he is entitled, with the help of drugs and surgery (surgery in such instances is purely palliative and entirely justified on this basis as it allows the sick person to live his remaining days in less discomfort), he will be offered the first and indispensable condition for a painless and peaceful death.

"A painless, peaceful death," are the words used in the dictionary to define euthanasia, which is at other times vividly described as "mercy killing." In August 1967 a young man killed his mother who was dying of leukemia. "She reportedly had begged him to kill her, and even as he was arrested, his mother's sister embraced him saying, "God bless you" (Kinsolving, 1967). One can easily understand the pity that the doctor feels for a patient to whom he can no longer offer anything but a "painless, peaceful death." But one cannot help but be overwhelmed with the immense problems and responsibilities that euthanasia would present, even to those who would never kill in any other circumstance. For if euthanasia were to be considered acceptable in cases of terminal cancer, why should it not be acceptable as well in other painful illnesses which are not leading to death? In an editorial in *The Lancet* (Anon., 1961), we read that

> in his recent study, Exton-Smith found that unrelievable enduring pain and misery is worst not, as the public suppose, among patients dying of cancer whose pain, if present, he found controllable and relatively

short, but in the victims of locomotor disorders not essentially lethal. If "euthanasia" is granted to the first class, can it be long denied to the second?

Euthanasia is a "painless, peaceful death," and also "a means of producing it." Must this means be of necessity killing? Rarely can an easy and happy death be produced by killing, for, despite the hope of relief that the promise of death does bring, death by killing carries violence within itself. What if the patient who desired to die reconsidered at the last minute and nobody but himself was aware of his reconsideration? If euthanasia were ever to be legalized, would not the anguish of making such a decision add an insufferable weight to the already difficult task of facing an involuntary death? The task, by adding a new stress to the stress already existing, would make the act of deciding almost impossible.

But there are alternatives to the stark conception of euthanasia as "mercy killing." A painless, peaceful death can be given to people in the terminal stage of cancer. In a letter to the editor of *The Lancet* (1961), Cicely Saunders writes: "We are now always able to control pain in terminal cancer . . . and only very rarely indeed do we have to make (patients) continually asleep in doing so." And in a later editorial in the same medical journal (1961) one reads: "If euthanasia . . . were put on a par with, say, safe childbirth; if the known means to make death comfortable were applied by individual and collective effort with intelligence and energy, could not all but a few deaths be made at least easy?"

An important consideration is, is it desirable to prolong life when death is very near? A number of means to prolong life artificially do not add to the quality of life of a very sick person. According to one observer, J. W. Reid (1964), perhaps

> the patient . . lies in bed surrounded by standards from which dangle bottles of various solutions with tubing running to arms fixed to boards projecting on either side of the bed as though he were nailed to a cross. A nurse stands at one side, and the intern on the other side is injecting a new drug that has successfully prolonged life in a small series (of patients) for a few weeks and (the clincher) as long as a year in one authenticated case! The wife stands uncertainly in the doorway wanting to be with her husband in these last hours but diffident about pushing her way through the busy traffic around the bed.

The author goes on to say: "Is not all this activity to keep alive a dying man more often merely an educated cruelty?"

His opinion is echoed by many physicians. The prolongation of life often does more harm than good in the pursuit of a peaceful death. The quality of a human life, which at that stage is synonymous with physical comfort and mental peace, must be the only consideration.

Together with the problem of prolonging or not prolonging life, doctors face that of the free use of powerful drugs to relieve pain as completely as possible. Heroin and morphine are addictive drugs, but what is the importance of addiction at a stage of life when death is so near? The answer seems obvious. However, Dr. John Hinton expresses the opinion that "there is too much error on the side of caution." He believes that "given in adequate and frequent enough doses to begin with, so that the patient is confident that the pain is controllable, the need to increase the dose of morphia or heroin and the undue dependence of the patient on the drug do not often constitute a great problem in dying patients" (Hinton, 1967). This inducement of confidence in the patient seems extremely important, for if he knows from the very beginning that this physical pain will be controlled, his fear of future suffering will be greatly alleviated. The anticipation of pain is as difficult to bear as the pain itself, and more frightening. The certainty that one's doctor is able to control both of these by his skill in the handling of the drugs available, is deeply comforting to the dying patient. Such practices can result in true euthanasia, a means to a painless, peaceful death.

Finally, mental suffering often accompanies physical pain in terminal cancer. Sometimes psychiatric intervention is indispensable, perhaps more often than is the common practice. Its object is, as expressed by Weisman and Hackett (1961), "to help the dying patient preserve his identity and dignity as a unique individual, despite the disease, or, in some cases, because of it." They introduce the concept of "appropriate death." It is

> an aspect of euthanasia—death without suffering—for patients whose death is imminent . . . the conventional concept of euthanasia as the hastening of the death of the incurably ill patients is the antithesis of the appropriate attitude towards death which psychiatric intervention advocates. In conventional euthanasia the patient's personality is ignored; in the proposal of therapeutic dissociation of the patient from the disease, the personality in its unique dignity is enhanced.

Nonpsychiatrists express similar ideas when, like Dr. Cicely Saunders, they say (1961): "We try, and we believe very often with success, to enable our patients to remain themselves throughout their illness, to find their own key to the situation and to use it. They make of it (consciously or unconsciously) not just a long defeat of living but a positive achievement of dying."

All religions and most philosophies have recognized death as a challenge, as a beginning. In the words of Plato, "Those who tackle philosophy aright are simply and solely practicing dying, practicing death, all the time, but nobody sees it." One does not have to be religious, or a philosopher, to confront death in a manly way. One has only to be human, to realize that the acceptance of everything which is our lot is under the control of our intellect and of our sensibility. Everything which happens to us is ours if we make it so. It is within our power of understanding. This is where hope enters. It is when one may hear what W. H. Auden calls the "imaginary song":

> You, alone o imaginary song
> Are unable to say an existence is wrong

Our existence before death is worth living to the fullest. All of us, within limits, can measure up to last "failure." Jean Cocteau says that who does not understand failure is lost: he is lost to the hope and to the deepening of experience that failure offers. In the elation of success, when we ride the crest of the wave, our sense of power blinds us. Success is intoxicating, and the intoxication is authentic, as are all our experiences. But success is not the whole. In the hollow of the wave, in failure and in the approach of death, we can experience a humble power, and the knowledge of peace. Physicians and families care best for the dying patient by helping to make death an inevitable but positive experience, from which none of us is spared.

References

Alvarez, W. C. Care of the Dying. *Journal of the American Medical Association,* 1952, *150,* 89-91.

Anon. Euthanasia. *Lancet,* 1961, *1* (12 Aug.), 351–354.

Bell, Thomas. *In the Midst of Life.* New York: Atheneum, 1961.

Hillman, James. *Suicide and the Soul.* New York: Harper and Row, 1964.

Hinton, John. *Dying.* London: Penguin Books, 1967.

Kinsolving, Lester. Some Thoughts on Mercy Killing. *San Francisco Chronicle,* Aug. 26, 1967.

Reid, J. W. On the Road to the River. *Canadian Medical Association Journal,* 1964, *91,* 911-913.

Ross, W. S. *The Climate is Hope.* New York: Prentice-Hall, 1965.

Saunders, Cicely. Letter to the Editor. *Lancet,* 1961, *2* (2 Sept.), 548–549.

Weisman, Avery D., and Hackett, Thomas P. Predilection to Death. *Psychosomatic Medicine,* 1961, *23,* 232-256.

32 ·

Patient Autonomy and "Death with Dignity": Some Clinical Caveats

David L. Jackson and Stuart Youngner

Drs. David Jackson and Stuart Youngner practice and teach in the Division of Clinical Pharmacology and Critical Care Medicine of Case Western Reserve University and the University Hospitals of Cleveland. Their article deals with the necessity for maintaining sound clinical judgment in dealing with dying patients. The authors illustrate their argument with six case reports touching on the topics of patient ambivalence, depression, hidden problems, fear, differences in perception between patient and family, and staff misconceptions of the patient's concept of death with dignity.

Reprinted by permission of The New England Journal of Medicine *Vol. 301, No. 8 (1979): 404–8. Supported in part by NIMH Grant MH 15022–02.*

The rapid advance in medical technology over the past two decades has raised serious questions about patient autonomy and the right to die with dignity. This article will attempt to examine psychologic issues affecting decision making in these areas. Attempts to answer these questions have come from many quarters: legal, ethical and religious, as well as medical. The lay public and press have also participated actively in this dialogue.

Both legislatures and the courts have attempted to clarify these issues. Many states have enacted laws providing for "living wills"—legal documents that give patients the right to refuse heroic measures for their care when in a "terminal" condition.[1] Such laws also protect physicians from legal action by family members when they comply with such "wills." Both the courts and some state legislatures have recently attempted to provide legal definitions of death.[2] The courts have also ruled on who should make the final decisions when patients are not competent. Most recently, in the Saikewicz case,[3,4] the Supreme Court of Massachusetts asserted that all decisions about the institution or termination of life-prolonging measures must be made by the courts if the patient is not legally competent.

Physicians have approached the difficult problem of decision making for critically ill patients in various ways. Attempts have been made to establish reliable clinical criteria for predicting outcome in critically ill patients. This effort has been most successful in defining brain death, where clear-cut clinical criteria can predict with certainty a fatal outcome.[2] Efforts at predicting outcome in "vegetative" brain states and other serious "terminal" conditions have been less successful.

Another approach has been to develop systems for classifying patient-care categories.[5-7] This triage approach is designed to permit direction of maximal effort toward the care of "viable" patients, stressing daily reevaluation of medical status and treatment options and open communication among medical personnel, patient and family.

Many hospitals have established ethics or "optimal-care" committees that serve in an advisory capacity to physicians, patients and families when difficult decisions arise about stopping or withholding life-support systems.[8]

Imbus and Zawacki[8] described an approach for patients with "burns so severe that survival is unprecedented." When given a choice between "ordinary" care or "full treatment measures," twenty-one of twenty-four patients chose the former. The authors make a strong argument for an aggressive approach to preserve patient autonomy. They ask, "Who is more likely to be totally and lovingly concerned with the patient's best interest than the patient himself?"

Little has been written, however, about the specific clinical and psychologic problems that may complicate the concept of patient autonomy and the right to die with dignity. Cassem[9] has noted that in clinical situations where pain and depression are prominent features, "the physician ethically could proceed against the will of the patient." Rabkin and his colleagues[10] warn that "caution should be exercised that a patient does not unwittingly 'consent' to an ONTR [order not to resuscitate], as a result of temporary distortion (for example, from pain, medication or metabolic abnormality) in his ability to choose among available alternatives." They go on to say that "it may be inappropriate to introduce the subject of withholding cardiopulmonary resuscitation efforts to certain competent patients when, in the physician's judgment, the patient will probably be unable to cope with them psychologically." Unfortunately, the authors do not develop this concept in a detailed manner and therefore leave it open to criticism.[8]

The issues of patient autonomy and the right to die with dignity are without question important ones that require further discussion and clarification by our society as a whole. However, there is a danger that in certain cases, preoccupation with these dramatic and popular issues may lead physicians and patients to make clinically inappropriate decisions— precisely because sound clinical evaluation and judgment are suspended. This article will attempt to illustrate this concept by use of clinical examples from a medical intensive-care unit. Each case will demonstrate a specific clinical situation where concerns about patient autonomy and the right to die with dignity posed a potential threat to sound decision making and the total clinical (medical, social and ethical) basis for the "optimal" decision.

CASE REPORTS

CASE 1—Patient ambivalence

An eighty-year-old man was admitted to the Medical Intensive-Care Unit (MICU) with a three-week history of progressive shortness of breath. He had a long history of chronic obstructive lung disease. He had been admitted to a hospital with similar problems four years earlier and had required intubation, mechanical respiratory support and eventual tracheostomy. The patient remained on the respirator for two months before weaning was successfully completed. During the four years after discharge, his activity had been progressively restricted because of dyspnea on exertion. He required assistance in most aspects of self-care.

On admission, he was afebrile, and there was no evidence of an acute precipitating event. Maximum attempts at pulmonary toilet, low-flow supplemental oxygen and treatment of mild right- sided congestive heart failure and bronchospasm were without effect. After four days of continued deterioration, a decision had to be made about whether to intubate and mechanically ventilate the patient. His private physician and the director of the MICU discussed the options with this fully conversant and alert patient. He initially decided against intubation. However, twenty-four hours later, when he became almost moribund, he changed his mind and requested that respiratory support be initiated. He was unable to be weaned from the respirator and required tracheostomy—a situation reminiscent of his previous admission. Two months later, he had made no progress, and it became obvious that he would never be weaned from respiratory support.

Attempts were made to find extended-care facilities that could cope with a patient on a respirator. Extensive discussions with the patient and his family about the appropriate course to follow revealed striking changes of mind on an almost daily basis. The patient often expressed to the MICU staff his wish to be removed from the respirator and said, "If I make it, I make it." However, when his family was present, he would insist that he wanted maximal therapy, even if it meant remaining on the respirator indefinitely. The family showed similar ambivalence. The patient was regularly the center of conversation at the MICU weekly interdisciplinary conference (liaison among medical, nursing, social-work and psychiatric staff). There was great disagreement among MICU staff members concerning which side of the patient's ambivalence should be honored. Ultimately (after 4½ months on the respirator), the patient contracted a nosocomial pulmonary infection, became hypotensive and experienced ventricular fibrillation. No efforts were made at cardiopulmonary resuscitation. In this difficult case, the concept of patient "autonomy" became impossible to define.

CASE 2—Depression

A fifty-four-year-old married man with a five-year history of lymphosarcoma was admitted to the hospital intensive-care unit for progressive shortness of breath and a one-week history of nausea and vomiting. Over the past five years, he had received three courses of combination-drug chemotherapy, which resulted in remission. His most recent course occurred four months before admission. On admission, X-ray examination of the chest showed a diffuse infiltrate, more on the left than on the right. Eight hours after admission, he was transferred to the MICU because of hypotension and increasing dyspnea. Initially, it was not clear whether these findings indicated interstitial spread of lymphosarcoma or asymmetric pulmonary edema. Physical findings were compatible with a diagnosis of congestive heart failure, and he was treated for pulmonary edema, with good response. His neurologic examination was normal, except for a flat, depressed affect. Deep-tendon reflexes were 2+ and symmetric. Laboratory examination revealed only a mildly elevated blood urea nitrogen, with a normal creatinine and a slightly elevated calcium of 11.8 mg per deciliter (2.95 mmol per liter). There were no objective signs of hypercalcemia. His respiratory status improved rapidly.

The patient refused his oncologist's recommendation for additional chemotherapy. Although his cognitive abilities were intact, he steadfastly refused the pleas of his wife and the MICU staff to undergo therapy. Over the first six days in the MICU with treatment by rehydration, his calcium became normal, his nausea and vomiting slowly improved, and his affect brightened. At that time, he agreed to chemotherapy, stating that, "Summer's coming and I want to be able to sit in the backyard a little longer." During this course of chemotherapy, the patient discussed his previous refusal of therapy. In his opinion, the nausea and vomiting had made "life not worth living." No amount of reassurance that these symptoms were temporary could convince him that it was worthwhile to continue his fight. Only when this reassurance was confirmed by clinical improvement did the patient overcome his reactive depression and concur with the reinstitution of vigorous therapy.

CASE 3—Patient who uses a plea for death with dignity to identify a hidden problem

A fifty-two-year-old married man was admitted to the MICU after an attempt at suicide. He had retired two years earlier because of progressive physical disability related to multiple sclerosis during the fifteen years before admission. He had successfully adapted to his physical limitations, remaining actively involved in family matters with his wife and two teenage sons. However, during the three months before admission, he had become morose and withdrawn but had no vegetative symptoms of depression. On the evening of admission, while alone, he ingested an unknown quantity of diazepam. When his family returned six hours later, they found the patient semiconscious. He had left a suicide note.

On admission to the MICU, physical examination showed several neurologic deficits, including spastic paraparesis, right-arm monoparesis, cortical sensory deficits, bilateral ophthalmoplegia and bilateral cerebellar dysfunction. This picture was unchanged from recent neurologic examinations. The patient was alert and fully conversant. He expressed to the MICU house officers his strong belief in a patient's right to die with dignity. He stressed the "meaningless" aspects of his life related to his loss of function, insisting that he did not want vigorous medical intervention should serious complications develop. This position appeared logically coherent to the MICU staff. However, a consultation with members of the psychiatric liaison service was requested.

During the initial consultation, the patient showed that the onset of his withdrawal and depression coincided with a diagnosis of inoperable cancer in his mother-in-law. His wife had spent more and more time satisfying the needs of her terminally ill mother. In fact, on the night of his suicide attempt, the patient's wife and sons had left him alone for the first time to visit his mother-in-law, who lived in another city. The patient had "too much pride" to complain to his wife about his feelings of abandonment. He was able to recognize that his suicide attempt and insistence on death with dignity were attempts to draw the family's attention to his needs. Discussions with all four family members led to improved communication and acknowledgement of the patient's special emotional needs. After these conversations, the patient explicitly retracted both his suicidal threats and his demand that no supportive medical efforts be undertaken. He was discharged, to have both neurologic and psychiatric follow-up examinations.

CASE 4—Patient demands out of fear that treatment be withheld or stopped

An unmarried eighteen-year-old woman, twenty-four weeks pregnant and with a history of chronic asthma, was admitted to the hospital with a two-day history of increasing shortness of breath. She was found to have a left lobar pneumonia and a gram-negative urinary-tract infection. She was transferred to the MICU for worsening shortness of breath and hypoxia resistant to therapy with supplemental oxygen. Despite vigorous pulmonary toilet and antiasthmatic and antibiotic therapy, her condition continued to deteriorate. She was thought to require intubation for positive end-expiratory pressure respiratory therapy. Initially, she refused this modality of treatment. She was alert, oriented and clearly legally competent. After several discussions with physicians, nurses, family and friends, she openly verbalized her fears of the imposing and intimidating MICU equipment and environment. She was able to accept reassurance and consented to appropriate medical therapy. She showed slow but progressive improvement and was discharged eight days later.

CASE 5—Family's perception differs from patient's previously expressed wishes

A seventy-six-year-old retired man was transferred to the MICU four days after laparotomy for diverticulitis. Before hospitalization, he had enjoyed good health and a full and active life-style. He sang regularly in a barbershop quartet until one week before admission. The patient's hospital course was complicated by a urinary-tract infection, with sepsis and aspiration pneumonia requiring orotracheal intubation to control pulmonary secretions.

Before intubation, he had emphasized to the medical staff his enjoyment of life and expressed a strong desire to return, if possible, to his previous state of health. After intubation, he continued to cooperate vigorously with his daily care, including painful procedures (e.g., obtaining samples of arterial-blood gas). However, he contracted sepsis and became delirious, and at this time his wife and daughter expressed strong feelings to the MICU staff that no "heroic" measures be undertaken. Thus, serious disagreement arose concerning the appropriate level of supportive care for this patient. The professional staff of the MICU felt that the medical problems were potentially reversible and that the patient had both explicitly and implicitly expressed a wish to continue the struggle for life. Because this view conflicted with the family's wishes, the MICU visiting physician called a meeting of the Terminal Care Committee (a hospital committee with broad representation that meets at the request of any physician, nurse or family member who would like advice concerning the difficult decision to initiate, continue, stop or withhold intensive care for critically ill patients). Meeting with the committee were the private physician, the MICU attending physician, as well as representatives from the MICU nursing and house-officer teams. The family was given the opportunity to attend but declined. The committee supported the judgment of the MICU staff that because of the patient's previously expressed wishes and the medical situation, vigorous supportive intervention should be continued. A meeting was then held between medical staff and the patient's family, during which it was agreed by all that appropriate medical intervention should be continued but that the decision would be reviewed on a daily basis. Five days later, the patient contracted a superinfection that did not respond to maximal antibiotic therapy. He became transiently hypotensive and showed progressive renal failure. In the face of progressing multilobe pneumonia and sepsis caused by a resistant organism, the decision to support the patient with maximum intervention was reviewed. The family concurred with the professional staff's recommendation that cardiopulmonary resuscitation should not be attempted if the patient suffered a cardiopulmonary arrest. On the eighteenth day in the MICU, the patient died.

Decision making in this case became more difficult because the patient's deteriorating condition made him unable to participate. The advice of the Terminal Care Committee was critically important in this situation, where the family's perception of death with dignity conflicted not only with the patient's own wishes but also with the professional judgment of the MICU staff.

CASE 6—Misconception by some of MICU staff of patient's concept of death and dignity

A fifty-six-year-old woman was receiving chemotherapy on an outpatient basis for documented bronchogenic carcinoma metastatic to the mediastinal lymph nodes and central nervous system when she had a sudden seizure, followed by cardiorespiratory arrest. Resuscitation was accomplished in the outpatient department, and she was transferred to the MICU. She had been undergoing combination-drug chemotherapy as an outpatient for six months but continued to work regularly.

In the MICU, her immediate management was complicated by "flail chest" and a tension pneumothorax requiring the drainage of the chest. She was deeply comatose and hypotensive. Several MICU staff members raised questions about the appropriateness of continued intensive care. After initial medical stabilization, including vasopressor therapy and mechanical respiration, her clinical status was reviewed in detail with the family. Because of the patient's ability to continue working until the day of admission, her excellent response to chemotherapy and her family's perception of her often-stated wish to survive to see the birth of her first grandchild (her daughter was seven months pregnant), maximal efforts were continued. She remained deeply comatose for three days. Her course was complicated by recurrent tension pneumothoraces, gram-negative sepsis caused by a urinary-tract infection and staphylococcal pneumonia. She gradually became more responsive and by the seventh hospital day was able to nod "yes" or "no" to simple questions. Her hospital course was similar to that of many critically ill patients. As soon as one problem began to improve, a major setback occurred in another organ system. With each setback, there was growing dissension among the MICU staff about the appropriate level of supportive care. The vast majority of the MICU staff felt strongly that continued maximum intervention was neither warranted nor humane. A smaller group of staff, supported by the patient's daughter and (once she was able to communicate) the patient herself, felt that as long as there was any chance for the patient to return to the quality of life she had enjoyed before cardiorespiratory arrest, maximum therapy was indicated.

The patient was the subject of many hours of debate and was a regular topic of conversation at the weekly interdisciplinary conference. She survived all her medical complications and was discharged home after seven weeks in the MICU, awake, alert and able to walk and engage in daily activities around her home without limitation. She saw the birth of her granddaughter, and spent Thanksgiving, Christmas and New Year's Day at home with her family. She died suddenly at home eleven weeks after discharge.

DISCUSSION

Our purpose is not to refute the importance of patient autonomy or discredit the more complex concept of death with dignity. Rather, we have attempted to provide a specific clinical perspective that may help clarify the difficult and often conflicting factors underlying the decisions made daily at the bedsides of critically ill patients.

Veatch[11] has effectively argued that many of the decisions regarding the withholding or stopping of life-support systems are ethical, not medical and therefore not the exclusive responsibility of the physician. Capron and Kass[12] state, "Physicians *qua* physicians are not expert on these philosophic questions, nor are they experts on the question of which physiological functions decisively identify the 'living human organism.' " However, careful examination of the legal guidelines suggested by these authors or the living-will statutes enacted by several states reveals vague terms, such as "irreversible,"[11,12] "hopeless"[13] and "terminal condition."[14] As Cassem has pointed out,[9] "In most cases in intensive care units, the confidence with which these label(s) [sic] can be applied depends entirely on the clinical judgment of the primary doctor, along with the best consultations he is able to acquire." Public policy can establish useful guidelines when medical evidence is clear, when exact physiologic measurement is possible and when disease outcome is accurately predictable (e.g., criteria for brain death[2] or Imbus and Zawacki's burn patients[8]). But rigid guidelines are not useful in most clinical situations, where separation of medical from social or ethical responsibility is difficult or artificial.

We heartily support the plea by Imbus and Zawacki[8] for "more and earlier communication with the patient." However, their question, "Who is more likely to be totally and lovingly concerned with the patient's best interest than the patient himself?" may be somewhat naive and, in certain clinical situations, potentially dangerous. Physicians must not use "professional responsibility" as a cloak for paternalism, but they must be alert not to let the possibility of abuse keep them from the appropriate exercise of professional judgment. Physicians who are uncomfortable or inexperienced in dealing with the complex psychosocial issues facing critically ill patients may ignore an important aspect of their professional responsibility by taking a patient's or family's statement at face value without further exploration or clarification.

The cases presented in this article illustrate specific situations in which superficial preoccupation with the issues of patient autonomy and death with dignity could have led to inappropriate clinical and ethical decisions. They suggest a checklist that may aid the clinician in evaluating such difficult situations.

CASE 1—Patient ambivalence

One must be cautious not to act precipitously on the side of the patient's ambivalence with which one agrees, while piously claiming to be following the principle of patient autonomy. Ambivalence may not be detected if communication is not a continuing feature of the situation or if the physician makes clear to the patient the answer he expects to hear. Ideally, one hopes for resolution of the ambivalence through clarification of the issues or changes in the course of the illness. However, in some instances, ambivalence may not resolve despite a protracted course and maximal communicative efforts.

CASE 2—Depression

A patient's refusal or request for cessation of treatment may be influenced by depression. If the depression is adequately treated or, as is more frequently encountered, is reactive to physical discomfort that can be relieved, the patient may well change his or her mind. The astute clinician must be alert for a history of endogenous depression, vegetative signs of depression and any acute conditions to which the patient may be reacting. Vigorous attempts to treat the causes of the depression should be made before automatically acquiescing to the patient's wishes.

CASE 3—Patient who uses a plea for death with dignity to identify a hidden problem

As demands for autonomy and death with dignity become acceptable and even popular, patients may use them to mask other less "acceptable" problems or complaints. As Case 3 illustrates, a thorough psychosocial history and clinical interview with the patient and family may identify the real problem. If the MICU team can deal effectively with the underlying "real" problems, the plea for death with dignity may radically change.

CASE 4—Patient demands out of fear that treatment be withheld or stopped

Situations do exist in which fear is rational, unshakable and ultimately a reasonable basis for refusing treatment. On the other hand, fear is often transient and based on misperception or misinformation. When a patient refuses treatment, the physician should try to identify any fears that may underlie the refusal of therapy. The physician can attempt to overcome the fear by means of honest, open explanation and reassurance and by efforts from family, friends and members of the health-care team.

CASE 5—Family's perception differs from patient's previously expressed wishes

Case 5 illustrates this difficult problem. In the absence of a legal document specifically expressing the patient's wishes, who has the right to decide? Clearly, the family represents the interest of the patient, but must a physician comply if both his medical judgment and his assessment of the patient's wishes conflict with the family's view? Of course, the issue could be decided in court. Fortunately, in this case, consultation with the ethics committee of the hospital led to a compromise satisfactory to both family and the MICU staff.

CASE 6—Misconception by some of MICU staff of patient's concept of death with dignity

In Case 6, some of the MICU staff assumed that a comatose patient with metastatic cancer would not want intensive "heroic" treatment. They were mistaken. This patient's will to live was revealed in her desire to see her grandchild born. In such cases, efforts must be made to ascertain the patient's wishes, rather than to make assumptions by the test "what would I want." Questioning family or waiting until the patient can communicate are methods of discovering the wishes of the patient. Supportive therapy must be continued until this information can be gathered.

This checklist describes six patients we have seen in a busy MICU. It is by no means complete but we hope it will help to clarify situations in which superficial and automatic acquiescence to the concepts of patient autonomy and death with dignity threaten sound clinical judgment. As physicians, we strongly support the principles of patient autonomy and death with dignity and welcome any dialogue that promotes them. Spencer[15] highlighted the importance of judiciously balancing the role of patient and family input into these often difficult decisions with the exercise of sound professional judgment. We must continue to emphasize our professional responsibility for thorough clinical investigation and the exercise of sound judgment. Living up to this responsibility can only enhance the true autonomy and dignity of our patients.

References

1 Zucker KW: Legislatures provide for death with dignity. J Leg Med 5(8):21–24, 1977
2 Black PM: Brain death. N Engl J Med 299:338–344, 393–401, 1978
3 Curran WJ: The Saikewicz decision. N Engl J Med 298:499–500, 1978
4 Relman AS: The Saikewicz decision: judges as physicians. N Engl J Med 298:508–509, 1978
5 Grenvik A, Powner DJ, Snyder JV, et al: Cessation of therapy in terminal illness and brain death. Crit Care Med 6:284–290, 1978
6 Tagge GF, Adler D, Bryan-Brown CW, et al: Relationship of therapy to prognosis in critically ill patients. Crit Care Med 2:61–63, 1974
7 Critical Care Committee of the Massachusetts General Hospital: Optimum care for hopelessly ill patients. N Engl J Med 295:362–364, 1976
8 Imbus SH, Zawacki BE: Autonomy for burned patients when survival is unprecedented. N Engl J Med 297:308–311, 1977
9 Cassem N: When to disconnect the respirator. Psychiatr Ann 9:84–93, 1979
10 Rabkin MT, Gillerman G, Rice NR: Orders not to resuscitate. N Engl J Med 295:364–366, 1976
11 Veatch RM: Death, Dying, and the Biological Revolution. New Haven, Yale University Press, 1976
12 Capron AM, Kass LR: A statutory definition of the standards for determining human death: an appraisal and a proposal. University of Pennsylvania Law Review 121:87–118, 1972
13 Taylor LF: A statutory definition of death in Kansas. JAMA 215:296, 1971
14 West's Annotated California Codes: Health and Safety Code. Section SS7185, Vol 39A. Accumulated pocket part for use in 1979, page 46
15 Spencer SS: "Code" or "no code": a nonlegal opinion. N Engl J Med 300:138–140, 1979

Voluntary Euthanasia: The Ethical Aspect

W. R. Matthews

W. R. Matthews was Dean of St. Paul's in London from 1934 to 1967. In this selection, the Very Reverend Matthews makes a case for voluntary *euthanasia, based on what he describes as the Christian ethical "doctrine of the sacredness of the human personality."*

From Euthanasia and the Right to Death *edited by A. B. Downing, pp. 25–29. Copyright ©1970 by Nash Publishing Co. Reprinted by permission.*

The proposal to legalize, under stringent conditions, voluntary euthanasia, has called forth much criticism from Christians. We ought not to be surprised at this, because the sacredness of human life and personality is a fundamental tenet of the Christian faith. Some of its earliest battles against paganism were fought against customs which presupposed that human lives could rightly be disposed of according to the convenience or pleasure of the state, or of some other human institution, such as the family. From the first the church stood against the exposure of unwanted babies and against gladiatorial shows, in which human lives were sacrificed for the amusement of the populace. The racial theories and practices of the Nazis remind us that this emphasis on the sacredness of human personality is needed today, and I should like to make it quite clear that I have no sympathy whatever with any design either to breed or to destroy human beings for some purpose of the state. I hold firmly the doctrine of the sacredness of human personality.

When a Christian first hears of the proposal to legalize voluntary euthanasia he naturally thinks that it is a dangerous one, because it may weaken, or even seem to contradict, the principle of the sacredness of human personality. That was my own primary reaction and, therefore, I wish to treat opponents of voluntary euthanasia with respect and to recognize that they have a case. I have come, however, to believe that they are mistaken, and I will try to state briefly the reasons which have caused me to change my mind.

It seems plain to me that the principle of the sacredness of human personality cannot be stretched to cover the case of those whom the proposed legislation has in mind. We have to present to ourselves the condition of a man who is incurably ill and destined to a period of agonized suffering, relieved only by the administration of narcotic drugs. The situation here, in many instances, is that a disintegration of the personality occurs. Nothing could be more distressing than to observe the gradual degeneration of a fine and firm character into something which we hardly recognize as our friend, as the result of physical causes and of the means adopted to assuage intolerable pain. It is contended that the endurance of suffering may be a means of grace and no Christian would deny this, but I would urge that, in the case of a man whose existence is a continuous drugged dream, this cannot be alleged.

Though we must readily agree that endurance of suffering in the right spirit may be a means of grace for the deepening of the spiritual life, we are bound to hold that, in itself, suffering is evil. If it were not so, how could it be a duty to relieve it as far as we are able? We should all revolt against a person who complacently regarded the suffering of someone else as "a blessing in disguise" and refused to do anything about it on those grounds. It seems to be an incontrovertible proposition that, when we are confronted with suffering which is wholly destructive in its consequences and, so far as we can see, could have no beneficial result, there is a prima facie duty to bring it to an end.

We sometimes hear it said that voluntary euthanasia is an attempt to interfere with the providential order of the world and to cut short the allocated span of life. It seems to be assumed by those who argue in this way that God has assigned to each one a definite number of days—"the term of his natural life"—and that to take any measure to reduce this number must in all circumstances be wrong. But we must observe that this argument would cut both ways and would equally condemn any attempt to lengthen the term. All medical treatment, which after all is an interference with the natural processes, would on this assumption be wrong, and many of us who are alive now because doctors have saved our lives have in effect no right to continue to exist in this world. Surely this view of the providential order is not the true one. Worked out to its logical conclusion it would lead to intolerable absurdities and even to the doctrine that every human effort to lengthen life or improve its condition is to be reprobated as contrary to the will of God.

No one is really prepared to act on this assumption. I suggest that a truer view of the providential order would be as follows: The Creator has given man reason, freedom, and conscience and has left him with the possibility of ordering his own life within limits. He is to do the best he can with the material presented to him, and that means that it is the will of God that we should use our reason and conscience and our power to choose when we are faced with evils that have a remedy. My view of Providence then leads me to suppose that we are required by our belief in God to give the most earnest consideration to the proposal to legalize voluntary euthanasia. We are not at liberty to dismiss it on some preconceived prejudice.

The less reflective critics of voluntary euthanasia allege that it would be legalized murder, or suicide, or both. But surely before we fling these ugly words about we should be careful to inquire what we mean by them.

Legally, since the Suicide Act of 1961[1] (passed without any opposition), it is no longer a criminal offense for any person to commit suicide or to attempt to do so, although it remains an offense, punishable by heavy penalities, to assist a suicide. Morally the act of the suicide may be wrong because he takes his own life solely on his own judgment. It may be that he does so in a mood of despair or remorse and thus evades the responsibility of doing what he can to repair the wrong or improve the situation. He may fling away his life when there is still the possibility of service and when there are still duties to be done. The proposals for voluntary euthanasia, as advocated by the contributors to this volume,[2] have nothing in common with this kind of suicide. The choice of the individual concerned—a person faced with hopeless and useless suffering—is submitted to the objective judgment of doctors, and his decision can only be carried out with their assistance.

Murder consists in the taking of the life of another person with deliberate intention, "with malice aforethought." Very few people are prepared to take the command. "Thou shalt not kill" as universally applicable and admitting no exceptions. If we did so, we should all have to be vegetarians. But supposing the command to apply only to human life, we can all imagine circumstances in which it would be a duty to kill. For example, if an innocent person is being murderously assaulted and there is no other way of defending him, we ought to try to kill the assailant. The suggestion that voluntary euthanasia. . .is murder seems to me absurd. The life which is abbreviated is one which the patient ardently wishes to resign; there is no malice in the hearts of those who cooperate, but rather love and compassion; the community is not deprived of any valuable service. None of the conditions which constitute the sin of murder are present in voluntary euthanasia . . .

Something must be said in reply to those who deprecate the raising of these questions and would prefer to leave things as they are. "Why not leave it to the doctor?" they cry, imagining—I do not know with what justification—that doctors often take measures to shorten the suffering of the hopelessly ill.

This attitude appears to me to be really immoral, because it is an excuse for shuffling off responsibility. By what right do we place this terrible burden on the individual doctor? We have to remember that, as the law stands at present, if he does not do all he can to preserve the tortured life up to the last possible gasp, he renders himself liable to grave penalties—even perhaps to the charge of murder. Is this a position in which one's conscience can be easy? The answer must be, no. There is no honorable way of dealing with the question except by making up our minds whether or not voluntary euthanasia under proper safeguards is ethically justifiable and, if we decide that it is, embodying that conclusion in the law. Moreover, if the legitimacy of properly safeguarded euthanasia at the request of a patient is accepted, every sufferer *in extremis* and in severe pain has a right to be able to choose it. It is unjust that he should have to depend upon the views of the individual doctor who happens to attend him.

I have met the argument that we can never be certain that any illness is incurable; that "while there is life there is hope." It is of course true that we hear of remarkable recoveries which confound the prognosis of the physician. I do not disregard the potentialities of "spiritual healing," nor would I exclude even the possibility of miracle, but I do not see how anyone who has had any experience of visiting the sick can question the proposition that there are cases where nothing but a miracle could restore the patient or stave off his dissolution within a brief period, and where nothing but useless agony can be anticipated. We cannot regulate our conduct at all unless we assume that it must be guided by the knowledge that we have. We take for granted that known causes will be followed by known effects in the overwhelming majority of cases. Any other assumption would strike at the roots of sanity.

The advance of medical science has changed the conditions of human life. It is true that the ultimate principles of Christian morals do not change. The root of all Christian morality is the injunction to love God and our neighbor, as St. Paul says, "love is the fulfilling of the law." But though the fundamental principles do not change, their application may differ as the needs of the time require. Rules which were once valid and useful may become obsolete and even an obstacle to the true "fulfilling of the law." We must beware lest, in holding fast to "the letter," we betray "the spirit." In my belief it is the vocation of the Christian to be alert to see where the law of love points to "new duties."

The great master principle of love and its child, compassion, should impel us to support measures which would make voluntary euthanasia lawful and which, as stated by the Euthanasia Society, "would permit an adult person of sound mind, whose life is ending with much suffering, to choose between an easy death and a hard one, and to obtain medical aid in implementing that choice."

Notes

1 Reverend Matthews is referring to the 1961 act passed in England.

2 The volume referred to is the book from which this selection is taken: A. B. Downing (Ed.), *Euthanasia and the Right to Death* (Los Angeles: Nash Publishing Company, 1970). The subtitle of that book is "A Case for Voluntary Euthanasia."

Appropriate and Appropriated Death

Avery D. Weisman

Avery D. Weisman has contributed much to our understanding of death and dying. One of his most felicitous contributions to the field of thanatology is the concept of an "appropriate death"—a consummatory end that each person would seek for himself were he able to do so. In this paper from his book On Dying and Denying, *Dr. Weisman contrasts appropriate death with appropriated death (suicide) and discusses how the dying may be helped toward achieving a more appropriate death.*

Every idea about death is a version of life. Concepts of heaven and hell, damnation and redemption, resolution of suffering, and rewards for deeds, good and ill, are simply extensions of what is already here. To look far into the future is largely an unrevealing pastime. Those events which we glimpse in the distant future are contemporary occasions, seen through the wrong end of a telescope. Even with thorough knowledge of someone's habits, thoughts, and style of life, we cannot accurately predict how and when he will come to the end of his life. Nor can we do this for ourselves. Like living, dying cannot be reduced to a small package of maxims. To tell another person what he ought to do, think, or be is an affront at any time; but to do this when he nears the end of life is sanctimonious cruelty.

We need not be very perceptive to realize that the unceasing destruction afflicting mankind supports the belief that death is senseless, unfair, painful, and tragic. Wars and calamities of nature somehow change our image of death, even giving it a bitter meaning. Where individual death is concerned, however, few of us would ever be prepared to die, if we did not die until we chose. Human beings struggle, suffer, falter, and ask for more. But when the margin between life and death blurs, as in many illnesses, people are then willing to slip quietly into oblivion. Indeed, were it possible for a few people in every generation to live on forever, we would soon cease thinking of them as members of the human race. This elite group might even be feared, like some monstrosity who could not die. Although in the flush of health, we may want to live on, and spontaneously assume that this is possible, the gift of immortality, were it available, might turn out to be a curse.

Appropriate death is a form of purposeful death, but not every instance of purposeful death is an appropriate death. To be willing to die does not mean that someone is able to die, or that his death would be appropriate. Death may be appropriate, but not acceptable; acceptable, but not appropriate. Obviously, appropriate death for one person might be unsuitable for another. Finally, what might seem appropriate from the outside, might be utterly meaningless to the dying person himself. Conversely, deaths that seem unacceptable to an outsider, might be desirable from the inner viewpoint of the patient.

APPROPRIATED DEATH

Appropriate death has a superficial resemblance to rational suicide, i.e., self-elected death compatible with the ego ideal. In olden times, suicide was an option that ensured honor for certain steadfast people. Many famous men took their own life, instead of surrendering their principles or compromising integrity. A legendary contrast in two manners of suicide is that of Seneca who chose death by his own hand, as opposed to his pupil, Nero, who had to be forced into suicide.

Actually, suicides of great men are often misinterpreted as great and rational deeds, worthy of the man. But we may forget that a great man may be subject to deep depressions and fully capable of destroying himself without the exoneration of "good reasons." The schoolbook jingle that "Lives of great men all remind us/We can make our lives sublime . . ." hides another fact, that the deaths of great men also show how mortal and fallible they can be. Who has the audacity to approve or disapprove of how anyone chooses to die, unless by his death, he nullifies whatever potential being alive holds? We can readily conjure up events that might justify self-destruction, but there are also circumstances in which murder could be condoned. An act of destruction might resolve conflict and relieve suffering, but for whom—the victim or the executioner?

It can be argued that to deprive man of his right to terminate life is an abridgement of his freedom. Yet, few suicides, rescued after an attempt, complain about their freedom, though they might regret being saved. The reasons that people assign to a suicide may be "good," but not the correct reasons. A man who is suicidal at 3 A.M. may find the idea unthinkable at 9 A.M., even though his reasons remain the same. One part of his personality decrees death for every other part. In a sense, suicide is an external agency that victimizes; the option to destroy oneself is not an expression of freedom, but one of despair. We lament a suicide; arguments for its freedom and rationality are only sophistries. Suffering of any origin is deplorable; any of us might choose to die before being completely tyrannized by disease or despotism. Few of us can predict with unerring certainty what we would do if . . . Suicide must be construed as an emergency exit, not the main approach to a style of life. The suicide, for his own private reasons and intentionality, appropriates death for himself; he does not seek appropriate conditions in which to die. His death usually negates his ego ideal, and in other respects, as well, may be the antithesis of the conditions and circumstances for an appropriate death.

It is conceivable that at at the very end of life, people can undergo changes in outlook, so that the meaning of having existed acquires a special significance. Appropriate death does not require complete knowledge about the dying person; few of us could satisfy these preconditions, even about ourselves! Appropriate death does require that we understand the contemporaneous experience that we call dying-in-the-here-and-now. The Greek word *kairos*, an auspicious moment that leads to a decisive change, can also be applied to the event called dying. It is not an idealized image of death, nor does it delete the painful implications of dying to and from a number of things. The here-and-now significance of dying is very concrete, and should not be confused with the imaginary then-and-there of a "promised land." The dying person can, at best, only foresee a wisp of future time. Hence, the now-and-here has a pungency that draws upon every level and period of his existence. Like some memento, it is a unit of reality that may encompass a lifetime.

CONDITIONS OF AN APPROPRIATE DEATH

Someone who dies an appropriate death must be helped in the following ways: He should be relatively pain free, his suffering reduced, and emotional and social impoverishments kept to a minimum. Within the limits of disability, he should operate on as high and effective a level as possible, even though only tokens of former fulfillments can be offered. He should also recognize and resolve residual conflicts, and satisfy whatever remaining wishes are consistent with his present plight and with his ego ideal. Finally, among his choices, he should be able to yield control to others in whom he has confidence. He also has the option of seeking or relinquishing significant key people.

Obviously, these conditions of an appropriate death are like the highest aspirations of mankind! Few people are ever fortunate enough to realize these goals. Consequently, it may seem most unlikely that people about to die could reach or even care about appropriate death, if the requirements are so unrealistic. On the other hand, our preconception that death can *never* be appropriate may be a self-fulfilling idea. If we believe that death is bad, and dying people, by a magical contagion, are tainted, then appropriate deaths are never possible. By discouraging therapeutic intercessions, therefore, we may contribute deep alienation, hopelessness, and loneliness.

Given a measure of consciousness, control and competence to work with, we can encourage appropriate death, or at least a purposeful death. Patients can, for example, be protected from needless procedures that only dehumanize and demean, without offering suitable compensation. We can, moreover, ask people how much consciousness is desirable. Some patients prefer solitude toward the end in order to collect their thoughts. Others, more gregarious, need family and friends. As life ebbs away, some patients want to doze, while others prefer to be alert, and to simulate the regular periods of sleep and wakefulness that healthy people enjoy.

If we refuse to think of appropriate death as a quixotic vision beyond reach, we will protect the patient's autonomy and personal dignity. Much, of course, depends upon the concern of the key participants. Although most people tremble at the notion of dying, it is wholly practical that they can offer a substantial contribution to the mutual task. An appropriate death, in brief, is a death that someone might choose for himself—had he a choice. The central idea, of course, is that to foster an appropriate death, one must realize that death is not an ironic choice without an option, but a way of living as long as possible. Our task is therefore to separate death and its prejudices from each other.

35· A Psychiatrist's Response to a Life-Threatening Illness

Lauren E. Trombley

Lauren E. Trombley, a young psychiatrist, died some eight months after he discovered that he was suffering from leukemia. The poignant, personal document reproduced here is Dr. Trombley's account of his psychological journey to death written during the last two months of his life.

From Life-Threatening Behavior, *Vol. 2, No. 1, 1972. Reprinted by permission.*

The idea of this essay was conceived in November of 1966 but lay fallow until May of the following year because of my inability to delineate clearly both the objective and content of this paper. The passage of time has, of itself, provided some jelling of the ideas and content which, for a time, were so amorphous and jumbled in my mind.

My reasons for writing this essay are to objectify and clarify my own feelings regarding my illness, to help crystallize my perspective on matters of living and dying, and to inform others in a subjective way about the psychological processes that take place in a person who has a life-threatening disease. This does not mean that such information is not available, although it is difficult to find in the psychiatric literature. One would have to look in works of fiction for the most part and, I suppose, in some essays of a philosophical nature by nonmedical authors to find the same kind of information but, of course, couched in much different terms. The problems encompassed by the therapist's efforts to understand himself in relation to his life-threatening disease, his shifting relationships to his family, his patients, and his colleagues as he is grappling with his problem have not been explored in any systematic way. I have not yet found any enlightenment as to why people in our profession do not write about this.

A narration of the chronological events pertaining to my predicament is in order to keep the reader properly oriented. In November, I discovered that I had acute myelogenous leukemia. This discovery was quite by accident and did not occur because of any perception of anything seriously amiss. I had noticed one evening that I had a number of petechiae. [Small spots on a body surface, such as the skin or a mucous membrane, caused by minute hemorrhages.] The following day I saw a physician who was a friend, and he recommended, after examining me and finding nothing unusual, that some blood tests be performed. This led to the ultimate diagnosis by bone marrow examination of the true picture. The next day the hematologist who had subsequently examined me and examined the slides of blood and bone marrow very reluctantly told me that I had this disease.

My initial reactions are difficult to describe and still more difficult to recall accurately. However, I do remember feeling that somehow the doctor's remarks could not be directed to me but must be about some other person. Of course, I shook off that feeling very soon during this conversation, and the full realization of the import of this diagnosis struck me. I was steeped in a pervasive sense of deep and bitter disappointment. I thought that I had been maliciously cheated out of the realization of all the hopes and aims that I had accrued during my professional career. I was in the third year of my psychiatric residency and on the brink of fully developing a professional identity. Further, and more important, I was also on the threshold of developing a true sense of personal maturity and personal identity. I felt now that this would all be denied me and that I would never live to realize the fruit of the struggles in which I had been engaged for so long a time. I immediately went to see my department chief and discovered that he had already been informed. He was most kind and gracious and extremely helpful in setting my skewed perspective back on the right track. For that matter, from that moment onward I never wanted for good counsel and enormous equanimity and maturity from my supervisors and teachers, without whom I doubt I could have rallied as well as I did.

The next subjective feeling I can clearly identify is that I was increasingly apprehensive following the diagnosis about my inevitable decreasing body efficiency and thus very likely my decreasing efficiency and interest in my work. This engendered some little guilt over my anticipating not being able to do the job I had been doing. Indeed, because of the drugs it was necessary to take for the illness and not really because of the illness itself, the capability of my usual performance was sharply curtailed. Luckily when I expressed such feelings of guilt over not pulling my weight in the organization, this was immediately squelched by my teachers who were able to assuage my unnecessarily hypertrophied superego, which has since become of a much more manageable size. Nonetheless, I did have pangs of remorse when I finally had to stop seeing long-term patients because my physical symptoms interfered too much with appointments. Surprisingly, I did not feel consciously angry or frightened by the knowledge that I had a life-threatening illness.

I was gravely disappointed and terribly annoyed that this thing inside my body would interfere with my life. But at no time did I really feel, as one might put it, "angered at the gods" for having such sport with me. Nor did I find that I used denial as a defense to any extent early in the course of the illness, as I did later on when it appeared that some of the chemotherapeutic measures were having considerably good effect and I began to feel that I could go on interminably from drug to drug and not die of my disease. Instead my attention was directed away from my illness in its early phases by some very practical matters that might be called "setting my affairs in order." I was so busy with this that it served quite well to focus on an aspect of dying that is not connected with the disease process itself and thus considerably decreased my own anxiety. There was an enormous mobilization of energy to get things accomplished in this regard by both me and my wife. There were a number of changes we needed to make in our lives in order to fulfill sooner than we had anticipated some of the expectations we had about how we would live. Although a great many things actually transpired I shall mention only two or three here as examples. We first moved from a small rented apartment that was adequate for our needs at the time to a larger house and we purchased additional furniture. Because I was deeply interested in music and particularly in composing, we borrowed a grand piano from friends who were extremely gracious in allowing us to use it while they were living in the area and did not find as much use for it as they had in the past. My wife undertook practically all of the details of this move herself and also redecorated one of the three bedrooms we had in the home so that I might have a private study and library. When we got all these things accomplished, we took stock of the situation and came to the realization that it had not really required a serious illness to do these things because we had not overextended ourselves in any financial sense and we could have done all this before I got sick if we had really set our minds to it. Sometimes it takes a crisis in an individual's life to get him to do the things that he could well have done to change his life for the better. We had, in effect, denied ourselves some of the comfort of a real home and space in which to work for no valid practical reason.

My parents expressed shock, grief, and disbelief over the situation. They worried about such things as how one gets such an illness or, perhaps more cogently, why one *should* get such an illness, reflecting, I suppose, a very common fantasy that such a thing must be some kind of a punishment—just or unjust—visited upon the victim.

When it came to the question of informing my three young children (by a previous marriage) about my illness, I was met with the question based on the precept "How could you do this to them just before Christmas?" I explained that it was far better for the children to understand precisely what it was that was going on, rather than permit them to develop their own fantasies about it which could very easily be far worse than the truth. The fact that it was close to Christmas was quite beside the point. As a matter of fact, the holiday gave me an opportunity to fly to my former home state and visit with both my parents and the children and to clarify personally some of the confusion I was sure existed about the nature of this disease. Indeed, there were a number of fantasies, doubts, and fears that very much needed to be dispelled. The children were prepared to some extent for a not-very-well father who had an illness that might easily take his life in a short period of time. One fantasy they all had (unexpressed except through probing) was, "Is this thing contagious? Will I get it if I am close to you?" As soon as this was corrected the children found themselves able to be much closer to me than they had been when we first met at the airport. As it turned out later nearly all of the children with whom I had therapeutic contact had this same fantasy.

Some of my colleagues may very well have had similar fantasies. If they did, I have not discovered it but can only surmise it because there have been practically no contacts at all with some of the people with whom I worked since the inception of my illness. There has been some speculation on my part (reinforced to some extent by conversations with supervisors) that some of the people with whom I have had fairly close contact in the past found it almost impossible to deal with me and my illness because of their own fears and fantasies concerning death. One almost amusing idea came to light through one of my supervisors, namely, that some of my colleagues might very well be wishing that I would drop dead and get it over with rather than continue to torment them as I was. For others there was a heightened awareness of a close relationship that had never been verbalized in the past. This occurred with two or three of my fellow residents, and certainly we were all the better for it. Not only was there some clarification of feelings and a chance to discuss them openly between us, but also this produced a closer relationship.

At all times I tried to make it clear that I in no way wanted to avoid open discussion of my illness. I did not want to play any games of pretending that I was better than I was (although I am prone to do so), nor did I want to avoid responding to questions about how I was from day to day under the assumption that to be reminded of my illness might hurt me. On the contrary, I felt somehow annoyed if I was not asked how things were going with me because I wanted to share with others feelings about my illness. One of my friends and teachers commented that one of the things tbat bothered him most was the destruction of his fantasies of omnipotence by the knowledge of my illness. In other words, there was nothing he could do to change the situation, although he wanted to very much. I imagine that many of my fellow residents felt the same way, and they responded to this in a very constructive manner. They were discussing this one day among themselves, and one of them suggested they donate blood, which most certainly I would eventually need, as a means of doing something positive and relieving the terrible feeling that there was nothing that could be done. This was, I think, of enormous help to them and, of course, to me too. This concrete measure proved to be so popular with all of my acquaintances in the Department of Psychiatry that the blood bank was soon swamped with individuals wishing to donate blood in my behalf.

All this took place in the first few weeks of my illness. During this time, I was also increasingly apprehensive about my ability to continue the program. I was vastly reassured when the acting department chief asked me, "What is it that the residency can do for you?" I was also repeatedly assured by my division chief that I should assume only the work that I felt really capable of doing efficiently. He would rather, he said, that I did less than I had been doing and do a good job of that, than try to put in a full day and have to drag around looking rather dreary, reminding other people that I was sick. This made good sense to me so I was able to stay home part of the time after I started to feel less well without feeling guilty about it. I have been enormously buoyed up by the generous support of the staff, and I hope they know how deeply grateful I am to them. At this point I was feeling very dismal about my prospects for any longevity, and I was very glad to get all the support that I did. I did not enter the hospital but continued working and began a program of medication as an outpatient. This was a very important step because otherwise I might have been compelled to concentrate almost exclusively on the internal workings of my disabled body and would not have been able to continue working. As it turned out, this was one of the most important features of the total adaptation to this disease, because everybody made me feel that I was not giving up, despite the reduction in the time I actually spent at work.

The relationship between me and my wife was also exceedingly important at this time. At first, of course, she responded with remorse, sympathy, and total understanding. As time progressed and it appeared that I was evincing some durability and I was pretty much my old self despite the shadow I lived under, she was able to express some of the deeper feelings concerning me and my illness which were not really seen by her as separate entities. Since then we have been able to share feelings, more openly than ever before, never to the detriment of either of us. People wrongly assume that a sick person should be "protected" from strong, and particularly negative, feelings. The truth is that there is probably no more crucial time in a person's life when he needs to know what's going on with those who are important to him.

Some special problems arose in the therapeutic relationship with child patients. On occasion, I would be absent either because I did not feel well or because it was necessary for me to be hospitalized briefly for some special treatment or because some complication had developed. The children were apprised of the reason for my absence without elaboration, and they rarely would press for information beyond what was given to them. One child in particular, a ten-year-old boy with a borderline psychosis, continued his relationship to me with little allusion to my impairment resulting, for example, in my not going outside with him to play games, realizing that I had some limitations because I did not feel well. Although he did not ask for any further explanation, it evolved later on when he was transferred to another therapist that he understood (how I am still not clear) that I had a serious illness and that the transfer was necessary because of this. He was not able to express (or else I could not permit him to express) his feelings regarding this during the time that we had our relationship. The reason given for transferring him to another therapist was my needing to reduce my schedule because I was going to be more involved with teaching and could not continue with some patients. This, in fact, was true, but it did not offer the real underlying explanation for the reduction in my therapy time with patients.

This illustrated for me two things about working with children: *(a)* they are extraordinarily perceptive and will pick up difficulties in a nonverbal way that the therapist is struggling with even though he may be trying to hide them; and *(b)* even borderline children are quite adaptable and will readily accept the limitations of the therapist, providing he is quite clear about them. It is rare that the child will press to see whether or not the therapist is indeed as limited as he indicates. There were occasions in the treatment of the two borderline children I was seeing when they sought to understand whether or not I was strong enough to be able to control them. I handled this in several ways, one being to indicate to them that if things were going to continue to be as upsetting as they were, probably we should terminate the hour and continue again next time. Or more frequently, and usually at least as effectively, I would indicate to the child that I was not up to wrestling with him or having to assume control over him and I would have to depend upon his own ability to conform to the limits I had set without my needing to restrain him physically. Somewhat to my surprise this was often readily accepted by the child who would comment, "OK, I'll stop," and the rest of the hour would be much more manageable for both of us. Eventually, every therapist experiences, somewhat to his astonishment, the ability of even very sick patients to protect the therapist under certain circumstances.

On a number of occasions I have found it necessary either to change or cancel an appointment with the mother of a certain patient who was being seen in the clinic. This particular patient had a great deal of difficulty in expressing any overt anger or hostility. It was a constructive experience for both of us to be able to get this patient to see that I was perfectly capable (sick or not) of tolerating her annoyance with my not being present at an expected time and that I would still see her and not hate her for having such negative feelings about me, although I could not help the fact that I could not meet with her at that specific time. Here, perhaps, is one of the few times the countertransference needs of the therapist were beneficial to the patient. In other words, because of the guilt I felt in not being able to meet with the patient because I was under the weather, I really needed her to be angry with me in an open and direct way. By getting her to understand that I would be much relieved in knowing precisely what her feelings were, she was able to tell me, still in a tentative way, that she was angry. This marked, I believe, a significant turning point for this patient who is probably one of the most inhibited women in her affective life that I have dealt with.

In the several months since the inception of my illness I became increasingly aware of a new sensitivity that had gradually but progressively developed in my interpersonal relationships, both with patients and with all my acquaintances. The sensitivity of which I speak is rather elusive insofar as a clear definition is concerned, but perhaps I can resort to describing it in terms of its effect. One thing I noticed most pointedly was that I was very much more tolerant of the vagaries and inconsistencies of other people's attitudes and behavior than I had ever been before. Perhaps "tolerant" is not a very good word. It might be better to use the word "understanding," because many times I have found myself perceiving very quickly what lay beneath a particular person's attitude or affect which did not seem altogether appropriate to the situation. Thus I found myself much more at ease with people whom I had found difficult to tolerate in the past. Some people commented that they found it easy to be with me because I openly invited questions about my illness.

This heightened awareness of affect in others also extended to myself, and I found that my own feelings were much more accessible to my conscious recognition than they had been in the past. I also found that all of my senses seemed more acute, though I believe that really I simply paid more attention to what was going on around me and, in a way, I found myself hungering for every sensory experience that I could absorb. In many ways the world seemed to offer more beauty, and there was a heightened awareness of sounds and sights, which in the past I may have only casually observed or simply not have paid much attention to at all. This kind of experience was by no means unique to me. It has, for example, been quite accurately described by Hans Zinnser in his autobiography, *As I Remember Him*. But aside from the sensory and affective sensitivity that I had seemed to acquire, there appeared to me to be a culmination of all the learning experience that I had in my professional career which, in a compressed space of time, became the foundation for practically a new way of life. Another way to put this is that there was quite suddenly an integration of all the values and understanding I had of human experience into some kind of cohesive whole which, although difficult to describe, made extremely good sense to me.

This brings me to a question that I had earlier put aside: What happened to all the anger and depression that should have occurred after the news of my illness? I think I know. It would seem that the struggles I had with myself had not been in vain, and it was fortunate that I was where I was at the time all this happened, since I had a great deal of psychological help available to me. At any rate, it would appear that the peace I made with myself during my illness, and the maturing ability that I was developing to cope with life crises like this one, arose from several dynamic factors. One was the increasing capacity to sublimate the rage and aggression engendered by the impotency I felt regarding this invasion from within. Instead of striking blindly outwardly or, probably more likely, addressing the anger inward and thus becoming depressed, I became intensely involved in musical composition and composed practically like a madman for the first several weeks of my illness, completing one lengthy work and two smaller ones which represented in that space of time more output in this field of art than I had ever been able to accomplish in the past. This outlet proved so effective that it was very seldom that I was conscious of any feelings of despair or depression. Indeed, I suspect that when they began to reach consciousness I would begin furiously (and I use the word quite deliberately) to become creatively involved, and thus dispel the unpleasant affect. One other possibility as to my rather benign attitude was the simple reversal of affect, though I doubt that played as large a part as sublimation. Certain instruments lend themselves to this kind of alteration in the discharge of affect better than others. For example, the percussion instruments, which in a sense include the piano, are really excellent ways to deal with the aggressive energy present in everyone. But it is revealing to cite the ways I thought of working with music in these past few months. I would attack the piano, I would literally hammer out a new piece. I think that further illustrations are not necessary because it is obvious now how music and I served each other in this regard now that I am able to look at this in retrospect.

Certainly there are rewarding aspects of facing a life-threatening illness. I have learned much about the alterations in my own internal psychological processes, and the subtle metamorphosis in interpersonal relationships that have occurred and are still occurring. I wish that other people in my position would also write subjectively about this. Perhaps this paper may encourage it.

By way of completing this little essay I might comment that the Eastern or Oriental view of the life cycle of constant renewal and death as not being clear endings or beginnings to anything has been extremely useful to me. In a way I have, at least intellectually, accepted and I hope that I can wholeheartedly embrace the idea that the death of any individual is really no more nor less than a punctuation mark in the endlessly fascinating conversation amongst all living things.

36· St. Christopher's Hospice

Cicely Saunders

Dame Cicely Saunders, Medical Director of St. Christopher's Hospice near London, has waged a lifelong war against the needless pain and indignity which so often surround death. This selection, which is excerpted from her annual report of St. Christopher's, reviews some of the ways in which a contemporary institution is developing programs for helping terminally ill patients achieve a decent and "appropriate" death.

From St. Christopher's Hospice Annual Report 1971–72. Reprinted by permission.

WHAT IS A HOSPICE?

In one sense, St. Christopher's was founded when a patient left us the first gift of all, back in 1948, but in a deeper one, it belongs to a tradition stretching back to the hospices of the Middle Ages which welcomed the pilgrims who arrived hungry, tired, and sore as they crossed Europe on the way to the various sites of pilgrimage. The word continued to be used in France and was extended to hospices for the elderly, the incurable and for foundlings (enfants trouvés). Mother Mary Aidenhead then took up the title when she founded the Irish Sisters of Charity in the middle of the last century, although the hospice at Harold's Cross, Dublin, was only dedicated especially to the care of dying patients sixty-seven years ago. Her foundation has long extended to several hospices, mainly concerned with the care of the dying and the long-term sick. St. Joseph's Hospice, Hackney, was founded in 1905, but before it opened its doors the sisters were visiting the sick in their homes, thus foreshadowing the domiciliary work we have now started at St. Christopher's over the past three years.

The other tradition from which St. Christopher's springs is that of the medieval hospital. Apart from the hospices which followed the pilgrim routes and which were primarily for hospitality, there came to be others, located in towns, "for the sick and poor" who were literally dying in the streets through cold and malnutrition, and who were picked up from the gutters and brought in for care and treatment. It was when these began to be staffed by professional physicians and surgeons that they took the name "hospital." The rich were nursed and died at home, although at times they made arrangements to spend their old age in a hospital, praying and preparing their souls for death; a hospital would often have a special wing for such patients with private rooms and many amenities. Poor patients, on the other hand, arrived *in extremis* because they had nowhere else to go. Medical treatment was still limited, and the chief comfort they could be offered was a religious consolation; they could contemplate the crucifix—"He suffered as I suffer now."

So the word originates back in time with the stopping places for pilgrims and extends through the French hospices and above all through the work of the Irish Sisters of Charity, to the present day. All the groups we have mentioned are gathered within our walls: the elderly residents in the Drapers' Wing; the Playgroup members—not foundlings but the children of staff—who come and cheer us all by their noisy play; those who need longer-term nursing than can be carried out in an ordinary hospital, and who make their home with us and give us all so much in friendship and life; and the very ill to whom we can give a great deal of treatment, often unexpected remission or even cure, but always, we hope, something of real comfort. The staff is, no doubt, more numerous than the monks of the hospice in the St. Bernard Pass, but I think that the way they involve themselves so deeply in the lives and problems of the patients and their families, the way they stay with us and bring their own families and friends to see us, and the way in which students come and come again combine to give us something of the busy, many-sided life of the medieval pilgrimage and its resting places.

The life of St. Christopher's is illustrated by the variety of announcements on the notice board. There is a diagram of the way the hospice finances have gone during these five years, with the mounting expenses (mainly consisting of the payments for salaries and wages of staff) met partly by monies from the regional board and the teaching hospitals and fully supplemented by the many good gifts we receive. There are frequent announcements of the birth of a baby to an ex-staff member, often set alongside the list of the anniversaries of patients who died during the same week a year ago. There is the chapel diary and notices of social and more serious meetings, and sometimes extras such as one never-to-be-forgotten notice, "As you know, the goldfish pond needs restocking . . ." Small things are very important. . . .

THE WORKING OF ST. CHRISTOPHER'S

People often ask us about the waiting list and are concerned at the number of applications they feel we must have to refuse. The situation has changed surprisingly little over the five years since we opened, and numbers have remained fairly constant. We have about 1,500 enquiries a year. Some 500 of these are about patients for whom St. Christopher's care has not been designed. We are often able to make suggestions about other organizations who may be able to help them. Sometimes we have heard that the chance to talk on the telephone has been all that was needed to help people to sort out their problems.

We help approximately two-thirds of the roughly 1,000 patient enquirers which remain. Most of those at home are visited before admission, and it is rare that we fail to admit a patient who is in distress which cannot be helped at home. Some of those who are never admitted include people who, having been given assurance that St. Christopher's will help if the time comes, remain well cared for in their own homes. One of the local family doctors has repeatedly said that he puts his patients on our list as a sort of insurance because he has found that the fact that the family are aware that St. Christopher's is in the background often means that admission will not be necessary.

The number of people we have been able to help has been increasing. During the first full year (1968) we admitted 380 patients, and during 1971 we admitted 489; during 1972, 519; and during 1973, 579.

The first voice on the telephone answering an enquiry from a member of family or the first person seen at the hospice is of great importance. The stewards and everyone at reception are the first people who are met as the hosts at St. Christopher's. The many jobs that they and the maintenance staff do around the hospice in keeping everything as a good gift should be kept is important, but their availability to meet any members of families, visitors, or any other enquirer who comes in is rightly put first by them. We have always tried to make it possible for each patient to see a doctor every day. . . .

All analgesics for patients with malignant pain should be given regulary, usually four hourly. The aim is to titrate the level of analgesia against the patient's pain, gradually increasing the dose until the patient is pain-free. At this stage the dose of analgesic will be given before the effect of the previous one has worn off and therefore before the patient may think it necessary. It is thus possible to erase the memory and fear of pain.

Since the opening of St. Christopher's Hospice considerable interest has been stimulated among nursing staff about the care of the dying and those with chronic pain, and we find that trained staff want to come and work with us to further their experience in this type of nursing. Obviously these trained nurses are not going to stay indefinitely, and therefore it means that we always have a need for this type of staff. One interesting fact has emerged and that is that there is an obvious place here for the young, who show a great interest and an amazing capacity for understanding the needs of our patients. Again, they do not stay longer than about a year as they either marry or move on.

The fact that we have a playroom for the children of the staff has played an enormous part in maintaining a continuity of staffing. This enables a married person, trained or untrained, who has a desire to come back to nursing or care for people, to return to a field of nursing where she has a tremendous amount to give and also finds satisfaction.

There have been times when in order to keep the wards running as they should we have been extended as far as we are able, but help has always come just when we were getting desperate. We have not employed agency nurses—the gaps that occur at holiday periods have been filled by volunteers or by the students and others who do much of their learning by working. . . . People often say, "How can you work at St. Christopher's Hospice? It must be so depressing." This is just not true. It is a very happy place, but, of course, it has its moments of tension, its moments of distress; but amongst all this there is also joy and fulfillment. The work is hard and heavy, both physically and emotionally, but also very satisfying. Over the past five years the demands on the nursing staff have increased. When we started we based our ratio of staff on a 1–1 basis over twenty-four hours, but that has now been increased to 1.25–1 over twenty-four hours on a year-round basis. I think the fact that fourteen nurses have been with us for over five years and another twelve nurses for over four years emphasizes that there are people who really do want to nurse and that this type of nursing is rewarding. . . .

Referrals come to the staff medical social worker from the doctors, ward and clinic sisters, other staff, from patients themselves and their families, or from the social worker who arranges the admission. Numbers remain steady, at around ninety a year, with proportionately more men than women. Many contacts are necessarily short, and help when needed must be given immediately. Needs vary and are often practical—fares for visiting relatives can be heavy—advice over sorting personal and legal affairs is often needed, and a few patients and residents have been helped to have a holiday. But help is not only of a material kind. As with all the staff, the social worker's job is to listen, support, and counsel.

The social worker also organizes the Family Service Project, a study of the effects of bereavement, which is directed by Dr. Murray Parkes, and was started in May 1970. The purpose is to identify and offer help to any recently bereaved families or friends who may prove unlikely to be able to cope unaided with their grief and the stresses of life caused by their loss. Staff and volunteers visit to assess the need and to offer support, and if more specialized help is indicated, this can be arranged.

The work involved in keeping the records and arranging visits is cumulative. Out of approximately 750 records reviewed since the project started, 118 people have been visited or offered help, and once contact has been established by a visitor, it may continue over several months or occasionally years. . . .

It is good to know that we still have twenty-six volunteers who came to us soon after the hospice opened, and although many volunteers have had to leave us during the past five years, we have been able to maintain a steady flow of new helpers, and our numbers stay at around 100 to 110.

We use voluntary help in every department of the hospice, and this has now been extended to making the curtains and assembling the library for the new teaching and residential block. A team of volunteers also help to get the news letters distributed three or four times a year. . . .

TEACHING

During the year, we have been watching with interest developments on the second site and the rapid rise of the teaching and residential unit down the road. Even more important, though less spectacular, has been the steady growth in the amount of teaching undertaken in the hospice itself. More time has been spent over in-service training for new members of the staff and voluntary workers. We have had in all 2,383 visitors either for a day or for an afternoon visit. This number includes doctors, nurses, social workers, priests, and students of all sorts. There have been over 100 residential visitors

—people who have lived and worked with us and who have been able to learn from the patients and their families the problems of long-term illness and ways of coping.

All the members of the Hospice staff are involved in one way or another with the teaching. As the program develops it will still be based on experience in the wards. Nothing else can take the place of such experience. . . .

CLINICAL STUDIES AND RESEARCH

Our Department of Clinical Studies is gradually extending its work. The evaluation of analgesic (pain relieving) drugs continues, and one of the ward staff nurses has now joined the team as nurse observer. This is enabling us to look at well-established drugs and their use while patients are fully relieved and comfortable and to plan the treatment that suits them best. At the same time a number of other symptoms and their treatment are being considered. This is a long-term project which will eventually be fully reported in the medical press.

A marathon task is undertaken by the recorder (one of the doctors on our council) in making precis of the notes of all the patients who have been in the hospice. This enables us to keep records on a punch card system and to review the many facets of our work year by year. It gives valuable information on the demands for our care as well as our success in giving it, and the statistics compiled from these records have been used by the groups who are planning to enter this field.

Some people with cancer spend most of their illness in hospital, some are cared for at home, and others spend part of their time at home and part in hospital. Each pattern of care has advantages and disadvantages for the patient and for the family. We have been trying to assess these by visiting the surviving spouses of people who have died of cancer in two London boroughs and asking them for their opinion about eacb phase of the illness. Our analysis to date indicates that although patients are often sent into hospital because of painful symptoms, those who die at home will have more pain than those who die in hospital. From the relative's point of view nursing someone at home is often a time of severe stress, but there is reason to believe that, in the long term, people who have been able to care for someone in this way may find themselves coping with life rather better after bereavement than those who have never had the opportunity to do so.

This study is also enabling us to discover the comments, criticisms, and general attitudes of family members toward various aspects of the care provided by St. Christopher's Hospice. These comments are of particular value in helping us to improve our standards of care. . . .

TWO STORIES

Mr. P. was fifty-two and a proofreader for a national newspaper. He came to us from a teaching hospital with an unsolved problem of pain, unhappy and breathless.

He quickly settled to our regime of drugs, and pain was never a problem again. Mr. P. used the ten weeks he was with us to sort out his thoughts on life and faith, and he found his own way into peace. He was quiet and self-contained, but he enjoyed meeting students and visitors and he made good friends in the ward.

After Christmas I took him some copies of a photograph I had taken of him at one of our parties. I wanted to give it to him, he wanted to pay for it. We ended by each accepting something from the other. As we were discussing this I held my hand out. At this he held both his, palms upwards, next to mine and said, "That's what life is about, four hands held out together." After that we could discuss anything. Once I asked him what he thought about heaven. "If you believe in Him there's just no question," he said promptly. Pressed to go further he added, "It's not as if I could think of Him—like a breathing person—it's the same when you are going on a holiday—you don't know what it will be like when you get there, you just hope it will be nice."

Mr. P. became weary before he died, and though he was somewhat confused for a day or two, this quickly disappeared, and he was very peaceful till he died in his sleep one morning without a sign of distress, not even a sigh. I will never forget the picture of the hands he gave us. I cannot think of a better symbol for our aims for St. Christopher's.

Mr. A., a bricklayer of sixty-one came to the ward after Mr. P. left us. He had been visited at home for fifteen weeks before his admission. He was not very keen to let anyone into his flat, where he lived alone, protecting his independence even from his daughter. Throughout the weeks of his stay in St. Christopher's we had to help him maintain his fight for independence. Short of breath as he was, he would stamp up and down the stairs to the garden or the Pilgrim Room, pausing to look very critically at the progress of the Play Group Wing building on the way. He made many friends and established himself as escort and guide to a blind patient in his bay. His relationships with the other patients were often colourful but always kind. Bed was definitely not on his schedule, and he sat out beside it till his last day surrounded by the *Daily Mirror*, well spread out, ashtrays with endless cigarette ends and ash everywhere.

On his last day he was still in charge, dictating what he would let us give him and very much himself. In the evening he checked that Sister had his sons' phone number correctly. When the night nurses came on he said, "I may give you trouble tonight." He died quietly in his sleep early next morning.

37· I Want to Die While I'm Still Alive

Sylvia Lack

Dr. Sylvia Lack is the medical director of a hospice in New Haven, Connecticut. This selection—first presented at the 1976 Conference on Death and Dying in Orlando, Florida—enumerates the characteristics and goals of a hospice program of care.

From Death Education *Vol. 1, No. 2 (1977): 165–176. Reprinted by permission of the publisher.*

I want to talk about the hospice program of care as it has been developed in Britain and is now being developed in the United States. I want to talk about the characteristics that go into a hospice program of care because I know there are a number of people who are specifically interested in setting up their own hospice programs.

You need to know at the outset that all programs that care for the dying and their families are not necessarily hospice programs. There has been an explosion of interest in death and dying over the last few years and there have been many people who have heard that hospices work in England. They would like to set up one of their own in America, but they really have very hazy ideas of what goes into a hospice except that it does care for the dying. So, I want to run through some of the essential characteristics of a hospice program, which are:

1. Coordinated home care—inpatient beds under a central autonomous hospice administration
2. Physician directed services
3. Control of symptoms (physical, sociological, psychological, spiritual)
4. Provision of care by an interdisciplinary team
5. Services available on a twenty-four-hour-a-day seven-day-a-week on-call basis with emphasis on availability of medical and nursing skills
6. Patient/family regarded as the unit of care
7. Bereavement follow-up
8. Utilization of volunteers as an integral part of the interdisciplinary team
9. Structured staff support and communication systems
10. Patients should be accepted to the program on the basis of health needs, not ability to pay

The hospice program of care does care for the dying and their families. The emphasis of that care is on improving the quality of remaining life, and hence the title of this paper, which comes from a patient at St. Christopher's Hospice in England. When asked about her hopes for the future, with ten days to live, she said, "Well, I want to die while I'm still alive, if you know what I mean."

The emphasis on fulfilling that goal for many of our patients is to concentrate on them as people and to allow them to express themselves as human beings. We are not involved in killing people, and I would like to make that very clear, since there is a Florida-based group planning to set up in Central America and ship terminal patients down there and give them drugs to kill them.

So, I would like to make it quite clear that we are not in the business of killing people. We are in the business of improving the quality of remaining life, which involves making the distinction between appropriate and inappropriate treatment for patients. This distinction means concentration on control of symptoms when definitive treatment for disease is no longer possible. The best way this can be done has been found to be with a centrally coordinated service of inpatient beds and a home care program under an autonomous hospice administration. Although this definition sounds rigid, it in fact embraces a tremendous variety of methods of delivering hospice care.

We in New Haven currently have a home care program and we are planning a free-standing forty-four-bed hospital, which is the model that has proven successful in Britain. There are, in addition, hospice groups in this country and in Canada that are putting the same principles into operation using different methods. An example is the Palliative Care Unit in Montreal, which is a twelve-bed unit within an acute tertiary care hospital. This unit concentrates on delivering hospice care in coordination with a home care program within an acute general hospital.

Another group using different methods is St. Luke's in New York City. They have a hospice interdisciplinary team, consisting of doctors, social workers chaplains, and nurses, who work as a team, visiting terminal patients within the hospital. They also work with those on the staff who are working with the patient. The team and the staff will work to improve symptom control, to provide family care, home care, and twenty-four-hour coverage, and to take care of all the other facets that go into a hospice program. Many of the rules inappropriate for a terminal patient are waived for hospice patients within St. Luke's Hospital. Here again is an extremely interesting and relatively inexpensive way of putting into practice what has been learned in the free-standing hospices like St. Christopher's and St. Joseph's in England. There must be an expertise, interest, and concentration of symptom control if the aim is to improve the quality of life for people. To "live until they die," they must have good quality symptom control.

It is very difficult to be yourself and relate to other people if you are in severe pain. Those who are involved in caring for dying patients and have seen a patient who is in severe pain know the truth of this. The same applies to many other types of distress—vomiting, nausea, incontinence—that beset the dying patient. We hear far too much about counseling for the dying patient and not enough about giving the physical care. Over and over again we have the same experience in New Haven. We go into a home where all is chaos. The original request was for support and counseling for the patient and the family. We go in and find the patient has faecal incontinence because he is impacted. Nobody has bothered to give him a rectal exam. We find that it is the incontinence that is disrupting the family, and not the dying. Once the physical problems are under control—with the patient in a dry bed, relaxed, and free of pain—the same person who did the disimpaction can have meaningful conversation with the patient.

I am not saying that counseling is not important. But I am saying that physical care and symptom control are vital first steps. This means that a hospice program must have medical direction and must have the involvement, cooperation, and support of the medical community. There are hospice groups in America right now who are floundering because they neglected this tremendously important first step. The hard fact of setting up a successful health care program is that you must have the doctors on your side and in a leadership position.

The interdisciplinary team approach is another important characteristic. Again, what goes into the team depends on the needs of the local community; different hospices will have different interdisciplinary teams. The problems a dying patient and his family face are myriad and no one person is going to be able to deal with all of them. A comprehensive interdisciplinary team to tackle all the problems is needed.

Volunteers must play an integral part in the team. An important facet of the hospice movement has been the use of volunteers. They are important because they relate to the patient and the families on a totally different level from that of professionals. Over and over again we have situations where the person that the patient and family talk to about their deepest concerns is not the psychiatrist, the doctor, or the R.N. (who is now also acquiring the image of being too busy just like the doctors), but the volunteers, who are seen as people who have time and understanding. So volunteers are an extremely important group. Also, they are vital in keeping costs down, and that is an important aspect of a hospice.

Patients are accepted on the basis of health-care need, not on ability to pay. No British hospice discriminates against patients because of their financial status, and American hospices must also strive to uphold this high standard of care. We cannot avoid our responsibility in this area by reference to socialized medicine. Most of the hospices in Britain are not under the National Health Service. They are financed by a combination of charitable donations, patient contributions, and government reimbursement.

The family is going through a grief process as well as the patient, and they need as much care as the patient. Not only do family members need care, but they also need to be involved in care giving. They do wish to look after their relatives at home if that is possible, and if the patient is admitted to an inpatient facility they want to be involved in giving the care there. Bereavement follow-up is extremely important in any program of care directed to the dying and their families. We often forget that after the death has taken place there is a family that lives on—and it is not only the family. There is also a hospice staff that lives on. Some kind of bereavement follow-up program must be part of looking after the family as the unit of care. Some kind of organized staff support system must be part of the program.

St. Christopher's Hospice in England was built in 1967 to serve the dying and their families. The medical director, Dr. Cicely Saunders, explains the term *hospice* referring to the medieval hospices, which were places of hospitality run by religious groups where pilgrims could find rest and comfort on their journey to the Holy Land. Dr. Saunders speaks of the journey that the dying take on their way from one life to the next. This concept is symbolized by the statue of St. Christopher, the patron saint of travellers, which greets visitors to the hospice.

Also greeting visitors to St. Christopher's is a sign, "St. Christopher's Hospice—IN." At the end of the driveway is another sign, "St. Christopher's Hospice—OUT." A hospice is not just a one-way street where you go in to spend your last hours or days and never come out into the world again. Patients are admitted for symptom control, and discharged to go home feeling more comfortable than they came in. A patient can come to St. Christopher's to give the family a rest from the care at home. This hospice is a place where pain control is a specialty, and where patients can attend a pain clinic for expert advice. It is also a place where lives come to a close in peace and dignity, and where the families are cared for in their bereavement.

It is important to look at the environment that patients are in—the geographical situation that you put them in, and the influence that architecture can have on their lives. St. Joseph's Hospice in London has beautiful floor-to-ceiling windows overlooking the gardens and a busy street beyond. Thus, even bedridden patients can enjoy the view and feel a part of their community. So many facilities have windows beginning half way up the wall, which is fine if you are able to stand, but restrictive if you can only look up at the sky from your bed. Being bedbound should not restrict your mobility to one room. In a hospice, beds move freely from the ward to the chapel, and from the recreation room out to the yard.

Giving is part of being human and the patient needs to be allowed to give as well as to receive. Thus a watchmaker is given his own area in the hospice where he can mend the watches of staff and visitors. So many people come to the end of a chronic illness with a sense that they have lost their place of usefulness in the world. Their dependent position is accentuated by the generous personalities of many health-care workers and we need to learn afresh that sometimes the greatest gift we can give another is, in fact, to receive.

When a person s life is in its last hours, that person needs a quiet place in which to die naturally. Most patients in a hospice die peacefully with no IV injections or gastric tubes. If such treatment is appropriate, it is used, but most people can be kept comfortable by slow, skillful oral feeding. The symptoms of dehydration are usually combated by frequent mouth washes and vaseline on the lips.

Options for very sick people are drastically reduced, and a hospice program must seek to extend these options as far as possible. Many people want to stay at home if there is nothing more that the hospital can offer them, but most cannot stay at home because the care they need in terms of symptom control, medical attention, nursing expertise, and social-work help, is all hospital based. If you can take this care into the home, then families do the most amazing things. They want to help, and they ask for the support to enable them to do what they want to do. The consistent pattern that I have seen in Britain and in New Haven is that a large number of families want to care for their dying relatives at home, and a large number of dying people want to stay at home right up until the end. What they need is the support to enable them to do that.

What do I mean by support? A lady whose father had just died defined it as, "hospice was my backbone. They held me up so that my hands were free to care for my father."

Who are the people that we care for? If you think of the aims of health care very broadly, you can divide them into two categories. One aim is to cure the disease, and the other, if cure is not possible, is to palliate. One can further divide palliative treatment into treatment designed to increase the length of survival or treatment to improve the quality of life.

Our patients fall into this last category. Specific therapies to produce a cure or remission have been exhausted. Treatment is now directed toward improving the quality of life. Here, I am discussing the care of those dying of a chronic degenerative disease. For most people entering the health care system the classic goals of investigation, diagnosis, treatment, and cure are most appropriate, and it is quite correct that the mainstream of medicine continues to forge in this direction. However, we must remember that some people do not fit into this orientation and a different care plan with goals appropriate for the dying is required.

Many practicalities flow from the decision that a person has a terminal illness. The patient will be shielded from the intense battery of complicated investigations that are the necessary lot of the acute patient. History, thorough clinical exam, and simple noninvasive tests are usually sufficient to determine symptom etiology. A primary physician and multidisciplinary team should be the main providers of care at this point. This type of team can tackle the social, spiritual, physical, interpersonal, and financial pain of the situation. The usual array of medical specialists, none of whom are accustomed to holistic or family care, are not best equipped to support the dying.

The symptoms that loom so large in the lives of patients must receive a proportionate amount of attention. The problem-oriented approach makes this easier. We concentrate on the problems, treating each one almost as a disease in itself. If you avoid the practice of simply ignoring patients' symptoms, you can become quite successful at dealing with them. When you ask patients what you can do for them, they almost never say, "Save my life," or "I don't want to die." They say, "When can you get rid of the pain?" What's going to happen to the family?" These are the kinds of things they ask you to do. "Will you help me with all these insurance papers? I've got a pile of paper on the kitchen table a mile high and I just can't get to it." And so one needs to concentrate on providing the expertise to deal with these problems.

I will illustrate this approach by a discussion of the problem of pain. When you are talking about controlling the pain of a terminal patient, you need to remember that it is not just a physical pain. By the time the patient has reached the terminal stages of his disease, he is suffering from many other types of pain, including mental, financial, interpersonal, and spiritual. You need to pay attention to the whole person if you are going to bring the physical complaints of pain under control.

The aims of treatment are:

1. To identify the etiology
2. To prevent pain
3. To help the patient be alert
4. To maintain normal affect
5. To maintain easy administration

Identification of the etiology is a clinical diagnosis and investigations should be limited to a basic few, but always remember that not all pain suffered by the cancer patient is due to the cancer.

We want to control the pain so that it will not return. We are aiming to get steady pain control. When we are controlling the blood sugar of diabetics, we don't wait for them to go into a coma before insulin is given. Instead, we find out how much insulin they need to prevent acute manifestations of their disease and then give it to them on a regular basis. The same principle is used in pain control.

In providing pain control we want to maintain alert patients, not sedated ones. We want a normal affect. We are not aiming to put everybody on a high, but instead want to have them able to relate normally with their families and friends.

Finally, we are looking for a treatment that is easy to administer. If we give patients pain control on a continuous IV morphine infusion, we are limiting their options in terms of where they go for the rest of their lives. So ideally we want to give them a treatment that will give them the greatest ease and freedom of movement.

Forty percent of all cancer patients can be expected to have severe pain. We think of such pain in terms of physical pain, anxiety, depression, and insomnia, and unless we look at pain with all these components in mind, then we are not likely to get on top of it. Anxiety and depression are part of the chronic nature of the pain. The patient is anxious about the pain coming back. He is anxious because of the meaning of pain. This is not acute pain that you and I think of as pain. It is not like a toothache or childbirth or appendicitis. These acute pains have a foreseeable end. The pain is serving a purpose by alerting you to something going on in your body that may need attention. Pain for the cancer patient has a sinister meaning. If you wake up with a stiff neck in the morning, you assume you left the window open and slept in a draft. The cancer patient wakes up with a stiff neck and assumes she has metastases. The degree of perceived pain is totally different in these two situations. You must take into account the anxiety that these patients are suffering. Chronic depression is caused by chronic pain. Depression must be carefully evaluated as it may be an appropriate phase of the patient's grief process.

We are not afraid to use narcotics for severe physical pain, and the point at which we start to use narcotics is when nonnarcotic medication used correctly is failing to control the pain. We don't wait until the patient has only hours or days to live. We use narcotics when other medications and other pain control measures, such as a spinal block or traction, have failed. We almost always combine our narcotics with phenothiazine. The one we use routinely is Compazine or prochlorperazine. We use phenothiazines with the narcotic for several reasons. First, it potentiates the narcotic so that you can use a lower dosage of narcotic if you use phenothiazine with it. Second, it is an antiemetic. We are using narcotics orally, so we use phenothiazine as an antiemetic. Finally, they are tranquilizers, which help with the anxiety component of pain. Other anxiolytic drugs are the benzodiazepines such as Valium and Librium and we may use those either in combination with a phenothiazine, or, very rarely, alone with the narcotics. And we use tricyclics as antidepressants. Elavil is probably the one people know best. You need judgment and experience in the area of treating the depression of a patient with a terminal disease, because depression may be a perfectly appropriate and necessary reaction or stage that the patient is going through—a response to the realization that he is dying. Just because somebody is depressed, you don't automatically rush in with an antidepressant. But if depression is an identifiable component of physical pain, you may find that the addition of a tricyclic antidepressant gets rid of that last bit of pain.

The way in which we use narcotics is to find the dose that controls the pain but doesn't sedate the patient, and this may be a very fine dosage range. If you are used to seeing narcotics being increased in jumps of ten milligrams, you may miss this gap because a one or two milligram adjustment of dose may be needed. One of the reasons why we give our narcotics as an oral liquid is because you can titrate the dose of a liquid more finely than you can with tablets. There are two ways in which this can be done. If the patient is in severe pain and we need to be on top of the pain immediately, even at the cost of sedation, we start off with a high dose of narcotics. Inform the patient and the family that sedation is expected for two to three days. Then gradually reduce the narcotic until the pain returns. Increase it a little bit, and then we are in the pain-free interval. The more usual way of accomplishing this especially on home care is to start with a low dose of narcotic and build up gradually. The sedative effect of the narcotic wears off in twenty-four hours, sedation is largely avoided, and we gradually arrive at an appropriate dosage.

In New Haven, we are using morphine dissolved in cherry syrup combined with a phenothiazine. This is called the "Hospice mixture." We don't have the cocaine, alcohol, or chloroform water included in the Brompton's cocktail, and find they are not necessary to our goal. In particular, please note that we consider heroin unnecessary for good pain control in most cases. Morphine is a satisfactory substitute for use in this country.

A British patient in severe pain with spinal metastases from breast carcinoma was on forty milligrams of heroin orally every four hours, which is equivalent to eighty milligrams of morphine every four hours, plus a phenothiazine, benzodiazipine, and antidepressant. This was six weeks after she was admitted. Her pain was controlled sufficiently for her to be up and walking, dressed and planning to go home, but she still had some pain. She was tense with anxiety, and we recognized it was the anxiety component of the pain that was causing the problem, but we couldn't get at the cause of the anxiety, much less deal with it. It was only after she had been with us for six weeks that she developed enough trust to tell us what was troubling her. Ours is a long-term involvement—you can't just walk into patients' rooms, sit down, and expect them to trust you and tell you everything that is bothering them right away. This lady took six weeks before she told the orderly that her greatest fear about having cancer was that the chest wall secondaries she had would spread upwards and she would die like a leper with tumors all over her face. The underlying anxiety caused her pain to continue. After she had expressed her fears to an orderly, the doctor spoke to her about the fact that it just wasn't going to happen. When her psychological concerns were taken care of in combination with the physical symptom control, her pain disappeared and she went home.

Other less specific aspects of pain control are important, such as providing distraction and other activities. Pain control isn't just a matter of the doctor writing out the prescriptions. "The only drug which gives me any relief is my CB radio," says one of our new home care patients. Every member of the team must be involved with an understanding of what the treatment is all about. One doubting individual can destroy the patient's trust and confidence. The basic innner belief that the team won't let the patient down is crucial to effective pain management.

What people need most when they are dying is relief from distressing symptoms of disease, the security of a caring environment, sustained expert care, and assurance that they and their families will not be abandoned. "It's so good to know someone else is on my side—before it was only me."

38· Epilogue to *A Very Easy Death*

Simone de Beauvoir

Simone de Beauvoir is an internationally famous author, best known, perhaps, for her three books, The Mandarins, The Second Sex, *and* Coming of Age. *The title of her book* A Very Easy Death*—from which this selection is taken—appears to be sardonic inasmuch as the book is a description of the difficult, tortuous death of her mother. In the final passages of the book, reproduced here, de Beauvoir reviews her feelings about her mother's death, sees death in a new form, and reaches a shattering conclusion.*

Why did my mother's death shake me so deeply? Since the time I left home I had felt little in the way of emotional impulse towards her. When she lost my father the intensity and the simplicity of her sorrow moved me, and so did her care for others—"Think of yourself," she said to me, supposing that I was holding back my tears so as not to make her suffering worse. A year later her mother's dying was a painful reminder of her husband's: on the day of the funeral a nervous breakdown compelled her to stay in bed. I spent the night beside her: forgetting my disgust for this marriage-bed in which I had been born and in which my father had died, I watched her sleeping; at fifty-five, with her eyes closed and her face calm, she was still beautiful; I wondered that the strength of her feelings should have overcome her will. Generally speaking I thought of her with no particular feeling. Yet in my sleep (although my father only made very rare and then insignificant appearances) she often played a most important part: she blended with Sartre, and we were happy together. And then the dream would turn into a nightmare; why was I living with her once more? How had I come to be in her power again? So our former relationship lived on in me in its double aspect—a subjection that I loved and hated. It revived with all its strength when Maman's accident, her illness and her death shattered the routine that then governed our contacts. Time vanishes behind those who leave this world, and the older I get the more my past years draw together. The "Maman darling" of the days when I was ten can no longer be told from the inimical woman who oppressed my adolescence; I wept for them both when I wept for my old mother. I thought I had made up my mind about our failure and accepted it; but its sadness comes back to my heart. There are photographs of both of us, taken at about the same time: I am eighteen, she is nearly forty. Today I could almost be her mother and the grandmother of that sad-eyed girl. I am so sorry for them—for me because I am young and I understand nothing; for her because her future is closed and she has never understood anything. But I would not know how to advise them. It was not in my power to wipe out the unhappiness in her childhood that condemned Maman to make me unhappy and to suffer in her turn from having done so. For if she embittered several years of my life, I certainly paid her back though I did not set out to do so. She was intensely anxious about my soul. As far as this world was concerned, she was pleased at my successes, but she was hurt by the scandal that I aroused among the people she knew. It was not pleasant for her to hear a cousin state, "Simone is the family's disgrace."

The changes in Maman during her illness made my sorrow all the greater. As I have already said, she was a woman of a strong and eager temperament, and because of her renunciations she had grown confused and difficult. Confined to her bed, she decided to live for herself; and yet at the same time she retained an unvarying care for others—from her conflicts there arose a harmony. My father and his social character coincided exactly: his class and he spoke through his mouth with one identical voice. His last words, "You began to earn your living very young, Simone; your sister cost me a great deal of money," were not of a kind to encourage tears. My mother was awkwardly laced into a spiritualistic ideology; but she had an animal passion for life which was the source of her courage and which, once she was conscious of the weight of her body, brought her toward truth. She got rid of the ready-made notions that hid her sincere and lovable side. It was then that I felt the warmth of an affection that had often been distorted by jealousy and that she expressed so badly. In her papers I have found touching evidence of it. She had put aside two letters, the one written by a Jesuit and the other by a friend; they both assured her that one day I should come back to God. She had copied out a passage from Chamson in which he says in effect, "If, when I was twenty, I had met an older, highly regarded man who had talked to me about Nietszche and Gide and freedom, I should have broken with home." The file was completed by an article cut out of a paper—*Jean-Paul Sartre has saved a soul.* In this Rémy Roure said—quite untruthfully, by the way—that after *Bariona* had been acted at Stalag XII D an atheistical doctor was converted. I know very well what she wanted from these pieces—it was to be reassured about me; but she would never have felt the need if she had not been intensely anxious as to my salvation. "Of course I should like to go to Heaven: but not all alone, not without my daughters," she wrote to a young nun.

Sometimes, though very rarely, it happens that love, friendship or comradely feeling overcomes the loneliness of death: in spite of appearances, even when I was holding Maman's hand, I was not with her—I was lying to her. Because she had always been deceived, gulled, I found this ultimate deception revolting. I was making myself an accomplice of that fate which was so misusing her. Yet at the same time in every cell of my body I joined in her refusal, in her rebellion: and it was also because of that that her defeat overwhelmed me. Although I was not with Maman when she died, and although I had been with three people when they were actually dying, it was when I was at her bedside that I saw Death, the Death of the dance of death, with its bantering grin, the Death of fireside tales that knocks on the door, a scythe in its hand, the Death that comes from elsewhere, strange and inhuman: it had the very face of Maman when she showed her gums in a wide smile of unknowingness.

"He is certainly of an age to die." The sadness of the old; their banishment: most of them do not think that this age has yet come for them. I too made use of this cliché, and that when I was referring to my mother. I did not understand that one might sincerely weep for a relative, a grandfather aged seventy and more. If I met a woman of fifty overcome with sadness because she had just lost her mother, I thought her neurotic: we are all mortal; at eighty you are quite old enough to be one of the dead . . .

But it is not true. You do not die from being born, nor from having lived, nor from old age. You die from *something*. The knowledge that because of her age my mother's life must soon come to an end did not lessen the horrible surprise: she had sarcoma. Cancer, thrombosis, pneumonia: it is as violent and unforeseen as an engine stopping in the middle of the sky. My mother encouraged one to be optimistic when, crippled with arthritis and dying, she asserted the infinite value of each instant; but her vain tenaciousness also ripped and tore the reassuring curtain of everyday triviality. There is no such thing as a natural death: nothing that happens to a man is ever natural, since his presence calls the world into question. All men must die: but for every man his death is an accident and, even if he knows it and consents to it, an unjustifiable violation.

I

LIFE AFTER DEATH?

"To be or not to be" seems to be an almost simple question compared with "Do we continue after death?" These questions (of eschatology, survival after death, reincarnation, resurrection, immortality) all seem to be basic issues of any organized religious system.

As an introduction to the five selections of this section, here are three different views by important twentieth-century thinkers—de Beauvoir, Unamuno, and Freud.

In Simone de Beauvoir's memoir of her mother's death—the epilogue of which is reprinted in the previous section—she says: "Religion could do no more for my mother than the hope of posthumous success could do for me. Whether you think of it as heavenly or earthly, if you love life, immortality is no consolation for death."

Miguel de Unamuno, the Spanish philosopher, had a tragic and obsessive hunger for immortality. In his famous work The Tragic Sense of Life, *first published in 1921, he wrote: "For the sake of a name, man is ready to sacrifice not only life but happiness—life as a matter of course: 'Let me die, but let my fame live! Death is bitter, but fame is eternal.'" Unamuno seemed to be obsessed with immortality. A Catholic, he wrote: "If we all die utterly, wherefore does everything exist?" And "If there is no immortality, of what use is God?" He said further: "It is impossible for us, in effect, to conceive of ourselves as not existing, and no effort is capable of enabling consciousness to realize absolute unconsciousness, its own annihilation."*

This statement is all the more remarkable in that Unamuno, perhaps as far in his beliefs from a psychoanalytic orientation as any twentieth-century thinker could be, practically repeats one of Freud's most quoted statements about death and immortality: "Our own death is indeed unimaginable, and whenever we make an attempt to imagine it we can perceive that we really survive as spectators. Hence the psychoanalytic school could venture on the assertion that at bottom no one believes in his own death, or to put the thing in another way, in the unconscious everyone of us is convinced of his own immortality." These two statements present an amazing parallel of thought from two distinguished thinkers approaching the beguiling topic of immortality at about the same time from very different philosophic positions.

One of the most soothing strategies for dealing with the concept of death is simply to deny that death means the end of the individual (a concept that, in one form or another, is implied in several of the categories described by Toynbee).

This is perhaps one of the most "durable" views of death. Both the Heywood and the Russell selections emphasize that survival after death is, of necessity, based on belief; but Heywood sees "evidence" to support such a belief, while Russell sees logic as refuting the whole concept. Heywood's selection is included because this volume is a sampler of current thought, presenting both scientifically oriented positions and avowedly mystical, religious or parapsychological, even where the data seem to be shaky.

In 1975, Raymond A. Moody, Jr., then a medical student, wrote a thanatological best-seller, Life After Life. *Moody's book contains reports of over 100 subjects who purportedly died and returned to life and related their after-death experiences. In the foreward to the book, Dr. Kübler-Ross commends Moody's courage and says that he "will have to be prepared for a lot of criticism." The third selection in this section is from "Questions," a chapter of Moody's book, in which he attempts to answer the questions most often asked about survival-of-death experiences.*

Virginia Hine's paper raises the interesting question whether dramatically altered states of consciousness—drug induced, achieved through mental discipline such as yoga, or resulting from physical trauma—might not create thorough-going changes in an individual's attitude toward his or her own death. Hine also notes that the final hours of the dying process themselves often appear to be an altered state of consciousness in which dying people "withdraw" as wounded animals do. Whether or not death is the finality of the conscious life of an individual or a transition to some other form or level of postmortem consciousness, it nonetheless seems sensible to state, as Hine does, that the "further exploration of altered states of consciousness would seem to be useful" in relation to helping people die better.

Holck's paper, "Life Revisited: Parallels in Death Experiences," can be read as an extended footnote to Raymond Moody's reports on his interviews with people who claim to have experienced temporary death. Holck relates Moody's anecdotal reports to comparable reports in the long history of canonical and other religious writings and in the legends of different cultures. The fact that one finds these accounts in historical writings is seen by some as evidence of their truth and by others as evidence simply of the pervasiveness of folklore.

Bertrand Russell was one of the most intellectually gifted minds of this century. His thoughts and writings have illuminated mathematics, science, philosophy, and morality. His brief essay, "Do We Survive Death?" is written in typically pungent Russellian prose, putting to rest (for any logical mind that dares to follow his reasoning) the vexing notion of survival after death and its beguiling twin, immortality.

The attempt to put all these views together reinforces our sense of the oxymoronic quality of death. Death is destroyer and redeemer; the ultimate cruelty and the essence of release; universally feared but sometimes actively sought; ubiquitous yet unique; the end yet certainly a kind of beginning for the survivors, if not the decedent; of all phenomena, the most obvious and the least reportable; feared yet fascinating; a permanent solution and an endless puzzle.

39·

Death and Psychical Research: The Present Position Regarding the Evidence of Survival

Rosalind Heywood

Rosalind Heywood is Member of Council of the Society for Psychical Research in England. This selection, which first appeared in Man's Concern with Death *edited by Professor Toynbee, is one of a number of articles in that volume on psychical research, a study that is particularly popular in England. It has been included as representative of the kind of data upon which many psychical researchers base their approach to the age-old question of survival after death.*

From the point of view of the investigator, then, the findings of psychical research in relation to death seem to amount to something like this. On the one hand the apparent potentialities of ESP make it hard to conceive what kind of evidence could give coercive proof of survival —evidence that could not at a pinch be ascribed to some combination of telepathy, clairvoyance, precognition or retrocognition in relation to events in this world. As against this, the more we learn about the range of these capacities, about man's apparent power to transcend the limitations of the known senses and of time and space as presented to him by those senses, the less inconceivable it may be that the early researchers were on the right track in surmising that there could be something in him—what Professor C. D. Broad discreetly calls some psi component—which might be able to function independently of a physical body.

In a book concerned with attitudes to death some reference should perhaps be made not only to the attitude of the scientific researcher as regards the possibility of survival, but also to those of people who have themselves had ESP-type experiences connected with death. It may be guessed that most actively religious Christians who have such experiences accept them for what they appear to be, and that a number of the non-Christians who have them join some group, such as the theosophists or spiritualists, into whose beliefs their experiences will fit, for this gives them peace of mind. But how many people are there like the flight lieutenant, who appeared to talk quite normally with his dead fellow pilot and yet had no framework of belief which would hold his experience? Judging from the many cases sent to Dr. Louisa Rhine and to other writers of seriously intentioned books on psi, there must be an appreciable number, and owing to the present orthodox belief that death is the end, it looks as if some of them dare not mention such experiences for fear of being thought out of their minds. Some even wonder, could that perhaps be true? "Can you possibly explain this?" they write, "I have never dared ask anyone before. Do you think I could be mad?"

The experiences most often reported, incidentally, as with most of the authenticated cases in the annals of psychical research, are far removed from the headless, chain-clanking "ghosties and ghoulies" of fiction and Christmas Numbers. Apart from the apparently aimless haunting type, modern "ghosts" usually seem to want to help, or warn, or merely to appear to a loved friend or relative. And sometimes they are not distinguished from living persons until they vanish.

For those of us, then, who are conditioned by the widespread belief that mind and body die together, and who yet have apparent contacts with the purposeful discarnate, what is our rational attitude towards those contacts, especially as they are admittedly sporadic, fleeting, and not to be repeated to order? Perhaps I may be forgiven a personal summarized illustration of this dilemma, since it is not easy to describe other people's experience as if from the inside.

In the 1950s the expected death occurred of an inventor friend, with whom, as we both accepted that death was the end, I had shortly before agreed regretfully that he would never be able to bring to fruition the ideas still seething in his brain. About ten days after his death I was astounded and delighted to "meet," quite naturally, his apparently living personality, and to be assured with emphasis that we had been quite mistaken; he now had scope and opportunity beyond his wildest dreams. In some imageless way I seemed able to participate in his awareness of scope and opportunity and I was rejoicing in this when it flashed across my mind that I ought to ask for evidence of his splendid liberation. But the reply he made was, "I can't give you any evidence. You have no concepts for these conditions.[1] I can only give you poetic images." Which he did. But quite soon I realized that I could not hold the state into which, unexpectedly, my consciousness had switched, so I said, "Goodbye, I must drop now." And I "dropped" at once to ordinary awareness of mundane surroundings.

Although this experience does not appear to be very exceptional, there is not a shred of evidence to support my account of it, and investigators will therefore—and quite rightly—feel it their duty to dismiss it as a mere anecdote. But again, what is the rational attitude for the people who have such experiences, sometimes repeatedly? Should we discard them all as illusions, in obedience to orthodoxy? Should we even suspect our own sanity? (I asked two eminent psychiatrists to check on mine and they both gave me a clean bill of health. But one did say sadly, "I'm *afraid* you're quite sane.") Or should we defy the voice of contemporary science and bet on the reality of our own experiences, however fleeting and unpredictable?

On one thing, perhaps, the psi-experiencing agnostic can afford to bet

—that were the whole of humanity to have experiences similar to his own, of the occasional momentary, purposeful presence of discarnate persons he had known in life, it would not occur to them, however mistaken they might be in fact, to doubt the reality of survival. As things are, however, the only place where his reason can feel at ease and honest is on the fence. And there he will at least be encouraged to find a number of distinguished scholars who have thought it worthwhile to study the evidence for survival for many years. This is how three among them summed up their conclusions in the 1960s. First, the well-known American psychologist Professor Gardner Murphy.

> Where then do I stand? To this the reply is: what happens when an irresistible force strikes an immovable object? To me the evidence cannot be bypassed, nor, on the other hand, can conviction be achieved . . . Trained as a psychologist and now in my sixties, I do not actually anticipate finding myself in existence after physical death. If this is the answer the reader wants, he can have it. But if this means that in a serious philosophical argument I would plead the antisurvival case, the conclusion is erroneous. I linger because I cannot cross the stream. We need far more evidence; we need new perspectives; perhaps we need more courageous minds.[2]

Next, the doyen of British psychologists, Professor Sir Cyril Burt.

> The uncertainty leaves the matter open in *both* directions. On the one hand the theoretical psychologist (and that includes the parapsychologist) should, on this particular issue, preserve a strict agnosticism, pressing physicalistic interpretations as far as they will go, and even if in the end he feels compelled to adopt the hypothesis of a surviving mind, he must remember that it is, like the ether of old, no more than a hypothesis. On the other hand, those who, from reasons of faith, metaphysics, or what they take to be personal revelation, still wish to believe in survival for themselves or those they love, need have no grounds for fearing scientific censure. Thus our verdict on the whole matter must be the same as that pronounced by Plato two thousand years ago—the reply he puts into the mouth of Socrates while waiting to drink the hemlock. "I would not positively assert that I shall join the company of those good men who have already departed from this life; but I cherish a good hope." Hope implies not the virtual certainty of success but the possibility of success. And it is, I think, one important result of recent psychological and parapsychological investigations to have demonstrated, in the face of the confident denials of the materialists and the behaviourists, *at least the possibility* of survival in some form or other, though not necessarily in the form depicted by traditional piety or fourth century metaphysics.[3]

And finally, Professor C. D. Broad, sometime Knightbridge Professor of Moral Philosophy at Cambridge. He, incidentally, does not hide the fact that he does not want to survive.

> The position as I see it is this. In the known relevant normal and abnormal facts there is nothing to suggest and much to countersuggest, the possibility of any kind of persistence of the psychical aspect of a human being after the death of his body. On the other hand, there are many quite well-attested *paranormal* phenomena which strongly suggest such persistence, and a few which strongly suggest the fullblown survival of a human personality. Most people manage to turn a blind eye to one or the other of these two relevant sets of data, but it is part of the business of a professional philosopher to try to envisage steadily both of them together. The result is naturally a state of hesitation and scepticism (in the correct as opposed to the popular sense of that word). I think I may say that for my part I should be slightly more annoyed than surprised if I should find myself in some sense persisting immediately after the death of my present body. One can only wait and see, or alternatively (which is no less likely) wait and not see."[4]

It looks then as if at the present time to step off the fence on either side as regards survival entails an act of faith. On one side we can believe—but cannot prove—that men of science already know enough about the nature of things to be able to assert with safety that it is impossible; on the other we can believe—but equally cannot prove—that certain phenomena demonstrate that it is a fact.

Notes

1 In an article in *The New Scientist* for August 30th, 1962, Dr. Richard Gregory has suggested that travellers in space might be faced with a similar problem. "Suppose," he says, "we were to meet something really odd—say a new life form—could we see it properly? The perceptual system is a computer, programmed by evolutionary experience and by our own personal experience of the world. A new kind of object requires the perceptual computer to solve a new problem with an old programme, which may be neither adequate nor appropriate."

2 *Challenge of Psychical Research,* Harpers, New York, 1961, p. 273.

3 *Article,* "Psychology and Parapsychology" in a symposium *Science & E.S.P.,* edited by J. R. Smythies, International Library of Philosophy and Scientific Method, Routledge and Kegan Paul, p. 140.

4 *Lectures on Psychical Research,* International Library of Philosophy and Scientific Method, Routledge and Kegan Paul, 1962, p. 430.

40· Questions

Raymond A. Moody, Jr.

Raymond Moody wrote his book, Life After Life, *while he was a medical student in Georgia. In that book he recounts many anecdotes of individuals who were thought to have died and then returned to life. With four discursive omissions, the chapter called "Questions" is reproduced below.*

By now, many doubts and objections will have occurred to the reader. In the years that I have been giving talks, in private and public, on this subject, I have been asked many questions. In general, I tend to be asked about the same things on most occasions, so I have been able to compile a list of those questions which are asked most frequently.

Are you just making all this up?

No, I'm not. I very much want to pursue a career in the teaching of psychiatry and the philosophy of medicine, and attempting to perpetrate a hoax would hardly be conducive to that aim.

Also, it has been my experience that anyone who makes diligent and sympathetic inquiries among his own acquaintances, friends, and relatives about the occurrence of such experiences will soon have his doubts dispelled.

But aren't you being unrealistic? After all, how common are such experiences?

I am the first to admit that, due to the necessarily limited nature of my sample of cases, I am unable to give a significant numerical estimate of the incidence or prevalence of this phenomenon. However, I am quite willing to say this: The occurrence of such experiences is far more common than anyone who hasn't studied them would guess. I have given many public lectures on this subject, to many kinds and sizes of groups, and there has never been an instance in which someone there didn't come up afterward with a story of his own, or even, in some cases, tell it publicly. Of course, one could always say (and truly!) that someone with such an experience would be more likely to come to a lecture on such a topic. Nonetheless, in many of the cases I have encountered, the person involved did not come to the lecture because of the topic. For example, I recently addressed a group of thirty persons. Two of them had had near-death experiences, and both were there just because they were members of the group. Neither knew the topic of my talk beforehand....

How do you know that all these people aren't just lying to you?

It is quite easy for persons who have not listened and watched as others have related near-death experiences intellectually to entertain the hypothesis that these stories are lies. However, I find myself in a rather unique position. I have witnessed mature, emotionally stable adults—both men and women—break down and weep while telling me of events that happened up to three decades before. I have detected in their voices sincerity, warmth, and feeling which cannot really be conveyed in a written recounting. So to me, in a way that is unfortunately impossible for many others to share, the notion that these accounts might be fabrications is utterly untenable.

In addition to the weight of my own opinion, there are some strong considerations which should rule heavily against the fabrication hypothesis. The most obvious is the difficulty of explaining the similarity of so many of the accounts. How is it that many people just happen to have come up with the same lie to tell me over a period of eight years? Collusion remains a theoretical possibility here. It is certainly conceivable that a nice elderly lady from eastern North Carolina, a medical student from New Jersey, a Georgia veterinarian, and many others several years ago banded together and conspired to carry out an elaborate hoax against me. However, I don't regard this to be a very likely possibility!

If they are not overtly lying, perhaps they are misrepresenting in a more subtle way. Isn't it possible that over the years, they have elaborated their stories?

This question points to the well-known psychological phenomenon in which a person may start with a fairly simple account of an experience or event and over a period of time develop it into a very elaborate narrative. With each telling, a subtle detail is added, the speaker coming eventually to believe it himself, until at last the story is so embellished as to bear little resemblance to the original.

I do not believe that this mechanism has been operative to any significant degree in the cases I have studied, however. In the first place, the accounts of persons whom I have interviewed very soon after their experience—in some cases, while they were still in the hospital recovering—are of the same type as those of people who have recounted experiences which took place decades ago. Further, in a few cases, persons whom I have interviewed wrote down descriptions of their experiences shortly after they happened and read to me from their notes during the interview. Again, these descriptions are of the same sort as experiences which are recounted from memory after lapses of some years. Also, there is the fact that quite often I have been only the first or second person to whom an experience has been related, and then only with great reluctance, even in cases where the experience happened some years before. Though there has been little or no opportunity for embellishment in such cases, these accounts, again, are no different as a group from those accounts that have been retold more often over a period of years. Finally, it is quite possible that in many cases, the reverse of embellishment has taken place. What psychiatrists call "suppression" is a mental mechanism whereby a conscious effort is made to control undesired memories, feelings, or thoughts or to conceal them from awareness. On numerous occasions in the course of interviews, persons have made remarks which are strongly indicative that suppression has occurred. For example, one woman who reported to me a very elaborate experience which took place during her "death" said, "I feel that there is more to it, but I can't remember it all. I tried to suppress it because I knew people weren't going to believe me anyway." A man who suffered a cardiac arrest during surgery for major wounds received in Viet Nam related his difficulty in dealing with his out-of-body experiences emotionally. "I get choked up by trying to tell about it even now. . . . I feel that there is a lot I don't remember about it. I have tried to forget it." In short, it seems that a strong case can be made that embellishment has not been a very significant factor in the development of these stories.

Did all these people profess a religion before their experiences? If so, aren't the experiences shaped by their religious beliefs and backgrounds?

They seem to be to some extent. As mentioned earlier, though the description of the being of light is invariable, the identity ascribed to it varies, apparently as a function of the religious background of the individual. Through all of my research, however, I have not heard a single reference to a heaven or a hell anything like the customary picture to which we are exposed in this society. Indeed, many persons have stressed how unlike their experiences were to what they had been led to expect in the course of their religious training. One woman who "died" reported: "I had always heard that when you die, you see both heaven and hell, but I didn't see either one." Another lady who had an out-of-body experience after severe injuries said, "The strange thing was that I had always been taught in my religious upbringing that the minute you died you would be right at these beautiful gates, pearly gates. But there I was hovering around my own physical body, and that was it! I was just baffled." Furthermore, in quite a few instances reports have come from persons who had no religious beliefs or training at all prior to their experiences, and their descriptions do not seem to differ in content from people who had quite strong religious beliefs. In a few cases, someone who had been exposed to religious doctrines but had rejected them earlier in life acquired religious feelings with new depth after the experience. Others say that although they had read religious writings, such as the Bible, they had never really understood certain things they had read there until their near-death experiences. . . .

Do you have any cross-cultural cases?

No, I don't. In fact, one of the many reasons I say that my study is not "scientific" is that the group of individuals to whom I have listened is not a random sample of human beings. I would be very interested in hearing about the near-death experiences of Eskimos, Kwakiutl Indians, Navahos, Watusi tribesmen, and so on. However, due to geographic and other limitations, I have not been able to locate any.

Are there any historical examples of near-death phenomena?

As far as I know, there are not. However, since I have been fully occupied with contemporary instances, I have simply not had the time adequately to research this question. So I would not at all be surprised to find that such reports have been recounted in the past. On the other hand, I strongly suspect that near-death experiences have been vastly more common in the past few decades than in earlier periods. The reason for this is simply that it has only been in fairly recent times that advanced resuscitation technology has been available. Many of the people who have been brought back in our era would not have survived in earlier years. Injections of adrenalin into the heart, a machine which delivers a shock to the heart, and artificial heart and lung machines are examples of such medical advances.

Have you investigated the medical records of your subjects?

In so far as possible, I have. In the cases I have been invited to investigate, the records have borne out the assertions of the persons involved. In some cases, due to the passage of time and/or the death of the persons who carried out the resuscitation, records are not available. The reports for which substantiating records are not available are no different from those in which records are available. In many instances when medical records have not been accessible, I have secured the testimony of others—friends, doctors, or relatives of the informant—to the effect that the near-death event did occur.

I have heard that, after five minutes, resuscitation is impossible, yet you say that some of your cases have been "dead" for up to twenty minutes. How is this possible?

Most numbers and quantities one hears quoted in medical practice are means, averages, and are not to be taken as absolutes. The figure of five minutes which one often hears quoted is an average. It is a clinical rule of thumb not to attempt resuscitation after five minutes because, in most instances, brain damage from lack of oxygen would have occurred beyond that time. However, since it is only an average, one would expect individual cases to fall on either side of it. I have in fact found cases in which resuscitation took place after twenty minutes with no evidence of brain damage.

Were any of these people really dead?

One of the main reasons why this question is so confusing and difficult to answer is that it is partly a semantic question involving the meaning of the word "dead." As the recent heated controversy surrounding the transplantation of organs reveals, the definition of "death" is by no means settled, even among professionals in the field of medicine. Criteria of death vary not only between laymen and physicians, but also among physicians and from hospital to hospital. So, the answer to this question will depend on what is meant by "dead."

. . .One must remember that even though this is in part a semantic dispute, it is nonetheless an important issue. Even in those cases in which the heart was not beating for extended periods, the tissues of the body, particularly the brain, must somehow have been perfused (supplied with oxygen and nourishment) most of the time. It is not necessary that one assume in any of these cases that any law of biology or physiology was violated. In order for resuscitation to have occurred, some degree of residual biological activity must have been going on in the cells of the body, even though the overt signs of these processes were not clinically detectable by the methods employed. However, it seems that it is impossible at present to determine exactly what the point of no return is. It may well vary with the individual, and it is likely not a fixed point but rather a shifting range on a continuum. In fact, a few decades ago most of the people with whom I have talked could not have been brought back. In the future, techniques might become available which would enable us to revive people who can't be saved today.

Let us, therefore, hypothesize that death is a separation of the mind from the body, and that the mind does pass into other realms of existence at this point. It would follow that there exists some mechanism whereby the soul or mind is released upon death. One has no basis upon which to assume, though, that this mechanism works exactly in accordance with what we have in our own era somewhat arbitrarily taken to be the point of no return. Nor do we have to assume that it works perfectly in every instance, any more than we have to assume that any bodily system always works perfectly. Perhaps this mechanism might sometime come into play even before any physiological crisis, affording a few persons a brief glimpse of other realities. This would help to account for the reports of those persons who have had flashbacks of their lives, out-of-body experiences, etc., when they felt certain that they were about to be killed, even before any physical injury occurred.

All I ultimately want to claim is this: Whatever that point of irretrievable death is said to be—whether in the past, present, or future—those with whom I have talked have been much closer to it than have the vast majority of their fellow human beings. For this reason alone, I am quite willing to listen to what they have to say.

In the final analysis, though, it is quite pointless to cavil over the precise definition of "death"—irreversible or otherwise—in the context of this discussion. What the person who raises such objections to near-death experiences seems to have in mind is something more basic. He reasons that as long as it remains a possibility that there was some residual biological activity in the body, then that activity might have caused, and thus account for, the experience.

Now, I granted earlier that there must have been some residual biological function in the body in all cases. So, the issue of whether a "real" death occurred really reduces to the more basic problem of whether the residual biological function could account for the occurrence of the experiences. . . .

41• Altered States of Consciousness: A Form of Death Education?

Virginia H. Hine

Virginia Hine works at the Center for Continuing Education at the Miami-Dade Community College in Miami, Florida. Ms. Hine suggests that there is a link between adaptive attitudes toward death and the experience of dramatically altered states of consciousness whether the altered state of consciousness is drug induced, is achieved through various spiritual disciplines, or results from physical trauma in a "clinical death." She explores the implications for death education.

From Death Education *Vol. 1, No. 4 (1978): 377–396. Reprinted by permission of the publishers.*

It is no coincidence that the so-called consciousness revolution, with its smorgasbord of techniques for exploring altered states of consciousness, has swept the country at the same time as the subject of death and dying has come "out of the closet" and into the open. It would seem that the same shifts in cultural values that are freeing us to exercise a long-suppressed aspect of our human potential are also releasing us from the limitations of a death-denying world view. If there is a link between a more adaptive attitude toward death and the experience of nonordinary modes of awareness, then it would have important implications for death education. I would suggest, first, that there is such a link and, second, that it can be utilized not only to enhance objective understanding of death but to enrich or reorient the subjective experience of the dying process.

Behavioral scientists are busy coining terms to refer to nonordinary modes of thinking and experiencing. Indeed, George Leonard points out that the very paucity of commonly accepted vocabulary for radical changes in consciousness is an indication of the extent to which modern Western culture exercises effective censorship over this type of experience (1). The phrase that seems to have gained the widest acceptance is *altered states of consciousness,* which Charles Tart defines as "a qualitative alteration in the overall pattern of mental functioning, such that the experiencer feels his consciousness is radically different from the way it functions ordinarily" (2). (Such a definition would hardly be necessary in Tibetan, in which language there are 120 terms for different states of being!) Abraham Maslow used the term B-cognition, or Being-cognition, to describe a radically different sort of consciousness during times of "peak experiences" (3). Lawrence LeShan takes the position that there are not only two modes of consciousness, but that each mode is a means of perceiving two different levels of reality. During moments of ordinary perception and awareness, he suggests, we are operating in what he calls "sensory reality" and in moments of paranormal perception we are responding to a different level of reality that he calls "clairvoyant reality" (4). Carl Jung also insisted upon the objective reality of those levels of the unconscious he believed to be transpersonal and which he referred to as archetypes. In personal conversations with his biographer, Jung described his own experience of these two types of reality almost as if there were two different selves perceiving and acting. He "appeared to himself to be two distinct persons, to whom he gave the sober, empirical baptism, of personalities. No. 1 and No. 2" (5). Physician Andrew Weil, much less reverently, writes about "straight thinking" and "stoned thinking" regardless of whether drugs are used to break through the confines of normal perception (6). Carlos Castenada, a nonordinary anthropologist, recorded his long apprenticeship in the Yaqui way of knowledge and has made the concept of "a separate reality" familiar to millions of previously unidimensional Americans (7).

The new willingness to explore altered states of consciousness is being encouraged by a wide range of available techniques from the mild, nonmystic stress reduction offered by Transcendental Meditation (TM) (dubbed by some the McDonald's of the consciousness circuit), to the major life changes required by some mental and physical disciplines transplanted from the Eastern traditions. However, it is the most radically altered states of consciousness that seem to involve permanent changes in attitude toward death, in reduction of fear and need for denial. If this link is to be useful in death education, either as personal preparation for death or as increased understanding on the part of families and health professionals around dying people, we must focus on those alterations in consciousness that lead experiencers into changed perceptions of the meaning of death. These reports are coming from two directions. One is from people who seek, by one means or another, altered states of consciousness as part of spiritual development. The other is from people who have been subjected to physical trauma and have survived clinical death or near-death experiences. The link is obvious in the fact that people trying to describe the "bliss" of some altered states of consciousness frequently use death and dying imagery to do so. Conversely, those who have survived clinical death or can verbalize their experience as they approach actual death frequently use descriptive imagery used by seekers of cosmic consciousness or mystical union with God—often images used in spiritual traditions with which the dying person has had no familiarity or contact. Further, the experience, whether the result of a spiritual quest or a close encounter with physical death, seems to produce lasting changes in attitudes toward death.

Altered states of consciousness reported from a variety of cultural settings show interesting parallels not only in the use of death imagery in attempts to describe them, but in the positive attitudes toward death that accompany them. A few examples will suffice.

Abraham Maslow was one of the first behavioral scientists to recognize the significance of what he called peak experiences and to note that they need not occur within the framework of a religious belief system. According to Maslow (3), even those from a nontheistic background of scientific rationalism reported peak experiences that involved

> such emotions as wonder, awe, reverence, humility, surrender and even worship before the greatness of the experience. This may go so

far as to involve thoughts of death in a peculiar way. Peak-experiences can be so wonderful that they can parallel the experience of dying, that is of an eager and happy dying. It is a kind of reconciliation and acceptance of death. Scientists have never considered as a scientific problem the question of the "good death"; but here in these experiences, we discover a parallel to what has been considered to be the religious attitude toward death, i.e., humility or dignity before it, willingness to accept it, possibly even a happiness with it.

One of the classic descriptions of a peak experience, a radically altered state of consciousness, interpreted within a conventional religious belief system was written by Charles G. Finney. This early nineteenth century evangelist reported his conversion experience in the following words

> The waves (of joy and love) came over me, and over me, and over me, one after the other, until I recollect I cried out, "I shall die if these waves continue to pass over me." I said, "Lord, I cannot bear any more," yet I had no fear of death. How long I continued in this state I do not know, but it was late in the evening when a member of my choir came to see me . . . He found me in this state of loud weeping, and said, "Mr. Finney, what ails you?" I could make him no answer for some time. He then said, "Are you in pain?" I gathered myself up and replied, "No, but so happy that I cannot live."

During several years of research into the structure and functioning of the Pentecostal movement and its rapid spread into all major denominations and among all socioeconomic groups in this country, I recorded nearly 100 similar accounts of what participants term the "baptism of the Holy Spirit." All of these experiences involve some degree of alteration in state of consciousness. Many accounts, usually those involving more radical alterations in mode of awareness, included references to waves of love and joy or images of electric currents and brilliant light and the sensation that the experience was either like a death or that death would come if the experiencer remained long in this state. Radical alterations in both attitudes and behavior patterns were documented during the research and it was found that these were significantly related to systematic practice in altered states of consciousness. For many participants, one of the important attitude changes was a reduction in fear of death and a more positive orientation toward the experience of death.

The link between altered states of consciousness and positive attitudes toward death can be picked up in a variety of cultural settings. It is very clear in the Yaqui Indian framework of beliefs as described and experienced by anthropologist Carlos Castenada (7). Don Juan, the Yaqui sorcerer and spiritual adept, uses the term *impeccable warrior* to describe a person who lives his life, whatever his role or station, victoriously and effectively. To do this one must learn to perceive and work with nonordinary reality from which comes knowledge and power. To learn to "see" is to learn to perceive the separate reality that surrounds and is in and through ordinary reality. A man of knowledge can "see" his own death, always just behind his left shoulder, and guides his life according to its dictates. To move in that other dimension, utilizing a different mode of cognizing and experiencing, is to acquire power. This requires confronting one's own death as a personified reality, accepting it as an ally, and recognizing it as an integral component of living "impeccably" day by day.

The experience of altered states of consciousness resulting in positive orientations toward death is a constant theme in traditional Eastern cultural belief systems. In this cultural context a radical alteration in state of consciousness reinforces experientially the perception of the physical body and the world of social reality as confining and limiting, a prison from which one longs to be free. Paramahansa Yogananda, son of a wealthy, high-caste Hindu family who chose the religious life, was one of the early leaders in bringing Eastern systems of thought and disciplines to the Western world. In his autobiography, Yogananda (9) describes this sort of perception of death resulting from his guru's having led him into a total experience of "cosmic consciousness." "My body became immovably rooted; breath was drawn out of my lungs as if by some huge magnet. Soul and mind instantly lost their physical bondage and streamed out like a fluid, piercing light from every pore. The flesh was as though dead, yet in my intense awareness I knew that never before had I been fully alive." He goes on to describe a change in his perception of his surroundings in which his "ordinary frontal vision was now changed to a vast spherical sight, simultaneously all-perceptive," and he experienced himself as permeating and being permeated by the totality of the cosmos. At the end of the experience, "suddenly the breath returned to my lungs. With a disappointment almost unbearable, I realized that my infinite immensity was lost. Once more I was limited to the humiliating cage of my body, not easily accommodative to the spirit. Like a prodigal child, I had run away from my macrocosmic home and had imprisoned myself in a narrow microcosm."

The link between death and experience of altered states of consciousness is explicit, of course, in the Kriya Yoga doctrine that Yogananda (9) taught. Disciplines enhancing the capacity for altered states of consciousness are viewed as preparation for dying as an effortless transfer: "Prepare yourself for the coming astral journey of death by riding daily in a balloon of divine perception . . . Cease being a prisoner of the body; learn to escape into the spirit!"

The concept of death as a transition to a desirable state, even preferable to life, is not limited to those socialized into Indian cultural assumptions. Even Westerners who begin outside of any conventional religious tradition have experienced radically altered states of consciousness in which loss of the body can be contemplated without the usual fear of annihilation. Franklin Merrill-Wolff was an early rebel against both religious and academic orthodoxy during the 1930s. The burgeoning concern with nonordinary modes of awareness has sent many a modern inner space "cosmonaught," including John Lilly, to seek out first his writings and then the man himself, who has become a sort of Western style guru. Merrill-Wolff (10) uses the term *the recognition* to describe his experiences of higher states of consciousness. The recognition, he says, is "a kind of dying proceeding in the midst of continued bodily existence." His explanation of the shift in attitude from fear and denial to acceptance of death suggests that an experience of radically altered states of consciousness leads the experiencer to accept a different definition of reality in which death plays a positive rather than a negative role.

> It is difficult for the average individual, caught in the hypnotic glamour of embodied consciousness, to understand the attitude toward physical embodiment which recognition induces in the realized man. Let me assure the reader that this position is not artificial, nor forced, nor due to pessimism. It is just as natural as the distaste the normal man would feel for life in a front line trench during a modern war. Cheerfully he may choose to accept his tour of duty in the front lines because he feels that his country needs his service there, but wholeheartedly he abominates this life. He will not feel it a hardship when circumstances so change that he will not be needed at the front. Well, let me assure anyone who doubts that the inward life is so immeasurably richer than outer life that the keenest sensual enjoyment is relatively pain. Hence a tour of duty in gross physical embodiment is relatively like a period of life at the front during warfare. There are other worlds, more subtle than this outer field of life, where consciousness is also embodied and the life there is immeasurably richer than the life here below. Therefore why cling to the false glamour of life cast in the dregs?

This sort of overly positive attitude toward death so violates conventional scientific assumptions that many "objective" observers are impelled to explain radically altered states of consciousness in terms of the three D's—deprivation, disorganization, or deviancy. The experiencer must be socially, economically, or (if these conditions obviously do not pertain) emotionally deprived; a victim of social disorganization and alienation; or display some psychological disorder. A recent statement by the Group for Advancement of Psychiatry (11) presents the current surge of interest in mysticism and practice of altered states of consciousness as the result of a "general cultural crisis," which drives those in "a state of marginal health" to "turn aside from the difficult problems of the mundane by what amounts to a flight through introversion." Somewhat uncomfortable with their conventional conclusions, the authors note certain "creative" aspects of altered states of consciousness, and touch lightly, without analyzing, the fact that similar states can be induced physiologically through drugs.

Whatever the "explanations" for radically altered states of consciousness, death educators must face the discomfiting fact that a human capacity, viewed negatively within conventional scientific and rational frameworks, seems to produce positive results in terms of adaptive attitudes toward death. Increasingly this appears to be true whether the change originates with systematic attempts to alter the state of consciousness through one spiritual tradition or another, or with an experience of physiological intervention. The physiologically produced state that results in a permanent reorientation toward death may be drug-induced or part of "clinical death," the near-death experiences which have received so much attention recently.

The link between altered states of consciousness and the experience of dying has occurred spontaneously to many users of LSD, most of whom have come to the experience lacking any ready-made belief system which would predispose them to approach death positively. Many, like the more disciplined seekers after cosmic consciousness, emerge from their altered states of consciousness with a radically altered attitude toward their own dying. A common comment is that the hallucinatory experience was a death experience that prepared the individual to accept actual death without fear. Indeed some reorder their life planning accordingly. One young man who confronted his own immortality for the first time in an impressively penetrating way during an LSD trip, spent several months afterward reexamining his goals in life and his plans for implementing them. He planned in ten-year increments, reserving the last ten years for focusing entirely on "preparation for leaving the body."

The potential of LSD-induced altered modes of perception for changing not only attitudes toward death but the actual experience of death has been utilized in experiments on psychedelic therapy with dying patients. Eric Kast (12) used LSD with terminal cancer patients at the Chicago Medical School in the early 1960s to test its analgesic properties and found it significantly superior to morphine and demerol. He also discovered that it lessened fear of death. Sidney Cohen (13) confirmed Kast's findings two years later. Subsequently systematic work in LSD-assisted psychotherapy has been conducted at Spring Grove in Baltimore in cooperation with the Maryland Psychiatric Research Center and Sinai Hospital (14). Researchers found the expected relief of depression, anxiety, sense of isolation, and insomnia. An unexpected result in some patients was alleviation or even disappearance of severe physical pain. The most remarkable effect of psychedelic therapy, according to the report, has been a dramatic transformation of the concept of death. Along with this have come specific changes in value judgments that eased the encounter with death: "These involved a shift from the rumination on the past and apprehension about the future toward greater emphasis on the here and now. There was also a definite trend toward losing interest in status, money, possessions, and ambitions and an increased appreciation of the simple things in life." These types of value changes are also associated with the experiences of altered states of consciousness encouraged in classical religious traditions, both Eastern and Western. One patient in the Spring Grove program experienced clinical death during the process of his dying from cancer. He reported close parallels between the near-death experience and the LSD-induced state: "He found the experience of actual dying extremely similar to his psychedelic experiences and considered the latter an excellent training and preparation."

Recent exploration of near-death experiences has inspired a rash of popular accounts of the images and visions of dying people as well as of survivors of "clinical death." These accounts are variously interpreted as "proof" of life after death Christian style, or reincarnation Eastern style. They are also interpreted by the physiologically minded as anoxia, insufficient supply of oxygen to body tissues, common in dying people and mechanically induced by some aboriginal peoples who use smoke inhalation, near drowning, prolonged holding of the breath or hanging upside down to induce altered states of consciousness. Some psychologically minded observers tend toward explanations in terms of sensory deprivation and isolation research (itself an unexplained phenomenon) or "delusions" and "hallucinations" or the intrusion of Jungian "archetypes"—somewhat unsatisfactory attempts to explain by means of label switching. An attempt to explore the link between positive orientation toward death and altered states of consciousness requires noting the wide range of conflicting "explanations" without getting trapped in any of them. The implications for death education lie in tracing the common themes in the content of the experience that alters attitudes and in attention paid to the variety of ways in which the experience might be usefully encouraged by death educators.

A classical example of a near-death experience that permanently alters perception of the meaning of death is that of Carl Jung. His description (15) of the experience illustrates the recurrent images that are commonly used regardless of the socioeconomic or cultural background of the experiencer. During a serious heart attack in 1944, while he was unconscious, Jung had an experience that he described in terms familiar to students studying Christian mysticism, *The Tibetan Book of the Dead,* classical Hindu mythology, and a variety of current "schools" of research into psychic phenomena. While Jung was familiar with all of these traditions, similar images and even phraseology are used by less famous survivors of clinical death and many hallucinogenic trippers who were "unbelievers" or unfamiliar with these bodies of knowledge. Jung's description included sensations of weightlessness, or floating in space, of panoramic vision, identification with the universe, great illumination, indescribable bliss, a sloughing off of the "trappings" of earthly existence, meetings with "people to whom I belonged," and communication as a nonverbal, instantaneous kind of thought exchange: "This is eternal bliss, I thought. This cannot be described, it is far too wonderful."

Jung also experienced the return to ordinary perception as a depressing loss and described existence within a physical body as being confined within a "box."

> In reality a good three weeks were still to pass before I could truly make up my mind to live again. Disappointed, I thought "Now I must return to the box system again." For it seemed to me as if behind the horizon of the cosmos a three-dimensional world had been artificially built up, in which each person sat by himself in a little box. And now I should have to convince myself all over again that this was important! Life and the whole world struck me as a prison, and it bothered me

> beyond measure that I should again be finding all that quite in order. I had been so glad to shed it all, and now it had come about that I—along with everyone else—would be hung up in a box by a thread.

Raymond Moody's *Life After Life* (16) burst upon the national scene just as death-popularizer Elisabeth Kübler-Ross shifted her focus from the process of dying, studied from a rationalist "death-is-the-end" assumption, to the experience of death itself. This occasioned a reversal in her assumptive position. Her unequivocable statements in the media as well as in the Introduction to Moody's book refer to this collection of clinical data as "proof" of life after death and "confirmation" of Christian affirmations. As she predicted, this has cost her the support of a large segment of the scientific community, which is undoubtedly made quite bearable by the immensity of her popular support! This popular support ought not to be dismissed as faddism or as wishful thinking by serious students of death education who do wish to approach the phenomena on a scientifically sound basis. Most of the dying is being done by the great public who are responding to Moody's book and Kübler-Ross's lectures and TV appearances with joyous relief that it is now acceptable to recount their own (or their Aunt Minnie's) similar experiences. If indeed experiences involving nonordinary modes of perception do alter cultural assumptions about death and dying, then, "unscientific" or no, such experiences further the goals of death educators.

Moody (16) summarizes the seemingly permanent effects on the lives of survivors of near-death experiences that involved radically altered states of consciousness. One effect is a new view of death.

> As one might reasonably expect, this experience has a profound effect upon one's attitude towards physical death, especially for those who had not previously expected that anything took place after death. In some form or another, almost every person has expressed to me the thought that he is no longer afraid of death. This requires clarification, though. In the first place, certain modes of death are obviously undesirable, and secondly, none of these persons is actively seeking death. They all feel that they have tasks to do as long as they are physically alive and would agree with the words of a man who told me, "I've got quite a lot of changing to do before I leave here." Likewise, all would disavow suicide as a means by which to return to the realms they glimpsed during their experiences. It is just that now the state of death itself is no longer forbidding to them.

In exploring the link between altered states of consciousness and attitudes toward death, I am assuming that death educators hold the following to be true:

1. Conventional cultural avoidance and denial patterns must be challenged.

2. We must find ways of reducing the fear of death both in ourselves and others.
3. We should find some framework of thought in which death can be viewed more positively as part of life.

It is clear that with very little help from the scientific community these goals are being accomplished for a large and growing number of people. Can we afford to ignore the method through which this is happening even if it has been called "unscientific?" If we were to take seriously this link between altered states of consciousness and more adaptive orientation toward death, we would have to first try to identify which of the many types of alterations in consciousness result specifically in changed attitudes toward death. There is a large body of literature which would provide a background for this sort of investigation, starting with Charles Tart's classic (17), moving into the somewhat less orthodox field of parapsychology, and then on into the wholly unorthodox literature of the "consciousness revolution." In addition, there are hundreds of people in any community who would be willing informants for such research. The second major task would involve finding ways to encourage and support those modes of perception that are linked with positive attitudes toward death.

The method of altering attitudes toward death that has gained such popularity in recent months, the clinical death experience, is hardly one a death educator would want to offer his students! This, however, is only one of the three major paths to those states of awareness that we have discussed in this article. Some work has been done with drug-induced alterations in consciousness, a method that is far more familiar to and consistent with our basic cultural patterns than the alternatives—meditative states, "possession" experiences, and autohypnotism. Researchers whose work has already been cited (12–14) are convinced that the use of LSD, or certain substitutes, particularly when combined with psychotherapy, can transform the experience of dying, reducing fear, making pain manageable, and offering the dying person a way of discovering meaning and even joy in the act of death. There are, however, problems with this way of utilizing alterations in consciousness to provide the opportunity for the good death. Restrictive legislation and popular paranoia with respect to hallucinogens are not the only hindrances to using this access to altered modes of perception. Other death researchers are wary of relying too heavily on drugs as a substitute for the type of close personal interaction that also prevents anxieties and alleviates anguish (18, 19). Those who have disciplined themselves to go into altered states of consciousness at will also warn against "instant bliss" circumvention of the spiritual development they consider to be the preparation that culminates in the good death. Perhaps the work that has been done with LSD is sufficient to point us off in a new direction, even though further work may not find support or funding. One of anthropologist Castenada's hardest lessons with his Yaqui mentor was to accept the fact that mescalin and other hallucinogens were used only to break through the cultural definitions of reality. The real work of learning to draw power from altered states of consciousness began when the drugs were no longer needed. Dr. Stanislav Grof (14), one of the leading researchers in use of LSD with terminal patients, suggests that "there is now hope that one day it will be possible to transform radically the experience of dying, by chemical means or by some powerful nondrug techniques."

One advantage of "nondrug" techniques for entering altered states of consciousness is that they can be used with nonterminal people in a longer range effort to alter perceptions of death, not only as education for one's own death with dignity but as education for more helpful participation in the deaths of others. While such an approach to death education is obviously outside the comfortable confines of conventional science, there is at least one scientific work that could provide a reputable basis for further investigation. A positive correlation between reduced death anxiety and long-term systematic experience in consciousness alteration was found in a study comparing members of five "subcultures"—graduate students in psychology, graduate students in religion, psychedelic drug users, Zen meditators, and American-born disciples of Tibetan Buddhism. Using a combination of clinical interviews, psychometric testing, and psychophysiological measurements, the investigator found a significantly lower level of death-related fear in subjects with extensive experience in altered states of consciousness than in the two student groups (25).

The problem with exploring nondrug techniques is that it plunges the researcher into the seething world of parapsychology, transplanted Swamis, and high-powered hawkers of short cuts to samadhi. However, it is quite possible to thread one's way through the mazes of the "consciousness circuit" and find effective, socially acceptable, and psychologically sound ways to experiment with altered states of consciousness. The number of nondrug techniques for altering consciousness that are available in a community of any size these days is mind boggling. Few, if any, groups engaged in developing such techniques do so with the idea of altering attitudes toward death or personal preparation for a creative death experience. The task of research in this area would involve adapting a number of techniques for this purpose.

There is one very successful use of this approach in altering both attitudes toward and the experience of aging. A group called SAGE (Senior Acutalization and Growth Exploration) involves older people in three settings (independent, retirement home, and nursing home) in a freely adapted conglomeration of techniques designed especially for the needs of each individual. Both physical and mental training exercises are taught without any of the current labels indicating their origin as Tai-Chi, yoga, zazen, or meditation. Leaders search out personal experiences of a wide range of approaches (easy to do in Berkeley, California!) and then adapt them for participants in the program. The program is by nature difficult to fund, requires a research team who dares to participate in the research as subjects, and is subject to all of the disasters and defeats inherent in a truly pioneer effort. The rewards are interaction with people who are learning to age victoriously.

A similar smorgasbord of physical and mental mind-altering techniques could be developed to experiment with perceptions of death. Instructors come in all sizes and shapes from genuine Swamis to printed guides to inner space such as a "how-to book of mental exercises for achieving altered states of consciousness without the use of drugs or mysticism" (20). Every pioneer in such an approach to death education would have to make his or her own combination of techniques. To put this approach into the context of acceptable death education orientation, it can be seen as an attempt to develop what Robert J. Lifton (21) would call a new "death imagery," utilizing states of "experimental transcendence." He asserts that psychological health requires the acceptance of some mode of "symbolic immortality." Since World War II, death imagery has become largely imagery of extinction. In his view, we have lost faith in traditional modes of symbolic immortality that served us as a culture until that time, and the mode of experiential transcendence "has had to be discovered anew in the face of doubts about the other four modes."

A second approach to encouraging those states of consciousness that are linked with positive attitudes toward death would be a careful study of such alternatives to the hospital environment for dying as is being proposed by former psychologist Dr. Richard Alpert, now known as Ram Dass. In his recent book (22), he recounts a variety of impressive incidents in which he was able to use his highly developed capacity to go into altered states of consciousness and induce it in others to alter the quality of the dying experience. Ram Dass is using precisely what the Grofs (14), researchers in LSD therapy, have called "powerful nondrug techniques." Ram Dass is also in the process of creating a center for dying "where people could come to die consciously, surrounded by other beings who were not freaked by death." Ram Dass is supportive of the hospice movement but conceptualizes his center as serving a specific and even smaller group—those who have a certain orientation toward the nature of both life and death and who have been systematically utilizing altered states of consciousness in their own development. "They are beings who, because of their state of evolution, wish to use their death to help themselves awaken into the spirit." The kind of interaction that Ram Dass and his associates who can act as "guides" to a conscious death have with dying people, and the kind of training in altered states of consciousness that they can provide, is worth examination by death educators.

A third approach to studying the link between altered states of consciousness and adaptive perspectives on death is to utilize the natural occurrence of these altered states in dying people. Deathbed "hallucinations" are widely reported and as widely ignored except by those few who have caught their meaning. Much can be learned from the dying about those alterations in consciousness at the very end of life. Those who have taken the trouble to listen, record, respect, and try to understand these verbalizations of the dying have come away with far more positive perceptions of death and have served the dying by giving them dignity. To dismiss this material as delusion, mind wandering, wool gathering, or hallucination is to allow a rich source of information on the nature and meaning of death to be wasted.

It has been suggested that the terminally ill are subject, because of the disease process, to some of the same physiological changes that characterize primitive methods of inducing trance, and that the alterations in perception are similar to those of subjects on LSD, or to those of practitioners of deep meditation or mystical states. Indeed, the visions and imagery used by persons in all three conditions are remarkably similar. They are also remarkably similar to imagery identified by cross-cultural studies of mythologies and religious traditions as recurrent themes. Like all imagery, deathbed experiences have a symbolic quality with a hidden meaning. Psychologist Ira Progoff (23) following in Jung's footsteps, has developed a method of training people in recognizing, interpreting, and producing mental imagery as a way of getting in touch with the deeper levels of one's own self as well as inner access to "transpersonal" knowledge and experience. According to both Jung and Progoff, this kind of experience is ineffable, hence expressible only in terms of imagery. Therefore, like the Delphic oracles or religious scriptures, it must be interpreted. Progoff's approach to encouraging and using symbolic imagery would be very useful in a systematic study of the visions and imagery used by the dying to communicate their experiences.

Recognition of deathbed visions and imagery as meaningful not only confers dignity upon the dying person, but also suggests new ways of perceiving death for survivors. Doris Lund (24) describes her teenage son's distress in his final moments as "having to get to Westport" and "not being able to find the way," and asking for his mother's help. Responding as if his questions were meaningful, though she didn't quite understand, she assured him that he would find the way. Suddenly it flashed through her mind that Westport was the scene of his soccer team's hard-won victories and that he was experiencing death as an act to be well performed, a game to be played well and won. The insight enabled her to speak words that appeared to ease her son, and gave her a view of death that would totally transform our handling of dying patients were it to become a generally accepted notion. The image of not being able to find the way, of having to climb yet another hill, or, in the case of the death of a member of my family, "not being able to find the handle on the door," is a fairly common theme in anecdotes of deathbed utterances. Our family, unaware of Lund's book, came to the same conclusion—that death is something you do rather than something that happens to you, and this has made a great difference in our attitudes toward our own deaths. A systematic recording of the imagery used by dying people would undoubtedly reveal recurrent, shared themes that might bring new insights into the nature of death itself. The presence of beings invisible to others, sometimes long-dead relatives of the dying, sometimes more archetypal figures of Death or Love, is such a common experience that it warrants more respect and curiosity than is accorded by the evasive label, *hallucinations*. Demeaning treatment of the dying is one of the trends we are trying to reverse. To ignore or belittle what is clearly a deeply significant part of the subjective experience of dying is to reduce the dignity and meaning of death. Death itself involves some form of altered consciousness even in individuals who have had no previous experience with it. Untutored in the language appropriate to other modes of perception, many professionals, families, and even the dying themselves, view with discomfort the "degenerative" mental functioning of the dying. Given recognition as potentially valid communication of the death experience, interpreted by rules of thumb that Jungian psychologists in particular have developed for interpreting symbolic imagery, deathbed "hallucinations" could turn out to be a crucial source of information for death educators. They are also, if accepted with sensitivity, a potential form of communication between the dying and their loved ones through which the dying become less isolated and the survivors acquire deepened understanding.

SUMMARY

I have explored ways in which some forms of radically altered states of consciousness result in adaptive changes in attitude toward and perception of death. I have also suggested that these states constitute a form of education for facing one's own death with courage and acceptance as well as for reducing the fear and denial that distort relationships between dying people, their families, and members of the helping professions. In addition, I have suggested that for most people, the final stages of the dying process are experienced in an altered state of consciousness, a different mode of perception, whether this is the result of little-known psychological changes, physiological changes caused by the disease process itself, or drugs used to control pain. It has already been shown that the same mode of altered consciousness seems to come about triggered by drugs, physiological trauma, or mental and spiritual disciplines. It is important also to note that reports by survivors of clinical death suggest that even under heavy sedation and prolonged comatose conditions, it is possible to be experiencing through a different mode of consciousness, though the capacity to communicate this to others has been lost.

It can be said without fear of successful contradiction that the event of death is the ultimate in altered states of consciousness, whether one holds the assumption that death is the extinction of the individual consciousness or a transition to some other form of consciousness. Not nearly enough attention has been paid to the effect of these assumptions on research in the field of dying and death. Inherent in the nature of basic assumptions is the fact that they can be neither proved nor disproved. While scientists pay lip service to the ideal of spelling out assumptions so that bias can be considered, few actually do, mostly because, like members of any culture primitive or modern, they take their basic assumptions as fact. Many social scientists involved in death research assume the humanists' "extinction" theory and feel so certain that this assumption represents an evolutionary step up from superstition or wishful thinking, that they do not seriously question the possible imbalance in their selection of research areas or the probable bias in their interpretation of data. The only way to cope with this problem is to look at the subject of study first through the lens of the "extinction" assumption and then through that of the "transition" assumption.

If one assumes that death is the extinction of the individual consciousness, an important goal of death education becomes preparing oneself and assisting others to face death as the final life experience—an act of completion and fulfillment. If that final act is likely to involve some form of altered states of consciousness, one would not want to face a totally unexplored region of the self at the last minute.

If one assumes that death is a transition to some other form or level of consciousness, a goal of death education becomes some kind of experience of the self outside of time-space limitations, in order to reduce fear and increase one's capacity to cope with the kinds of perceptions and the different order of reality to be experienced, both during the dying process and in the after-death, bodiless state.

Given either of these mutually contradictory assumptions, it would seem that further exploration of altered states of consciousness would be useful both as preparation for one's own dying and as a means of insight into the kind of encouragement and support needed by those in whose dying we are likely to participate.

References

1 Leonard G. B. Language and reality. *Harper's Magazine*, Nov., 1974.
2 Tart, C. T. States of consciousness and state specific sciences. *Science*, June 1972, 1203–1210.
3 Maslow, A. *Religions, values and peak experiences*. Columbus: Ohio State University Press, 1964.
4 LeShan, L. *The medium, the mystic, and the physicist*. New York: Viking, 1974.
5 Van der Post, L. *Jung and the story of our time*. New York: Vintage, 1975.
6 Weil, A. *The natural mind: A new way of looking at drugs and the higher consciousness*. Boston: Houghton-Mifflin, 1972.
7 Castenada, C. *A separate reality*. New York: Simon and Schuster, 1971.
8 Finney, C. G. *An autobiography*. London: Hodder and Stroughton, 1892.
9 Yogananda, P. *Autobiography of a yogi*. Los Angeles: Self-Realization Fellowship, 1973.
10 Merrill-Wolff, F. *Pathways through to space: A personal record of transformation in consciousness*. New York: Julian, 1973.
11 Group for advancement of psychiatry, committee on psychiatry and religion. *Mysticism: Spiritual quest for psychotic disorder?* Volume 9, No. 97, November 1976. New York: Mental Health Materials Center.
12 Kast, E. LSD and the dying patient. *Chicago Medical School Quarterly*, 1966, 26, 80.
13 Cohen, S. LSD and the anguish of dying. *Harper's Magazine*. 1965, 231, 69, 77.
14 Grof, S., & Halifax-Grof, J. Psychedelics and the experience of death. In A. Toynbee & A. Koestler (Eds.), *Life after death*. London: Weidenfeld & Nicolson, 1976.

15 Jung, C. G. *Memories, dreams, reflections.* New York: Vintage, 1965.

16 Moody, R. A. *Life after life.* New York: Bantam, 1976.

17 Tart, C. T. (Ed.). *Altered states of consciousness: A book of readings.* New York: Wiley, 1969.

18 Hinton, J. *Dying.* Baltimore: Penguin, 1967.

19 Kübler-Ross, E. On the use of psychopharmacologic agents for the dying patient and the bereaved. In Goldberg, I. K. et al. (Eds.), *Psychopharmacologic agents for the terminally ill and bereaved.* New York: Columbia University Press, 1973.

20 Masters, R., & Houston, J. *Mind games.* New York: Dell, 1972.

21 Lifton, R. J. The sense of immortality: On death and the continuity of life. In Fulton, R. (Ed.), *Death and identity.* Bowie, Md.: Charles Press, 1976.

22 Dass, R. *Grist for the mill,* Santa Cruz, Calif.: Unity, 1977.

23 Progoff, I. *The symbolic and the real.* New York: McGraw-Hill, 1963.

24 Lund, D. *Eric.* New York: Lippincott, 1974.

25 Garfield, C. A. Psychothanatological concomitants of altered state experiences: An investigation of the relationship between consciousness alteration and fear of death. Doctoral dissertation, University of California, 1974.

42. Life Revisited: Parallels in Death Experiences

Frederick H. Holck

Frederick Holck is a member of the faculty of the Department of Religious Studies at Cleveland State University. *This selection is a paper Dr. Holck presented at the annual midwest meeting of the American Academy of Religion in Chicago in 1977. In the paper Dr. Holck investigates canonical literature and other religious writings and folklore for parallels to the descriptions of death experiences undergone by those who have been (or seemed to have been) temporarily clinically dead.*

From Omega, *Vol. 9, No. 1 (1978–79): 1–11. ©1978 by Baywood Publishing Co., Inc. Reprinted by permission.*

Since Elisabeth Kübler-Ross published her book, *On Death and Dying,* an unprecedented interest in this matter emerged. Prior to her publication, dealing with death was widely considered taboo and left to the few in whose professional domain it lay. Now almost every supermarket shopper is able to identify the five stages of the dying process conceptualized by Dr. Kübler-Ross. Since then a plethora of books has been appearing on the market which deal with death and dying from a variety of angles and that reflect many academic disciplines. In some schools, centers of thanatology have been established to carry out research projects and teaching. Research and writing up to now has focused mainly on events and experiences preceding death and on postmortem issues that relate to the grief process, or to economic, social, legal, and axiological questions. However, as a result of her many years' work with dying patients, Dr. Kübler-Ross has opened another area that so far has not been investigated by the academic disciplines. It deals with an exceptional subject which requires unusual methods of investigation: life beyond death or, perhaps more accurately, conscious existence during the death experience.

It is surprising to hear a physician respond to the question of whether or not there is life after death with: "Yes, beyond the shadow of a doubt." In her lectures, TV appearances, and other statements, she reports that she has found a remarkable similarity in the experiences of many who have been pronounced clinically dead and have been resuscitated. At this time, the results of her research (based on approximately two hundred cases) have not been published. According to her own remarks they can be expected this year. However, another author, Raymond A. Moody, a physician and a Ph.D. in philosophy, reported his investigations of "survival of bodily death" in his book *Life After Life* [1]. It is not surprising to find that Dr. Kübler-Ross supports his findings in a friendly foreword.

The purpose here is neither to criticize Dr. Moody's book nor to accept his findings as convincing proof of conscious human continuation after the experience of clinical death. In fact, Dr. Moody himself is cautious enough to state that he is "not trying to construct a proof of the ancient doctrine of the survival of bodily death." Rather, he evaluates his findings in terms of *subjective, psychological* considerations rather than logical ones. While physicians and scientists may question his methodology, and theologians his intentions, as a historian of religion I am interested in his presentation of case studies which can be related to comparable phenomena in the history of religion.

I have searched through the canonical literature and other pertinent writings of religious movements and through the folklore of different cultures for parallels in the description of death experiences. The purpose of this inquiry was to find out whether or not it is feasible to establish a certain affinity of type among death experiences in the history of religions. If these experiences (to paraphrase the late Dr. Radhakrishnan) are a genuine part of human nature, they ought to assume the same general forms [2].

To begin, I shall briefly summarize characteristic features of Dr. Moody 's report of death experiences. Some of the following elements are shared by all cases and therefore constitute an "ideal" experience [1]. It should be kept in mind, however, that all the reporting individuals have indicated that our language is not adequate to describe experiences that lie outside established areas; an important consideration when comparing and evaluating the statements.

1. At the moment of clinical death the dead person begins to hear an uncomfortable noise, a loud ringing or buzzing.

2. Simultaneously he experiences himself moving rapidly through a long dark tunnel.
3. Thereafter he finds himself outside his own physical body, although in the same environment, and perceives this body as an onlooker. In some cases the dead observe resuscitation attempts.
4. He realizes that he still has a body, though of a different nature.
5. He is not alone; he is met by dead relatives or friends who assist him.
6. He feels the presence of a loving, warm spirit, a being of very bright light with whom he communicates nonverbally. He experiences joy, love, and peace.
7. He views a panoramic, instantaneous playback of the major events of his life which enables him to evaluate it.
8. Eventually he approaches some kind of border indicating a dividing line between earthly life and the next life.
9. He realizes that he must return to his earthly existence because the time for his death has not yet come.

Again, this is only a model. In each case there are remarkable similarities; yet no two of them are identical, nor are all elements necessarily present, and, the order of events may vary. It must also be stated that some of the interviewed people resuscitated after clinical death did not report any of these experiences at all.

Let's now look at some material gathered from folklore and from the history of religions and view it against the background of the model just mentioned. Among the historical sources that elaborate on the dying process there are few references dealing with the first category of the Moody model: the experience of uncomfortable noises such as a loud ringing or buzzing. An experience that comes closest to this is contained in the *Bardo Thödol, The Tibetan Book of the Dead* which is briefly referred to by Moody in his short chapter on parallels [3]. At the moment of death a lama reads the *Thödol* to a dying person; this tells him about the events that will take place and explains their meaning. The purpose of the instruction is to guide the dead and impart liberating knowledge. He is told that "the natural sound of Reality reverberating like a thousand thunders simultaneously sounding, will come. That is the natural sound of thine own real self. Be not daunted thereby, nor terrified, nor awed." [3] These sounds are in reality a person's own thought forms.

Auditory sensations are not always unpleasant according to Moody's case studies. One woman recalls "music of some sort, a majestic, really beautiful sort of music." [1] An impression similar to this is given in the *Dream of Scipio,* the conclusion of Cicero's treatise *On the Republic* (VI, 18). There Scipio relates his experience: "When I had recovered from my astonishment over this panorama, and had come to myself, I asked; 'Tell me, what is this loud, sweet harmony that fills my ears?' His dead ancestor, Scipio Africanus the Elder, replied, "This music is produced by the impulse and motion of the spheres themselves ... Skillful men reproducing this celestial music on stringed instruments have thus opened the way for their own return to the heavenly region. . . .' " [4]

The second category of the Moody model, the dark tunnel sensation, including the experience of voidness, vacuum, darkness, can also be found in historical sources. In fact, it is one of the main features in Eastern tradition. Here, however, one has to be very cautious when identifying these phenomena because of the philosophical connotation of voidness *(Shūnyatā)* in the East. Some, but by no means all, of the available contemporary reports correspond to the Eastern experience of voidness. These appear to share several of the same characteristics. One contemporary states: "I was in an utterly black dark void. It is very difficult to explain, but I felt as if I was moving in a vacuum." Another remembers: "I was so taken up with this void that I just did not think of anything else." Another tells about his experience: "This was the most wonderful, worry-free experience you can imagine." And a woman reports, "There was a feeling of utter peace and quiet, no fear at all."[1]

When comparing these statements with some of those from the Eastern tradition the parallels become immediately apparent. In *The Tibetan Book of the Dead* a lama addresses the dying person: "Thy [nonphysical] body is a body of propensities, and void. Voidness cannot injure voidness; the qualityless can not injure the qualityless . . . That voidness is not of the nature of the voidness of nothingness, but a voidness at the true nature of which thou feelest awed." This nonphysical existence is to the knowing one blissful consciousness in its purest form "wherein all things are like the void . . . and the naked, spotless intellect is like unto a transparent vacuum without circumference or center." Those, however, who are ignorant will perceive a dull white or smoke-colored light, and become attracted by it [3]. This will lead to a fall into the hell worlds, accompanied by unbearable misery.

Another account that may fit into this second category appears in *Brhad Āranyaka Upanishad.* There the dying person's "self departs either through the eye or through the head or through other apertures of the body." . . . When life thus departs, all the vital breaths depart after him. He becomes one with intelligence. What has intelligence departs with him." [5]

And in the same Upanishad a different passage relates the "tunnel experience" as follows: "Verily when a person departs from this world, he goes to the air. It opens up out there for him like the hole of a chariot wheel . . . He goes to a world free from grief, free from cold. . ." In *De Genio Socratis,* Plutarch describes the experience of Timarch whose soul traveled through the heavenly spheres after it had left the body through the seams of his skull [6].

The features most widely shared belong to the third and fourth categories of the Moody model: the out-of-the-body experience, and, connected with it, the awareness of a "spiritual body." In almost every tradition, we find plenty of evidence to this effect. In one contemporary case a resuscitated person states: "A solid grey mist gathered around me and I left my body. I had a floating sensation as I felt myself get out of my body, and I looked back and I could see myself on the bed below . . ." A car accident victim reports: "I lost touch with my body. My being or myself or my spirit, or whatever you would like to label it—I could sort of feel it rise out of me, out through my head." This "being" is characterized as "nothing really physical," yet as having a density that could be likened to a cloud [1].

Among the Indian tribes of the Argentine and Bolivian Chaco, the belief is held that the human soul leaves the body at the moment of death and continues an independent state of being. The soul "at first hovers about its old abode, the dead body and the house where the departed lived . . . ." [7]

In Zoroastrian tradition the *Bundahishn* describes in detail the experience of the soul immediately following death: "When men die the soul sits for three days near the place where his head was . . . During the three nights, when cutting and dissolution come upon the body, then there seems to him to be as much distress as there does to a man when his house is destroyed. During those three days the soul sits near the head with the hope that it may so happen that the blood may be warmed up and breath may enter the body so that I may be able to go once more [into the body]." [8]

Similarly, the *Bardo Thödol* states that the consciousness (i.e. "soul") of the deceased hovers "within those places to which its activities had been limited." It is able to see "its relatives and connections as it had been used to seeing them before. It even hears the wailings." [3] The sensation of hovering or floating is a common feature in historical sources as well as in contemporary case studies. The Karelian Finns held the belief "that in the hour of death the soul does . . . become detached from the body . . . departs through the mouth and remains floating in the air near the body." [9, 10]

Since experience after clinical death appears to be—at least in regard to perception—so close to that in life, occasionally a person may not be fully aware of his new mode of existence, and confusion may result. He may ask "Am I dead or am I not dead? I cannot determine." In the same source the dead is cautioned to adapt himself to the new environment [3]. In St. Paul's vision, though not related to the dying process—a similar experience is expressed: "I knew a man in Christ above . . . whether in the body, I cannot tell, or whether out of the body, I cannot tell . . . Such an one caught up to the third heaven" (II Cor. 12:2).

Another feature of these categories is the inaudibility and invisibility of the nonmaterial entity as stated in several Moody cases: "I saw them resuscitating me . . . I was on a pedestal, just . . . looking over them. I tried talking to them, but nobody could hear me, nobody would listen to me." [1] Similar out-of-the-body experiences are described in numerous records. The *Encyclopedia of Religion and Ethics* contains such a story in which a slain Chippewa chief is carried home without being able to make himself heard. At home he shouts to his mourning wife: "I am hungry ! I am thirsty!" to no avail. In his frustration he returns to the battlefield. On his way "he finds a fire in his path . . . thwarting his approach. In despair he cries, 'I am seeking to return into my body' . . . and with a desperate effort he darts into the flame, to awake as from a long trance in his own weakened body." The same source refers to cases where "there are stationed on the road to the home of the dead, wardens whose business it is to turn back souls which are leaving the body before the appointed hour, while, again, a man may, by desperate effort, recover his own departing soul." [10]

Another interesting story is found in Lithuanian folklore where a man expresses a curiosity about death and life thereafter. It so happens that he gets ill and falls into a coma. He then is described as awakening from sleep without any pain left. He leaves his bed and sits near a stove. When his wife enters the room, she starts screaming: "He is dead, he is dead." He tries to calm her down: "Why are you crying? Look at me, I am here." But she continues to cry, standing near his bed. Suddenly he sees a body lying there. When his children enter the room, they join their mother in crying. Since no one listens to him, he leaves the house and attempts to communicate with his neighbors. They do not respond either. Later, when he returns home, he sees his relatives preparing the body for the funeral. Thereafter they kneel and pray and he joins them in their prayers. Two days later they take the body to the cemetery and he walks right along with them. At the graveside his wife kisses the body goodbye and he, too, kisses the body. Suddenly he grasps what is going on and he fully realizes his identity with the body. At this moment, it appears, he reenters his body, sits up, leaves the grave, and returns home with his family. The story indicates that he has now an understanding of the events following death. In this story we find, in addition to most of the common features in out-of-the-body experiences, the frequently reported experience of locomotion and the characteristic of confusion when the dead is ignorant of his new mode of existence [11].

Another interesting phenomenon which deserves mentioning is the recalling of the dead. The *Encyclopedia of Religion and Ethics* (IV, 415) relates some attempts to thwart the separation of the soul and body in cases of sickness and death by catching or recalling the escaping soul. Among the Tongking tribes in North Vietnam it was customary to accomplish the return of the soul by shouting after it. The Dayaks of Borneo used the more formal message of priestly incantations. A practice reminiscent of these customs was observed in Europe at the occasion of the departure of a Pope or of a Spanish king. It was traditional that death was certified only after a high official had shouted three times the dead monarch's name without receiving any response [10].

A recent case of "recalling" was brought to my attention by a scientist-colleague of mine who had just returned from the funeral of his mother. Due to the distance involved he arrived at the hospital too late, minutes after his mother had been pronounced dead on the basis of the absence of heart beat, breath, blood pressure, and reflexes. He remained beside her body talking to her, expressing his love for her for the last time while holding her hand. Then suddenly he perceived a slight pressure in her hand, a smile on her face, while she briefly opened her eyes. An attending physician checked her pulse and blood pressure and confirmed the brief rally before final death occurred.

The fifth category of the Moody model deals with the experience of meeting others. Adolf E. Jensen in his book, *Myth and Cult Among Primitive Peoples,* makes a statement which can be supported by a number of contemporary case studies as well as historical sources. He describes the journey into death as "a reunion with departed tribal or clan members, especially union with the deity that receives the deceased in the land of the dead." [12] In one of the Moody cases a dying woman reports that she recognized dead relatives and friends who welcomed her as if she were coming home. Others referred to angelic beings who helped them in their transition or who informed them that their time of death had not yet come [1].

The idea of guiding the soul to the underworld by a shaman can be found in a Siberian (Goldi) funerary ceremony. When the shaman and the deceased have reached the underworld ". . . the dead gather and ask [for the name] of the newcomer . . . The shaman . . . searches through the crowd of spirits for the close relatives of the soul he is conducting so that he may entrust it to them." [4] And Paul Radin tells of the spirit-road of the Winnebago tribe: "All your relatives who died before you will be there . . . There will be a bridge . . . You will be able to cross it safely, for you have all the guides . . . They will take you over and take care of you." [4]

In Chinese tradition during a funeral a liturgy was sung, addressed to the deceased, where a demon, in this case a benevolent spirit, "leads the soul on its way. It guides to the edge of a pool. You see that there it is also raining and the demon then says to you, 'It is not raining, it is the tears that your descendents are weeping.' Then the demon will lead you to a great rock. You will hear the thunder and the rain resounding. Then the demon will say, 'You need not fear. This is your descendents playing the *liu sheng*, and there is also the noise of the beating of a drum. Those noises are partners to you.' Then the demon will lead you along to your ancestors. The ancestors will guide you to Ntzï's place. This place is happy land. You must not be sad." [13]

In Islamic tradition al Nasā'ī mentions that the souls of the faithful in paradise welcome the incoming soul with great joy and guide him on his path to heaven [14]. The same expērience is continued in Lithuanian folklore where "the dying see their former dead friends, various spirits or saints, who come to visit or take them away." [15]

As a final example of this category I shall refer to Plato. In the *Republic* he tells of the hero Er, who was killed in battle, yet returned to life twelve days later. Er reports that "when his soul left the body he went on a journey with a great company." At their ascent they were met by those who had died before. "Those who knew one another embraced and conversed . . . and [those] from above were describing heavenly delights and visions of inconceivable beauty." [16]

The sixth category of the Moody model relates probably to the most common experience in the dying process: the encounter with a Being of Light. It may be perceived as personal or impersonal, and is found in almost all contemporary case studies and historical sources. In one of the Moody cases the light experience is described as "a pure crystal clear light . . . It was beautiful and so bright, so radiant . . . It's not any kind of light you can describe on earth. I didn't actually see a person in this light, and yet it has a special identity . . . It is a light of perfect understanding and perfect love." [1] The above-mentioned Er characterizes the light experience in impersonal terms as "a line of light, straight as a column . . . in color resembling the rainbow, only brighter and purer." [16]

In Indian tradition an incident is recorded in the *Bhāgavata Purāna* (X, I) which, though not related to death itself, describes an experience of similar nature. A couple, Vasudeva and Devaki, praying for divine protection, fall into a swoon. "In the gloom of that unconsciousness a light suddenly flashed; and in that light the thick, dark cloud of misery vanished, and with it the accumulated sorrows of recent years. The sun of gladness and peace, the Lord of Love, appeared before them . . . with his benign smile." [17] Raphael Karsten observed, among the Chaco Indians, the belief that the souls of the dead Tobas on their arrival in the heavenly resting place encounter an ever-shining sun. "Night and darkness do not exist there, day and sunshine continually reign." [7]

In Jewish tradition the *Apocalypse of Abraham* gives a description of his ascent to heaven where "he beheld amidst a radiant light the four holy creatures of Ezekiel carrying the throne chariot of God." In the same tradition the *Book of the Secrets of Enoch* makes several references to immeasurable light in heaven, as does the *Testament of the Twelve Patriarchs* [18]

Of the numerous references in Buddhist literature, two passages should suffice. The first is from *Saddharma—smrityupasthāna Sūtra* (Chapter 34): ". . . as the time of [a person's] death approaches he sees a bright light, and being unaccustomed to it at the time of his death he is perplexed and confused." [4] The second is from the *Bardo Thödol:* "The wisdom of the Dharma—Dhātu, blue in color, shining transparent, glorious, dazzling . . . will shoot forth and strike against thee with a light so radiant that thou wilt scarcely be able to look at it." [3]

The remaining categories of the Moody model, with the exception of number 8, are only slightly, if at all, identifiable in most historical sources. Some of the contemporary cases that describe panoramic reviews of major events in individuals' lives (category 7) are closely linked to the "light experience." One account states: "I didn't actually see the light as I was going through the flashbacks. He disappeared as soon as he asked me what I had done . . . The whole thing was really odd . . . I was actually seeing these flashbacks . . . it was so fast. Yet, it was slow enough that I could take it all in . . . It seems that it was less than five minutes and probably more than thirty seconds." Another survivor reports: "I can't exactly describe it to you . . . It was just all there at once . . . everything at one time . . ."[1]

The only historical parallel I could find that comes close to these experiences is contained in the *Bardo Thödol* where, according to Buddhist teachings, the sum total of an individual's actions are expressed in terms of his *Karma*. There the dead will face his good deeds being represented by the *Good Genius* who counts them out with white pebbles and his evil deeds by the *Evil Genius* who likewise counts them out with black pebbles. The dead person will be terrified and tremble. Denial is out of the question, because "the Lord of Death will say, 'I will consult the Mirror of

Karma! . . . He will look in the Mirror, wherein every good and evil act is reflected. Lying will be of no avail." [3] The essential point here is the presence in immediacy of all past actions.

There are, of course, numerous passages in the sacred literature of other religious traditions where, in the context of a postmortem judgment, one's life is scrutinized, such as, for instance, in Zoroastrianism. There the soul of the pious dead for three nights "experiences as much joy as all that which (he experienced as) a living being [8] or, as in Ancient Egypt, in the *Papyrus of Ani,* the dead Ani declares to Osiris his innocence by way of a negative confession. These and many other instances that relate to past actions do lack a panoramic aspect and should, therefore, not be counted with the "flash-back experiences."

Less generally encountered, or at least less often reported in contemporary cases, is the experience of a dividing line between terrestrial and postterrestrial existence (category 8). Moody relates a few accounts where this dividing line was manifested as "a body of water, a grey mist, a door, a fence across a field or simply a line." Perhaps the most interesting account recorded by Moody is one that has an almost unlimited number of parallels in the history of religions, mythology, and folklore. A woman suffering a severe hemorrhage lost consciousness and experienced annoying sounds. She told the interviewer: ". . . it seemed as if I were on a ship or a small vessel sailing to the other side of a large body of water. On the distant shore, I could see all my loved ones who had died . . . They seemed to be beckoning me to come over, and all the while I was saying '. . . I'm not ready to go' . . . Finally the ship almost reached the far shore, but just before it did it turned around and started back. . ." [1]

An experience with almost identical features is described by a Maori servant whose aunt had come back to life and told about her journey into the netherworld. When she had left her body she eventually reached a sandy beach where she found an old man with a canoe. He ferried her to the other side of the river, showing her the road to her dead ancestors. Upon her arrival she was welcomed by her dead father and other close relatives. "When her father had asked about his living relatives and especially about her own child, he told her she must go back to earth, for no one was left to take care of his grandchild." He therefore guided her back to the other side of the river where, after some incidents, she came to life again in her own house [4].

Similar ideas do appear among the Thompson River Indians of British Columbia. On their way to the netherworld the departed souls reach a river which they cross. Before moving on they leave their clothes behind. Three netherworld guardians prevent those souls from proceeding to the realm of the dead whose time to die has not yet come. The others are individually welcomed with joy by their dead relatives at the entrance door to the netherworld [4].

The Mesopotamian *Epic of Gilgamesh* may serve as a final random example of the almost unlimited number of cases that fit this category. Gilgamesh, King of Uruk, mourning for his dead friend Enkidu, attempts to overcome death of which he is afraid. He seeks a way to cross the waters of death to reach Dilmun, the Sumerian paradise of everlasting life. Urshanabi, a ferry man, brings him to Utnapishtim who resides in Dilmun. However, the courageous king cannot stay and has to sail back as a mortal to his own city until his appointed time of death. Although in this myth the land of immortal life is not accessible to humans after death, it is nevertheless separated from this earthly life by a large body of water which constitutes the dividing line [19].

All three preceding cases have another feature (category 9) in common with the contemporary Moody cases: the realization that a return to this human existence is necessary, for their time on earth has not yet run out. What may we conclude from the data of this investigation within the methodological constraints of our discipline? As indicated above, our intent was to determine whether or not it is possible to establish a certain affinity of type between the death experiences in contemporary case studies and those gathered from literary sources. It is apparent that there are general forms that can be identified from the random selection of source material used in this study. This strongly suggests that these phenomena manifest themselves universally and that they are part of the experience of the human race.

In summary, it can be stated that the most common of these general forms are:

1. an out-of-the-body experience combined with an awareness of a 'spiritual body'
2. a reunion with ancestors and departed friends
3. a 'light' experience
4. the encounter of a dividing or border line.

This, of course, leaves open the question of interpretation: whether these experiences are archetypal in nature in the sense of Jungian symbolism or whether they are to be understood as statements of factual events.

References

1 R. A. Moody, *Life After Life,* Mockingbird Publishing, Covington, Ga., 1975.

2 Dr. Radhakrishnan, *Eastern Religions and Western Thought,* Oxford University Press, New York, 1959.

3 *Bardo Thödol, The Tibetan Book of the Dead,* W. Y. Evans-Wentz, ed., Oxford University Press, Oxford, 1960.

4 M. Eliade, *From Primitives to Zen,* Harper & Row, New York, 1967.

5 *Brhad Āranyaka Upanishad,* Harper Torch, New York, 1963.

6 W. Bousset, *Die Himmelsreise der Seele,* Wissenschaftl. Buchgesellschaft, Darmstadt, 1960.

7 R. Karsten, *Indian Tribes of the Argentine and Bolivian Chaco,* Societas Scientiarum Fennica, Helsinfors, 1932.

8 J. D. C. Pavry, *The Zorastrian Doctrine of a Future Life*, AMS Press, New York, 1965.
9 K. Achte, Death and Ancient Finnish Culture, *Omega*, 7, pp. 249–259, 1976.
10 *Encyclopedia of Religion and Ethics*, Scribners, New York, 1928.
11 J. Basanaviĉius, *Iŝ Gyvenimo—V̄eliu Bei Velnu*, Turtu in Spaudo, Chicago, 1903.
12 A. E. Jensen, *Myth and Culture Among Primitive Peoples*, University of Chicago Press, Chicago, 1963.
13 D. C. Graham, ed., *Songs and Stories of the Ch'uan Miao*, Smithsonian Institution, 123.
14 R. Eklund, *Life Between Death and Resurrection According to Islam*, Dissertation, Almqvist and Wiksells, Uppsala, 1941.
15 J. Balys, *Motif—Index of Lithuanian Narrative Folk-Lore*, Tautosakos Darbai II Archyvo Leidinys, Kaunas, 1936.
16 Plato, *Republic*, Modern-Library, New York, 1934.
17 S. Prabhavananda, trans., *The Wisdom of God*, G. P. Putnams, New York, 1968.
18 K. Kohler, *Heaven and Hell in Comparative Religion*, Macmillan, New York, 1923.
19 M. K. Sandars, *The Epic of Gilgamesh*, Penguin Books, Baltimore, 1964.

43· Do We Survive Death?

Bertrand Russell

Bertrand Russell, British philosopher, mathematician, and essayist, was one of the most intellectually gifted individuals of our century. His many works, characterized by wit, clarity, and vivid metaphor, are known throughout the world. In this selection, taken from his book Why I Am Not A Christian, *Russell, in his typical no-nonsense, pungent prose, attacks the notion of survival after death.*

Before we can profitably discuss whether we shall continue to exist after death, it is well to be clear as to the sense in which a man is the same person as he was yesterday. Philosophers used to think that there were definite substances, the soul and the body, that each lasted on from day to day, that a soul, once created, continued to exist throughout all future

EDITOR'S NOTE *This is the only selection in this volume that violates our own canon of limiting all pieces to those published in the last fifteen years. The reasons for including this piece—as a counterfoil to the previous one—were persuasive enough to bend our rule. This piece was first published in 1936 in a book entitled* The Mysteries of Life and Death. *The quotations of Bishop Barnes in Russell's selection are from an article that appeared in the same work.*

time, whereas a body ceased temporarily from death till the resurrection of the body.

The part of this doctrine which concerns the present life is pretty certainly false. The matter of the body is continually changing by processes of nutriment and wastage. Even if it were not, atoms in physics are no longer supposed to have continuous existence; there is no sense in saying: this is the same atom as the one that existed a few minutes ago. The continuity of a human body is a matter of appearance and behavior, not of substance.

The same thing applies to the mind. We think and feel and act, but there is not, in addition to thoughts and feelings and actions, a bare entity, the mind or the soul, which does or suffers these occurrences. The mental continuity of a person is a continuity of habit and memory: there was yesterday one person whose feelings I can remember, and that person I regard as myself of yesterday; but, in fact, myself of yesterday was only certain mental occurrences which are now remembered and are regarded as part of the person who now recollects them. All that constitutes a person is a series of experiences connected by memory and by certain similarities of the sort we call habit.

If, therefore, we are to believe that a person survives death, we must believe that the memories and habits which constitute the person will continue to be exhibited in a new set of occurrences.

No one can prove that this will not happen. But it is easy to see that it is very unlikely. Our memories and habits are bound up with the structure of the brain, in much the same way a river is connected with the riverbed. The water in the river is always changing, but it keeps to the same course because previous rains have worn a channel. In like manner, previous events have worn a channel in the brain, and our thoughts flow along this channel. This is the cause of memory and mental habits. But the brain, as a structure, is dissolved at death, and memory therefore may be expected to be also dissolved. There is no more reason to think otherwise than to expect a river to persist in its old course after an earthquake has raised a mountain where a valley used to be.

All memory, and therefore (one may say) all minds, depend upon a property which is very noticeable in certain kinds of material structures but exists little if at all in other kinds. This is the property of forming habits as a result of frequent similar occurrences. For example: a bright light makes the pupils of the eyes contract; and if you repeatedly flash a light in a man's eyes and beat a gong at the same time, the gong alone will, in the end, cause his pupils to contract. This is a fact about the brain and nervous system—that is to say, about a certain material structure. It will be found that exactly similar facts explain our response to language and our use of it, our memories and the emotions they arouse, our moral or immoral habits of behavior, and indeed everything that constitutes our mental personality, except the part determined by heredity. The part determined by heredity is handed on to our posterity but cannot, in the individual, survive the disintegration of the body. Thus both the hereditary and the acquired parts of a personality are, so far as our experience goes, bound up with the characteristics of certain bodily structures. We all know that memory may be obliterated by an injury to the brain, that a virtuous person may be rendered vicious by encephalitis lethargica, and that a clever child can be turned into an idiot by lack of iodine. In view of such familiar facts, it seems scarcely probable that the mind survives the total destruction of brain structure which occurs at death.

It is not rational arguments but emotions that cause belief in a future life. The most important of these emotions is fear of death, which is instinctive and biologically useful. If we genuinely and wholeheartedly believed in the future life, we should cease completely to fear death. The effects would be curious, and probably such as most of us would deplore. But our human and subhuman ancestors have fought and exterminated their enemies throughout many geological ages and have profited by courage; it is therefore an advantage to the victors in the struggle for life to be able, on occasion, to overcome the natural fear of death. Among animals and savages, instinctive pugnacity suffices for this purpose; but at a certain stage of development, as the Mohammedans first proved, belief in Paradise has considerable military value as reinforcing natural pugnacity. We should therefore admit that militarists are wise in encouraging the belief in immortality, always supposing that this belief does not become so profound as to produce indifference to the affairs of the world.

Another emotion which encourages the belief in survival is admiration of the excellence of man. As the Bishop of Birmingham says, "His mind is a far finer instrument than anything that had appeared earlier—he knows right and wrong. He can build Westminster Abbey. He can make an airplane. He can calculate the distance of the sun . . . Shall, then, man at death perish utterly? Does that incomparable instrument, his mind, vanish when life ceases?"

The bishop proceeds to argue that "the universe has been shaped and is governed by an intelligent purpose," and that it would have been unintelligent, having made man, to let him perish.

To this argument there are many answers. In the first place, it has been found, in the scientific investigation of nature, that the intrusion of moral or aesthetic values has always been an obstacle to discovery. It used to be thought that the heavenly bodies must move in circles because the circle is the most perfect curve, that species must be immutable because God would only create what was perfect and what therefore stood in no need of improvement, that it was useless to combat epidemics except by repentance because they were sent as a punishment for sin, and so on. It has been found, however, that, so far as we can discover, nature is indifferent to our values and can only be understood by ignoring our notions of good and bad. The universe may have a purpose, but nothing that we know suggests that, if so, this purpose has any similarity to ours.

Nor is there in this anything surprising. Dr. Barnes tells us that man "knows right and wrong." But, in fact, as anthropology shows, men's views of right and wrong have varied to such an extent that no single item has been permanent. We cannot say, therefore, that man knows right and wrong, but only that some men do. Which men? Nietzsche argued in favor of an ethic profoundly different from Christ's, and some powerful governments have accepted his teaching. If knowledge of right and wrong is to be an argument for immortality, we must first settle whether to believe Christ or Nietzsche, and then argue that Christians are immortal, but Hitler and Mussolini are not, or vice versa. The decision will obviously be made on the battlefield, not in the study. Those who have the best poison gas will have the ethic of the future and will therefore be the immortal ones.

Our feelings and beliefs on the subject of good and evil are, like everything else about us, natural facts, developed in the struggle for existence and not having any divine or supernatural origin. In one of Aesop's fables, a lion is shown pictures of huntsmen catching lions and remarks that, if he had painted them, they would have shown lions catching huntsmen. Man, says Dr. Barnes, is a fine fellow because he can make airplanes. A little while ago there was a popular song about the cleverness of flies in walking upside down on the ceiling, with the chorus: "Could Lloyd George do it? Could Mr. Baldwin do it? Could Ramsay Mac do it? Why, NO." On this basis a very telling argument could be constructed by a theologically minded fly, which no doubt the other flies would find most convincing.

Moreover, it is only when we think abstractly that we have such a high opinion of man. Of men in the concrete, most of us think the vast majority very bad. Civilized states spend more than half their revenue on killing each other's citizens. Consider the long history of the activities inspired by moral fervor: human sacrifices, persecutions of heretics, witch-hunts, pogroms leading up to wholesale extermination by poison gases, which one at least of Dr. Barnes's episcopal colleagues must be supposed to favor, since he holds pacifism to be un-Christian. Are these abominations, and the ethical doctrines by which they are prompted, really evidence of an intelligent creator? And can we really wish that the men who practiced them should live forever? The world in which we live can be understood as a result of muddle and accident; but if it is the outcome of deliberate purpose, the purpose must have been that of a fiend. For my part, I find accident a less painful and more plausible hypothesis.

PART FIVE

SELF-DESTRUCTION

SELF-DESTRUCTION

Ordinarily, we tend to think of death as a biological or adventitious event. Suicide falls outside that pattern, and for those reasons, is generally the most cryptic of all modes of death. In the last twenty years, the number of books and articles written about suicide has increased enormously. A whole new field of specialization—suicidology—has arisen. Numerous suicide prevention centers, now around 200 in this country, have been established. Nonetheless, a suicidal death remains the most stigmatizing (to the survivors, of course) of all deaths.

Six recent selections comprise this section on Self-Destruction—three of them by the editor. The first is an article, entitled "Suicide," from the 1973 edition of Encyclopaedia Britannica. *It gives a general overview of the concept of suicide as well as several newer subconcepts, such as lethality or subintention, that might be used to increase our understanding of suicidal phenomena.*

The second selection, "Feelings." is from A. Alvarez's book The Savage God: A Study of Suicide. *Alvarez is a poet and literary critic who knew and wrote about Sylvia Plath, including her suicide. In this selection, Alvarez states that the various theories of suicides say very little about "how it feels." As a man who openly admits (in his book) to being "a failed suicide," Alvarez speaks with deep conviction of the suicidal person's "closed world with its own irresistible logic." In his extraordinary chapter, he outlines several different types of suicide. In his own straightforward and poetic way, Alvarez tells us a great deal about self-destruction.*

The third selection, "Suicide among the Gifted," is an empirical study of extensive life histories—a relatively rare type of study in this field. It is a scientific study—as psychology appropriately defines science—in that the experimenter was "blind" to the identity (suicidal or nonsuicidal) of each of the persons who was studied. Of the two main results—the first, that a suicidal outcome in a life could definitely (beyond any chance expectation) be assessed from case history data—was no great surprise; but the second finding, that these determinations could accurately be made for men of fifty-five before their thirtieth birthdays, was a finding with many important implications for the fixity of personality and the efficacy of psychotherapy.

The fourth selection, "Self-Destruction: Suicide Notes and Tragic Lives"—from the recent book Voices of Death*—considers the relationship of suicide notes to suicidal acts. The selection examines the notion that suicide notes (written as they are in the very context of the deed) are the "royal road to the understanding of suicidal phenomena." It also examines the counternotion* *that suicide notes, written as they are in a severely constricted psychological state, cannot be expected to contain profound psychodynamic insights and explanations. Finally, a third notion (the author's current position) is discussed: that suicide notes are best understood and studied within the context of the full life history of the person who wrote the note. A suicide note illuminates a life history, and conversely an extensive life history throws light on the inner meanings of the note. The two are integral parts of each other.*

The fifth selection is by Jean Baechler, a French political scientist, from his recent book Suicides. *In a somewhat iconoclastic way, Baechler clears the air of practically all previous suicidological theorizing—especially that of Durkheim, Halbwachs, and parts of Freud—and proposes to base his argument on the following definition: "Suicide denotes all behavior that seeks and finds the solution to an existential problem by making an attempt on the life of the subject." For Baechler, the central question is this: "What people seek what solutions to what problems by means of suicide?" His bare-bone approach, supported by his thoughtful exploration of the logical implications of his own position, leads Baechler to posit some new and thought-provoking ideas about the constancy and nature of suicidal phenomena and their place in the human condition.*

In the last selection, Dr. Calvin Frederick touches upon a fascinating and widespread aspect of suicide, namely indirect self-destructive behavior, sometimes referred to as subintentioned death. Dr. Frederick writes specifically about drug addiction as an example of such unconsciously motivated behavior. The piece treats of drug addiction as a serious problem in its own right, and of the universality of subintentioned deaths—not only through drug abuse, but also through alcoholism, excessive risk-taking, disregard of life-extending medical regimens, imprudent behavior, and all the ways in which human beings indirectly shorten or truncate their own lives.

44· Suicide

Edwin S. Shneidman

In this selection from the Encyclopaedia Britannica, *Shneidman provides a definition of suicide and discusses suicide in relation to society, religion, law, and the arts. The author outlines the main threads of the study of suicide and the psychological characteristics of suicide and suggests some methods of prevention, intervention, and postvention.*

No one really knows why human beings commit suicide. Indeed, the very person who takes his own life may be least aware at the moment of decision of the essence (much less the totality) of his reasons and emotions for doing so. At the outset, it can be said that a dozen individuals can kill themselves and "do" (or commit) twelve psychologically different deeds. Understanding suicide—like understanding any other complicated human act such as drug or alcohol misuse or antisocial behavior—involves insights drawn from many fields that touch on man's entire psychological and social life.

DEFINITION OF SUICIDE

In this article the definition of suicide will be treated in two ways: first, a definition is put forward and, then, some of the difficulties and complexities involved in defining the term are discussed. Briefly defined, suicide is the human act of self-inflicted self-intentioned cessation.

Suicide is not a disease (although there are those who think so); it is not, in the view of the most detached observers, an immorality (although, as noted below, it has often been so treated in Western and other cultures); and, finally, it is unlikely that any one theory will ever explain phenomena as varied and as complicated as human self-destructive behaviors. In general, it is probably accurate to say that suicide always involves an individual's tortured and tunneled logic in a state of inner-felt, intolerable emotion. In addition, this mixture of constricted thinking and unbearable anguish is infused with that individual's conscious and unconscious psychodynamics (of hate, dependency, hope, etc.) playing themselves out within a social and cultural context, which itself imposes various degrees of restraint on, or facilitation of, the suicidal act,

This definition implies that committing suicide involves a conceptualization of death; that it combines an individual's conscious wish to be dead and his action to carry out that wish; that it focuses on his intention (which may have to be inferred by others); that the goal of action relates to death (rather than self-injury or self-mutilation); and that it focuses on the concept of the cessation of the individual's conscious, introspective life. The word "suicide" would seem to be clear enough, although such phrases as "self-inflicted" (in the incident in which Saul asked another soldier to kill him) and "self-intentioned" (when Seneca was ordered by Nero to kill himself) add to the complications of finding a clear-cut definition of suicide.

Complexities and difficulties with definitions

If the definition of suicide is complicated, there are even more confusions of meaning when the adjective "suicidal" is used. Some of the current confusions relating to the term "suicidal" are as follows:

(1) The word "suicidal" is used to cover a number of categories of behaviour. For example, it may convey the idea that an individual has committed suicide, attempted suicide, threatened suicide, exhibited depressive behaviour—with or without suicidal ideation—or manifested generally self-destructive or inimical patterns.

(2) There also is confusion with respect to the temporal aspects of suicidal acts. One sees "suicidal" used to convey the information that an individual was self-destructive, is currently self-destructive, or will be so. Most diagnoses in this field are post hoc definitions, labeling an individual as "suicidal" only after he or she has attempted or committed suicide.

(3) Serious confusion relating to suicidal phenomena may occur if the individual's intentions in relation to his own cessation are not considered. "Suicide" may be defined for medical, legal, and administrative purposes. In the United States and Great Britain (and most of the countries reporting to the World Health Organization), suicide is defined (by a medical examiner or coroner) as one of four possible modes of death. There are 140 possible causes of death but only four modes. An acronym for the four modes of death is NASH: natural, accident, suicide, and homicide. This traditional fourfold classification of all deaths leaves much to be desired. Its major deficiency is that it emphasizes relatively adventitious details in the death. Whether the individual is invaded by a lethal virus (natural), or a lethal bullet (homicide), or a lethal steering wheel (accident) may be a trivial difference to the deceased, who may be more interested in the date of his death. More importantly, the NASH classification of death erroneously treats the human being in Cartesian fashion, as a biological machine, rather than appropriately treating him as a motivated psychosocial organism. It also obscures the individual's intentions in relation to his own cessation and, further, completely neglects the contemporary concepts of psychodynamic psychology regarding intention, purpose, and the multiple determination of behavior including unconscious motivation.

It may make more sense eventually to eschew the category of suicide entirely—along with the other NASH categories—and instead to classify all deaths in terms of the role of the individual in his own demise: (1) intentioned, (2) subintentioned—cases in which an individual has played partial, latent, covert, or unconscious roles in hastening his own demise—or (3) unintentioned. The problems of certification would then be no more difficult than they are at present, but such a classification would serve to put man back into his own dying and death and, in addition, would reflect the twentieth century view of man that emphasizes both the conscious and unconscious aspects of his intentionality.

The word

Suicide is a relative recent word. According to *The Oxford English Dictionary*, the word was first used in 1651 by Walter Charleton when he said, interestingly enough, "To vindicate ones self from . . . inevitable Calamity, by Sui-cide is not . . . a Crime." The exact date of its first use is open to some question. Edward Phillips in the 1662 edition of his dictionary, *A New World in Words*, claimed invention of the word: "One barbarous word I shall produce, which is suicide." Curiously enough he does not derive it from the death of oneself but says it "should be derived from 'a sow' . . . since it is a swinish part for a man to kill himself."

The British poetry critic Alfred Alvarez in 1971 claimed that he found the word was used even earlier, in Sir Thomas Browne's *Religio Medici*, written in 1635 and published in 1642, in the following passage: "Herein are they not extreme that can allow a man to be his own assassin and so highly extoll the end by suicide of Cato."

The word "suicide" does not appear in Robert Burton's *Anatomy of Melancholy* (1632 edition) or in Samuel Johnson's *Dictionary* (1755). Before the introduction of the word, other terms, mostly circumlocutions and euphemisms relating to self-murder, were used—among them self-destruction, self-killing, self-slaughter, *sibi mortem consciecere* (to procure one's own death), *vim sibi inferre* (to cause violence to oneself), and *sui manu cadere* (to fall by one's own hand). Burton's phrases for suicide include "to make way with themselves" and "they offer violence to themselves." The traditional (and current) German term is *Selbstmord*—self-murder.

It may well be that in light of current concepts and facts about human self-destruction a new (and more accurate) term may eventually come into general usage. In the 1960s a relatively new word, suicidology, was introduced. *Suicidologie* was used in a text by a Dutch professor, W. A. Bonger, in 1929, but did not become widely known. Independently, the word used by Edwin S. Shneidman in a book review (1964) and then in the *Bulletin of Suicidology* (1967) and at the first convention of the American Association of Suicidology, which met in 1968. Since then the word has come into general use. Suicidology is defined as the scientific study of suicidal phenomena.

MAIN THREADS OF SUICIDAL STUDY

The modern era of the study of suicide began around the turn of the twentieth century, with two main threads of investigation, the sociological and the psychological, associated with the names of Emile Durkheim (1858–1917) and Sigmund Freud (1856–1939), respectively. Much earlier, during classical Greek times, suicide was viewed in various ways, but in classical Rome, in the centuries just before the Christian era, life was held rather cheaply and suicide was viewed either neutrally or even positively. The Roman Stoic Seneca said: "Living is not good, but living well. The wise man, therefore, lives as well as he should, not as long as he can . . . He will always think of life in terms of quality not quantity . . . Dying early or late is of no relevance, dying well or ill is . . . even if it is true that while there is life there is hope, life is not to be bought at any cost."

Historically it seems that the excessive martyrdom and penchant toward suicide of the early Christians frightened the church elders sufficiently for them to introduce a serious deterrent. That constraint was to relate suicide to crime and the sin associated with crime. A major change occurred in the fourth century with a categorical rejection of suicide by St. Augustine (354–430). Suicide was considered a crime, because it precluded the possibility of repentance and because it violated the Sixth Commandment relating to killing. Suicide was a greater sin than any sin one might wish to avoid. This view was elaborated by St. Thomas Aquinas (1225–74), who emphasized that suicide was a mortal sin in that it usurped God's power over man's life and death. Although neither the Old nor the New Testament directly forbids suicide, by 693 the Council of Toledo proclaimed that an individual who attempted suicide was to be excommunicated. The notion of suicide as sin took firm hold and for hundreds of years played an important part in Western man's view of self-destruction.

The Christian injunctions against suicide seemed paradoxically to rest on a respect for life (especially the life of the soul in the hereafter) and were a reaction to the light way in which life was held by the Romans. If those were the church's original motivations, however, they went awry and the results were excessive and counterproductive, and resulted in degrading, defaming, impoverishing, torturing, and persecuting individuals (who had attempted suicide, committed suicide, or were the survivors) whom they had originally tried to protect and succor.

The French philosopher Jean Jacques Rousseau (1712–78), by emphasizing the natural state of man, transferred sin from man to society, making man generally good (and innocent) and asserting that it is society that makes him bad. The disputation as to the locus of blame—whether in man or in society—is a major theme that dominates the history of suicidal thought. David Hume (1711–76) was one of the first major Western philosophers to discuss suicide in the absence of the concept of sin. His famous essay "On Suicide," published in 1777, a year after his death, was promptly suppressed. That well-reasoned essay is a statement of the Enlightenment position on suicide. The burden of the essay is to refute the view that suicide is a crime; it does so by arguing that suicide is not a transgression of our duties to God, to our fellow citizens, or to ourselves. He states that ". . .prudence and courage should engage us to rid ourselves at once of existence when it becomes a burden. . . . If it be no crime in me to divert the Nile or Danube from its course, were I able to effect such purposes, where then is the crime in turning a few ounces of blood from their natural channel?"

Whereas Hume tried to decriminalize suicide, Rousseau turned the blame from man to society. In the twentieth century, the two giants of suicidal theorizing played rather different roles: Durkheim focused on society's inimical effects on the individual, while Freud—eschewing the notions of either sin or crime—gave suicide back to man but put the locus of action in man's unconscious.

Durkheim's best-know work, *Le Suicide* (1897), established a model for sociological investigations of suicide. There have been many subsequent studies of this genre. The monographs and books by R. S. Cavan on suicide in Chicago (1926), of Calvin F. Schmid on suicide in Seattle (1928) and Minneapolis (1933), of Peter Sainsbury on suicide in London (1955), of Louis I. Dublin and Bessie Bunzel (1933), and of Andrew F. Henry and James F. Short, Jr,, on suicide in the U.S. (1954) all fall within the sociological tradition of taking a plot of ground—a city or a country—and figuratively or literally reproducing its map several times to show its socially shady (and topographically shaded) areas and their differential relationships to suicide rates.

According to Durkheim suicide is the result of society's strength or weakness of control over the individual. He posited three basic types of suicide, each a result of man's relationship to his society. In one instance, the "altruistic" suicide is literally required by society. Here, the customs or rules of the group demand suicide under certain circumstances. Hara-kiri and suttee are examples of altruistic suicides. In such instances, however, the persons had little choice. Self-inflicted death was honourable; continuing to live was ignominious. Society dictated their action and, as individuals, they were not strong enough to defy custom.

Most suicides in the United States are "egoistic"—Durkheim's second category. Contrary to the circumstances of an altruistic suicide, egoistic suicide occurs when the individual has too few ties with his community. Demands, in this case to live, do not reach him. Thus, proportionately, more individuals, especially men, who are on their own kill themselves than do church or family members.

Finally, Durkheim called "anomic" those suicides that occur when the accustomed relationship between an individual and his society is suddenly shattered. The shocking, immediate loss of a job, a close friend, or a fortune is thought sufficient to precipitate anomic suicides; or, conversely, poor men surprised by sudden wealth also have been shocked into anomic suicide.

The students and followers of Durkheim include Maurice Halbwachs in France and Ronald W. Maris and Jack D. Douglas in the United States Douglas, especially, has argued that Durkheim's constructs came not so much from the facts of life and death as from official statistics, which themselves may distort the very facts they are supposed to report.

As Durkheim detailed the sociology of suicide, so Freud fathered psychological explanations. To him, suicide was essentially within the mind. Since men ambivalently identify with the objects of their own love, when they are frustrated the aggressive side of the ambivalence will be directed against the internalized person. The main psychoanalytical position on suicide was that it represented unconscious hostility directed toward the introjected (ambivalently viewed) love object. For example, one killed oneself in order to murder the image of one's loved-hated father within one's breast. Psychodynamically, suicide can be seen as murder in the 180th degree.

In an important exegesis of Freud's thoughts on suicide by Robert E. Litman (1967, 1970), he traces the development of Freud's thoughts on the subject, taking into account Freud's clinical experiences and his changing theoretical positions from 1881 to 1939. It is evident from Litman's analysis that there is more to the psychodynamics of suicide than hostility. These factors include the general features of human condition in Western civilization, specifically, suicide-prone mechanisms involving rage, guilt, anxiety, dependency, and a great number of specifically predisposing conditions. The feelings of helplessness, hopelessness, and abandonment are very important.

Psychodynamic explanations of suicide theory did not move too much from the time of Freud to that of Karl Menninger. In his important book *Man Against Himself* (1938), Menninger (in captivating ordinary language) delineates the psychodynamics of hostility and asserts that the hostile drive in suicide is made up of three skeins: (1) the wish to kill, (2) the wish to be killed, and (3) the wish to die. Gregory Zilboorg refined this psychoanalytic hypothesis and stated that every suicidal case contained strong, unconscious hostility combined w1th an unusual lack of capacity to love others. He extended the concern from solely intrapsychic dynamics to the external world and maintained that the role of a broken home in suicidal proneness demonstrated that suicide has both intrapsychic and external etiological elements.

In addition to the sociological and psychological approaches to the study of suicide, there is a third main contemporary thrust that might be called the philosophical or existential. Albert Camus, in his essay *The Myth of Sisyphus,* begins by saying: "There is but one serious philosophic problem and that is suicide." The principal task of man is to respond to life's apparent meaninglessness, despair, and its absurd quality. Ludwig Wittgenstein also states that the main ethical issue for man is suicide. To Camus, Wittgenstein, and other philosophers, however, their ruminations were never meant as prescriptions for action. Arthur Schopenhauer (1788–1860), the philosopher of pessimism, lived to a fairly ripe age and died of natural causes.

Suicide has been related to many emotions: hostility, despair, shame, guilt, dependency, hopelessness, ennui. The traditional psychoanalytic position, first stated by Wilhelm Stekel at a meeting in Vienna in 1910, is that "no one kills himself who has not wanted to kill another or at least wished the death of another." This thought became translated into the psychoanalytic formulation that suicide represented hostility toward the introjected (ambivalently identified) love object. Currently, even psychodynamically oriented suicidologists believe that although hostility can be an important psychological component in some suicides, other emotional states—especially frustrated dependency and hopelessness and helplessness—often play the dominant role in the psychological drama of suicide. If there is one general psychological state commonly assumed to be associated with suicide it is a state of intolerable emotion (or unbearable or "unrepeatable despair")—what Herman Melville, in his masterpiece on self-destruction, *Moby Dick,* called "insufferable anguish."

Over and above the emotional states related to suicide, there are three important general psychological characteristics of suicide:

(1) The first is that the acute suicidal crisis (or period of high and dangerous lethality) is an interval of relatively short duration—to be counted, typically, in hours or days, not usually in months or years. An individual is at a peak of self-destructiveness for a brief time and is either helped, cools off, or is dead. Although one can live for years at a chronically elevated self-destructive level, one cannot have a loaded gun to one's head for too long before either bullet or emotion is discharged.

(2) The second concept is ambivalence. Few persons now dispute that Freud's major insights relating to the role of unconscious motivation (and the workings of what is called the unconscious mind) have been one of the giant concepts of this century in revolutionizing our view of man. The notion of ambivalence is a critical concept in twentieth century, psychodynamically oriented psychiatry and psychology. The dualities, complications, concomitant contradictory feelings, attitudes, and thrusts toward essentially the same person or introjected image are recognized hallmarks of psychological life. The dualities of the mind's flow constitute a cardinal feature of man's inner life. One can no longer ask in a simple Aristotelian way, "Make up your mind." To such a question a sophisticated respondent ought to say: "But that is precisely the point. I am at least of two, perhaps several, minds on this subject." A law has equal force whether it is passed in the Senate by a 100–0 or a 51–49 vote; so has a bullet. The paradigm of suicide is not the simplistic one of wanting to or not wanting to. The prototypical psychological picture of a person on the brink of suicide is one who wants to and does not want to. He makes plans for self-destruction and at the same time entertains fantasies of rescue and intervention. It is

possible—indeed probably prototypical—for a suicidal individual to cut his throat and to cry for help at the same time.

(3) Most suicidal events are dyadic events, that is, two-person events. Actually this dyadic aspect of suicide has two phases: the first during the prevention of suicide when one must deal with the "significant other," and the second in the aftermath in the case of a committed suicide in which one must deal with the survivor-victim. Although it is obvious that the suicidal drama takes place within an individual's head, it is also true that most suicidal tensions are between two people keenly known to each other: spouse and spouse, parent and child, lover and lover. In addition, death itself is an extremely dyadic event.

The cold sociological truth is that some modes of death are more stigmatizing to the survivors than are other modes of death and that, generally speaking, suicide imposes the greatest stigma of all upon its survivors. The British physician John Hinton deals with this in his book *Dying* (1967). Hinton also comments that the notes left by the suicidal subject often cause further anguish.

Suicide notes provide an unusual window into the thoughts and feelings of a suicidal person. Various surveys in different places indicate that about 15 percent of individuals who commit suicide leave suicide notes—although the actual range is from 2 to 30 percent. By the 1970s fewer than twenty systematic studies of suicide notes had been completed. One of the first scientific studies of suicide notes was by W. Morgenthaler (1945) in a monograph that reported forty-seven suicide notes (in German) from Bern, Switz. The best-known reports in the United States are by Edwin S. Shneidman and Norman L. Farberow (1947, 1970) in their studies of genuine suicide notes and elicited matched notes written by nonsuicidal persons. Suicide notes have been subjected to a number of types of analyses: by emotional states, logical styles, "reasons" stated or implied death wishes, language characteristics, relations to persons, and by computer count of key "tag words." In general these analyses indicate that (1) it is possible to distinguish between genuine and simulated suicide notes, and, more importantly, (2) genuine suicide notes are characterized by dichotomous logic, greater amount of hostility and self-blame, use of very specific names and instructions to the survivor, more decisiveness, less evidence of thinking about thinking, and more use of the various meanings of the word "love."

The two fundamental aspects of death and suicide

Twentieth-century philosophers, especially Percy Bridgman (1938), pointed out that there is an epistemological characteristic unique to death, specifically that there are two fundamental aspects of death: the private aspect, as an individual lives it himself (my death); and the public aspect, as one can experience, in reality, the death of another (your death). In death (and suicide) there is a key difference between the principal actor and the observer. One major implication of this key difference is that I can observe and experience your death (just as you can observe and experience my death), but I can never experience my own death for if I could, I should still be alive.

Some of this kind of thinking operates in suicide, especially when it is seen as a psychologically magical act. Just as Melville wrote that "All evil, to crazy Ahab, were visibly personified and made practically assailable in Moby Dick," so to the suicidal mind, using this same tortured logic, the whole world is "made practically assailable" and can be thought to be expunged by destroying oneself.

The fantasies of one's own suicide can represent the greatest possible combination of omnipotence and potential realization of effectiveness—greater even than one's fantasies of the assassination of another, group revenge, mass murder, or even genocide. Any "average" individual can say: "From my point of view, suicide destroys all"—and it can be done.

These inferred psychodynamics of suicide (relating to delusions of annihilation) are thought by psychoanalysts to have their origins in the earliest notions of an individual's infantile omnipotence. The literature of suicide in Western man, however, continually emphasizes that suicide can be an individual's final act, his final escape hatch, his final revenge—often misconstrued as a final "right." This unique epistemological dual characteristic of death (the difference between my death and your death) is fundamental to an understanding of suicide.

ATTEMPTED SUICIDE

Although it is obvious that one has to "attempt" suicide in order to commit it, it is equally clear that often the event of "attempting suicide" does not have death (cessation) as its objective. It is an acknowledged fact that often the goal of "attempted suicide" (such as cutting oneself or ingesting harmful substances) is to change one's life (or to change the "significant others" around one) rather than to end it. On the other hand, sometimes death is intended and only fortuitously avoided. After that, one's life—what has been called "a bonus life"—is forever somewhat different. Alfred Alvarez, who himself made a serious suicide attempt, said that survivors have a changed life, with entirely different standards.

Erwin Stengel, a student of attempted suicide, in his arguments and statistical presentations, seems to suggest, in the main, that persons who attempt suicide and those who commit suicide represent essentially two different "populations"—with admittedly some overflow from the first to the second. It is useful to think of two sets of overlapping populations: (1) a group of those who attempt suicide, few of whom go on to commit it, and (2) a group of those who commit suicide, many of whom have previously attempted it. A great deal has to do with the lethality of the event. Lethality is roughly synonymous with the "deathfulness" of the act and is an important dimension in understanding any potentially suicidal person. Avery D. Weisman in 1972 distinguished three aspects of lethality: that of intention (ideation and involvement); that of implementation (risk and rescue); and that of intercession (resources, relief, and reorientation). The ratio between suicide attempts and commits is about eight to one—one committed suicide for every eight attempts.

Suicide attempts have many meanings and, whatever their level of lethality, ought to be taken seriously. A person who attempts suicide because he believes that there is no use living may not necessarily mean that he wants to die but that he has exhausted the potential for being someone who matters.

PARTIAL DEATH AND SUBSTITUTES FOR SUICIDE

Sometimes the very life-style of an individual seems to truncate and demean his life so that he is as good as dead. Often alcoholism, drug addiction, mismanagement of physical disease (such as diabetes or Buerger's disease), and masochistic behaviour can be seen in this light. A study of gifted individuals (with IQ's over 140) indicated that conspicuous failure in adult life—a kind of "partial death"—was sometimes the "price" for life as a substitute for overt suicide.

The chief theorist of the concept of partial death is Karl Menninger. Much of his conception is explicated in *Man Against Himself.* Menninger writes of (1) chronic suicide, including asceticism, martyrdom, neurotic invalidism, alcohol addiction, antisocial behaviour, and psychosis; (2) focal suicide—focused on a limited part of the body—including self-mutilations, malingering, multiple surgery, purposive accidents, impotence, and frigidity; and (3) organic suicide, focusing on the psychological factors in organic disease, especially the self-punishing, aggressive, and erotic components. In the 1970s, the focus was on concepts such as indirect self-destructive behaviour. There have been many studies of alcoholism and drug addiction and diabetes and on aspects of homicide (on both the murderer and the victim) as suicidal equivalents. In relation to the role of the homicidal victim in his own death, the work of Marvin Wolfgang (1958) has been particularly interesting.

A related concept is that of "subintentioned death." That concept asserts that there are many deaths that are neither clearly suicidal nor clearly accidental or natural but are deaths in which the decedent has played some covert or unconscious role in "permitting" his death to occur, sort of "accidentally," or by "inviting" homicide, or, by unconsciously disregarding what could be life-extending medical regimen, and thus dying sooner than "necessary." Losing the "will to live" and so-called voodoo deaths—as well as many deaths in ordinary society—can be viewed as subintentional deaths (Shneidman, 1963). Obviously, this view of death changes the nature and statistics of suicide dramatically.

This concept of a reduced level of life as a substitute (or psychological "trade") for suicide itself presents fascinating philosophic, social, psychological, and moral questions that relate to whether or not there actually is an irreducible suicide rate among human beings. Is there a price for civilization? Indeed, a price for life? Litman, reflecting on Freud's work, agrees with Freud's general schematic view and that there is a suicidal trend in everyone.

This self-destructiveness is controlled through constructive habits of living and loving, but when they break down, the individual may easily be forced into a suicidal crisis. To keep alive one must keep his thoughts, feelings, and aspirations in a vital balance.

SUICIDE AND RELIGION

In the Western world it has been traditionally said that the suicide rate is higher among Protestants than among Catholics or Jews and that the latter group shows significantly low suicidal figures. By the 1970s it was known, however, that the role of religion in relation to suicide is more complicated and that religious affiliation serves both to inhibit and, at other times, to facilitate suicide. At the outset it is important to distinguish between religious beliefs and religious (social) affiliation. Durkheim not unexpectedly emphasized the sociological aspects of religion. He stated: "If religion protects one from the desire for self-destruction, it is not because it preaches to him, with elements of religious origin, respect for one's person: it is because it forms a social group." A nationwide study in the United States indicated that the pro rata suicide rate among veterans—a fairly representative group of United States citizenry—for Catholics and Protestants was about equal to the numbers (and percentages) of Protestants and Catholics in the country generally. Much more important than nominal religious affiliation would be a number of subtlties of religious belief: the feeling of group belongingness, belief in an omnipotent God, belief in the efficacy of prayer, belief in a hereafter or existence after death, and other issues relating to death in general. Results of a national U.S. survey of 30,000 persons reported by Shneidman in 1970 indicated that a sizable percentage (57 percent) of individuals of all religious backgrounds (and with a variety of intensities of religious belief) did not believe in any life after death and that over one-third indicated that religion had played either a relatively minor role or no role at all in the development of their attitudes toward death (and toward suicide). Just as in the twentieth century there has been an enormous "secularization" of death—the physician and hospital in many ways replacing the clergyman and the church in relation to the anxieties surrounding death—so too has there been a secularization of suicide. Few of the current debates about suicide are on primary religious grounds; when the ethics of suicide are debated, those usually are in terms of such concepts as "freedom" and "life," *i.e.,* how free an individual should be to take his own life and how far "benign intervention" should go in an attempt to save an individual's life before the intervention is intrusive and robs him of more than his life is worth.

When Durkheim spoke of religion as a source of social organization (holding individuals together with common beliefs and practices), he was not only speaking of social integration but he was also, from a psychological point of view, referring to personal identification. Walter T. Martin and Jack P. Gibbs (1964) proposed a theory relating status integration with suicide and Henry and Short (1954) discussed the positive relationship between suicide and status and the negative relation between suicide and the strength of a relational source. In general it appears that a person who is uneasy in his religion (or in his irreligion) or changes his religion several times (like a person who is uneasy in his marriage or has several marriages) is more likely to commit suicide, not so much on purely religious (or marital) grounds but because of his general perturbation and lack of good self-concept, which underlie his uneasy search for certainty and stability in his life.

SUICIDE AND THE LAW

Not surprisingly, the history of suicide and the law closely parallel and reflect—often with significant lags—the major cultural and philosophic attitudes toward suicide. Probably the most important single legal change was the passage of the Suicide Act in England in 1961 that (1) finally abolished criminal penalties for committing suicide—considering that in the nineteenth century (as late as 1823), a London citizen who committed suicide was buried at a crossroads in Chelsea with a stake pounded through his heart; (2) no longer made survivors of suicide attempts liable to criminal prosecution; and (3) as a kind of quid pro quo for the liberalization of the first two measures, increased the penalties (up to fourteen years' imprisonment) for aiding and abetting a suicidal act. Earlier, the Homicide Act of 1957 changed the charge against a survivor of a suicide pact from murder to manslaughter.

In the United States, most aspects of suicide are not against the law. As of the early 1970s a comparatively small number of states (nine) listed suicide as a crime, although no penalties (such as mutilation of bodies or forfeiture of estates) were exacted. In such states suicide attempts are either felonies or misdemeanours and could result in jail sentences, although such laws are selectively or indifferently enforced. Two states (Nevada and New York) repealed such laws, stating in effect that although suicide is "a grave social wrong" there is no way to punish it. Eighteen states—Alaska, Arkansas, California, Florida, Kansas, Louisiana, Michigan, Massachusetts, Minnesota, Mississippi, Missouri, Montana, Nevada, New Mexico, New York, Oregon, Wisconsin, and Wyoming—have no laws against either suicide or suicide attempts but specify that to aid, advise, or encourage another person to commit suicide is a felony. In the more than twenty other states, there are no penal statutes referring to suicide.

In the early 1970s, especially in Great Britain, there was some movement (among some eminent lawyers, theologians, philosophers, and physicians) toward the legalization of voluntary euthanasia; proposals were to repeal the aiding and abetting aspect of suicide laws so that a physician might, on a patient's request, assist him to his own voluntary death.

SOME ODDITIES OF SUICIDE

The lore about suicide contains a large number of interesting and esoteric items about various cultures. Suicide was thought, for example, to be absent among so-called primitive cultures, but it is evident that this is not so. Studies were made of suicide in Africa (Paul Bohannan, 1960), India (Verrier Elwin, 1943; Upendra Thakur, 1963), Hong Kong (Yap Powmeng, 1958), and Japan (Ohara, 1961). Practically every popular article on suicide routinely contains a statement about the kamikaze pilots who flew and died for Japan in World War II. Also, in relation to Japan, one often reads of the practice of hara-kiri or seppuku, which is the ritual act of disemboweling onself and was limited to the samurai warrior and noble classes. General Tojo, who attempted hara-kiri at the end of World War II, was saved by United States doctors, only to be hanged later by a military tribunal. In 1970 the well-known Japanese author Mishima Yukio . . . committed seppuku (with ritual self-disemboweling and decapitation) at the age of forty-five. In general, however, suicide in contemporary Japan is more "Western" than otherwise—often done with barbiturates. In a discussion of suicide in nineteenth-century India one finds references to suttee, the custom in which Hindu widows threw themselves onto the funeral pyres of their husbands.

Six suicides are recorded in the Old Testament: Abimelech, Samson, Saul, Saul's armour bearer. Ahithophel, and Zimri. The most famous and among the most frequently cited suicides perhaps, are Socrates' drinking hemlock and Cato's throwing himself upon his sword. The apocryphal stories of Bismarck's contemplating suicide, Napoleon's attempting suicide, Washington's despondency, and Lincoln's depression keep reappearing in articles on suicide—including this one.

Myths of suicide—

Following is a summary of some of the more outstanding misconceptions of suicide:

Fable: Persons who talk about suicide do not commit suicide. *Fact:* Of any ten persons who will themselves commit it, eight have given definite warnings of their suicidal intentions.

Fable: Suicide happens without warning. *Fact:* Studies reveal that the suicidal person gives many clues and warnings regarding his suicidal intentions.

Fable: Suicidal persons are fully intent on dying. *Fact:* Most suicidal persons are undecided about living or dying, and they "gamble with death," leaving it to others to save them. Almost no one commits suicide without letting others know how he is feeling.

Fable: Once a person is suicidal, he is suicidal forever. *Fact:* Individuals who wish to kill themselves are suicidal only for a limited period of time.

Fable: Improvement following a suicidal crisis means that the suicidal risk is over. *Fact:* Most suicides occur within about three months following the beginning of "improvement," when the individual has the energy to put his morbid thoughts and feelings into effect.

Fable: Suicide strikes much more often among the rich, or, conversely, it occurs almost exclusively among the poor. *Fact:* Suicide is neither the rich man's disease nor the poor man's curse. Suicide is represented proportionately among all levels of society.

Fable: Suicide is inherited or "runs in the family." *Fact:* It follows individual patterns.

Fable: All suicidal individuals are mentally ill, and suicide always is the act of a psychotic person. *Fact:* Studies of hundreds of genuine suicide notes indicate that although the suicidal person is extremely unhappy, he is not necessarily mentally ill.

Romantic suicide and the artist—

Since at least the sixteenth century, specifically in the Italian commedia dell'arte, there has been a character named Harlequin who typically wears a multicoloured suit and a black mask—and has a connection with death. Indeed to be loved by Harlequin was to be married to death. This is the idea of death as a lover; it relates to the romanticization of death itself. As a refinement of this idea, suicide has historically been thought to be a romantic kind of death. One specific myth is that suicide is caused by unrequited love. Suicide pacts (portrayed romantically in *Mayerling* and in *Elvira Madigan)* are depicted as the essence of intense love. One result of this mystique is a belief that especially sensitive people, artists—poets, painters, and writers—are unusually prone to commit suicide and, indeed, add to their reputations as artists by committing suicide. Perhaps the best-known novel of this genre is Goethe's *The Sorrows of Young Werther,* published in 1774 when the author was twenty-four years old and credited, in the mythology of suicide, with having created a veritable epidemic of romantic suicides throughout Europe. By the 1970s the list of suicides of artists was sufficiently long and vivid to persuade an uncritical student of suicide that the sensitivity of the artist is somehow related to the special nature of a romantic suicidal death. The list includes Van Gogh, Virginia Woolf, Hart Crane, the Italian writer Cesare Pavese, Randall Jarrell, Modigliani, Jackson Pollock, Mark Rothko, Ernest Hemingway, John Berryman, Sylvia Plath, Mishima, and Kawabata Yasunari. Perhaps the best description and analysis of suicide and the creative literary artist is by the English poetry editor and critic Alfred Alvarez in his book *The Savage God:* (1971). One of the most romanticized suicides in Western literature is that of the English poet Thomas Chatterton (1752–70), who took poison at the age of seventeen. This particular death illustrates the notion (or myth) "that those with more life and passion go soon"—that the best die young. It reminds one of those who have died "too young"—Byron, Shelley, Keats, Mozart—and the particular poignancy of an untimely death of an especially beautiful or gifted person. We tend to be essentially undemocratic about death and suicide—because we tend to believe that some deaths level (or elevate) certain people more than others.

STATISTICS ON SUICIDE

The demographic use of statistics on suicide perhaps were given their greatest impetus by John Graunt and Johann Peter Sussmilch. Graunt was a London tradesman who, in 1662, published a small book of observations on the London bills of mortality. He separated various bits of information contained in these rolls of names of the dead into separate categories and organized the information systematically, finally constructing mortality tables—the first attempt to organize data in that manner. Of great significance was his success in demonstrating the regularities that can be found between medical and social phenomena when one deals with large numbers. He demonstrated how an analysis of the mortality statistics could be used to the advantage of physicians, businessmen, and government.

Much of what is known today as statistical information came into existence with the work of Sussmilch, a Prussian clergyman who in 1741 in his analyses of vital data from church registers created political arithmetic, or what is now called vital statistics. It is important to keep in mind that statistics, particularly statistics on suicide, are in part socially manufactured data—mostly by coroners and physicians. Suicidal deaths are notoriously underrepresented and obviously vary from country to country dependent not only on the number of suicides that in fact occur in each country but also on deeply ingrained cultural folkways relating to the social, cultural, and religious attitudes of that country.

There are several sources of suicide statistics. Louis Dublin's text, *Suicide* (1963), is a standard source; the World Health Organization (WHO) booklet, *The Prevention of Suicide* (1968), is another. *Suicide in the United States, 1950–1964* (1967) and *The Facts of Life and Death* (1970), both published by the United States Department of Health, Education, and Welfare, are standard sources in the United States. In general, the reported suicide rate for the United States is between 10 and 12 per 100,000 which places the United States about in the middle of the countries that report to the United Nations. Austria, West Germany, Hungary, Japan, Czechoslovakia, Denmark, Finland, Sweden, and Switzerland report rates of over 25 per 100,000 population, and Italy, the Netherlands, and Spain report rates under 10 per 100,000. The number of suicides in the United States per year is given at about 22,000 but many experts believe the actual number to be at least twice as high.

In any discussion of the statistics of suicide—keeping in mind their tenuous character—it is important to distinguish among rank, rate, and number. Currently, in the United States, suicide is ranked among the first five causes of death for white males from ten to fifty-five. For example, suicide is the second-ranked cause of death for white males age fifteen to nineteen, but one must appreciate that the first leading cause of death, accidents, yields 627 chances in 100,000 of the individual dying from that cause, while suicide yields (only) 88 chances in 100,000. Generally, in the early ages when suicide is high, it occupies that rank because the other killers like heart disease, malignant neoplasms (cancer), vascular lesions of the central nervous system (stroke) and cirrhosis of the liver are not then common.

In general, statistics on suicide in the nineteenth and twentieth centuries indicate that more men than women commit suicide (about three to one) and that more women than men attempt suicide (again about three to one). In the early 1970s there was evidence that the ratio for committed suicide seemed to be changing, moving toward (but not yet achieving) an equal proportion between the sexes. Statistics relating to race and ethnic origin seem to be undergoing changes, probably reflecting general changes in attitude toward the concept of race and ethnicity. In the United States it was reported for years that Caucasian suicides far outnumbered Negro suicides, but the rate for Negros seems to be changing, moving closer to that for Caucasians. Whether this reflects the effects of urban ghetto living, the effects of identifying with "the white man's problems," or simply better and more accurate record keeping are all issues for further study. Some studies (conducted in England and Australia) that followed individuals who emigrated either to the United States or to Australia seem to indicate that the suicide rates of specific groups such as Hungarians, Italians, Poles, and Irish appear, for a generation or so, to be closer to the rates of the homeland than to the rates of the adopted country. In these data, there are many methodological issues that are also yet to be resolved.

In relation to suicide statistics, a standard textbook on sociology published in 1972 reported that sociologists still made continuous reference to the work of Durkheim. Rates derived from Durkheim's studies show that suicide rates for Protestants have been consistently higher than those for Jews or Catholics. In the early part of the twentieth century the Jewish rate in the Netherlands was higher than the Protestant, and during the depression, in Toronto, Canada, Catholic rates also were higher than Protestant. The inference is that the time, the place, and the social circumstances are all important factors.

In the matter of comparative national statistics, Alvarez points out that United States President Dwight D. Eisenhower blamed the high Swedish suicide rate on what too much social welfare can do. But the present rate in Sweden, Alvarez notes, is about the same as it was in 1910, before comprehensive social welfare programs were begun and is actually ranked ninth on a table published by WHO. The countries of Central Europe show the highest rates: Hungary has the highest national rate; Austria and Czechoslovakia are third and fourth. The highest suicide rate in the world is that of West Berlin; its rate is more than twice that of West Germany as a whole. The city, it has been suggested, is a model of what Durkheim called anomie—alienated not only geographically but also in cultural, social, and political aspects. Countries like Ireland and Egypt, where suicide is considered by many a mortal sin, have rates among the lowest in the world, bearing out Stengel's conclusion that highly industrialized and prosperous countries tend to have comparatively high suicide rates. Alvarez concludes that official statistics reflect only a fraction of the true figures, which a number of authorities reckon to be anywhere from a quarter to a half again as large. Because of religious and bureaucratic prejudices, family sensitivity, differences in the proceedings of coroners' hearings and postmortem examinations, the shadowy distinctions between suicides and accidents—in short, the unwillingness to recognize the act for what it is—knowledge of the extent to which suicide pervades modern society is diminished and distorted.

A certain sizable percentage of deaths that are certified by coroners or medical examiners—estimated to be between 10 and 15 percent—are equivocal as to what the actual mode of death ought to be; this uncertainty usually lies between suicide or accident. A procedure, labelled by Shneidman the "psychological autopsy," has been developed to deal with these equivocal deaths. Essentially, the psychological autopsy involves the use of social and behavioural scientists (psychologists, psychiatrists, social workers, and other trained personnel) who interview relatives and friends of the decedent with the goal of developing information about the decedent's intention vis-à-vis his own death in the days just before the death. Clues—verbal ("You won't be seeing me around"); behavioural (*e.g.*, giving away prized possessions or marked changes in patterns of eating, sexuality, interests); or situational (*e.g.*,the loss of a loved one)—are deemed to point more to suicide than to accident. In the absence of such clues, a recommendation for a nonsuicidal or "undetermined" mode of death should be made to the certifying official.

SUICIDE VENTION (PREVENTION, INTERVENTION, POSTVENTION)

The Latin word *venire* means "to come" or "to do." In relation to any event (*e.g.*, suicide) one can act before, during, or after—corresponding to prevention, intervention, and postvention. These terms also correspond roughly to the public health concepts of primary, secondary, and tertiary prevention.

Prevention

If, as this article has suggested, suicidal phenomena are existential-social-psychological-dyadic events, then obviously primary prevention is enormously complicated—almost tantamount to preventing human unhappiness. Some students of human nature believe that the urge toward self-destruction is ubiquitous and that a certain amount of it is an inevitable and constant price of civilization, if not of life itself. Primarily prevention would relate to the principles of good mental hygiene in general.

Intervention

Intervention relates to the treatment and care of suicidal crisis or suicidal problems. On this score, suicide prevention centers could be more accurately labeled suicide intervention centers. A great deal has been learned about practical techniques for effective suicide intervention. There is a vast literature on therapy and treatment of suicidal persons in various settings—in the community, in suicide prevention and crisis intervention centers, in poison-control centers, in outpatient offices, and in both medical and mental hospitals. In general, most of the suggestions for care have in common the stressing of good rapport, working with the "significant others" in the suicidal person's life, using the available community resources for referral (for emotional support, legal aid, financial help, employment, individual and group psychotherapy, hospitalization), and focusing on the reduction of the person's "lethality" during the period of suicidal crisis. Much of the suicide prevention work borrows from the theory of crisis intervention developed by Erich Lindemann (1944) and Gerald Caplan (1964). In the United States, the theoretical and empirical work of the Los Angeles Suicide Prevention Center, established in 1955, and in Great Britain, the work of the Samaritans, established in 1953, has been widely emulated.

In 1960 there were fewer than a half-dozen suicide prevention centers in the United States: a decade later there were over 200. Typically there are telephone-answering centers; maintaining twenty-four hour service, they serve as short-term resources, are theoretically modeled in terms of the concept of crisis intervention, and use both professional and lay volunteer staff.

Suicide is best understood as a socio-psychological, existential human event that calls for compassionate response to an individual in an emotional and philosophic crisis. Obviously suicide is not solely a medical problem and many kinds of persons including volunteers—provided they are carefully selected, well-trained, and continuously supervised—can serve as lifesaving agents in the prevention of suicide. The lay volunteer has been described as probably the most important single discovery in the history of suicide prevention. Nonetheless, professionally trained persons—psychologists, psychiatrists, social workers—continue to play the primary roles in suicide prevention and especially in research.

Postvention

Postvention, a term introduced by Shneidman in 1971, refers to those things done after the dire event has occured that serve to mollify the aftereffects of the event in a person who has attempted suicide, or to deal with the adverse effects on the survivor-victims of a person who has committed suicide. It is offering psychological services to the bereaved survivors. It includes work with the surviving children, parents, and spouses. Much of postventive work has been focused on widows. Studies show that survivors are apt to have a higher morbidity and mortality rate in the year following the death of their loved one than comparable persons who are not survivors of such a death. It may well be that the major public mental-health challenge in suicide lies in offering postventive help to the survivor-victims. The development of postvention is part of the current new view of the special psychological needs relating to death.

Bibliography

Emile Durkheim, *Suicide* (1897; Eng. trans. by J. A. Spaulding and G. Simpson, 1951).

Sigmund Freud, "Mourning and Melancholia" (1917), in *The Standard Edition of the Complete Psychological Works*, vol. 14 (1965).

Karl A. Menninger, Man Against Himself (1938).

Edwin S. Shneidman and Norman L. Farberow (eds.), *Clues to Suicide* (1957). *The Cry for Help* (1961).

Glanville Williams, *The Sanctity of Life and the Criminal Law* (1957).

Louis I. Dublin, *Suicide: a Sociological and Statistical Study* (1963).

Erwin Stengel, *Suicide and Attempted Suicide* (1964).

Paul Friedman (ed.), *On Suicide* (1967).

Jack D. Douglas, *The Social Meanings of Suicide* (1967).

Robert E. Litman, "Sigmund Freud and Suicide," in E. S. Shneidman (ed.), *Essays in Self-Destruction* (1967).

U.S. Public Health Service, *Suicide in the United States, 1950–1964* (1967).

Arnold Toynbee *et al., Man's Concern with Death* (1969).

World Health Organization, *Prevention of Suicide* (1968).

E. S. Shneidman, "Orientations Toward Death: A Vital Aspect in the Study of Lives," in R. W. White (ed.), *The Study of Lives* (1963).

Edwin S. Shneidman, "Suicide, Lethality and the Psychological Autopsy," in E. S. Shneidman and M. Ortega (eds.), *Aspects of Depression* (1969).

N. L. Farberow, *Bibliography on Suicide and Suicide Prevention* (1969).

E. S. Shneidman (ed.), *On the Nature of Suicide* (1969).

E. S. Shneidman, N. L. Farberow, and R. E. Litman, *The Psychology of Suicide* (1970).

A. Alvarez, *The Savage God: a Study of Suicide* (1971).

Jacques Choron, *Suicide* (1972).

45 • Feelings

A. Alvarez

*A. Alvarez is not a professional suicidologist. He is a poet and drama critic. He has edited and written several books, of which the most interesting and important for this anthology is his book about suicide—*The Savage God*—in which, as perhaps only a literary man can, he discusses suicide in a broadly humanistic and deeply personal way.*

The psychoanalytic theories of suicide prove, perhaps, only what was already obvious: that the processes which lead a man to take his own life are at least as complex and difficult as those by which he continues to live. The theories help untangle the intricacy of motive and define the deep ambiguity of the wish to die but they say little about what it means to be suicidal, and how it feels.

First and most important, suicide is a closed world with its own irresistible logic. This is not to say that people commit suicide, as the Stoics did, coolly, deliberately, as a rational choice between rational alternatives. The Romans may have disciplined themselves into accepting this frigid logic, but those who have done so in modern history are, in the last analysis, monsters. And like all monsters, they are hard to find. In 1735 John Robeck, a Swedish philosopher living in Germany, completed a long Stoic defense of suicide as a just, right and desirable act; he then carefully put his principles into practice by giving away his property and drowning himself in the Weser. His death was the sensation of the day. It provoked Voltaire to comment, through one of the characters in *Candide:* ". . . I have seen a prodigious number of people who hold their existence in execration; but I have only seen a dozen who voluntarily put an end to their misery: three Negroes, four Englishmen, four Genevois, and a German professor called Robeck." Even for Voltaire, the supreme rationalist, a purely rational suicide was something prodigious and slightly grotesque, like a comet or a two-headed sheep.

The logic of suicide is, then, not rational in the old Stoic sense. It scarcely could be, since there is almost no one now, even among the philosophers, who believes that reason is clean and straightforward, or that motives can ever be less than equivocal. "The desires of the heart," said Auden, "are as crooked as corkscrews." To the extent that suicide *is* logical, it is also unreal: too simple, too convincing, too total, like one of those paranoid systems such as Ezra Pound's Social Credit, by which madmen explain the whole universe. The logic of suicide is different. It is like the unanswerable logic of a nightmare, or like the science-fiction fantasy of being projected suddenly into another dimension: everything makes sense and follows its own strict rules;

yet, at the same time, everything is also different, perverted, upside down. Once one decides to take his own life he enters a shut-off, impregnable but wholly convincing world where every detail fits and each incident reinforces his decision. An argument with a stranger in a bar, an expected letter which doesn't arrive, the wrong voice on the telephone, the wrong knock at the door, even a change in the weather—all seem charged with special meaning; they all contribute. The world of the suicide is superstitious, full of omens. Freud saw suicide as a great passion, like being in love: "In the two opposed situations of being most intensely in love and of suicide, the ego is overwhelmed by the object, though in totally different ways." As in love, things which seem trivial to the outsider, tiresome or amusing, assume enormous importance to those in the grip of the monster, while the sanest arguments against it seem to them simply absurd.

This imperviousness to everything outside the closed world of self-destruction can produce an obsession so weird and total, so psychotic, that death itself becomes a side issue. In nineteenth-century Vienna a man of seventy drove seven three-inch nails into the top of his head with a heavy blacksmith's hammer. For some reason he did not die immediately, so he changed his mind and walked to the hospital, streaming blood.[1] In March 1971 a Belfast businessman killed himself by boring nine holes in his head with a power drill. There is also the case of a Polish girl, unhappily in love, who in five months swallowed four spoons, three knives, nineteen coins, twenty nails, seven window bolts, a brass cross, one hundred and one pins, a stone, three pieces of glass and two beads from her rosary.[2] In each instance the suicidal gesture seems to have mattered more than its outcome. People try to die in such operatic ways only when they are obsessed more by the means than by the end, just as a sexual fetishist gets more satisfaction from his rituals than from the orgasm to which they lead. The old man driving nails into his skull, the company director with his power drill and the lovelorn girl swallowing all that hardware seem to have acted wildly out of despair. Yet in order to behave in precisely that way they must have brooded endlessly over the details, selecting, modifying, perfecting them like artists, until they produced that single, unrepeatable happening which expressed their madness in all its uniqueness. In the circumstances, death may come but it is superfluous.[3]

Without this wild drama of psychosis, there is a form of suicide, more commonplace but also more deadly, which is simply an extreme form of self-injury. The psychoanalysts have suggested that a man may destroy himself not because he wants to die, but because there is a single aspect of himself which he cannot tolerate. A suicide of this order is a perfectionist. The flaws in his nature exacerbate him like some secret itch he cannot get at. So he acts suddenly, rashly, out of exasperation. Thus Kirillov, in Dostoevsky's *The Possessed,* kills himself, he says, to show that he is God. But secretly he kills himself because he knows he is not God. Had his ambitions been less, perhaps he would have only attempted the deed or mutilated himself. He conceived of his mortality as a kind of lapse, an error which offended him beyond bearing. So in the end he pulled the trigger in order to shed this mortality like a tatty suit of clothes, but without taking into account that the clothes were, in fact, his own warm body.

Compared with the other revolutionaries in the novel, Kirillov seems sane, tender-hearted and upright. Yet maybe his concern with godhead and metaphysical liberty consigned him, too, to the suburbs of psychosis. And this sets him apart from the majority of the inhabitants of the closed world of suicide. For them, the act is neither rash nor operatic nor, in any obvious way, unbalanced. Instead it is, insidiously, a vocation. Once inside the closed world, there seems never to have been a time when one was not suicidal. Just as a writer feels himself never to have been anything except a writer, even if he can remember with embarrassment his first doggerel, even if he has spent years, like Conrad, disguised as a sea dog, so the suicide feels he has always been preparing in secret for this last act. There is no end to his sense of *déjà vu* or to his justifications. His memory is stored with long, black afternoons of childhood, with the taste of pleasures that gave no pleasure, with sour losses and failures, all repeated endlessly like a scratched phonograph record.

An English novelist who had made two serious suicide attempts said this to me:

> I don't know how much potential suicides *think* about it. I must say, I've never really thought about it much. Yet it's always there. For me, suicide's a constant temptation. It never slackens. Things are all right at the moment. But I feel like a cured alcoholic: I daren't take a drink because I know that if I do I'll go on it again. Because whatever it is that's there doesn't alter. It's a pattern of my entire life. I would like to think that it was only brought on by certain stresses and strains. But in fact, if I'm honest and look back, I realize it's been a pattern ever since I can remember.
>
> My parents were very fond of death. It was their favorite thing. As a child, it seemed to me that my father was constantly rushing off to do himself in. Everything he said, all his analogies, were to do with death. I remember him once telling me that marriage was the last nail in the coffin of life. I was about eight at the time. Both my parents, for different reasons, regarded death as a perfect release from their troubles. They were very unhappy together, and I think this sunk in very much. Like my father, I have always demanded too much of life and people and relationships—far more than exists, really. And when I find that it doesn't exist, it seems like a rejection. It probably isn't a rejection at all; it simply isn't there. I mean, the empty air doesn't reject you; it just says, "I'm empty." Yet rejection and disappointment are two things I've always found impossible to take.
>
> In the afternoons my mother and father both retired to sleep. That is, they retired to death. They really died for the afternoons. My father was a parson. He had nothing to do, he had no work. I begin now to

> understand how it was for him. When I'm not working, I'm capable of sleeping through most of the morning. Then I start taking sleeping pills during the day to keep myself in a state of dopiness, so that I can sleep at any time. To take sleeping pills during the day to sleep isn't so far from taking sleeping pills in order to die. It's just a bit more practical and a bit more craven. You only take two instead of two hundred. But during those afternoons I used to be alive and lively. It was a great big house but I never dared make a sound. I didn't dare pull a plug in case I woke one of them up. I felt terribly rejected. Their door was shut, they were absolutely unapproachable. Whatever terrible crisis had happened to me, I felt I couldn't go and say, "Hey, wake up, listen to me." And those afternoons went on a long time. Because of the war I went back to live with them, and it was still exactly the same. If I ever bumped myself off, it would be in the afternoon. Indeed, the first time I tried was in the afternoon. The second time was after an awful afternoon. Moreover, it was after an afternoon in the country, which I hate for the same reasons as I hate afternoons. The reason is simple: when I'm alone, I stop believing I exist.

Although the speaker is well into a successful middle age, the injured and rejected child she had once been still lives powerfully on. Perhaps it is this element which makes the closed world of suicide so inescapable: the wounds of the past, like those of the Fisher King in the legend of the Holy Grail, will not heal over—the ego, the analysts would say, is too fragile—instead, they continually push themselves to the surface to obliterate the modified pleasures and acceptances of the present. The life of the suicide is, to an extraordinary degree, unforgiving. Nothing he achieves by his own efforts, or luck bestows, reconciles him to his injurious past.

Thus, on August 16, 1950, ten days before he finally took sleeping pills, Pavese wrote in his notebook: "Today I see clearly that from 1928 until now I have always lived under this shadow." But in 1928 Pavese was already twenty. From what we know of his desolate childhood—his father dead when he was six, his mother of spun steel, harsh and austere—the shadow was probably on him much earlier; at twenty he simply recognized it for what it was. At thirty he had written flatly and without self-pity, as though it were some practical detail he had just noticed: "Every luxury must be paid for, and everything is a luxury, starting with being in the world."

A suicide of this kind is born, not made. As I said earlier, he receives his reasons—from whatever nexus of guilt, loss and despair—when he is too young to cope with them or understand. All he can do is accept them innocently and try to defend himself as best he can. By the time he recognizes them more objectively, they have become part of his sensibility, his way of seeing and his way of life. Unlike the psychotic self-injurer, whose suicide is a sudden fatal twist in the road, his whole life is a gradual downward curve, steepening at the end, on which he moves knowingly, unable and unwilling to stop himself. No amount of success will change him. Before his death Pavese was writing better than ever before —more richly, more powerfully, more easily. In the year before he died he turned out two of his best novels, each in less than two months of writing. One month before the end he received the Strega Prize, the supreme accolade for an Italian writer. "I have never been so much alive as now," he wrote, "never so young." A few days later he was dead. Perhaps the sweetness itself of his creative powers made his innate depression all the harder to bear. It is as though those strengths and rewards belonged to some inner part of him from which he felt himself irredeemably alienated.

It is also characteristic of this type of suicide that his beliefs do not help him. Although Pavese called himself a Communist, his politics permeate neither his imaginative work nor his private notebooks. I suspect they were merely a gesture of solidarity with the people he liked, against those he disliked. He was a Communist not because of any particular conviction, but because he hated the Fascists who had imprisoned him. In practice, he was like nearly everybody else in this present time: skeptical, pragmatic, adrift, sustained neither by the religion of the Church nor by that of the Party. In these circumstances, "this business of living"—the title of his notebooks—becomes peculiarly chancy. What Durkheim called "anomie" may lead to a social conception of man infinitely more impoverished than any religious formulation of his role as a servant of God. Yet since the decline of religious authority,[4] the only alternative to the ersatz and unsatisfactory religions of science and politics has been an uneasy, perilous freedom. This is summed up in an eerie note found in an empty house in Hampstead: "Why suicide? Why not?"

Why not? The pleasures of living—the hedonistic pleasures of the five senses, the more complex and demanding pleasures of concentration and doing, even the unanswerable commitments of love—seem often no greater and mostly less frequent than the frustrations—the continual sense of unfinished and unfinishable business, jangled, anxious, ragged, overborne. If secularized man were kept going only by the pleasure principle, the human race would already be extinct. Yet maybe his secular quality is his strength. He chooses life because he has no alternative, because he knows that after death there is nothing at all. When Camus wrote *The Myth of Sisyphus*—in 1940, after the fall of France, a serious personal illness and depressive crisis—he began with suicide and ended with an affirmation of individual life, in itself and for itself, desirable because it is "absurd," without final meaning or metaphysical justification. "Life is a gift that nobody should renounce," the great Russian poet Osip Mandelstam said to his wife when, in exile after his imprisonment, she proposed that they commit suicide together if Stalin's secret police took them again.[5] Hamlet said that the only obstacle to self-slaughter was fear of the afterlife, which was an unconvinced but Christian answer to all those noble suicides which the heroes of Shakespeare's Roman plays performed so unhesitatingly. Without the buttress of Christianity, without the cold dignity of a Stoicism that had evolved in response to a world in which human life was a trivial commodity, cheap enough to be expended at every circus to amuse the crowd, the rational obstacles begin to seem strangely flimsy. When neither high purpose nor the categorical imperatives of religion will do, the only argument against suicide is life itself. You pause and attend: the heart beats in your chest; outside, the trees are thick with new leaves, a swallow dips over them, the light moves, people are going about their business. Perhaps this is what Freud meant by "the narcissistic satisfactions [which the ego] derives from being alive." Most of the time, they seem enough. They are, anyway, all we ever have or can ever expect.

Yet such "satisfactions" can also be very fragile. A shift of focus in one's life, a sudden loss or separation, a single irreversible act can suffice to make the whole process intolerable. Perhaps this is what is implied by the phrase "suicide when the balance of mind was disturbed." It is, of course, a legal formula evolved to protect the dead man from the law and to spare the feelings and insurance benefits of his family. But it also has a certain existential truth: without the checks of belief, the balance between life and death can be perilously delicate.

Consider a climber poised on minute holds on a steep cliff. The smallness of the holds, the steepness of the angle, all add to his pleasure, provided he is in complete control. He is a man playing chess with his body; he can read the sequence of moves far enough in advance so that his physical economy—the ratio between the effort he uses and his reserves of strength—is never totally disrupted. The more improbable the situation and the greater the demands made on him, the more sweetly the blood flows later in release from all that tension. The possibility of danger serves merely to sharpen his awareness and control. And perhaps this is the rationale of all risky sports: you deliberately raise the ante of effort and concentration in order, as it were, to clear your mind of trivialities. It is a small-scale model for living, but with a difference: unlike your routine life, where mistakes can usually be recouped and some kind of compromise patched up, your actions, for however brief a period, are deadly serious.

I think there may be some people who kill themselves like this: in order to achieve a calm and control they never find in life. Antonin Artaud, who spent most of his life in lunatic asylums, once wrote:

> If I commit suicide, it will not be to destroy myself but to put myself back together again. Suicide will be for me only one means of violently reconquering myself, of brutally invading my being, of anticipating the unpredictable approaches of God. By suicide, I reintroduce my design in nature, I shall for the first time give things the shape of my will. I free myself from the conditioned reflexes of my organs, which are so

> badly adjusted to my inner self, and life is for me no longer an absurd accident whereby I think what I am told to think. But now I choose my thought and the direction of my faculties, my tendencies, my reality. I place myself between the beautiful and the hideous, the good and evil. I put myself in suspension, without innate propensities, neutral, in the state of equilibrium between good and evil solicitations.[6]

There is, I believe, a whole class of suicides, though infinitely less gifted than Artaud and less extreme in their perceptions, who take their own lives not in order to die but to escape confusion, to clear their heads. They deliberately use suicide to create an unencumbered reality for themselves or to break through the patterns of obsession and necessity which they have unwittingly imposed on their lives.[7] There are also others, similar but less despairing, for whom the mere idea of suicide is enough; they can continue to function efficiently, and even happily, provided they know they have their own, specially chosen means of escape always ready: a hidden cache of sleeping pills, a gun at the back of a drawer, like the wife in Lowell's poem who sleeps every night with her car key and ten dollars strapped to her thigh.

But there is also another, perhaps more numerous class of suicide to whom the *idea* of taking their own lives is utterly repugnant. These are the people who will do everything to destroy themselves except admit that that is what they are after; they will, that is, do everything except take the final responsibility for their actions. Hence all those cases of what Karl Menninger calls "chronic suicide"—the alcoholics and drug addicts who kill themselves slowly and piecemeal, all the while protesting that they are merely taking the necessary steps to make an intolerable life tolerable. Hence, too, those thousands of inexplicable fatal accidents—the good drivers who die in car crashes, the careful pedestrians who get themselves run over—which never make the suicide statistics. The image recurs of the same climber in the same unforgiving situation. In the grip of some depression he may not even recognize, he could die almost without knowing it. Impatiently, he fails to take the necessary safety measures; he climbs a little too fast and without working out his moves far enough in advance. And suddenly, the risks have become disproportionate. For a fatal accident, there is no longer need of any conscious thought or impulse of despair, still less a deliberate action. He has only to surrender for a moment to the darkness beneath the threshold. The smallest mistake—an impetuous move not quite in balance, an error of judgment which leaves him extended beyond his strength, with no way back and no prospect of relief—and the man will be dead without realizing that he wanted to die. "The victim lets himself act," said Valéry, "and his death escapes from him like a rash remark . . . He kills himself because it is too easy to kill himself."[8] Whence, I suppose, all those so-called "impetuous suicides" who, if they survive, claim never to have considered the act until moments before their attempt. Once recovered, they seem above all embarrassed, ashamed of what they have done, and unwilling to admit that they were ever genuinely suicidal. They can return to life, that is, only by denying the strength of their despair, transforming their unconscious but deliberate choice into an impulsive, meaningless mistake. They wanted to die without accepting the responsibility for their decision.

Every so often the opposite of all this occurs: there is a cult of suicide which has very little to do with real death. Thus early-nineteenth-century romanticism—as a pop phenomenon rather than as a serious creative movement—was dominated by the twin stars of Thomas Chatterton and Goethe's Young Werther. The ideal was "to cease upon the midnight with no pain" while still young and beautiful and full of promise. Suicide added a dimension of drama and doom, a fine black orchid to the already tropical jungle of the period's emotional life. One hundred years later a similar cult grew up around the *Inconnue de la Seine.* During the 1920s and early 1930s, all over the Continent, nearly every student of sensibility had a plaster cast of her death mask: a young, full, sweetly smiling face which seems less dead than peacefully sleeping.

The girl was in fact genuinely *inconnue.* All that is known of her is that she was fished out of the Seine and exposed on a block of ice in the Paris morgue, along with a couple of hundred other corpses awaiting identification. (On the evidence of her hair style, Sacheverell Sitwell believes this happened not later than the early 1880s.) She was never claimed, but someone was sufficiently impressed by her peaceful smile to take a death mask.

It is also possible that it never happened at all. In another version of the story a researcher, unable to obtain information at the Paris Morgue, followed her trail to the German source of the plaster casts. At the factory he met the *Inconnue* herself, alive and well and living in Hamburg, the daughter of the now-prosperous manufacturer of her image.

There is, however, no doubt at all about the cult around her. I am told that a whole generation of German girls modeled their looks on her.[9] She appears in appropriately aroused stories by Richard Le Gallienne, Jules Supervielle and Claire Goll, and oddly enough, since the author is a Communist, was the moving spirit behind the heroine of *Aurélian,* a long novel which Louis Aragon considers his masterpiece. But her fame was spread most effectively by a sickly though much-translated best seller, *One Unknown,* by Reinhold Conrad Muschler. He makes her an innocent young country girl who comes to Paris, falls in love with a handsome British diplomat—titled, of course—has a brief but idyllic romance and then, when milord regretfully leaves to marry his suitably aristocratic English fiancée, drowns herself in the Seine. As Muschler's sales show, this was the style of explanation the public wanted for that enigmatic, dead face.

The cult of the *Inconnue* seemed to attract young people between the two world wars in much the same way as drugs call them now: to opt out before they start, to give up a struggle that frightens them in a world they find distasteful, and to slide away into a deep inner dream. Death by drowning and blowing your mind with drugs amount, in fantasy, to the same thing: the sweetness, shadow and easy release of a successful regression. So the cult flourished in the absence of all facts, perhaps it even flourished because there were no facts. Like a Rorschach blot, the dead face was the receptacle for any feelings the onlooker wished to project into it. And like the Sphinx and the Mona Lisa, the power of the *Inconnue* was in her smile—subtle, oblivious, promising peace. Not only was she out of it all, beyond troubles, beyond responsibilities, she had also remained beautiful; she had retained the quality the young most fear to lose—their youth. Although Sitwell credits to her influence an epidemic of suicide among the young people of Evreux, I suspect she may have saved more lives than she destroyed. To know that it can be done, that the option really exists and is even becoming, is usually enough to relieve a mildly suicidal anxiety. In the end, the function of the romantic suicide cult is to be a focus for wandering melancholy; almost nobody actually dies.

The expression on the face of the *Inconnue* implies that her death was both easy and painless. These, I think, are the dual qualities, almost ideals, which distinguish modern suicide from that of the past. Robert Lowell once remarked that if there were some little switch in the arm which one could press in order to die immediately and without pain, then everyone would sooner or later commit suicide. It seems that we are rapidly moving toward that questionable ideal. The reason is not hard to find. Statistics, for what they are worth, show that in Great Britain, France, Germany and Japan there has been an enormous increase in death by drugs. In a brilliant essay entitled "Self-Poisoning," Dr. Neil Kessel has written:

> In every century before our own, poisons and drugs were dissimilar. Poisons were substances which should not be taken at all, the province not of physicians but of wizards. Their properties verged upon the magical. They were, indeed, "unctions bought of mountebanks." By the second half of the nineteenth century, science had displaced sorcery and poisons were purchased from the chemist, not the alchemist. But they still differed from drugs. Drugs, with few exceptions, though recognized to produce undesirable actions if taken in excess, were not considered lethal agents and were not used to kill. The growth of self-poisoning has come about in the train of a rapid rise in the number of highly dangerous preparations employed therapeutically, together with a great contemporaneous increase in prescribing.
>
> The effect of this medical resolution has been to make poisons both readily available and relatively safe. The way has thus been opened for self-poisoning to flourish . . . Facilities for self-poisoning have been placed within the reach of everyone.[10]

Along with the increase in suicide by drugs has gone a proportionate decrease in the older, more violent methods: hanging, drowning, shooting, cutting, jumping. What is involved, I think, is a massive and, in effect, a qualitative change in suicide. Ever since hemlock, for whatever obscure reason, went out of general use, the act has always entailed great physical violence. The Romans fell on their swords or, at best, cut their wrists in hot baths; even the fastidious Cleopatra allowed herself to be bitten by a snake. In the eighteenth century the kind of violence you used depended on the class you belonged to: gentlemen usually took their lives with pistols, the lower classes hanged themselves. Later it became fashionable to drown yourself, or endure the convulsions and agonies of cheap poisons like arsenic and strychnine. Perhaps the ancient, superstitious horror of suicide persisted so long because the violence made it impossible to disguise the nature of the act. Peace and oblivion were not in question; suicide was as unequivocally a violation of life as murder.

Modern drugs and domestic gas have changed all that. Not only have they made suicide more or less painless, they have also made it seem magical. A man who takes a knife and slices deliberately across his throat is murdering himself. But when someone lies down in front of an unlit gas oven or swallows sleeping pills, he seems not so much to be dying as merely seeking oblivion for a while. Dostoevsky's Kirillov said that there are only two reasons why we do not all kill ourselves: pain and the fear of the next world. We seem, more or less, to have got rid of both. In suicide, as in most other areas of activity, there has been a technological breakthrough which has made a cheap and relatively painless death democratically available to everyone. Perhaps this is why the subject now seems so central and so demanding, why even governments spend a little money on finding its causes and possible means of prevention. We already have a suicidology; all we mercifully lack, for the moment, is a thorough-going philosophical rationale of the act itself. No doubt it will come. But perhaps that is only as it should be in a period in which globle suicide by nuclear warfare is a permanent possibility.

Notes

1 See S. A. K. Strahan, *Suicide and Insanity* (London, 1893), p. 108.

2 See G. R. Fedden, *Suicide: A Social and Historical Study* (London: Peter Davies, 1938), p. 305.

3 A perfect example of a suicide which summed up a man's whole life and yearnings occurred in March 1970. A body was found jammed in a crevice one hundred feet down the sheer cliffs near Land's End. It was dressed in full "City gentleman's" uniform: pinstriped trousers, black jacket, polished shoes and bowler hat. Over the dead arm was a neatly rolled umbrella. The man, who carried no identification, was looking westward, out to sea. He had died from an overdose of sleeping pills. The police eventually discovered that he was a much Anglicized and Anglophile American who had lived and worked in London for a long time. His marriage had gone on the rocks and he had finally left his wife. He had chosen Land's End to die because that was the point nearest America. By jamming himself in the rock, he was able to gaze west toward the States until he lost consciousness.

Another, though less odd example is that of a young American climber, very gifted and graceful, who was badly depressed at breaking up with his girl. One Saturday morning he called on friends who lived near the Shawangunks, a popular outcrop north of New York City. He seemed quite relaxed and played in the garden with the friends' small children, of whom he had always been fond. Then he drove over to the cliffs, which are vertical and between two and three hundred feet high, and jumped off. Physical perfectionist to the last, he performed as he fell an immaculate swan dive.

4 "What undermined the Christian faith was not the atheism of the eighteenth century or the materialism of the nineteenth—their arguments are frequently vulgar and, for the most part, easily refutable by traditional theology—but rather the doubting concern with salvation of genuinely religious men [like Pascal and Kierkegaard], in whose eyes the traditional Christian content and promise had become 'absurd.' " (Hannah Arendt, *The Human Condition* [Chicago, 1958, and London, 1969–1959], p. 319.)

5 Mandelstam was, in fact, rearrested and died in a forced-labor camp somewhere in Siberia. Yet right up to the end he refused his wife's alternative: "Whenever I talked of suicide, M. used to say: 'Why hurry? The end is the same everywhere, and here they even hasten it for you.' Death was so much more real, and so much simpler than life, that we all involuntarily tried to prolong our earthly existence, even if only for a brief moment—just in case the next day brought some relief! In war, in the camps and during periods of terror, people think much less about death (let alone about suicide) than when they are living normal lives. Whenever at some point on earth mortal terror and the pressure of utterly insoluable problems are present in a particularly intense form, general questions about the nature of being recede into the background. How could we stand in awe before the forces of nature and the eternal laws of existence if terror of a mundane kind was felt so tangibly in everyday life? In a strange way, despite the horror of it, this also gave a certain richness to our lives. Who knows what happiness is? Perhaps it is better to talk in more concrete terms of the fullness or intensity of existence, and in this sense there may have been something more deeply satisfying in our desperate clinging to life than in what people generally strive for." (Nadezhda Mandelstam, *Hope Against Hope* [New York, 1970], p. 261.)

6 *Artaud Anthology*, ed. by Jack Hirschman (San Franciso, 1965, and Great Horwood, 1967), p. 56.

7 Perhaps the most famous example is that of the distinguished scholar who had worked for years on the definitive edition of one of the gloomier American novelists. Maybe the long, deadening grind and obsessional detail got to him in the end. Add to that the even deeper gloom of McCarthyism and vague hints of a private scandal. It doesn't matter. One afternoon he finally put all his papers in order, paid every bill to the last cent, wrote farewell letters to all his friends saying he was sorry, put out food and milk for his cat, packed an overnight case and carefully locked his apartment. Down in the street he mailed the letters—they would arrive too late—and then took a taxi downtown. He checked into a scruffy hotel and took a room on an upper floor. Every last meticulous detail had been attended to; he had added the final footnote to his own life. Then his whole obsessionally controlled, minutely organized universe exploded like a grenade. He hurled himself across the room and crashed through the window he hadn't even bothered to open. He burst, lacerated, into free space and smashed onto the sidewalk.

8 Paul Valéry, *Oeuvres* (Paris, 1962), Vol. II, pp. 610–11.

9 I owe this information to Hans Hesse of the University of Sussex. He suggests that the *Inconnue* became the erotic ideal of the period, as Bardot was for the 1950s. He thinks that German actresses like Elisabeth Bergner modeled themselves on her. She was finally displaced as a paradigm by Greta Garbo.

10 Neil Kessel, "Self-Poisoning," in E. Shneidman, (Ed.), *Suicidology: Contemporary Developments* (New York: Grune & Stratton, 1976), p. 346.

46• Suicide Among the Gifted

Edwin S. Shneidman

In this selection from the journal Life-Threatening Behavior, *Shneidman reports on a study in which a "blind analysis" was conducted of thirty cases—five suicides, ten natural deaths, and fifteen living persons. The analysis was conducted in terms of perturbation and lethality. The results indicated that suicide is a discernible part of a life-style and can be predicted in a person of fifty-five by the time that individual is thirty years old. Various psychodynamic hypotheses are offered to account for these findings.*

From Life-Threatening Behavior *Vol 1, No. 1, Spring 1971. Reprinted by permission.*

INTRODUCTION AND BACKGROUND

The two principal assertions in this paper are (a) that discernible early prodromal clues to adult suicide may be found in longitudinal case history data and (b) that it is useful to conceptualize these premonitory clues in terms of *perturbation* and *lethality.*

The data from which evidence for these assertions was obtained are those of the longitudinal study of 1,528 gifted people initiated by Lewis M. Terman in 1921.[1] Terman and his coworkers searched the public schools of the cities of California for exceptionally bright youngsters. His purposes were "to discover what gifted children are like as children, what sort of adult they become, and what some of the factors are that influence their development" (Oden, 1968). That study, begun over a half-century ago, continues to this day.

Of the original 1,528 subjects, 857 were males and 671 were females. The sample was composed of children (mean age 9.7 years) with Stanford-Binet IQs of 140 or higher—the mean IQ was over 150—and an older group of high school students (mean age 15.2 years) who scored within the top 1 percent on the Terman Group Test of Mental Ability. The present analysis will be limited to male subjects, of whom approximately 80 percent were born between 1905 and 1914.

An enormous amount of data has been collected. At the time of the original investigation in 1921–22, the information included a developmental record, health history, medical examination, home and family background, school history, character trait ratings and personality evaluations by parents and teachers, interest tests, school achievement tests, and the like. Subsequently, there has been a long series of systematic follow-ups by personal field visits: in 1924, 1925, 1936, 1940, 1945, 1950, 1955, and 1960. Another follow-up study is planned for the near future. In the field studies (1921, 1927, 1940, and 1950), subjects and their families were interviewed, and data from intelligence tests, personality tests, and questionnaires were obtained.

The Terman studies have catalyzed two generations of thought, research, attitudinal changes, and educational developments. Detailed descriptions of the subjects at various ages, as well as summaries of the important findings, are available in a series of publications authored by Professor Terman and his chief coworker, Melita Oden (Oden, 1968; Terman, 1925, 1940; Terman & Oden, 1947, 1959). Among longitudinal studies (Stone & Onque, 1959) the Terman Study is unique in many ways, including the extent to which its staff has continued to maintain contact with the subjects for over half a century. As of 1960, only 1.7 percent of the 1,528 subjects had been lost entirely.

Almost everyone in the psychological and pedagogical worlds now knows the basic findings of the Terman Study: that intellectually gifted children —far from being, as was once thought, spindly, weak, and maladjusted or one-sided—are, on the whole, more physically and mentally healthy and successful than their less-than gifted counterparts. An unusual mind, a vigorous body, and a well-adjusted personality are not incompatible.[2]

A mortality summary for the Terman gifted group is as follows: In 1960 —when the median age was 49.6—there had been 130 known deaths, 83 male and 47 female. The mortality rate was 9.8 percent for males and 7.2 percent for females—8.6 percent for the total group. According to Dublin's life tables (Dublin, Lotka, & Spiegelman, 1949), 13.9 percent of white males, 10.1 percent of white females, and 12 percent of a total cohort who survive to age eleven will have died before age fifty. In 1960, the figures indicated a favorable mortality rate in the Terman group lower than the general white population of the same age.

By 1960, 110 of the 130 Terman group deaths—61 percent—had been due to natural causes. (Cardiovascular diseases ranked first with males, and cancer was first among females.) Accidents accounted for nineteen male deaths, while only five females died in accidents. Five men had lost their lives in World War II. There were no homicide victims. One death was equivocal as to mode and could not be classified. As of 1960, suicide was responsible for fourteen male and eight female deaths; by 1970 there were twenty-eight known deaths by suicide—twenty men and eight women.

An inspection of the listing of suicidal deaths (table 1) suggested that there were several subgroups: student suicides, thirty- and forty-year suicides, and middle-age suicides. Among the twenty-eight suicides—of both sexes, ranging in age from eighteen to sixty-three (a forty-five-year span), year of death from 1928 to 1968 (forty years), using a variety of lethal methods (pills, poison, drowning, guns)—there was a subgroup of five persons—numbers 14 to 18—all of whom were male, Caucasian, with IQ's over 140, born about the same time (between 1907 and 1916), four of whom committed suicide within a year of each other (1965 or 1966), were in the "middle period" of their lives (ages at death forty-three, fifty, fifty-one, fifty-three, and fifty-eight), and used the same method (all gunshot). This special subgroup seemed to offer a unique opportunity for an especially intensive investigation.[3]

A listing of all those subjects who had died indicated that there were ten other males, born about the same time (1910 to 1914) as the five suicides, who had died of natural causes (either cancer or heart disease) during the same years that four of the five suicides had killed themselves (1965–66). The opportunity for a natural experiment, using blind analyses, was evident.

TABLE 1
THE TWENTY-EIGHT SUICIDES AS OF 1970

	Age at suicide	Year of birth	Year of suicide	Marital status	Education	Occupational level	Method of suicide
Men							
1.	18	1910	1928	S	High school	Student	Poison
2.	19	1916	1935	S	2 years college	V	Gunshot
3.	24	1908	1932	S	AB +	Graduate student	Drowning
4.	28·	1910	1938	S	MA	II	Poison
5.	33	1913	1946	M^2, D	High school	III	Barbiturate
6.	34	1913	1947	S	2 years college	III	Carbon monoxide
7.	35	1904	1939	S	Ph.D.	I	Gunshot
8.	37	1909	1946	M	1½ years college	II	Poison
9.	42	1905	1947	M	2 years college	II	Not known
10.	42	1916	1958	M^2, D^2	AB + 3 years	I	Barbiturate
11.	45	1911	1956	M	3 years college	II	Barbiturate
12.	45	1911	1956	M	AB, MA, LLB	IV	Carbon monoxide
13.	45	1913	1958	M	MD +	I	Poison
14.	43	1910	1953	M^4, D^4	2 years college	II	Gunshot
15.	50	1916	1965	M, D	BS	—	Gunshot
16.	51	1915	1966	M^2, D^2	High school	III	Gunshot
17.	53	1913	1966	M	LLB	I	Gunshot
18.	58	1907	1966	M^3, D^2	2 years college	I	Gunshot
19.	61	1905	1966	S	MA	I (retired)	Barbiturate
20.	63	1905	1968	M^2, D^1	Ph.D.	I	Barbiturate
Women							
1.	22	1914	1936	S	2 years college	Student	Gunshot
2.	30	1905	1935	S	AB	Librarian	Carbon monoxide
3.	30	1913	1943	M	2 years college	Housewife	Gunshot
4.	32	1917	1949	W	3 years college	Physical therapist	Barbiturate
5.	37	1916	1953	M^5, D^4	2 years college	Writer	Barbiturate
6.	40	1915	1955	M, D	3 years college	Housewife	Barbiturate
7.	44	1910	1954	M	MA	Housewife	Barbiturate
8.	44	1910	1954	M, D	BS	Social Worker	Barbiturate

I. Professional; II. Official, managerial, and semiprofessional; III. Retail business, clerical, sales, skilled trades, and kindred; IV. Agricultural and related; V. Minor business, minor clerical, and semiskilled occupations.

Thirty cases were selected to include the five suicides, the ten natural deaths, and fifteen individuals who were still alive. The latter two subgroups were matched with the five suicides in terms of age, occupational level, and father's occupational level. That these three subgroups are fairly well matched is indicated by the information in table 2. (The reader should keep in mind that all thirty subjects were male, Caucasian, Californian middle- and upper-middle-class, had IQ's over 140, and were members of the Terman Gifted Study.) Each folder was edited by Mrs. Oden so that I could not tell whether the individual was dead or still alive. (Death certificates, newspaper clippings, and other "death clues" were removed.) The cases came to me, one at a time, in a random order. Although I was "blind" as to the suicide-natural death-living identity of each case, I did know the total numbers of cases in each subgroup.

TABLE 2
OCCUPATIONS AND AGES FOR THE SUICIDE, NATURAL DEATH, AND LIVING SUBJECTS

	Suicide (N=5)	*Natural (N=10)*	*Living (N=15)*
Occupational level			
I — Professional	2	5	7
II — Official, managerial, semiprofessional	2	4	6
III — Retail business, clerical and sales, skilled trades	1	1	2
Fathers' occupational level			
I — Professional	–	2	5
II — Official, managerial, semiprofessional	4	6	6
III — Retail business, clerical and sales, skilled trades	–	1	4
IV — Agricultural and related occupations	–	–	–
V — Minor business or clerical and semiskilled	1	1	–
Year of birth			
1907	1	–	–
1908	–	–	–
1909	–	–	–
1910	1	1	3
1911	–	3	3
1912	1	1	4
1913	–	2	1
1914	–	3	3
1915	1	–	1
1916	1	–	–

RATING OF PERTURBATION (THE LIFE CHART)

The cases were analyzed in terms of two basic continua (by which every life can be rated): perturbation and lethality. Perturbation refers to how upset (disturbed, agitated, sane-insane, discomposed) the individual is—rated, let's say, on a 1 to 9 scale[4]—and the latter to how likely it is that he will take his own life. (Lethality is discussed in the next section below.) For each of the thirty cases a rough chart of the individual's perturbation in early childhood, adolescence, high school, college, early marriage, and middle life was made. Clues were sought relating to tranquility-disturbance especially evidences of any *changes* and variations in the levels of perturbation. An attempt was made to classify the materials under such headings as "Early prodromata," "Failures," and "Signatures"—each explained below.

A "life chart" was constructed for each case, roughly following the procedures developed by Adolf Meyer (1951, 1952). In each case the folders were examined more or less chronologically in an attempt to order the materials in a temporal sequence while keeping in mind a number of related skeins.

One example of perturbation (from an individual who turned out to be among the five homogeneous suicides): A high school counselor wrote about one young man that he was "emotionally unstable, a physical roamer and morally erratic, excellent to teachers who treat him as an adult but very disagreeable to others." At the same time, the home visitor wrote: "I like him tremendously; he is better company than many teachers." Ten years later the subject himself wrote: "My gifts, if there were any, seem to have been a flash in the pan."

Early prodromata

Under this category were included early important interpersonal relationships, especially with the subject's father and mother. The folder materials contained ratings by the subject of his attitudes and interactions with each of his parents. Some information relating to relationships with parents may be of special interest. In the 1940 questionnaire materials—when the modal age of the male subjects was 29.8 years—there was a series of questions concerning earlier conflict and attachment to mother and father. The responses of the five individuals who, as it turned out, made up the homogeneous suicide group seemed to have three interesting features: (a) in answer to the question "Everything considered, which was your favorite parent—father, mother, had no favorite?" only one of the five answered "father"; (b) in answer to the question about the amount of conflict between the individual and his father and the individual and his mother, two of the five indicated moderate to severe conflict with the mother; (c) the one suicide who was most obviously rejected by his father (and who indicated that he had had conflict with him) was the only one (of the five) to indicate that "there has been a person . . . who had had a profound influence on his life." He wrote: "My father, I think, has been responsible for a code of ethics stressing honesty and fair dealing in all relations." It was this man's father who insisted that he come into the family business and then called him stupid when he, for reasons of his own temperament, did not show the same amount of aptitude for business that his (less bright) older brother demonstrated.

In general, for the five suicidal subjects, for reasons that are not completely clear, it seemed that the relationships with the father were more critical than the relationships with the mother. It may be that any exceptionally bright, handsome young child tends to be mother's darling and, for those same reasons, tends to be father's rival—hence the built-in psychological tendency for there to be more friction between father and son than between mother and son. (It all sounds vaguely familiar: I believe that there is a Greek play about this theme.)

In the perusal of the records, evidence of trauma or stress in early life was sought: the death of a parent, divorce of the parents, stress (either overt or subtle) between the parents, or rejection of the subject by either parent. In retrospect, I had in mind a continuum ranging from tranquil and benign at one end to stressful and traumatic at the other.

The folder materials indicated that at the time the study began practically all of the subjects were described in essentially positive terms. For example, among the five subjects who, as it turned out, were the five homogeneous suicides, the following early descriptions by the home visitor appeared: "Attractive boy, well built, attractive features, charming." "Round chubby boy; very sweet face." "Winning little fellow, very fine all-around intelligence. The mother has excellent common sense and much is due to her." "Friendly, cheerful, freckled boy." "Tall for his age."

At the beginning, the psychological picture for most Terman youngsters was benign. However, in two of five homogeneous suicide cases there were, at an early age, already subtle prodromal clues of things to come: "He is the constant companion of his father but he is not his father's favorite." (A few years later, at age fourteen, a teacher wrote about this child: "This boy's parents are of two minds; his mother is for college, his father thinks that college is of no value to a person who expects to take up the business. The boy does not show very much hardmindedness. His type is more the theoretical, he prefers ideas to matter.") During the same year, his mother wrote that the child's worst faults were "his lack of application and irresponsibility"—perhaps not too unusual at age fourteen.

Another example: A child is ranked by his mother as "average" in the following traits: prudence, self-confidence, optimism, permanence of mood, egotism, and truthfulness. We do not know, of course, how much of this is accurate perception or how much is self-fulfilling prophecy.

Still another example: At age fourteen there is a series of letters from the head of his boarding school. (The parents were away on an extended trip.) The headmaster wrote letters having to do with the boy's veracity, perhaps revealing his own special emphases: "We have every hope of making him a straightforward young man. We are people he cannot bluff, and with consistent vigilance the boy will be able to overcome his difficulties." A few years later his mother wrote: "His success will depend a good deal on his associates."

Least successful

In Melita Oden's (1968) monograph she presented a number of measures and comparisons between the 100 Terman subjects ranked as most successful and an equal number adjudged to be least successful. For each of the thirty cases that I have analyzed, I tried to make some judgment along a success-failure continuum. In the end, eight cases were labeled as conspicuous successes and five cases as failures. As it turned out, none of those cases rated by me as "most successful" subsequently committed suicide, whereas three of the cases rated as "least successful" killed themselves.[5]

An example: a very bright young boy (IQ 180) who did very well in high school, both academically and in extracurricular activities. When he was fifteen years old Professor Terman wrote of him: "I think there is no doubt that he would make a desirable student at Stanford." Within a year, at age sixteen, he had entered Stanford and flunked out. Eventually, after working as a clerk, he returned to college after one year and graduated. He earned a law degree going to an evening law school. He then became an attorney in a large law firm. He was described as unsocial and shy. In his forties he says he was inclined to drink rather heavily, but not sufficiently to interfere with his work. His wife is described as vivacious and he as withdrawn. After a heart attack, his income suddenly became half of what he had been earning. He described himself as much less interested than his peers in vocational advancement or financial gain.

Signatures

In each case I looked for some special (albeit negative) indicators that might in themselves, or in combination, be prodromatic to suicide. For example, alcoholism, homosexuality, suicide threats, conspicuous achievement instability, depression, neurasthenia, and dyspnea could be listed. All five of the homogeneous suicides had one or more of these signature items. An additional eight (of the thirty cases) also had signature items. These items in themselves did not necessarily point to suicide, but when taken in combination with other features in the case they constituted an important aspect of the total prodromal picture.

Another example, this one emphasizing the lifelong instability of the individual: At age seven his mother wrote that "he is inclined to take the line of least resistance." At the same time, the teacher rated him high in desire to excel, general intelligence, and originality; average in prudence, generosity, and desire to know; and low in willpower, optimism, and truthfulness. She indicated that, though he came from a good home, he was inclined to be moody and sulky. At age eight his mother said he was strong-willed and liked to have his own way, that school was easy, and that he was making excellent grades. At age ten his parents divorced. At age twelve the teacher reported that he was not a very good student and was only doing fair work, that he had rather lazy mental habits. At age sixteen he graduated from high school with a C average. He did not attend college. In his twenties he became an artist. He was married. During World War II he was in the army. After the service he was unemployed and was described by his wife as "immature, unstable, irresponsible and extravagant." Because of his many affairs his wife, although stating she was fond of him, left him. She called him impulsive, romantic, and unstable. In his thirties he worked for a while as a commercial artist. He wrote to Professor Terman: "I am a lemon in your group." He indicated, as a joke, that his "hobby" was observing women from a bar stool. He remarried. He wrote to Professor Terman in relation to his art work that he "received much acclaim from those in the immediate audience," but that his works had not yet been displayed in any shows. His life was a series of ups and downs, some impulsive behaviors, and lifelong instability, although his status improved markedly in the late 1950s.

Apropos "up and downs" in general, any sudden *changes* in life status or life-style can be looked upon as suspicious (i.e., prodromal to suicide), especially a change which marks a decline of status, position, or income. Generally, in suicide prevention work, one views any recent changes in life-style as possible serious indicators of suicidal potential.

RATING OF LETHALITY (THE PSYCHOLOGICAL AUTOPSY)

In addition to the life chart, the second procedure employed was one that I had some years before labeled "the psychological autopsy." This procedure is a retrospective reconstruction of an individual's life that focuses on lethality, that is, those features of his life that illuminate his intentions in relation to his own death, clues as to the type of death it was, the degree (if any) of his participation in his own death, and why the death occurred at that time. In general, the main function of the psychological autopsy is to help clarify deaths that are equivocal as to the *mode* of death—usually to help coroners and medical examiners decide if the death (which may be clear enough as to cause of death, e.g., asphyxiation due to drowning or barbiturate overdose) was of an accidental or suicidal mode. Clearly, the *psychological* autopsy focuses on the role of the decedent in his own demise.

In the last few years, a number of individuals have written on this topic: Litman and his colleagues (Litman, Curphey, Shneidman, Farberow, & Tabachnick, 1963) have presented a general overview of its clinical use; Curphey (1961) has written of the use of this procedure from the medicolegal viewpoint of a forensic pathologist; and Weisman and Kastenbaum (1968) have applied this procedure to study the terminal phase of life. Elsewhere (Shneidman 1969b), I have indicated that three separate types (and uses) of the psychological autopsy can be discerned. Each is tied to answering a different primary question as follows: (a) why did the individual commit suicide? (b) why did the individual die at this time? and (c) what is the most accurate mode of death in this case? Given a death which is clear as to *cause* of death but which is equivocal as to *mode* of death, the purpose of this type of psychological autopsy is to clarify the situation so as to arrive at the most accurate or appropriate mode of death—what it "truly" was. This original use of the psychological autopsy grew out of the joint efforts of the Los Angeles County chief medical examiner-coroner (then Dr. Theodore J. Curphey) and the staff of the Los Angeles Suicide Prevention Center as an attempt to bring the skills of the behavioral sciences to bear relevantly on the problems of equivocal deaths. In those 10 percent of coroner's cases where the mode of death is questionable or equivocal, this equivocation usually lies between the modes of accident and suicide. Here are three simplified examples:

1. *Cause of death:* asphyxiation due to drowning. Woman found in her swimming pool. Question: did she "drown" (accident), or was it intentional (suicide)?
2. *Cause of death:* multiple crushing injuries. Man found at the foot of a tall building. Question: did he fall (accident), or did he jump (suicide)? Or, even, was he pushed or thrown (homicide)?
3. *Cause of death:* barbiturate intoxication due to overdose. Woman found in her bed. Question: would she be surprised to know that she was dead (accident), or is this what she had planned (suicide)?

An outline for a psychological autopsy is presented in table 3.

TABLE 3
OUTLINE FOR PSYCHOLOGICAL AUTOPSY

1. Identifying information for victim (name, age, address, marital status, religious practices, occupation, and other details)
2. Details of the death (including the cause or method and other pertinent details)
3. Brief outline of victim's history (siblings, marriage, medical illnesses, medical treatment, psychotherapy, previous suicide attempts)
4. "Death history" of victim's family (suicides, cancer, other fatal illnesses, ages at death, and other details)
5. Description of the personality and life-style of the victim
6. Victim's typical patterns of reaction to stress, emotional upsets, and periods of disequilibrium
7. Any recent—from last few days to last twelve months—upsets, pressures, tensions, or anticipations of trouble
8. Role of alcohol and drugs in (a) overall life style of victim and (b) in his death
9. Nature of victim's interpersonal relationships (including physicians)
10. Fantasies, dreams, thoughts, premonitions, or fears of victim relating to death, accident, or suicide
11. Changes in the victim before death (of habits, hobbies, eating, sexual patterns, and other life routines)
12. Information relating to the "life side" of victim (upswings, successes, plans)
13. Assessment of intention, i.e., role of the victim in his own demise
14. Rating of lethality
15. Reactions of informants to victim's death
16. Comments, special features, etc.

In the usual application of the psychological autopsy, the procedure is to interview close survivors (relatives and friends) of the decedent in order to reconstruct his role in his own death. In the present study, I was, of course, limited to an examination of folder materials.

All the criteria that have been discussed above—perturbation, including early prodromata, failure, and signatures—were combined into one judgment of that individual's lethality, that is, the probability of his committing suicide in the present or the immediate future. In this process of judgment I was guided by two additional governing concepts: (a) the key role of the significant other and (b) the concept of a partial death (or chronic suicide or "burned out" life).

The crucial role of the significant other

In an adult who is suicide prone, the behavior of the significant other, specifically the wife, seems either lifesaving or suicidogenic. My reading of the cases led me to feel that the wife could be the difference between life and death. In general, a wife who was hostile, independent, competitive, or nonsupporting of her husband who had some of the suicidal prodromata seemed to doom him to a suicidal outcome, whereas a wife who was helpful, emotionally supportive, and actively ancillary seemed to save a man who, in my clinical judgment at least, might otherwise have killed himself.

To the extent that these global clinical impressions of the important role of the spouse, in some cases, are correct, then, in those cases, there is an equal implication for suicide prevention, specifically that one must deal actively with the significant other. A regimen of therapy or a program of education must not fail to include the spouse; indeed it might be focused primarily on the spouse and only secondarily on the potential suicide victim. Of course, the conscious and unconscious attitudes of the wife toward her husband must be carefully assessed. In a situation where the wife is deeply competitive (and might unconsciously wish him dead), using her as an auxiliary therapist would at best be an uphill climb. It is possible that in some cases a separation might be a lifesaving suggestion. All the above is not to impugn the wife; rather it is to involve her appropriately. It could very well be that, had the study focused on female suicides, the above prescription would be in relation to the complementary role of the husband.

The concept of a partial death

This concept is well known in suicidology. In the technical literature it was given its most well known presentation by Karl Menninger (1938) in *Man against Himself.* On valid psychological grounds it denies the dichotomous nature of psychological death and asserts that there are some lives that are moieties and only partial existences. Henry Murray (1967) expands this theme in his paper "Dead to the World":

> When I chose the phrase "dead to the world," I was thinking of a variety of somewhat similar psychic states characterized by a marked diminution or near-cessation of affect involving both hemispheres of concern, the inner and the outer world. Here it is as if the person's primal springs of vitality had dried up, as if he were empty or hollow at the very core of his being. There is a striking absence of anything but the most perfunctory and superficial social interactions; output as well as intake is at a minimum . . .

> I have been talking about a diminution or cessation of feeling, one component of consciousness, on the assumption that this condition is somewhat analogous to a cessation of the whole of consciousness. If the cessation of feeling is temporary it resembles sleep; if it is permanent (a virtual atrophy of emotional life) it resembles death, the condition of the brain and body after the home fires of metabolism in the cortex have gone out. In a feelingless state the home fires are still burning but without glow or warmth.

That last statement about the home fires burning led me to think of a "burned out" person—a person whose whole life was a kind of chronic suicide, a living death, a life without ambition and seemingly without purpose.

In the lethality ratings of the thirty cases, those that gave me the greatest difficulty were the chronic, nonachieving, "partial death" lives. I decided that I would rate this type of person among the first twelve in lethality, but not among the first five. I did this with the conviction that this very style of living was in itself a kind of substitute for overt suicide; that in these cases, the *raison d'être* for committing overt suicide was absent, in that the truncated life itself was the significant inimical act (Shneidman, 1963).

RESULTS OF BLIND CLINICAL ANALYSES

On the day that I completed the blind analysis of the thirtieth case I wrote a memorandum to Professor Sears that included the following:

> My analysis of the data and possibly the data themselves do not permit me to state with anything like full confidence which five cases were suicidal. The best that I can do—from my subjective ratings of each individual's perturbation and lethality—is to rank order eleven of the cases as the most likely candidates for suicidal status. I should be somewhat surprised if any of the other nineteen individuals committed suicide. The rank order for suicide potential is as follows . . .

Then we—Mrs. Oden, Mrs. Buckholtz, and I—met to "break the key."

The facts revealed that the individual whom I had ranked as number 1 had, in fact, committed suicide, my number 2 had committed suicide, number 3 was living, number 4 had committed suicide, number 5 had committed suicide, and number 6 had committed suicide. Numbers 7 and 9 were living; numbers 8, 10, and 11 had died natural deaths. For the statistical record, the probability of choosing four or five of the five suicide cases correctly by chance alone is 1 out of 1,131—significant at the .000884 level. Obviously, the null hypothesis that there are no discernible prodromal clues to suicide can be discarded with a fair degree of confidence.

Table 4 presents a summary of the blind analysis data in terms of a brief vignette, signature items, success-failure ratings, perturbation ratings, lethality ratings, and suicide probability ranking for all thirty subjects. (The "Postscript" information was not available to me when I made these ratings and was added to the chart after all the other ratings and rankings had been made.)

Much of my analysis of these thirty cases was inferential, sometimes even intuitive—which is to say that not every clue or cognitive maneuver can be recovered, much less communicated. But for what it is worth, I deeply believe that a number of experienced professional persons could have done as well. Indeed, I feel that the volumes of information generated in the past twenty years by suicidologists furnish the working concepts and the background facts for making precisely this kind of (potentially lifesaving) judgment every day of the year in the practical clinical situation. Knowledge of this sort is now an established part of the new discipline of suicidology.

One striking result was that among those who committed suicide in their fifties, the pattern of life consistent with this outcome seemed clearly discernible *by the time they were in their late twenties.* The data subsequent to age thirty served, in most cases, primarily to strengthen the impression of suicidal outcome that I had formulated at that point. Those relatively few cases in which this earlier impression was reversed in the thirties and forties had one or two specific noteworthy elements within them: (a) a psychologically supporting spouse or (b) a "burning out" of the individual's drive and affect. In the latter cases, this condition of psychological aridity and successlessness seemed to be the price for continued life.

What were some of the main clinical impressions relating to adult suicide in this gifted male group? In the briefest possible vignette, my main overall clinical impression might be formulated in this way: the *father*, even in his absence, *starts* the life course to suicide; *school and work* (and the feelings of inferiority and chronic low-grade hopelessness) *exacerbate* it; and the *wife* can, in some cases, effect the *rescue* from it (or otherwise play a sustaining or even a precipitating role in it).

Among the five homogeneous suicides, three types of suicidal prodromata—relating to instability, trauma, and control—could be differentiated.

Instability

In general, suicide is more likely to occur in a life where there has been instability (rather than stability). As used here, instability is practically synonymous with perturbation.

Chronic instability Evidences of chronic, long-term instability would include neuropsychiatric hospitalization, talk or threat of suicide, alcoholism, multiple divorces, and any unusually stressful psychodynamic background—even though these bits of evidence occurred in as few as one of the five cases. Examples: Mr. A: NP hospitalization, divorce, talk of suicide at 15 and at 20; Mr. B: unstable personality, divorced, flighty behavior, few stabilizing forces; Mr. C: unhappy man, rejected by father, always second-best, four marriages, highly perturbed.

TABLE 4

BLIND RATINGS AND OUTCOMES FOR THIRTY MATCHED MALE SUBJECTS

No.	*Notable characteristics*	*Signatures*	*Life success*	*Perturbation*	*Lethality*	*Suicide rank*	*Postscript*
1	NP hospitalization; divorced; great perturbation: talks of suicide at 15 and 20	Suicide threats	C-	7-8	High	1	Committed suicide
2	Deaf; professional; low drive for worldly success	Nonachiever	C	3-4	Low	12+	Living
3	Flunked out of college; obtained LLB; shy; ups and downs; drop in income; alcohol	Alcohol; ups and downs	C	6-7	High	2	Committed suicide
4	Insurance man in heart attack rut	–	B	3-4	Low	12+	Died—heart
5	Ambitious bank officer	–	B	3-4	Low	12+	Died—cancer
6	Brilliant professor of medicine; textbook author; good life	–	A	1-2	Low	12+	Died—cancer
7	Set back at adolescence by home stresses; obese; no college aspirations; withdrawn; low-level job; underachiever; stabilized	Underachiever; stabilized	C-	6-7	?	11	Died—heart
8	Physician; too high standards for people; tones down	–	B+	5-6	Low	12+	Died—heart
9	Hard-driving rancher; dominated by mother	–	B	5-6	Low	12+	Died—cancer
10	Stable geologist; steady life	–	A	1-2	Low	12+	Living
11	Lithographer; brilliant; no family back-up; underachiever	Underachiever	C	5-6	Low	12+	Living
12	Multimarried, emphysemic; inventor; ups and downs	Dyspnea; failure	C	6-7	High	4	Committed suicide
13	Scion of business fortune; straight success line; father helpful and supportive	–	A	4-5	Low	12+	Living
14	Quietly successful in own small business; tranquil life	–	B	3-4	Low	12+	Living
15	Had all advantages; did rather well but not superlatively	–	B	3-4	Low	12+	Living
16	Neurasthenic; esoteric mother; underachiever; chronic suicide	Depression; neurasthenia	C-	6-7	?	7	Living

17	Artist; unstable; flighty; impetuous; willful	Instability	B-	7-8	?	5	Committed suicide
18	Insurance man; stable life; interesting siblings	–	B	3-4	Low	12+	Living
19	Brilliant child and siblings; needed a father; stabilized by second wife	–	B	4-5	Low	12+	Living
20	Pleasant man; pleasant life; pleasant family; likes work	–	B	2-3	Low	12+	Living
21	Early genius; hiatus; never fully recovers; wife commits suicide	–	B	5-6	Mdn	12+	Died—heart
22	Shy, depressed artist; multiple illnesses; making it	Depression; ill	B	6-7	?	9	Living
23	Unhappy; forced into father's business; rejected by father; always second to sibling 4 divorces; unstable; downhill; alone	Depression; instability	B+	7-8	?	6	Committed suicide
24	Average school administrator; ordinary stresses	–	B	4-5	Low	12+	Living
25	Well-adjusted, stable attorney; great relationship with father; good life success	–	A	2-3	Low	12+	Living
26	Depressed engineer; hypomanic wife; his job holds him	Depression	B	6-7	Mdn+	8	Died—cancer
27	Scientist; brilliant beginning; wife drains him; good but not great	–	B+	3-4	Low	12+	Living
28	Engineer; overcame adolescent crisis and parents' divorce; good marriage; has grown steadily	–	B	4-5	Low	12+	Died—heart
29	Author; asthmatic; depressed; strong support from wife	Dyspnea; depression	A-	5-6	?	10	Died—cancer
30	Professional; stormy life; alcoholic; competing wife	Alcohol; instability	B-	6-7	?	3	Living

Recent downhill course A recent downhill change that occurs in a career marked by ups and downs, that is, a generally unstable life course, was characteristic of suicidal persons. Specifically, these changes include a marked sudden decrease in income, sudden acute alcoholism, a change in work, and divorce or separation, especially where the wife leaves the husband for another man. In general, a sudden, inexplicable change for the worse is a bad augury. This means that in an individual with an up-and-down history, the most recent bit of information can be singularly irrelevant, if not outright misleading. Examples: Mr. D: highly recommended for university, flunked out of college, went back to school, earned an LL. B. degree, shy, alcoholic, sudden drop in income, up and down course, does not "burn out"; Mr. E: inventor, multiple marriages, up and down course, severe emphysema. (N.B., dyspnea can be an especially incapacitating symptom and has been related to suicide in special ways [Farberow, McKelligott, Cohen, & Darbonne, 1966].)

Trauma

Early childhood or adolescent trauma Examples would include acute rejection by one or both parents, lack of family psychological support, and separation or divorce of the parents. A crisis in adolescence can turn a life toward lower achievement.

Adult trauma This includes poor health, such as asthma, emphysema, severe neurosis, obesity, and multiple illnesses. Another major type of adult trauma relates to the spouse, either rejection by the wife for another man or being married to a hyperactive (and competing) wife, who has changed from the woman he married. Examples: Mr. F, a depressed engineer whose top security job in aerospace holds him together; and Mr. G, who has a complicated, hypomanic, and successful wife toward whom he is deeply ambivalent.

Controls

Outer controls These are the compensations or stabilizing influences in individuals who, without these assets from other than within themselves, would be more perturbed than they are and might commit suicide. Examples: the stabilizing work of Mr. F, mentioned above; the stabilizing wife of asthmatic Mr. H, a woman who nurses him and keeps the world from inappropriately intruding upon him or exhausting him. She husbands his limited energies.

Inner controls These inner controls are not the usual strengths or positive features or assets of personality or character. They are the negative inner controls of default. One such is what occurs in some individuals who are perturbed early in their lives, who, if they survive, stabilize or simmer down or "burn out" in their fifties or sixties.

Examples: Mr. J: He was psychologically traumatized during adolescence by home stresses. He has no hobbies, no college aspirations, is withdrawn, and works as a mechanic and caretaker. Mr. K: Extremely high IQ. He is neurasthenic, has a mother with esoteric tastes, experiences back and shoulder pains just like his father, and is unable to hold a job as a professional. He calls himself "an unsuccessful animal." He ends up working as a clerk in a large company. His stance is that—to use an example from Melville—of a contemporary Bartleby ("I prefer not to"), what Menninger (1938) has called a "chronic suicide," where the truncated life itself can be conceptualized as a partial death.

DISCUSSION

Whereas the clinical challenge is to be intuitive, to display diagnostic acumen, and to manifest therapeutic skill, the scientific challenge is to state theory and to explicate facts in a replicable way. I feel obligated to address myself to the theoretical side of this issue.

I shall begin with low-level theory, that is, an explication of the specific items that guided my thinking in choosing the individuals whom I believed had committed suicide. Some ten items were in my mind: (1) early (grammar school, adolescence, or college age) evidences of instability, including dishonesty; (2) rejection by the father; (3) multiple marriages; (4) alcoholism; (5) an unstable occupational history; (6) ups and downs in income; (7) a crippling physical disability, especially one involving dyspnea; (8) disappointment in the use of one's potential, that is, a disparity between aspiration and accomplishment; (9) any talk or hint of self-destruction; and (10) a competitive or self-absorbed spouse. In summary, this low-level theoretical explication states that a bright male Caucasian who committed suicide in his fifties was apt to be: rejected by his father, adolescently disturbed, multimarried, alcoholic, occasionally unsettled or unsuccessful, disappointed in himself and disappointing to others, unstable, lonely, and perturbed with a penchant for precipitous action.

At a somewhat deeper level, and thus more theoretical, are the elements of rejection, disparity between aspiration and accomplishment, instability, and perturbation. At a still deeper level (and even more theoretical) is the notion that the suicidal person is one who believes that he has not had his father's love and seeks it symbolically without success throughout his life, eventually hoping, magically, to gain it by a singular act of sacrifice or expiation. The most theoretical formulation might be stated as follows: those gifted men who committed suicide in their fifties did not have that internalized viable approving parental homunculus that—like a strong heart—seems necessary for a long life.

It is interesting to reflect that the five gifted suicidal persons of this study constituted an essentially nonpsychotic group. This assertion is not to gainsay that each of them was severely perturbed at the time of the suicide, but they were not "crazy"; that is, they did not manifest the classical hallmarks of psychosis such as hallucinations, delusions, dereistic thinking, and the like.

Their perturbation took the form—prior to the overt suicidal act—of alcoholism, other than one marriage (single, divorced, or multiple marriages), and chronic loneliness, occupational ups and downs, impetuosity and impulsivity, and inner (as well as overt) agitation. Although, as it is in most suicidal persons, one can suppose that their thought processes were circumscribed ("tunnel vision") and tended to be dichotomous ("either a happy life or death"), there was no direct evidence to indicate that they were psychotically bizarre or paleological (Shneidman, 1969a).

As has been noted by Oden (1968), the "magic combination" for life success among the gifted is not a simple one. For suicide also the equation is a combination of obvious and subtle elements. Many factors, none of which alone seems to be sufficient, appear to coexist in a suicidal case. And, as in any equation, there are factors on both the positive (life-loving, biophilic, suicide-inhibiting) and the negative (death-loving, necrophilic, suicide-promoting) sides.

In the algebra of life and death, the wife may play an absolutely vital role, holding her spouse to life or, at the worst, stimulating or even provoking him to suicide. Every suicidologist knows that suicide is most often a two-person event, a dyadic occurrence, and for this reason, if no other, the management and prevention of suicide almost always has to involve the significant other. With high suicide risk gifted males, my impression is that the most important lifesaving task is not directly to the potentially suicidal person, but through the wife—especially in concert with the family physician.

Currently, there is a small number of retrospective studies seeking to establish some of the early precursors of suicide among special populations presumed to be intellectually superior, specifically physicians and university graduates. A few words about each.

Blachly and his colleagues (Blachly, Disher, & Roduner, 1968) have made an analysis of 249 suicides by physicians reported in the obituary columns of the *Journal of the American Medical Association* between May 1965 and November 1967. Deaths from suicide exceeded the combined deaths from automobile accidents, airplane crashes, drowning, and homicide. The mean age of the suicidal group was forty-nine. Blachly and his associates mailed questionnaires to the next of kin (usually the widow); about 30 percent of the inquiries were returned, many with extensive comments. The suicide rate varied greatly among the medical specialties, ranging from a low of 10 per 100,000 among pediatricians to a high of 61 per 100,000 among psychiatrists. A résumé of Blachly's main findings is presented in table 5.

Paffenbarger and his associates (Paffenbarger & Asnes, 1966; Paffenbarger, King, & Wing, 1969) have completed analyses of over 50,000 medical and social histories (including physical and psychological evaluations) of former male students at the University of Pennsylvania and at Harvard covering a thirty-four-year period from 1916 to 1950. Their original focus was on individuals who subsequently died of coronary heart disease. The data drew their attention to those who had committed suicide—whom they then compared with their nonsuicidal cohorts. The 4,000 known deaths included 225 suicide deaths. Their findings relative to suicide point to paternal depri-

TABLE 5

SUMMARY OF FINDINGS OF THREE STUDIES OF PRECURSORS OF SUICIDE

*Present clinical impressions**	*Blachly's tabular results*	*Paffenbarger's statistical findings*
a. early (before 20) evidences of instability, including dishonesty	a. mentally depressed or disturbed	a. college education of father
b. actual or felt rejection by the father	b. prior suicidal attempt or statement of suicidal intent	b. college education of mother
c. multiple marriages	c. heavy drinker or alcoholic	c. father professional
d. alcoholism	d. drug addiction or heavy drug user	d. father died
e. an unstable occupational history	e. "inadequate" financial status	e. parents separated
f. ups and downs in income (not to mention ups and downs in mood)	f. death of close relative in decedent's childhood	f. cigarette smoker in college
g. a crippling physical disability, especially one involving dyspnea	g. suicide of relative	g. attended boarding school
h. disappointment in the use of potential, i.e., a disparity between aspiration and accomplishment	h. seriously impaired physical health	h. college dropout
i. any talk or hint of self-destruction		i. nonjoiner in college
j. a competitive or self-absorbed spouse		j. allergies
		k. underweight
		l. self-assessed ill health
		m. self-consciousness
		n. subject to worries
		o. feelings of being watched or talked about
		p. insomnia
		q. secretive-seclusiveness
		r. "anxiety-depression" index (including nervousness, moodiness, exhaustion, etc.)

*Of course, not all of these features occurred in any suicidal case; conversely, some of these features occurred in as few as one suicidal case. It was the "total impression" that counted most.

vation through early loss or death of the father, loneliness and underjoining in college, dropping out of college, and feelings of rejection, self-consciousness, and failure during the college years.

Dr. Caroline Thomas (1969)—like Paffenbarger, a cardiologist—studied the causes of death among 1,337 former medical students of the Johns Hopkins University School of Medicine from 1948 to 1964. Her project—as did Paffenbarger's—began as a study of the precursors of coronary heart disease but, in light of the data (fourteen suicides among the thirty-one premature deaths shifted to include precursors of suicide.

What may be of especial interest in table 5 are the common elements or threads in the findings of these three projects and the clinical findings of this present study. To what extent these findings relate only to the intellectually superior and to what extent they are ubiquitous is a matter for further study; nonetheless it is not premature to say that, on the basis of currently known data, it would appear that the common findings would seem to have general application.

Notes

1 This study was conducted while the author was a Fellow at the Center for Advanced Study in the Behavioral Sciences, 1969-70. Arrangements were made for confidential access to the research records by Professor Robert R. Sears who, with Professor Lee J. Cronbach, is one of the two scientific executors of the Terman Study. The data themselves are the property of Stanford University. The author is especially grateful to Mrs. Melita Oden and Mrs. Sheila Buckholtz, long-time staff members of the Gifted Study, for their extensive help in preparing relevant data for his use and for advice and guidance along the way.

2 As part of the Terman Study of the Gifted, Catharine M. Cox (1926) completed a comprehensive retrospective study of the childhood intelligence of 301 historically eminent men born after 1450. Of the individuals discussed in her study, 119 were thought to have I.Q.'s of 140 or higher. (As examples, here are some names—1 person in each of the five-step I.Q. intervals from 140 to 190: Carlyle, Jefferson, Descartes, Hume, Pope, J. Q. Adams, Voltaire, Schelling, Pascal, Leibnitz, and J. S. Mill.) As to suicide among this extraordinary group, so far as can be ascertained, only 1 of the 301 eminent men died by killing himself—Thomas Chatterton, at age 17.

3 In the technical literature on suicide, one does not find many anamnestic or case history reports for individuals who have *committed* suicide. (Materials for attempted suicides are another story; the data for them are far more plentiful.) Only four sources—spread over a half-century—come to mind: Ruth Cavan's (1928, pp.198–248) extensive diaries of two young adults, Binswanger's (1958) detailed report of 33-year-old Ellen West, Kobler and Stotland's (1964, pp. 98–251) extensive reports of four hospitalized patients—ages 23, 34, 37, and 56—in a "dying hospital," all of whom committed suicide within the same month, and Alvarez' (1961) annotated bibliography.

4 The following point must be strongly emphasized: a basic assumption in this entire scheme is that an individual's orientations toward his cessation are biphasic; that is, any adult, at any given moment, has (a) more or less long-range, relatively chronic, pervasive, habitual, characterological orientations toward cessation as an integral part of his total psychological makeup (affecting his philosophy of life, need systems, aspirations, identification, conscious beliefs, etc.); and (b) is also capable of having acute, relatively short-lived, exacerbated, clinically sudden shifts of cessation orientation. Indeed, this is what is usually meant when

one says that an individual has become "suicidal." It is therefore crucial in any complete assessment of an individual's orientation toward cessation to know both his habitual *and* his at-that-moment orientations toward cessation. (Failure to do this is one reason why previous efforts to relate "suicidal state" with psychological test results have been barren.)

5 Among the twenty men who committed suicide, at least three were considered outstandingly successful by gifted group standards: two in the 1960 study and one who died in 1938 who had a brilliant record until his death at the age of twenty-eight. Conversely, three were considered least successful: two in 1940 (they had died before 1960) and one in the 1960 evaluation (Oden, 1968).

References

Alvarez, W. C. *Minds That Came Back.* Philadelphia: Lippincott, 1961.

Binswanger, L. The Case of Ellen West. In R. May, E. Angel, & H. F. Ellenberger (Eds.), *Existence.* New York: Basic Books, 1958. Pp.237–364.

Blachly, P. H., Disher, W., & Roduner, G. Suicide by Physicians. *Bulletin of Suicidology.* December 1968, 1–18.

Cavan, R. S. *Suicide.* Chicago: University of Chicago Press, 1928.

Cox, C. M. The Early Mental Traits of Three Hundred Geniuses. *Genetic Studies of Genius.* Vol. 2. Stanford: Stanford University Press, 1926.

Curphey, T. J. The Role of the Social Scientist in the Medicolegal Certification of Death from Suicide. In N. L. Farberow & E. S. Shneidman (Eds.), *The Cry for Help.* New York: McGraw-Hill, 1961.

Dublin, L. I., Lotka, A. J., & Spiegelman, M. *Length of Life.* New York: Ronald Press, 1949.

Farberow, N. L., McKelligott, W., Cohen, S., & Darbonne, A. Suicide among Patients with Cardiorespiratory Illnesses. *Journal of the American Medical Association,* 1966, 195, 422–28.

Kobler, A., & Stotland, E. *The End of Hope.* New York: Free Press of Glencoe, 1964.

Litman, R. E., Curphey, T. J., Shneidman, E. S., Farberow, N. L., & Tabachnick, N. D. Investigations of Equivocal Suicides. *Journal of the American Medical Association,* 1963, 184, 924–29.

Menninger, K. A. *Man against Himself.* New York: Harcourt, Brace, 1938.

Meyer, A. The Life Chart and the Obligation of Specifying Positive Data in Psychopathological Diagnosis. Reprinted in E. E. Winters (Ed.), *The Collected Works of Adolf Meyer.* Vol. 3. Baltimore: Johns Hopkins Press, 1951. Pp. 52–56.

Meyer, A. Mental and Moral Health in a Constructive School Program. Reprinted in E. E. Winters (Ed.), *The Collected Works of Adolf Meyer.* Vol. 4. Baltimore: Johns Hopkins Press, 1952. Pp. 350–70.

Murray, H. A. Dead to the World: The Passions of Herman Melville. In E. S. Shneidman (Ed.), *Essays in Self-Destruction.* New York: Science House, 1967.

Oden, M. H. The Fulfillment of Promise: 40-year Follow-Up of the Terman Gifted Group. *Genetic Psychology Monographs,* 1968, 77, 3–93.

Paffenbarger, R. S., Jr., & Asnes, D. P. Chronic Disease in Former College Students. III. Precursors of Suicide in Early and Middle Life. *American Journal of Public Health,* 1966, 56, 1026–36.

Paffenbarger, R. S., Jr., King, S. H., & Wing, A. L. Chronic Disease in Former College Students. IX. Characteristics in Youth that Predispose to Suicide and Accidental Death in Later Life. *American Journal of Public Health,* 1969, 59, 900–908.

Shneidman, E. S. Orientations toward Death: A Vital Aspect of the Study of Lives. In R. W. White (Ed.), *The Study of Lives.* New York: Atherton Press, 1963. Reprinted, with discussion, in *International Journal of Psychiatry,* 1966, 2, 167–200; and in Shneidman, E. S., Farberow, N. L., & Litman, R. E., *The Psychology of Suicide.* New York: Science House, 1970.

Shneidman, E. S. Logical Content Analysis: An Explication of Styles of "Concludifying." In G. Gerbner et al. (Eds.), *The Analysis of Communication Content.* New York: John Wiley & Sons, 1969(a).

Shneidman, E. S. Suicide, Lethality and the Psychological Autopsy. In E. S. Shneidman & M. J. Ortega (Eds.), *Aspects of Depression.* Boston: Little, Brown & Co., 1969(b).

Stone, A. A., & Onque, G. C. *Longitudinal Studies of Child Personality.* Cambridge: Harvard University Press, 1959.

Terman, L. M. *Genetic Studies of Genius: I. Mental and Physical Traits of a Thousand Gifted Children.* Stanford: Stanford University Press, 1925.

Terman, L. M. Psychological Approaches to the Biography of Genius. *Science,* October 4, 1940, 92, 293–301.

Terman, L. M., & Oden, M. H. *Genetic Studies of Genius: IV. The Gifted Child Grows Up.* Stanford: Stanford University Press, 1947.

Terman, L. M , & Oden, M. H. *Genetic Studies of Genius: V. The Gifted Child at Mid-Life.* Stanford: Stanford University Press, 1959.

Thomas, C. B. Suicide among Us: Can We Learn to Prevent It? *Johns Hopkins Medical Journal,* 1969, 125, 276–85.

Weisman, A. D., & Kastenbaum, R. The Psychological Autopsy: A Study of the Terminal Phase of Life. *Community Mental Health Journal Monograph,* 1968, 4, 1–59.

Self-Destruction: Suicide Notes and Tragic Lives

Edwin S. Shneidman

In this selection, a theory about the importance and usefulness of suicide notes is developed. Three positions are outlined. The first (called the thesis) is that suicide notes—written as they are in the context of the deed itself—are, by themselves, the royal road to the understanding of suicidal phenomena; the second (called the antithesis) is that suicide notes—written as they are in a state of psychological constriction—cannot, by themselves, be useful psychological documents; and the third position (the synthesis) is that suicide notes, when placed within the context of a detailed case history of that same person—of which they are obviously a part—can, in many useful ways, illuminate the case history just as the details of the case history can illuminate the note itself.

There is probably no description of suicide that contains as much insight in as few words as that found in the opening paragraph of *Moby Dick:* ". . . a damp, drizzly November in my soul." In its essence, that is what most suicide is: a dreary and dismal wintry storm within the mind, where staying afloat or going under is the vital decision being debated. In about one fourth of these occasions where a suicide is going to be committed, the individual will write something about that debate. Those documents—suicide notes—have something of the fascination of a cobra: they catch our eyes, yet we are ever conscious that some serious threat may lurk in them.

Suicide notes are cryptic maps of ill-advised journeys. A suicide note, no matter how persuasive it seems within its own closed world, is not a model for conducting a life. When one examines suicide notes, one can only shudder to read these testimonials to tortuous life journeys that came to wrecked ends. They fascinate us for what they tell us about the human condition and what they warn us against in ourselves.

My own long-term sustained study of them is admittedly a somewhat arcane pursuit. It would be like someone's contemporary fascination with alchemy, phlogiston, or the inheritance of acquired characteristics, or with the notion that the world is flat, or that the earth is the center of the universe, or the proof that Bacon really wrote Shakespeare's plays—all flawed ideas. The difference that may make my obsession with suicide notes seem legitimate is that I know that suicide notes—like the many schizophrenic diaries I have read—are flawed documents. I have never read a suicide note that I would want to have written.

But what can we actually learn about suicide from suicide notes? In the last twenty-five years, my answers to this question have undergone some radical changes. I have held three different positions on the relationship of suicide notes to suicidal phenomena.

My original view on the value of suicide notes dates from that special day in 1949 when I unexpectedly came across several hundred suicide notes in the vaults of a coroner's office. Since then, almost without a flagging of interest, I have been fascinated with suicide notes as perhaps the best available way of understanding suicidal phenomena. I believed that it was possible to unlock the mysteries of suicidal phenomena by using suicide notes as the keys. When one addresses the question: "Why do people take this trip?" (i.e., commit suicide), one can reasonably look upon suicide notes as psychological data and search them for clues as to how the tragic outcome of that life's voyage might have been averted. It would seem that suicide notes, written as they are in the very context of the suicidal act, often within a few minutes of the death-producing deed, would offer a special window into the thinking and the feeling of the act itself. In no other segment of human behavior is there such a close relationship of document to deed.

My subsequent counterreaction to that view was a (somewhat exaggerated) jump to an almost opposite position. In that position I believed that suicide notes, written as they were by individuals in a state of psychological constriction and of truncated and narrowed thinking, could hardly ever—by virtue of the state in which they were composed—be illuminating or even important psychological documents. Admittedly, that point of view had a touch of "overkill" in it.

I now believe that suicide notes, by themselves, are uniformly neither bountiful nor banal, but that they definitely can have a great deal of meaning under certain circumstances, specifically when they are put into the context of the detailed life history of the individual who both wrote the note and committed the act. In those instances—where we have both the suicide note and an extended life history—the note will then illuminate many aspects of the life history, and conversely, the life history can make many key words of the note come alive and take on special meanings that would otherwise have remained hidden or lost. My present view is thus an amalgamation of my two previous views.

To readers who know their philosophy, this process will remind them of the ideas of the German philosopher Georg Wilhelm Friedrich Hegel. Hegel believed that all thought and development of ideas proceeded in a certain way. Specifically, the process begins with an affirmation of an idea (which he called the "thesis"), then it gives way to its opposite (the "antithesis"), and then the two are united by a new idea which combines them (the "synthesis"). This process (which may take minutes or years or decades or centuries), repeated over and over, endlessly, Hegel called the "dialectic." (This idea influenced Friedrich Engels and Karl Marx in their "dialectical materialism.") What has happened over the last quarter century in relation to my own thoughts about suicide notes has unconsciously mirrored some aspects of this basic dialectical process and might be called a "dialectical suicidology."

I

The findings of many previous investigations over the past century—starting with Brierre de Boismont's systematic study in 1856—have been extraordinarily diverse and diffuse. As a whole, these studies of suicide notes tell us that the suicidal person—specifically as compared with the nonsuicidal person—is likely to think in terms of dichotomous logic, separating everything in his world into two mutually exclusive categories (like perfect and nothing, life and death), and to be constricted and focused in his suicidal thinking; to think in terms of specific instructions (as opposed to broad or philosophic generalizations), writing to his survivors-to-be as though he were going to be alive to supervise his wishes; to avoid intellectualizing (i.e., to avoid thinking about how he is thinking), dealing more with raw feeling than with rational thought; to be concerned with blaming, both others (the expression of hostility) and oneself (the expression of guilt or shame); and to be concerned with love—the various aspects, nuances, and shading of affection, affiliation, devotion, and either romantic or erotic love.

The figures vary as to the percentage of individuals who commit suicide who also leave suicide notes, ranging from 15 percent to over 30 percent. Who, among those who commit suicide, writes suicide notes? Except for knowing that note writers and non-note writers are essentially similar in terms of all the major demographic variables—age, race, sex, employment status, marital status, physical condition, history of mental illness, place of suicide and history of previous suicidal attempts—we know very little about the psychology of suicide-note writing. The distinguished suicidologist Erwin Stengel, in his scholarly book *Suicide and Attempted Suicide,* said: "Whether the writers of suicide notes differ in their attitudes from those who leave no notes behind, it is impossible to say. Possibly they differ from tne majority only in being good correspondents." That sounds like as reasonable an explanation as any.

Studies of suicide notes have dispelled at least one myth about suicide: that suicidal acts are uniformly motivated by a single formula. Of course, no one commits suicide who is not, in some way and to some heightened extent, intellectually or emotionally distraught, but these perturbations can take the form of the passions of unrequited love, intellectual self-assertion, shame and guilt related to disgrace, the wish to escape from the pain of insanity, the wish to spare loved ones from further anguish, and a sense of inner pride and autonomy connected to one's own fate and the manner of one's own death. All these psychological trends, and more, are found in suicide notes.

Suicidal acts are very complicated psychological events—never mind their social, sociological, or anthropological components. "Just" from a psychological point of view, there are many underlying, resonating, and sustaining causes (together with a multiplicity of precipitating events) that come together in each suicidal event. Nevertheless, we occasionally find a suicide note in which one particular emotional state will figure so clearly that it will seem to characterize (or at least to dominate) that particular suicidal act. In these cases we are almost beguiled into believing that this single emotion was the sole (if not the primary) cause of the act itself. Here are some examples.

Hate

In the now famous meeting of Freud and others in Vienna in 1910—the only meeting of the psychoanalytic group specifically on the topic of suicide —Wilhelm Stekel enunciated what was to become the orthodox psychoanalytic view. He said: "No one kills himself except as he wishes the death of another."[1] Suicide was seen by the early psychoanalysts primarily as hostility directed toward the ambivalently viewed loved person who had been introjected into one's own unconscious mind—what I have called "murder in the 180th degree."

It is certainly not difficult to find evidence of hostility in contemporary suicide notes that would seem to support this hypothesis. The following hate note is from a most unusual set of suicide notes. Between 1934—the year after Fiorello La Guardia became mayor of New York City and began to reform the police department—and 1940, in a half-dozen years, ninety-three New York City policemen committed suicide. (Only two papers have been written about this strange epidemic.)[2] Among these ninety-three police suicides, nineteen left suicide notes. Here is one of the shortest and one of the angriest, written by a thirty-seven-year-old patrolman who was in a bar waiting for his sergeant, whom he had planned to kill. After a long wait, he wrote this hate-laden note and then shot himself.

> To whom concerned: Goodbye you old prick and when I mean prick you are a prick. Hope you fall with the rest of us, you yellow bastard. May the precinct get along without you.

Love

Currently, most suicidologists believe that suicide is not motivated by hostility alone, but that there are many other emotional states—such as dependency, shame, guilt, fear, despair, frustration, loss of autonomy and especially feelings of hopelessness and helplessness—that can be the basic psychological ingredients of suicide. Love, especially frustrated love, seems to play as great a role in as many cases of suicide as does hate. A young man of thirty-five wrote the following contemporary note:

> My Darling, To love you as I do and live without you is more than I can bear. I love you so completely, wholeheartedly without restraint. I worship you, that is my fault . . . Without you life is unbearable. This is the best way. This will solve all our problems. . . . If it is possible to love in the hereafter, I will love you even after death. God have mercy on both our souls. He alone knows my heartache and love for you.

Here is a love suicide note from a European woman of the last century who was the daughter of a very famous man. Consider in the following brief suicide note by Eleanor Marx,[3] the youngest of Karl Marx's three daughters

—whose sister also committed suicide—the complicated and overladen meanings of the word "love." One needs to keep in mind her tremendously complicated and psychologically tortured relationship with her famous father. For example, she did not learn until she was an adult that her father had had an illegitmate son by one of the dear friends of the family—and she immediately had to make a close psychological relationship with that person. Also keep in mind that her suicide note is addressed to her lover of several years, an unpredictable person who had had numerous affairs with other women, which she tolerated because she loved him. But there was a last straw which broke her heart. This man, Edward Aveling, had, without telling her, secretly married another woman. For Eleanor, that was the ultimate betrayal and rejection. Her note reads:

> Dear, It will soon be over. My last word to you is the same that I have said during all these long, sad years—love.

She drank prussic acid in her apartment. It is unclear today whether Aveling arranged for her to have the poison or whether there was a suicide pact, from which he fled. What is clear is the ambiguity of that key word, "love." It can be read to mean bitterness, regret, accusation, disappointment, tenderness, nostalgia, impotent rage, or helplessness at being duped or traduced.

An important key to suicide is to recognize that its cause is neither love nor hate; rather, it is the simultaneous presence of *both* of them as well as other emotions. This state of being able to experience contradictory emotions at the same time toward the same person, called *ambivalence*, is illustrated in this short suicide note:

Dear Betty:
I hate you.
Love,
George

Shame and disgrace

Some suicides seem to be related particularly to a sense of shame, "loss of face," disgrace or a sense of dereliction of duty. Prideful people especially seem vulnerable to these emotions. An example is the suicide of Dr. Paul Kammerer, an eminent Viennese biologist. His experiments with alytes, the midwife toad (called that because the male toad wraps the fertilized eggs around his legs and carries them until they are hatched), attempted to prove the inheritance of certain acquired characteristics, specifically friction (or nuptial) pads on the front paws of the male toad, which helped him hold the female during mating. He had done fifteen years of very careful work, breeding and observing these toads, when it was discovered that injections of India ink had been made into the paws of the demonstration specimens, thus producing false results. Although it is not known whether he, or a laboratory assistant attempting to be helpful, did the forging, Kammerer was a ruined man.

In the woods near Vienna, in 1926, six weeks after he was accused, Kammerer shot himself through the head. Here is a translation of the suicide note found beside his body:

> Letter to whosoever finds it:
>
> Dr. Paul Kammerer begs not to be brought to his home so that his family might be spared the sight. It would be the simplest and cheapest way to use the body in a dissecting laboratory of a university. This would also be most agreeable to me since, in this way, I would render science at least a small service. Perhaps my esteemed colleagues will discover in my brain a trace of the qualities they found absent in the expressions of my intellectual activities while I was alive. Whatever happens to the corpse—burial, cremation or dissection—its owner belonged to no religious denomination and wishes to be spared any kind of religious ceremony which would probably be refused to him in any event. This is not animosity against any individual priest who is as human as the rest of us and often a good and noble person.[4]

There are several interesting details in this lugubrious document. The sense of shame, repentance and restitution are evident. His attitude toward himself as already a corpse is striking, but his inability to see himself as dead—Freud had written that no one can truly imagine his own death, but always remained a spectator—is seen in the contradiction that he does not care what happens to the corpse, but that he (the living man? the corpse? and if the corpse, what difference does it make?) wishes to be spared a religious ceremony. And there is a sense of counteraction: he rejects others before they reject him, as in his phrase ". . . which would probably be refused to him in any event."

And what is not in the note: statements of affection and wishes for forgiveness from his family, warmth, love. The note is largely a set of instructions: to the person who finds his body, to the pathologist who dissects his brain and to the priest who may or may not be good enough to conduct a tender ceremony. Finally, one can also infer that on an unconscious level, he views himself as a kind of priest of science who is as human as anyone and is really a good and noble person.

It seems to make most sense to view Kammerer's suicidal act as an overwhelming concatenation, in a disturbed individual, of several emotional surges in addition to the overarching shame: anxiety, anger, depression, hopelessness, guilt, rejection; in other words, heightened general perturbation. All suicidal deaths are complicated events, but Kammerer's suicide seems more complex and more mysterious than most.

Fear—specifically of recurring insanity

Occasionally we find a suicide note that is rational in its irrationality, reflecting an act that we regret but nonetheless can understand. Virginia Woolf drowned herself in a small river, the Ouse, near her home in Sussex, England. She was a gifted woman, a literary celebrity, author of several novels in her special style emphasizing the flow of consciousness. She was also an editor, the founder, with her husband, of the Hogarth Press (which, among other famous books, printed Freud's works in English) and a key member of the so-called Bloomsbury group—a veritable who's who of creative individuals all concerned with the search for things good, true and beautiful.

In short, she was the hub of a radiant literary-philosophic wheel. But with all this, she still suffered—whether from genes or psychodynamics one cannot tell—crippling periods of mental incapacitation. In anyone, especially in a mature intellect, one of the most awesome fears is the niggling threat of losing one's hold on reality, of losing one's mind or going crazy. In 1941, these symptoms or presentiments began to reappear in Virginia Woolf. What they foreboded was simply too much for her to contemplate enduring, for herself and others. Here is her suicide note, addressed to her husband of almost thirty years:

> Dearest,
>
> I feel certain I am going mad again. I feel we can't go through another of those terrible times. And I shan't recover this time. I begin to hear voices, and I can't concentrate. So I am doing what seems the best thing to do. You have been in every way all that anyone could be. I don't think two people could have been happier till this terrible disease came. I can't fight any longer. I know that I am spoiling your life, that without me you could work. And I know you will. You see I can't even write this properly. I can't read. What I want to say is that I owe all the happiness of my life to you. You have been entirely patient with me and incredibly good. I want to say that—everybody knows it. If anybody could have saved me it would have been you. Everything has gone from me but the certainty of your goodness. I can't go on spoiling your life any longer.
>
> I don't think two people could have been happier than we have been.[5]

That note is both fearful and tender. She cannot bring herself to live through another period of psychosis, and more than that, she does not wish to burden her dear husband. The note, beginning with the reason for her desperate act, is then filled with feelings of hopelessness, concern, gratitude, and love. The negative emotions are sparked by the desperation relating to her fears of her imminent madness. A significant part of that kind of malady is the inability to share one's secret terror—itself a symptom of the disturbed state of mind—with those who might have been the rescuers.

Traumatic rejection and self-abnegation

The sense of total rejection, in a personality that already deprecates itself, is often a root cause of self-destruction. The cast of characters in the following tragedy is as complicated as it is well known. Fanny Imlay, later Fanny Imlay Godwin, had a star-crossed life seemingly from the moment she was conceived. Her genealogy is a bit complicated but bears careful tracing. She was born in 1794, the illegitimate daughter of Mary Wollstonecraft, who was a famous feminist—the author of *The Rights of Women*—and of an American Revolutionary War captain named Imlay. Her mother then married William Godwin, a famous pamphleteer and political philosopher and novelist (he wrote *Caleb Williams*), and died a few days after having given birth to Fanny's half-sister, Mary Wollstonecraft Godwin (later the author of *Frankenstein*), who became the second wife of the poet Percy Bysshe Shelley. Thus Fanny was Shelley's half-sister-in-law—and in love with him. All her short life she was the odd one: illegitimate, half orphaned, excluded from the excitement of her half-sister's life, unnoticed or rejected by the beautiful Shelley, unemployed because of her famous but unsavory relatives, and living with the legacy of her own mother's suicide attempt when she was a young woman. In 1816, at age twenty-two, Fanny Godwin poisoned herself in an inn at an English seaside resort. This is her suicide note:

> I have long determined that the best thing I could do was to put an end to the existence of a being whose birth was unfortunate and whose life has only been a series of pains to those persons who have hurt their health in endeavoring to promote her welfare. Perhaps to hear of my death may give you pain, but you will soon have the blessing of forgetting that such a creature ever existed.[6]

The key words in this painful note are "being" and "creature." She is not a woman or a person or a human; she is just a biological thing that never should have been born. This is a note filled with nothingness; an overpowering sense of void and worthlessness. And to her mind, without love to fill that void, she might as well be dead.

In 1817, the year after Fanny's suicide, Shelley wrote a poem entitled "On Fanny Godwin."

> Her voice did quiver as we parted,
> Yet knew I not the heart was broken
> From which it came, and I departed
> Heeding not the words then spoken.
> Misery—O Misery,
> This world is all too wide for thee.

"Credo" suicide notes

Some few suicide notes are written as creeds. They are essays about suicide itself, specifically about a man's moral and legal right to take his own life if he so chooses. The most famous piece of "credo" suicidal writing is not contained in a suicide note but in the essay "On Suicide" by the eighteenth-century Scottish philosopher David Hume. So controversial was it considered that it was not published until a year after his death.

In his essay, Hume—who died a natural death (apparently of cancer) at age sixty-five—sought to decriminalize suicide. In current terms, he might say that where the victim is oneself, it is an act within a consenting adult, and thus there is, in either the legal or the moral sense, no victim. Hume asserted that suicide is no crime; that there is no culprit; and certainly, there is no sin.

Elton Hammond was an English eccentric who committed suicide at age thirty-three in 1819. Hammond was on the fringe of the literary life of eighteenth-century England.[7] He was somewhat peculiar, perhaps even insane. (He once announced to his sister that he was going to be greater than Jesus Christ.) But the main point here is not Hammond's mental health, but the clear way in which, in his suicide note, he stated a man's right to ownership of himself. It is an anticlerical antiauthoritarian credo.

It is likely that a man like Hammond would have known of Hume's essay. The similarities in thought and language between the two documents strongly suggest this possibility. But Hammond goes Hume one better; he is not only writing about his beliefs about suicide, he is putting his life where his mind is. Here is his suicide note.

TO THE CORONER AND THE GENTLEMEN
WHO WILL SIT ON MY BODY

Norwood, 31st Decr. 1819.

Gentlemen,

To the charge of self-murder I plead not guilty. For there is no guilt in what I have done. Self-murder is a contradiction in terms. If the king who retires from his throne is guilty of high treason; if the man who takes money out of his own coffers and spends it is a thief; if he who burns his own hayrick is guilty of arson; or he who scourges himself of assault and battery, then he who throws up his own life may be guilty of murder,—if not, not.

If anything is a man's own, it is surely his life. Far, however, be it from me to say that a man may do as he pleases with his own. Of all that he has he is a steward. Kingdoms, money, harvests, are held in trust, and so, but I think less strictly, is life itself. Life is rather the stewardship than the talent. The king who resigns his crown to one less fit to rule is guilty, though not of high treason; . . . the suicide who could have performed the duties of his station is perhaps guilty, though not of murder, not of felony. They are all guilty of neglect of duty, and all, except the suicide, of breach of trust. But I cannot perform the duties of my station. He who wastes his life in idleness is guilty of a breach of trust; he who puts an end to it resigns his trust—a trust that was forced upon him,—a trust which I never accepted, and probably never would have accepted. Is this felony? I smile at the ridiculous supposition. How we came by the foolish law which considers suicide as felony I don't know; I find no warrant for it in philosophy or scripture.

I would rather be thrown naked into a hole in the road than that you should act against your consciences. But if you wish to acquit me, I cannot see your calling my death accidental, or the effect of insanity, would be less criminal than a jury's finding a £10 Bank of England note worth thirty-nine shillings, or premeditated slaying in a duel simple manslaughter, both of which have been done. But should you think this is too bold a course, is it less bold to find me guilty of *felo de se* when I am not guilty at all, as there is no guilt in what I have done? I disdain to take advantage of my situation as culprit to mislead your understandings, but if you, in your consciences, think premeditated suicide no felony, will you, upon your oaths, convict me of felony? Let me suggest the following verdict, as combining liberal truth with justice:—"Died by his own hand, but not feloniously." If I have offended God, it is for God, not you, to enquire. . . . I am free today, and avail myself of my liberty. I cannot be a good man, and prefer death to being a bad one—as bad as I have been and as others are.

I take my leave of you and of my country condemning you all, yet with true honest love. . . . God bless you all!

Elton

As a footnote to this suicide document, it is sad to relate that the coroner's jury did not accede to Hammond's request; they rendered a verdict of suicide by virtue of insanity—exactly what Hammond did not wish. (But this was done, in part, because Hammond's friend Henry Crabb Robinson did not turn over Hammond's letter to the jury, hoping, perhaps, to save his reputation.)

II

We have raised the question: What can we learn from suicide notes? Obviously, they often contain a great deal of interesting descriptive material, particularly of emotional states. But are they the full and explicating documents that would satisfactorily "explain" a suicide? The fact that a dozen and a half research studies by a score of qualified investigators over the past twenty years have *not* produced the new, important breakthroughs of information that one could legitimately expect from that amount of effort raises questions about their usefulness.

Overall, one might say that suicide notes are relatively barren compared with what we had hoped to find in them.[8] It seems as though we tend to confuse the drama of the suicidal situation with our own expectations that there be some dramatic psychodynamic insights in the communications written during the moments of that drama. But the fact remains that memorable (authenticated) words uttered *during* battle or *on* one's deathbed are rare. It seems to be true also of suicide notes. Understandably, however, we continue to hope that even an ordinary individual, standing on the brink of what man has always conceptualized as life's greatest adventure and mystery, ought to have some special message for the rest of us. Western civilization has for centuries romanticized death; we tend to read with special reverence and awe *any* words, however banal, that are part of a death-oriented document.

Perhaps suicide notes, by themselves, cannot be what we wanted them to be—for the plain and simple reason that they are written by a person whose mind (by virtue of being suicidal) is usually tunneled, overfocused, constricted, and narrowed on a single goal.

A tragically precise and insightful description of tunneling and constriction is contained in the verbalization of the young woman who jumped from a balcony.

> . . . I went into a terrible state. . . . I was so desperate . . . That's the *only* way to get away from it. The *only* way to lose consciousness. . . . everything just got very dark all of a sudden, and *all* I could see was this balcony. Everything around it just *blacked out*. It was just like a *circle*. That was *all* I could see, just the balcony . . . and I went over it. . . . [Italics added.]

As we read these chilling words we can practically visualize the constriction of her mind's focus, almost as the diaphragm of a fine camera closes down to its essential linear circle. And while this is happening, the mind's lens is adjusting to sharpen the focus on but a single objective. The objective is escape, specifically escape from intolerable emotion. It is at that precise moment of maximum constriction and focus that the picture is snapped; it is at that same moment when, as it were, the mind snaps and the act occurs.

Several suicidologists and literary writers have commented on the role of constriction in suicide. Margarethe von Andics[9] wrote a book about suicide (one hundred suicide attempts in Vienna in the 1940s) in which she emphasized the narrowing of the scope of consciousness that was characteristic of the suicidal state; Erwin Ringel, also of Vienna, has written extensively, since 1958, of what he calls the presuicidal syndrome, placing great emphasis on constriction.[10]

The contemporary English poet, novelist and critic A. Alvarez, who wrote an excellent book on suicide, *The Savage God*, has described what he calls "the closed world of suicide" in the following way:

> Once a man decides to take his own life he enters a shut-off, impregnable but wholly convincing world . . . where every detail fits and every incident reinforces his decision. . . . Each of these deaths has its own inner logic and unrepeatable despair. . . . [Suicide is] a terrible but utterly natural reaction to the strained, narrow, unnatural necessities we sometimes create for ourselves.[11]

Boris Pasternak, the famous author, writing of the suicide of several young Russian poets, has stated:

> A man who decides to commit suicide puts a full stop to his being, he turns his back on his past, he declares himself bankrupt and his memories to be unreal. They can no longer help or save him, he has put himself beyond their reach. The continuity of his inner life is broken, and his personality is at an end. And perhaps what finally makes him kill himself is not the firmness of his resolve but the unbearable quality of this anguish which belongs to no one, of this suffering in the absence of the sufferer, of this waiting which is empty because life is stopped and can no longer feel it.[12]

Because this sense of constriction exists in the suicidal person, is it any wonder that suicide notes, written at the very moment when an individual has lost touch with his own past, are taken up with minutiae and are in other ways relatively arid and psychologically barren?

Thus we see the relative barrenness of many—but not all—suicide notes can be psychologically explained. In order for a person to kill himself, he has to be in a special state of mind, a state of relatively fixed purposes (not to deny an ever-present ambivalence) and of relative constriction of the mind. It is a psychological state that, while it permits (indeed, facilitates) suicide, obviously militates against good insight or good communication. In other words, that special state of mind necessary to perform the suicidal deed is one which is essentially incompatible with an insightful recitation of what was going on in one's mind that led to the act itself. Suicide notes often seem like parodies of the postcards sent home from the Grand Canyon, the catacombs, or the pyramids—essentially *pro forma,* not at all reflecting the grandeur of the scene being described or the depth of human emotions that one might expect to be engendered by the situation.

To state the case strongly: In order to commit suicide, one cannot write a meaningful suicide note; conversely, if one could write a meaningful note, one would not have to commit suicide. Or to put it in another way: In almost every instance, one has to be relatively intoxicated or drugged (by one's overpowering emotions and constricted logic and perception) in order to commit suicide, and it is well nigh impossible to write a psychologically meaningful document when one is in this disordered state.

Suicide notes, *by themselves,* may not tell us everything we want to know. Life is like a long letter and the suicide note is merely a postscript to it and cannot, by itself be expected to carry the burden of substituting for the total document.

III

There is a vital reciprocity between suicide notes and the lives of which they are a part. This statement—my current position—is the synthesis of my two previous attitudes: the thesis that suicide notes by themselves are uniformly bountiful; and the antithesis that suicide notes have to be constricted and pedestrian documents. Suicide notes definitely can have a great deal of meaning (and give a great deal of information) when they are put in the context of the life history of the individual who both wrote the note and committed the act. In this situation—where we have *both* the suicide note and a *detailed* life history—then the note will illuminate aspects of the life history, and conversely, the life history can make many key words and ideas of the suicide note come alive and take on special meanings that would otherwise have remained hidden or lost. It is close to the art of biography.

Here are five suicide notes written by one woman (who committed suicide by barbiturate overdose) and many details of her life, to which these notes were but the final words.

In this case—Natalie, who killed herself at age forty—there were, in addition to her suicide notes, literally hundreds of separate personal documents and other records. They included the following: Early school records, teachers' notes to her parents, school physicians' reports, school evaluations, college records, several psychological tests, numerous questionnaires which she had completed, dozens of her letters and miscellaneous personal documents by the score. In all, there were over one hundred separate documents, including her suicide notes. (It took me many months to find them.)

We begin at the tragic end, with excerpts from the police report of her death:

> On arrival, went through house into bathroom where victim was observed lying on the floor, head resting on a pillow, toward the west, feet pointed toward the east. Victim was dressed in a green bathrobe; was cold to the touch, rigor mortis having started to set in. On the pillow it was noted there was a stain, caused by a purge from the victim's mouth. Photographs of the scene were taken.
>
> There was one small brown bottle with the label bearing prescription number and "One capsule at bed time . . ." This bottle was empty. Also a small plastic container was received with the label inside the cover reading "One tablet 4 times daily, regularly . . ." This container was also empty.
>
> Undersigned spoke to [name and address], who stated he was victim's father. He further said that approximately two weeks ago, victim told him that she was going to commit suicide. He said he talked her out of the notion at that time, and did not figure she would make any further attempt on her life. He further said victim had been in ill health since her divorce and had been treated by a psychiatrist, address unknown; also that the victim had filed a will which is currently in the possession of her attorney.
>
> While at location, victim's husband, [name], who gave address same as victim's, employed at Eastern Steel Corp., arrived and stated he would take care of his two children, Betty, fifteen years; and Nancy, ten years.

The investigating officer reported finding five suicide notes. I have made a few changes in identifying details:

1. To her adult friend:

   Rosalyn—Get Eastern Steel Co.—Tell them and they will find Bob right away. Papa is at his business. Betty is at the Smiths—Would you ask Helene to keep her until her Daddy comes—so she won't know until he comes for her. You have been so good—I love you—Please keep in touch with Betty—Natalie

2. To her eldest daughter:

   Betty, go over to Rosalyn's right away—Get in touch with Papa.

3. To her ex-husband, from whom she was recently divorced:

   Bob—I'm making all kinds of mistakes with our girls—They have to have a leader and everyday the job seems more enormous—You couldn't have been a better Daddy to Nancy and they do love you—Nancy misses you so and she doesn't know what's the matter—I know you've built a whole new life for yourself but make room for the girls and keep them with you—Take them where you go—It's only for just a few years—Betty is almost ready to stand on her own two feet—But Nancy needs you desperately. Nancy needs help—She really thinks you didn't love her—and she's got to be made to do her part for her own self-respect—Nancy hasn't been hurt much yet—but ah! the future if they keep on the way I've been going lately—Barbara sounds warm and friendly and relaxed and I pray to God she will understand just a little and be good to my girls—They need two happy people—not a sick mixed-up mother—There will be a little money to help with the extras—It had better go that way than for more pills and more doctor bills—I wish to God it had been different but be happy—but please—stay by your girls—And just one thing—be kind to Papa [*his* father]—He's done everything he could to try to help me—He loves the girls dearly and it's right that they should see him often—Natalie

   Bob—this afternoon Betty and Nancy had such a horrible fight it scares me. Do you suppose Gladys and Orville would take Betty for this school year? She should be away from Nancy for a little while—in a calm atmosphere.

4. To her ex-father-in-law:

   Papa—no one could have been more kind or generous than you have been to me—I know you couldn't understand this—and forgive me—[The lawyer] has a copy of my will—Everything equal—the few personal things I have of value—the bracelet to

Nancy and my wedding ring to Betty—But I would like Betty to have Nana's diamond—have them appraised and give Betty and Nancy each half the diamonds in the band. Please have somebody come in and clean—Have Bob take the girls away immediately—I don't want them to have to stay around—You're so good Papa dear—

5. To her two children:

My dearest ones—You two have been the most wonderful things in my life—Try to forgive me for what I've done—Your father would be so much better for you. It will be harder for you for awhile—but so much easier in the long run—I'm getting you all mixed up—Respect and love are almost the same—Remember that—and the most important thing is to respect yourself—The only way you can do that is by doing your share and learning to stand on your own two feet—Betty, try to remember the happy times—and be good to Nancy. Promise me you will look after your sister's welfare—I love you very much—but I can't face what the future will bring.

A number of sad observations can be made about these suicide notes. The despairing writer of them seems so pushed, so weary, so harried, so beaten by life. She has capitulated. Not atypically, the notes—especially the first two—contain directions, words like "get," "ask," "tell," "go." The disposition of affection is curious: It can be seen in different forms of the salutation and the complimentary close. The only use of "dear" or "dearest" is with her children and her ex-father-in-law. Words of love are reserved only for her neighbor-friend and for her children. There is no note to either of her living parents, both of whom resided nearby.

Her note to her ex-husband is a painful *mea culpa*. She takes all blame and pleads to him—a man who drank quite a bit and was impossible for her to live with—to be good to their children. In an amazing turnabout, she asks that the new stepmother and her ex-husband provide a stable home for her girls.

Her life can be retraced from the available materials. The conditions of her birth were noted as "absolutely normal." She was breast fed until she was two months old. As an infant, she slept soundly.

At the age of five and a half she was given dancing lessons. There is a note that she was very enthusiastic and showed decided ability. When Natalie was six, her mother wrote to a friend that "Edgar Guest's poems are her great favorites." In that same letter, the mother wrote: "I have tried to use a lot of common sense and have answered every question to the best of my ability because she is an understanding child and will listen to reason. I have not had to stimulate a desire to learn because she always wanted to know everything her older playmates knew and she would try to learn voluntarily."

She had a brother, who was eight years older than she. Later she would say about him that "he could never make a living."

When Natalie was six years old, in the first grade, she was given an individual intelligence test. One item that she missed—although she scored extremely high overall, with an IQ of over 153, which put her in the extremely superior category—was this one: "Yesterday the police found the body of a girl cut into eighteen pieces. They believed that she killed herself. What is foolish about that?" Her nonprophetic answer was "She wouldn't kill herself." The psychologist noted, however, her general alertness and her extremely logical mind.

A very important event occurred in Natalie's life when she was seven: her father deserted her mother. Later in her life, she noted, with obvious sadness, that *"My father never came to see me except once."*

The records of her childhood medical examinations are interesting. One, written by a school physician when she was eight, states that she was "somewhat nervous, bordering on irritability," and that she had some loss of hearing in her right ear. A school record when she was eleven notes that her last name had been changed to reflect the fact that her mother had divorced and remarried. The teacher's report states that she was a "youngster with an understanding and reasoning little mind that at times surprises her family" and that "her courtesy and tact are remarkable."

At age twelve there are several items of interest. She suffered from numerous headaches and had glasses prescribed. She reported that she still had disburbing eye strain even with glasses. She experienced her menarche; she was a straight A student (in the seventh grade) and indicated that she wanted to go to college and that she would also like to be a dancer. Her hearing loss had increased and she was somewhat sensitive about it; she would not admit this difficulty to any of her teachers. Her main teacher reported that although she was extremely bright, she "shrinks from opportunities for leadership." At about this time, she wrote a letter in which she indicated that her new stepfather was devoted and kind to her and her brother. Perhaps this helps to explain her unusual attitude to her girls' new stepmother (in the note to her ex-husband).

She finished high school and went on to college for three years but did not graduate. At college she developed a close, lasting student-teacher relationship with a distinguished professor; she wrote detailed letters to him for years. At the age of twenty-five, having, in her own words, been "an unsuccessful secretary," her "ultimate goal" was to "be a successful homemaker." She married and in the two following years lived in five different cities. Understandably, she wrote that "it is hard to develop interests in any one place." She became pregnant almost immediately after getting married.

There is a gap in the records for five years. At age thirty she had two children and reports a "great tendency to worry and extreme nervousness." Her husband was drinking rather heavily. There was a dramatic change in her own physical and psychological state. She reported that she was "too tired even to wash the windows." She also reported a sharp pain in her side, which her doctor told her was due to "neurotic tendencies." She wrote that she was "chronically worn out and tired and very unhappy in the marriage."

There is a painful letter to her favorite college professor, written when she was about thirty-five:

> . . . Until I was twenty-five I didn't know there were such things as problems in this world, but since then with the exception of my two lovely children and my perfect relationship with my mother, I've had just one struggle after another, made one blunder after another. My husband and I bicker constantly. I've wanted to divorce him a thousand times and still I know that is not the solution. We were both raised in broken homes and we both love our children too much. He comes home drunk at night far too often. He can't afford it. He refuses to look at the bills and says "Why haven't you saved money?" I have no one to talk to. I feel like I'm cornered. . . . My mother's youngest brother and my nearest neighbor both committed suicide in one month [about a year before].

In this same communication, writing about her misfortunes in general, she said this about her father: "I adored my father from afar. Our occasional meetings were unsatisfactory. My father is a very brilliant man—however *he has little use for me*—He lives twenty minutes away but has been in our home only once for a few minutes in the past two years." Those lines strike a key theme in her broken life. She said that she was reading Menninger's *Man Against Himself*—a book about suicide.

In another letter she wrote of her children:

> Our little ones are nice, but the eldest still bites her fingernails and fights constantly with her younger sister. She is the result of my selfishness. . . . Well, I've poured out my heart and I'm a little ashamed. In my heart I've never doubted that I can be a happy, relaxed, useful human being, but it's taking such a long time to get there.

Four years later, when Natalie was thirty-nine, she separated from her husband, because—from another letter—of "his violent temper, his selfishness and his drinking." Nine months later she was divorced. Four months after the divorce was final (and he had already remarried), she was dead of suicide.

What deep psychological strains motivate such an act? When we read about her life, especially the subtleties of interaction with her father, we can see the malignant beginnings of her self-abnegating attitudes. At the end, she is so frantic that she will give anything, make any votive offering, including her life, to achieve the feeling of childhood love.

In her suicide she reenacted her own earlier life drama—the childhood yearning for her parents to be together—and in this misdirected symbolic sacrifice, instead of giving her children a (seemingly) united home, she, in the most traumatic way possible, deprived them of their own mother. Her aspirations—to be her father's favorite, to be accepted and not abandoned, to care for and not reject her own children (as she had been rejected and not cared for), to be symbolically reunited with her father in a happy home, to sacrifice herself so that some of the problems of her children might be solved—were no better realized in her death than they were in her life.

Natalie's suicide note to her children is filled with contradictions and inconsistencies. (We remember that when she was tested as a child, the psychologist called her extremely logical.) In the suicide note, the implicit logical arguments flow back and forth, between assertion and counterassertion, never with any resolution. Here are some examples: She says, in effect, you will stay with your father, you should love your father, I know that you cannot love your father but at least you must respect him. She then almost free associates to the word "respect" and argues, rather lamely, that love and respect are almost the same anyway, and in case that argument is not persuasive (which it is not), then one should, at least, respect oneself. The logic wanders.

Another sad example: She says to her children, You must stand on your own two feet, but she also implies that the point of her removing herself from their lives is so that they can be reunited with their father—as, probably, she unconsciously yearns to be reunited with her father.

To tell one's children in a suicide note to remember the happy times certainly has some contradictory element in it, on the very face of it. I love you so much, she says, but the end result of her actions is to make them orphans. She adds, I can't face what the future will bring, but she then takes her life largely because of the haunting, inescapable past. And finally, there is her statement, "I'm getting you all mixed up," which obviously betokens the confusion not in their minds but in her own.

The connections between suicide notes and other aspects of a life seem inescapable with Natalie. The first has to do with Natalie's passivity, her fear of aggression and her fear of violence. In her suicide note she says that the children have to have a leader; when she was twelve, her teacher reported that she shrank from opportunities for leadership. It would appear that all her life she wanted love given to her; in her childhood, and as a wife and mother, she was afraid to stand up for her legitimate rights. She feared and hated quarreling. In the note she said, about the girls, that one afternoon they had "such a horrible fight it scared me." Indeed it must have—adding to her feelings of helplessness and hopelessness, feelings that are part of the suicidal scene.

Another connecting thread can be found between the poignant item contained in the letter she wrote around age thirty-five in which she says, "I adored my father from afar. . . . however *he has little use for me,*" and all the pleading for her children in her suicide notes. In her note to her friend she says: "Please keep in touch with Betty"; and to her ex-husband: "Nancy misses you so . . . [and] needs you desperately . . . [and] really thinks you didn't love her . . . be good to my girls." If one substitutes her name for her girls', one can read the notes as though they were addressed to her own father, whom she could not bring herself—out of a mixture of hostility, rejection and yearning—to contact. At the end, her love is expressed to her ex-father-in-law: "You're so good Papa dear." Finally, in a state of psychological bankruptcy, she tells her children: "Your father would be so much better for you." She is depleted, tired, exhausted, burned out. "I can't face what the future would bring," she says. For her, it would be more of the same. The notes *and* the life both tell us so.

It should now be evident that suicide notes, written, as they are, as part of the life that they reflect, can have a great deal of meaning (and give us a great deal of scientific and clinical information) when they are examined in light of the details of the full life history of which they are the penultimate act. By putting a suicide note within the context of the life history of the individual (who both wrote the note and committed the act), one can find that many words, ideas, emotional proclivities, styles of reaction, modes of thinking, etc., that characterized that life are reflected in the specific details of the suicide note. And conversely, many words, phrases, ideas, passions, emphases, etc., contained in the suicide note are extensions of those very same threads that had previously characterized the life. Living or dying, a particular individual has a certain consistency, a certain "unity thema," a certain "trademark," which he or she will show in work-style, in play-style and in life-style, whether celebrating life in a poem of love or contemplating death in a note of suicide.

There is a bizarre but fascinating and incredibly inventive novel, *The Dwarf,* by the contemporary Swedish author Pär Lagerkvist—winner of the 1951 Nobel Prize in literature—about an aberrant and evil dwarf (in a medieval Italian prince's court), which, by sheer coincidence, contains uncanny and tragic parallels to an actual contemporary case that I know. Indeed the gruesome similarities (in what a sadistic monster can do to a sensitive child) between that honored work of fiction and the actual case are so striking that I have decided to present the two in tandem. My purpose is not to focus on the monsters, but rather on their victims. First, let us read some passages from the novel. It begins:[13]

> I am twenty-six inches tall, shapely and well proportioned, my head perhaps a trifle too large. My hair is not black like the others', but reddish, very stiff and thick, drawn back from the temples and the broad but not especially lofty brow. My face is beardless, but otherwise just like that of other men. My eyebrows meet. My bodily strength is considerable, particularly if I am annoyed. When the wrestling match was arranged between Jehoshaphat and myself I forced him onto his back after twenty minutes and strangled him. Since then I have been the only dwarf at this court.

One of the several subplots in *The Dwarf* concerns the prince's young daughter, Angelica. Here is an excerpt:

> There is a great difference between dwarfs and children. Because they are about the same size, people think that they are alike, and that they

suit each other; but they do not. Dwarfs are set to play with children, forced to do so. It is nothing less than torture to use us dwarfs like that. But human beings know nothing about us.

> My masters have never forced me to play with Angelica, but she herself has done so. That infant, whom some people think so wonderful with her round blue eyes and her little pursed mouth, has tormented me almost more than anyone else at court.
>
> We visit her dolls which have to be fed and dressed, the rose garden where we have to play with the kitten. . . . She can sit and play with her kitten for ages and expect me to join in. She believes that I too am a child and with a child's delight in everything. I! I delight in nothing.

And then the dwarf's revenge on the child:

> Once I crept into her room as she lay sleeping with her detestable kitten beside her in bed and cut off its head with my dagger. Then I threw it into the dungheap beneath the castle window. She was inconsolable when she saw that it was gone, and when everybody said that of course it must be dead, she sickened with an unknown fever and was ill for a long time, so that I, thank goodness, did not have to see her.

And finally, the dwarf's ultimate revenge on Angelica when she has grown up to be a young woman: He informs the prince, his master, that Angelica is being visited by a lover, who is, of all people, the scion of the prince's hated rival family. The prince is furious.

> "Impossible!" he maintained. "Nobody can come into the town over the river, between the fortresses on both banks where archers keep watch night and day. It is absolutely unthinkable!" . . .
>
> "Yes, it is unthinkable," I admitted . . . but think if the criminal had already slipped away! Or if both had fled! The horrible suspicion sent me flying over the courtyard as fast as my legs could carry me, and up the stairs to Angelica's door.
>
> I put my ear against it. No sound within! Had they fled? I slipped inside and immediately recovered my composure. To my joy I saw them sleeping side by side in her bed, by the light of a little oil lamp that they had forgotten to extinguish.
>
> Now I heard the Prince and his men on the stairs, and presently he came in followed by two sentinels. Livid with wrath he snatched the sword from one of the sentinels and with a single blow severed Giovanni's head from his body. Angelica woke up and stared with wild dilated eyes as they dragged her gory lover from her couch and flung him on to the muckheap outside the window. Then she fell back in a swoon and did not recover consciousness as long as we remained in the room.

In the town there is a plague; Angelica suffers a rather peculiar and different malady:

> Angelica cannot be sick of this plague. Her malady is the same as that which she once had as a child. I do not quite remember when, nor the exact circumstances. She has always been rather sickly, for reasons which could not possibly affect anybody else's health. Ah, now I remember. It was when I cut off her kitten's head.

Finally, Angelica is driven to despair:

> Angelica has drowned herself in the river. She must have done it yesterday evening or last night, for nobody saw her. She left a letter behind which leaves no doubt that she killed herself in that manner. Throughout the day they have been searching for her body, all the length of the river where it flows through the beleaguered city, but in vain. Like Giovanni's it must have been carried away by the tides.
>
> There is a great to-do at the court. Everybody is upset and cannot realize that she is dead. I see nothing extraordinary about the letter, and it changes nothing—certainly not the crime which was committed and which everybody condemned unanimously. It contains nothing new.
>
> I had to hear it again and again until I know it almost by heart. It runs something like this:
>
>> I do not want to stay with you any longer. You have been so kind to me, but I do not understand you. I do not understand how you could take my beloved away from me, my dear one who came so far from another country to tell me that there was a thing called love.
>>
>> As soon as I met him, I knew why life had been so strangely difficult up to then.
>>
>> Now I do not want to stay here, where he is not, but I shall follow him. I shall just lay myself down to rest on the river, and God will take me where I am to go.
>>
>> You must not believe that I have taken my life, for I have only done as I was told. And I am not dead. I have gone to be joined forever to my beloved.
>>
>> I forgive you with all my heart.
>>
>> Angelica.
>
> The Princess is convinced that she is the cause of Angelica's death. This is the first time I have ever known her to take any interest in her child. She scourges herself more than ever to efface this sin, eats nothing at all, and prays to the Crucified One for forgiveness.
>
> The Crucified One does not answer.

Now let us turn to a real-life tragedy: the suicide of a twenty-three-year-old woman. I shall call her Dolores. This occurred in the 1970s, in a large city in the United States, in a motel room. She had brought with her a copy of Alvarez's *The Savage God* (in which he discusses the suicide of the poet Sylvia Plath). She registered under the name "Marilyn Plath." She hanged herself from the shower. She left this suicide note:

> Forgive me. It was too late for me to be repaired. No one is to blame. I love you all. I want to be buried here. I am a broken doll. I have been to too many doll hospitals. They couldn't repair me. So dear doctor and Gregor, you were working against the impossible. How can a doll that has been through a mangler be repaired? I love you all for your great loving effort. Remember me with happiness for now I shall have no more pain.

Some few weeks before that eventful day, she had spontaneously written another personal document, a sort of essay of anguish, which she had entitled "What Is Depression?" Here it is, verbatim:

> Depression is feeling revulsion from one's mother as a child. Depression is hoping to be the greatest love in someone's life and realizing it will never be so. Depression is knowing that although Maria, my nana as a child, loved me she went along all the way with the very strong mistress of the house, my charming mother, who constantly punished me for small reasons and instructed my nana to do the same. Depression is knowing that my family loved me but was told how bad I was, so love was limited. Depression is fear of having wanted to reach out to my mother and getting rejection in return. Depression is caring but beginning to stop reaching out. Depression is being a showpiece, the best dressed little girl. Who could say she hadn't the perfect mother? She dressed you so well—you have the nicest clothes—what a lucky girl you are to have such a wonderful mother. Depression is being noticed by my mother in public and ignored by her in private. Depression is knowing that I am being blackmailed by a little brother who knows he is the chosen one and having to do as he says. Depression is knowing that father loved me but never stood up for me—my mother was the master of the house. Depression is hearing over and over the story of my birth. The disappointment experienced by my mother of having had a girl. Depression is not really knowing if I was such an awful child—not being certain I couldn't have been such a revulsion without doing some great wrong. Depression is not remembering the wrong things My father slept with a gun under his pillow—my mother told me I had access to it one day—that I pointed it at my mother and that it was taken away. I was about three and don't remember. *Depression was the killing of my dog and the murder of my doll by my brother.* [Italics added.] Depression is the development of hate, knowing that whatever I do I won't be loved. Depression was the encouragement of

> my parents telling my teacher to constantly punish me if I did anything incorrectly. Depression was being caned at school and beaten at home for having had to be caned at school. Depression is doing everything to be loved—but my mother saw to it that no one was going to love me. Depression is seeing love happening and suddenly disappearing. Depression is hearing that my brother makes my family so happy and I am a constant crown of thorns. Depression is my brother convincing me that if I put sugar in my hands bees will make honey for me—Depression is being stung and having my mother laugh heartily for my brother's cleverness and my stupidity. Depression is hearing this hilarious story repeated over and over. Depression is the fright of being stung by a bee for the first time and wanting to be held and comforted and receiving laughter at my stupidity. Depression is knowing in life there is no real love—that love will die or the person will leave me.
>
> There is so much more but I don't want to think anymore right now—but I hate her and all the people who couldn't love me just for me. They would just begin to love me and then they would meet her and the love for me would stop almost immediately. I am never going to let her take anyone from me again. I will do anything however wrong to prevent this—however drastic. I will stop at nothing.

This remarkable psychological document is a painfully shrill cry of hate and hurt. It is the wail of the psychologically rejected child; the lament of the unfavorite sibling.

Dolores was born in a major city in South America. Her parents were well-to-do and sent her to a fancy school—where she was beaten. After she finished high school in her native country, she came to the United States, attended a large university and had a lover, named Gregor. He was a tender man and extremely solicitous of Dolores's feelings. For some months before she died she was in psychotherapy. The following is a summary of some of her early memories as related to me by her therapist:

> When she was born, in the hospital, her mother refused to look at her because she was not a boy. Dolores knew this well because her mother reminded her of it again and again, but also because she was also told this by the nurse when she was old enough to remember. Her mother did not look at her until she brought her home and then she was taken care of by this nana. Dolores has distinct memories back to about the age of four. Those crucial memories were somewhere between four and six. The critical memory is that she had a doll. It was an ordinary doll, nothing very special about it, but she absolutely adored it. One day she couldn't find this doll. They lived in a large house which had a walled-in garden and wooden pickets all the way around the garden, and she couldn't find her beloved doll and went out and there she saw, on top of one of those pickets, just

> the head of her doll impaled on the fence. The rest of it her impish brother had destroyed. [The brother verified that memory to the therapist.] But her feeling was that he had killed her doll and her dog and she said that over and over.
>
> There is another memory which goes back to that time. These memories were also verified by her brother. This other memory—which dates back to a very young age—is of her grandmother's house, which was apparently not too far from their house. Across from her grandmother's house there was a cemetery. Dolores remembers going often to the cemetery when she was very despairing, having been punished by her mother. At the age of four or five she would go to the cemetery whenever there was a funeral and she would sit and watch the mourners and all the beautiful flowers and she would say to herself, Oh, I wish someone would love me enough to care. She remembers her feelings of rejection as early as that.

The skeins of death were interwoven into her life almost from the beginning. Could it be that she was responding to her mother's unconscious (or even conscious) messages that things would be better if she, Dolores, were dead? A miserable childhood and the subtle parental cruelties of a lifetime can be a lethal potion.

When she was a young adult, her lover's concern and devotion could not pierce the impenetrable wall of Dolores's fixed feelings of being unlovable. In her distorted view of life, no one could give her enough love. Even her intense positive relationship with her psychotherapist was, not unexpectedly, contaminated with a fatal drop of deep childhood ambivalence.

The key imagery is that of the broken doll. The "broken doll" in the suicide note directly parallels the "murder of my doll" in the life history. In the same sense that the doll of her childhood was hopelessly destroyed and could never be repaired, she felt that neither could she—another broken doll that had been through life's mangler—be propped up enough to live.

Although there was no actual dwarf in her life, her mischievous little brother, encouraged by her mother, was the impish and sadistic figure in her childhood. Like the dwarf, he was a monster. There were also other symbolic monsters in her life (such as her unbearable feelings of rejection), which finally broke her delicate spirit.

In these two cases, then, we can begin to appeciate the reciprocal relationship between the suicide notes and the lives themselves.

Notes

1 Paul Friedman, ed., *On Suicide* (New York: International Universities Press, 1967).

2 Paul Friedman, "Suicide Among Police: A Study of 93 Suicides Among New York City Policemen, 1934–1940," in Edwin S. Shneidman, ed., *Essays in Self-Destruction* (New York: Science House, 1967); and Michael F. Heiman, "Police Suicides Revisited," *Suicide*, Spring 1975, Vol. 5, No. 1, pp. 5–20.

3 Yvonne Kapp, *Eleanor Marx* (New York: Pantheon, 1977).

4 From Arthur Koestler, *The Case of the Midwife Toad* (New York: Random House, 1972).

5 From Quentin Bell, *Virginia Woolf—A Biography* (London: Hogarth Press, 1972; New York: Harcourt, Brace, Jovanovich, 1972).

6 From Walter Edwin Peck, *Shelley: His Life and Work*, Vol. I, p. 493 (Boston: Houghton, Mifflin Co., 1927· London: Chatto and Windus, Ltd).

7 A fascinating account of Elton Hammond's life, together with a series of his letters and his suicide note, appear in *The Diary, Reminiscences and Correspondence of Henry Crabb Robinson*, Vol. III, Chap. 5 (London: Macmillan and Co., 1869).

8 Edwin S. Shneidman, "Suicide Notes Reconsidered," *Psychiatry*, November 1973, Vol. 36, No. 11, pp. 379–394.

9 Margarethe von Andics, *Suicide and the Meaning of Life* (London: William Hodge & Co., 1947).

10 Erwin Ringel, "The Presuicidal Syndrome," *Suicide and Life-Threatening Behavior*, Fall 1976, Vol. 6, No. 3, pp. 131–149.

11 From A. Alvarez, *The Savage God: A Study of Suicide* (New York: Random House, 1972).

12 From Boris Pasternak, *I Remember: Sketch for an Autobiography* (New York: Pantheon, 1959).

13 Selections from *The Dwarf* by Pär Lagerkvist, translated from the Swedish by Alexandra Dick. Copyright ©1945 by L. B. Fisher Publishing Corp. Renewed Copyright ©1973 by L. B. Fisher Publishing Corp. (now a division of Farrar, Straus & Giroux, Inc.).

48· A Strategic Theory [of Suicide]

Jean Baechler

Jean Baechler is a French social scientist who has come recently to the study of suicide. This selection outlines his new approach to the definition of suicide and the implications that his definition has for the study and prevention of suicidal deaths. His approach cuts through much of the theorizing of the past and has important implications for the practice of the future,

DEFINITION

We begin this analysis with the observation that suicide is an unusual event. Accordingly, one can assume the existence of neither an external suicide-generating wave nor an internal suicidal force. How useful, how universal is such a wave or force if it carries off "only" about 10,000 Frenchmen a year? Even if one does not compare this figure to all living Frenchmen but only to those who die during a given year, that still gives us a proportion on the order of one in fifty. This is certainly not negligible, but it is insufficient to constitute proof of a force or a wave.

The contrary opinion, which I recognize results from an initial skepticism, is here based on a solid foundation. Assuming that social variables do have some influence—and at this stage I cannot say whether or not they do—it is certain that this influence can only be indirect, that it must be "mediated." In this respect, the argument of Achille-Delmas, that the number of those who are not affected by the factor considered is greater than its putative victims, is entirely convincing.

The hypothesis of a death wish or an impulse to die is of a kind with that of excess population, at least to the extent that both are too ethereal to be based on facts. The burden of proof belongs to anyone who advances an hypothesis of this kind. At best, it can perhaps explain death but certainly not suicide. As for the partial hypotheses of psychoanalysis, I would call them specific interpretations of suicide; if we take them as explanations of one form of suicide (for example, grief as the murder of an internalized object), we cannot yet decide on their validity. On the other hand, as soon as one tries to generalize them (so that *every* suicide must be the murder of an internalized object), they miscarry, for the number of exceptions to this postulated mechanism exceeds the number of cases that verify it.

Finally, it seems just as impossible to link suicide to a determinative mental illness as to consider it a form of mental derangement. If suicide is neither an illness nor the result of an illness, that does not mean that it simply occurs in any population whatsoever, that a suicidal population has no particular psychological characteristics to distinguish it from a nonsuicidal one.

In short, it seems to me beyond doubt that the problem of suicide must be taken up again on an entirely new basis. The least bad starting point is to fix on a definition of the object to be studied. With respect to the whole question of definitions, I must confess to a thoroughgoing nominalism: each of us can adopt the definition that appeals to him, provided that it allows him to specify, to arrange, and, finally, to conceptualize an object, My nominalism admits of at least one exception for suicide. In fact, the definitions adopted by earlier writers on the subject are not simply arbitrary (as is every definition within a nominalist conception); they sometimes involve the entire theory of an author. A few examples will make this clear.

Here is Durkheim's definition: "The term suicide is applied to all cases of death resulting directly or indirectly from a positive or negative act of the victim himself, which he knows will produce this result."[1] This is when first examined unexceptionable, and one's reaction is "Why not?"; in fact it is full of restrictions that entirely falsify its proper scope. "All cases of death" implies that one may not include in the category of suicide all those acts that have not resulted in an actual death—in short, all attempted suicides are excluded. I do not know whether Durkheim excluded attempted suicides on purpose or inadvertently; the fact is, however, that by doing so he compromised a great deal. In fact if he had had to take attempted suicides into consideration, his entire method would have collapsed, for there are no reliable statistics on genuine attempted suicides. To say nothing of the pseudoproblem that would have to be raised: are attempted suicides genuine or fake?

Undertaken by "the victim himself" eliminates the cases where the person who committed suicide dies by the hand of another—for example, the person who goes to war searching for death, or one who avoids facing a great disappointment by agreeing to die in a surgical procedure that he knows will be fatal.[2] It matters little whether the number of cases is great or small: the statistical method requires they be ignored because they do not count statistically.

"Which he knows will produce this result" reveals an entirely rationalist conception, where the behavior of every man is perfectly transparent to himself. Even if this prejudice were shared by the entire nineteenth century, it is no less prejudice. I will argue shortly that there are suicides that are in a way automatic, where a part of one's consciousness and one's will is nullified; above all, there are suicides whose sought-for result, which we call "death," is open to a whole series of interpretations and quite different representations.

The definition chosen by Halbwachs also is prejudiced in a certain way: "By suicide one means every case of death that results from an act undertaken by the victim himself with the intention, or with a view to, killing himself, and *which is not a sacrifice.*"[3] The opening part of the definition follows Durkheim and is open to the same criticism. The distinction introduced between "with the intention, or with a view to" seems to indicate that Halbwachs nourished some doubts about the deliberate nature of the suicidal act. The last detail marks an intentional break with Durkheim. By getting rid of sacrifice, he put an end to altruistic suicide as well. Chiefly, however, he was forced to do so because of his theory. In effect, for Halbwachs, suicides are the consequence of the greater or lesser "complexity" of society. The more complex a society, the greater the rate of failures. If one were to admit of "positive" suicides, it would be necessary to abandon the hypothesis of "complexity." Because, in spite of everything, the distinction can be shown to be arbitrary (do the Christian martyrs represent failures of Roman socialization or sacrifices?), Halbwachs produced an "objective" criterion that should be cited: "We believe that a sociological definition must principally account for the attitude of society and the different judgments that it brings to externally similar acts. From the moment that society is held to be the instigator and responsible agent for these acts and considers other ones as purely individual, even though society may have suggested, advised, and approved them, two different categories are involved."[4] This society that instigates, suggests, advises, approves, considers, and so forth is very odd. After all, Bayet has shown that "society," that is, individuals who speak and write, does not have *an* ethics of suicide, but two, and that these two are juxtaposed and combined in different ways.

Here is how Dr. Achille-Delmas enters the lists: "Suicide is the act by which a fully competent man kills himself; he is able to live but he chooses, without any moral obligation, to die."[5] For this author, suicide is a characteristic result of manic-depressive hyperthalmia and hypertension. In this respect it is a definition that serves him quite well. "Kills himself" eliminates anything tentative. The author strongly holds the opinion that it is all quite simple: "of course, it is necessary to distinguish all fake attempts undertaken for reasons of concern, sympathy, or blackmail, which are nothing but phony suicide-attempts revealing vainglorious, perverse, or covetous mythomania."[6] "Fully competent" excludes suicidal persons who are demented, who kill themselves for unconscious motives, and accidental suicides that result from errors. "Able to live but chooses to die" allows one to ignore both coerced suicides (where the choice between life and death does not exist) and euthanasia (by which one seeks to escape a more terrible death). "Without any ethical obligation" intends that we should eliminate "ethical suicides" (where one dies in order to fulfill an heroic or sacred duty). All these qualifications, which amount to exclusions, are arbitrary, not to say inconsistent because discrimination among these various forms of death is rigorously maintained only in the author's passion for classification. To have wished fondly to distinguish pseudosuicides, Achille-Delmas produced a definition that was, quite simply, absurd, even from his own point of view. One would like to know the degree of competence of a manic-depressive or a person with hypertension at a moment of crisis. One would like to encounter a suicide who, *at the moment of his suicidal action,* has the *genuine* (that is, for him and not for the external observer) choice between living and dying: if life were really a possible outcome, no one would ever die! There is no suicide save when death appears as the *only* outcome.

After these definitions that say too much, let us conclude with one that does not say enough. Here is Dr. Deshaies': "We define suicide as the *act of killing oneself* in an *habitually* conscious way, by taking death as a *means* or as an *end.* This is initially a genetic definition that allows one to avoid the arbitrariness of a prior choice of facts."[7] The rhetorical caution of the second sentence mitigates the inconsistency of the first. Besides, even this initial definition does not avoid being arbitrary, for "the act of killing oneself" ignores attempted suicides. It is true that the author tries to take them into account later. What must one understand by "conscious" and who will believe the incongruity of that "habitually"? "Death as a means or as an end" introduces something completely new by suggesting that the suicidal person intends something. But the formulation is far too vague, at this stage, to be of any use.

It would be tedious to multiply examples; besides, I would give the impression of wishing to avoid criticism myself by postponing the moment of producing my own definition. Well, no longer: we must take the plunge. In the remainder of this book, I will base my argument on the following definition: *Suicide denotes all behavior that seeks and finds the solution to an existential problem by making an attempt on the life of the subject.* Each word in this definition deserves a careful analysis, with the purpose of avoiding any unintentional ambiguities and drawing the first outlines of the argument to be developed subsequently.

ANALYSIS OF THE DEFINITION

Suicide is a *behavior* rather than an act because only rarely is it circumscribed by the precise moment when it is accomplished. More generally, the fatal result is preceeded by an evolution that can be traced back to its first beginnings and various appearances (for example one or several depressions, mental troubles, aberrant conduct, etc.) that, properly speaking, neither foreshadow nor determine the suicide but are alternative solutions to a fundamental problem and less injurious to the subject. On the other hand, the word "act" objectifies suicide and detaches it from the one who commits it, whereas one must insist on the importance of the personalities who make up their minds to do it.

Suicidal behavior is a response to a *problem*, by which I refer to the whole situation that obliges the subject to take up a position and find a way out. Thus, the loss of a dear one, an incurable illness, or an imminent defeat all force a subject to reconsider the way his life is arranged and to undertake, in one way or another, a reorganization of the terms of his life. The problem may be *internal*, that is, presented in terms of dealing with impulses or requests (a strong superego can produce an intense feeling of guilt), or *external*, that is, prompted by real changes (which appear as modifications in the eyes of a neutral observer) in the environment of the subject. The preceding distinction, however fuzzy it may be (for an "external" problem becomes a problem only from the moment it is perceived, internally, as one), has its own importance because it serves immediately to indicate a difficulty that it will be necessary later on to deal with directly: the elucidation of external factors that contribute to suicide can have a bearing only on those cases where the problem has an external origin, and not on other kinds, unless one assumes that these factors influence the personality directly. I shall return to this. One is tempted to introduce a second distinction according to which the problem is *real* or *imaginary*. There is a difficulty here, however: for the subject considering suicide, the problem is always "real." For one who is jealous and who, in a fit of passion, kills the one he loves before killing himself, the other's betrayal is a certainty or a tormenting possibility, whatever the contradictory protestations may be. In the same way, the madman who hears voices that command him to kill himself does not doubt the reality of these voices even if, for the analyst, they are the imaginary product of an aggravated guilt. In other words, to give any degree of consistency to this distinction, it is necessary to introduce a neutral observer who could make it because, as uncertain as it may be, it is indispensable for anyone who wishes to account for the mechanisms of suicide. For example. the infirmities of age are a real problem; in certain societies where the surplus is limited and the effort of each person is indispensable for the survival of all, a feeble old person very quickly becomes an insupportable burden. Frequently, he kills himself to spare his family or society this added weight. In cases of this kind, the interpretation is easy, for the reality of the problem confers a kind of rationality on the behavior. Because rational conduct—defined here as the adequacy of means to end—

is the most widely shared thing in the world, it is always possible, whatever the distance between civilizations, to go over the chain of propositions that led to the ultimate decision. On the other hand, when the problem is imaginary, the neutral observer is helpless, for he cannot put himself in the place of the subject; he is forced to look for a specific "logic" or, better (since there is but one logic), to explain the genesis of the illusions that produced the problem. In the first case, it is sufficient to be human to understand; in the second, it is necessary to be armed with scientific theories. And anyhow, the neutral observer is only relatively neutral. He is neutral insofar as he does not personally participate in the problematic situation with which the subject is struggling. He is not neutral insofar as he necessarily forms a certain idea of the situation. A medieval observer who believed in higher powers, the devil, and sorcerers would not have the same neutrality as a contemporary psychiatrist. The same difficulty arises in connection with a third useful distinction, which bears on the *variable seriousness* of a real problem. Within Ringel's sample of suicide victims can be found, on the one hand, a woman who lost her husband and three children and, on the other, a schizophrenic who lost a canary. It goes without saying that for the subject the problem is always real and vital. The neutral observer, however, must be able to distinguish insignificant problems because he is interested in finding out why this insignificance assumed a vital importance for certain people. No absolute criterion of the seriousness of a problem has been set out. One must be satisfied with a criterion that makes use of "averages," that is, the mean response given by the majority of people to a given problem. The afflictions of love are common enough between the ages of fifteen and twenty-five; rare are they who kill themselves for love, the vast majority consoling themselves by establishing new ties. The loss of a husband or wife is, after sixty or seventy years, a frequent misfortune and statistically almost inevitable: nearly all the widows and widowers survive. Consequently, the observer is forced to admit, however troublesome it may be to do so, that a broken heart and widowhood are not "serious" problems. It follows that a suicide brought on by a deception or a loss must be explained by the peculiarities of the subject who suffers them. From the outside, the problem becomes one of an internal reality that is to some extent imaginary. It is clear that, as a result of this criterion, "serious" problems can surface only in extreme situations (an accumulation of misfortunes) or in social cataclysms (war or revolution). From which follows a new difficulty in determining the value of social factors in suicide: we take it to be probable, from now on, that they are perceptible only in atypical situations and crises and that they remain hidden, if not dormant, in the normal condition of a society.

The problems are termed *existential* in order to indicate that they concern the whole of the subject's situation and are at the same time internal and external. One does not kill oneself for an idea unless this idea focuses on one's aspirations or conflicts. One can reason about suicide and even convince oneself rationally of its desirability, but it is more than probable that no one has ever killed himself for an abstract reason.

In one sense the *solution* that suicide brings to a problem is always sufficient. For the subject, the problem provided no alternative solution; otherwise he would not have killed himself. In order to be able to distinguish between the adequacy or inadequacy of suicide as a solution, it is necessary once again to appeal to a neutral observer. By taking account of all the data, he can decide whether the subject was forced to give up or whether he could have continued. Moralists are not in error to pose as neutral observers and to show that nobody has ever been "right" to kill himself. For the analyst, the certainties of the moralist incline him precisely to think that the point of view of the neutral observer is without interest to him. From the very fact that the subject has reached the conclusion that the *sole* solution to his problem is death, the only *instructive* position is to show why and how the subject has been driven to this end. In other words, the only scientifically useful hypothesis is to consider that, for the subject as he is, the solution is actually adequate, that, in terms of the way the problem is posed, the subject finds a "good" solution.

Yet this solution must be available. I would insist that suicide be included among the solutions that may be proposed to a person concerning the conduct of his life. This is actually the case. Speaking in terms of ideal types, there are five ways of resolving any existential problem whatsoever. The first solution can be called rational, and consists in changing the given conditions of the problem in such a way as to adjust the means to the sought-for end. Of course, one must include the subject as part of the given conditions. That is, if the world cannot be transformed in accord with one's desires, one can modify or reduce one's desires in order to obtain a satisfactory solution. A kind of bargaining is set up between the objective conditions and the aspirations of the individual or group, which ends up producing a compromise solution that contents the vast majority. The second solution consists in the imaginary obliteration of the objective data: the subject cuts his ties to what is real and constructs his private reality. The third solution is, in a sense, the opposite of the second: when faced with the impossibility of modifying the objective conditions, one removes, either really or in fantasy, one of the central data of the situation, namely, the subject himself. The fourth solution consists in removing one or several elements of the situation in order to arrange it in the subject's favor: one may call this a crime or misdemeanor. The final solution may be called an apocalypse: the pure and simple suppression of all the data, including the subject.

These five solutions are always available whenever a problem must be resolved. Let us take the game of chess. The rational solution consists in keeping to the rules of the game, considering the moves of one's opponent in order to develop a victorious strategy, and not to forget that one can lose. The unreal solution would be to play only imaginary games against imaginary opponents. The suicidal solution would be to refuse to play or to quit. The "criminal or unlawful" solution consists in cheating or not playing by the rules. And finally, the apocalyptic solution would be to throw the chessboard to the ground. Here is a more serious example: unrequited love, love that is not returned. The subject can—at least in theory—adopt five solutions: renounce his affections and bestow them elsewhere, convince himself that he is loved but that the lover is forbidden to declare it, kill himself, kill the other, kill the other and then kill himself.

Not much would be served by multiplying examples; each reader can make up his own. He will satisfy himself that these five solutions are logical, that is, that they entirely resolve the problem, which is not to say that they are rational. Only the first is rational in the sense that it considers all the data and uses them to maximize the satisfactions and to minimize the discomforts for the subject. But—and this is the important point—because they are logical, these five solutions have never had to be invented: they have been available ever since the first rational being appeared. Consequently, wherever there are people, there are people who seek to solve their problems by suicide.

This analysis leads to two important consequences. The first, clearly, is that there is no need to assume the existence of an internal or an external force in order to acknowledge something as untoward as suicide. But suicide is not queer: it is simply one way of resolving a problem, one logical and universal way among others. The mystery of suicide appears to me to be in this way entirely removed or, more exactly, there is really no mystery. The fact that something like suicide exists is perfectly natural. That does not mean that our task is finished. On the contrary, it is just beginning, but on a solid basis because the question that will henceforth be at the center of our investigation will be expressed in the following terms: *what people seek what solutions to what problems by means of suicide?* Thus, the emphasis is to be placed first on recruitment of the suicidal person (whether the factors involved are internal or external), next on the meaning of the suicidal act, and last on the factors that can influence the formation of problems and situations where the suicidal solution will be probable.[8]

The second consequence is less obvious. Because the number of available solutions is limited to five and the number of problems to be resolved is indefinite, it follows that totally different problems may receive an identical solution. Let us take an extreme example. Everyone ends up dying; the roads that lead to death are multiple: yet there is but one result. Here the situation is so clear that the idea never occurs to anybody to use the common nature of the result as the basis for assuming an identity of ways of gaining it. With respect to suicide, the situation is exactly the same, even if it is more complicated. Suicide also is the unique result whenever other solutions are excluded (it does not matter why they were excluded); nothing forces us to assume that the roads that lead to it are identical. Let us say that an individual has experienced successive and ever more serious misfortunes and defeats; a moment may arrive when all hope to change the situation is lost: he stops taking part by killing himself, and in a way, he takes flight. Let us take another person who has a violent grudge against someone close to him; he cannot kill him or seriously harm him, we will say, because his conscience forbids it; he kills himself in order to inflict an insuperable grief on the other: he has taken his revenge. Or finally, let us consider a career soldier raised in an aristocratic, military tradition; for him, fleeing and surrender are out of the question: he kills himself rather than surrender. One could multiply examples in order to show that, if suicide is singular in terms of its consequences, it is multiple in terms of its agents and meanings. The second part of this study will deal wholly with the meanings of suicide. Let us say, from now on, that one can find dozen of types of suicide, each one having its own mechanism. If suicide is a unique means, it may be put to the service of multiple and heterogeneous ends.[9]

An unsympathetic reader might object: "why in the world study, in the same book, patterns of behavior that you admit are heterogeneous?" I could reply, as I have every right to do: *sic enim mehi placuit*, "because such is my pleasure." Instead, I would reply more pedantically: war is a means of gaining glory, territory, or security. These three ends are heterogeneous and correspond to three different logics. If one takes each goal in isolation, one discovers that war is but one means among others of attaining them. In other words, human and social phenomena can always appear within two different problematics: within one, they are the common denominator of a whole series of phenomena (war with respect to glory, territory, security); within the other, they are one means against others (one can obtain glory by thought, art, crime, war, etc.). The same thing is true for suicide On the one hand, it is the common denominator for a whole series of behavioral patterns. On the other, it is one of a number of behavioral patterns serving a single end: one can run away by using drugs, drinking, becoming a hermit, or killing oneself; one can take revenge by hurting, spoiling, killing, or by committing suicide. I believe it is "interesting" to consider the entire series where the pattern "by committing suicide" appears and analyze them in terms of their common denominator.[10]

I deliberately chose to use a term as vague as *"attempt on the life"* because of the ways by which a suicide can be accomplished are extremely variable. One can try to conceptualize the variations by means of oppositely paired concepts: if one is both clear and thorough, one risks being overwhelmed with facts, for reality rarely conforms to conceptual purity.

Suicide can be successful or *symbolic*, with all gradations in between. It is successful if death—defined by a flat electroencephalogram reading—is its consummation. It is symbolic or verbal if the subject dreams of suicide or threatens to kill himself. Between the idea or the threat of suicide and the successful suicide may be placed the suicidal *gesture* (swallowing aspirins or giving the appearance of being ready to throw oneself out the window); the *serious attempt*, where a fatal outcome is very probable; and the *self-indulgent attempt*, where a fatal outcome is excluded either because the method used is known to be ineffective or because the subject knows he will be discovered in time. Of course, a successful suicide can be transformed into an attempted suicide if the subject fails for reasons outside his control. Later we shall see how central these distinctions are and how they are logically inscribed in intelligible conduct. In particular, we will show that the distinction between (successful) *suicide* and *attempted suicide* (from failed suicide to the gesture and threat) has nothing to do with the subject's seriousness or lack of it. Suicidal behavior, whatever its importance, is *always* serious because it intends to gain a specifiable end by adequate means.

Suicide can be *direct* or *indirect.* It is direct when the subject brings about the fatal outcome by making a positive gesture (hanging himself, throwing himself in the water, swallowing barbiturates, etc.). I would include among direct suicide cases where death is inflicted by another at the request of the subject. I mean by *indirect* suicide all behavior that is bound to provoke a homicidal reaction in another. That is, provocation pure and simple. Examples abound in the hagiography of the early centuries. Here is a particularly clear-cut case that happened in Palestine in the seventh century: Pierre of Capitolias, a married priest (who nevertheless succeeded in sending all his family to a convent) was haunted by martyrdom. In order to achieve it, he made a series of offensively rude remarks about the Muslim religion. In spite of the authorities' astonishing forebearance (in order not to have to punish him, they made him out as a madman), he ended up obtaining his wish and died in great pain.[11] Here is a literary example borrowed from Tolstoy's *War and Peace:* During a battle that was going badly for the Russians, the brave general, Bagovout, was violently taken to task by a superior. Highly incensed, he plunged into the battle, making his answer his determination to be killed.

Indirect suicide can take the most incredible detours. Sometimes people are consciously looking for capital punishment: to expiate who-knows-what shortcoming, they kill in order to be killed. A criminal who recently provided a diversion for French journalism gives a shocking illustration of this. Condemned for murder to life imprisonment at hard labor (whereas he openly demanded the death penalty), Claude Buffet murdered two hostages during an attempted escape. His case is interesting because he quite consciously developed a "theory" of indirect suicide. If one can rely on newspaper reports, he reasoned as follows: Christ gave everyone the right to live or die, but he forbade suicide; the only solution, if one is tired of living, is to kill in order to be killed; murder, therefore, becomes the only way to leave this intolerable world and gain eternal life.[12] What is involved here is, of course, a particularly primitive ideological rationalization, but it is symptomatic.

Suicide can be of the *present* time or *long term.* It belongs to the *present* if the consequences of behavior must be fatal in the short term. In the case of suicide by shooting, the result is almost instantaneous, whereas it can take several weeks to die by a hunger strike. I call every suicide that takes the form of a progressive destruction of the subject a *long-term* suicide whether or not a terminal point to the process can be given or even clearly indicated. I am thinking here of all kinds of toxicomania, especially alcoholism.

Suicide can be *absolute* or *relative.* This distinction may appear obscure or subtle, but it is very real. Edwin Shneidman drew our attention to this problem.[13] To say that a suicide is looking for "death" is to rest content with a most imprecise statement. Shneidman distinguished four modes of death:

1. *Cessation:* that is, "an end to the possibility of any subsequent conscious experience."[14] This is what I would call absolute suicide

since the subject intends a total and definitive annihilation.

2. *Termination:* that is, "the cessation of physiological functions of the body."[15] This suicide is only relative since the subject retains the hope of an afterlife. This hope can take all kinds of different forms, such as survival in the memories of friends or the remembrance of mankind.
3. *Interruption:* that is, "the cessation of consciousness, generally accompanied by the expectation of later conscious experience."[16] Suicide must lead to a state that actualizes sleep, anesthesia, alcoholic stupor, diabetic coma, epileptic fit, amnesia, and so on. What is involved here is sort of a temporary closing down, a bypassing of the subject. The suicide is relative.[17]
4. *Continuation:* that is, "the person does not have the intention of actually dying but of obliterating certain internal or external aspects of life.[18] The subject does not intend to disappear, but would like to be rid of some things that he finds intolerable.

To be sure, the absolute or relative nature of the subject's intentions in each case brings about the same real result, death. These distinctions are useful, provided they are used prudently. When dealing with factual material, it is rarely possible to observe them rigorously. Generally, the suicidal person is undecided among several intentions. Frequently, a serious attempt is followed by the subject's thanks that his life has been saved for him. It seems clear that a decision as serious as killing oneself cannot avoid bringing about a great disturbance at the moment it is undertaken: it is improbable that the subject knows the kind of death he intends; it is the neutral observer who in most cases is in a position to decide.

Suicide may be *total* or *partial.* It is *total* if the behavior must lead immediately or eventually to death, as we discussed above. It also can be partial. In order to resolve a problem, the subject adopts a behavior that constitutes a fraction of, or a substitute for, death. I am thinking, for example, of self-mutilations. As Freud and Menninger showed so well, what is involved may be (these authors would say, rather, that it always is) self-punishment. Flagellation, abstinence, all the manifestations of asceticism can be taken as attentuated or symbolic forms of relative suicide. Entering a convent is another: one commonly calls this act a "death to the world." Let us be clear that we are not affirming that all asceticism or every monastic vocation is a partial suicide. Nevertheless, it is important to retain these formal distinctions because we shall see that they can represent either alternative solutions or attempted solutions within a suicidal process. No doubt, one must be careful and not fall into the trap that Menninger did: biting one's nails is a form of self-mutilation so removed from total suicide that there is something arbitrary about keeping it in a study of suicide. As ever, it is a question of degree.

Suicide can be *deliberate* or *involuntary.* This division is too clear-cut, and one must introduce a whole set of gradations. What may be involved is a deliberation in the strong sense of the term, where the subject draws up a balance sheet: on the debit side, he puts all the inconveniences he would have if he were to continue living, on the credit side, the joys he can hope yet to draw from life. It is probable that a good number of suicides by the elderly are of this type. On the other side of the scale, one finds brutal suicides committed under the pressure of an acute rupture in equilibrium, under the effect of fear (for example, a soldier who has been subjected to a long and intense artillery barrage), of pain, or of anger (thus, Tolstoy's brave general, Bagovout). One can even point to cases of automatic suicide: drowning persons who are saved but who are unable to explain why they jumped into the water or even to remember having done so.[19] These are exceptions; the general case involves deliberation. Of course, this deliberation can take delirious forms and may establish a balance sheet that, in the eyes of a neutral observer, is aberrant. Deliberation may be prolonged for years or decades, or then again, it may start just at the last moment. This is important because it allows us to provide for "ideas and threats of suicide." Contrary to common opinion, which holds that those who speak of suicide never kill themselves, one must take them very seriously. Anamnesis of numerous survivors shows that they nourished ideas of suicide over long periods and were occasionally quite open about informing their friends of it.

Suicide can be *intended* or *ventured.* It is intended when the subject uses a method that, except for luck, must lead to death. To shoot oneself in the head, to hang oneself, or to jump from the Eiffel Tower is seldom anything but final. On the other hand, methods that leave something to chance —throwing oneself into a river or, especially, swallowing barbiturates— contain a genuine chance of being saved. Sometimes—as when the subject takes care to alert a third party to his act or to commit it with the certainty of being discovered in time—the suicide is frankly simulated. We will see that behavior of this type is not to be disregarded because it is characteristic of certain types of suicide (I call them appeal suicides). I mean by ventured suicide, all conduct where, without being a certainty, there is a very high probability of death. The best example is Russian roulette, where one has one chance in six or seven of killing oneself. Generally speaking all dangerous activities (for example, auto racing, mountain climbing, acrobatics, etc.) *could* reflect suicidal tendencies. There is no question of considering all race car drivers as suicidal but simply of having available a form of suicidal behavior that is revealed in taking risks. We will see how useful this distinction is for interpreting suicides by the young.

Finally, suicide can be *chosen* or *imposed.* Generally speaking, suicide is chosen. I mean by this rather inaccurate term that the subject "chooses" one solution from a range of possible solutions. As we already have said, the several possibilities exist objectively, that is, for the neutral observer, even if for the suicidal person all other outcomes are closed off. One may understand better what I have in mind by considering imposed suicide. When the Roman emperor condemned a grandee to death, he allowed him to kill himself; only if he refused would the executioner intervene. In several archaic societies, the leader is followed into the tomb by his wives, slaves, and dependents. The question is whether they are to be seen as suicides. When one asks: "what would happen if the subject refused to kill himself?" and when the answer is: "he would be put to death," one is correct in considering that this is not a suicide but a form of execution. Having said that, I am inclined for two reasons not to eliminate imposed suicides. In the first place, these modes of execution are symptomatic of a civilization: it is not the same thing to allow a person condemned to death to swallow a cup of hemlock rather than forcibly slice his head off; the two practices reveal different conceptions of punishment.[20] The second, more decisive reason is that all imposed suicides are an institutionalization of chosen suicides—more particularly, of suicides as mourning and as punishment. We will see that these kinds of suicides can be institutionalized, and in fact have been by certain societies.

The last part of my definition is the *subject*. He is found at the center of this recital; he "decides" the outcome and commits his whole personality and experience to it. Suicide is the total act par excellence. That is why all the explanations of its common meaning miss their goal. One does not commit grief suicide, but a determinate individual shows his grief, in a determinate way, and finds a determinate outcome in death. The total nature of the act has three consequences:

1. It is extraordinarily difficult, not to say impossible, to give an exhaustive account of a single case of suicide. It would have to be possible to retrace minutely the smallest details of a person's evolution and to show how it led him to perceive an existential problem in such a way that his response had to be death.
2. It is impossible to weigh accurately any single factor, whether internal or external. It is always necessary to take account of a group of factors and to show how they combine with one another.
3. As the subject is the center of the whole thing, the transition to the act of suicide obviously depends on him. Now, there is a gulf between the accumulation of factors that make suicide probable and the transition to the act. Of two individuals confronted with the same problems and armed with the same general psychic dispositions, one kills himself, the other does not. No doubt, it is always legitimate to say that the identity was not absolute and that there certainly was a difference that distinguished them. The objection does not hold for the case of a single individual who now and then over the years thinks of suicide and then, one fine day, decides on it without knowing why himself. Suicide, considered as a precise action, has the ontological status of an event. Just as one can accumulate factors that explain that an insurrection or a revolution happens within a given society without being able to show precisely why it took place on this day and in this manner, so too the act of suicide remains mysterious *hic et nunc*. In spite of every explanation, it remains true that it could have happened either sooner or later or not

at all. In other words, however far it is pushed, explanation always comes up against an unknown: the transition to the act itself. That is the element of freedom and creativity that is left to man, even in suicide.

THEORETICAL IMPLICATIONS

The definition we have adopted contains a number of theoretical implications.

The first is the distinction between the *I* and the *Me.* It is the exclusive privilege of man, because he is self-conscious, to be able to divide himself between an *I*—an abstract and empty instance but nevertheless an affirmation of an identity irreducible to others—and a *Me*—composed of states of consciousness and unconsciousness, values it makes use of, and norms it obeys; in short, a personal mixture of received characteristics, idiosyncracies of the species, and particularities of the group to which it belongs. This distinction alone makes it possible to conceive of oneself as a means with respect to an end: with suicide, the *I* uses the *Me,* even if it is to get rid of it, just as an investor can gain control of a business in order to shut it down. This conception of suicide is paradoxical only as far as one continues to impose moral prohibitions on it. It is only from an ethical perspective that gives an absolute value to life that suicide seems to be an absolute defeat. In fact, even for adherents to this position, Bayet has shown it is difficult to hold to consistently: a more subtle ethics always appears to justify certain suicides that turned out well. For those of us who, as men of science, do not have to make value judgments, suicide always is an adequate solution, however little one is able to account for all the data *as they are perceived by the subject.* Only the neutral observer is in a position to decide that the perception of the subject is inadequate. But the neutral observer has a strictly functional role in scientific procedure: he serves to determine to what extent the objective situation (that is, for an average population) admits of no other outcome or has been closed off by the mental state of the subject.

The second implication is that the life of a man is neither the automatic unfolding of a program that has been decided in advance nor the arithmetic result of forces that bear on an individual: *life is a struggle.* From the moment he is born, each individual is faced with problems to be resolved. He must first of all struggle *against himself,* against his own aggressive and libidinal impulses that ceaselessly throw up obstacles against reality. He must struggle *against his parents.* I am not yet convinced of the universal reality of the Oedipus complex. The confirmations that are brought to us from psychoanalysis are burdened with a twofold inconvenience: they deal with selected individuals, those who have a smattering of psychoanalysis. One would like analysts to show more theoretical inventiveness and to construct scenarios other than the Oedipal. Rather than conceive of relations within the family configuration strictly in sexual terms, one could interpret them differently. One could say, for example, that even though the child is weak and helpless, he still must assert himself. In order to do so, he must develop a strategy that cannot be the same toward both mother and father because their roles are different (at least they are in all known civilizations); this strategy cannot for every long be the same because of the sex of the child since very soon the child is urged towards different ends according to whether it is a boy or a girl. Now, the habitual arrangement is that the weak point in the opposite camp is the mother, while the strong point is the father. Against the weak point, one will use devious means more effectively (illness, obvious weakness, tears, smiles, and caresses); against the strong point, more direct and aggressive means are required. In other words, there is no need to maintain that the infant desires to possess his mother and castrate his father in order to understand certain constant factors within family relations. That does not mean that predominantly sexual scenarios are not encountered. It is possible that certain children have received a particularly strong share of sexuality that forces them to adopt a properly sexual strategy. Strategies other than those based on the will to power or sexuality are equally conceivable, but it is probable that the number is quite limited, just as limited as the number of fundamental drives that set them in motion.

Specialists will not fail to find these remarks naive. No doubt they are right, for it is always imprudent to venture outside one's own area of professional competence. I feel more confident in asserting that the struggle begins against oneself and against one's parents and is followed throughout one's life *against others.* Whether it be in the realm of economics or politics, occupational, ideological, or sexual life, it is necessary to struggle ceaselessly against someone or something in order to obtain anything. It is necessary, finally, to struggle *against the human condition,* against sickness, misfortunes, limitations of all kinds, and death.

The third implication is that the personality of an individual is formed by these experiences of struggle and by the memory of his own behavior as well as by the results he obtained. Of course, one does not engage in all possible struggles, and each of us cannot live out every destiny. The range of choice is limited from the start by individual inclination: family milieu, social group, and type of society. It is clear that the range is not the same for a young Roman and a young Parisian, a workman's son and the son of an engineer, a child raised in a united family without major problems and another who must put up with quarreling alcoholic parents, an imbecile and an intelligent child, a pretty girl and an ugly one. Gradually, as experiences mount up, the range of choice ceaselessly contracts, at first quite quickly with the entrance into adult life and then more slowly until old age and death. In other words, a personality is constituted bit by bit, as much in a positive way, by lived experiences, as in a negative way, by lost opportunities. Now, since each experience is a response made to a problem and since one ever-possible response is the obliteration of the subject, it follows that suicide is at every moment an objective possibility for every person. This objective abstract possibility will have a higher probability of being actualized if unsuccessful experiences accumulate or are particularly serious.

The fourth implication is concerned with populations rather than with individuals. Within any given society, and even more within any given social group, the number and type of problems and conflicts that affect individuals are limited in number and are found in a kind of typical configuration. Hence, the solutions to them also are typical. Consequently, the part that an individual personally adds to the solution of his own problems, the inventions that the novelty of a situation demands of him, are reduced to practically nothing. Quite soon after early infancy, a person experiences very severe limitations placed on his initiative. Present opinion tells us to deplore this situation, but the opposite view also can be maintained, perhaps more justifiably because, if typical solutions are given to typical problems, an enormous amount of energy and individual effort are saved. Imagine a man permanently confronted with new problems and forced to invent solutions for them each time: no one could hold up for long, everyone would quickly give up, and the myth of Sisyphus, a mortal Sisyphus this time, would become the fate of us all. The present situation contains the additional advantage that risks of defeat are reduced to a minimum. In fact, since typical problems receive typical solutions, it is improbable that in the long run very many defeats will occur; the opposite would be true if neither the problems nor the solutions were typical. Defeats can occur only under exceptional circumstances, when the regular rhythm of work and daily life is interrupted or when an individual is unable to understand and practice the rules of the game.

This brings us to a fifth and final implication. If all members of a given population were always and at every moment capable of understanding and acting on the rules of the game, that is, if they conduct the struggle of their lives by giving typical solutions to typical problems, they only suicides would correspond to situations where the typical outcome is the disappearance of the subject (for example, the refusal to admit defeat in a fight), which, we shall see, can occur only rarely. Then there would be numerous suicides only in exceptional periods, during severe crises, and there would be mass suicides when a society underwent rapid and prolonged transformations. The first hypothesis is weakened by the nonnegligible number of suicides, the second by a remarkably permanent suicide rate, and the third by the absence of a massive increase during historical upheavals.

The only theoretical solution to this contradiction seems to me to be the following: it is necessary to *assume* that every individual does not have the same weapons available for carrying on the struggle of life. By weapons, we mean the individual's inner ability to find responses to problems that allow him to continue to live by integrating himself into a network of typical solutions. *This ability can reveal itself as deficient either by a shortcoming or by excess.* If it appears as a shortcoming, it condemns the individual to live perpetually below the level of his real possibilities, it renders him incapable of seizing the opportunities available to him, and it prevents him from creating a personality that would allow him to make his way within the career he has embarked on. Here we encounter Ringel's notion of *Fehlentwicklung*, developmental failure. These are all the cripples of life, incapable of creating solid and satisfactory bonds, of succeeding in their job, of making their way in the world. If there is an excess of vital energy, the consequences are no better; in fact, the individual is obliged to live below his potential, to go off the beaten track, and to make his way as a renegade. As he is no longer supported and helped by the net of typical solutions, he is forced to invent a personal plan for life and to expend considerable energy bringing it about. The risks of defeat are enormous because he is forever running into real obstacles, and he may lack the energy to fulfill his destiny. Of course, these two categories are not condemned to suicide; several outcomes are always open to them and not just those of renunciation or ambition. Nevertheless, the probability is higher that they will seize on a fatal outcome because there is a higher probability that they will find themselves up against "unforeseen" problems whose adequate solution is suicide.

Where do these differences in "vital capacity" as compared with the majority come from? No doubt they arise neither from social milieu nor from the experiences of early childhood. Besides, the forces generated by the social milieu are far too powerful and general to explain the appearance of a distinct minority, and anyway, for individuals of the same social origin placed in the same situation, only a minority respond by suicide. As for early childhood experiences, it is clear that they act differently on different individuals. Even if a lack of maternal love or the absence of a father always has injurious consequences, the damage is not identical for all the children in such families. One must conclude from this that vital capacity is an original datum, that it is inscribed in the genetic code. Recent progress in theoretical biology and the echo that it is beginning to have in public opinion have taught us to be shocked no longer when we learn that men are not genetically identical. Nevertheless, this progress simply gives a scientific foundation to a conviction that only a fanatical egalitarianism could reverse.

Let us be clear about this. I nowhere claim that suicide is inscribed in one's genetic code. I do say that it is likely that men are born with unequal capacities for life, that some are deficient, and that others have too much. Only life itself, by the accumulation of experiences, may reveal these original defects and may *eventually* lead to suicide. Supposing that one day a suicide-producing chromosome were discovered, just as a superfluous and possibly "crime-producing" chromosome was discovered; that would not mean that the subject was condemned to a suicidal or criminal career. It only indicates that certain subjects meet with a greater difficulty than others in integrating themselves normally (i.e., like the majority) into a social system and that they have a greater chance of running into trouble. That does not exclude the possibility either that other subjects will not turn out badly or that subjects so identified necessarily will. This is a question of greater or smaller probability, all other things being equal.

CONSEQUENCES

The preceding analyses enable us now to tie up certain loose ends and to lay the groundwork for later arguments.

As with psychiatric theories, one cannot study suicide without considering the role of *mental illness*. Even if one does not admit that every suicide must be the result of an illness, it is impossible not to recognize that a *certain* proportion of suicidal persons is sick. We notice, however, that the figures differ considerably with the authors involved. Explanation according to mental illness suits just about everyone, friends and family, journalists, civil and religious authorities. It goes without saying that it does not satisfy the scholarly investigator. For him, two series of questions are raised:

1. What might be the kinds of relations between a mental illness and suicide? Psychiatrists tend to hold that illness is by nature conducive to suicide (for example, melancholia). The theory that I am trying to defend excludes that sort of statement: suicide neither necessarily prefigures nor is a consequence of mental illness; suicide and illness are on the same level, both being responses to a problem. This clarification is important because it suggests that an analysis of cases must weigh all the factors, that is, collect together all the alternative solutions adopted by the subject to resolve his fundamental problem.
2. As a general rule, mental troubles precede suicide: such troubles must, therefore, constitute a less desperate solution, whereas suicide implies a worsening of the situation. Consequently, the very fact of mental illness takes some part in the etiology of suicide. In my interpretation, this may be easily explained, at least on the level of principles. Mental illness, in fact, may act in two convergent ways. By the very fact that it signifies, to a greater or lesser extent, a loss of contact with reality, the perception that the subject has of himself and his situation is eclipsed. With the aid of fantasies, the real situation is slowly replaced by a more and more frightening imaginary one. Simultaneously, and for the same reasons, the capacity to respond rationally to a problem diminishes and then disappears. Little by little suicide constitutes the only solution left. In certain cases, this progressive reduction of alternatives to a single and obligatory solution takes the form of a somehow detached injunction, a voice that clearly commands the subject to kill himself.

These two remarks, brief as they may be, are sufficient to lead the uninitiated to suspect that there must be a positive correlation between suicide and mental illness. Because suicide is a solution brought to bear on a problem, one may justifiably doubt that a subject, whose ability for improvising adequate solutions to new problems is limited, is likely to hit on a fatal solution when his problem has been transformed by fantasies. Let me repeat, these notations are intended to establish signposts for later development in detail; here they serve merely as rough indicators.

The theory we have adopted allows us to deal with the problem of suicide rates. I will not come back to this again: the *stability of suicide rates* clearly has a statistical origin. In a given population, it is probable that a determinate number of individuals will find the solution to their problems in suicide or in attempted suicide, exactly as the number of deaths, accidents, marriages, births, and so forth may be determined. All these indicators are likely to vary over time, but the variations are slow and reflect the interaction of a multiplicity of variables. Society does not demand of its members that they produce a determinate number of children, neither does it exact its tribute of suicides: the figures are the statistical summary of complex individual adventures.

One cannot deduce a suicide rate but only verify and interpret it retrospectively. However, I believe that one can deduce the *deficiencies of suicide rates*. The evidence shows that, in countries where reliable statistical services are maintained, the rates vary between 10 and 40 per 100,000 population. They never show a rate of 1 per 1,000 and above. First of all, then, save under exceptional circumstances, suicide can become a real solution only for a small minority: the vast majority resolve their typical problems by means of typical solutions without having to conceive of suicide as anything but an ever-present theoretical outcome. In other words, there is always a way of coping with any situation whatsoever, and most people find it.[21] It follows, naturally enough, that the probability of suicide must gradually increase with age as the subject gains the experience of his own insufficiencies, the discomforts of his situation, and the diminished chances of a favorable reversal. But from the very fact that the subject advances in age, death becomes more and more probable anyway. It becomes, so to speak, less and less necessary to delay the call. We will see that the facts entirely confirm this hypothesis: the percentage of suicides increases with age within the population of suicides, but the percentage of suicide among all causes of death declines constantly with age. In other words, the more one ages, the more the number of suicides increases, but the chances of death by any illness whatsoever also increase. These two facts, that the human condition is always nearly tolerable for the majority and that eventually one dies anyway, are enough to explain why suicide rates are uninformative.

One can verify these assertions by considering evidence from extreme situations. When conditions of life are brutally transformed and human beings are plunged into situations that are universally considered as exceeding the capacity to resist, it is to be expected that mass suicides would occur if the means of killing oneself were readily available. Take, for example, the Nazi concentration camps.[22] Clearly, there are no statistics available, but individual testimony does exist.[23] One has the impression that, although suicides were frequent and certainly more numerous than outside the camps, they never attained massive proportions. Now, if it is unnecessary to recall the way out reserved for most of these unfortunates, it must be remembered that, contrary to the general law of the world of prisons, where everything is arranged to remove every material aid to killing oneself, suicide in concentration camps was particularly easy: it was enough to throw oneself on the electrified barbed wire or to hang oneself at night in the barracks. Why did only a minority make use of these facilities? First, because, in a situation of extreme deprivation, the level of one's aspirations collapses. All vital energy is concentrated on the search for food, a less exacting labor, a less uncomfortable place in the dormitories, and so on. Each success in this incessant quest produces a "satisfaction," which provides a new reason to continue. And what is most important, death is probable in any case. As one person testified: "the detainee does not kill himself, he is allowed to die."[24] Finally—and this sentiment is appropriate to the camps—suicide is avoided because survival is the highest form of challenge: precisely because the executioners want your death, the simple fact of not dying or of hanging on as long as possible allows one to continue the struggle, which is a kind of victory. This element of defiance clearly emerges from the testimony of an escapee from the hell of hells.[25] Marched off to Treblinka and thereby selected to live a bit longer, he recalls: "Men were crying in the darkness. Then the sound of a box overturning and a death rattle. Someone began praying. A suicide. I made up my mind not to let life ebb away on its own, not to settle for a cowardly death. They were taking our lives; it meant that our lives were jewels. My people were dead; I held their lives in trust. They'd bequeathed me their past, what they could have become and what they had known of joy and sorrow. Through me alone, Senatorska Street might live on . . . Through me vengeance would live on. I'd decided to live. I *would* escape—for those I loved."[26] And then, a little further on:

> There was still escape by death. That night more men hanged themselves in the hut. When, for the third time, I heard a man dragging the box to help a friend die, I dashed over, grabbed him by the shoulders, and shook him.
>
> "But they *want* us to die!"
>
> "If we all die, all of us, what'll we do?"
>
> . . . I was fighting that black wave. I had only one recourse: saying over to myself, I must live, for those I loved, live to avenge myself and tell the world that Treblinka meant death. . . . Live, escape, proclaim, avenge.[27]

A third consequence deserves some attention. From all that has been said to this point, it follows that suicide must be an *inelastic* phenomenon. I am borrowing this term from political economy to express the idea that suicide must be, as a statement about society, quite insensitive to the variations in factors that influence it. Let us assume a given society is characterized by a suicide rate of 30 per 100,000 and let us ask under what conditions this rate could vary strongly in one direction or another—to move, for example, to 15 or to 45 per 100,000. To make this example even clearer, we shall consider only the case of an increase; in the case of a decrease, one would simply reverse the arguments. In terms of the definition adopted, suicide rates could appreciably and permanently vary only under the effects of three fundamental modifications:

1. *A narrowing of possible solutions,* more precisely, of rational solutions, and in such a way that suicidal ones benefit. It would be necessary to admit that over a long period and without untoward accidents, a society proves to be incapable of producing normal conditions, that is,

conditions that the majority can support. This situation would weaken what I hold to be a fundamental psychological law: the extreme elasticity of men with respect to change (whether favorable or unfavorable) that operates by the mechanism of levels of aspirations.In contrast, it is conceivable that a severe crisis touching an entire population could, for a brief time, increase the probability of a suicidal solution. Political conditions (revolution, war, and terrorist regimes) are the most likely to lead to such a consequence.

2. *An increase in the number and severity of problems* that the individual must face. This is just as improbable as the preceding case, again with the exception of political crises. I would even add that the number and severity of problems that an individual must face are a constant governed by a *natural* capacity to "stand it." One of the common interpretations of modernity is that contemporary human beings live in a world so complex that they are unable to understand it all; they give up hope of doing so and sink into madness or annihilate themselves by suicide. To begin with, I would like to have explained to me how one calculates the degree of complexity of a society. Next, I would like it specified whether the complexity concerns the entire society as it is observed from the outside or the circumstances that impinge on an individual on the inside. On the first point, one would tend to think that all societies are equally complex and that the social sciences give us the key neither to Kwakyutl, nor Chinese, nor contemporary Western society. Whether one considers the political, economic, religious, ideological, moral, or whatever sphere, the complexity is always the same, infinite. If one takes the point of view of thc individual, it is probable that the situation is always everywhere equally simple and clear: the number of typical situations is 'imited, and the solutions to them are well known. One could, at most, support the idea that complexity has declined today; it is easier and takes less time and effort to become a specialized worker than it does to become a peasant; knowledge today is greater, although it must necessarily be left to specialists; in a prescientific society, it is necessary to know how to get along with natural and supernatural forces. I would not pursue this simple parallel much further but suggest only that one can without difficulty maintain an interpretation that is the opposite of the habitual one. I take it as highly probable that it is neither more nor less difficult to live one's life in the Cro-Magnon caves or on the sampans of Bangkok than it would be in Leptis Magna or La Garenne-Colombes.

3. *A diminution of vital capacity.* As mentioned earlier, by this term I mean the genetically determined capacity to confront typical problems and to find typical solutions within a given society. By nature, it is outside any social determination because of the nontransmitability of acquired characteristics. In fact, only one external variable can, over the very long term, affect it negatively: it is possible that the massive decline in

infant and juvenile mortality is accompanied in the long run by a deterioration of human material. One can conceive that it may end up multiplying the number of life's cripples and that the legions of suicide would be substantially increased. Of this suicidal prospect, I would say that, for the past and the present, nothing allows us to assume a mutation of this type.

These commonsensical reflections, in short, lead me to believe that suicide must be a universal constant. In the absence of universal figures, I cannot propose a direct proof. Thus, I must have recourse to indirect proof by showing that, if the phenomenon of suicide were elastic, one would find enormous variations under the effect of the massive changes that take place in society. It is admitted by all the specialists that a suppressed aggression, for which no external outlet exists, will have a tendency to turn against the subject and to translate itself into suicide. Consider the evolution of aggression in Western civilization.[28] Up to about the fifteenth century, before the establishment of centralized states, daily life was (for us) extraordinarily violent. The lay elite passed their time at war, hunting, or in tournaments; the people had extremely primitive manners and customs, and fights were a common occurrence; insecurity was widespread and one risked one's life on leaving one's own village. The chronicles are full of stories of assassination, massacre, pillage, and destruction. At least until the eighteenth century, manners slowly evolved and tended to reduce violence to the point where it practically disappeared from daily life. This evolution was instigated by the establishment of centralized states. The aristocracy was domesticated by court life: it was forced to give up its personal wars and to adopt new rules for the social game where aggression appeared as intrigue and no longer as violence. Manners and customs were "civilized" at the top and, by imitation, won over larger and larger sections of the population. The progress of royal administrative control brought security to the countryside and put an end to private violence. By the nineteenth century, the situation had stabilized: courtly manners and customs spread to the whole population by way of democratization and public instruction; the civil bureaucracy, police, and judiciary grew more effective and consistent; a pluralist political regime opened the possibility of a nonviolent resolution of conflict. In fact, violence no longer appeared virulent, save on two occasions, in war or in riots and revolutions. In short, the West has succeeded in beating the odds against humanizing war, at least as wars have developed among Westerners, and riots have likewise become less and less bloody.[29] Since war and riot are not our daily fare, where has violence gone? It has not disappeared purely and simply, for as soon as an occasion arises when man can express his primitive savagery he is not found wanting. Very simply, it has been contained and mastered by each individual. In psychoanalytic terms, one would say that social development in the West (this is true for all nation-states) has tended ceaselessly to reinforce the superego in order to master aggressive forces. Now, this considerable transformation within the economy of aggressive forces has not in the least precipitated an avalanche of suicides. To be sure, I have no figures to support this claim (and neither do proponents of the other position), but if repressed aggression has led to correspondingly intense disruptions, the message would get around: there would not be 10,000 suicides in France but hundreds of thousands.

Another indirect proof? Nothing could be easier. The most decisive characteristic of modern Western civilization is plurality of choice. Whether at an individual or a collective level, the range of choice has ceaselessly grown larger. An individual can choose among an infinity of trades and occupations; there are a great number of ways of dressing, loving, and amusing oneself; one may change one's mind about such matters repeatedly. Collectivities have available different ways of dividing up their wealth, power, and prestige; one can establish different priorities; one imagines several ways of living together; there are diverse solutions to the problem of finding a place in the international system. Our civilization is the first to define itself by change, instability, and the absence of an unopposed sense of purpose. We said that one of the reasons why the suicide rate is maintained at a low level is that individuals can give typical solutions to typical problems. But social pluralism disturbs one's tranquility because it obliges people to invent, in a way, their own lives by choosing themselves within the vast range of options open to them. If suicide were elastic, the suicide rates would show great jumps and would reflect a great anxiety in the face of life's insoluble problems. It goes without saying that epidemics of suicide are periodically proclaimed. However, nothing, strictly nothing, appears to confirm these fantasies. Men have adapted themselves to a new situation, have succeeded in accommodating themselves to it, and have found more reasons to live than to die—as they always do.

Let us push the irreducible pessimists to their last line of defense. Let us examine their use of suicide rates in France over the last century and a half and try to demonstrate its inelasticity. Two features leap before our eyes: the rate increases regularly up to the end of the nineteenth century, then remains at a standstill and fluctuates slowly around what appears to be an equilibrium point. Short-term variations are so weak as to be insignificant and may be neglected. I would add that these two factors are valid not only for France but for all countries whose civilizations are closely comparable. One can formulate seven explanatory hypotheses and definitely eliminate five of them.

1. *Increased urbanization* of French society was identified by Halbwachs as a cause. In fact, this amounts to a pedantic treatment of a very old myth that maintains that the city, especially the large city, must be a place of perdition for the unfortunate country folk who answer its call and succumb to its charms. A fascinating study could be made of the endurance of these myths in the teeth of contradictory evidence. It is simply false that the newly urbanized necessarily flounder in crime, madness, and suicide. No doubt one could admit that, during periods of

anarchic and intensive urbanization, the accumulation of a floating population in the suburbs and in certain overpopulated areas favors criminal activities, but it is a kind of collective criminality that reflects not an individual abnormality but an adaptation to an abnormal situation.[30] Over the long term, solid arguments favor another position. First of all, it is evident that, from the very fact that large masses are grouped together, deviant behavior is more frequently and more easily perceived than in smaller communities. This point is reinforced by the great ease with which the authorities become acquainted with factual information: what police force informs us of the crimes perpetrated in the provinces of the ancien régime? One also must remember that those who hold cities in such contempt are themselves not rustics but city dwellers;[31] The *O beatos nimium agricolas* are chanted by intellectuals who so well defend the drudgery of plow and harrow and personally cultivate the pleasures of the countryside during their short visits passed in comfort and idleness. But after all, let us admit that life in tentacular cities drives people to suicide. Unfortunately, the data in no way support this contention. In fact, the increase in the suicide rate in the nineteenth century is in no way comparable to the massive changes that have led increasing proportions of French peasants to the cities. Even more, the curve levels off in the twentieth century, whereas urbanization continues. It has declined slowly since 1945, even though cities underwent a new phase of accelerated growth. This is so clear that one can take it as certain that—assuming that urbanization has some influence on suicide, which I doubt—it is so weak as to be negligible.

2. One can draw the same conclusion from the second hypothesis: *industrialization.* It is said to have either a direct influence on suicide, by making conditions of life worse, or an indirect one, by introducing constant changes: being forced ceaselessly to adapt to ever-new conditions and give meaning to a life that is split in several directions (especially between occupation and family), the unfortunate individual is unable to find himself in such a society. I have already suggested that, from the point of view of an individual, it is unlikely that lives are more or less complex in different civilizations. It hardly matters anyway: the incontestable fact is that the data in no way reflect these changes. Since 1945, the period charcterized by a new phase of French industrialization, this is particularly clear. If the hypothesis were correct, one has had to deal, if not with hecatombs, at least with an upward swing of the curve. Nothing of the kind happened, only a miserable stagnation.

3. *Anomie,* so dear to Durkheim, resists examination no better. It is beyond dispute that the material condition of Frenchmen has been raised, and it is more than probable that it has contributed to an expansion of desires beyond real possibilities of satisfying them. One may doubt, however, that this catastrophe has led very many people to kill themselves. To be serious, one must be an intellectual, comfortably ensconced

in one's life, and convinced that the disappearance of scarcity, famine, epidemics, infantile mortality, premature death, and aggression on every side, in exchange for certainty as to where one's next meal is coming from, improved health, more comfortable lodgings, greater freedom, and so on, are insufferable changes and incite some people to kill themselves. Intellectuals give the impression of finding it intolerable that people no longer perish from hunger; some do so because suffering no longer sanctifies creation; others because a prosperous people no longer revolt (which is false anyhow). In any event, the curve of suicides again goes in the opposite direction to the one describing a rise in the standard of living.

4. As far as I know, an *increase in life expectancy* has not yet been singled out. The correlation, however, would be entirely intelligible. In fact, the relation of age and suicide rate is constant. One could expect that the number of suicides increases in proportion to the number of people attaining an advanced age. Alas! no; the French have been able to withstand this blow; otherwise, the curve would have continued to rise in the twentieth century.
5. The *lowering of infant mortality* is a more subtle and no longer exploited hypothesis. One could argue that lower infant mortality has multiplied the number of physically weak and therefore the chances that they will break under the strains of life. One cannot dispute this hypothesis with the available data. In fact, in order for modifications to occur in such a way that natural selection induces perceptible consequences within an entire population, numerous generations are required.[32] We must wait for several centuries to verify this hypothesis.
6. The sixth hypothesis has the triple merit of being elegant, founded on fact, and new. It starts from the general argument that suicide rates sharply fall off during periods of *war*. The argument that imputes a lowering of rates to deficiency in the collection of statistics during wartime or to the possibility open to potential suicides to get themselves killed in combat fails because the same lowering occurs among neutrals. In the same way, the argument that actual suicidal individuals, being mobilized, have no time to think about their problems runs afoul of the fact that the decline affects women as much as men. Let us take the fact as established. An hypothesis that immediately comes to mind would relate the suicide rate to the long period of peace in Europe between 1815 and 1914. The argument would be as follows: within any given society, a determinate quantity of aggressiveness exists. It must be expressed one way or another, and the best way possible is war. When no war occurs for a long period, it is internalized and is reflected by a host of deviant phenomena—crime, rebellions, internal conflicts, and so forth. Thus, suicide is the outlet chosen by a minority. The hypothesis seems satisfactory enough, especially since the twentieth century with its thirty years of war (1914–1945) effectively reversed the nine-

teenth-century trend. In fact, I believe that some suicides are explainable, *in the last analysis* (that is, by abstracting from a series of mediations that have their own importance), by a peace that lasts too long. Certainly not all suicides, nor even a majority, can be explained this way; otherwise, the rates would fall even more sharply during wartime. On the other hand, the hypothesis as is, is based on a very coarse interpretation of suicide as aggression directed against the subject because he is prevented from being aggressive toward others. We must refine these propositions.

7. The seventh hypothesis is easily the most convenient. The suicide curve reflects the *progress in maintaining statistical data,* which reached a certain plateau at the end of the nineteenth century. This is a convenient hypothesis because it is confirmed in an intelligible way by three series of nineteenth-century peculiarities. First is the victory of the "calculators" and "rationalists," whom Burke deplored: the state became accustomed to calculating and accounting. Next came the increase in state apparatus that, by means of the civil bureaucracy and the judiciary, was able to obtain a more and more precise idea of reality. Finally, secularization made it less and less obnoxious to admit that one of one's friends or relatives was suicidal. These three peculiarities took nearly a century to develop all their ramifications. Does this mean that twentieth-century data exactly reflect reality? That is unlikely; there will always be camouflages and disguises (above all, accidental ones). What is the proportion of them? I have no idea, and I do not really care. I am inclined to think, however, that it is quite low, almost negligible. It is not less than the proportion that is indeterminate, which completely obliterates all the analyses based on variations in rates.

If the phenomenon of suicide is insensitive to such unprecedented upheavals as urbanization, industrialization, and demography, one may say that it is inelastic. I just spoke of *constant rates.* Clearly, I was not thinking of something like Planck's constant, an immutable number. I am thinking of weak variations about a rate on the order of 20 to 30 per 100,000, which must be found in nearly all societies. When the data fall sharply below this, it is necessary to see in it an absence or a deficiency of statistical information.[33] I would equally maintain that this elasticity exclusively concerns *successful suicides.* I will show that *attempted suicides,* in the strong sense of suicides perpetrated without the intention of going through to a fatal outcome, have, on the contrary, the possibility of being very elastic: it is probable that attempted suicides show a certain sensitivity to external factors.

THE PREVENTION OF SUICIDE

The inelasticity of suicide will allow me to make the terms of this question a bit more precise so as not to have to come back to it later. Traditionally, books on suicide close with some recommendations, or rather exhortations, on the need for mankind to get rid of such calamities. Of course, such pieties change not a whit the reality of suicide, no more than the incessant advertisements in newspapers and on radio and television influence the number of highway accidents. Doctors and psychiatrists are in a way led by their position to undertake this rite of adjuration: for them, death always means a defeat, even more so a voluntary death. Sociologists and psychologists believe themselves obliged to prove the impossible, that their research serves something: without exception, they serve at best only to clarify, which constitutes a necessary and sufficient justification. As for bureaucrats, it seems that they must be mixed up with everything, even what does not concern them. Personally, I would maintain that this book, if it is read, will have not the slightest influence on suicide; that, from the point of view of the individual, it is necessary to defend fiercely the right to abandon voluntarily one's life; that it is an inalienable human privilege; and that, from the point of view of society, it is not at all certain that suicides represent something harmful simply because they concern a population with problems.

This is my personal position, and no one need share it. But let us say that we must eliminate suicide as one of the solutions available to people. How does one go about it? If one begins with the hypothesis that suicide is a consequence of modernity, it would be necessary to return to an agrarian society and to renounce the triumphs of science, technology, and political freedom. Assuming that such a reverse evolution were even possible, it would be undertaken by a formidable means of repression during which one can be certain that there would occur many occasions for suicide. Anyhow, suicide is not at all a modern phenomenon: to return to barbarism would not deliver us from this evil but probably would make it neither more nor less frequent.

Perhaps one holds the opposite view, that suicide survives only because it is tied to an imperfect state of society and that an ideal society would render men so happy that they would cease to think of killing themselves. To link individual happiness to the favorable organization of society seems to me quite simply to be stupid. I cannot see how losing a dear one could become a pleasure or why growing up would be easier....

There remains the possibility of acting on the genetic stock so as to produce only individuals who withstand everything. It would be necessary to begin by isolating the elements of the genetic code that determine one's vital capacity. We are not yet at that point. And fortunately not, because I have a repugnance for all biological manipulations.

These remedies are not serious; otherwise, they rapidly would become frightening. It is not very likely that suicide will ever become so great a problem as to force political leaders to such extremes. It is more likely that it will remain a subject of fascination for journalists and writers. One point seems to me to be solidly established: whatever our future may be, there will always be suicides, and they will be a nearly constant proportion of the population. One can deplore it, but one also can consider it as the price we pay for being human, that suicide is one of the illustrations of humanity.

1 E. Durkheim, *Suicide: A Study in Sociology*, trans. John A. Spaulding and George Simpson (Glencoe: The Free Press, 1951), p. 44.

2 See for example, Blaise Cendrars, *L'Homme foudroyé* (Paris: Livre de Poche, 1960), pp. 322–323.

3 M. Halbwachs, *Les causes du suicide* (Paris: Alcan, 1930), p. 479. Emphasis added by the author.

4 Ibid., p. 480.

5 F. Achille-Delmas, *Psycho-pathologie du suicide* (Paris: Alcan, 1932), p. 104.

6 Ibid., p. 20.

7 G. Deshaies, *Psychologie du Suicide* (Paris: P.U.F., 1947), p. 5. Emphasis added by the author.

8 This is why I have called the proposed theory "strategic." I would like to suggest that suicide is a means put to the service of an end and that, in suicide, the individual sets forces into motion with a view to attaining a certain objective. In this regard, I must pay my respects to Douglas, who in the last part of his book develops a similar account of the problem.

9 This is why this book is not called *Suicide*, but *Suicides*.

10 At this stage of the analysis I am not yet able to introduce a more solid justification. If the construction of types gives mentally satisfying results, it is much more difficult to find the pure state in real cases, since overlapping always occurs. But one thing at a time.

11 See Alain Ducellier, *Le Miroir de l'Islam* (Paris: Julliard, 1971), pp. 99–103.

12 *Le Monde*, 29 June 1972. Friedrich Hacker declared: "our clinical evidence allows us to establish that 28 murderers plausibly have assured us that they have killed other people in order to be executed themselves." *Aggression-violence dans le Monde moderne* (Paris: Calmann-Lévy, 1972), p. 146. After his second trial Buffet was, in fact, executed (Dec. 1972). In a letter addressed to the President of France, he demanded to receive at once the "grace" of the guillotine: "To kill in order to commit suicide, that's my morality!" *Le Monde*, 15 December 1972.

13 E. S. Shneidman, "Orientations toward Death: A Vital Aspect of the Study of Lives" in R. W. White, ed. *The Study of Lives* (New York: Atherton Press, 1963), pp. 201–237. (Reprinted in *International Journal of Psychiatry* 2[1966]:167–200.)

14 Ibid., p. 210.

15 Ibid., p. 210.

16 Ibid., p. 211.

17 Here is a good example: Madame F, twenty-one years old, hospitalized in a psychiatric ward. She is intelligent and competent but finds herself confronted by a whole series of problems: exhausting work, tiny living quarters, young children, financial problems. One evening when she is alone she takes forty poisonous tablets. When she wakes up in the hospital she declares that she had for a long time dreamed of going to sleep free from care: "I wished to cure myself by sleeping; the sick look so happy when they sleep." (Case cited in S. Casabon, *La Tentative de Suicide (Etude statisique et psychologique)* (thèse de médecine, Bordeaux, 1964).

18 Ibid., p. 211 [i.e., Shneidman, "Orientations toward Death"].

19 See H. Henseler, who cites several cases in "Der unbewusste Selbstmordversuch," *Nervenarst* 42 (1971):595–598.

20 It is evidence of the degree to which we have been influenced by Christianity that in discussions for or against capital punishment no one has ever suggested a third solution: to allow the condemned person to kill himself. Quite the contrary, the cells on "death row" are constructed so as to make suicide impossible and their inmates placed under constant surveillance.

21 The most effective and most constant mechanism is to desire only what one can get: each individual learns very soon to seek only what is available in the station to which he was born. Only when this "rational" mechanism becomes impossible do "irrational" ones intervene.

22 P. Citrone, *Le Suicide dans les Camps de Concentration* (thèse de médecine, Paris, 1948); idem. "Le Suicide dans les camps de concentration," *Cahiers internat. sociol.* 12 (1952):147–149.

23 Seven such accounts deal with suicide in *Documents pour servir à l'Histoire de la Guerre*, vol. 4, Office d'Editions, 1945.

24 Ibid., p. 83.

25 Martin Gray and Max Gallo, *For Those I Loved*, trans., Anthony White (Toronto: Little, Brown, 1972).

26 Ibid., p. 129

27 Ibid., pp. 131–132.

28 I am relying on the analysis of Norbert Elias, *La Civilisation des Moeurs* (Parks: Calmann-Lévy, 1973), pp. 279–297.

29 On the first point, the extension of a single diplomatic and strategic system to the whole world reintroduced violent warfare and pushed it to its extreme. One has moved from a homogeneous international system to a heterogeneous system. See Jean Baechler, "Un Système international hétérogéne?" *Contrepoint* 7–8 (1972):27–42. Internally, violence seems to continue to decline. The events of May 1968 saw extraordinarily little violence: compared to the past, if only to the nineteenth century, they gave the impression of a game where what was involved was not to kill one's opponent but, by cornering him, to force him to give up and surrender all claims to the use of force.

30 An abnormal situation of this kind has been minutely studied, with respect to Paris of the Restoration and the July Monarchy, by Louis Chevalier, *Classes laborieuses et classes dangereuses à Paris pendant la première moitié du xixe siècle*, 2nd ed. (Paris: Plon, 1969).

31 It is rare that it is necessary to force peasants to move towards cities. The benefits of all kinds, material, moral, and intellectual, that they provide are so obvious that they are irresistibly attracted to them as soon as an urban civilization is established.

32 According to Jacques Monod, *Chance and Necessity*, trans. A. Wainhouse (New York: Knopf, 1971), it is necessary to wait for about fifteen generations. On the other hand, it certainly seems that the decline in infant mortality must be immediately reflected in an increase in the number of handicapped babies. This can be explained: in this second case what is involved is the viable maintenance of genetic accidents; in the first, it is a question of modifying the genetic stock of humanity.

33 Who could take seriously the official Egyptian suicide rate for the period 1961–1963 as 0.2 per 100,000?

49• Drug Abuse as Indirect Self-Destructive Behavior

Calvin J. Frederick

Calvin J. Frederick is the chief of Disaster Assistance and Emergency Mental Health, National Institute of Mental Health, Rockville, Maryland, and Professor of Medical Psychology at the George Washington University School of Medicine. Dr. Frederick has worked in the fields of overt suicide and indirect self-destructive behavior for a number of years.

DEFINITION AND CONCEPTUALIZATION

There is little doubt that drug abuse and self-destructive behavior are related problems in society today. The main question is the extent to which drug abuse may be a causal factor in precipitating self-destructive acts. The personal conflicts and tensions which give rise to such aberrant behavior may be expressed through different avenues. There are growing indications, however, that drug abuse itself can be a precipitator of self-destructive behavior. Deliberate drug overdoses demonstrate this convincingly, but less obvious indicators, such as feelings of haplessness and helplessness, signify a loss of hope and are a result of the addictive process.

Indirect self-destructive behavior, by definition, is covert rather than overt or direct, with latent and subtle signs. The author views self-destructive behavior as on a continuum between self-assaultive on one end, and overt, unmistakable suicide on the other. The degree of personal awareness varies directly with the clarity of the behavioral act in the direction of suicide. Self-assaultive behavior is characterized by personal abuse of oneself, without total awareness of its life-threatening components. Anorexia nervosa and picking at a melanoma would constitute illustrations of self-assaultive behavior, assuming an absence of knowledge about the dangers of such phenomena. Self-destructive acts fall between the two ends of the continuum and suggest relatively more conscious understanding of one's behavior. It may be seen in people who possess a known physical problem but neglect proper health care. Specific instances are smoking after developing emphysema, overeating by cardiac patients, and neglect of medication in the presence of severe diabetes mellitus. Direct suicidal behavior involves an overt act with a relatively clear plan and intent to end one's life. Even though not so classified initially, self-assaultive and self-destructive acts can easily become suicidal.

Numerous psychological equivalents of suicide occur in everyday life without being recognized. In addition to the neglect of medical illnesses like those just cited, frequent reckless and inebriated driving and certain aspects of drug abuse can constitute suicidal behavior. Like such clinical syndromes as suicidal behavior and alcoholism, drug abuse and addiction are not unitary problems, and addicts and abusers do not compose a homogeneous population. At least four groups of persons engage in drug abuse and addiction: (1) those who are thrill-seekers and become addicted adventitiously; (2) those with various personality disorders; (3) rebellious youth; and (4) those who become addicted medically. It has not been fully determined, as yet, whether or not certain personality types become addicted to particular kinds of drugs. In the author's experience, rebellious young persons are more likely to use hallucinogenic drugs, whereas those less militant are inclined to use marijuana. Although additional data are needed to confirm this phenomenon, it has become increasingly apparent that addicts often ingest alcohol and then move into drug addiction, and vice versa. It is also now apparent that many persons become alcoholics as well as drug addicts at different ages of entry.

One of the difficult problems in today's society is that psychotropic drugs are prescribed medically in increasing numbers. About one fifth of all prescriptions written in the last few years have been for psychotropic agents. Hypnotic drugs, which for our purposes will include amphetamines, stimulants, short-acting barbiturates, and glutethimides, are the most frequently used. Tranquilizers and antidepressives must be viewed separately for several reasons. First, the chemical and physiological reaction is not the same as in the other drugs noted. Second, no law prohibits the use of such drugs when medically prescribed. Third, there is no strong evidence to indicate the presence of physical addiction or habituation to them. Nevertheless, there is a serious problem with the use of all dangerous drugs, and it is generally agreed that no drug is entirely safe. Twenty-five percent of the United States population uses sedatives, stimulants, or tranquilizers, according to the 1975 White Paper on Drug Abuse. Many drug deaths from these substances are listed as accidental overdoses rather than suicides.

METHODS OF SUICIDE IN THE UNITED STATES

It might be helpful to look at the methods used in suicide over the past several decades to note how drugs have been used in direct suicide deaths (Table 1). Until the mid-twentieth century, breathing domestic coal gas was a frequent method of suicide. This was related to the use of coal for heat by most of the United States. After the introduction of natural gas into North American homes, the number of expirations from gas decreased dramatically, since natural gas is not poisonous if adequate oxygen is supplied with it. The dramatic decline in suicidal deaths from 1950 to 1960 no doubt reflects this changeover from coal to natural gas. In addition, deaths by hanging and strangulation decreased during the third quarter of this century, but the number of suicides from firearms and poison by other gases rose markedly. In the last twenty-five years, deaths from firearms and explosives have increased 28 percent, poison by other gases 61 percent, and solid and liquid substances (drug abuse) by 31 percent. Poison by domestic gas has decreased by 98 percent, whereas suicides from hanging and strangulation have declined by 36 percent. The noticeable rise in poisoning by gases other than the domestic type is due to motor vehicle exhaust intoxication, which accounts of 82 percent of self-inflicted deaths in this category.

TABLE 1
PERCENTAGE OF SUICIDAL DEATHS IN THE UNITED STATES, BY METHOD: 1950, 1960, 1964, AND 1975

Method	*1950*	*Percent* *1960*	*1964*	*1975*	*25-year percent change*
Solid and liquid substances	10.5	12.4	15.7	13.8	+31
Domestic gas	6.5	1.0	0.4	0.1	−98
Poisoning by other gases	6.2	9.4	10.8	10.0	+61
Hanging and strangulation	21.0	17.7	14.6	13.5	−36
Drowning	3.9	3.2	2.6	2.0	−49
Firearms and explosives	43.0	47.4	47.6	55.0	+28
Cutting and piercing	3.1	2.6	1.9	1.4	−59
Jumping	3.7	3.7	3.7	2.7	−27
Other and unspecified causes	2.1	2.7	2.7	1.5	−29

SOURCE: National Center for Health Statistics, Mortality Statistics Branch.

The largest category of suicide fatalities in the United States involves *firearms and explosives.* The percentage of death from firearms has continued to rise, due in all likelihood to the easy access to guns in this country. When a gun is used, the chances of the suicidal act resulting in a fatality are much greater than when other methods are employed, such as poisons or cutting and piercing instruments. The probability of rescue in time to save a life is increased with the use of less lethal means. In contrast to the United States, most European countries reveal low suicide rates by firearms. Suicide is committed in those countries principally by hanging or poison.

DRUG ADDICTION AS INDIRECT SELF-DESTRUCTION

In recent years, professionals have become more aware of the indirect or latent aspects of suicidal behavior. *Indirect suicide is rarely obvious to the unskilled observer or to the potential victim.* A variety of terms has been used to describe behavior of this nature, such as: psychological equivalents of suicide; hidden suicide; latent suicide; covert suicide; and indirect self-destruction. Although patterns may vary, as a rule, the following comprise the prominent characteristics of indirect suicide: (1) there is lack of full awareness of the consequences; (2) the behavior is rationalized, intellectualized, or denied; (3) the onset is gradual, even though the death may appear to be precipitous; (4) open discussion seldom occurs, in contrast to obvious "cries for help" is direct suicide; (5) long suffering, martyrlike behavior often appears; (6) secondary gain is obtained by evoking sympathy and expressing hostility via the process; and (7) the death is often seen as accidental. Meerloo (1968) has spoken of hidden suicide in discussing some specific attitudes toward self-chosen death. Many people seem to move toward death without being fully aware that they are doing so. These incidents are never shown in the published statistics on suicide. In some parts of the world, people indicate a greater dread of life than a fear of death. Although life for the suicide attempter generally suggests a state of insecurity, death may hold the hope of eternal relief.

Hillman (1965) noted that Freud put death at the center of existence and observed that "all death is suicide," whether by an airplane crash, heart attack, or by an evident method called suicide. He commented further that "suicide is the urge for hasty transformation." There is little doubt that each suicide attempt suggests an experience approaching death. Hendin (1974) states that some young people present a bland front that conceals self-destructive impulses probably stemming from early painful relationships and anxiety related to their mothers. Many people who have been deprived of emotions early in life feel alive only when they experience some unusual thrill, become anxious, or feel pain. The life-and-death struggle seems to heighten the sensations and the feelings which some people need.

The interaction of youngsters with monsters, horror movies, books, etc. represents one dimension of the life-and-death struggle. The thrill of being "scared to death" exemplifies this symbolically. The idea of being able to come to grips with one's innermost fears provides reassurance in the life-and-death struggle, even at an early age. The religious notion of being born again is another aspect of the same phenomenon. It helps to bear the anxiety associated with the reality of death. Religion provides a structure for dealing with the overwhelming anxiety of life in all its destructive aspects. On the other hand, fear of the unknown and resignation in the acceptance of death is a source of periodic turmoil in us all, as Shakespeare wrote so colorfully in his famous soliloquy in *Hamlet*.

Drugs can bring psychological as well as physical relief to people who are in mental anguish or bodily pain. Such relief leads to tension reduction and becomes automatically reinforcing, in keeping with one of the basic principles of learning theory. Any anxiety-reducing process is a strong reinforcement for the accompanying response. The probability of repeating such an act on subsequent occasions increases markedly thereafter. Thus, it is easy to see how drug addiction can be quickly learned. The relief which it offers initially becomes a way of "ending it all" on a temporary basis. In the psychoanalytic sense it is, to begin with, an offering of a portion of one's life, or body, as a symbolic payment in death for the value received from the drug. It stems from the old biblical notion that it is better to "cut off thy right arm rather than that thy whole body shall perish." Such an effective temporary sacrifice then makes it easier to give one's self up entirely to the anticipated effects of heavy drug use. One of the insidious aspects of the addictive process is that, initially, relief comes readily, but later a tolerance for drugs often develops, and increased dosages are required to bring relief. As drug abuse develops, it becomes easier and easier to ingest an overdose, either accidentally or "accidentally on purpose." Escape from stress into sleep brings a death equivalent temporarily, or an actual death permanently.

The dramatic increase, recently, in the use of the drug phencyclidine (PCP) warrants special mention. It became known through the drug subculture, initially in 1967, as the "PeaCe Pill" or "peace pill," but a more commonly used term since the mid-1970s has been "angel dust." It can be administered intravenously as well as in powder or pill form. It has become a new drug of choice because of its ready availability and the belief that it will bring about exotic effects similar to other psychedelic drugs like lysergic acid diethylamide (LSD), mescaline, and psilocybin. Without the user's knowledge, the drug is sometimes sold to him or her as a substitute for other drugs, but in many instances it is taken deliberately. In powder form, it is sniffed, and potentially lethal aspects have not deterred many users. During 1975, in the city of Detroit alone, PCP was reported as the most common drug found in emergency overdose management. Burns and Lerner (1976) note that the increasing availability of his "enigmatic psychoactive agent" is likely to expand its abuse and continue to challenge the medical community. Some of the first symptoms noted are alterations in body image, such as an elongation or floating away of arms and legs, and/or the contraction and extension of body size. These experiences resemble the psychedelic highs which the user often seeks. Unfortunately, the serious and potentially lethal side effects include high blood pressure, extreme temperature, seizures, coma, and cardiac arrest. Showalter and Thornton (1977) comment that the body-image distortions noted are often incorrectly interpreted as hallucinations by both patients and physicians. Instead, these symptoms are aspects of psychological impairment. Feelings of progressive depersonalization, isolation, and depresson are likely to occur and last for hours. One of the most common presenting symptoms is severe anxiety. Along with disorganized thought, concrete thinking, mental blocking and use of neologisms, increased dosages bring negativism, hostility, and apathy. The stage before coma is one of catalepsy, or "dissociative anesthesia," found in both humans and animals. Originally PCP was used to achieve this state during surgical procedures at both the human and infrahuman levels; but the drug was abandoned for administration to humans, and today it is legitimately available only for use by veterinarians.

There is general agreement among professionals and in the drug community alike that the potentially lethal aspects of PCP are such that a massive educational campaign is needed to help prevent its broad dissemination and use. Those who still wish to take chances with the drug are indirectly suicidal and should be encouraged to obtain professional help. For further information, the reader is referred to Fauman et al (1976), Lundberg et al. (1976), and Balster and Chait (1976).

Drug abuse may overlap with other types of indirect self-destruction associated with psychophysiological disorders, such as colitis, ulcers, and dysmenorrhea, since a heavy ingestion of drugs invariably takes its toll on gastric function and renal efficiency. Other physiological systems are affected, as well, including both the central and autonomic nervous systems. The side effects from chronic drug ingestion may result in such phenomena as nasal and lacrimal irritability, gastric distress, and constipation. The insidiousness of drug abuse is that the drug helps overcome the discomfort the person endures as a result of such side effects. A self-destructive quality can also be noted in the fact that the drug abuser is willing to undergo the secondary physical stresses of repeated drug abuse.

The phenomenon of suicidal contagion may spread through some high-risk members of the drug-abuse population, but there is no evidence to support it as a major contributor to the incidence of suicide. In some instances, publicity about the suicidal deaths of such well-known figures as Marilyn Monroe and Freddie Prinze has been thought to evoke a temporary increase in suicide, but this has not been related to drug abuse per se.

SELECTED RESEARCH RELATED TO DRUG ABUSE AND INDIRECT SELF-DESTRUCTION

Clinicians have long stated that, although behavior can be defined as suicidal only when an *intentional* act of self-destruction is performed, there are subintentioned deaths as well. In the last two decades research studies have begun to emerge which bear on this issue. Shneidman (1963) has proposed three essential orientations toward death in addition to the classical, basic categories of natural, accidental, suicidal, and homicidal. These are: subintentioned, intentioned, and unintentioned. It was his belief that subintentioned death comprised the vast majority of deaths. By definition, in the subintentioned death, the decedent plays some role, even though covert or unconscious, in hastening his or her own demise. Such behavior is obviously risk-taking and shows a disregard for ordinary prudence in one's behavior. The behavior usually demonstrates narrowly focused judgment, which is indicated by the fact that such persons themselves facilitate, foster, or exacerbate their own deaths. Both research and clinical evidence suggest that addiction and drug abuse can be equivalent to suicide.

A number of key points warrant discussion regarding whether or not addiction is self-destructive. In the first place, one must accept the concept of subintentional death, and the view that much of the behavior leading to it may not be fully conscious. In the second place, it is unclear whether or not there are certain personalities which are suicidal and employ addiction as a form of self-destruction. Third, it must be demonstrated that addiction is followed by self-destruction. Once addiction has taken place, does it bring out or heighten self-destructive tendencies? While it appears that many addicts behave in self-destructive ways—such as deliberately taking bad doses of drugs, or becoming overdosed—more research is needed to answer these questions definitively.

Self-destructive behavior is not uncommon when LSD is used. Incidents of actual death, the requirement of forcible restraint to prevent suicide, visual hallucinations of seeing oneself dead, and delusions of immunity to dangerous acts have all been reported. Robbins et al. (1969) have noted that many heroin drug abusers begin with tobacco and alcohol and then move to amphetamines, barbiturates, tranquilizers, and ultimately to illicit drugs. Such a sequence has frequently included marijuana, despite the contention that marijuana does not lead to heroin addiction.

In a research study performed in the District of Columbia and vicinity, Frederick et al. (1973) showed that many drug addicts had depressive personality traits and had attempted more suicides than might be expected in comparable age groups of nonaddicts. Moreover, this study demonstrated that: (1) addicts, in general, are more depressed than nonaddicts, particularly in younger age groups, whether on methadone or abstaining from it; (2) addicts are more self-destructive than nonaddicts; (3) addicts have more aberrant attitudes toward life and death than nonaddicts; (4) methadone appeared to act essentially as a palliative rather than as a cure; and (5) the problem of addiction is heightened among certain minority groups. Depression was found in 39 percent of the "attempt" population still on methadone and rose to 60 percent in the group abstaining from methadone.

These findings underscored the presence of depression and were supported later by Weissman et al. (1976) in a study of lower-social-class males who were participating in a methadone maintenance program. They found approximately one-third of the subjects to be suffering from moderate to severe depression. The depressive symptoms were associated with a decrease in social functioning, an increase in stress in the preceding six-month period, and a history of alcohol abuse. It was emphasized that since the combination of depression and drug abuse creates a high risk for suicide, depressive symptoms require early detection and treatment. The treatment of most secondary depressions requires considerably more attention, particularly in the testing of psychotropic drugs in controlled medical trials.

Lester et al. (1976) obtained data on more than 200 suicide cases in Philadelphia in 1972, to discover additional correlates of choice of the method of suicide. Among the 25 variables used for comparison, 26 percent used coma-producing drugs, 26 percent died by hanging, 19 percent used firearms; 8 percent employed jumping as a method, and 6 percent died from drowning. The choice of method was differentially related to age, sex, race, marital status, and employment status. Moreover, suicides who used drugs had been psychiatrically hospitalized more often than those who employed hanging or firearms. Suicides using drugs or hanging had more previous attempts and threats and had abused drugs more often than those using firearms. Both the psychological and demographic factors are useful for exploring this problem in greater depth.

Schuman and Polkowski (1975) studied sixty-two secondary school students in their classrooms over five weeks in an intensive drug-information program, looking for within-group changes in their perceptions. Peer pressure and "kicks" were cited as reasons for beginning the use of drugs, but peer pressure had relatively greater strength for girls than for boys. Boys and girls differed in reasons for stopping drug use. Peer-group and professional help was instrumental in the cessation of drug use for girls, while punishment was more effective for boys. In rating the relative dangers and pleasures of marijuana and heroin, most students did not discriminate effectively between the two drugs, although ratings of marijuana dangers decreased. Unexpectedly, responses concerning the health hazards of heroin did not increase. Thus, it may be inferred that, in some instances, the potentially dangerous aspects of hard-core drugs may not be perceived accurately by many teenagers. This would lend support to the notion that there are, indeed, indirect aspects to self-destructive behavior in the sense that overdoses may be taken as a gamble, for "kicks," or as an attention-getting threat.

Data from the National Center for Health Statistics reveal the startling increase in suicides among younger age groups, between fifteen and twenty-five years of age over a period of twenty years, as shown in Figure 1. The overwhelming majority of overt deaths from drug addiction occurs among the younger age groups, but the indirect aspects of drug abuse as a form of

FIGURE 1
AGE-SPECIFIC SUICIDE RATES BY FIVE-YEAR AGE GROUPS: 1955, 1965, 1975

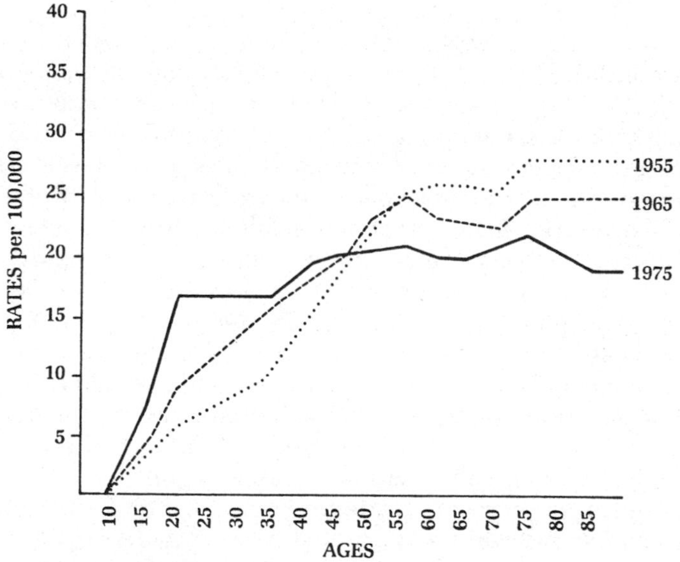

SOURCE: National Center for Health Statistics, Mortality Statistics Branch.

self-destruction also seem much more apparent in the younger ages.

Suicide by overdose is not confined to the young, as shown by Benson and Brodie (1975), who cited the elderly as a high-risk population in both the United States and Great Britain. The older white male is a particularly high risk. Besides physical and mental illness, barbiturates and psychotherapeutic agents contribute to suicide. These drugs are often accessible to older persons for misuse. Suicidal acts are nearly always very serious among the elderly because of their physical states and psychological attitude. There are a few so-called suicidal gestures among the elderly. Because depression is common among older persons, the onset of declining income and prestige combined with a loss of mental and physical abilities make drug abuse and suicide easy routes to take for respite from their problems.

Overdosing with hard-core drugs as a method of suicide has now appeared with such frequency that addiction must be seriously considered as a contributing factor to suicide. Braconnier and Olievenstein (1974) reported a study of thirty-five drug addicts, fifteen to twenty-four years of age, who made one or more suicide attempts. The subjects had all begun to abuse drugs between the ages of fifteen and twenty-one. Among the twenty-nine males and six females, in all of the families studied, one or both parents had taken psychotropic drugs or were alcoholics. A majority of the subjects used several drugs; hashish, LSD, barbiturates, solvents, amphetamines, and opiates were the most common. Six attempts were made under the actual influence of a drug, and four cases attempted suicide while using LSD. Thirty-one persons had made more than one attempt, and eight had made five or more. The most frequent methods used were ingestion of one or more medications or an overdose of heroin. In some instances, the consumption of alcohol was associated with drug ingestion.

Friedman et al. (1973) explored the relationship between drug overdose, depression, and suicide in 103 patients in a methadone maintenance clinic. A survey of these subjects disclosed that 33 had taken heroin overdoses. Reconstruction of the events leading to suicidal behavior indicated that most overdoses were covert or indirect suicide attempts. Thirty-eight percent of these covert attempts were related to incarceration, and 12 percent were accidents due to variability in street samples of the drug. Incarceration in jail should not be overlooked as a contributing factor in such instances.

A study by Jacobson and Tribe (1972) showed a suicide attempt rate of 112 per 100,000 population, and a female-male ratio of 2:1 in a predominantly urban sample. Among the 254 cases admitted to a psychiatric emergency unit, most patients were suffering from depression and had been admitted because of deliberate self poisoning with barbiturates. It was thought that, psychodynamically, this was a cry for help in a dramatic attempt to draw attention to personal conflicts. This information is consonant with the clinical studies and experiences of the author (Frederick et al., 1973), Tobias (1972) and Weissman et al. (1976).

Some recent data gathered by Barton (1974) summarizes the essence of drug-related mortality in the United States. Vital certificates were used as source documents to analyze a sample of 5,138 drug-related deaths in 1963 and then to compare them with a sample of 9,920 drug-related deaths in 1971. The data revealed a 36 percent increase in deaths in which there was drug dependence, a 42 percent increase in deaths due to accidental poisoning, a 13 percent increase in deaths due to suicide by drugs, and a 36 percent increase in drug deaths listed as undetermined accident or suicide. It was emphasized that vital-statistics data are, in many instances, only estimates of the true cause of death, since the psychological factors are not usually explored in listing the mode of death.

The chronic use of either habit-forming medication or hard-core narcotics falls into the range of indirect suicide and self-assaultive behavior, whereas deliberate overdoses are direct suicidal acts.

References

Balster R. L., and Chait, L. D. The behavioral pharmacology of phencyclidine. *Clinical Toxicology,* 9:513–528, 1976.

Barton, W. I. Drug-related mortality in the United States, 1963–1971. *Drug Forum,* 4(1):79–89, 1974.

Benson, R. A., and Brodie, D. C. Suicide by overdoses of medicine among the aged. *Journal of the American Geriatrics Society,* 23:304–308, 1975.

Braconnier, A., and Olievenstein, C. Attempted suicide in actual drug addicts. *Revue de neuropsychiatrie infantile et d'hygiene mentale de l'enfance,* 22:677–693, 1974.

Burns, R. S., and Lerner, S. E. Perspectives: Acute phencyclidine intoxication. *Clinical Toxicology,* 9:477–501, 1976.

Fauman, B., Aldinger, G., Fauman, M., and Rosen P. Psychiatric sequelae of phencyclidine abuse. *Clinical Toxicology,* 9:529–538, 1976.

Frederick, C. J. Drug abuse as self-destructive behavior. *Drug Therapy,* 2:49-68, 1972.

Frederick, C. J., Resnik, H. L., and Wittlin, B. J. Self-destructive aspects of hard core addiction. *Archives of General Psychiatry,* 28:579–585, 1973.

Friedman, R. C., Friedman, J. G., and Ramirez, T. The heroin overdose as a method of attempted suicide. *British Journal of Addiction,* 68:137–143, 1973.

Hendin, H. Students on heroin. *Journal of Nervous and Mental Disease,* 158:240–255, 1974.

Hillman, J. *Suicide and the Soul.* New York: Harper and Row, 1965.

Jacobson, S., and Tribe, P. Deliberate self-injury (attempted suicide) in patients, admitted to hospital in Mid-Sussex. *British Journal of Psychiatry,* 121:379–386, 1972.

Lester, D., Beck, A. T., and Bruno, S. Correlates of choice of method for completed suicide *Psychology,* 13:70–73, 1976.

Lundberg, G. D., Gupta, R. C., and Montgomery, S. H. Phencyclidine: Patterns seen in street drug analysis. *Clinical Toxicology,* 9:503–511, 1976.

Meerloo, J. A. Hidden suicide. In H. L. P. Resnik, ed., *Suicidal Behaviors: Diagnosis and Management.* Boston: Little, Brown, 1968, pp. 82–89.

Robbins, E., Gassner, S., Kayes, J., Wilkinson, R. H., and Murphy, G. E. The communication of suicidal intent: A study of 134 cases of successful (completed) suicides. In W. A. Rushing, ed., *Deviant Behavior and Social Process.* Chicago: Rand McNally, 1969, pp. 251–269.

Schuman, S. H., and Polkowski, J. Drug and risk perceptions of ninth-grade students: Sex differences and similarities. *Community Mental Health Journal,* 11:184–194, 1975.

Shneidman, E. S. Orientations toward death: A vital aspect of the study of lives. In R. W. White, ed., *The Study of Lives.* New York: Atherton, 1963.

Showalter, C. V., and Thornton, W. E. Clinical pharmacology of phencyclidine toxicity. *American Journal of Psychiatry,* 134:11, 1977.

Tobias, J J. Overdosing and attempted suicide among youth in an affluent suburban community. *Police Journal,* 44:319–326, 1972.

Weissman, M. M., Slobetz, F., Prusoff, B., Mezritz, M., and Howard, P. Clinical depression among narcotic addicts maintained on methadone in the community. *American Journal of Psychiatry,* 133:1434-1438, 1976.

POETIC EPILOGUE

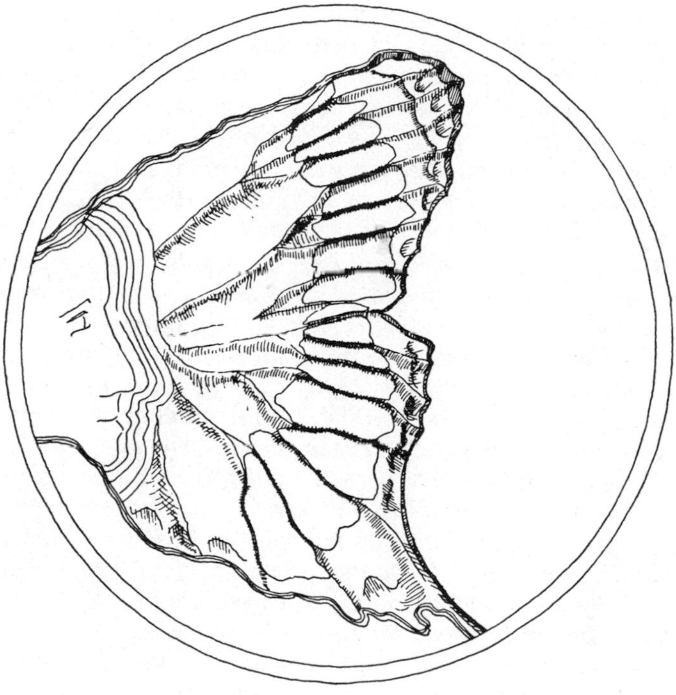

POETIC EPILOGUE

This selection—a poem about a person's own impending death—can legitimately be thought of as a "personal document" in the sense that Gordon Allport, the famed psychologist, called diaries, letters, and journals personal documents. (see The Use of Personal Documents in Psychological Science. *New York: SSRC, 1942.) Apart from the poetry of death, other examples of death-oriented personal documents are, of course, suicide notes, and "death journals," (as they might be called), accounts written in the context of the author's actually dying. Recent examples of this latter genre would include "Notes of a Dying Professor,"* Pennsylvania Gazette, *March, 1972; Betty Harker, "Cancer and Communication Problems: A Personal Experience,"* Psychiatry in Medicine, *Volume 3, 1972; and Lauren Trombley, "A Psychiatrist's Response to a Life-Threatening Illness," (included as a selection in this volume). In each of these, the writer expresses feelings and experiences of the last few months of life. There are many poems about death. The reader interested in this fascinating but lugubrious topic may wish to peruse Corliss Lamont's edited book* Man Answers Death: An Anthology of Poetry, *which contains 302 poems from the early Greeks and Romans to contemporary times.*

Perhaps almost every person thinks in some artistic or romantic way about his or her death, but only a very few of us are able to put organized thoughts on paper in moving poetry. Ted Rosenthal was very lucky that he could. He was very unlucky that he was dying of leukemia. Like some other potentially great young poetic voices (he died in 1972 when he was 34), he had just begun to speak his mind. The threat of death seemed to catalyze his talents. He was able to communicate to us all what the essence of the pain of dying is like. (There is a remarkable film of Ted Rosenthal which is available from Eccentric Circle Cinema Workshop of Evanston, Illinois.) His book of poetry (like the film) is called, poignantly, How Could I Not Be Among You? *The lines that comprise this Epilogue represent a portion of the first stanza of that work, plus the nine concluding stanzas.*

50. How Could I Not Be Among You?

Ted Rosenthal

My name is Ted Rosenthal.
I am 31.
I live in Berkeley where I have
Lived for the last 10 years.
I was born and raised in New York City.
So I am 31.
I lived well into my thirties.
I can always say that. . . .

Though you may find me picking flowers
Or washing my body in a river, or kicking rocks,
Don't think my eyes don't hold yours.
And look hard upon them
and drop tears as long as you stay before me
Because I live as a man who knows death
and I speak the only truth
to those who will listen.

Never yield a minute to despair, sloth, fantasy.
I say to you, you will face pain in your life
You may lose your limbs, bleed to death
Shriek for hours on into weeks in unimaginable agony.
It is not aimed at anyone
but it will come your way.
The wind sweeps over everyone.

You will feel so all alone, abandoned,
come to see that life is brief.
And you will cry, "No, it cannot be so,"
but nothing will avail you.
I tell you never to yearn for the past.
Speak certain knowledge.
Your childhood is worthless.
Seek not ritual. There is no escape in Christmas.
Santa Claus will not ease your pain.
No fantasy will soothe you.

You must bare your heart and expect nothing in return.
You must respond totally to nature.

You must return to your simple self.
I do not fool you. There lies no other path.
I have not forsaken you, but I cannot be among you all.
You are not alone
so long as you love your own true simple selves.
Your natural hair, your skin, your graceful bodies,
your knowing eyes and your tears and tongues.

I stand before you all aching with truth
Trembling with desire to make you know.
Eat, sleep, and be serious about life.
To be serious is to be simple;
to be simple is to love.
Don't wait another minute, make tracks, go home.
Admit you have some place to return to.
The bugs are crawling over the earth, the sun shining over everyone.
The rains are pounding, the winds driving.
The breeze is gentle and the grass burns.
The earth is dusty. Go ankle deep in mud.

Get tickled by the tall cattails.
Kick crazily into the burrs and prickles.
Rub your back against the bark, and go ahead, peel it.
Adore the sun.
O people, you are dying! Live while you can.
What can I say?
The blackbirds blow the bush.
Get glass in your feet if you must, but take off the shoes.
O heed me. There is pain all over!
There is continual suffering, puking and coughing.
Don't wait on it. It is stalking you.
Tear ass up the mountainside, duck into the mist.

Roll among the wet daisies. Blow out your lungs
among the dead dandelion fields.
But don't delay, time is not on your side.
Soon you will be crying for the hurt, make speed.
Splash in the Ocean,
leap in the snow.
Come on everybody! Love your neighbor
Love your mother, love your lover,
love the man who just stands there staring.
But first, that's alright, go ahead and cry.
Cry, cry, cry your heart out.
It's love. It's your only path.

O people, I am so sorry.
Nothing can be hid.
It's a circle in the round.
It's group theater,
no wings, no backstage, no leading act.
O, I am weeping, but it's stage center for all of us.
Hide in the weeds but come out naked.
Dance in the sand while lightning bands all around us.

Step lightly, we're walking home now.
The clouds take every shape.
We climb up the boulders; there is no plateau.
We cross the stream and walk up the slope.
See, the hawk is diving.
The plain stretches out ahead,
then the hills, the valleys, the meadows.
Keep moving people. How could I not be among you?

ANNOTATED BIBLIOGRAPHY

Recently, the British-American psychiatrist, Michael A. Simpson, published Dying, Death and Grief: A Critically Annotated Bibliography and Source Book of Thanatology and Terminal Care (New York and London: Plenum Press, 1979). *The main part of the book consists of several hundred annotated references on death and dying. Simpson has evaluated each of these by awarding them from one to five stars, where five stars means "highly recommended; buy and read." Below are reproduced the 33 (of 708) books to which he has given this highest rating. The citations and comments are arranged alphabetically by author from Simpson's book, which itself deserves a five-star rating.*

A Death in the Family. James Agee. Bantam, New York. PB $1.50.

Pulitzer Prize-winning novel dealing with the effects of the sudden death of a young father on a close-knit family.

Kinflicks. Lisa Alther. Chatto & Windus, London, 1976. Penguin 1977. PB 95 pence. A. A. Knopf, NY (Random House Canada) 1975. Signet, NY 1977 $2.25. Also 'Haut-Kontakte' Ullstein Verlag, Berlin, 1977.

"My family has always been into death," it begins. At long last someone who had something new to say about death in America and a sparkling style to say it in. The story of Ginny Babcock is not merely brilliantly funny and poignant as a novel (It's a cliché for a reviewer to admit to laughing aloud, but the occurrence is still rare enough to be worth recording). It is also a fine account of varying responses to death; and of the dying, from idiopathic thrombocytopenic purpura, of Ginny's mother, for whom death was a demon lover for whose assignation one must be ready. "The trick was in being both willing to die and able to do so at the same time. Dying properly was like achieving simultaneous orgasm."

The Savage God. A. Alvarez. Weidenfeld & Nicolson, London 1972. 250pp. £3.50. Bantam, NY. PB $1.95.

A study of attitudes toward suicide and death through history and literature, and the fascination this theme has had for writers at all times. Includes an account of his relations with Sylvia Plath, and her suicide and his own suicide attempt.

Ethical Decisions in Medicine. Howard Brodie. Little, Brown & Co., Boston. 1976. 340 pp. $9.95, £6.70.

Probably the best available book on medical ethics. Soundly organized with clearly stated objectives and self-evaluation components. Proposes a concise method for dealing with ethical problems and provides many lucid examples of its use. It examines key issues including informed consent, determination of the quality of life, ethical participation, allocation of scarce resources, euthanasia, and allowing to die. As some recent thanatology research has breached some of the principles of ethical research in human beings, everyone involved in this area could benefit from reading this book, which will also provide a valuable basis for teaching the subject.

The Sanctity of Social Life: Physicians' Treatment of Critically Ill Patients. Diana Crane. Russell Sage Foundation, N.Y. 1975. 286 pp. $13.50.

A uniquely valuable study based on extensive interviews, observations, hospital record audit, and detailed questionnaires. Rather than pontificating on what ought *to be done, Crane describes what doctors* actually *do for the critically ill. She shows that while withdrawal of treatment is widespread in some types of case, positive euthanasia is rare. Both adults and children seem to be regarded as "treatable" while they retain the potential for interacting in some meaningful way with others. A much-needed antidote to the usual speculative literature on this subject, with commendable detail and objectivity.*

A Very Easy Death. Simone de Beauvoir. Penguin Books, Harmondsworth. 1969. 92 pp. 85¢. Celo Press, NC. 1965. 139 pp. $1.25. Warner PB, NY. 1973. $1.25. 65 pence, U.K.

Unreservedly recommended. A brilliant and unforgettable account of her mother's death in France, a death that was anything but easy. Deeply moving description of a proud woman's clinical humiliation and the conflicting love and hostility her daughter experienced in confronting the death.

New Meanings of Death. Ed. Herman Feifel. McGraw-Hill, N.Y., 1977. 357 pp. $11.95. Also in PB.

A splendid volume—even more interesting and accessible than Feifel's 1959 classic. Includes Feifel on death in contemporary America; Kastenbaum on death and development through the life span; Bluebond-Langner on meanings of death to children; Shneidman on death and the college student; Weisman on the psychiatrist and the inexorable; Garfield on the personal impact of death on the clinician; Saunders on St. Christophers Hospice; Kelly on Make Today Count; Kalish on death and the family; Leviton on death education; Lifton on immortality, Simpson on death and poetry; Gutman on death and power; Shaffer and Rodes on death and the law.

A Bibliography on Death, Grief and Bereavement 1845--1973. Compiled by Robert Fulton. 3rd revised edition. 1973. Center for Death Education and Research, Minnesota. 173 pp. PB

Quite simply the very best and most comprehensive bibliography on the subject available. Lists 2,639 items, and efficiently cross-references them in a useful index. Not fully comprehensive, but has only relatively minor omissions and errors. Generally excludes journalistic, literary and principally theological works, and much of the material on suicide. Very useful for any serious student of the subjects.

Death, Grief & Bereavement: A bibliography 1845–1975. Compiled by Robert Fulton with others. Arno Press, New York, 1976. 253 pp. $20.00

The most comprehensive and reliable bibliography of the literature on death, grief and bereavement in print. Some 4,000 entries, mainly journal articles, indexed by subject, with nearly eighty classifications.

Talking About Death. E.A. Grollman. Beacon Press, Boston, 1970. 30 pp. $1.95 PB.

Strongly recommended. A beautiful book, probably the best available for use in discussing death with children. Well-illustrated and constructed; simple, direct, honest.

Talking About Death: A Dialogue Between Parent & Child. Earl A. Grollman. Beacon Press, Boston. 1976. 98 pp. $3.95.

Simply, excellent. A new edition of the excellent earlier version with a greatly expanded guide to parents on how to use it and to discuss death with children. Lists some resources such as organizations, cassettes, films, books. Explicit and observant.

Dying. John Hinton. Pelican Books, Harmondsworth & Baltimore. 1967. 2nd edition 1972. 220 pp. $2.95; 90 p.

Succinct and highly capable review of existing knowledge on attitudes to death, what dying is like, terminal care and mourning based on a thorough review of the literature up to the 1960s and the author's own experience. Compact.

Gramp. Mark and Dan Jury. Grossman Publishers (Viking Press), New York. 1976. 152 pp. Illustrated. $5.95. PB.

Simply, superb. A moving, honest and direct account of the dying of Frank Tugend, as recorded in photographs and words, by a family who made his death an act of love. Arteriosclerotic dementia led to a gruelling three-year

deterioration. On February 11, 1974, aged eighty-one, he removed his false teeth and announced that he was no longer going to eat or drink. The family decided to respect his wishes and not hospitalize him. Three weeks later, he died at home. Death with dignity? Perhaps, though not how most people picture it. An invaluable, unromanticized corrective to the stickily sentimental nature of too much death literature.

The Psychology of Death. Robert Kastenbaum and Ruth Aisenberg. Springer Publishing Co. N.Y. 1972. 500 pp. $11.95. Duckworth, London. 1974. £8.95. Concise Edition, Springer, N.Y. 1976. 434 pp. PB. $9.95.

Quite simply the very best book on the psychology of death, and one that is unlikely to be improved on for some time. Very well organized and highly useful to any professional or scholar involved in work related to death. A truly critical review; stimulating, eclectic and honest. Looks at concepts of and attitudes towards death, developmentally and clinically, and the relevant cultural milieu; also thanatomimesis, longevity, suicide, murder, accidents and illness. Stylish, yet straightforward and not self-conscious. Strongly recommended.

Catastrophic Diseases: Who Decides What? A Psychosocial and Legal Analysis of the Problems Posed by Hemodialysis and Organ Transplantation. Jay Katz and Alexander Morgan Capron. Russell Sage Foundation, N.Y. 1975. 295 pp. $10.00.

A highly able explanation of important issues, extending and complementing both Katz's earlier work (Experimentation with Human Beings, 1972) and Fox and Swazey's recent book (1974). The authors explore the nature and effects of catastrophic illness, and such goals and values as the preservation of life, reduction of suffering, personal integrity and dignity, pursuit of knowledge, economy and public interest. There's a cogent account of the development and present status of the technical procedures and a study of the characteristics, authority and capacity of the physician-investigators and patient-subjects, the functions of informed consent, and limitations of consent. The stages of decision making are reviewed, the activities of professional and public institutions involved; and proposals for the formulation of policy regarding the allocation of resources and selection of donors, the administration of such major medical interventions at local and national levels, with a review of decisions and consequences. Lucid, readable, fascinating and challenging.

On Death and Dying. Elisabeth Kubler-Ross. Macmillan, NY. 1968. $7.95, $2.25 PB. 250 pp. Tavistock, London, 1973 paperback edition £1.30.

Strongly recommended. A classic and highly influential work, in which Dr. Ross advanced her model of the "five stages" in the progress of the dying patient. Interesting and humane, with sound practical advice and transcripts of some interviews.

A Grief Observed. C. S. Lewis. Faber and Faber, London. 1961/1973. 60 pp. PB. 45 pence. Seabury Press, NY. $4.50.

"No one ever told me that grief felt so much like fear" . . . An outstandingly honest, naked observation of a widower's grief. Begun, without plans for publication, as a means of self-therapy, written informally in odd notebooks, during his first weeks alone. Unique, moving, memorable.

The American Way of Death. Jessica Mitford. 1963. 280 pp. Simon and Schuster, New York, 1963. Fawcett/Crest PB $1.95.

Justly famous, witty, well-documented and merciless exposure of the multimillion dollar death industry and American funeral practices.

Death and the Family: The Importance of Mourning. Lily Pincus. Pantheon Books, New York. 1974. 278 pp. $8.95. Vintage PB, 1976, $2.95. Faber, London, £4.50.

Written by a social worker with great experience in marital and family therapy; a brilliant book, sensitive and well written, always readable, wise and human. A genuine, fresh and substantial contribution to the understanding and therapy of bereavement and the dying family. Highly recommended.

The Bell Jar. Sylvia Plath. Bantam, NY. PB $1.75

A brilliant novel, autobiographical in many respects, about a nineteen-year-old girl who attempts suicide, finding life difficult to bear. One of the best evocations of suicidal thinking in literature.

Jewish Reflections on Death. Jack Riemer. Schocken Books, NY. 1974. 184 pp. $7.95, $3.45 PB.

An eloquent anthology of great interest and value to Jew and non-Jew alike. The laws of Judaism, especially with regard to bereavement, show great psychological and spiritual wisdom, giving a structure to grief that relates to death firmly and realistically as a normal part of life. These essays give a clear account of the beauty and insight of the traditional procedures for the business of mourning and also explore the modern problems relating to death, from the Jewish experience, of suffering and solace. An unusually interesting book. A short glossary of Hebrew terms used would aid the comprehension of non-Jewish readers.

Loss and Grief: Psychological Management in Medical Practice. Ed. B. Schoenberg, A. C. Carr, D. Peretz, and A. H. Kutscher. Columbia University Press, NY. 1970. PB 400 pp. $4.95. £5.80.

Strongly recommended. Deals with the broader issues of reactions to loss of different kinds, including loss of limb, organ, sensory loss or loss of sexual function; also with the reactions to death in the patient, family, and the health care team. A very high standard of contributions from a distinguished group of authors. A forty-five item annotated bibliography.

Death: Current Perspectives. Ed. E. S. Shneidman. Mayfield Publishing Co., Palo Alto. 1976. 547 pp. $12.50, $8.95 PB.

A bright and highly personal selection of extracts from published works on death, selected and arranged with great skill. A potentially valuable college text. Though some sources are overworked, those most highly recommended in this bibliography are well represented: Toynbee, Gorer, Ariès, Gil Elliot, Sudnow, Glaser and Strauss, Shneidman, Kübler-Ross, Hinton, Kastenbaum, Feifel, Saunders and Weisman. A great smorgasbord.

The Facts of Death. Michael A. Simpson. Spectrum/Prentice-Hall, 1979. 250 pp. approx.

An eloquent and warm practical book for families and helpers. Reviews succinctly what we know about the nature of death and dying, patient's rights, how to manage one's own death and to cope with the dying of another; death and children; suicide; how to cope with a suicidal person, and with one's own suicidal impulses; bereavement and grief; funerals, and how to plan one's estate and funeral, and how to avoid the Terminal R.I.P.-off. Maybe they told you the facts of life: this is what they left out.

Cancer Ward. A. Solzhenitsyn. Bantam, New York. 1969. 560 pp. $1.25.

A great novel, about life in the cancer ward of a Russian hospital, that defies any brief review.

Death Inside Out. Ed. P. Steinfels and R. M. Veatch. Hastings Center Report. Harper Forum Books. Harper and Row, New York. Fitzhenry and Whiteside, Canada. 1975. 150 pp. PB $7.30.

One of the more refreshing books on death. Elegant, clear thinking, critical, thoughtful and stimulating. Principally concerned with philosophical, ethical and historical issues rather than practical and personal problems. One of the comparatively few books of genuine intellectual interest in the field. Includes Ariès "Death Inside Out," again, and Ivan Illich on tbe political uses of natural death; Eric Cassell on dying in a technological society; William May on the metaphysical plight of the family (the great family secret: God is dead); Robert Morison on death: process or event? Paul Ramsey on the indignity of "death with dignity"; David Smith on letting some babies die; and other works by Leon Kass and Tristram Engelhardt.

Passing On: The Social Organization of Dying. David Sudnow. Prentice-Hall, Englewood Cliffs, NJ. 1967. 176 pp. $4.20 PB.

Excellent sociological study of death in a county hospital and its management by the staff; including counting of deaths and their visibility, social death, preparing and moving bodies, how we announce death and bad news; uses of a corpse, etc. Fascinating reading, introducing a new way of looking at what we do. Strongly recommended.

The Death of Ivan Illych. Leo Tolstoy. New American Library, New York. PB $1.25 and other editions.

Strongly recommended. Brilliant account of the death of a bourgeois Russian judge, with probably more insight into the psychology of death than any other major author.

Man's Concern with Death. Arnold Toynbee et al. Hodder and Stoughton, London. 1968. 280 pp. £2.25.

One of the early and persisting classics of the death literature. Among its competent chapters are several by Ninian Smart on philosophical and religious concepts, Keith Mant on the medical definition of death, Simon Yudkin on death and the young, and Eric Rhode on death in twentieth century fiction. But best of all are the splendid chapters by Arnold Toynbee, erudite and elegant and superbly literate. The epilogue, a moving account of Toynbee's personal experience and his feelings about the imminent prospect of death, is especially poignant reading.

Johnny Got His Gun. Dalton Trumbo. Bantam, NY. $1.50.

A powerful antiwar novel; a nineteen-year-old World War I veteran has been left, after multiple injuries; blind, speechless, and limbless. He beats out messages on his pillow with his head, begging to be taken out of his hospital room, to show the world a survivor of Every War.

The Book (On the Taboo Against Knowing Who You Are). Alan Watts. Vintage Books, NY. 1972. 146 pp. $1.65 PB.

A classic, elegantly, lucidly and wittily written book. Dealing with the delusion of the lonely separate ego alienated from the universe, with his usual skillful understanding of Eastern and Western religions and philosophies. Offers a coherent philosophical style which genuinely deals with fear of death and a manner of coming to terms with life. Highly recommended.

On Dying and Denying. Avery Weisman. Behavioral Publ., New York. 1972. $12.95.

A very significant study of "terminality," concentrating on the central role of denial. Very competent and illustrated with many clinical examples. Of the highest quality both intellectually and practically.

Helping Your Children to Understand Death. Anna M. Wolf. Revised edn. 1973. Child Study Press, NY. 64 pp. $1.50 PB.

Possibly the best book available to help parents and children talk about death. Simple but not simplistic, wise but not know-all, and soundly practical. Well grounded in child development and family dynamics, it deals sensibly with the common questions of children and parents. Issues of faith, inescapable in this area, are considered from the viewpoint of the major faiths; other matters covered include suicide, assassination and war, and hypocrisy. Very highly recommended to all who deal with children, have children, or have been children.

NAME INDEX

Page numbers in italic indicate a selection by this author.

SUBJECT INDEX